Before Elvis

The Prehistory of Rock 'n' Roll

Larry Birnbaum

THE SCARECROW PRESS, INC.
Lanham • Toronto • Plymouth, UK
2013

Published by Scarecrow Press, Inc.
A wholly owned subsidiary of The Rowman & Littlefield Publishing Group, Inc.
4501 Forbes Boulevard, Suite 200, Lanham, Maryland 20706
www.rowman.com

10 Thornbury Road, Plymouth PL6 7PP, United Kingdom

British Library Cataloguing in Publication Information Available

Library of Congress Cataloging-in-Publication Data

Birnbaum, Larry.
Before Elvis : the prehistory of rock 'n' roll / Larry Birnbaum.
p. cm.
Includes bibliographical references and index.
ISBN 978-0-8108-8638-4 (cloth : alk. paper) — ISBN 978-0-8108-8628-5 (pbk. : alk. paper) — ISBN 978-0-8108-8629-2 (ebook) 1. Popular music—United States—1931-1940—History and criticism. 2. Popular music—United States—1941-1950—History and criticism. 3. Popular music—United States—1951-1960—History and criticism. 4. Rhythm and blues music—History and criticism. 5. Rock music—United States—To 1961—History and criticism. I. Title.
ML3477.B47 2013
781.640973'0904—dc23
2012032269

The paper used in this publication meets the minimum requirements of American National Standard for Information Sciences Permanence of Paper for Printed Library Materials, ANSI/NISO Z39.48-1992.

Printed in the United States of America

To my wife, Marianna, and my mother, Paula.

Contents

Introduction

Considering that rock 'n' roll is little more than fifty years old, its origins are remarkably obscure. For all the books, magazines, newspaper articles, movies, radio and television programs, websites, college courses, and even museums devoted to rock 'n' roll and its exponents, few attempts have been made to trace the roots of the music back much further than the end of World War II, less than ten years before the emergence of Elvis Presley.

Although there is no consensus as to what the first rock 'n' roll record is, it is generally agreed that rock music grew out of postwar rhythm-and-blues. Thanks to the revival of swing dancing, there's been a growing awareness of the "jump" music that preceded R&B, but jazz historians still give short shrift to the bluesy side of the swing era. The boogie-woogie craze of the late 1930s and early 1940s has only been sketchily described, and the development of the boogie beat, the basis for early rock 'n' roll (and for ska, the predecessor of reggae), remains little known.

The influence of country, pop, and Caribbean music on early rock 'n' roll has likewise been acknowledged but not closely examined. The interaction of country music with jazz and R&B is especially important, but though western swing—country music's string-powered response to big-band jazz—has been extensively researched, the "hillbilly boogie," which bridged the gap between western swing and the rockabilly, has been virtually ignored.

Until now, rock 'n' roll has largely been viewed as a bolt from the blue, an overnight revolution provoked by the bland pop that preceded it and created through the white appropriation of music that had previously been played only by and for blacks. But the roots of rock can be tracked all the way back to the minstrel and "coon" songs of the nineteenth and early twentieth centuries, which were written and performed by whites and blacks alike. The notion that Presley was the first white artist to perform African

American music with a semblance of authenticity could hardly be further from the truth. Following a tradition dating back to colonial America, white musicians sang and played black music throughout the recorded era, some so convincingly that both white and black listeners misjudged their race. Much of modern rock and pop, from Elvis to Eminem, can be regarded as a latter-day extension of blackface minstrelsy, with a harder beat but without the burnt cork.

The prehistory of rock 'n' roll was not just an underground phenomenon, confined to the back streets and byroads of blues and country music. Besides such unsung characters as Goree Carter, Hardrock Gunter, and the Harlem Hamfats, the list of rock forerunners includes such household names as Bing Crosby, Roy Rogers, and Ella Fitzgerald. Broadway reviews showcased ragtime and jazz, Hollywood musicals and animated cartoons helped popularize swing, and singing cowboy movies created a national audience for country music. "Blueberry Hill" became a rock classic at the hands of Fats Domino in 1956, but the song, a No. 1 pop hit for Glenn Miller in 1940, was sung by Gene Autry in the 1941 western *The Singing Hill* and recorded in 1949 by Louis Armstrong.

It is widely believed that rock music is derived from the blues and that the blues, based on dimly remembered African models, began in the Mississippi Delta. In fact, the evidence for the Delta origin of the blues is tenuous, and the connection between rural blues and early rock 'n' roll is oblique, mediated by jazz and country music. For the most part, the blues found its way into rock music through jazz, which has incorporated blues since jazz began. With rare exceptions, country blues had little impact on rock 'n' roll before the British Invasion of the mid-1960s. In any case, the form followed by such rock classics as Bill Haley's "Rock Around the Clock" and Carl Perkins's "Blue Suede Shoes" is not the blues but the verse-and-refrain hokum song.

The evolutionary paths of jazz, blues, country, pop, and gospel music were closely intertwined. The New Orleans–born singer and banjo player "Papa" Charlie Jackson helped spark a trend for bawdy hokum songs with his 1925 hit "Shake That Thing." Jackson's "Salty Dog Blues," recorded the previous year, became a standard of both Dixieland jazz and bluegrass. Thomas A. Dorsey, who helped lead the hokum movement under the name Georgia Tom, went on to found modern gospel music. Jimmie Davis, a white country singer who recorded such risqué hokum songs as "Tom Cat and Pussy Blues," also cut a version of "Salty Dog" with the black guitarists Oscar "Buddy" Woods and Ed "Dizzy Head" Schaffer, a rare example of a racially integrated southern session. After popularizing "You Are My Sunshine," which became a hit for Gene Autry and for Bing Crosby in 1941, Davis appeared in singing cowboy movies and, after serving two terms as governor of Louisiana, spent the final years of his career performing mostly gospel songs.

During the swing era, big bands such as Count Basie's, Benny Goodman's, and Tommy Dorsey's picked up the boogie-woogie, while blues and country music took on a jazzy feel. Artists such as the Kansas City blues shouter Big Joe Turner brought the earthy sounds of the Southwest to nationwide attention; Turner's first record, "Roll 'Em Pete," made in 1938 with the boogie-piano master Pete Johnson, embodies the spirit of what was to become rock 'n' roll. Early 1940s jump bands such as Lucky Millinder's and Louis Jordan's—with their shouted vocals, shuffle rhythms, boogie bass lines, and honking saxophones—laid the foundation for rhythm-and-blues.

With the postwar decline of the big bands, singers and small combos came to the forefront. Among the leaders of the burgeoning R&B movement were Roy Milton, Roy Brown, Joe and Jimmy Liggins, and Amos Milburn—all nearly forgotten today. Wynonie Harris, who made his first record in 1945 as the vocalist with Lucky Millinder's band, cut the smash hit "Good Rockin' Tonight" in late 1947, launching a cascade of similar "rock" songs with lyrics about whiskey, women, and automobiles. This first wave of rock 'n' roll had all but ended by the time young whites discovered the music and claimed it as their own.

Country musicians kept abreast of African American trends, adapting to every new style from ragtime to R&B. Western swing, born in 1930 when singer Milton Brown joined fiddler Bob Wills's band in Fort Worth, grew increasingly sophisticated through the early 1940s, paralleling developments in big-band jazz. The hillbilly boogie emerged after the war, paving the way for rockabilly and rock 'n' roll. It's fairly well-known that Elvis Presley's "Hound Dog" is based on Big Mama Thornton's rhythm-and-blues original, but few are aware that there were half a dozen white country versions of the song before Presley recorded it.

The roots of rock run through mainstream pop as well, from Irving Berlin's early coon songs to the Andrews Sisters' harmonized boogie-woogies and the R&B-flavored belting of Frankie Laine and Johnnie Ray. Before Elvis Presley or Bill Haley had a hit, the pop singer Kay Starr made the Top 20 with her cover version of the Clovers' 1951 rhythm-and-blues chart-topper "Fool, Fool, Fool."

Rock 'n' roll's long, gradual evolution can be heard through successive versions of songs such as "Keep A Knockin'." Before Little Richard turned it into a rock 'n' roll anthem in 1957, "Keep A Knockin'" was recorded by James "Boodle It" Wiggins and by Bert Mays in 1928, by Lil Johnson in 1935, by Milton Brown in 1936, by Louis Jordan and by Jimmy Dorsey in 1939, and by Jimmy Yancey in 1950, among others. The original melody, published by J. Paul Wyer as "The Long Lost Blues" in 1914 and recorded by W. C. Handy's band in 1917, is a variation of "Bucket's Got a Hole in It," said to have been played in the early 1900s by the New Orleans cornetist Buddy Bolden.

Most existing rock 'n' roll histories begin with the late 1940s or early 1950s and proceed through the familiar developments of the following decades. Only a few, such as Ed Ward, Geoffrey Stokes, and Ken Tucker's *Rock of Ages: The Rolling Stone History of Rock & Roll* or Robert Palmer's *Rock & Roll: An Unruly History* (both out of print), even refer to the music of the first half of the twentieth century. Pop music histories such as Ian Whitcomb's *After the Ball: Pop Music from Rag to Rock* or Larry Starr and Christopher Waterman's *American Popular Music: From Minstrelsy to MTV* deal with ragtime, blues, jazz, country, and Tin Pan Alley but don't systematically relate these genres to the evolution of rock. Perhaps the best explanation of the origins of rock is still to be found in Charlie Gillett's *The Sound of the City* (first published in 1970), one of the only books to recognize the link between rock and big-band swing.

One writer who has traced some of the various musical strains that found their way into rock 'n' roll is Nick Tosches, whose books *Unsung Heroes of Rock 'n' Roll, Country,* and, most recently, *Where Dead Voices Gather* make some of the same sorts of connections that *Before Elvis* does. But Tosches makes no attempt to be comprehensive, presenting the material in fragmented fashion and giving it a highly personal spin. Other writers view rock history through the prism of sociology or personality rather than focusing on the music itself.

I have long been curious about the origins of rock music and skeptical about the prevailing ideas on the subject. Since I began researching and writing *Before Elvis,* my enthusiasm for the book has only grown. Over the last decade or so, there has been a surge of publishing activity in the fields of blues, jazz, country, and other genres that fed into the development of rock. The past few years alone have seen the origin of the blues radically reexamined in a number of books, journal articles, and dissertations.

But while the facts are available to those who pursue them, the conventional mythology about rock's origins persists. To mark the fiftieth anniversary of Elvis Presley's first commercial recording, for example, *Time* magazine's website ran a story, under the headline "Elvis Rocks. But He's Not the First," that recycled such common misconceptions as that Jackie Brenston's "Rocket 88" was the first rock 'n' roll record, that rock was a direct offshoot of the blues, and that Presley hung out in black nightclubs while he was still in high school.[1] I feel it's time to set the record straight.

Chapter One

That's All Right

A WHITE MAN SOUNDS BLACK

On the summer Saturday in 1953 when Elvis Presley first walked into the Memphis Recording Service, ostensibly to make a record for his mother, he chose to sing a pair of lugubrious pop ballads—"My Happiness," a 1948 hit for Jon and Sandra Steele, the Pied Pipers, Ella Fitzgerald, the Marlin Sisters, and John Laurenz, and "That's When Your Heartaches Begin," a 1940 recording by the Ink Spots that had been reissued in 1952 and remade by the white pop singer Bob Lamm in 1951 and by the black doo-wop group Billy Bunn and His Buddies in 1952.[1] While cutting the double-sided acetate disc for Presley, Marion Keisker, the office manager, surreptitiously taped his performance in order to play it for Sam Phillips, who owned Sun Records as well as the Memphis Recording Service.

"Over and over I remember Sam saying, 'If I could find a white man who had the Negro sound and the Negro feel, I could make a billion dollars,'" Keisker later said. "This is what I heard in Elvis . . . this Negro sound."[2] Both she and Phillips heatedly denied the remark as Albert Goldman quoted it in his 1981 book *Elvis*: "If I could find a white boy who could sing like a nigger, I could make a million dollars."[3] Phillips also disputed Keisker's claim to have recorded the disc, saying that he was the one in the control booth.[4]

In 1957, Presley rerecorded "That's When Your Heartaches Begin" as the flip side of "All Shook Up," with the Jordanaires adding vocal harmonies. In 1960, a teenage band from Liverpool, not yet called the Beatles, made a rehearsal tape of the song, which eventually surfaced on bootleg cassettes and CDs. Presley's original acetate sides turned up in the attic of one of his high school friends in 1988 and were released on CDs in the 1990s.[5]

Listening to these earliest Elvis recordings today, it is nearly impossible to understand Keisker's reaction: the eighteen-year-old Presley does not sound black at all. At times he does seem to be imitating the Ink Spots' lead singer, Bill Kenny, but like many African American singers who successfully crossed over into the mainstream pop market, Kenny sounded white, scrupulously enunciating his words and rolling his *r*'s in a way that seems strained and artificial today.

Presley returned to the Memphis Recording Service in January 1954 and paid four dollars to record another pair of gooey ballads, both coauthored by the prolific Nashville songwriter Fred Rose. "I'll Never Stand in Your Way," written with Hy Heath, was a 1953 pop hit for Joni James. "It Wouldn't Be the Same (without You)," written with the singing movie cowboy Jimmy Wakely, was recorded between 1950 and 1952 by Al Rogers and the Rocky Mountain boys, Dude Martin and His Roundup Gang, and Lily Ann Carol, who'd sung with Louis Prima's band.

When Phillips finally had Keisker call Presley to audition for Sun at the end of June 1954, it was to record a ballad. Phillips had received a demo disc of a song called "Without You" that, according to Keisker, had been cut by "a Negro kid hanging around the studio."[6] But Phillips told Presley's biographer Peter Guralnick that the demo had been made by an inmate at the Tennessee State Penitentiary. Guralnick compares the voice on the demo to "a cross between the Ink Spots and a sentimental Irish tenor," adding that "there could have been nothing less overtly African-American-sounding than this particular acetate or this particular song."[7] In any case, Presley never recorded "Without You," but Phillips was sufficiently impressed with his failed audition to offer him another chance.

At his first meeting with guitarist Scotty Moore and bassist Bill Black, on July 4, 1954, Presley sang country, pop, and R&B ballads. His first two commercial studio recordings, made the following evening, were in the same vein. "Harbor Lights," a song introduced in 1937 by Rudy Vallee, had been revived in 1950 by Sammy Kaye, Guy Lombardo, Bing Crosby, and others. "I Love You Because" was a big country hit in 1950 both for its author, the blind Texas singer-songwriter Leon Payne, and for the great honky-tonk singer Ernest Tubb.

Presley evidently aspired to be a country-pop crooner, and though he earned the title King of Rock 'n' Roll with up-tempo rockers such as "Hound Dog" and "All Shook Up," he continued to sing and record ballads throughout his career. The vapid material of his later years is often ascribed to the malign influence of his manager, Col. Tom Parker, but before there was anyone to guide him, Elvis displayed a penchant for the syrupy and maudlin. If anything, it was Sam Phillips who steered him toward R&B and blues, which Phillips had been recording since he opened his studio in 1950.

Before he became a recording artist, Presley showed no inclination to sing rhythm-and-blues, other than ballads by the likes of the Ink Spots and Billy Eckstine. He would serenade his first girlfriend with Lonnie Johnson's ballad "Tomorrow Night," a No. 1 R&B hit in 1948 that crossed over to the pop charts, but he was doubtless unaware of Johnson's early blues recordings. He apparently amassed a considerable collection of rhythm-and-blues records, but it's not clear whether he acquired them before or after his first recording session.[8] Published reports that Presley frequented blues clubs on Beale Street in Memphis while still in high school were debunked by both Albert Goldman and Peter Guralnick.[9] He probably made his first visits to the clubs in 1955, and the striking photographs of Elvis with the Beale Street luminaries B. B. King, Bobby Bland, and Junior Parker were taken in 1956 and 1957, after Presley had already achieved stardom.

Presley's early exposure to live music came mainly through shows by white gospel quartets such as the Blackwood Brothers and the Statesmen. Although they were influenced to some extent by contemporary black gospel groups such as the Soul Stirrers, they sounded more like barbershop quartets, at least on their records. Months before his first visit to the Memphis Recording Service, Elvis began attending the church that the Blackwood Brothers belonged to, occasionally sneaking out to hear the service at a black church nearby. It was only when he began to record for Sun that he abandoned his dream of joining the Songfellows, a youthful quartet formed by a nephew of James Blackwood.

Radio was Presley's primary source of musical inspiration, but though he surely tuned in to the pioneering Memphis rhythm-and-blues station WDIA, his pre-Sun repertoire was largely drawn from pop singers such as Kay Starr, Teresa Brewer, Jo Stafford, Bing Crosby, Dean Martin, Eddie Fisher, and Perry Como, as well as country singers such as Hank Williams, Eddie Arnold, and Hank Snow.[10] By Scotty Moore's account, it was an inspired fluke that Presley's first release—the record that put him on the map—was an up-tempo R&B song. Having already cut "Harbor Lights" and "I Love You Because" on the evening of July 5, 1954, Presley, Moore, and Black were taking a midnight break when Elvis spontaneously began singing "That's All Right," a song recorded in 1946 by the Mississippi bluesman Arthur "Big Boy" Crudup. Black and Moore joined in, and Sam Phillips had the musicians start the number again so he could record it.[11]

In 1956, Presley told an interviewer for the British magazine *Hit Parade* that he "dug the real low-down Mississippi singers, mostly Big Bill Broonzy and Big Boy Cruddup [sic], although they would scold me at home for listening to them." He added that it was Phillips who suggested he do Crudup's material. "We talked about the Cruddup records I knew—'Cool Disposition,' 'Rock Me, Mama,' 'Hey, Mama,' 'Everything's All Right' [actually

'Hey Mama, Everything's All Right'], and others, but settled for 'That's All Right,' one of my top favourites."[12]

The same year, Presley told a reporter from the *Charlotte Observer*: "Down in Tupelo, Mississippi, I used to hear old Arthur Crudup bang his box like I do now, and I said if I ever get to the place where I could feel all old Arthur felt, I'd be a music man like no one ever saw."[13] A reluctant stage performer, Crudup had to be coaxed by Elmore James and Sonny Boy Williamson (Aleck "Rice" Miller) into playing a few club dates with them in Mississippi.[14] It's hardly possible that Elvis saw Crudup perform in Tupelo—clear across the state from Crudup's home in Silver City—before the Presley family moved from there to Memphis in 1948, when Elvis was thirteen. (The rhythm-and-blues singer Roy Brown went so far as to claim that the young Presley sang with Brown's band in Tupelo and then followed them to Tennessee.)[15]

Elvis may have heard "That's All Right" on the radio, but unlike Crudup's "Keep Your Arms Around Me," "I'm Gonna Dig Myself a Hole," or "So Glad You're Mine," it didn't make the national R&B charts.[16] Perhaps he heard the song at Charlie's, a record shop in Memphis where he would hang out.[17] Sam Phillips was certainly aware of Crudup, a forerunner of the electrified Delta blues that became popular among African Americans in the early 1950s, when Phillips began to record artists such as Howlin' Wolf.

Crudup's style was already anachronistic when he made his first record, "If I Get Lucky," in 1941. Commercial blues recordings had become polished and homogenized, but though he tried to keep up with contemporary trends and was one of the first bluesmen to play electric guitar, Crudup was essentially a throwback to the raw country blues of the 1920s. (Ironically, Crudup had been signed to the Bluebird label, RCA's "race" subsidiary, by Lester Melrose, the white artist-and-repertoire man chiefly responsible for the urbane blues sound of the swing era.) Still, his records were strong sellers, especially his 1945 hit "Rock Me Mamma." That song, based on Big Bill Broonzy's "Rockin' Chair Blues," from 1940, was recorded as "Rock Me Mama" by Big Joe Turner in 1941, as "Roll Me, Baby" by Tommy McClennan in 1942, as "Rockin' and Rollin'" by Lil' Son Jackson in 1951, as "Rock Me" by Muddy Waters in 1956, and as "Rock Me Baby" by B. B. King in 1964.

Crudup recycled the same melodies and lyrics over and over. "If I Get Lucky" begins with the line "That's all right, mama, that's all right for you," lifted from Blind Lemon Jefferson's 1926 classic "That Black Snake Moan." (Practically the same line appears on Little Brother Montgomery's "Something Keeps A-Worryin' Me," from 1936, Count Basie's "Boogie Woogie [I May Be Wrong]," from 1937, Big Joe Turner and Pete Johnson's "It's All Right Baby," from 1938, and Louis Jordan's "It's a Low Down Dirty Shame," from 1942.) Crudup's "Mean Old Frisco Blues," from 1942, has the same basic tune as "That's All Right," as does "Dirt Road Blues," from 1945, where Crudup alternates the title line, taken from Charlie Patton's 1929 recording of "Down the Dirt Road Blues," with the verses of "That's All Right." At one point, Crudup sings "big road" instead of "dirt road," an apparent reference to Tommy Johnson's 1928 "Big Road Blues."

Crudup's "That's All Right" is more of a bluesy R&B song than a true blues, as it doesn't quite follow the conventional twelve-bar blues structure. Crudup's voice is high and piercing, and he accompanies himself with jangling, choppy guitar chords over a rapid drumbeat and the surging pulse of an upright bass. Presley's drumless version is sweeter and more melodious, with a pronounced country-western flavor. Elvis stays close to the original lyrics but makes a few changes, substituting "Son, that gal you foolin' with, she ain't no good for you" for Crudup's "The life you livin', son, now women be the death of you." Contrary to some descriptions, Presley's tempo is no faster than Crudup's, and Crudup rocks harder.

Three nights after Presley cut "That's All Right," the disc jockey Dewey Phillips, Sam Phillips's friend and former business partner (but no relation), played an acetate advance pressing on his WHBQ radio show. Years later Dewey Phillips told an interviewer that "a lot of people listening had thought [Elvis] was colored."[18] If they did, it was probably because Phillips, although he was white himself, normally played only R&B records by black artists. The finished record was sent to country-western stations, which played mostly the flip side, a rocked-out take on Bill Monroe's bluegrass standard "Blue Moon of Kentucky." When Sam Phillips asked Fats Washington, a black R&B disc jockey, to play "That's All Right," Washington obliged but then said on the air that "this man should not be played after the sun comes up in the morning. It's so country."[19]

Each of Presley's next four Sun singles followed the same formula—an R&B song coupled with a country or pop song. "Good Rockin' Tonight," which Presley recorded in September 1954, had been a No. 1 rhythm-and-blues hit for Wynonie Harris in 1948. Although Harris's rendition is a cover of Roy Brown's 1947 original, it's often cited as the first rock 'n' roll record. Elvis's version, omitting the last two verses, was a local country hit but did not sell as well as "That's All Right."[20]

Presley's "Milkcow Blues Boogie," recorded in December 1954, is ultimately based on Kokomo Arnold's 1934 recording of "Milk Cow Blues" and not on any of the different songs with the same title recorded previously by Freddie Spruell, Sleepy John Estes, and Big Bill Broonzy. Arnold's song was popular enough to be covered not only by such bluesmen as Josh White and Bumble Bee Slim (both in 1935) but by the western-swing bandleader Cliff Bruner (in 1937) and the swing bandleader Bob Crosby (in 1938). On Johnnie Lee Wills's 1941 western-swing version, fiddler Cotton Thompson sings a jumbled abridgement that's the same as Presley's except for the final verse.

But Elvis most likely heard the very similar 1947 rendition recorded exclusively for radio play by Johnnie Lee's better-known older brother, bandleader Bob Wills, where all the verses match Presley's.

Presley's hiccuping, high-spirited "Baby Let's Play House," recorded in February 1955, easily outshines the Nashville bluesman Arthur Gunter's laid-back original, his only R&B hit, recorded just a few months earlier (and covered by a doo-wop group, the Thunderbirds, even before Elvis got to it). Although Gunter's song was inspired mainly by Eddie Arnold's "I Wanna Play House with You," a No. 1 country hit in 1951, it shares an insistent refrain—"Come back baby, come"—with Doctor Ross's "Come Back Baby," which Sam Phillips had produced in 1953. But Arthur Crudup had recorded a nearly identical "Come Back Baby" in 1946, on the same date he recorded "That's All Right."[21] In any event, "Baby Let's Play House" was Elvis's first national hit, reaching the Top 10 on *Billboard* magazine's country chart.

Presley's last Sun single, recorded in July 1955, was "Mystery Train," which Junior Parker had cut for Sun in October 1953 with his band the Blue Flames. As Greil Marcus points out in his 1975 book *Mystery Train,* the first line of the song—"Train I ride, sixteen coaches long"—is found on the Carter Family's 1930 country classic "Worried Man Blues."[22] The line also turns up on various recorded versions of traditional country ballads such as "In the Pines," "Nine Hundred Miles," and "Who Will Shoe Your Pretty Little Foot," with the number of coaches ranging from fifteen to one hundred.

The Carter Family is said to have learned "Worried Man Blues" from its composer, Esley Riddle, a black musician who would accompany the family patriarch, A. P. Carter, on his regular expeditions in search of folk songs to record.[23] But another song with the same title, including the signature line "I'm worried now but I won't be worried long," was recorded in 1927 by an obscure blues singer named John D. Fox, accompanied on guitar by Crying Sam Collins.

The label on Presley's "Mystery Train" gives the songwriting credits to Junior Parker and Sam Phillips, but Parker was probably the sole author. Producer Johnny Vincent claimed to have recorded the song with Parker in 1952 for the Champion label, but no copy of that record has ever surfaced.[24] Parker's first Sun single, "Feelin' Good," was an R&B hit, but "Mystery Train" (credited only to Parker on the label) was not, and Parker signed a contract with the Duke label shortly after its release. In response, Phillips successfully sued Duke's owner, Don Robey, acquiring half the publishing royalties to "Mystery Train" at around the same time.[25]

Years later Phillips told interviewers it was Parker's "Mystery Train" that first attracted Presley to Sun Records, although this seems unlikely, given Elvis's original choice of ballad material.[26] Presley's "Mystery Train" is smoother, faster, and more mellifluous than Parker's, dispensing with the Blue Flames' chugging rhythm and train-whistle sax. It was a hit on country radio, but the flip side, "I Forgot to Remember to Forget," a mawkish C&W ballad written by the steel guitarist Stan Kesler and the rockabilly singer Charlie Feathers, propelled the single to No. 1 on the national country charts.[27]

Reviewing "That's All Right" in August 1954, a *Billboard* writer described Presley as "a potent new chanter who can sock over a tune for either the country or the r.&b. markets."[28] But though he subsequently visited a few blues clubs, Elvis was marketed strictly as a country artist, performing on the *Grand Ole Opry* and *Louisiana Hayride* radio shows and touring the South with Hank Snow and the group that succeeded the Carter Family—the Carter Sisters and Mother Maybelle. Not until after he'd left Sun did Presley cross over to the pop and rhythm-and-blues charts with his first RCA single, "Heartbreak Hotel," a torchy rhythmic ballad loosely based on Roy Brown's No. 1 R&B hit from 1950, "Hard Luck Blues."

ROCK 'N' ROLL ARRIVES

Nevertheless, Greil Marcus asserts in *Mystery Train* that "Elvis was the first young Southern white to sing rock 'n' roll, something he copied from no one but made up on the spot."[29] The qualifier "southern" is apparently meant to exclude the Michigan-born Bill Haley, who in June 1951 covered "Rocket 88," a No. 1 R&B hit earlier that year for Jackie Brenston and His Delta Cats. It was Sam Phillips who recorded Brenston's hit, but since Phillips had yet to found the Sun label, he sent the master disc to Chess Records in Chicago. Like Wynonie Harris's "Good Rockin' Tonight," Brenston's "Rocket 88" is often cited as the first rock 'n' roll record, although it is also adapted from an earlier song, in this case Jimmy Liggins's "Cadillac Boogie."

Like Scotty Moore and Bill Black, who were in a group called the Starlite Wranglers when they met Presley, Haley performed western swing before turning to rock 'n' roll. Inspired by singing cowboys such as Gene Autry and Elton Britt, he learned to yodel and formed a band in Chester, Pennsylvania, called the Four Aces of Western Swing, later changing the name to the Saddlemen. His first recordings, for Jack Howard's Cowboy label in 1948, were strictly country, including songs by Hank Williams and Red Foley. After cutting his steel-guitar-flavored "Rocket 88" at the instigation of producer Dave Miller, Haley continued to record in a "hillbilly boogie" style, or as Haley called it, "cowboy jive."[30]

In early 1952, Haley covered another R&B song, "Rock the Joint," a 1949 hit for Jimmy Preston that's apparently based on Nelson Alexander's "Rock That Voot," from the previous year. Both songs are in the same mold as

"Good Rockin' Tonight," but "Rock the Joint" is considerably more raucous. Haley heard Preston's record while working as a disc jockey at a Chester radio station, where another white disc jockey was using it as the theme for his rhythm-and-blues show.[31]

By the time Haley recorded "Rock the Joint" for Dave Miller's fledgling Essex label, it had already been covered by Chris Powell and the Five Blue Flames, a black group from Philadelphia (in late 1949), and by Jimmy Cavallo and His House Rockers, a white group from upstate New York (in 1951). Powell and Cavallo both copied Preston's original more closely than Haley, who countrified and bowdlerized the lyrics, replacing Preston's "We're gonna hucklebuck, we're gonna jitterbug" with "Do an Old Paul Jones and a Virginia reel" and excising such lines as "Just keep on drinkin', we're gonna ball tonight."

Haley's "Rock the Joint," much stiffer than Preston's but with a bracing slap-bass rhythm and a hot guitar solo by Danny Cedrone, was released as the B-side of the country ballad "Icy Heart," but it got so much airplay that Haley abandoned his cowboy outfits and changed his band's name from the Saddlemen to the Comets. He scored a Top 20 pop hit the following year with his own R&B-style composition "Crazy Man, Crazy," also on Essex; the flip side, "Whatcha Gonna Do," foreshadows Carl Perkins's "Blue Suede Shoes" with the opening line "One for the money, two for the show, three to get ready, and here I go." Also in 1953, Haley wrote "Rock-a-Beatin' Boogie" for Danny Cedrone, who recorded it with his own band, the Esquire Boys; a black rhythm-and-blues group, the Treniers, covered it the same year.

James Myers, a Philadelphia music publisher and promoter, offered Haley a song he claimed to have cowritten under the pen name Jimmy DeKnight with lyricist Max Freedman, but Freedman was likely the sole composer.[32] Freedman had previously cowritten "Sioux City Sue" with singer Dick Thomas, who scored a No. 1 country hit with it in 1945. The following year, Gene Autry made a movie titled after that song, but by then there were so many versions of "Sioux City Sue" in circulation, including a Top 10 pop hit by Bing Crosby, that Autry's soundtrack rendition was not released on record.[33] The name "Sioux City Sue" appears in the lyrics of "Good Rockin' Tonight" (though not in Presley's abridged version), together with those of the song-title heroines "Sweet Lorraine," "Sweet Georgia Brown," and "Caldonia."

Myers and Freedman's song, "Rock Around the Clock," is essentially a reworking of "Rock the Joint," with lyrics seemingly adapted from Wynonie Harris's 1945 record "Around the Clock." (Harris's song also inspired Arthur Crudup's "So Glad You're Mine," from 1946, which Elvis Presley covered ten years later, and Chuck Berry's "Reelin' and Rockin'," from 1958.) The melody on the verses of "Rock Around the Clock" is almost identical to the one on Hank Williams's first hit, "Move It On Over," from 1947, which Williams may have taken from the country singer Buddy Jones's 1941 recording of "Red Wagon." That song is based on the black bandleader Richard M. Jones's composition "Little Red Wagon," which the blues singer Georgia White recorded in 1936 with Jones on piano and Les Paul on guitar. Charlie Patton's "Going to Move to Alabama," recorded in 1929, has a similar melody, based in turn on the tune of the 1927 hit "Jim Jackson's Kansas City Blues."

Arthur Crudup borrowed Jones's title line for his own blues "That's Your Red Wagon" in 1945, and Bob Wills cut Jones's song in western-swing style as "It's Your Red Wagon" on a radio-play-only disc in 1946. In 1947, two years after Jones's death, two white songwriters, Gene DePaul and Don Raye, adapted his song as "Your Red Wagon," which was sung by Marie Bryant in the Nicholas Ray–directed film noir *They Live by Night* and recorded by Ray McKinley, the Andrews Sisters, and Count Basie with Jimmy Rushing, among others.

Two R&B records titled "Rock Around the Clock" had previously been released, Hal "Cornbread" Singer's in 1950 and Wally Mercer's in 1952. Mercer's is an entirely different song, but Singer's "Rock Around the Clock," cowritten by Singer and Sam Theard, resembles Myers and Freedman's and contains the line "One for the money, two for the show, three make ready, four let's go." Haley performed "Rock Around the Clock" in clubs in 1953, but because Dave Miller disliked James Myers, he would not allow Haley to record it on Essex. "Three times I took the tune into the recording studio and put it on the music rack, and every time Miller would see it, he'd come in and tear it up and throw it away," Haley recounted.[34]

In early 1954, Myers produced a callow, amateurish recording of "Rock Around the Clock" by Sonny Dae and His Knights, led by a Philadelphia drummer whose real name was Paschal Vennitti. In March, after it was released on Jack Howard's Arcade label, *Billboard,* in its Reviews of New R&B Records, commented, "Effort has an insistent beat. . . . Could attract some juke coin."[35] But the disc got only regional exposure and quickly disappeared. When Haley's contract with Essex expired the following month, he signed with Decca Records; on April 12, three months before Elvis Presley cut "That's All Right," he recorded "(We're Gonna) Rock Around the Clock" in New York, with Danny Cedrone duplicating his guitar solo from "Rock the Joint." But though Decca was a major label, "Rock Around the Clock"—released as the B-side of "Thirteen Women," Haley's cover of an R&B record by Dickie Thompson—did not sell as well as "Crazy Man, Crazy," at least initially.

Haley's next single, recorded in June 1954, was a cover of Big Joe Turner's "Shake, Rattle and Roll," a No. 1 R&B hit recorded a few months earlier. The song had been written under the name Charles Calhoun by the

Atlantic Records composer-arranger Jesse Stone, a black man born in 1901 who began singing in his family's traveling minstrel act when he was four years old. Stone may have been familiar with Memphis Minnie and Kansas Joe's 1931 record "Shake Mattie," with the chorus, "Shake, Mattie, shake, rattle, and roll / I can't get enough love, satisfy my soul." He could have remembered a shimmy-era number called "Shake, Rattle and Roll" that was written and recorded in 1919 by Al Bernard, a white singer from New Orleans who performed in blackface.[36] He might even have heard the ragtime hit "You Got to Shake, Rattle and Roll," published in 1910 by the African American vaudeville singer and comedian H. Franklin "Baby" Seals. (Both Bernard's and Seals's songs refer to shooting craps.)

At the behest of the Decca producer Milt Gabler, Haley changed Stone's lyrics to eliminate anything that might deter pop radio programmers, who were touchier than their R&B counterparts. "I believe to my soul you a devil in nylon hose" became "I believe you're doin' me wrong and now I know." But Haley was truer to the original than he'd been on "Rock the Joint." Gabler, who had produced records by Louis Jordan and the Ink Spots, gave "Shake, Rattle and Roll" a crisp, horn-heavy arrangement that was closer to genuine rhythm-and-blues than anything Haley had recorded before. "We'd begin with Jordan's shuffle rhythm," Gabler remembered. "I'd sing Jordan riffs to the group that would be picked up by the electric guitars."[37] Turner's record crossed over to the pop charts in August 1954 but was quickly eclipsed by Haley's, which reached the Top 10. (Elvis Presley recorded a rapid-fire rockabilly take on "Shake, Rattle and Roll" for RCA in February 1956, including both the "nylon hose" and "now I know" lines, but it never charted.)

The movie *Blackboard Jungle* was released in March 1955, with Haley's "Rock Around the Clock" blaring over the opening credits. Based on a semi-autobiographical novel by Evan Hunter, the film tells the story of an inner-city high school teacher beleaguered by student hoodlums. In a memorable scene, another teacher brings his valuable collection of jazz records to class; when he plays Bix Beiderbecke's "The Jazz Me Blues," one student protests, "How 'bout some bop?" Others demand Frank Sinatra or Joni James. The lead delinquent begins smashing the brittle 78s, reading the titles—"Cow-Cow Boogie," "Cherokee," "Clap Hands, Here Comes Charlie," "Blue Moon"—before throwing them against the wall. Another ruffian puts what sounds like a Stan Kenton record on the turntable (it's not Kenton's "Invention for Guitar and Trumpet," which is listed in the credits), and the students dance and drum to the rhythm. But though the pioneering disc jockey Alan Freed was already calling his rhythm-and-blues radio show a *Rock 'n' Roll Party* and hosting concerts under the rock 'n' roll rubric, no one requests any R&B records or uses the term "rock 'n' roll."

By the summer of 1955, "Rock Around the Clock" topped the pop charts. This was the moment when rock 'n' roll exploded into the national consciousness, and also the moment when the music became firmly associated with adolescent rebellion. Riots broke out at theaters where *Blackboard Jungle* was screened and at concerts where Haley appeared, and rock 'n' roll was denounced as vulgar and immoral by politicians, clergymen, psychologists, white racists, and older musicians who—rightly, as it turned out—feared for their livelihoods.

At a time when Elvis Presley's music had scarcely been heard outside the South, "Rock Around the Clock" defined the sound of rock 'n' roll in the minds of the general public. With its one-note saxophone riffs over crude approximations of a boogie-woogie bass line and a shuffle drumbeat, the song is a tame imitation of rhythm-and-blues. Billy Williamson's steel guitar is hidden under Joey D'Ambrosio's tenor sax, masking its C&W flavor; only Danny Cedrone's fleet guitar solo offers any semblance of virtuosity. Haley's plain-vanilla vocals are as nonthreatening as they are unconvincing, and the lyrics ("Put your glad rags on, join me, hon") pointedly avoid African American slang. But the mix is unusually hot for its time, with Billy Gussak's splashy, oddly accented drumming right up front. (Haley only added a drummer after recording "Rock the Joint" in 1952; Presley used drummers on his last two Sun singles in 1955, but only on the country sides.)

Black jump-blues and doo-wop hits, from Lucky Millinder's "Who Threw the Whiskey in the Well" in 1945 to the Dominoes' "Sixty-Minute Man" in 1951 and the Chords' "Sh-Boom" in 1954, had occasionally crossed over to the pop charts. The Crew-Cuts' painfully white cover version of "Sh-Boom" had been a No. 1 pop hit in 1954, as had the Fontane Sisters' cover of the Charms' "Hearts of Stone" in early 1955. But Haley's "Rock Around the Clock" kicked the door wide open for black and white rockers alike. Between July 1955 and January 1956, Fats Domino's "Ain't It a Shame," Chuck Berry's "Maybellene," and Little Richard's "Tutti-Frutti" all crossed over, although the first and last of these were outsold by Pat Boone's lame cover versions. Presley's "Heartbreak Hotel" hit the pop charts in March 1956, at the same time as Carl Perkins's "Blue Suede Shoes." The Everly Brothers' "Bye Bye Love," Jerry Lee Lewis's "Whole Lot of Shakin' Going On," and the Crickets' "That'll Be the Day" (featuring Buddy Holly) followed in 1957.

In December 1955, Haley cut his last Top 10 hit, "See You Later, Alligator," originally recorded earlier that fall as "Later Alligator" by the Cajun singer Bobby Charles, who may have adapted it from the New Orleans bluesman Guitar Slim's 1954 single "Later for You Baby." (Charles's record briefly made the R&B charts, although he was white.) Haley then gradually faded away, although he remained popular in England. John Lennon, in his final interview, told the *Playboy* magazine writer David Sheff that "Rock Around the Clock" had inspired him to pursue a musical career. "I enjoyed

Bill Haley, but I wasn't overwhelmed by him," Lennon added. "It wasn't until 'Heartbreak Hotel' that I really got into it." It was Lennon, of course, who is said to have said, "Before Elvis, there was nothing," although this widely circulated quotation appears to be apocryphal.

But Haley may not have been the first white rock 'n' roll singer, nor Presley the first young southern white rock 'n' roll singer, unless one simply defines rock 'n' roll as the music they sang. In 1950, at the age of twenty-five, the Alabama-born Hardrock Gunter released "Gonna Dance All Night," with the refrain "We're gonna rock and roll while we dance all night." With Gunter talk-singing the lyrics like a square dance caller, the song is mediocre, enlivened only by intermittent boogie piano. It doesn't really rock in a modern sense, and neither does the speedier, jazzier update Gunter recorded for Sam Phillips, which was released on Sun in May 1954, two month's before Presley's "That's All Right." (In August 1951, two months after Bill Haley cut "Rocket 88," Gunter covered the Dominoes' "Sixty-Minute Man," including the line "I'll rock 'em, roll 'em all night long," as a duet with Roberta Lee.)

Gunter's first "Gonna Dance All Night" was the follow-up to his 1950 debut record, "Birmingham Bounce," on the Bama label. When Bama refused an offer from Decca to buy or lease that record, Decca had Red Foley cover "Birmingham Bounce"; Foley's version, a fairly close copy of Gunter's, became a No. 1 country hit and crossed over to the pop charts. More than twenty other versions followed, by artists such as Lionel Hampton, Tommy Dorsey, Pee Wee King, Tex Williams, and Amos Milburn. While Milburn's breathless R&B rendition swings fiercely, driven by frantic saxophones, Gunter's "Birmingham Bounce" is just a better-than-average example of post–World War II hillbilly boogie. But with its boogie bass line, muted backbeat, and lyrics featuring the words "boogie," "jump," and "rockin'," it might qualify as rock 'n' roll, if only barely.

By the early 1950s, hillbilly boogies were no longer novel. Boogie-woogie fever had swept America in the late 1930s and early 1940s, as swing bands adopted the rhythmic bass lines popularized by black piano players a decade earlier. Western swing, country music's fiddle-driven answer to big-band jazz, followed suit. In 1941, a western-swing combo called the Village Boys recorded "Boogie Woogie in the Village," an instrumental featuring pianist Mancel Tierney. Several country boogies came out in 1945, including Arthur Smith's "Guitar Boogie," which inspired the Delmore Brothers "Hillbilly Boogie" the following year. Boogie tunes proliferated on the country charts in the late 1940s, culminating in the tremendous success of Red Foley's "Chattanoogie Shoe Shine Boy," which topped both the country and pop charts in early 1950, just before Gunter cut "Birmingham Bounce."

Bill Haley's "Green Tree Boogie," from 1951, and "Sundown Boogie," from early 1952, are typical of the genre, and both prefigure "Rock Around the Clock." "Sundown Boogie," Haley's last record before "Rock the Joint," opens with the words, "Takes a rockin' chair to rock, takes a rubber ball to roll," a line that appears on Ma Rainey's 1924 recording "Jealous Hearted Blues" and on "Jim Jackson's Kansas City Blues" (Jackson's song also shares its twelve-bar verse-and-refrain structure with "Rock Around the Clock"). The main differences between Haley's songs before and after "Rock the Joint" are the addition of drums and the increasing use of words such as "rock" and "gone," as in "real gone." Still, these incremental changes, if only for lack of anything more substantial, can be interpreted as marking the approximate moment when white rock 'n' roll was born.

But while rock today is as nearly all-white as country music, rock 'n' roll is unquestionably an African American invention. One may agree with the bandleader Louis Jordan, one of the music's true forefathers, who in 1973 told the author Arnold Shaw, "Rock 'n' roll was not a marriage of rhythm and blues and country and western. That's white publicity. Rock 'n' roll was just a white imitation, a white adaptation of Negro rhythm and blues."[38] Or one may accept the more equivocal view of Nick Tosches, who writes in his book *Unsung Heroes of Rock 'n' Roll* that "rock 'n' roll was not created solely by blacks. . . . It evolved slowly, wrought by blacks and by whites."[39] But even if one acknowledges that whites made important contributions to the development of rock and that blacks assimilated many elements of white music—or at least reappropriated white borrowings—it is incontrovertible that black rhythm-and-blues formed the primary basis for what became known as rock 'n' roll.

The term "rock 'n' roll" was given currency by Alan Freed, who introduced it as a substitute for the racially identified label "rhythm-and-blues." A number of other white disc jockeys (as well as black ones), mostly in the South, had been broadcasting R&B radio programs even before 1949, when *Billboard* replaced the word "race" with "rhythm-and-blues" on its black music charts. In 1951, Freed began hosting a rhythm-and-blues show in Cleveland, playing records almost exclusively by black artists. Among the exceptions were Johnny Otis, a white bandleader who passed for black, and Louis Hardin, a blind, eccentric composer and street musician whose 1950 recording of "Moondog's Symphony," featuring a wolf baying over clattering percussion, became the background music over which Freed announced the opening of his show.

Hardin, who routinely stood at attention on a Manhattan street corner dressed as a Viking, had adopted the name Moondog, as did Freed, who called his program the *Moondog House*. After Freed began broadcasting from New York in September 1954, Hardin sued him over the use of the name and won, forcing Freed to retitle his show. Seeking to reach young whites, he named it the *Rock 'n' Roll Party*, although he still referred to the music he played as "blues and rhythm."[40]

While still in Cleveland, Freed began promoting concerts such as the "Biggest Rhythm and Blues Show" in 1953, which featured Wynonie Harris, Ruth Brown, the Clovers, Buddy Johnson and His Orchestra, and the jazz saxophonist Lester Young. The concerts, like Freed's radio show, attracted almost entirely black audiences.[41] Not until January 1955, when Freed presented his first New York concert, the "Rock 'n' Roll Jubilee Ball," did significant numbers of whites turn out, although the artists on that bill—including Fats Domino, Big Joe Turner, Clyde McPhatter and the Drifters, Ruth Brown, Charles Brown, Varetta Dillard, Dakota Staton, Danny Overbea, Red Prysock, the Clovers, the Harptones, the Moonglows, and Ella Johnson with Buddy Johnson and His Orchestra—were all black.[42]

Ten years later, none of the "Jubilee Ball" performers but the Drifters (minus Clyde McPhatter) could be found on the pop or R&B charts; with a few exceptions, the only black artists still associated with the term "rock 'n' roll" were oldies acts. Just one week after Freed's historic New York concert, Ray Charles's "I've Got a Woman" entered *Billboard*'s R&B chart, quickly becoming Charles's first No. 1 hit. It was based on a gospel record Charles heard on the radio, probably the Southern Tones' "It Must Be Jesus," from 1954. Black gospel songs and spirituals had influenced both black and white secular music since Reconstruction, but by the end of the 1960s, the sacred-turned-profane style that Charles helped pioneer so dominated the rhythm-and-blues scene that *Billboard* replaced the heading "R&B" with "soul" on its black music charts.

Early rock 'n' roll was praised and denounced for promoting racial integration, especially in the South, where segregation laws were still in force. But after a brief period during which young Americans seemed to share a common enthusiasm for the music—Presley's "Hound Dog," for example, topped the pop, country, and R&B charts simultaneously in 1956—blacks largely abandoned it, as did country musicians and fans. Rock 'n' roll was initially embraced by working-class teenagers across the racial spectrum, but with the British Invasion of the mid-1960s, "rock music," as it was increasingly called, acquired upward mobility, appealing to a new generation of college students whose immediate predecessors had strummed folk guitars or grooved to cool jazz.

A scene from Presley's 1957 movie *Jailhouse Rock* illuminates the class conflict inherent in early rock 'n' roll. Presley's character, an ex-convict turned rock singer named Vince Everett, is taken to a party given by the parents of his manager/girlfriend, whose father is a college professor. The guests discuss modern jazz, mentioning Dave Brubeck, Paul Desmond, and Lennie Tristano. "I say atonality is just a passing phase in jazz music," says one woman. "What do you think, Mr. Everett?" Elvis responds, "Lady, I don't know what the hell you talkin' about," and storms out of the house. In his "Rock and Roll Music," released a month after Presley's film and its title song, Chuck Berry offers a more nuanced opinion: "I have no kick against modern jazz / Unless they try to play it too darn fast / And change the beauty of the melody / Until it sounds just like a symphony."

For the folkies of the early 1960s, rock 'n' roll represented commercialism at its crassest. Peter, Paul and Mary, the most popular group in America when the Beatles arrived in early 1964, released the double-album *In Concert* later that year, including a comedy treatment of "Blue," an anonymous folk song found among whites and blacks in the South under such titles as "Old Blue," "Oh, Blue," and "Old Dog Blue." Peter Yarrow introduces it as a children's song, and the three singers harmonize the line "I had a dog and his name was Blue / I betcha five dollars he's a good dog, too" with their usual high-spirited insipidity. Suddenly, Yarrow interrupts, asking, "What if this song were to be changed, modified by an unscrupulous modifier of folk songs, whose business it is to make this type of song palatable for the teenage, delinquent, mother-my-dog instinct? And then it would be a rock 'n' roll song." The trio breaks into a doo-wop parody, complete with a spoken interlude in which Paul Stookey asks, "Why did you leave me, sweetheart? / Blue, you promised to write."

The performance drips with inadvertent irony. *In Concert* was a Top 10 album, outselling most rock records of the day. The song itself has been the subject of many commercial recordings, beginning with Jim Jackson's "Old Dog Blue" in February 1928, which appears on the landmark 1952 compilation *Anthology of American Folk Music*. Other versions include blues (Furry Lewis, Lonnie Pitchford), bluegrass (the Dillards), country (T. Texas Tyler, Grandpa Jones, Willie Nelson), pop (Frankie Laine), and rock interpretations (the Byrds, J. J. Cale), in addition to renditions by folk revivalists such as Pete Seeger, Burl Ives, Joan Baez, Dave Van Ronk, Ian and Sylvia, Odetta, Tom Rush, Bob Gibson and Bob Camp, Glenn Yarbrough, and Ramblin' Jack Elliott. But Peter, Paul and Mary leave out the poignant verses, found even in children's versions, that describe the dog's illness, death, and burial.

Bob Dylan's controversial plugged-in appearance at the 1965 Newport Folk Festival turned the musical tide, and by September 1967, PP&M were eating crow and liking it with their Top 10 single "I Dig Rock and Roll Music." A month later, the first issue of *Rolling Stone* magazine hit the racks; its cofounder, the longtime *San Francisco Chronicle* jazz and pop music columnist Ralph Gleason, was one of the few critics who had not dismissed rock 'n' roll out of hand in the 1950s. *Crawdaddy!* a self-described "magazine of rock and roll criticism," had made its debut in February 1966. Before that, rock was generally held to be beneath serious criticism.

Rock critics of the late 1960s were in the vanguard of the "new journalism," in which pretensions of omniscient objectivity gave way to first-person, often-drug-enhanced perceptions expressed through the techniques of fiction. It was in this heady atmosphere that rock 'n' roll acquired a consciousness of its history, viewed through psychedelic lenses and filtered through the radical sensibilities of the day. In his 1969 book *The Story of Rock,* one of the earliest histories of the music, the Brandeis University professor Carl Belz characterizes rock 'n' roll as a "folk idiom" born out of the integration of pop, country, and rhythm-and-blues.[43] In *Rock: From the Beginning,* published the same year, the British writer Nik Cohn describes rock as "a mixture of two traditions—Negro rhythm 'n' blues and white romantic crooning."[44]

The notion that Jackie Brenston's "Rocket 88" was the first rock 'n' roll record came up around that time. "The first rock record is the original version of 'Sh-Boom' by the Chords," Belz asserts. Although he notes that the Crows' "Gee," a similar doo-wop record, crossed over to the pop charts earlier in 1954, Belz does not mention "Rocket 88" at all—or, for that matter, Wynonie Harris's "Good Rockin' Tonight."[45] But in his 1970 history, *The Sound of the City,* Charlie Gillett, who gives "Good Rockin' Tonight" only a passing mention, describes "Rocket 88" as "a fast boogie dance song that is one of the several records that people in the music business cite as 'the first rock 'n' roll record.'"[46]

Brenston himself made no claims of originality, admitting to the writer Jim O'Neal: "I come up with 'Rocket 88' because I had been doing a thing Jimmy Liggins had did some years ago called 'Cadillac Boogie.' So if you listen to the two, you'll find out they're both basically the same. The words are just changed."[47] Brenston was the baritone saxophonist with Ike Turner's Kings of Rhythm when he cut his only hit. Although the band was from Clarksdale, Mississippi, the musicians tried to emulate the jump blues of Louis Jordan and other urban bandleaders. Brenston would probably not have sung on "Rocket 88" if the Kings' regular singer, Johnny O'Neal, hadn't just left the group, which was renamed the Delta Cats for the occasion.

As the band arrived at the Memphis Recording Service, guitarist Willie Kizart's amplifier fell and broke. "I stuffed a little paper in there where the speaker cone was ruptured, and it sounded good," Sam Phillips later told the critic Robert Palmer.[48] Kizart's distorted guitar, playing a boogie riff handled by the horn section in "Cadillac Boogie," became the vamping backbone of "Rocket 88." Besides the switch from Cadillac to Oldsmobile (which introduced its "rocket" V-8 engine in 1949), Brenston's song is distinguished from Liggins's chiefly by its crudity. The five Delta Cats sound ragged and raw compared to Liggins's sleekly arranged eight-piece Drops of Joy, with the Cats' Raymond Hill blowing a rough, squealing tenor-sax solo in place of Harold Land's sophisticated quasi-bebop break. While the gravel-throated Liggins spouts hepcat jive ("Keep rollin', jack, makin' time / That cat's purrin', got eight kittens cryin'), Brenston keeps it down-to-earth ("Goin' round the corner and get a fifth / Everybody in my car's gonna take a little nip").

Recorded in November 1947, between Roy Brown's and Wynonie Harris's "Good Rockin' Tonight" sessions, "Cadillac Boogie" has a similar melody. Released as the flip side of Liggins's Top 10 R&B hit "Teardrop Blues," it's all but forgotten today, while Brenston's "Rocket 88" is still widely regarded as the fountainhead of rock 'n' roll. One of the reasons is surely that Kizart's broken amp anticipated the sound of the fuzz box, which was in its heyday when "Rocket 88" was rediscovered, having been popularized by Davie Allan and the Arrows' recording of "Blue's Theme" for the soundtrack of the 1966 biker movie *Wild Angels*.

THE MEANING OF ROCK

The idea that the term "rock 'n' roll" originated as a sexual euphemism is also a product of the 1960s, when Americans discovered sex in something like the sense that Columbus discovered America. Sex surpassed drugs, rock 'n' roll, and revolutionary politics as the leading obsession of the decade, and sexual implications were perceived even where none existed. But in the case of rock 'n' roll, the connotation was real. Henry Glover, who produced many of Wynonie Harris's records for the King label, said, "They had a definition in those days of the word 'rock' meaning the sex act."[49] Ralph Bass, another King producer at the time, concurred: "We weren't talkin' about rock 'n' rollin'; we were talkin' about sex."[50]

The first reference to "rockin' and rollin'" in recorded music, however, occurs in the pseudo-religious context of "The Camp Meeting Jubilee," recorded on a one-sided ten-inch disc for the Victor Talking Machine Company's Monarch label in 1904 by one of the most popular vocal-harmony groups of the barbershop era, the Haydn Quartet, who were known for, among other things, minstrel-show songs. The performance is a crude white parody of a black revival meeting, complete with mock preaching and call-and-response singing, and it includes the rousing chorus "Keep on rockin' and rollin' in your arms / Rockin' and rollin' in your arms / Rockin' and rollin' in your arms / In the arms of Moses." The same song was recorded around 1916 by a company called Little Wonder, which put out a line of cheap, short (five and a half inches) one-sided discs in tacit collaboration with Columbia Records, using some of Columbia's big-name artists without crediting them. The "Male Quartette" cited on the label of Little Wonder's "The Camp Meeting Jubilee" has been identified as the Peerless Quartet, another leading white harmony group.[51]

The first recorded pop song to include the words "rock" and "roll" was Trixie Smith's bluesy "My Man Rocks Me (with One Steady Roll)," from

1922, and here the meaning is plainly sexual. (Smith also anticipates "Rock Around the Clock" with such lines as "I looked at the clock and the clock struck one / I said, 'Now, daddy, ain't we got fun.'") But on "Moonshine Blues," recorded the following year, Ma Rainey sings, "You'll find me reelin' and a-rockin', howlin' like a hound," describing her inebriated condition. On "Leavin' This Morning," from 1928, Rainey sings, "See me reelin' and rockin', drunk as I can be."

Lil Johnson's "Rock That Thing," from 1929, is a variation of "Papa" Charlie Jackson's 1925 hit "Shake That Thing," an influential number (covered the same year by Ethel Waters, thirty years later by Wynonie Harris, and many times in between) that prefigured the hokum songs of the late 1920s and early 1930s. But whether the word is "rock" or "shake," the reference is to dancing rather than sex, even though hokum songs were filled with lascivious double entendres and Lil Johnson practically made a career out of them.

In 1926, Clara Smith, billed as "The World's Champion Moaner," recorded "Rock, Church, Rock," a slow drag with the refrain "Rock, church, rock, everybody start reelin'." Closer to blues than to gospel, the song has little religious content beyond the word "church," but there are no obvious sexual overtones to the word "rock." In 1928, Blind Willie Davis cut "Rock of Ages"—not the familiar English hymn with words written in 1776 by Augustus Montague Toplady and music added in 1830 by Thomas Hastings, which was made into a hit record in 1914 by the famed soprano Alma Gluck, but an American folk version found among both blacks and whites. Powered by plangent guitar chords similar to those of Appalachian folk singers, Davis's record could surely be said to rock, but not to a rock 'n' roll beat. (The British band Def Leppard did record a rock 'n' roll treatment of Toplady and Hastings's "Rock of Ages" in 1983.)

A number of religious songs using the word "rock" or "roll" predate the recorded era. "Rock o' My Soul" and "Roll, Jordan, Roll" are both included in *Slave Songs of the United States,* the groundbreaking compilation of African American spirituals and folk songs published in 1867. (Peter, Paul and Mary recorded "Rock o' My Soul" on their *In Concert* album as "Oh, Rock My Soul," copyrighted in Peter Yarrow's name.) In 1959, the eminent folklorist Alan Lomax recorded a group led by Willis Proctor on the Georgia Sea Island of St. Simons singing "Daniel," with the line "Rock, believer, rock." The intensely rhythmic call-and-response chant, accompanied by handclapping that brings to mind Afro-Cuban percussion, is apparently a surviving example of the "shout," a circle dance dating back to the era of slavery and first described in 1845 near St. Simons.[52]

A variation of the same chant was recorded for the Library of Congress in the late 1920s under the title "Rock Daniel," with the singer credited only as H. Jones.[53] Another variation, performed by a group led by the Rev. C. H. Savage, was recorded in Coahoma County, Mississippi, in 1941 by Alan

Lomax, John W. Work, and Lewis Jones. Work wrote: "The favorite pastime of the religious was the Rock Daniel. At church entertainments, after the quilting, or at parties given by religious people, the rock was a prominent feature. A man and a woman facing each other would place their hands on each other's shoulders and rock, while singing familiar religious songs. Sometimes at the conclusion of a church service, the members would remain and have a rock."[54]

Also in 1941, Sister Rosetta Tharpe, a gospel singer who played bluesy, jazzy guitar, recorded "Rock Daniel" in swing style with Lucky Millinder's big band. She sings the introductory line "We are going to learn a new thing, a rhythm and a rock" and later plays a guitar solo that anticipates Chuck Berry. Tharpe also recorded four versions (one with just her guitar, the other three with Millinder's band) of Thomas A. Dorsey's "Rock Me," where she prays, "Rock me in the cradle of thy love." Reviewing her first version with Millinder for *Billboard* in 1942, Maurie Orodenker writes, "It's Sister Rosetta Tharpe for the rock-and-roll spiritual singing."[55] (More than any other single figure, it was Dorsey, formerly a hokum singer known as Georgia Tom, who brought jazz and blues into African American church music and popularized the term "gospel song.")[56]

The words "rock" and "roll" appeared in the titles or lyrics of blues, jazz, and gospel songs throughout the 1920s and 1930s. The married couple Coot Grant and Kid Wilson recorded the vaudeville-style "Rock, Aunt Dinah, Rock" in 1925, the Four Harmony Kings recorded the spiritual "Rolling and Rocker Dem in His Arms" in 1926, and Sadie McKinney recorded the flowery, mournful "Rock Away" in 1927. "Rockin' on the Hill Blues," by the Beale Street Sheiks; "Rolled from Side to Side Blues," by Little Hat Jones; "Roll That Jelly," by Buddy Burton; and "Rock Me Mama," by Banjo Ikey Robinson's Bull Fiddle Band (with the singer Frankie "Half-Pint" Jaxon), all date from 1929.

In 1930, Robinson's Knights of Rest, a blues trio comprising guitarist Scrapper Blackwell, pianist Jimmy Blythe, and clarinetist Bob Robinson, recorded "Rocking and Rolling."[57] In 1934, the Boswell Sisters, a jazzy white vocal trio, sang "Rock and Roll" (referring to the "rollin', rockin' rhythm of the sea") in the movie *Transatlantic Merry-Go-Round* and recorded it for the Brunswick label.[58] A couple of weeks after the Boswells' recording, the Eton Boys, a white vocal quartet, cut the same song; a few days later, Joe Haymes and His Orchestra, one of the first white bands to adopt the swing format, followed suit, with trumpeter Cliff Weston singing. "Rock and Roll" was also recorded in 1934 by the American bandleader Harry Reser and the British bandleader Harry Roy.

In 1939, the country singer Buddy Jones recorded "Rockin' Rollin' Mama"; the same year, Merline Johnson, known as the Yas Yas Girl, did "Rock and Rollin' Daddy," but the record was not released. There were blues songs like Bo Carter's "Rolling Blues" in 1936 and Curtis Jones's "Roll Me Mama" in 1939, as well as big-band jazz tunes like Duke Ellington's "Rockin' in Rhythm" in 1931, Don Albert's Rockin' and Swingin' in 1936, and Erskine Hawkins's "Rockin' Rollers Jubilee" in 1938.

Some songs, such as Blind Willie McTell and Ruby Glaze's "Rollin' Mama Blues," from 1932, or Georgia White's "Rock Me Daddy," from 1937, are openly sexual. Glaze pleads, "Oh, roll me on my belly, babe, feed me with your chocolate tongue," while White begs, "Rock me, daddy, till you hear me moan." But others are wholly innocent. "(When) Satan starts to hound you, commence to rock and roll," sings the New Orleans trumpeter Henry "Red" Allen on "Get Rhythm in Your Feet (and Music in Your Soul)," from 1935; the song was quickly covered by Benny Goodman with the singer Helen Ward and by the sweet-band leader Freddy Martin. Tampa Red sings, "When you're out for a lovely evening, forget about your daily blues, and rock it in rhythm," on "Rock It in Rhythm," from 1938. Red helped shape the Chicago blues sound but performs "Rock It in Rhythm" in swing style, accompanied by a trumpet and saxophone. Ella Fitzgerald swings in a slower tempo with Chick Webb's band on "Rock It for Me," also from 1938, singing, "It's true that once upon a time the opera was the thing / But today the rage is rhythm and rhyme / So won't you satisfy my soul with the rock and roll?"

The 1940s brought a steady stream of similar songs, including Harlan Leonard's "Rockin' with the Rockets," "Rock and Ride," and "Keep Rockin'," all in 1940; Sweet Georgia Brown's "Rock Me in the Groove," in 1941; Cab Calloway's "I Want to Rock," in 1942; Hadda Brooks's "Rockin' the Boogie," in 1945; and Benny Goodman's "Rattle and Roll" (with a shout chorus surprisingly similar to Haley's "Rock Around the Clock"), in 1946. Wild Bill Moore recorded "We're Gonna Rock" on December 18, 1947, but it was Wynonie Harris's "Good Rockin' Tonight," cut ten days later, that opened the floodgates. For the next couple of years, the rhythm-and-blues scene was deluged with songs such as Joe Lutcher's "Rockin' Boogie," from 1948; Goree Carter's "Rock Awhile," from 1949; Connie Jordan's "I'm Gonna Rock (till My Rocker Breaks Down)," from 1950; and H-Bomb Ferguson's "Rock H-Bomb Rock," from 1951. Johnnie Lee Wills jumped on the bandwagon from the country side in 1951 with "The Band's A-Rockin'."

Some of these songs are "Good Rockin'" knockoffs, some are reworkings of old blues themes, some are piano boogies or honking saxophone instrumentals. Many allude to sex with a wink and a nod, but most are about dancing, rhythm, and having a good time. On Paul Bascomb's frenetic "Rock and Roll," from 1947 or 1948, Bascomb, singing under the name Manhattan Paul, hollers, "I'm crazy 'bout my baby 'cause she loves to rock and roll," adding, "She's built so fine, she makes my love come tumblin' down." On Wild Bill Moore's "Rock and Roll," from 1948, the singer (probably Scatman Crothers) shouts, "You jump right back, you do the boogie, too / You move right up, you do the Susie Q," ending with "Look out, mama, wanna do the rock and roll." But on the laid-back "Let's Rock a While," recorded in 1950, Amos Milburn croons, "I saw you boogie-woogie, jitterbug, and stuff / Now that things are groovy, I think you've jumped enough," explaining, "I just want to hold you, and we don't need to dance."

On Roy Brown's original "Good Rocking Tonight," which Wynonie Harris follows closely (although "Rocking" is changed to "Rockin'" on the label), Brown sings, "Yes, I'm gonna hold my baby as tight as I can / Tonight she'll know I'm a mighty, mighty man." But he adds, "I want you to bring my rocking shoes," and says that "Deacon Jones and Elder Brown, two of the slickest cats in town" would be "stomping and jumping at the jamboree," along with Sioux City Sue and the other song-title women. Ironically, the records inspired by "Good Rockin' Tonight" are less likely to use the word "rock" in a specifically sexual sense than those made earlier.

Rather than simply signifying sex, "rock" and "roll" were ambiguous terms, typical of slang in general and African American slang in particular. Compare the verb "to ball," which among hippies in the late 1960s had an exclusively sexual meaning. That usage originated in the expression "have a ball," which, of course, came from "ball," a formal dance. When Little Richard screamed, "Good golly, Miss Molly, sho' like to ball," in 1958, he was referring to dancing. As late as 1965, Willie Tee, on his New Orleans R&B record "Thank You John," could sing "I know that you've been ballin'"—meaning drinking and partying—in describing a woman's rejection of a man's sexual advances. The word "party" itself, used as a verb, has since acquired the same sort of sexual connotation.

Sexual expression has always been more overt in African American jazz, blues, and R&B than in mainstream white pop; traditional jazz and, later, swing were condemned by both white and black moralists. As rhythm-and-blues grew more popular, the criticism mounted, cresting in 1954 and 1955, when R&B radio stations and jukebox operators, responding to articles in trade publications such as *Billboard* and *Variety,* agreed not to broadcast or distribute sexually suggestive records.[59] But white rock 'n' roll, while sometimes decried as salacious, was more often associated with juvenile violence and crime.

THE REVOLUTION THAT WASN'T

More problematic than rock 'n' roll's sexual implications is the commonly accepted view that it represented a musical revolution—a sharp break with past styles and a leap into uncharted territory. Nik Cohn portrays the pre-rock era as a musical desert: "There was no such thing as teenage music then, nothing that kids could possibly identify with."[60] It's true that the pop charts of the early 1950s were dominated by bland singers such as Perry Como, Eddie Fisher, and Jo Stafford, but these were among the performers that the teenage Elvis Presley admired and emulated, even though he was also exposed to country music and rhythm-and-blues.

In fact, the rock 'n' roll music that teenagers adopted in the 1950s grew directly out of the swing music their parents had listened to when they were teenagers. The roots of rock are audible on "Boogie Woogie," which Count Basie recorded with a small combo in 1936 and with his big band in 1937 (both versions featuring singer Jimmy Rushing), and which Tommy Dorsey recorded as an instrumental in 1938. These recordings, as well as Benny Goodman's similar "Roll 'Em," from 1937, were based on "Pine Top's Boogie Woogie," recorded by pianist Clarence "Pinetop" Smith in 1928, although their immediate inspiration may have been pianist Cleo Brown's slicked-up 1935 cover of Smith's song. Dorsey's "Boogie Woogie" is to Smith's as Pat Boone's "Tutti-Frutti" is to Little Richard's, and it likewise outsold the original.

Boogie-woogie fever peaked with "Beat Me Daddy (Eight to the Bar)," a big hit for both Will Bradley's band and the Andrews Sisters in 1940, the same year that Frank Sinatra made his first records with Tommy Dorsey. Singing with Harry James's band the previous year, Sinatra had shared the bill with the Boogie Woogie Trio—Albert Ammons, Pete Johnson, and Meade "Lux" Lewis—at the Hotel Sherman in Chicago. The trio's radio broadcasts from the hotel, as well as the records they cut earlier in 1939 with some of James's musicians, helped introduce a wider public to authentic boogie piano. In 1949, Sinatra covered Paul Williams's R&B chart-topper "The Huckle-Buck"; in 1950, he covered Red Foley's "Chattanoogie Shoe Shine Boy"; in 1951, he covered Johnny Hodges's R&B hit "Castle Rock"; and in 1955, he covered the Charms' doo-wopping "Two Hearts."

So it's all the more surprising that Sinatra, in a short essay for a European magazine in 1957, described rock 'n' roll as "the most brutal, ugly, degenerate, viscious [sic] form of expression it has been my displeasure to hear." He added: "It fosters almost totally negative and destructive reactions in young people. It smells phony and false. It is sung, played and written for the most part by cretinous goons and by means of its almost imbecilic reiterations and sly, lewd—in fact plain dirty—lyrics . . . it manages to be the martial music of every sideburned delinquent on the face of the earth."[61]

The British-born jazz critic Leonard Feather composed Dinah Washington's first R&B hits, "Salty Papa Blues" and "Evil Gal Blues," recorded in 1943 with members of Lionel Hampton's band. But in 1956, Feather wrote that "rock 'n' roll bears the same relationship to jazz that wrestling bears to boxing" and scornfully singled out Hampton for his "willingness . . . to cater to the atavistic demands of youthful rock 'n' roll audiences."[62] Hampton, however, was no mere bandwagon jumper; notwithstanding his solid jazz credentials, he was a pioneer of rhythm-and-blues and rock 'n' roll whose 1942 recording of "Flying Home," featuring a ferocious tenor saxophone solo by Illinois Jacquet, spawned a whole school of honking R&B saxophonists, among them Paul Williams, Wild Bill Moore, and Paul Bascomb.

Duke Ellington took a more inclusive view in an article for *Music Journal* in 1962. "Rock 'n' Roll is the most raucous form of jazz, beyond a doubt," he wrote. "It maintains a link with the folk origins, and I believe that no other form of jazz has ever been accepted so enthusiastically by so many."[63] Although he may have been stretching the point, Ellington was on the right track: elements of blues and boogie-woogie—"the folk origins"—certainly passed through and intertwined with big-band swing, and the resulting jump-blues style—truly a "raucous form of jazz"—evolved into rhythm-and-blues and rock 'n' roll.

Some older musicians condemned rock 'n' roll as trite and repetitious. "The so-called 'tunes' are monotonous with a similarity that is often ridiculous," wrote Bob Crosby, one of the first swing bandleaders to add boogie-woogies to his repertoire.[64] But the shocked incomprehension with which rock was generally greeted is inexplicable in purely musical terms. It's as if a sudden collective amnesia had erased all memory of the links between rock 'n' roll or rhythm-and-blues and the music that preceded them.

Stranger still is the notion that Elvis Presley's appropriation of black music represented anything new or different. The assimilation of African American music by whites is virtually the story of American popular music, from the eighteenth century onward. The first American blackface stage performance is thought to be Lewis Hallam Jr.'s 1769 portrayal of the slave Mungo in composer Charles Dibdin and librettist Isaac Bickerstaffe's comic opera *The Padlock,* which had premiered in London the previous year with Dibdin in the blackface role. According to the author Russell Sanjek, "The songs Dibdin wrote for Mungo, including the hit 'Dear heart, what a terrible life I lead,' were not true black music, only a white man's perception of what such exotica should sound like, but they set the pattern for all future such characterization."[65]

In 1799, the German-born classical musician Gottlieb Graupner is said to have sung his own composition "The Gay Negro Boy," accompanying himself on banjo, in a Boston production of Thomas Southerne's 1696 play *Oroonoko* (based on Aphra Behn's 1688 novella *Oroonoko: or, the Royal Slave*).[66] Black-dialect songs had been published in England since the late eighteenth century; the earliest one known to have been published in the United States, "Backside Albany," was written by Michael "Micah" Hawkins, a white man who had learned to play the violin from a family slave, and first performed in 1815 by Hopkins Robinson, whom Sanjek describes as "the founding father of theatrical burnt-cork minstrelsy."[67]

Like Robinson, George Washington Dixon, "the first popular blackface singing actor to give performances of what became known as 'plantation melodies,'" got his start as circus clown.[68] By the 1830s, minstrel songs such as Dixon's "Zip Coon" (later known as "Turkey in the Straw") and Thomas "Daddy" Rice's "Jump Jim Crow" were all the rage.[69] The peculiar limp of a disabled slave was the source of Rice's "Jim Crow" song-and-dance routine, which created a sensation in both the United States and England. The 1843 debut of Dan Emmett's Virginia Minstrels in New York touched off the era of the minstrel show, which lasted well into the twentieth century. Christy's Minstrels, founded by Edwin P. Christy three years later, popularized Stephen Foster's "Ethiopian" songs, including "Oh! Susanna," "Camptown Races," and "Old Folks at Home."

Although the minstrel shows borrowed elements of African American culture, especially the banjo, the music was mainly of European origin, often adapted from English, Irish, or Scottish folk songs. Black minstrel troupes, which had been formed as early as 1849, proliferated after the Civil War, with African American performers in black makeup singing in the white minstrel style.[70] The most renowned black composer of minstrel songs, James A. Bland, wrote "Carry Me Back to Old Virginny" and "Oh, Dem Golden Slippers" in the late 1870s.

Not until the Civil War was white America widely exposed to genuine African American music, beginning with the publication of the slave spiritual "Go Down, Moses" in 1861. Having reluctantly added black spirituals to their original repertoire of white parlor songs, a student choir from Fisk University, founded in Nashville by white missionaries to educate newly freed slaves, gained national stardom after appearing at a festival in Boston in 1872. The stirring harmonies of the Fisk Jubilee Singers (the name they took after newspapers referred to them as "nigger minstrels") inspired an ongoing tradition of American popular harmony singing that extends from barbershop to gospel, jazz, and R&B.[71]

As minstrel shows gave way to vaudeville and burlesque, concurrently with the rise of Tin Pan Alley, a more aggressively mocking, syncopated variation of the minstrel song came into vogue. J. P. Skelley's "The Dandy Coon's Parade," from 1880, and J. S. Putnam's "New Coon in Town," from 1883 (sometimes attributed to Paul Allen), launched the craze for "coon songs," which reached its height between 1895 and 1905. Although most coon songs are blatantly racist by today's standards—filled with stereotypical depictions of razor-toting, chicken-stealing, watermelon-eating blacks—many of them were written by African Americans, including Sam Devere's "The Whistling Coon," from 1888, and Ernest Hogan's "All Coons Look Alike to Me," a huge hit in 1896. But with such exceptions as Bert Williams and George W. Johnson, nearly all the best-known performers of coon songs and black dialect comedy were white.

The most famous "coon shouter" was a white woman, May Irwin, who introduced her biggest hit, "The Bully Song," in the 1895 Broadway production *The Widow Jones.* The song's composer, Charles Trevathan, claimed to have learned it from blacks in Tennessee, but he may have taken it from a black brothel singer in St. Louis named Mama Lou, who has also been cited as the uncredited source for the songs "Ta-ra-ra-boom-de-ay" and "There'll Be a Hot Time in the Old Town Tonight."[72] W. C. Handy claimed to have heard laborers singing "The Bully" on the levee at St. Louis around 1892, and the song was mentioned in the December 8, 1894, edition of the *Leavenworth Herald.*[73] In a 1907 recording of "The Bully," Irwin sings, "I'm a Tennessee nigger, an' I don't allow / no red-eyed river roustabout with me to raise a row." Despite the perfunctory dialect, however, she makes no real attempt to sound black.

The word "rag" first appeared on sheet music to describe the accompaniment to an optional chorus of "All Coons Look Alike to Me." To the turn-of-the-century public, coon songs and the syncopated music that accompanied them were one and the same. Even Irving Berlin's 1911 mega-hit "Alexander's Ragtime Band," with such lines as "it's de bestest band what am," would have qualified as a coon song, and it was first popularized by the coon shouter Emma Carus.[74] Only in retrospect was a distinction made between the scurrilous coon songs and the sublime ragtime instrumentals of Scott Joplin and others. Sophie Tucker began her career as a coon shouter and sang blues songs after abandoning blackface, while Al Jolson continued to perform in burnt cork long after it fell from fashion.

The minstrel show, which had originated in the North, lasted longest in the South, where coon songs passed into the repertoire of white and black musicians and were later sometimes mistaken for folk songs. The Georgia-born comedian and singer Emmett Miller toured the South with minstrel troupes in the 1920s and performed in blackface as late as the 1950s. He began recording in 1924 and the following year cut "Lovesick Blues," a Tin Pan Alley song written by Irving Mills and Cliff Friend and first recorded in 1922 by the vaudeville singer Elsie Clark. In 1928, Miller rerecorded "Lovesick Blues" in New York with a group of jazz musicians including trombonist Tommy Dorsey, saxophonist Jimmy Dorsey, and guitarist Eddie Lang.

Rex Griffin's 1939 cover of Miller's "Lovesick Blues" is the basis for Hank Williams's 1949 version, the biggest hit of Williams's career. Miller's distinctive yodeling style may also have influenced Jimmie Rodgers, the father of modern country music, and it definitely inspired the influential western-swing singers Milton Brown and Tommy Duncan. Miller's 1928 "Lovesick Blues" opens with a comic dialogue between Miller and the minstrel veteran Dan Fitch, similar to the routines on Freeman Gosden and Charles Correll's *Amos 'n' Andy* radio show, which made its debut the same year. The way Miller sings the song itself will seem strikingly familiar to anyone who's heard Williams's rendition, except that Miller's voice is even more nasal and he affects a convincing African American accent, sounding much blacker than Elvis Presley ever did. Reviewing a 1927 performance, the *Macon Telegraph* wrote, "Miller plays the part of a negro as few have done."[75]

Other white country artists recorded coon songs into the 1920s and 1930s. For example, "Dat's de Way to Spell 'Chicken,'" copyrighted in 1902 by Sidney Perrin and Bob Slater, was recorded as "C-h-i-c-k-e-n Spells Chicken" in 1926 by Sam and Kirk McGee, who claimed to have learned it from a harmony quartet in their native Tennessee. A fragment of the same song, omitting the original references to "darkies" and "pickaninnies," was recorded in the mid-1960s as "The Chicken" by Mississippi John Hurt, a black songster in the pre-blues tradition who had been rediscovered by folk revivalists. (The McGee brothers, by contrast, replace the word "pickaninny" with "nigger.")

Another country duo from Tennessee, the Allen Brothers, began recording for Columbia in 1927 but cut only three singles before quitting the label in a huff because one of their records had been issued as part of Columbia's race series instead of its hillbilly series.[76] The mistake was probably made with their second record, "Chattanooga Blues," where Austin Allen sounds black enough singing the blues and even blacker in a short spoken interlude. The confusion was surely compounded by the brothers' instrumentation of guitar, banjo, and kazoo, which made them sound like one of the popular black jug bands of the day.

Bing Crosby, the biggest-selling recording artist before Elvis Presley, was influenced by Al Jolson and by the minstrel songs he heard in his youth.[77] Crosby got his first taste of stardom after Paul Whiteman, the most popular bandleader of the 1920s, hired him and his singing partner Al Rinker in 1926. With the addition of Harry Barris, the duo became a threesome, the Rhythm Boys, whose first recordings with Whiteman in 1927 included Barris's "Mississippi Mud," featuring some minstrel-like dialogue and the refrain "just as happy as a cow chewin' on a cud / when the darkies beat their feet on the Mississippi mud." The dialect became more emphatically black when a hoarse-voiced Crosby rerecorded the song the following year with Whiteman's celebrated saxophonist Frankie Trumbauer.

Mildred Bailey, Al Rinker's sister, joined Whiteman's band in 1929. Inspired by Ethel Waters and Bessie Smith, she was—along with Connie Boswell—not only one of the first female jazz singers of note but one of the first nonblack singers to master the feeling of swing (she and Rinker were of mixed white and Native American ancestry). Bailey scored hits throughout the 1930s, recording mostly with white bands such as those of the Dorsey Brothers, Benny Goodman, and her husband, vibraphonist Red Norvo. But she also recorded with Teddy Wilson, John Kirby, members of Count Basie's band, and the Delta Rhythm Boys, a black vocal group. On Bailey's version of "Rock It for Me," recorded shortly after Ella Fitzgerald's, she sounds less vibrant than Fitzgerald but no less black.

Kay Starr, also part Native American, followed in Bailey's bluesy footsteps but switched from jazz to pop and became one of the most successful singers of the early 1950s. Although she sang everything from standards to polkas to country and rhythm-and-blues songs, her smoky voice resembled Dinah Washington's even on such unlikely material as "Lovesick Blues." Starr and Washington both recorded "Wheel of Fortune" around the beginning of 1952, but while Washington's version made the R&B Top 5, Starr's had a ten-week run at the top of the pop charts. Other white singers of the period affected African American mannerisms, among them Connie Boswell, Ella Mae Morse, Anita O'Day, Louis Prima, Frankie Laine, and Harry "the Hipster" Gibson. But with the possible exception of Boswell, whose peak years came earlier, none was as popular as Starr, who Billie Holiday reportedly said was the only white woman who could really sing the blues.[78]

In January 1952, Anita O'Day recorded her own composition "Rock and Roll Blues," but despite hot solos by saxophonist Budd Johnson and trumpeter Roy Eldridge and the rollicking chorus "We gonna rock, we gonna roll," it was not a hit. Two months later, Starr recorded a cover version of the Clovers' No. 1 R&B hit "Fool, Fool, Fool," with credible doo-wop harmonies supplied by the Lancers, a white male vocal quartet. Although she omits the line "When you walked down the street, I said, 'There goes my meat,'" Starr, like O'Day, makes a much more convincing rhythm-and-blues artist than Bill Haley, who recorded "Rock the Joint" at about the same time. On the flip side, "Kay's Lament," the Lancers chant, "Rock, Sister Katie; rock it, Sister Katie," while she shouts the blues with authority on lines like "Sometimes I think I will and then again I think I won't," a lift from Wynonie Harris's "Around the Clock" that would turn up again on Chuck Berry's "Reelin' and Rockin'." Both sides of the single made the pop Top 20, a year before Haley's "Crazy Man, Crazy."

According to Peter Guralnick, Elvis Presley "sang quite a few of Kay Starr's songs" while still in high school, but these were probably ballads. "Fool, Fool, Fool"/"Kay's Lament" has been overlooked by compilers of possible first rock 'n' roll records, and though the Oklahoma-born Starr was a "white" southerner who scored pop hits singing rhythm-and-blues in an authentic style before Presley or Bill Haley, she has so far escaped consideration as the first rock 'n' roll singer (as has O'Day), because of her sex, perhaps, or because she never returned to the idiom again. She did score a No. 1 pop hit in 1956 with "Rock and Roll Waltz," but that was an adult-oriented novelty about parents trying to waltz to a rock song.

At any rate, Presley was not the first white person or white southerner to sing rock 'n' roll, much less to sing African American music. He became a superstar because he arrived at the right time and place with the look, moves, style, and attitude that the youthful public was waiting for, not because he was what Sam Phillips was supposedly looking for—"a white man who had the Negro sound and the Negro feel." The rock 'n' roll revolution, sparked by the inclusion of "Rock Around the Clock" on the soundtrack of *Blackboard Jungle,* was already under way by the time Presley scored his first pop hit. Although he gave the music a major push, it would probably have run a similar course without him.

Chapter Two

The Train Kept A-Rollin'

STROLL ON

A scene near the end of Michelangelo Antonioni's 1966 movie *Blow-Up* captures a pivotal moment in rock 'n' roll history. The film's protagonist, a London fashion photographer played by David Hemmings, glimpses the mysterious woman played by Vanessa Redgrave, pulls his Rolls Royce convertible to the curb, and follows a howl of amplifier feedback into a trendy nightclub. Inside, motionless fans stare glassy-eyed at the stage, where the Yardbirds are performing a song called "Stroll On."

Guitarist Jeff Beck, annoyed by a crackling noise coming from his amplifier, smacks his instrument against a speaker, throws it to the floor, and smashes it with his foot. He tosses the broken-off guitar neck into the crowd, touching off pandemonium, then picks up a new guitar in time to join the band's other guitarist, Jimmy Page, in a series of devastating power chords. Hemmings's character comes up with the severed fretboard, fights his way through a clutching mob, runs out of the club with his prize, and casually discards it on the sidewalk.

Besides making a cryptic statement about the anomie beneath the sleek surface of Swinging London, the scene captures one of England's most innovative rock bands at the peak of its creative power, during the brief stretch in late 1966 when the two guitar gods, Page and Beck, played together in the Yardbirds. The wall of feedback that opens "Stroll On" is revolutionary, as are the jarringly dissonant chords that announce the instrumental break and the twining guitar duet that follows Beck's distorted, blues-edged solo. The music anticipates the psychedelic and heavy-metal movements soon to come (Led Zeppelin, the definitive metal band, originated as the New Yardbirds under Page's leadership in 1968), and its influence echoes through punk and grunge to the latest retro-rock.

While pointing to the future, the song also reflects the past. The guitar riff in the intro and the drum roll at the break respectively suggest a train whistle and the chug of a locomotive, and the twin-guitar part owes a lot to Chuck Berry.

But like so much in cinema, the scene is not all it appears to be. The music was recorded at one studio and the stage performance filmed at another. The version on the soundtrack album is played twice in a row in the movie, and two guitars are heard while Beck is shown breaking his. In any event, the guitarist known for smashing his instrument on stage was not Jeff Beck but Pete Townshend of the Who, the band the scene was written for; when the Who could not be contracted, Antonioni had Beck do Townshend's routine. Keith Relf, the Yardbirds' singer, reportedly said that the other guitarist on the soundtrack is not Page but Chris Dreja, who plays bass on screen (Page had in fact joined the band as its bassist before switching instruments with Dreja).[1]

"Stroll On" is a reworded version of a song the Yardbirds had recorded without Page a year earlier, "The Train Kept A-Rollin'," for which the movie rights could not be obtained. Though not nearly as wild as "Stroll On," the group's first recording of "The Train Kept A-Rollin'" is a rock-music milestone in itself. There's no feedback, and the track begins immediately with the train-whistle guitar riff, followed by the same minor-key fuzz-tone vamp that propels "Stroll On." There are two instrumental breaks instead of one, both featuring Relf's double-tracked harmonica as well as Beck's incendiary guitar, but instead of crashing power chords, there's a fuzz-tone bass. Building to frenzied intensity, the extended breaks—shorter versions of the onstage instrumental jams the band called "rave ups"—represent some of the earliest psychedelic blues-rock, antedating Jimi Hendrix and Cream (whose guitarist, Eric Clapton, had preceded Beck in the Yardbirds).

The Yardbirds recorded "The Train Kept A-Rollin'" in September 1965, on the last leg of their first tour of the United States, and it was released on their second U.S. album, *Having a Rave Up with the Yardbirds* (on the Epic label). Beck recalls that the session took place at Sam Phillips's studios in Memphis, but Giorgio Gomelsky, the Yardbirds' manager and producer at the time, says it was at the Columbia Recording Studios in New York.[2] The double tracking of Relf's harmonica and vocal parts may have been the idea of the Columbia staff engineer Roy Halee, who went on to produce Simon and Garfunkel's albums. Doubling the same track to reinforce a voice or instrument was a common technique, but on "The Train Kept A-Rollin'," two different Relf takes, with different words, are superimposed, making the lyrics hard to understand.

According to Gomelsky, the Yardbirds were inspired to record "The Train Kept A-Rollin'" by the legendary American blues harmonica player Sonny Boy Williamson (Aleck "Rice" Miller), whom the group had backed when he toured England in 1963. "Sonny Boy Williamson was doing all these train tunes with the mouth organ," Gomelsky says. "Harmonically, that was the perfect instrument to imitate a train. So I guess it just came about because of that somehow. We were traveling [in the U.S.], and we took some train journeys. And then we were in New York, it was the last week of the tour, and it was sort of a recap of all the journeys we did."[3]

The group may well have been aware of a recording of "The Train Kept A-Rollin'" made for the British CBS label just a few months earlier by Screaming Lord Sutch and the Savages. Beck had cut a single ("Dracula's Daughter," backed with "Come Back Baby") as a member of the Savages the previous year, before joining the Yardbirds. The self-dubbed Lord Sutch was a bizarre entertainer-cum-politician who combined humor, horror-movie imagery, and rockabilly music in an act inspired by the American rhythm-and-blues singer Screamin' Jay Hawkins. Produced by Joe Meek, a progenitor of the pre-psychedelic British "freakbeat" sound, Sutch's "The Train Kept A-Rollin'" is a weird parody of early-1960s rock 'n' roll that manages to sound corny and avant-garde at the same time. It has little in common with the Yardbirds' version besides the chugging drums and the opening train-whistle lick, played by the future Deep Purple guitarist Ritchie Blackmore, who also contributes a feverish solo.

Lord Sutch could not have been aware of a recording of "The Train Kept A-Rollin'" made in early 1959 by Connecticut's Bob Vidone and the Rhythm Rockers but first issued on the 2003 Norton Records compilation *The Raging Teens, Volume 4*. Hearing it, however, one would swear that Sutch had somehow got hold of Vidone's unreleased demo disc. Among other similarities, the two-note horn blasts that punctuate the first line—"I caught a train, *bop bop,* I met a dame, *bop bop*"—are nearly identical, and they are not found on any other version of the song. Vidone, who released a couple of obscure singles in the late 1950s, prefigured the "psychobilly" music of the early 1980s with such songs as "Madness" and "Weird."

Sutch's "The Train Kept A-Rollin'," like Vidone's, is apparently based on the rockabilly version recorded on July 2, 1956, by the Johnny Burnette Trio. Sutch's and Burnette's arrangements are completely different; the only obvious borrowing is the drawn-out final word, which Burnette renders as "go-oh-oh-oh-oh" and Sutch as "go go go go go." But both versions were released on singles with the same song on the flip side, "Honey Hush," which had been a No. 1 rhythm-and-blues hit for Big Joe Turner in 1953. (Vidone actually quotes from "Honey Hush" at the end of his "Train Kept A-Rollin'.")

As a youth, Jeff Beck had been captivated by rockabilly; his guitar hero was Cliff Gallup of Gene Vincent's Blue Caps. Beck maintains that the Yardbirds covered Burnette's "The Train Kept A-Rollin'" at his instigation. "They just heard me play the riff, and they loved it and made up their version of it," he says. "We didn't bother to make any references to the original record."[4]

Singer-guitarist Johnny Burnette had formed his trio in 1953 with his brother Dorsey Burnette on standup bass and Paul Burlison on lead guitar. The three had grown up in Memphis and were acquainted with Elvis Presley, who drove a truck for the same company, Crown Electric, that employed Burlison and Dorsey Burnette. There is some debate about who influenced whom: the trio is said to have played in an R&B-flavored hillbilly-boogie style even before Presley made his first commercial recordings in 1954, but Johnny Burnette's first record ("You're Undecided," backed with "Go Mule Go"), made for the Mississippi-based Von label before the end of 1955, is strictly country.[5]

In early 1956, the Burnette brothers and Burlison traveled to New York City and won the televised competition on *Ted Mack and the Original Amateur Hour*, which led to a contract with Decca Records' Coral subsidiary. They cut their first Coral single, the rockabilly romp "Tear It Up," backed with "You're Undecided," in New York in May, then went on tour, adding a drummer. Before one show, Burlison accidentally jarred a tube loose while moving his amplifier; he liked the resulting distortion so much that he began loosening the tube deliberately.

The trio's next recording session, at the producer Owen Bradley's studio in Nashville, yielded "The Train Kept A-Rollin'," featuring Burlison's groundbreaking fuzz-tone guitar on the repeated three-note minor-key riff that serves as the song's instrumental break. Burlison played the same fuzzy figure more extensively on the following day's recording of "Honey Hush."[6] His loose tube paved the way for the development of the fuzz box, a custom-made version of which Beck was using as early as 1963.[7]

There is no train-whistle effect on the trio's "Train Kept A-Rollin'," nor is there anything like Beck's riveting, relatively complex solos. Burlison's simple, buzzing licks lend the record a raw, primitive feel, but it's Johnny Burnette's yelping, hiccuping vocal that gives the song its frantic energy. The appropriation of black jive talk by white southerners is a rockabilly hallmark, and Burnette hollers the story of meeting a "real gone dame" on a train with much greater authenticity than the comparatively stilted-sounding Keith Relf, whose dame is "cool" rather than "gone."

Despite television appearances on Dick Clark's *American Bandstand,* Steve Allen's *Tonight Show,* and Perry Como's *Kraft Music Hall,* plus a spot in the movie *Rock, Rock, Rock!* the Johnny Burnette Trio enjoyed only regional success, and "The Train Kept A-Rollin'," the group's biggest seller, never made the national charts. Perhaps the sound was just too crude; Gene Vincent's smoother "Be-Bop-A-Lula," recorded two months earlier, was a Top 10 smash. The trio had disbanded by the end of 1957, but Burnette reinvented himself as a teen-pop crooner and scored a pair of string-smothered hits on the Liberty label in 1960, "Dreamin'" and "You're Sixteen," the latter covered by Ringo Starr in 1974.

Burnette's early trio sides were virtually forgotten in the United States (though not in Britain) until the rockabilly revival of the late 1970s, and practically all of the many covers of "The Train Kept A-Rollin'" are modeled on the Yardbirds' version. The original recording of the song, made by Tiny Bradshaw on July 25, 1951, remained even more obscure, although it had been reissued by King Records in 1959, shortly after Bradshaw's death, on the LP *A Tribute to the Late Tiny Bradshaw, the Great Composer.*

Born in Youngstown, Ohio, in 1909, Bradshaw began his career singing with Horace Henderson's Collegians, whose leader was the brother of the renowned jazz musician Fletcher Henderson. Moving to Harlem, Bradshaw sang and played drums with jazz groups such as the Savoy Bearcats, Marion Hardy's Alabamians, the Mills Blue Rhythm Band, and Luis Russell's Orchestra. In 1934, he formed his own big band and recorded eight sides for Decca in a swinging style modeled after Cab Calloway's; the following year, his band backed Ella Fitzgerald on her first professional gig.

Unlike Calloway, who helped popularize jive talk among whites, even publishing a *Hepster's Dictionary,* Bradshaw was relegated to the chitlin circuit. He did not record again until 1944, by which time he had a different band and was playing in a jump-blues style (Bradshaw preferred the term "bounce") influenced by Louis Jordan, who like Calloway was a showman who could sell black music to white audiences. In March 1947, even before Wynonie Harris's seminal recording of "Good Rockin' Tonight," Bradshaw cut "Take the Hands Off the Clock" for Savoy. Cowritten by singer Sam Theard and Bradshaw's trumpeter at the time, Henry Glover, the song contains the lyrics "Let 'em rock . . . I mean, everybody rock."

In 1949, Bradshaw started recording for King, a Cincinnati label founded six years earlier by Syd Nathan. King had expanded from country music to rhythm-and-blues and by the early 1950s was well on the way to dominating the R&B market, with artists such as Bull Moose Jackson, Earl Bostic, and Wynonie Harris. Nathan encouraged his country artists to record R&B material and vice versa, especially if he held the copyrights. To build his rhythm-and-blues catalog, he hired Henry Glover as an artist-and-repertoire man; soon Glover was writing songs and producing sessions for both country and R&B artists. Nathan had Glover arrange the saxophonist Paul Williams's 1949 R&B hit "The Huckle-Buck" as a country song for the Delmore Brothers under the title "Blues Stay Away from Me," which Dorsey and Johnny

Burnette covered in rockabilly style on the same date they recorded "The Train Kept A-Rollin'."

Bradshaw made his commercial breakthrough in 1950 with his second King single, the rollicking "Well Oh Well." Credited to Bradshaw, Henry Bernard (Glover's pseudonym), and Lois Mann (Nathan's pseudonym), it's an answer song to "San Fernando Valley," which had been introduced by Roy Rogers in the movie of the same title in 1943. The following year, Bing Crosby turned "San Fernando Valley" into No. 1 pop hit, and Bradshaw recorded it for the Armed Forces Radio Service's black-oriented Jubilee program series. But on "Well Oh Well," instead of "hittin' the trail to the cow country" and moving to California as Rogers and Crosby do, Bradshaw decides to "forget the trail to the cow country" and "stay right here where I'm at." And while Rogers and Crosby croon in decorous two-step rhythms to the accompaniment of violins, Bradshaw shouts over a slamming backbeat, pushed by jazzy horns.

Although it never crossed over to the pop charts, "Well Oh Well" was a major rhythm-and-blues hit. Bradshaw went on a national tour, then returned to his new home in Cincinnati and performed mostly in the Midwest. Of his subsequent King singles, only "Soft," a saxophone-driven instrumental from late 1952, approached the success of "Well Oh Well," but that was enough to land Bradshaw gigs on R&B package shows around the country. In 1954, a few months after appearing with Ruth Brown and the Clovers on a show staged in Cleveland by Alan Freed, he suffered a debilitating stroke. In 1958, he recorded his last single, a cover of the Royal Teens' "Short Shorts."

Released in early 1952, Bradshaw's "The Train Kept A-Rollin'" never made the national R&B charts. It's a vibrant mid-tempo song with a boogie-woogie bass line and a shuffling drumbeat, lively enough but not nearly as frenetic as Burnette's or the Yardbirds' renditions. Bradshaw scat-sings the introduction, then shouts the tale of the "gone dame" (who "was a hipster" rather than the "hepster" she became in later versions) with a hearty, grainy ease that makes even Burnette sound affected. When Bradshaw sings "the train kept a-rollin'," a chorus finishes the line with "all night long"; curiously, Lord Sutch uses the same call-and-response on the refrain. The band—three horns and a four-piece rhythm section—is tight and swinging, and as the drummer shifts into a heavy backbeat, Red Prysock brings the performance to a climax with a brawny, bluesy tenor sax solo in the honking style of the day. There is no train-whistle or locomotive mimicry, nor is the distinctive minor-key riff of the Burnette and Yardbirds versions anywhere to be heard.

The song is credited to Bradshaw, Lois Mann, and Howie Kay. Mann's name was plainly added to allow Syd Nathan to siphon off a share of the publishing royalties, as label owners routinely did in those days; as for Kay, his identity remains a mystery. But like "Well Oh Well," the "The Train Kept

A-Rollin'" is an adaptation of an earlier song, in this case "Cow-Cow Boogie," a Top 10 pop hit for the Freddie Slack Orchestra with vocalist Ella Mae Morse in 1942 and for Ella Fitzgerald with the Ink Spots in 1944.

COW-COW BOOGIE

On "Cow-Cow Boogie," instead of meeting a dame on a train who "was pretty, from New York City," Morse and Fitzgerald meet a cowboy who sings "a ditty he learned in the city." Although not specifically identified as a "hipster," the cowboy is described as a "swing half-breed" who "was raised on loco weed" and has "a knocked-out western accent with a Harlem touch." Where Bradshaw sings "Get along, sweet little woman," Morse and Fitzgerald quote the cowboy singing "Get along, get hip, little dogie," an allusion to a line published in 1910 by John A. Lomax in the traditional cowboy song "Whoopee Ti Yi Yo, Git Along Little Dogies" and popularized in 1933 by Billy Hill's composition "The Last Round-Up (Git Along, Little Dogie, Git Along)."

Both "The Train Kept A-Rollin'" and "Cow-Cow Boogie" are set in the Southwest: Bradshaw's train stops in Albuquerque and El Paso, while Morse and Fitzgerald meet their cowboy "out on the plains near Santa Fe." But what clinches the connection between the two songs is Morse's line "he trucked 'em on down the old fairway" (recited by the Ink Spots' bass singer, Orville "Hoppy" Jones, on Fitzgerald's version), which Bradshaw renders as "she trucked on down the old fair lane." (The verb "truck" had entered the pop lexicon via the 1935 dance hit "Truckin'," which was recorded by Fats Waller, Duke Ellington, and the Mills Blue Rhythm Band, among others.)

"Cow-Cow Boogie" was actually written for Ella Fitzgerald to sing in the 1942 Abbott and Costello movie *Ride 'Em Cowboy.* In this inane musical comedy, the slapstick duo play New York hot-dog and peanut vendors who run afoul of their boss, hop a train, and wind up working on a western dude ranch. The singing cowboy Dick Foran costars as Bronco Bob Mitchell, an author of western stories who's not the rodeo rider he's cracked up to be. Fitzgerald—playing Ruby, a maid at the ranch—is featured in two musical numbers. First she sings "A-Tisket, A-Tasket," the 1938 hit that made her a star; later she performs "Rockin' and Reelin'," a song in the same vein as "Cow-Cow Boogie," which Fitzgerald is said to have filmed but which didn't make the final cut.[8]

At a square dance on the ranch, the Merry Macs, a three-man, one-woman white vocal group, interrupt the caller, telling him, "Don't be a chump, do a square dance but make it jump." They launch into "Rockin' and Reelin' (Rockin' around the Square)," with lines such as "make the old Virginia reel really hop" and "do the boogie if the beat is in eight." They call on Ruby to "give the calls, make 'em up, do it in jive, and break 'em up," and Fitzgerald, doffing her maid's apron, delivers a jive-talking proto-rap, promising to "show you how they rock the square, you know, back in Harlem on Sugar Hill." A three-couple black dance troupe briefly demonstrates the Lindy hop, exiting before the dance floor fills with jitterbugging whites, as Fitzgerald and the Merry Macs trade verses to the offscreen accompaniment of a brassy big band.

"Rockin' and Reelin'" is not listed in the credit crawl, which attributes the film's other original songs to composer Gene DePaul and lyricist Don Raye. Most likely, Benny Carter also had a hand in "Rockin' and Reelin'"; he undoubtedly cowrote "Cow-Cow Boogie" with DePaul and Raye, but his name was left off the early editions of that song for contractual reasons.[9]

Carter helped shape the swing era as a trumpeter, alto saxophonist, arranger, composer, and bandleader. It was Carter's band that accompanied Fitzgerald when she won the Amateur Night contest at Harlem's Apollo Theatre in November 1934 by singing a pair of songs in the style of her idol, Connie Boswell of the Boswell Sisters. Carter became Fitzgerald's friend and mentor; he's said to have recommended her to the bandleader Chick Webb (with whom she recorded "A-Tisket, A-Tasket") following her week-long stint with Tiny Bradshaw.[10] In October 1941, Carter's band recorded his own "Back Bay Boogie," a much more dynamic arrangement than Slack's "Cow-Cow Boogie." After World War II, Carter moved to Hollywood, where he wrote many film and television scores, occasionally joining Fitzgerald for concerts and recordings.

Don Raye was a vaudeville song-and-dance man who turned to songwriting. In 1939, he and Frances Faye wrote "Well All Right (Tonight's the Night)," a hit for the Andrews Sisters, who expanded on the jazzy harmonies of the Boswell Sisters to become the best-selling female vocal group of the pre-rock era. The following year, Raye was invited to Hollywood to write for the Andrews Sisters' movie debut in the Ritz Brothers comedy *Argentine Nights.* Together with Hughie Prince, Raye composed "Rhumboogie" ("It's Harlem's new creation / with a Cuban syncopation"), which the Andrews Sisters perform in the movie and the Ritz Brothers mime in a drag impersonation of the sisters.

Raye knew trombonist Will Bradley and drummer Ray McKinley, who since late 1939 had co-led a band (under Bradley's name) that included pianist Freddie Slack. A national boogie-woogie craze was underway—sparked by the performances of pianists Pete Johnson, Albert Ammons, and Meade "Lux" Lewis at the impresario John Hammond's first "From Spirituals to Swing" concert at Carnegie Hall in December 1938—and Slack was one of the few whites to master the style. The Bradley band had already recorded "Rhumboogie" when Raye and Prince stopped by to hear the group at the Famous Door on New York's Fifty-second Street in 1940, around the time that Fitzgerald performed there.

As the band played one of its boogie numbers, "there was one part where I had a drum break," McKinley later recounted. "And for some reason or other that night, instead of playing the break, I sang out, 'Oh, Beat Me, Daddy, Eight to the Bar!' After the set, Hughie called me over to the table and asked if they could write a song using that break. I told them to go ahead, and they offered to cut me in on the tune."[11] Because he was under contract to a different publisher than Raye and Prince, McKinley used the name of his first wife, Eleanore Sheehy, on the song.

Released later the same year, Bradley's recording of "Beat Me Daddy (Eight to the Bar)"—featuring Slack's piano, along with McKinley's vocal about a boogie pianist "in a little honky-tonky village in Texas"—became the band's biggest hit, reaching No. 2 on *Billboard* magazine's newly established Best Selling Records chart. That fall, the Andrews Sisters' sleekly harmonized version also reached No. 2.[12] Bradley's band followed up with Raye's "Scrub Me, Mama, with a Boogie Beat," which the Andrews Sisters also covered. The song, about a rhythmic Harlem washerwoman, was made into a stereotypically racist cartoon by the animator Walter Lantz, of Woody Woodpecker fame.

The next Raye hit was "Down the Road a Piece," recorded by the Will Bradley Trio, comprising McKinley, Slack, and bassist Doc Goldberg. McKinley and Raye banter in Amos 'n' Andy–style dialect over Slack's lukewarm boogie piano before McKinley sings the lyrics about a place with a band that's "better than chicken fried in bacon grease." The long instrumental break includes whistling and a delicate duet between Goldberg on bass and Slack on celesta (Meade "Lux" Lewis had introduced both whistling and the celesta to the boogie-woogie).

Like "The Train Kept A-Rollin'," "Down the Road a Piece" evolved into a rock 'n' roll standard, covered by the R&B pianist Amos Milburn in 1946, the hillbilly-boogie pianist Merrill Moore in 1955, Chuck Berry in 1960, and the Rolling Stones in 1964. Milburn's is easily the hardest-rocking version, with heavy, driving piano rhythms that make Slack's playing sound flowery by comparison. Except for the whistling, Milburn follows the original closely, recording with just bass and drums and imitating the celesta part on piano; he even repeats the opening dialogue, but with a natural delivery that strips away any racist implications. As with "The Train Kept A-Rollin'," the lyrics of "Down the Road a Piece" become increasingly garbled on each successive version. Milburn nearly nails the line about "eight-beat Mac, . . . Doc and ol' 'Beat Me Daddy' Slack," but by the time the Rolling Stones get to it, the reference is to "Charlie McCoy . . . that rubber-legged boy," with Mick Jagger affecting a less credible African American accent than McKinley's.

In 1941, the Andrews Sisters made three movies with Abbott and Costello. The first, *Buck Privates,* made the comedy duo famous and showcased the three sisters singing Raye and Prince's "Boogie Woogie Bugle Boy," which was nominated for an Academy Award, made into a Walter Lantz cartoon (again with stereotypical black characters), and revived some thirty years later as a camp anthem by Bette Midler. The second, *In the Navy,* marked the beginning of Raye's decade-long collaboration with Gene DePaul.

Before heading for Hollywood, DePaul, a native New Yorker, had played piano in Jan Savitt's swing band, known for its shuffle rhythms and for its male vocalist, George "Bon Bon" Tunnell, perhaps the first full-time black singer in a white group. After Raye's retirement, DePaul and lyricist Johnny Mercer wrote the scores to the movie musical *Seven Brides for Seven Brothers* and the Broadway show *Li'l Abner.*

In 1942, when Mercer cofounded Capitol Records in Hollywood, one of the first artists he signed was Freddie Slack. The previous year, Slack had left Bradley and formed his own trio, backing Big Joe Turner on a couple of records. With Mercer's help, he organized a big band and hired Ella Mae Morse, a seventeen-year-old singer from Texas who had briefly performed with Jimmy Dorsey's band three years earlier, when Slack was Dorsey's pianist.

Recorded on May 21, 1942, "Cow-Cow Boogie" was Capitol Records' second release and first million-seller, establishing the label as a viable competitor to the New York–based majors—Columbia, Victor, and Decca—and even crossing over to the R&B charts. Walter Lantz made the song into a cartoon, this time with animated cattle and a Meade "Lux" Lewis piano solo. Dorothy Dandridge performed it in a Soundie—the celluloid ancestor of the music video—as a miniskirted cowgirl in a barroom full of black cowboys. And Morse sang it with Slack's band in the movie *Reveille with Beverly,* which also featured Frank Sinatra, the Mills Brothers, and the bands of Duke Ellington, Count Basie, and Bob Crosby, Bing's younger brother.

Ella Fitzgerald's career had stalled after Chick Webb died, and she had been touring and recording with a vocal-instrumental quartet called the Four Keys before she recorded "Cow-Cow Boogie" for Decca in late 1943; by that time, the Four Keys had been drafted, so the Ink Spots were enlisted to sing their parts.[13] She scat-sings softly under Hoppy Jones's recitation on her relaxed rendition, which sold about as well as Slack and Morse's. It was Fitzgerald's first hit in three years, paving the way for her triumphant comeback.

Morse had signed a personal contract with Mercer on the day she cut "Cow-Cow Boogie"; after two more hits with Slack's band, including the R&B-chart-topping "Mr. Five by Five," she left Slack to pursue a solo career on Capitol.[14] She recorded pop hits through the early 1950s, including two, "Shoo-Shoo Baby" in 1943 and "Buzz Me" in 1946, that crossed over to the

R&B charts. She reunited with Slack in 1946 to record "The House of Blue Lights," a sophisticated update of "Down the Road a Piece" that made the pop Top 10. On "The House of Blue Lights," written by Slack and Don Raye, Morse sings and scats like Fitzgerald, and her jiving dialogue with Raye—seemingly cribbed from the *Hepster's Dictionary*—is refined past the point of racial offensiveness. It's been reported that Sammy Davis Jr. was surprised, upon meeting Morse, to discover that she was white. "Ella, baby, I thought you were one of us!" he said. "I am," she replied.[15]

Backed by pianist Eddie Heywood Jr.'s sextet, a black group, the Andrews Sisters scored a hit with "The House of Blue Lights" later in 1946; the former Glenn Miller saxophonist Hal McIntyre recorded it with his own band at about the same time. Merrill Moore cut it 1953, and Chuck Miller, another white pianist, made the pop Top 10 with it in 1955. Chuck Berry's 1958 version, incorporating Morse's scatted finale as well as a garbled line from "Down the Road a Piece," was not released until 1974; Jerry Lee Lewis's mid-1970s version was not released until after he rerecorded the song for his 1995 album *Young Blood.* "The House of Blue Lights" was also recorded by Canned Heat, Asleep at the Wheel, Commander Cody and the Lost Planet Airmen, George Thorogood and the Destroyers, the Flamin' Groovies, and the Meat Puppets, among others. Little Richard mentions that "they caught Miss Molly dancin' at the House of Blue Lights" on his 1958 rock 'n' roll classic "Good Golly Miss Molly," and Huey "Piano" Smith approximates Slack's keyboard intro on his 1957 New Orleans R&B hit "Rockin' Pneumonia and the Boogie Woogie Flu."

"Cow-Cow Boogie" had its own recorded posterity, apart from "The Train Kept A-Rollin'," through covers by such artists as Glenn Miller, Maxine Sullivan, Mel Tormé, and the Judds. There's even a jived-up variation in Slim Gaillard style ("vootedy bootedy bootie macscootie, get along dogerini") recorded in 1946 by Louis Prima with the Riders of the Purple Sage under the title "Vout Cowboy." But the most intriguing version is on an acetate disc (the kind once used for home recordings) made around 1943 by Charles "Cow Cow" Davenport, who claimed authorship of the song and is credited in *The Encyclopedia of Popular Music* as its "sole composer."[16]

On the disc, released as part of the 1997 Document Records CD *Cow Cow Davenport, Volume 3: The Unissued 1940s Acetate Recordings,* Davenport sings "Cow-Cow Boogie" with practically the same words and melody as on the Slack-Morse version. But the absurd lyrics about a hip cowboy are quite unlike those of his other songs, on the same CD or elsewhere. He seems to mock the lines subconsciously with the slightly altered wording "For a cowboy song, just too much . . . / Yeah, that guy must've been full of them loco weed."[17]

As he sings, his left hand repeats the rolling piano riff with which Slack opens his "Cow-Cow Boogie." The riff can also be heard beneath Slack's band at times, but Davenport plays it throughout the song, adding chords very sparingly with his right hand. After he finishes singing, he keeps playing the riff for a while, then goes into a spoken monologue. "Now listen to that beat," he begins, referring to the piano riff. "That's a strange beat. That beat, I'd like to tell you somethin' about it. It was 1910 . . . when that beat was originated."

Davenport proceeds to relate how his career began, giving musical demonstrations along the way. His rambling narrative continues through three more tracks of the CD, each representing a different one-sided acetate disc. He begins by saying that his mother had a love of music, not mentioning that his father was a Baptist minister.

> Quite naturally, she belonged to the choir, for singin'. She was assistant piano; she would play when the other piano player wasn't there to play. . . . So she would practice . . . and one day she was practicin' Stephen Foster's "Swanee River." I never will forget it. In fact, I can see her playin' now. [Davenport plays a stately version of "Old Folks at Home."] Yeah, she was playin' "Swanee River." I'd stand around the piano, listenin'. . . . But when she'd get up off the piano, and as quick as she'd gotten away from the house, I would come in, sit down, and play. I'd play my version of "Swanee River" like *I* wanted to play.

At this point Davenport plays "Old Folks at Home" with the "strange beat" from 1910 in the bass, as well as a few eight-to-the-bar boogie rhythms. But he doesn't explicitly claim that he invented the riff or wrote "Cow-Cow Boogie"; instead, he immediately shifts into the story of how his grandmother prompted him to come up with the term "boogie-woogie."

> She'd walk in and say, "Stop that ol' boogie music!" "Grandma, why you call that 'boogie music'?" "'Cause that's the devil's music!" Well, that's the same thing that my mother was playin', so I asked her, "Why you call my music 'boogie music'?" Then she said, "Well, when I was a child, my parents used to tell me and all the children, if they were bad, the boogieman would get them." And the boogieman was the devil. He rode a big horse, and you could hear his feet go boogedy boogie, boogleedy woogie, boogleeda woogie, boogleeda woogie. So that's where I got the name of boogie music.

Davenport then illustrates "what I call boogie beat," playing two twelve-bar blues choruses using the "Cow-Cow Boogie" riff. He tells how he left home because his grandmother objected to his music and hints at how he got his nickname. Before hopping a freight train to Atlanta, he observed that "They had two cowcatchers on that train, and that brakeman sure could catch that cowcatcher. . . . Then my mind got on that cowcatcher, and I knew I could make something out of that."

He says that on arriving in Atlanta, he made his way to a succession of "joints" until he found one with a pianist, who let him sit in. He plays the "Cow-Cow Boogie" riff again, demonstrating how, with his grandmother in mind, he sang: "Mama don't 'low no music playin' in here / Grandma don't 'low no music playin' in here / I don't care what she don't 'low, play my music anyhow / Mama don't 'low no music playin' in here." The song, of course, is "Mama Don't Allow," a standard of blues, bluegrass, and Dixieland jazz alike.

Davenport's acetate narrative doesn't quite jibe with the published accounts of his life, beginning with the interviews he gave in the 1940s to Art Hodes, a white pianist active in the traditional-jazz revival movement.[18] Born in Anniston, Alabama, in 1894, Davenport was a member of the first generation of boogie-woogie pianists. He took piano lessons at the age of twelve and taught himself ragtime. His disapproving father sent him to the Alabama Baptist Normal and Theological School in Selma, where he continued to play rags. After leaving school, he performed in the honky-tonks of Birmingham, then joined a traveling carnival.[19]

He was working as a blackface minstrel when he met singer Dora Carr, with whom he toured the South for the recently formed Theatre Owners Booking Association. After a sojourn in New Orleans, the two recorded Davenport's signature song, "Cow Cow Blues," for the OKeh label in 1925. The original title was "Railroad Blues," and Davenport recorded the same song under that name in 1938. Like many blues of its era, it has a chugging rhythm and lyrics about a train that "carried my man away." But the line that stuck to both the tune and its composer was "Ain't nobody rock me like Papa Cow Cow do."

After Carr left him for another man, Davenport teamed with singer Ivy Smith in a new touring act called the Chicago Steppers. In Pittsburgh, he met pianist Clarence "Pinetop" Smith, to whom he claimed to have introduced the term "boogie-woogie."[20] It was Smith's "Pine Top's Boogie Woogie," recorded on December 29, 1928, that gave the genre its name and formed the model for most of the boogies that followed, including "Down the Road a Piece" and "The House of Blue Lights." It also contains the piano flourish that Freddie Slack and Huey Smith used as an introduction.

A financially disastrous tour of the South ended with Davenport spending six months in an Alabama prison, where, he said, "I caught pneumonia. It must have settled in my right arm."[21] He moved to Cleveland and in 1938 secured a recording contract with Decca in New York, but his playing was still impaired, so Sammy Price handled the keyboard parts while Davenport sang. Davenport suffered a stroke later that year and never recovered the full use of his right hand.

Davenport returned to New York around 1941 and attempted to collect royalties for songs he claimed to have written. But even after the successes of

Bob Crosby's big-band version of "Cow Cow Blues" in 1941 and Slack's "Cow-Cow Boogie" the following year, Davenport got no further in the music scene than a job as a men's room attendant at the Onyx Club on Fifty-second Street. Then he was discovered by Art Hodes, who featured Davenport on his radio program and in the magazine he edited, *The Jazz Record*. In 1944, Davenport recorded eight sides for the independent Comet label, which were reviewed in *Down Beat* magazine.

In December 1945, *Down Beat* ran an article by Carlton Brown in support of Davenport's copyright claims. Citing a photostat of a signed agreement with the State Street Music Company as well as receipts in Davenport's possession, Brown writes that in 1929 Davenport signed away the rights to many of his compositions, including "Cow Cow Blues," "Mama Don't Allow No Easy Riders Here," and "You Rascal You," for as little as two dollars each.[22]

The State Street Music Company was owned by J. Mayo Williams, an influential black producer and A&R man who was running Vocalion's "race" division when Davenport recorded for that label in 1928 and 1929. (Davenport claimed to have recommended Pinetop Smith to Williams, who produced "Pine Top's Boogie Woogie" for Vocalion.) Among Davenport's recordings for Williams are two virtually identical solo piano renditions of "Cow Cow Blues," one released on Vocalion and the other on its parent label, Brunswick. One of those recordings, either of which is now regarded as the definitive version, was reissued in the early 1940s on the Brunswick Collector's Series album *Boogie Woogie Piano: Historic Recordings by Pioneer Piano Men*. Brown notes in his *Down Beat* article that "Davenport gets composer's credit on the label but no royalties."

Davenport's piano accompanied Lovin' Sam Theard's vocal on a 1929 Brunswick recording of "You Rascal You." That song became a hit for Red Nichols, Cab Calloway, and Louis Armstrong successively in late 1931 and an even bigger hit for the Mills Brothers in early 1932. Whether or not Theard received royalties, he is credited as the song's composer, and neither the melody nor the lyrics resemble any that Davenport is known to have written.

As for Davenport's June 1929 Vocalion recording of "Mama Don't Allow No Easy Riders Here," it's a vocal-less piano rag with little melodic similarity to "Mama Don't Allow" as it is generally known today or as it was demonstrated on acetate by Davenport. The Chicago-based singer-pianist John Oscar cut "Mama Don't Allow No Easy Riders Here" for Brunswick just four days later, using Davenport's melody and adding such lyrics as "I don't care what mama don't allow, I'm gonna have my easy rider anyhow." Tampa Red's Hokum Jug Band recorded an antic version of the same song for Vocalion the following month, with Davenport playing piano and Frankie "Half-Pint" Jaxon singing. Tampa Red redid it as a duet with Georgia Tom later that year, and Jaxon recorded "Mama Don't Allow It" twice with a jazz band in 1933, using the melody that's now familiarly known.

But Papa Charlie Jackson had recorded "Mama Don't Allow It (and She Ain't Gonna Have It Here)," with a melody similar to that of "Salty Dog Blues," in 1925, and the white country guitarist Riley Puckett had cut "Mama Don't Allow No Low Down Riders Here" in 1928. It may be that "Mama Don't Allow" grew out of "Mister Crump," a song W. C. Handy said he wrote in 1909, although Handy's authorship is also questionable. A Memphis-based black vaudeville duo called the Too Sweets advertised the song "Mama Don't Allow No Easy Talking Here" in September 1912 and protested the following year that it had been stolen from its author, Lulu "Too Sweet" Perry.[23]

In 1941, Handy published his autobiography, *Father of the Blues,* in which he tried to buttress his longstanding claim to have written the first blues song. Handy's "The Memphis Blues" was copyrighted on September 27, 1912, but three other songs with the word "blues" in the title—Chris Smith and Tim Brymn's "I've Got the Blues but I'm Too Blamed Mean to Cry," H. Franklin Seals's "Baby Seals Blues," and Hart Wand's "Dallas Blues"—had come out previously that year. Handy explained that he had written "Memphis Blues" three years earlier for the campaign of E. H. Crump, a reform candidate for the Memphis mayoralty who was threatening to run pimps and gamblers out of town. The words, he said, were adapted from spontaneous comments made or sung by audience or band members when the tune was first played.[24]

On a reminiscence that Handy tape-recorded in 1952, he sings the more-or-less original lyrics, including the lines "Mr. Crump don't 'low no easy riders here. / We don't care what Mr. Crump don't 'low, / We gonna barrelhouse anyhow."[25] After Crump was elected, Handy says, he had to change the title, so he published the song as "The Memphis Blues." In fact, the first edition, an instrumental, was subtitled "Mister Crump," and new lyrics were added later; in his book *The Country Blues,* Samuel Charters suggests that Handy changed the title in response to the success of "Dallas Blues."[26]

In his liner notes to *Cow Cow Davenport, Volume 3: The Unissued 1940s Acetate Recordings,* David Evans speculates that Davenport, in the wake of Slack's "Cow-Cow Boogie," followed Handy's example in promoting himself as the father of boogie-woogie. Eventually he was admitted to the American Society of Composers, Authors and Publishers and collected some royalties. He was featured in a couple of prestigious New York concerts, made a few more records, and moved back to Cleveland, where he worked at a defense plant until his death in 1955.[27]

Davenport did pursue legal action over the rights to "Cow-Cow Boogie" but settled for five hundred dollars—not bad, considering that the song has no apparent musical tie to any of his known compositions."[28] The rolling riff that Slack plays on "Cow-Cow Boogie" and that Davenport demonstrates on the acetates is nowhere to be found on Davenport's previous recordings; in any case, it's hardly a real boogie-woogie bass line at all.

By contrast, "Cow Cow Blues" makes extensive use of boogie bass lines, although it also contains elements of ragtime. "Cow Cow Blues" was not without influence: figures from the tune turn up in such piano recordings as Albert Ammons's hypnotic "Bass Goin' Crazy," from 1939, and Big Maceo Merriweather's irresistibly swinging "Texas Stomp," from 1945. But those records made a negligible impact on mainstream pop music, though Merriweather's "Worried Life Blues" became a blues standard and was covered by Chuck Berry.

JOHNNY B. GOODE

A descending figure from "Cow Cow Blues" does foreshadow the opening guitar solo from Berry's 1958 rock classic "Johnny B. Goode." Jelly Roll Morton plays practically the same figure on his July 1923 recording of "New Orleans Joys," a tune notable for its use of the habanera or tango rhythm in the bass line. But on Davenport's May 1929 recording of "Texas Shout"—where he plays the descending figure at the beginning of the tune, preceded by a repeated note—the "Johnny B. Goode" connection is inescapable.

By his own admission, Berry lifted the first part of his solo from guitarist Carl Hogan's intro to Louis Jordan's "Ain't That Just Like a Woman," recorded in January 1946.[29] Hogan may have taken the motif from Count Basie's May 1940 recording of "Super Chief," where it's heard as a brassy shout chorus in the middle of the tune, and Basie may have got it from Andy Kirk's March 1936 recording of "Walkin' and Swingin'," where a shorter snatch of the same shout chorus appears. But the "Johnny B. Goode" motif also shows up, almost as Hogan plays it, in the ragtime-blues guitarist Blind Blake's "Too Tight," recorded around October 1926. Blind Lemon Jefferson plays practically the same riff on "Got the Blues," which he first recorded in March 1926. And Wilbur Sweatman's Jazz Orchestra, one of the first black jazz bands to make records, plays the "Johnny B. Goode" riff on its December 1918 recording of "Bluin' the Blues."

Although there is no direct musical link between Slack's "Cow-Cow Boogie" and Davenport's "Cow Cow Blues," there may be an indirect connection, however ephemeral. In the middle of Bob Crosby's "Cow Cow Blues," there is a brief piano figure that bears an uncanny resemblance to the "strange beat" Slack plays on "Cow-Cow Boogie."

Nine years Bing's junior, Bob Crosby was singing with the Dorsey Brothers Orchestra in 1935 when he was recruited to front a band formed by defectors from Ben Pollack's group (which launched the careers of Benny

Goodman, Jack Teagarden, Glenn Miller, and Harry James). With several New Orleanians among its members, the Crosby band helped lead the revival of traditional New Orleans jazz, by then considered passé. In 1938, even before the "From Spirituals to Swing" concert, the band added boogie-woogies to its repertoire, featuring pianist Bob Zurke, a white boogie master like Freddie Slack, on big-band arrangements of Meade "Lux" Lewis's "Yancey Special" and "Honky Tonk Train Blues."

The group also recorded contemporary swing charts and pop songs, the latter accounting for most of its hits. By September 1940, when Crosby's band cut "Cow Cow Blues," it had replaced Benny Goodman's band on *The Camel Caravan,* the most popular musical radio show of the day, but it was increasingly reliant on novelty effects and swing clichés.[30] Crosby based his "Cow Cow Blues" on Sammy Price's March 1940 septet version, which similarly alternates between boogie piano and swinging band sections. "It was my arrangement that I recorded, and later Bob Crosby took the whole arrangement, note for note, and didn't say a word to me," Price recounted, exaggerating somewhat. "Well, I didn't care, because I wasn't greedy and I was making money and I had gained recognition."[31] (Bob Zurke also recorded "Cow Cow Blues" with his big band in May 1940, but the arrangement is much different.)

Unlike Price's arrangement or Crosby's earlier boogie charts, which were reasonably faithful to their sources, Crosby's "Cow Cow Blues" goes off the rails, interjecting swing and Dixieland passages so exaggerated that they seem to spoof Davenport's original. Among the interpolations are a Louis Armstrong–style trumpet solo, a slightly sappy take on the "Johnny B. Goode" shout chorus from Basie's "Super Chief," and two measures' worth of the little piano figure, built on the same three notes as Slack's. The pianist, Jess Stacy, had left Benny Goodman to join Crosby after Bob Zurke formed his own band. His short solo, segueing from the rolling, western-flavored riff to classically tinged arpeggios, is eminently forgettable, but it could well have made an impression on Slack, who—like Carter, DePaul, and Raye—was probably familiar with Crosby's recording.

It's doubtful, however, that Benny Carter could have heard Crosby's "Cow Cow Blues" before October 1940, when he cut his own boogie adaptation of "Sugar Blues," a trad-jazz standard written by Clarence Williams and Lucy Fletcher in 1919. Among the artists who recorded "Sugar Blues" over the years were Leona Williams, Sara Martin, King Oliver, Johnny Dunn, Tommy Dorsey, Count Basie, Harry James, Bob Wills, Fats Waller, and Clarence Williams himself. On a piano roll of "Sugar Blues" made in April 1923, three months before Jelly Roll Morton recorded "New Orleans Joys," Williams plays the "Johnny B. Goode" riff with an opening trill instead of a repeated note, just as pianist Charlie Spand does on his August 1929 duo recording of "Hastings Street" with Blind Blake. (A similar riff turns up on

King Oliver's "Deep Henderson," from 1926, with clarinetist Albert Nicholas holding a high note in place of the piano trill before playing the descending figure.)

Ella Fitzgerald scored a minor hit with "Sugar Blues" in June 1940, and Johnny Mercer made the Top 5 with it in 1947, but the song is most closely associated with Clyde McCoy, a white trumpeter known for his growling wah-wah sound. McCoy had a big hit with "Sugar Blues" on the Columbia label in 1931 and another hit with a rerecording for Decca four years later. Decca, which also released Fitzgerald's "Sugar Blues," recorded Benny Carter for the first time in May 1940, allowing him to choose his own repertoire. But for his second Decca session, the label demanded more commercial material, including "Boogie Woogie Sugar Blues," which it issued over Carter's objections, prompting his defection to Bluebird. "I went along at first," Carter recalled, "but the results were just not what I wanted my orchestra to sound like."[32]

On "Boogie Woogie Sugar Blues," trumpeter Russell Smith emulates McCoy's wah-wah technique. More intriguingly, pianist Sonny White plays a slowed-down version of the "Pine Top's Boogie Woogie" bass pattern that strongly suggests Slack's "Cow-Cow Boogie" riff—the "strange beat" Davenport dated to 1910. Like Jess Stacy's "Cow Cow Blues" figure, White's bass line lacks the passing tone that gives Slack's figure its cantering feel. One of the early names for the boogie-woogie style was "fast western," and according to the critic Ernest Borneman, "The 'western' bass was an attempt to imitate the clipclop of horses' hooves; thus the similarity between the rhythm of a great many cowboy songs and 'fast western' blues."[33]

The first use of a western-style repeating bass figure may have occurred in Richard M. Jones's composition "Jazzin' Babies Blues," which Ethel Waters recorded without the figure in May 1922 and King Oliver's Jazz Band (including Louis Armstrong) recorded with the figure in June 1923. Jones himself also recorded the tune (sometimes confused with the New Orleans Rhythm Kings' similar-sounding "Tin Roof Blues") in June 1923 as a piano solo, clearly stating the bass figure in the introduction. Like Jess Stacy's or Sonny White's bass lines, it sounds like Freddie Slack's "strange beat" without the passing tone.

While "Cow-Cow Boogie" may not have any specific relationship to Davenport's music, it was certainly inspired by his nickname. The lyrics, with their peculiar juxtaposition of cowboy and hipster imagery, amount to an elaborate pun on the title of "Cow Cow Blues." Written for a musical comedy western at the height of the boogie-woogie craze just after the United States entered World II, the song reflects a confluence of pop-culture trends—singing cowboys, slapstick comedy teams, big-band swing, African American slang, the rediscovery of traditional jazz and blues—united by the common element of escapism.

If Freddie Slack's "Cow-Cow Boogie" represents the assimilation of black music by whites, Tiny Bradshaw's "The Train Kept A-Rollin'" exemplifies its reappropriation by blacks. However unknowingly, Bradshaw also reconnected the song to its railroad roots. On the original "Cow Cow Blues," with its locomotive rhythms, Dora Carr rattles off the names of southern rail lines—the Seaboard, the W&A, the Cannonball—and of course Papa Cow Cow took his moniker from a cowcatcher, not a cowpuncher. In the end, Giorgio Gomelsky's speculation that the song was "somehow" derived from a train imitation turns out to have merit, and not only as regards the Yardbirds version.

But "Cow Cow Boogie" didn't just start with the sound of a train. The descending figure that "Cow Cow Blues" shares with Jelly Roll Morton's "New Orleans Joys"—preceded by a repeated note, as it is on Wilbur Sweatman's "Bluin' the Blues," Blind Lemon Jefferson's "Got the Blues," Davenport's "Texas Shout," Blind Blake's "Too Tight," Count Basie's "Super Chief," Louis Jordan's "Ain't That Just Like a Woman," and Chuck Berry's "Johnny B. Goode"—can be heard in "A Bunch of Blues," published in 1915 by J. Paul Wyer and H. Alf Kelley (or Kelly) and recorded in 1916 by pianist W. G. Haenschen and drummer T. T. Schiffer, in 1917 by W. C. Handy's band, in 1918 by accordionist Charlie Klass, and in 1923 by the Original Memphis Five.[34]

As its title implies, "A Bunch of Blues" is a medley, comprising four different compositions: "The Weary Blues," "String Beans Blues," "Ship Wreck Blues," and the "The Long Lost Blues."[35] Wyer, who played violin in W. C. Handy's band around 1909, first collaborated with Kelley on the two-part "Long Lost Blues," published in 1914.[36] The second theme of "The Long Lost Blues" may mark the first written appearance of the melody later known as "Keep A Knockin'," the basis for Little Richard's 1957 rock 'n' roll hit by that title. Practically the same tune, however, is used for "Bucket's Got a Hole in It," a song performed by everyone from Buddy Bolden, generally regarded as the very first jazz musician, to Louis Armstrong, Hank Williams, and Ricky Nelson.

"The Weary Blues," published separately by Kelley in 1916, is not the same tune as the traditional jazz classic of that title published in 1915 by Artie Matthews, nor is "Ship Wreck Blues" the same tune as the "Shipwrecked Blues" recorded by Clara Smith in 1925 or the "Shipwreck Blues" recorded by Bessie Smith in 1931. Neither "Ship Wreck Blues" nor "String Beans Blues" seems to have been published outside of "A Bunch of Blues."

"String Beans Blues" is apparently a tribute to Butler "String Beans" May, a once-famous, now-forgotten African American vaudeville singer, pianist, and comedian who died in 1917 at the age of twenty-three. The Alabama-born May, one of the first popularizers of the blues, is not known to have copyrighted or published any of his compositions, but some of their titles have been preserved in reviews and advertisements in African American newspapers and in the reminiscences of musicians who saw May perform, such as Jelly Roll Morton. Among those titles are "The Whiskey Blues," "Low Down Jail House Blues," and "Hospital Blues" but not "String Beans Blues," indicating that that tune is not necessarily May's, although some of its elements might be.[37] And it is in the opening strain of "String Beans Blues" that the "Johnny B. Goode" riff is heard.

But the riff's first published and recorded appearance seems to have been made in the white songwriter Carey Morgan's popular "Trilby Rag," copyrighted in May 1915 (six months before "A Bunch of Blues"), introduced by the celebrated dance team of Vernon and Irene Castle, and waxed for Victor by Conway's Band in August of the same year.[38] And "Trilby Rag" is clearly the source of Cow Cow Davenport's "Atlanta Rag," which Davenport recorded on a piano roll in 1922 and which includes the "Johnny B. Goode" riff. "Atlanta Rag," in turn, forms the basis for both "Cow Cow Blues" and "Texas Shout."

The descending figure that follows the repeated note in the "Johnny B. Goode" riff and that appears without the repeated note in Davenport's "Cow Cow Blues" and Morton's "New Orleans Joys" can be traced back still further, though not with any degree of certainty. Morton, who recorded "New Orleans Joys" in 1923, later claimed that it was his first composition, written between 1902 and 1905 under the title "New Orleans Blues." "All the black bands in the city of New Orleans played . . . this tune," Morton told Alan Lomax.[39] (Morton also played a relatively modern-sounding blues for Lomax that he attributed to a New Orleans pianist called Game Kid and dated to around 1900; this "Game Kid Blues" opens with the complete Johnny B. Goode figure, followed by a chugging rhythm strikingly suggestive of Chuck Berry.)[40]

Morton's recollections, in this matter as in others, are open to challenge. Morton said he was born on September 20, 1885, but a baptismal certificate gives the date as October 20, 1890, which would mean he was no more than eighteen years old and perhaps only twelve when he wrote "New Orleans Blues."[41] And while there were songs with the word "blues" in the title before 1902—notably Chris Smith and Elmer Bowman's "I've Got de Blues," published in 1901—no title identifying the blues as a style of music or type of song, such as "Memphis Blues" or "Baby Seals Blues," is known to have been published before 1912.[42]

String Beans May was at least six years Morton's junior, but Morton saw him perform in the early part of May's career, around 1910, and got the idea to wear a diamond in his tooth from the younger entertainer.[43] A reviewer in 1914 compared Morton's comedic blackface stage act to May's, and Morton may well have been influenced by May's music.[44]

The Latin beat in "New Orleans Joys" would seemingly have dated from after 1913, when the tango first swept the United States, having emerged in Argentina a decade earlier. But the original tango rhythm (no longer heard in modern tangos) was derived from the habanera, or *danza,* which developed in Cuba in the early nineteenth century and became an international phenomenon after the publication of Sebastián Yradier's "La Paloma" around 1860. Mexican bands introduced the habanera to New Orleans in the 1880s, and Morton played "La Paloma" for Alan Lomax in 1938 to demonstrate how he put a "Spanish tinge" into "New Orleans Blues."[45] The habanera rhythm appears in a section of Bert Williams and George Walker's "My Little Zulu Babe," recorded in 1901. But the first African American musician said to have used habanera rhythms was the pianist Jesse Pickett, whom the ragtime pianist Eubie Blake met as a youngster when Pickett was playing in a brothel in Blake's native Baltimore. "He was an old pimp," Blake recalled. "He was pretty old already back in 1898."[46]

Pickett was known for the song "The Dream," also called "The Bull Diker's Dream," "The Bowdiger's Dream," "The Digah's Dream," or "The Ladies' Dream." Pianist James P. Johnson, ten years younger than Blake, attributed the song to John "Jack the Bear" Wilson, an opium-smoking vaudeville and bawdyhouse pianist whom Blake also met in Baltimore (but evidently not the same "Jack the Bear" whom Jelly Roll Morton met in Jackson, Mississippi).[47] Johnson recorded "The Dream" with his band in 1944 and as a piano solo in 1945, using a pronounced if not particularly authentic habanera figure in the bass. Blake recorded "Dream Rag" on his 1969 comeback album *The Eighty-Six Years of Eubie Blake,* saying, "I play it just as Jesse taught it to me over seventy years ago."[48] But despite its distinctive habanera rhythm, Blake's "Dream Rag" is hardly recognizable as the same tune as Johnson's "The Dream."[49]

As recorded by Blake, the song is a frilly precursor of ragtime rather than a genuine rag. It is of interest mainly for that reason, but in the middle of "Dream Rag" there is a brief series of triplets, virtually identical to the ones Cow Cow Davenport repeats at greater length over a boogie-woogie bass line in "Cow Cow Blues." Whether Davenport was familiar with Jesse Pickett's song or whether Blake really played the tune as Pickett did will never be known. Most likely the splashed triplets, and the descending bass figure in "Cow Cow Blues" and "New Orleans Joys," were simply floating folk strains—fragments of the common vocabulary shared by African American musicians of the 1890s. But if Eubie Blake is to be believed, "Cow Cow Blues"—and, by extension, "The Train Kept A-Rollin'"—can ultimately be grounded in the era of the coon song, a time when ragtime, blues, boogie-woogie, and jazz were just beginning to take form.

ROLLING ON

As the song evolved, its performers went through a remarkable number of racial alternations, from Jesse Pickett to Conway's Band to W. C. Handy to Charles Klass to Jelly Roll Morton to the Original Memphis Five to Cow Cow Davenport to Bob Crosby to Ella Fitzgerald to Freddie Slack to Tiny Bradshaw to Johnny Burnette. But from Burnette on, every artist who recorded "The Train Kept A-Rollin'," with the exception of the bluesman Honeyboy Edwards, was white. What alternation there was was between England and the United States.

One of the first post-Yardbirds recordings of "The Train Kept A-Rollin'" was by a trio from upstate New York called the Rogues, who released their version on the Audition label in July 1966 as the flip side of the single "You Better Look Now." Drenched in distortion, it sounds like a cross between the Yardbirds' "Train" and the Count Five's Yardbirds-inspired hit "Psychotic Reaction," which was released a couple of months later. In 1967, a Seattle band, Brave New World, cut a grungy, stomping demo of "The Train Kept A-Rollin'" that came to light on two different 2002 compilations from the vaults of Jerden Records (one on the British Big Beat label and the other on American Beat Rocket), both titled *Northwest Battle of the Bands, Vol. 3.* A third variation—swift and slick, with an actual train whistle dubbed in at the beginning and end—was recorded during the same period by Steve Walker and the Bold and issued on the 1996 Bomp collection *Pebbles, Vol. 10.*

The Yardbirds had recorded "The Train Kept A-Rollin'" again for BBC radio shortly after returning from their 1965 U.S. tour, but the performance—oddly fuzzless and, without the doubled vocal, easily comprehensible—was not released until the late 1990s. They made another recording of the song in March 1968, a year and a half after Beck left and a few months before the band broke up and Page hired Robert Plant, John Paul Jones, and John Bonham to fulfill its contractual obligations as the New Yardbirds. (At Page's suggestion, the first song the foursome played together was "The Train Kept A-Rollin'.") The old Yardbirds taped their concert at the Anderson Theater in New York but decided that the music was not worth releasing. Three years later, following Page's success with Led Zeppelin, Epic Records issued the performance, dubbing in additional crowd noises, on an LP and an eight-track cassette titled *Live Yardbirds! Featuring Jimmy Page*. Page went to court and had the album pulled from store shelves within a week, but several bootleg versions remain in circulation.[50]

Shortly before the Yardbirds' Anderson Theater concert, Nazz, a Philadelphia rock quartet led by Todd Rundgren, made a demo of "The Train Kept A-Rollin'." It's basically a copy of the Yardbirds' first version, with a speedy beat and a bass line that sounds almost electronic. Guitarist Rundgren sticks close to Beck's solos, and singer Robert "Stewkey" Antoni is double-tracked like Relf. But the recording was not issued until 1983, when it was included on the Rhino Records collection *The Best of Nazz*.

The Dallas-based Scotty McKay Quintet released "The Train Kept A-Rollin'" in 1968 as a single on the Falcon label. Although singer McKay had played guitar and piano as a member of Gene Vincent's Blue Caps in the late 1950s under his given name, Max Lipscomb, his "Train Kept A-Rollin'" betrays no familiarity with Johnny Burnette's. Instead, it combines the feedback and heavy chording of the Yardbirds' "Stroll On" with Keith Relf's muddled "Train Kept A-Rollin'" lyrics, which McKay further mangles while imitating Relf's voice and rudimentary harmonica technique. The long, biting guitar solo, which ends with a jarring tape edit, is in Jimmy Page's style, and McKay maintained that Page himself had dubbed the part in; the track is even included on the Page compilation *Have Guitar, Will Travel.*[51] But the solo is also claimed by Bobby Rambo, the regular guitarist with McKay's quintet, and by Blair Smith, the guitarist for another Dallas band, the Exotics.[52]

Haymarket Square, Chicago's short-lived answer to the Jefferson Airplane, recorded "The Train Kept A-Rollin'" as part of a performance for a 1968 art exhibit. The performance turned into the band's only album, *Magic Lantern* (on Chaparral Records), a rare collector's item until it was reissued on the Gear Fab label in 2001. Moody and amateurish, it's an artifact of the psychedelic era—acid-rock at its most elemental. At least two more American versions of "The Train Kept A-Rollin'" are known to have been cut in the late 1960s, one by the Cynics, from Fort Worth, Texas, and the other by the Precious Few, from Lynchburg, Virginia. Amazingly, the Precious Few's recording ends with a solo bass playing a simple western-flavored figure similar to Freddie Slack's "Cow Cow Boogie" riff.

The Denver-based group Sugarloaf released "The Train Kept A-Rollin'" on its self-titled 1970 debut album (on Liberty Records), following an extended version of its Top 5 hit "Green-Eyed Lady." Though obviously inspired by the Yardbirds, the band's mildly jazz-tinged "Train" shows a measure of originality; like "Green-Eyed Lady," it's a cheesy harbinger of progressive rock. The Welsh band Shakin' Stevens and the Sunsets released "The Train Kept A-Rollin'" on their 1970 debut album, *A Legend* (on EMI), and rerecorded the song for their 1973 album *Shakin' Stevens & Sunsets*. Virtually alone among "Train" covers, Stevens's is based on the Johnny Burnette version, albeit without the Paul Burlison guitar riff.

Along with the MC5 and, to a lesser extent, the Stooges, the Up was a part of the poet and musician John Sinclair's revolutionary circle in Detroit and Ann Arbor, Michigan, in the late 1960s and early 1970s. Sinclair claims that the quartet was a precursor of punk rock, and its only commercial single, "Just Like an Aborigine," does sound like a Ramones prototype.[53] (Its other single, "Free John Now," backed with the poet Allen Ginsberg's "Prayer for

John Sinclair," was handed out at a rally to protest Sinclair's imprisonment.) But the Up's "Train Kept A-Rollin'" is pure garage rock; recorded at a Columbus, Ohio, show in September 1972, it was finally released on the group's only album, *Killer Up!* produced by Sinclair in 1995 for his own Total Energy label.

The British blues-rock band Foghat set the lyrics of "Honey Hush" to the music of the Yardbirds' "Train Kept A-Rollin'" on its album *Energized* (on Bearsville), issued in January 1974. The version that secured the place of "Train Kept A-Rollin'" in the hard-rock mainstream, however, was the one on Aerosmith's second album, *Get Your Wings.* Released by Columbia in March 1974, the album helped propel Aerosmith to stardom and is still regarded as one of the band's best. "Train Kept A-Rollin'," the only non-original song on *Get Your Wings*, was released as a single a few months later. As if in emulation of the screen presentation of "Stroll On," it's played twice in a row, first to a strutting beat and then, following the dubbed-in cheers of a nonexistent audience, in a faster rhythm. Steven Tyler sings with rote, rasping efficacy, modifying the words to suit his personality. Nazz's Stewkey Antoni had already described the dame on the train as "handsome" rather than a "hepster"; Tyler makes the same error, adding, "We kind of looked the same."

But the track is essentially a guitar showcase, with no fewer than five solo spots, including the elaborate introduction. All the solos allude to Beck's, but the original phrases are embellished with flashy filigree and augmented with bravura blues licks, walking the line between hard rock and heavy metal. Though the playing substitutes fluid precision for Beck's raw edginess, it's still one of the most impressive displays of rock-guitar pyrotechnics in the period between the death of Jimi Hendrix and the emergence of Eddie Van Halen.

According to a chronology that's duplicated on numerous Aerosmith websites, the band Chain Reaction—featuring singer Steve Tally, who'd changed his name from Stephen Tallarico—had opened for the Yardbirds at the 1968 Anderson Theater show (Aerosmith's own published "autobiography" has Chain Reaction more plausibly opening for the Yardbirds at a Connecticut high school in 1966).[54] Tally later formed Aerosmith with guitarist Joe Perry and bassist Tom Hamilton and changed his name to Steven Tyler. In an interview for *Guitar World* magazine, Perry says that "The Train Kept A-Rollin'" was "the only song we had in common when we first got together. Steven's band had played 'Train' and Tom and I played it in our band. . . . It's a blues song, if you follow its roots all the way back. . . . I always thought if I could just play one song, it would be that one because of what it does to me."[55]

Yet the session guitarist Dick Wagner credibly claims that he and his frequent partner Steve Hunter played the solos on Aerosmith's "Train Kept

A-Rollin'," not Perry or the band's other guitarist at the time, Brad Whitford. Producer Bob Ezrin, who was also responsible for Wagner and Hunter's better-known associations with Alice Cooper and Lou Reed, hired them for *Get Your Wings.* "I was living at the Plaza Hotel in New York at the time, and I got a call to come over and play on this Aerosmith record," Wagner says. "I didn't know who they were. . . . I guess nobody did then. I played on 4 tracks and Steve played on a couple tracks. We weren't credited because the band didn't want anybody thinking that Joe Perry didn't play all those solo's [sic]!"[56]

Wagner says that he and Hunter both played on "Train Kept A-Rollin'," but it's hard to tell who plays what.[57] "We wanted to keep the solos equal so we'd sit down . . . and go through the material so it was totally even," Hunter explains. "We didn't want it to look like there was a rhythm guitar player and a lead guitar player, because that's what we both did."[58]

"The Train Kept A-Rollin'" is the final track on 1977's *Motörhead* (on Chiswick), the first album released, though not the first recorded, by the British heavy-metal trio of the same name. Motörhead's crude, pummeling sound—similar to the punk rock that emerged around the same time—paved the way for the thrash-metal of Metallica and a host of other bands. Like Aerosmith's "Train," Motörhead's draws from both the first Yardbirds recording and "Stroll On," but it's played only once through, with just two guitar solos, not counting the brief introduction. When he isn't cranking out power chords, the lone guitarist, "Fast" Eddie Clarke, plays lean but effective leads, tipping his hat to Beck before breaking into Chuck Berry riffs. Singer Lemmy Kilmister reduces the lyrics to Tarzan-movie basics: "I was alone, she was a woman / I was a man, I never knew her name," he grunts, dispensing entirely with the dame on the train. About all that's left is "she was pretty, New York City" and, ineluctably, "that old fair lane."

A recording of "The Train Kept A-Rollin'" made by the Long Island glam-metal band Twisted Sister at a 1979 show in Port Chester, New York, was tacked onto a tape of the group's 1984 London concert and issued on the 1994 CD *Live at Hammersmith* (on Spitfire Records). A ten-minute extravaganza, the track takes Aerosmith's version into Spinal Tap territory: following a prolonged feedback freakout by guitarist Eddie Ojeda, singer Dee Snider announces that "This train is goin' to cocaine land," and the rhythm kicks into overdrive. As on the Tiny Bradshaw and Lord Sutch versions, there's a call-and-response on the title line, but this time it's the audience that sings "all night long."

The Parisian post-punk band Métal Urbain recorded two demos of "The Train Kept A-Rollin'" in January 1979; released on the 2003 Acute Records CD *Les Hommes Morts Sont Dangereux*, they feature French-accented vocals and edgy guitars crisply punctuated by a drum machine.

Tav Falco's Memphis "punkabilly" band Panther Burns recorded "Train Kept A-Rollin'" on a 1980 EP and a 1981 single, both produced for the band's own Frenzi label by the former Box Tops and Big Star vocalist Alex Chilton, who also plays guitar on the sessions. An earlier Falco recording, made for a Memphis television station in 1979, surfaced on *It Came from Memphis, Volume 2* (on the Birdman label), a companion CD to Robert Gordon's 1994 book *It Came from Memphis.* Surprisingly, it shows no Yardbirds influence whatsoever, and while it's essentially in rockabilly style, it barely nods to Johnny Burnette. Instead, Falco drawls the lyrics over Chilton's minimalist strumming, adding abstract plinks and squeals on guitar. Like Chilton, Falco sojourned in New York the following year, hooking up with "no wave" musicians such as Arto Lindsay and James Chance. Chilton cut his own generic-sounding rockabilly version of "Train Kept A-Rollin'" on his 1982 album *Live in London* (on the British Aura label).

A recording of "The Train Kept A-Rollin'" made by the New York metal band Riot during a 1980 tour of England was released in 1993 on the album *Live Riot.* The group revs into full-blown thrash while singer Guy Speranza interpolates lyrics from "Honey Hush." Another recording of the song, made by the Finnish metal band Hanoi Rocks at the Marquee Club in London in 1983, was released in the United States in 1991 on the album *All Those Wasted Years*, half a decade after the group broke up. The New Jersey metal band Skid Row included a live performance of "The Train Kept A-Rollin'" in Alpine Valley, Wisconsin, sung by a prancing, shirtless Sebastian Bach, on its 1990 video *Oh Say Can You Scream.* A live rendition by the Canadian band the Tragically Hip, including a spoken digression by lead singer Gordon Downie, was recorded at a 1991 concert in Arizona and issued on a couple of bootleg albums. And the Canadian rocker Colin James released one of the few versions directly based on Tiny Bradshaw's on the 1993 album *Colin James and the Little Big Band.*

Two 1980s British psychobilly bands recorded "The Train Kept A-Rollin'"—Guana Batz on the 1984 various-artists compilation *Stomping at the Klub Foot* and the punkier King Kurt on its 1994 comeback album *Poor Man's Dream.* Two 1990s American cowpunk bands also cut the song—Kentucky's Nine Pound Hammer on its album *Live at the Vera,* recorded in Holland in 1994, and Maryland's Ironboss on the 2000 collection *Right in the Nuts: A Tribute to Aerosmith.* Not to be left out, the rockabilly revivalists Stray Cats did the song on their 1993 album *Original Cool.*

Aerosmith released a concert version of "The Train Kept A-Rollin'" on its 1978 album *Live! Bootleg,* and there are a number of actual bootlegs of other Aerosmith "Train" performances, plus a recording of Guns N' Roses playing the song with Steven Tyler and Joe Perry from a televised 1992 show in Paris. There are also bootlegs of Led Zeppelin performing "The Train Kept A-Rollin'" during tours of the United States and Europe in 1968, 1969, and 1980. Motörhead released several live "Train" recordings, notably the one on its 1981 album *No Sleep 'til Hammersmith.*

Jeff Beck recorded "The Train Kept A-Rollin'" with singer Andrew Roachford, keyboardist Tony Hymas, and drummer Peter Richardson for the 1988 movie *Twins,* starring Arnold Schwarzenegger and Danny DeVito. On screen, Beck appears with different musicians, backing singer Nicolette Larson on a country song. In a scene vaguely reminiscent of both *Blow-Up* and *Ride 'Em Cowboy,* a group of gangsters confronts Schwarzenegger and DeVito in a nightclub filled with cowboy-hatted dancers. While Beck looks on, DeVito grabs an acoustic guitar from the stage and knocks one of the thugs out with it, just as the band breaks into "The Train Kept A-Rollin'." Barely a snatch of the tune is heard in the film, but the complete track—a pumped-up, Aerosmith-informed update—appears on the soundtrack album and on the boxed set *Beckology.*

A re-formed Yardbirds, featuring only Chris Dreja and drummer Jim McCarty from the original lineup, redid "The Train Kept A-Rollin'" with Joe Satriani on guitar for the group's 2003 album *Birdland* (on Favored Nations Records). And Paul Burlison, at the age of sixty-eight, rerecorded "The Train Kept A-Rollin'" as the title track of his 1997 album on Sweetfish Records, with Johnny Burnette's son Rocky singing.

The Long Island retro-rocker Ralph Rebel cut an even more nostalgic version for his 2001 album *Big Town Boogie* (on Golly Gee). Rebel's "The Train Kept A-Rollin'" harks back to the brassy jump-blues style, but his tepid arrangement owes more to the swing-dance revival movement than to Tiny Bradshaw's original.

On the novelty side, there's the version on the 2001 album *5,000,000* (on IRS Records) by Dread Zeppelin, a group that covers songs by Led Zeppelin and other rock artists to a reggae beat, with vocals by an Elvis impersonator. There's a bluegrass version, recorded outside Nashville, on the 2000 album *Pickin' on Aerosmith,* part of CMH Records' extensive Pickin' On series of tributes to rock and country artists by top bluegrass musicians. Inevitably, there's a karaoke version—Aerosmith style—on *Party Tyme Karaoke: Rock Classics* (Sybersound), a special karaoke disc with lyrics that scroll on a monitor.

Arguably the most outlandish version, however, is the one by the late David "Honeyboy" Edwards on the 2001 tribute compilation *Sweet Emotion: Songs of Aerosmith,* the first and, it seems, last album in the Heavy Hip Mama label's projected Blues on Fire series, in which blues artists pay ironic homage to rock stars. A genuine Mississippi Delta blues legend, Edwards played with Charlie Patton, Tommy McClennan, Big Joe Williams, Big Walter Horton, and Robert Johnson. In 1942, Alan Lomax recorded him for the Library of Congress; in the 1950s, Sam Phillips and Leonard Chess recorded him for the Sun and Chess labels. But though he cut several albums in the

1960s, 1970s, and 1980s, Edwards won little recognition until the 1990s, by which time his ability to perform had markedly diminished.

On "Train Kept A-Rollin'," made when Edwards was eighty-five, the gritty tenor heard on his early recordings has deteriorated into a hoarse moan. At first he struggles with the lyrics, reciting them as though reading from cue cards; then he strikes up a four-to-the-bar boogie-guitar beat and sings, repeating the line "train keep rollin' all night long" until he works up a head of steam. He awkwardly mouths Steven Tyler's words "I'm in heat, I'm in love" a couple of times, but then, perhaps tapping into a distant memory, reverts to Tiny Bradshaw's "with a heave and a ho." The song ends and, after a pause, starts again and fades out.

Presumably, the producers didn't intend to create a demeaning lampoon of a feeble old bluesman, but that's what they accomplished, at least to an extent. It's to Edwards's credit that he is able to make the song his own for a few moments here and there, but "The Train Kept A-Rollin'" is just too much of a stretch for him. The recording, clearly not Edwards's idea, seems to be an attempt to reproduce the roots of rock as they are often imagined—a lone male black Mississippian growling rough blues stanzas while plucking primitive guitar licks. Ultimately, though, "The Train Kept A-Rollin'" is an outgrowth of the rowdy piano tradition of southern barrelhouses and tent shows rather than the keening guitar blues of the Delta cotton fields.

As on many of the albums where it appears, "Train Kept A-Rollin'" is the final track on *Sweet Emotion*—the culmination of what has come before. *Rock: Train Kept A-Rollin'* is also the title of one of a dozen genre-specific double CDs broken out of the twenty-six-disc 1999 boxed set *Sony Music 100 Years: Soundtrack of a Century*. Spanning more than three decades of music on Columbia and its affiliated labels, it includes artists ranging from Bob Dylan to Korn, among them the Yardbirds, Jeff Beck, and Aerosmith. It's a summation of an era, but it does not contain the song "Train Kept A-Rollin'."

As it evolved from ragtime through jazz, boogie-woogie, big-band swing, small-combo rhythm-and-blues, rockabilly, blues-rock, acid rock, heavy metal, punk, thrash, psychobilly, and points beyond, "The Train Kept A-Rollin'" became increasingly wild and dissonant, as if each performer were trying to surpass the intensity of the previous one. Through all the transformations, the essence of Bradshaw's original survives—a semblance of the melody, a smattering of the lyrics, and the immortal refrain "The train kept a-rollin' all night long," a cogent sexual metaphor for power and endurance. What few traces remain of "Cow-Cow Boogie" are harder to discern, but its conceptual core—the absorption of black blues and boogie-woogie, with a country-western tinge, into the white popular mainstream—is the basis for everything that follows.

As for "Cow Cow Blues," it's the impetus that set the entire sequence of musical events in motion. The strands of ragtime, blues, and boogie-woogie that found their way into "Cow Cow Blues" date back still further, to the late nineteenth century at least, but there the trail goes cold, and documentation gives way to speculation.

Chapter Three

One o' Them Things!

BIG BILL

According to the title of a Muddy Waters song, "The Blues Had a Baby and They Named It Rock and Roll." By 1976, when that song was recorded, it was widely accepted that rock 'n' roll was an offshoot of the blues—either the electric Chicago blues that Waters popularized in the 1950s or the Mississippi Delta blues that first inspired him in the 1920s.

Waters made the national R&B charts in 1948 singing pure Delta blues, accompanied only by his electric guitar and an upright bass. Lightnin' Hopkins and John Lee Hooker charted the following year singing unadulterated rural blues with just their own acoustic guitars. In the early 1950s, Waters and a few other blues singers, among them Howlin' Wolf and Elmore James, had R&B hits with electrified band arrangements of country-style blues. But with such exceptions as Big Boy Crudup's "That's All Right," which Elvis Presley adapted into his first record, country blues was not absorbed directly into rock music until the 1960s.

About the closest thing to a blues-to-rock crossover before then was Chuck Willis's "C.C. Rider," a No. 1 R&B hit that made the pop Top 20 in 1957. Willis was surely familiar with Wee Bea Booze's "See See Rider Blues," a No. 1 R&B hit that made the pop Top 20 in 1943. Booze's song is based on Ma Rainey's 1924 classic "See See Rider Blues," which also became a pop hit. The song was recorded in country-blues style by Blind Lemon Jefferson in 1926 (as "Corrina Blues"), by Big Bill Broonzy in 1934, by Leadbelly in 1935, and by Lightnin' Hopkins in 1948, but neither Rainey's version, featuring such musicians as Louis Armstrong and Fletcher Henderson, nor Booze's, with jazzy piano accompaniment by Sammy Price, comes close to country blues. And despite its twelve-bar form, Willis's rendition, with its marimba introduction and gospel-flavored Gene Barge saxophone solo, sounds more like soul music than blues or, for that matter, rock 'n' roll.[1]

Muddy Waters's "I'm Your Hoochie Coochie Man," a Top 5 R&B hit in 1954, made a quasi-crossover after the white songwriters Jerry Leiber and Mike Stoller appropriated its distinctive doomsday vamp for the Robins' "Riot in Cell Block #9" the same year. Just before two of its members left to form the nucleus of the Coasters, the Robins, a black vocal group, had a genuine crossover hit with Leiber and Stoller's "Smokey Joe's Cafe," but "Riot" never charted nationally and was only later rediscovered by rock fans. Its lyrics, however, form the apparent basis for Presley's 1957 smash "Jailhouse Rock," also written by Leiber and Stoller. In any case, "Hoochie Coochie Man" is not a twelve-bar blues but a sixteen-bar song written by Willie Dixon, who despite having been born in Mississippi was influenced more by the urbane music of Nat "King" Cole and the Ink Spots than by Delta blues.

Another near crossover was "All by Myself" (not the 1921 Irving Berlin standard), which Big Bill Broonzy recorded in 1941 and Fats Domino updated in 1955. Not a true blues, Broonzy's original harks back to the verse-and-refrain hokum songs of the late 1920s and early 1930s, while Memphis Slim's accompanying piano anticipates Domino's heavier second-line New Orleans beat. Domino substitutes teen-friendly lyrics ("Meet me in the parlor 'bout half past one / We're going out and have some fun") for Broonzy's raunchy ones ("Cross-eyed Sue told Popeye Jim / All Uncle Sam's soldiers, I can take care of them"). But though Domino's "All by Myself" was a No. 1 R&B hit, it didn't make the pop charts, unlike his previous release, "Ain't It a Shame." The Johnny Burnette Trio recorded a yelping rockabilly take on "All by Myself" on the same date they cut "The Train Kept A-Rollin'," but it was issued only as an album track.

In the 1950s, few identified the blues, as distinct from rhythm-and-blues, as the root form of rock 'n' roll. One of those few was the anonymous author of the 1958 paperback *Who's Who in Rock 'n Roll,* who refers to "Rock and Roll, as a direct linear descendant of the old-time blues."[2] Another was Big Bill Broonzy, who in 1957 said of Elvis Presley: "He's singin' the same thing I'm singin' now, and he knows it. . . . When I was a kid I used to hear 'em call it rockin' the blues. Well, that's what he's doin' now. . . . Rock and roll is a steal from the old original blues."[3]

Broonzy was introduced to the white listening public at John Hammond's first "From Spirituals to Swing" concert at Carnegie Hall in December 1938, booked as a substitute for Robert Johnson, who had been murdered that August. The program notes identified Broonzy both as a "farm hand" from an "Arkansas plantation" and as "a laborer in Chicago," while noting that "for years and years he has been the best-selling blues singer on Vocalion's 'race' records." In 1959, when a recording of the concert was released on a long-playing album, Hammond reminisced that "Broonzy was prevailed upon to leave his Arkansas farm and mule and make his very first trek to the big city."[4]

In fact, the Mississippi-born Broonzy had left Arkansas in 1920 and moved to Chicago, where he learned guitar with help from either "Papa" Charlie Jackson, the first self-accompanied solo bluesman to make records with any degree of success, or Jim Jackson, best known for "Jim Jackson's Kansas City Blues."[5] From 1927 until his death in 1958, Broonzy recorded prolifically while holding various nonmusical day jobs. In 1930, he recorded with Georgia Tom Dorsey in the Famous Hokum Boys, one of several Hokum Boys groups that sprang up after the huge success of Dorsey and Tampa Red's "It's Tight Like That." Discovered by Lester Melrose, Broonzy didn't come into his own until the mid-1930s, when he was about forty years old. Yet he became one of the most popular and widely imitated bluesmen of that decade, recording hundreds of sessions as a leader and sideman, his output rivaled only by his friend Tampa Red.

Many of Broonzy's ostensibly original compositions simply rework other musicians' country-, vaudeville-, or hokum-blues hits. Often accompanied only by a piano and his own guitar, he also recorded with instruments ranging from washboards, jugs, and kazoos to trumpets, clarinets, and saxophones. In January 1937, he cut "Let's Reel and Rock," featuring the jazzy trumpet of Alfred Bell. The song—apparently based on the Harlem Hamfats' "We Gonna Pitch a Boogie Woogie," recorded a couple of months earlier—contains only a brief snatch of boogie piano and does not rock in any modern sense. In 1941, Broonzy played guitar on Lil Green's "Why Don't You Do Right?" which became Peggy Lee's first hit after she recorded it with Benny Goodman's band in 1942. That song was based on "Weed Smoker's Dream," recorded in 1936 by the Harlem Hamfats, a Chicago-based combo whose blend of blues and jazz paralleled the country-jazz fusion of Bob Wills and prefigured the sound of postwar urban blues.

After his "From Spirituals to Swing" appearances in 1938 and 1939, Broonzy performed for white audiences at nightclubs such as Cafe Society in Greenwich Village while continuing to tour and record for the rhythm-and-blues market. Leadbelly had preceded him on the folk circuit, and Josh White and the team of Sonny Terry and Brownie McGhee followed shortly, Terry having also performed at the "Spirituals to Swing" concerts. But unlike these other bluesmen, Broonzy did not become a full-time folkie until the early 1950s, when his R&B career petered out.

In 1951, Broonzy made his first tour of Europe, particularly impressing a circle of British trad-jazz fans who would launch the London blues scene that nurtured Eric Clapton and the Rolling Stones. It was the Stones who made rock fans aware of Chicago blues, covering Muddy Waters's "I Want to Be

Loved" on the flip side of their very first British single in 1963. And it was Clapton who brought Delta blues into the rock scene three years later when he recorded songs by Robert Johnson with John Mayall's Blues Breakers and with the trio Cream.

In his last years, Broonzy became a folk icon, recording some two dozen albums in the United States and Europe. Dutifully assuming the role of rustic folk singer, he added older songs such as "John Henry" and "Bill Bailey, Won't You Please Come Home?" to his repertoire and gave interviews where he reminisced about his rural childhood and discussed, among other matters, the origin of the blues.

In 1959, the year after Broonzy's death, Samuel Charters published his pioneering study *The Country Blues,* bringing to light Broonzy's early career as a commercial blues singer. In conjunction with the book, Charters released an album by the same title on Folkways Records' subsidiary RBF label—the first twelve-inch, long-playing, various-artist reissue compilation of country blues. Title notwithstanding, both book and record included musicians who, like Broonzy, spent most or all of their careers in cities. But Charters and his fellow folk enthusiasts had little use for electric blues and less for rock 'n' roll.

HANDY VS. MORTON

No one, not even John Hammond, had more influence on the attitude of the folk establishment toward the blues than Alan Lomax, the son of the renowned folklorist John A. Lomax. At the age of seventeen, Alan Lomax had accompanied his father on the 1933 Library of Congress–sponsored expedition where they discovered Leadbelly at the Louisiana State Penitentiary. The following year, explaining why they made field recordings in segregated southern prisons, the Lomaxes wrote, "Our purpose was to find the Negro who had the least contact with jazz, the radio, and with the white man."[6]

White scholarly interest in African American folk music dates back at least to the 1860s.[7] In 1925, just after the first country blues records appeared, Howard W. Odum published *The Negro and His Songs,* in which he classifies the blues together with "modern 'Nigger songs' [and] popular 'hits'" rather than with genuine folk songs.[8] Two years earlier, Dorothy Scarborough had published her essay "The 'Blues' as Folk-songs," in which she first speculates that "Blues, being widely published as sheet music in the North as well as the South, and sung in vaudeville everywhere, would seem to have little relation to authentic folk-music of the Negroes."

"But in studying the question," she continues, "I had a feeling that it was more or less connected with Negro folk-song, and I tried to trace it back to its origins. Negroes and white people in the South referred me to W. C. Handy as the man who had put the blueing in the blues. . . . To my question, 'Have blues any relation to Negro folk-song?' Handy replied instantly. 'Yes—they are folk-music. . . . They are essentially racial, the ones that are genuine . . . and they have a basis in older folk-song. . . . Each one of my blues is based on some old Negro song of the South, some folk-song that I heard from my mammy when I was a child.'"

Accepting Handy's explanation, Scarborough adds, "Even though specific blues may start indeed as sheet music composed by identifiable authors, they are quickly caught up by popular fancy and so changed by oral transmission that one would scarcely recognize the relation between the originals and the final results. . . . Blues also may spring up spontaneously, with no known origin in print, so far as an investigator can tell. . . . The Texas Negroes are especially fond of blues, and have . . . been singing them for years, before Handy made them popular in print."[9]

Handy had been promoting himself as the composer of the first published blues since at least 1916, when he wrote an article for the African American weekly newspaper *New York Age* titled "How I Came to Write the 'Memphis Blues.'"[10] The year after that, the *Indianapolis Freeman,* an African American weekly that covered the national black entertainment scene, reported that "Mr. W. C. Handy . . . ushered into musical composition a new form. A style to which no man can lay earlier claim—the blues style."[11] And it is largely to Handy that we owe the idea that the blues originated as African American folk music in the Mississippi Delta.

Born in Florence, Alabama, in 1873, Handy was a classically trained African American musician who toured as far as Cuba, Canada, and Mexico with Mahara's Minstrels before assuming the leadership of a black Knights of Pythias band in Clarksdale, Mississippi, in 1903. Performing mostly for white social functions, "I came to know by heart every foot of the Delta," Handy would declare in his 1941 autobiography, *Father of the Blues*, although from the context it would seem that his knowledge was limited to the local railroad stops.[12]

Handy experienced a musical epiphany at a train station in Tutwiler, Mississippi, where "a loose-jointed Negro had commenced plunking a guitar beside me while I slept." Fretting his guitar with a knife, the man sang, "Goin' where the Southern cross the Dog," referring to the junction of the Southern Railway and the Yazoo Delta Railroad, the latter known as the Yellow Dog. "The singer repeated the line three times, accompanying himself on the guitar with the weirdest music I had ever heard," Handy recalled. "The tune stayed in my mind."[13]

Writing fifteen years before the publication of Handy's autobiography, his friend and collaborator Edward Abbe Niles, a white lawyer who moonlighted as a pop- and folk-music critic, describes the same incident with slight differences. He gives the words of the song as "Gwine where de

Southern cross de Yaller Dawg" and says that Handy jotted the tune down rather than simply remembering it. In his autobiography, Handy, never specifying exactly when the event took place, mentions it just after telling how he became familiar with the Delta and before relating a different incident in Cleveland, Mississippi, where he discovered that his white patrons would pay handsomely to hear raw African American folk music. Niles tells the Cleveland story first, placing the "Yaller Dawg" affair "a few weeks later."[14]

In his 1916 essay for the *New York Age,* Handy describes his Tutwiler and Cleveland experiences as follows: "On a plantation in Mississippi I was awakened by a Negro singing a typical 'Blues,' accompanying himself with a guitar tuned in a Spanish key and played in true Hawaiian style with a knife. It was entrancing. . . . Later, while playing an engagement in this same state, with a firstclass [sic] orchestra using New York hits, we failed to please. The local band was called in, only three in number, but how they could play the 'Blues!' They received more for the hour than we for the night. I then saw that the 'Blues' had a commercial value."[15]

In 1914, Handy wrote "Yellow Dog Rag," later renamed "Yellow Dog Blues," including the line "He's gone where the Southern cross the Yellow Dog." The song was recorded with jazz band accompaniment by Lizzie Miles in 1923 and by Bessie Smith in 1925. In 1927, Crying Sam Collins recorded a different, country-style "Yellow Dog Blues" with the line "I'm goin' where [the] Southern cross the Yaller Dog."

Born in Louisiana in 1887, Collins lived in southern Mississippi, far from the Delta, but on "Yellow Dog Blues" his plaintive falsetto and keening slide guitar—played with a knife, as in Handy's story—anticipate the classic Delta stylings of Robert Johnson and even Muddy Waters.[16] Collins's repertoire also included hokum and vaudeville-style material, and he made the first recording of "Midnight Special," which Leadbelly turned into a folk standard and the Weavers turned into a pop hit. On "Riverside Blues," from 1927, Collins sounds like the missing link between jazzy female blues singers like Bessie Smith and the father of modern white country music, Jimmie Rodgers, who made his first recordings a few months later.

In 1929, Charlie Patton, whom some have credited as the originator of the Delta blues, recorded "Green River Blues," repeating the line "I'm goin' where the Southern cross the Dog" three times, just as Handy said he heard it. Born sometime between 1887 and 1891, Patton began his career by 1909; although Handy did not publish his own music until after moving to Memphis, Patton knew of Handy's band when it was touring the Delta and must have heard Handy's famous compositions later on.[17] In their 1988 Patton biography, *King of the Delta Blues,* Stephen Calt and Gayle Dean Wardlow point out that Patton was a highly original musician whose guitar accompaniment on "Green River Blues" was particularly inventive. They argue that he was unconcerned with carrying on any folk tradition and note that he occasionally sang lyrics that had appeared earlier in published blues compositions.[18]

If Patton, Collins, or Handy took the line about the Southern crossing the Dog from African American tradition, it was not a very old tradition, since the Southern Railway was first established by J. P. Morgan in 1894. More importantly, Handy claimed to have used the tune that the "loose-jointed Negro" played as the basis for his first published song, "The Memphis Blues," which he said he wrote in 1909 under the title "Mr. Crump." Although "the melody of *Mr. Crump* was entirely my own," Handy said, "it was a weird melody in much the same mood as the one that had been strummed on the guitar in Tutwiler."[19]

Stack Mangham, a bank clerk in Clarksdale who played clarinet in Handy's band, had a slightly different recollection when he was discovered by Alan Lomax's colleague Lewis Jones in the early 1940s during their survey of folk music in Coahoma County. "I didn't pay much attention to the blues and that music until Handy came here. He didn't either at first," Mangham recounted. "I remember when we first became conscious of it. We were playing down at Cleveland for a dance and the people had been dancing, but they had gotten tired and sleepy and nobody was dancing much except a few couples on the floor. We took intermission and three fellows came in there with a guitar, a mandolin, and a bass violin, and started to play and the people began to get wild. Everybody woke up and got interested and began to dance. Handy got the idea. He went back in the corner and took his pencil and a piece of paper and copied a part of what they were playing. When Handy went from here to Memphis, he finished the piece after working on it for a couple of years and called it *Mr. Crump,* and later the *Memphis Blues.* It's the same thing we heard that night at Cleveland."[20]

After maintaining for many years that "The Memphis Blues" was the first published blues composition, Handy eventually conceded that "Baby Seals Blues" and "Dallas Blues" had been published slightly earlier.[21] Nonetheless, his unverifiable assertion that he wrote "Mr. Crump" three years before the publication of "Memphis Blues," basing it on a bluesy strain he heard in the Mississippi Delta around 1903, became the starting point that blues historians have referred to ever since.

Handy's claims did not go unchallenged. In 1938, after Robert Ripley's *Believe It or Not* radio show named Handy as the originator of both jazz and the blues, Jelly Roll Morton responded with an angry letter that was published in *Down Beat* magazine. In it he writes that "when I was eight or nine years of age, I heard blues tunes entitled *Alice Fields, Isn't It Hard to Love, Make Me a Palate* [sic] *on the Floor*—the latter of which I played myself on my guitar. . . . Mr. Handy cannot prove that he has created any music. He has possibly taken advantage of some unprotected material that sometimes floats around."[22]

In his native New Orleans, Morton adds, he had heard the blues "when I was knee-high to a duck. . . . I used to hear a few of the following blues players, who could play nothing else—Buddie Canter, Josky Adams, Game Kid, Frank Richards, Sam Henry and many more." He also names Happy Galloway (Morton spells it "Galloways"), Tig Chambers (he spells it "Tick"), and Bab Frank (he spells it "Bob") among the blues musicians of that time. "Later Buddy Bolden came along. . . . This man also wrote a *blues* that lived a very long time . . . under the name of *St. Louis Tickler* [actually 'St. Louis Tickle']."

Besides these musicians, Morton mentions that "Tony Jackson used to play the Blues in 1905, entitled *Michigan Water Tastes Like Sherry Wine.* He never sang anything else on the stage but Blues, such as *Elgin Movements in My Hips, with 20 Years' Guarantee.* Blues just wasn't considered music—there were hundreds, maybe thousands who could play blues and not another single tune." At least ten years older than Morton, Jackson—a popular New Orleans ragtime pianist, singer, and songwriter whose best-known tune is the pop standard "Pretty Baby"—was Morton's early idol.

In the same letter, Morton says he wrote "New Orleans Blues" in 1905 and "Alabama Bound" in 1907 but neglected to publish them, adding that "the first publication with a title 'blues' as far as I can remember was a tune written by Chris Smith." The reference is probably to Smith and Elmer Bowman's "I've Got de Blues," a coon song from 1901, but possibly to Smith and Tim Brymn's "I've Got the Blues but I'm Too Blamed Mean to Cry," from 1912. (Other songs with the word "blues" in the title date back at least as far as 1850, when Gustave Blessner and Sarah M. Graham published "I Have Got the Blues To Day!")

Handy indignantly responded that he had "had vision enough to copyright and publish all the music I wrote so I don't have to go around saying I made up this piece and that piece in such and such a year like Jelly Roll and then say somebody swiped it."[23] But Morton's letter, which also contained his famous boast that he invented jazz in 1902, helped revive public interest in his music, which by then was considered old hat.

Also in 1938, Alan Lomax recorded his historic interviews with Morton for the Library of Congress, in which Morton mentions other early blues musicians such as Brocky Johnny, Skinny Head Pete, Old Florida Sam, and Tricky Sam. Introducing his performance of "Mamie's Blues," Morton says, "Here's was among the first blues that I've ever heard, happened to be a woman that lived next door to my godmother's in the Garden District. Her name was Mamie Desdunes."[24] The following year, on a commercial recording of "Mamie's Blues" for the General label, Morton says, "This is the first blues I no doubt heard in my life. Mamie Desdunes, this is her favorite blues. She hardly could play anything else more, but she really could play this number."[25]

Trumpeter Bunk Johnson confirmed the existence of Mamie Desdunes, telling Alan Lomax that he'd "played many a concert with her singing those same blues," but Johnson often embellished his memories.[26] To judge from Morton's recordings, "Mamie's Blues" is too modern for the turn of the twentieth century; unlike other early blues, including Handy's, the song is in twelve-bar form throughout, complete with blue notes and a habanera bass line.

Morton did not get around to publishing "New Orleans Blues" until 1925. "Alabama Bound," which Morton told Lomax he wrote in 1905, was published in 1909 as "I'm Alabama Bound" by Robert Hoffman, a white Alabama native who lived in New Orleans. The same tune appears as part of "Blind Boone's Southern Rag Medley No. Two," published in 1909 by the African American piano prodigy John William "Blind" Boone.

Hoffman's composition (not to be confused with the 1925 Tin Pan Alley standard "Alabamy Bound") was recorded in 1910 by Prince's Band, Columbia Records' white house ensemble, and sung by both white and black vaudevillians after John J. Puderer added lyrics the same year.[27] In the 1920s, versions of the song were recorded in country-blues style, including Papa Charlie Jackson's "I'm Alabama Bound," Papa Harvey Hull and Long Cleve Reed's "Don't You Leave Me Here," Henry "Ragtime Texas" Thomas's "Don't Leave Me Here" and "Don't Ease Me In," and Charlie Patton's "Elder Greene Blues." The words differ, but the melody stays close to Hoffman's, especially on Jackson's 1925 rendition, the earliest to be recorded.

Although "Alabama Bound" is not a blues in structure or harmony, a parenthetical note on the cover of the first edition of Hoffman's song says that it is "also known as the Alabama Blues." This is perhaps the earliest printed reference to the blues as a musical genre, albeit a genre yet to be strictly defined, and it indicates that the tune existed before Hoffman wrote it down. Several variations of the song's text collected in 1915 or 1916 and published by the folklorist Newman I. White show some similarity to the later recordings, though not to Puderer's lyrics.[28] But one reported to Will H. Thomas and published in 1912 contains the couplet "Why don't you be like me, why don't you be like me / Quit drinking whisky, babe, let the cocaine be" in place of Puderer's "I done told you nigger for to be like me / Just drink good whiskey, let your cocaine be."[29] And Roy Carew, a white jazz fan who lived in New Orleans in the early years of the twentieth century and who later became Morton's friend and song-publishing partner, remembered an office boy in Gretna, Louisiana, singing, "Why don't you be like me? / Why don't you be like me? / Drink good whiskey boy, let the cocaine be" in 1904 or 1905.[30]

Other Morton claims are similarly moot. "Michigan Water Blues" was copyrighted in 1923 by Clarence Williams; although Williams had lived in New Orleans and was influenced by Tony Jackson, he later wrote, "I got the idea for the 'Michigan Water Blues' from a turpentine worker in Louisiana."[31] In an interview with Alan Lomax, Morton attributes the song "I Got Elgin Movements in My Hips, with a Twenty Year Guarantee" to String Beans May, a black vaudevillian billed as the "Elgin Movements Man," who performed the song as early as 1910.[32]

W. C. Handy appropriated the title line of "Make Me a Pallet on the Floor" for the chorus of his 1924 composition "Atlanta Blues." Howard Odum collected a folk text of "Make Me a Pallet on the Floor"—without the obscene verses Morton sang for Lomax—and published it in 1911, before the song was copyrighted or recorded.[33] A semblance of the melody appears in Blind Boone's "Southern Rag Medley No. One," published in 1908. "Make Me a Pallet on the Floor" is also said to have been performed by the New Orleans cornetist Buddy Bolden, whose career ended when he suffered a nervous breakdown in 1906.[34] But even if Morton heard the song as a child, it is not a true blues.

Several witnesses confirm that Bolden played blues, but his smutty theme song, "Funky Butt," which Morton recorded as "Buddy Bolden's Blues," is not formally a blues, even though Morton told Lomax it was "no doubt . . . the earliest blues that was the real thing," having been written "about nineteen-two."[35] It does appear as a strain in "St. Louis Tickle," a ragtime hit published in 1904 by the white songwriter Theron Bennett, as well as in "The Cakewalk in the Sky," published in 1899 by Ben Harney, a white singer-pianist who claimed to have invented ragtime. But it may have been composed by Willie Cornish, who played trombone in Bolden's band between 1897 and 1906.[36] On his 1939 General recording of "Buddy Bolden's Blues," Morton sings the line "Thought I heard Judge Fogarty say, / Thirty days in the market, take him away." In his 1928 book *American Negro Folk-Songs,* Newman White claims to have heard a similar line in Statesville, North Carolina, around 1903.[37]

BIRTH OF THE BLUES

Known as the Mother of the Blues, Ma Rainey was perhaps the greatest of the early blues singers. She began her career in 1900, at the age of fourteen; touring with minstrel troupes, she became a favorite on the southern black vaudeville circuit before making her first record in 1923. Rainey told the musicologist John W. Work that she first heard the blues in 1902 at a tent show in Missouri where she was performing. As Work relates in his 1940 book *American Negro Songs*: "She tells of a girl from the town who came to the tent one morning and began to sing about the 'man' who had left her. The song was so strange and poignant that it attracted much attention. 'Ma' Rainey became so interested that she learned the song from the visitor, and used it soon afterwards in her 'act' as an encore. The song elicited such response from the audiences that it won a special place in her act. Many times she was asked what kind of song it was, and one day she replied, in a moment of inspiration, 'It's the *Blues*.'" Later, Rainey added, she often heard others sing such songs, although they were not yet called blues.[38]

In 1927, the year before he cut such jug-band classics as "Minglewood Blues" and "Viola Lee Blues" (later transformed into rock songs by the Grateful Dead), Gus Cannon recorded "Poor Boy, Long Ways from Home" under the name Banjo Joe, accompanied on guitar by Blind Blake. In the early 1970s, Cannon told the researcher Bengt Olsson that he'd learned the song from an older guitarist, Alec Lee, in Clarksdale, Mississippi, around 1900. Howard Odum collected a version of the text that he published in 1911, commenting that the song was "sometimes sung with . . . knife instrumental music" and that "each stanza consists of a single line repeated three times."[39] Like others who recorded "Poor Boy"—including the Georgia bluesman Barbecue Bob Hicks, who cut the song a few months earlier in 1927—Cannon roughly adheres to Odum's model, fretting his banjo with a metal bar instead of a knife. In Cannon's version, as in Hicks's, the song follows the twelve-bar format but lacks the flatted third and seventh notes that give the blues its distinctive modality.

Other black Mississippi guitarists born around 1900 who were interviewed in the 1960s and 1970s by Calt and Wardlow did not recall hearing the blues, at least by that name, in the first years of the twentieth century. Sam Chatmon remembered songs such as "Bucket's Got a Hole in It" from his youth but said, "I ain't never heard nobody pick no blues till my brother Bud and Charlie Patton." Skip James heard songs such as "Alabama Bound" between 1908 and 1910 but said, "I hadn't heard of blues then." Robert Wilkins likewise heard only songs such as "Make Me a Pallet on the Floor," which he called rags, beginning around 1904.[40]

In 1942, Alan Lomax interviewed a blind gospel songwriter in Clarksdale, Mississippi, named Charles Haffer Jr., who recalled square dances where "the old fiddlers played *Old Hen Cackle; Shortnin Bread; Mississippi Sawyer; Bill Bailey, Why Don't You Come Home; It Ain't Gonna Rain No Mo* and all that stuff." Haffer said that before he embraced religion in about 1909, "I used to sing all the old jump-up songs—blues weren't in style then—we called them reels."[41]

In his autobiography, *A Blues Life,* Henry Townsend, a St. Louis musician born in Mississippi in 1909 and raised in Missouri and southern Illinois, says that in his childhood, "that word wasn't used, *blues*. I never heard that word used. They called them reels back then."[42] And in a taped interview that was included on his 1969 album *I Do Not Play No Rock 'n' Roll,* Mississippi Fred McDowell, who was actually from Tennessee, says, "the blues came from a reel. They changed it, just to say 'blues.'"[43]

But the distinction between blues and reels—the latter apparently a catch-all term for various ballads and dance tunes—was not altogether semantic. On April 17, 1908, a white classical musician from New Orleans, Anthony (or Antonio) Maggio, published an "Up-to-Date Rag" titled "I Got the Blues" (no relation to Smith and Bowman's "I've Got de Blues").[44] The first section prominently utilizes minor-third blue notes within a twelve-bar structure, making "I Got the Blues" the earliest known tune to link the word "blues" with music a modern listener could readily identify by that name. As Maggio recounted in 1955, he had been on the levee in the Algiers district of New Orleans in 1907 when "I heard an elderly negro with a guitar playing three notes. He kept repeating the notes for a long time. I didn't think anything with only three notes could have a title so to satisfy my curiosity I asked what was the name of the piece. He replied, 'I got the blues.'"[45]

Maggio based his "I Got the Blues" on the three-note figure (A#-B-G) and performed it with his quintet. "To my astonishment, it became our most popular request number," he said. "In a very short time all the negroes in New Orleans with street organs were playing the Blues." Maggio went on to say that W. C. Handy visited New Orleans in 1910 or 1911, when "I Got the Blues" could still be heard in the streets, and subsequently used the three-note figure in his own songs. Handy, who had previously said he'd heard a church elder sing the figure in Florence, Alabama, denied Maggio's claim, saying, "I haven't been in New Orleans since 1900."[46] But there is an unmistakable resemblance between the first section of "I Got the Blues" and the opening of "Jogo Blues," Handy's second blues composition, which he published in 1913. "Jogo Blues" sold disappointingly, so in 1914 Handy transferred the same basic motif to the chorus of his next published song, "St. Louis Blues," the sensational hit that entrenched the blues as a popular musical genre.

Roy Carew wrote of hearing R. Emmet Kennedy perform "Honey Baby," which Carew called "the first complete blues song I ever heard," at a concert in Algiers around 1906. Kennedy, a white man who collected African American folk songs, published "Honey Baby" in his 1925 book *Mellows: A Chronicle of Unknown Singers.* Responding to Carew's query, he wrote, "I feel certain that it goes back farther than 1905. I had known it for a long time before I arranged it for the piano."[47]

Charles Thompson, a ragtime pianist from St. Louis who was rediscovered in the 1960s, said that Louis Chauvin, an older St. Louis pianist, "was a ragtime player and he was a blues player too. He played real blues." Thompson must have heard Chauvin before 1906, by which time Chauvin had left St. Louis. But none of Chauvin's three published compositions—the best-known being "Heliotrope Bouquet," written in Chicago with Scott Joplin in 1907—shows the influence of blues. Thompson also named the obscure St. Louis pianists Conroy Casey, Raymond Hine, and Willie Franklin as "boys who played nothing *but* the blues—no songs, no rags, only blues. They played in the buffet flats and at the sporting houses you see, and in those places it was strictly blues all the way."[48]

A recognizable blues strain appeared in print as early as 1904, when the black St. Louis songwriters James Chapman and Leroy Smith published a "RagTime Two-Step" called "One o' Them Things!" Only the slightest blues modality can be heard, but the first section follows the twelve-bar form and approximates the typical harmonic progression of the blues (I-I-I-I/IV-IV-I-I/V-IV-I-I). Chapman died in 1905, just before the publication of his Scott Joplin–orchestrated march "Military Parade," but Leroy Smith continued to perform "One o' Them Things!"[49]

The British pianist and scholar Peter Muir points to an even earlier song, "I Natur'ly Loves That Yaller Man," from 1898, as "the only known example of the standard blues progression in published music before 1900." Written by the East Coast pianist "Jack the Bear" Wilson (whom James P. Johnson credited for the Latin-tinged rag "The Dream") and his vaudeville partner Lawrence Deas, it contains lyrics more typical of coon songs than of blues, such as the opening line, "White folks all say, and think they're right / all coons, to them, they look a-like!" But Muir maintains that the twelve-bar opening section—with its blues chord progression, minor-third blue notes, falling melody line, slow tempo, and call-and-response vocal-and-piano pattern—qualifies the song as an incipient blues.[50]

John Jacob Niles, a classically trained white singer from Louisville, Kentucky, who helped bring folk music to the concert stage, claimed to have heard a medicine show vocalist, Ophelia "Black Alfalfa" Simpson, perform a blues in 1898. But Niles would only have been about six years old in 1898, and the text of "Black Alfalfa's Jail-House Shouting Blues" that he supplies in his 1930 *Musical Quarterly* article "Shout, Coon, Shout!" is that of a relatively modern blues in both form and content.[51]

The author and educator William Barlow has pointed to the transcription of a work song titled "Nobody There," collected in 1890 by the folklorist Gates Thomas and published in 1926, as "the first written record of a blues song in Texas." But the song, as notated by Thomas, is not really recognizable as a blues.[52]

The first known newspaper account of a blues performance appeared in the April 16, 1910, edition of the *Indianapolis Freeman,* describing the intoxicated-dummy routine of a twenty-two-year-old ventriloquist, "Professor" Johnnie Woods, at a vaudeville theater in Jacksonville, Florida. "He uses the 'blues' for little Henry in this drunken act," the reviewer wrote.[53] On July 16, 1910, the *Freeman* reported that "Mr. Kid Love is cleaning with his 'Easton Blues' on the piano" at the Palace Theatre in Houston. In 1908 and 1909, H. "Kid" Love and his wife, Gussie, had performed together at theaters in Memphis, including the Lyric on Beale Street, just a couple of doors down from Pee Wee's Saloon, where W. C. Handy hung out.[54]

Another early vaudeville blues artist was the pianist and comedian H. Franklin "Baby" Seals, whose "Baby Seals Blues" is the only one of the groundbreaking blues published in 1912 to include lyrics. A native of Mobile, Alabama, Seals was performing on the southern black vaudeville circuit by 1909. In early 1910, he published "You Got to Shake, Rattle and Roll" in New Orleans, then moved on to Houston and Greenville, Mississippi, where he ran the Bijou Theater until the spring of 1911. On April 27, 1912, the *Indianapolis Freeman*, covering a performance of his in Louisville, Kentucky, noted that "Seals features 'Blues.'" The same edition contained an opinion piece by the vaudevillian Paul Carter dismissing the blues as "smut" and "junk."[55]

Chris Smith and Tim Brymn copyrighted "I've Got the Blues but I'm Too Blamed Mean to Cry," on January 12, 1912, but it is basically a rag with a faintly bluesy tinge. (The title is nearly identical to a line from a folk song, "I got the blues, but too damn mean to cry," collected by Howard Odum and published in 1911.)[56] On August 3, Seals copyrighted "Baby Seals Blues," subtitled "Sing 'Em, They Sound Good to Me," in an arrangement by Artie Matthews, who is sometimes mistakenly credited as the songwriter. Seals performed the song with his wife and stage partner, Floyd Fisher; by 1913 it had been taken up by other black vaudevillians, including Charles Anderson, a yodeling female impersonator who dressed as a "colored mammy," and Edna Benbow, who would record a couple of dozen blues in the early 1920s under the name Edna Hicks.[57]

Anderson's October 1923 recording of "Baby Seals Blues" (under the title "Sing 'Em Blues") with pianist Eddie Heywood offers an eccentric example of the early vaudeville blues style.[58] Strident and histrionic, it sounds hopelessly dated today, possessing none of the timeless majesty that distinguishes the Delta blues at its best. But while the song is not in twelve-bar form, its lyrics ("I've got the blues, I can't be satisfied . . . / I've got 'em bad, I want to lay down and die") and modality mark it as at least a quasi-blues.

On August 6, 1912, Hart Wand, a white violinist and bandleader from Oklahoma City, copyrighted "Dallas Blues." According to Samuel Charters, Wand had already published the song in March but did not copyright it until its third printing. Wand claimed that the melody was his own but that the title was suggested by a black porter who heard Wand play the tune and commented, "That gives me the blues to go back to Dallas."[59] With some irregularities, "Dallas Blues" roughly follows the twelve-bar form and standard blues chord pattern, complete with blue notes. Lloyd Garrett added lyrics in 1918, and the song became a belated hit in 1931 when it was recorded by the white bandleader Ted Lewis, with Fats Waller singing (one of his first recorded vocals) and playing piano.

In September 1912, W. C. Handy copyrighted "The Memphis Blues," which is melodically similar to "Dallas Blues" but contains both twelve- and sixteen-bar sections. Within weeks, Handy said, he was tricked into selling the copyright for fifty dollars to Theron Bennett, who commissioned George Norton, the lyricist of "My Melancholy Baby," to write new words extolling Handy and his band.[60]

On November 9, 1912, Lee Roy "Lasses" White, a white minstrel trouper from Texas who performed in blackface, copyrighted "Negro Blues," which was published in Dallas in July 1913 as "Nigger Blues." The song, also melodically similar to "Dallas Blues," not only follows the standard blues form but contains several verses that turn up on later country blues recordings. Among these are: "Oh! the blues ain't nothing but a good man feeling bad, / Oh! that's a feeling that I've often had"; "You can call the blues any old thing you please, / But the blues ain't nothing but the dog gone heart disease"; and "I'm goin' to lay my head down on some railroad line, / Let the Santa Fe try to pacify my mind." "Nigger Blues" was recorded in 1916 by George O'Connor, a white lawyer and minstrel singer in Washington, D.C., who is said to have entertained every American president from McKinley to Truman.[61] Lasses White went on to perform his burnt-cork comedy with the *Grand Ole Opry* and later appeared on screen as a sidekick to the movie cowboys Tim Holt and Jimmy Wakely.

RECORDING THE BLUES

The first blues recordings were of "The Memphis Blues," which was cut as an instrumental by the Victor Military Band on July 15, 1914, and by Prince's Band on July 24. Morton Harvey, a white minstrel-show entertainer, became the first singer to record a blues when he cut "The Memphis Blues" for Victor on October 2, 1914. The white minstrel comedy team of Arthur Collins and Byron Harlan recorded a more successful version the following year.

The fox trot, introduced in 1914, was danced to "The Memphis Blues" by Vernon and Irene Castle, who had brought the tango to the United States the year before. This dance connection helped propel the blues to mass popularity: between 1912 and 1920, more than seven hundred blues songs were copyrighted and over four hundred issued on sheet music. More than one hundred blues were captured on some four hundred records, with many songs recorded by more than one artist. In addition, hundreds of blues piano rolls were made.[62]

Many early blues recordings were instrumentals, including "Livery Stable Blues," which was cut by a white quintet from New Orleans, the Original Dixieland Jazz Band, on February 26, 1917, and issued on what is considered to be the first jazz record. While some instrumental blues recordings were by black bands such as James Reese Europe's, Wilbur Sweatman's, and Ford Dabney's, nearly all the early recorded blues vocals were by whites, among them Arthur Collins, Billy Murray, Vernon Dalhart, Al Bernard, Nora Bayes, Marie Cahill, and Marion Harris. Of Harris, W. C. Handy said, "She sang blues so well that people hearing her records sometimes thought that the singer was colored."[63]

The first blues recording featuring an actual black singer was made in England by the Ciro's Club Coon Orchestra, an African American ragtime combo led by the Jamaican-born pianist Dan Kildare that entertained British high society at Ciro's Restaurant in London until scandalized authorities shut the place down. In September 1917, the group recorded a snappy version of "St. Louis Blues" on which the vocal, probably by Louis Mitchell or Seth Jones, is smothered by a banjo and banjoline, an instrument with a mandolin neck and a banjo-like body.

The first American recording of a black man singing the blues was made by Bert Williams, the most famous African American entertainer of the early 1900s. A minstrel comedian who always wore burnt cork on stage, Williams popularized the cakewalk in the late 1890s with his vaudeville partner, George Walker, and became a Broadway star on his own after the ailing Walker retired in 1909. On November 24, 1919, Williams recorded the "I'm Sorry I Ain't Got It You Could Have It If I Had It Blues," a faintly bluesy thirty-two bar song in typical vaudeville style. Three weeks later the song was recorded as an instrumental by the Louisiana Five, a white New Orleans jazz band.

In August 1920, Mamie Smith became the first African American woman to record a blues. Smith was a protégée of the vaudeville veteran Perry Bradford, who persuaded OKeh Records to take a chance on a little-known singer at a time when black female recording artists were almost unheard of.[64] Accompanied by white musicians at her first session, in February 1920, Smith cut a pair of pop songs that Bradford had written. Backed by a black band at her second session, on August 10, she sang Bradford's "Harlem Blues," a song she'd performed in his 1918 review *Made in Harlem*. In an attempt to broaden the record's appeal, Bradford changed the title to "Crazy Blues."[65]

Though not as popular as Marion Harris's recording of "St. Louis Blues," made a few months earlier, "Crazy Blues" was a sizable hit. Like "St. Louis Blues," it includes both twelve- and sixteen-bar verses, with the twelve-bar sections containing three different lines of text rather than a repeated first line. But Smith's voice is recognizably black, and the raggedly improvised accompaniment, filled with slurs and growls, is authentically jazzy. Despite such provocative lines as "I'm goin' to do like a Chinaman, go and get some hop / Get myself a gun and shoot myself a cop," the song enjoyed sufficient mainstream popularity that the rising white vaudeville star Cliff "Ukulele Ike" Edwards featured it in his act.[66]

But it was the song's overwhelming success among blacks that revolutionized the recording industry, prompting major companies to establish subsidiary "race" labels and black entrepreneurs such as W. C. Handy's former publishing partner Harry Pace to create their own independent labels. Ultimately, "Crazy Blues" so completely overshadowed all previous blues recordings that it is often inaccurately cited not only as the first blues vocal record but as the first blues record, period.

The new race labels scrambled to sign black women saloon and vaudeville singers who could record blues songs, among them Lucille Hegamin, Alberta Hunter, Edith Wilson, and Ethel Waters. The vogue for blues records kicked into high gear in 1923, when Bessie Smith and Ma Rainey cut their first sides; but while these southern singers brought an earthier flavor to the blues, they were still accompanied mainly by jazz musicians. The jazzy, female-oriented vaudeville style dominated the blues market through the mid-1920s; in his influential 1946 jazz history *Shining Trumpets,* Rudi Blesh dubs it "classic" blues, a refined version of the "archaic" folk blues he presumes had preceded it. "The blues had undoubtedly appeared in their established form by 1870," Blesh asserts, adding that "the blues are a naturally evolved form and sophistication acts like a blight upon them."[67]

Bert Williams recorded two other blues-tinged songs, "Unlucky Blues" and "Lonesome Alimony Blues," in 1920. The same year, singer Noble Sissle recorded the barely bluesy "Broadway Blues" with his vaudeville partner, pianist Eubie Blake; the two made several other such records over the next couple of years, both before and after the 1921 Broadway première of their landmark musical comedy *Shuffle Along*. Similarly bluesy songs ("Cornfield Blues," "Monday Morning Blues," "Preacher Man Blues," and the twelve-bar "Jelly Roll Blues") were recorded in 1921 by the Norfolk Jazz Quartette, a black male vocal-harmony group.

On October 25, 1923, the day after he'd accompanied Charles Anderson on "Sing 'Em Blues," pianist Eddie Heywood backed vocalist Guilford "Peachtree" Payne on "Peach Tree Blues," a stagy number where Payne sings, talks, yodels, and mimics a child's voice, all while following the standard blues pattern. In early November 1923, a black male singer from the East Coast named Reese Du Pree recorded "Long Ago Blues" in New York for the OKeh label, with piano accompaniment.[68] While Du Pree's clear enunciation suggests a vaudeville background, the song itself is a fully developed blues in structure and harmony.

Around this time, record companies began to show an awareness of folk-style blues. In 1923, Harry Pace's Black Swan label advertised Josie Miles's record "Love Me in Your Old Time Way" with the copy: "Have you ever heard the snatches of songs sung by Negro section hands on Southern railroads? . . . Generally termed blues, yet how strongly contrasted are these songs springing from the depths of the laborer's soul to the commonplace dance tunes that we are accustomed to call BLUES."[69] Yet Miles's song is precisely such a "commonplace dance tune," sung in vaudeville style with jazz band accompaniment.

The first guitarist to record with a blues singer was Sylvester Weaver, who backed Sara Martin on "Longing for Daddy Blues" in October 1923. The following month, Weaver recorded a pair of slide guitar solos, one of which, "Guitar Rag," would become a country music standard after Bob Wills recorded it as "Steel Guitar Rag" (featuring guitarist Leon McAuliffe) in 1936. Weaver was not a rural musician—like Martin, he hailed from Louisville, Kentucky—but his unpolished, ragtime-influenced playing anticipates the style of country-blues guitarists who recorded after him.

In March 1924, the Pruitt twins—guitarist Miles and banjo player Milas—recorded the accompaniment for two blues by Ma Rainey, two by Ida Cox, and three by Lottie Kimbrough (recording under her married name, Lottie Beaman). But the Pruitts' jangling sound bears as much resemblance to old-time white country music as to country blues. In February 1924, Reese Du Pree became the first black male singer to record a blues with guitar accompaniment when he cut "Norfolk Blues" with a guitarist who sounds like Jimmie Rodgers.

The first black male singer-guitarist to record a blues was Ed Andrews, who cut "Barrel House Blues," backed with "Time Won't Make Me Stay," for OKeh in Atlanta in late March or early April of 1924. His simple strumming and thumb-picked bass runs on a twelve-string guitar are hardly distinguishable from the type of playing found on early white country recordings, but the songs are in orthodox blues form, and Andrews's down-home tenor has a hardscrabble purity that owes nothing to vaudeville. The earliest true country-blues record, it was a breakthrough for the genre but not for Andrews, who never recorded again.

In May 1924, Daddy Stovepipe, whose real name was Johnny Watson, cut "Stove Pipe Blues" for the Gennett label, accompanying himself on guitar and harmonica. Watson was born in Mobile, Alabama, on April 12, 1867, earlier than any other recorded bluesman, but "Stove Pipe Blues" is not particularly archaic. With its choppy strumming and lilting melody—not quite in twelve-bar form—it sounds like a folk musician's take on vaudeville blues. Daddy Stovepipe never got much recognition, though he continued to record occasionally until 1961, two years before his death at the age of ninety-six.

In August 1924, Papa Charlie Jackson, accompanying himself on a six-string banjo, recorded his first two sides, "Airy Man Blues" and "Papa's Lawdy Lawdy Blues." Although neither song is actually a blues, Paramount Records advertised him that month as "the famous Blues-singing–Guitar-playing Man" and the "only man living who sings, self-accompanied, for Blues records."[70] Said to be from New Orleans, Jackson was living in Chicago by the early 1920s; judging from his polished technique and ragtime-era repertoire, he was a veteran of the minstrel- and medicine-show circuits.

Jackson's second record, from September 1924, pairs "Salt Lake City Blues," a genuine twelve-bar blues, with "Salty Dog Blues," a string of eight-bar verse-and-refrain couplets that became a standard of jazz and country music alike. His biggest hit, "Shake That Thing," recorded in May 1925, uses twelve-bar couplets but is otherwise similar to "Salty Dog Blues," with lyrics not nearly as salacious as Jackson's leering delivery makes them seem. In the same vein is "All I Want Is a Spoonful," from September 1925, which Charlie Patton adapted into "A Spoonful Blues" in 1929; that song was the basis for Howlin' Wolf's 1960 "Spoonful," written by Willie Dixon, which Cream turned into a blues-rock anthem in 1966.

Jackson's records sold well, and he kept recording into the 1930s, on his own and as an accompanist to Ida Cox, Lucille Bogan, Ma Rainey, and others. In 1926, Jackson sang but did not play on a slowed-down version of "Salty Dog" by Freddie Keppard's Jazz Cardinals. A cornet player from New Orleans, Keppard was one of the founding fathers of jazz, with a style said to be like Buddy Bolden's; his collaboration with Jackson illustrates the close relationship between early jazz and blues as well as Jackson's essential urbanity.

Although his music was closer to vaudeville than to country blues, Jackson's success opened the door for other, more rural self-accompanied blues singers. His style inspired a lingering fad for bawdy, humorous songs, dubbed "hokum blues" after the Dallas String Band recorded a song by that title in December 1928. Rather than a typical verse-and-refrain hokum song, "Hokum Blues" is a mostly instrumental twelve-bar blues (with only two sung verses) that's given a hokum treatment with minstrel-like joking and a jug-band-style arrangement. The same month, Paramount began crediting Tampa Red and Georgia Tom's records to the "Hokum Boys."

One of the first hokum-style recordings after Jackson's was Ukulele Bob Williams's rendition of "Go 'Long Mule," a comic song published in 1924 by Henry Creamer, a black Broadway lyricist, and Robert A. King, a white Tin Pan Alley composer. By the time Williams cut his version in November of that year, the song had already been recorded by at least half a dozen other artists, including Arthur Collins, the Goofus Five, and Fletcher Henderson's Orchestra, featuring Louis Armstrong on trumpet. "Go 'Long Mule" entered the country-music tradition with a 1927 recording by Uncle Dave Macon and was eventually cut by Johnny Burnette at his very first studio session under the title "Go Mule Go."

Williams's ukulele accompaniment contains a four-note, one-measure riff (I-II-IIIb-II) that is also found in Anthony Maggio's "I Got the Blues" and on a 1921 recording of "There Ain't No Nothin' (Gonna Take the Place of Love)" by the Black Swan Dance Orchestra, with Fletcher Henderson on piano. The riff shows up on at least three solo piano records of the period: Eddie Heywood's "The Mixed Up Blues" (1923), Hersal Thomas's "Suitcase Blues" (1925), and Jimmy Blythe's "Jimmie Blues" (1925). It's also found on singer Pearl Dickson's "Little Rock Blues," from 1927, with twin-guitar accompaniment by Richard "Hacksaw" Harney and his brother Maylon. In simplified form (I-II-I-II), it provides the chugging beat of Johnnie Temple's "Lead Pencil Blues" in 1935 and of Robert Johnson's "I Believe I'll Dust My Broom," "Sweet Home Chicago," and "Rambling on My Mind" in 1936. The simplified figure became one of the rhythmic foundations of rock 'n' roll, courtesy of Chuck Berry, while both riffs endure as fixtures of modern electric blues.

The next male blues star to emerge after Papa Charlie Jackson was Lonnie Johnson, who was also from New Orleans and whose technique was even more refined. Johnson maintained that he was born in 1900, but other sources give the year as 1899, 1894, or 1889. In 1963, Johnson told Valerie Wilmer: "When I was fourteen years old I was playing with my family. They had a band that played at weddings—it was schottisches and waltzes and things, there wasn't no blues in those days, people didn't think about the blues."[71]

In 1960, he told the British blues scholar Paul Oliver, "Early days of the blues—as far back as I can get is 1914." Sometime after that, Johnson struck out on his own. "The blues was all the go and from then on I loved blues and I just continued to playing them. . . . Strictly blues all the way—on the violin. And I made several numbers on the piano—I used to play piano for a while, but only blues, no popular songs. Then I bought my guitar. I bought it in 1917."[72] After World War I, he moved to St. Louis, performing in nightclubs with his brother James and on Mississippi riverboats with trumpeter Charlie Creath's jazz band.

Johnson made his recording debut with Creath's Jazz-O-Maniacs in November 1925, singing and playing violin on "Won't Don't Blues." Days later, Johnson made his first record under his own name, playing violin on "Falling Rain Blues" and guitar on "Mr. Johnson's Blues." Immediately successful, he recorded prolifically into the early 1930s. He was a fine singer and songwriter with a distinctive voice and melodic feel, but it was his dazzling virtuosity as a guitarist that made his reputation. He recorded as a soloist with Louis Armstrong's Hot Five in 1927 and with Duke Ellington's Orchestra in 1928. He cut a series of duets with the white jazz guitarist Eddie Lang and recorded with Lang, King Oliver, and Hoagy Carmichael in a group called Blind Willie Dunn and His Gin Bottle Four. He accompanied "classic" blues singers such as Clara Smith and Victoria Spivey as well as the country blues singer Alger "Texas" Alexander.

Johnson had a profound influence on other guitarists, from Charlie Christian and Django Reinhardt to T-Bone Walker and B. B. King. Henry Townsend first saw him perform at a theater in St. Louis around 1920. "I wasn't playing no guitar then, and he was one of the people that made me really want to get into it," Townsend recalled.[73] Robert Johnson's 1937 recordings "Malted Milk" and "Drunken Hearted Man" clearly reflect Lonnie Johnson's style; Robert, whose middle name was Leroy, reportedly so admired the older guitarist that he told friends his middle initial stood for Lonnie.[74]

But while Lonnie Johnson helped shape the country blues, he was no country bluesman. "I sing city blues," he told Wilmer.[75] After the Great Depression interrupted his career, Johnson made a comeback, topping the R&B charts in 1948 with the ballad "Tomorrow Night," a 1939 hit for the pop bandleader Horace Heidt. Elvis Presley recorded the song for Sun in 1954, but his version was not released until 1965, when it appeared on the RCA album *Elvis for Everyone,* with overdubbed vocals by the Anita Kerr Singers.

The artist who established the country blues as a viable commercial genre was Blind Lemon Jefferson. Born in East Texas, he worked the streets and dives of Dallas, then traveled throughout the South, including the Mississippi Delta, before cutting his first blues records in March 1926. The second one to be released, "Got the Blues," backed with "Long Lonesome Blues," was a race-market smash, and Jefferson went on to record nearly a hundred sides before his death in 1929. His high, penetrating vocals and dexterous guitar work, alternating rhythmic strumming with intricate single-note runs, virtually defined the country blues, inspiring bluesmen as disparate as Lightnin' Hopkins, T-Bone Walker, John Lee Hooker, and Howlin' Wolf.

Although Jefferson's rough-hewn style betrays little trace of jazz or vaudeville, he shared material with more sophisticated performers. One of his biggest hits, "That Black Snake Moan," which he first recorded in November 1926, may have been adapted from "Black Snake Blues," recorded in May of that year by Victoria Spivey, a classic blues singer from Houston who had previously crossed paths with Jefferson in Texas. "Black Snake Blues," with the haunting line "Some black snake been suckin' my rider's tongue," was popular enough to be covered by Martha Copeland, Clarence Williams, and King Oliver, and Spivey redid it as a duet with Lonnie Johnson in 1928 under the title "New Black Snake Blues." "Black Snake Moan," with the more prosaic lyric "Black snake crawlin' in my room," was in turn covered by the classic blues singer Martha Copeland, who also recorded "Black Snake Blues" (and by Hack's String Band, a white group from Kentucky).

Another of Jefferson's hits, "Match Box Blues," from March 1927, takes its title line from "Lost Wandering Blues," recorded by Ma Rainey with the Pruitt twins in March 1924, where Rainey sings, "I'm standin' here wonderin', will a matchbox hold my clothes." Near the end of "Match Box Blues," Jefferson plays the same boogie-woogie run he'd used to open "Rabbit Foot Blues" three months earlier—the first recording of a boogie guitar line, which Jefferson evidently borrowed from piano boogies.

In 1934, Larry Hensley, a white Kentuckian, recorded a remarkably faithful copy of Jefferson's "Match Box Blues"; in 1935, the Shelton Brothers, from Texas, recorded a jazzier country version, reworded and heavily influenced by Jimmie Rodgers. Another Texas group, Roy Newman and His Boys, recorded a western swing version in 1938, closer in spirit to Big Bill Broonzy's "Match Box Blues" (from 1935) than to Jefferson's. In 1957, Carl Perkins recorded his classic rockabilly adaptation, "Matchbox," retaining only the title line from Jefferson's original. But Perkins's song did not become a hit until the Beatles covered it in 1964.

Jefferson rerecorded "Match Box Blues" in April 1927, adding the line "Brown 'cross town going to be my teddy bear / Put a string on me, I'll follow you everywhere." In June, accompanied by pianist George Perkins, he recorded "Teddy Bear Blues," with the line "I said, fair brown, let me be your teddy bear / Tie a string on my neck and I'll follow you everywhere." In January 1957, Elvis Presley recorded "(Let Me Be Your) Teddy Bear," by the Philadelphia songwriters Kal Mann and Bernie Lowe, with the line "Baby, let me be your lovin' teddy bear / Put a chain around my neck and lead me anywhere." By summer, the song, featured in Presley's movie *Loving You,* was a No. 1 hit, the third of four Presley would have that year.

In June 1926, three months after Jefferson's first blues session, Freddie Spruell made what is considered to be the first Mississippi Delta blues record, "Milk Cow Blues." According to his widow, Spruell had moved to Chicago as a boy from Lake Providence, Louisiana, just across the Mississippi River from the Delta.[76] His only musical links to the Delta are his crudely Charlie Patton–like guitar strumming and his 1928 recording "Low-Down Mississippi Bottom Man," which contains the lines "In the lowlands of Mississippi, that's where I was born" and "Way down in the Delta, that's where I long to be."

Spruell sold far fewer records than Blind Blake, a brilliant guitarist from Florida or Georgia who made his first solo recording—the Lonnie Johnson–styled "Early Morning Blues," backed with the instrumental rag "West Coast Blues"—in August 1926. Other popular country bluesmen of the period were Barbecue Bob Hicks and Blind Willie McTell, both Georgia natives who began recording in 1927; Hicks covered Blake's "Diddie Wah Diddie" as "Diddle-Da-Diddle," while McTell covered Blake's "Wabash Rag" as

"Georgia Rag." Blake, Hicks, and McTell all had varied repertoires that included spirituals and rags as well as blues.

In 1928, Tommy Johnson became the first major Delta-style bluesman to record, followed by Charlie Patton in 1929, Son House in 1930, and Skip James in 1931. In terms of record sales, only Patton had much success, although Johnson was locally popular and widely influential. But though Delta blues were not recorded until some twenty years after blues compositions were published in St. Louis and New Orleans—at a time when the first generation of Delta bluesmen were in their teens or younger—the notion persists that the Mississippi Delta was the cradle of the blues.

ROOTS OF THE BLUES

In the early years of the twentieth century, the Delta was not an isolated backwater where old traditions were likely to be preserved. On the contrary, the region had only begun to be settled in the late nineteenth century, as swampy woodlands were cleared for farming. The rich soil brought relative prosperity, attracting African American migrants and sojourners from poorer parts of Mississippi, such as Charlie Patton and Tommy Johnson. Barrelhouses, where sharecroppers could drink, dance, gamble, and consort with prostitutes, provided employment for musicians.

Virtually alone among blues historians, Stephen Calt and Gayle Dean Wardlow contend that, rather than originating on the plantations, "the so-called 'country blues' were ruralized blues, early 'country blues' being their adaptation as dance music by performers who took their musical cues from barrelhouse transients."[77] They speculate that these barrelhouse musicians included the kind of itinerant performers that W. C. Handy describes as having hung around Clarksdale—"blind singers and footloose bards that were forever coming and going."[78]

The consensus continues to be that the blues is of rural provenance, an outgrowth of earlier folk forms such as spirituals, work songs, and field hollers. The evidence for this is tenuous, since the earliest surviving noncommercial field recordings of African American folk music were not made until the mid-1920s, and most scholarly recordings are from subsequent decades.[79] Some black spirituals but hardly any work songs or field hollers were notated before such music was recorded in the field.

Stephen Calt has theorized that the blues derives from a single eighteenth-century British hymn, "Roll Jordan," written by Charles Wesley, the younger brother of the Methodist leader John Wesley. Calt bases his hypothesis on structural similarity, pointing out that each of the four-bar lines that make up "Roll Jordan" consists of a ten-beat verse followed by a six-beat refrain ("Roll, Jordan, roll") and that each of the three four-bar lines that make up a typical blues stanza consists of ten vocalized beats (blues lyrics, like Shakespeare's plays, being in iambic pentameter), followed by a six-beat instrumental fill. He observes that "Roll Jordan" was published in a Kentucky camp-meeting hymnal during the Great Revival of the early nineteenth century, when many black slaves were Christianized. While acknowledging that the well-known African American spiritual "Roll, Jordan, Roll," although based on Wesley's hymn, does not retain its original structure, he notes that the same or similar beat patterns were used in other spirituals. But even if one accepts the highly speculative premise that "Roll Jordan" is the source of what Calt calls the "blues phrase," there is no particular reason to believe that this line structure is the kernel from which all other blues characteristics sprouted.[80]

Field hollers, also called "levee camp hollers," "moans," and "arhoolies," are generally considered to be even more influential than spirituals; Alan Lomax wrote that "these songs were directly antecedent to the blues of the Delta country."[81] Son House lent credibility to this theory when he told the writer Julius Lester: "People wonder a lot about where the blues came from. Well, when I was coming up, people did more singing in the fields than they did anywhere else. . . . We'd call them old corn songs, old long meter songs. . . . Then they called themselves, 'got the blues.' That's what they called the blues. Them old long meter songs."[82] But House, born in Mississippi in 1902, was raised in Louisiana and did not work in the cotton fields, play guitar, or listen to the blues until he moved back to the Delta as an adult. Any field hollers he may have remembered from childhood were sung after the first commercially published blues strains had already appeared.

What has been cited as the earliest description of a field holler was given by Frederick Law Olmsted, the great landscape architect, who in 1853 observed a black worker in South Carolina delivering "a long, loud musical shout, rising and falling and breaking into falsetto."[83] The same vague description could apply to the "Levee Camp Holler" sung by a Mississippi convict called Bama and recorded by Alan Lomax in 1947. But like other recorded field hollers, Bama's is an individual expression, whereas Olmsted's Carolina shouter was part of a train-loading gang, and the other loaders took up the same wail, even singing it in chorus.

Many of the hollers that Lomax and other folklorists recorded contain lyrics found in songs that were commercially published or recorded earlier. And though they often contain commonly used floating verses, hollers did not follow a prescribed format; as Howlin' Wolf recalled, "They'd make these songs up as they go along. . . . They made up the work songs as they felt."[84] It is simply a leap of faith to assume that field hollers at the turn of the twentieth century, when the blues had barely begun to emerge, sounded the same as those recorded decades later, when the blues was at the height of its popularity.

While excavating Native American artifacts near Clarksdale, Mississippi, in 1901 and 1902, the Harvard University archaeologist Charles Peabody was intrigued by the singing of the black diggers he employed and the black farm workers tilling the surrounding fields. In 1903, he described their songs in the *Journal of American Folk-Lore,* giving examples of words and music. Peabody took some of "the long, lonely sing-song of the fields" to be "strains of apparently genuine African music. . . . Long phrases there were without apparent measured rhythm, singularly hard to copy in notes."[85] Nevertheless, Peabody gave sketchy notation for five of what are presumably field hollers. He observed that they were "based for the most part on the major or minor triad," and in fact only two of the five contain flatted third or seventh blue notes. Yet Alan Lomax maintained that Peabody's transcription unquestionably "contains the cadences peculiar to the levee-camp holler that my father and I so frequently recorded all across the Deep South during the 1930s and '40s."[86]

Among the other kinds of songs Peabody heard were "ditties and distichs" such as "They had me arrested for murder / And I never harmed a man." Practically the same couplet, "They have accused me of murder / And I haven't harmed a man," appears in "Levee Camp Moan Blues," a commercial recording made in August 1927 by the country blues singer Texas Alexander, accompanied on guitar by Lonnie Johnson. With its drawn-out, melismatic notes and free tempo, Alexander's song sounds like a field holler, and Elijah Wald identifies it as such in his book *Escaping the Delta,* although Peabody does not associate the "murder" couplet with the "lonely sing-song of the fields."[87]

Peabody recognized some of his workers' songs as popular "'ragtime' melodies," including "The Bully Song," introduced in 1895 by the white coon shouter May Irwin, and "Just Because She Made Dem Goo-Goo Eyes," written in 1900 by the white team of Hughie Cannon and John Queen and recorded in 1902 by Belle Davis, the first black woman to make records.[88] (Curiously, both of these songs use the twelve-bar form.) But Peabody listed the following verse among the folk texts he'd collected: "Some folks say preachers won't steal; / But I found two in my cornfield. / One with a shovel and t'other with a hoe, / A-diggin' up my taters row by row."

In 1896 or 1897, a similar verse—"Some folk say that a nigger won't steal, / But I caught a couple in my cornfield. / One had his shovel and the other had a hoe. / If that ain't a-stealin', why, I'd like to know"—had been recorded as the opening stanza of the song "Way Down Yonder in the Cornfield" by the Manhansett Quartette, a popular white vocal group. In 1894, "Way Down Yonder in the Cornfield" had been recorded by the Standard Quartette, a black group that gained fame with the touring show *South before the War,* but it is not known whether the singers substituted the word "preacher" for "nigger," because no copy of the wax cylinder has surfaced.[89]

"Way Down Yonder in the Cornfield" (not to be confused with a song by the same title written in 1901 by Gus Edwards and Will D. Cobb) was popular enough around the time of Peabody's excavations to have been recorded in 1900 by the Haydn Quartet (as part of their "Cornfield Medley") and in 1901 by the baritone J. W. Myers, two of the biggest acts of the day. Several other artists also recorded the song between 1895 and 1925; according to the black-music scholar Lynn Abbott, "'Way Down Yonder in the Cornfield' was the ultimate early barbershopping vehicle."[90] Carl Sandburg's 1918 poem "The Singing Nigger" contains the line, "I saw five of you with a can of beer on a summer night and I listened to the five of you harmonizing six ways to sing, 'Way Down Yonder in the Cornfield.'"[91]

Several variations of the opening stanza, most collected around 1915, appear under the title "Some Folks Say" in Newman White's *American Negro Folk-Songs*; another appears in Howard Odum's 1926 book *Negro Workaday Songs*.[92] This "cornfield" verse turns up in a number of other folk songs, especially "Run, Nigger, Run!" which was collected without the verse by Newman White and Dorothy Scarborough and with it by John and Alan Lomax.[93] Another folklorist, E. C. Perrow, published both the cornfield verse and "Run, Nigger Run!" in 1915.[94]

Alan Lomax made at least two field recordings of "Run, Nigger, Run!" one in 1933 with Moses "Clear Rock" Platt, a black Texas prison inmate, and another in 1937 with W. H. Stepp, a white Kentucky fiddler. But the song had already been recorded commercially in 1924 by Fiddlin' John Carson, one of the first white country musicians to make records; in 1925 by Uncle Dave Macon, the first star of the *Grand Ole Opry*; in 1927 by Gid Tanner and His Skillet-Lickers, a country string band whose rollicking version contains the cornfield verse; and in 1928 by Dr. Humphrey Bate and His Possum Hunters, the first string band to perform on the *Grand Ole Opry*.

Joel Chandler Harris, the white Georgia journalist who refashioned African American folk tales into children's stories narrated by the fictional Uncle Remus, mentions "Run, Nigger, Run!" in his first book, *Uncle Remus: His Songs and His Sayings* (1880), and gives a full text, including the cornfield verse, in *Uncle Remus and His Friends* (1892).[95] In 1876, Lafcadio Hearn, the journalist, folklorist, and Japanologist, published a version of the cornfield verse ("Some folks says that a rebel can't steal"), attributing it to a "colored laborer" in Cincinatti.[96] The inclusion in the 1867 compilation *Slave Songs of the United States* of a brief "Run, Nigger, Run!" collected in Arkansas and consisting largely of the cornfield verse, would seem to confirm the song's folkloric provenance.[97]

Newman White and the Lomaxes maintain that "Run, Nigger, Run!" originated after antebellum slave rebellions. But White cites as the possible source of the cornfield verse an early minstrel song, "Whar You Cum From," published around 1846 by J. B. Harper, "the Celebrated Delineator of Comic and Aethiopian characters," which contains the line "Some folks say dat niggers won't steal, / I kotch one in my cornfield."[98] And "Run, Nigger, Run!" without the cornfield verse, was published in 1851 in *White's Serenaders' Song Book,* by the prominent blackface minstrel Charles White.[99]

According to Robert Toll's 1974 history *Blacking Up: The Minstrel Show in Nineteenth-Century America,* "early minstrels used Afro-American dances and dance-steps, reproduced individual Negro's songs and 'routines' intact, absorbed Afro-American rhythms into their music, and employed characteristically Afro-American folk elements and forms."[100] Other writers have discounted the influence of genuine African American folk music on blackface minstrelsy because the early minstrels were northerners who had little or no contact with the plantation life they parodied. But in their book *Way Up North in Dixie,* Howard and Judith Sacks argue that Dan Emmett appropriated "Dixie," perhaps the most famous minstrel song, from the repertoire of the Snowden Family Band, free black neighbors of Emmett's in his home town of Mount Vernon, Ohio.[101]

If only because of its racist character, one can say with some confidence that the cornfield verse is of white authorship, a product of blackface minstrelsy. Adopted by blacks despite its derogatory nature, it passed back and forth between folk and commercial music over the course of a century. Charles Peabody was not the first to mistake minstrel songs for folk music: the Swedish novelist Frederika Bremer, after hearing a black banjo player sing such compositions as Stephen Foster's "Oh! Susanna" and "Old Uncle Ned" on a visit to South Carolina in 1850, described them as "negro songs universally known and sung in the South by the negro people, whose product they are."[102] The particular significance of Peabody's observations is that they were made at around the same time and place that W. C. Handy had his Tutwiler revelation and that they have since been used to buttress the case for the Mississippi Delta origin of the blues.

AFRICA, BRITAIN, AND VAUDEVILLE

While the birthplace of the blues is debatable, virtually no one today disputes that the music was created by African Americans and that it contains at least some African component. To the contrary, it is currently fashionable to believe that the blues was transplanted from Africa almost intact, a view stemming from the Western discovery, or rediscovery, of African music in the 1970s and 1980s. Westerners have studied African traditional music since the nineteenth century, and African songs such as "Skokiaan" and "Wimoweh" ("The Lion Sleeps Tonight") found their way onto the American pop charts as early as the 1950s. But Alex Haley's *Roots,* both the 1976 book and the 1977 television miniseries, awakened new interest in the Manding griot music of the Senegambia region. And the international emergence a decade later of Ali Farka Touré, a Malian guitarist who admired John Lee Hooker, gave the connection between Africa and the blues a contemporary human form.

The compilers of *Slave Songs of the United States* regarded the mostly religious material they collected as "the natural and original production of a race" whose members had "become imbued with the mode and spirit of European music—often, nevertheless, retaining a distinct tinge of their native Africa." They felt that some songs, especially the secular ones, contained passages that "may very well be purely African in origin."[103]

The idea that African American music came from Africa was challenged by the Austrian critic Richard Wallaschek, who wrote in 1893 that "these negro-songs . . . are mere imitations of European compositions." The numbers in *Slave Songs of the United States,* he added, "are unmistakably 'arranged'—not to say ignorantly borrowed—from the national songs of all nations, from military signals, well-known marches, German student-songs, etc."[104] The French musicologist Julien Tiersot likewise denied the African derivation of African American spirituals, writing in 1911 that "these songs have no distinctive character."[105]

The American critic Henry Krehbiel responded in 1914, declaring that "the songs of the black slaves of the South are original and native products. They contain idioms which were transplanted hither from Africa, but as songs they are the product of American institutions."[106] Krehbiel analyzed over five hundred African American songs, mostly spirituals. "For the majority of them," he concluded, "I have found prototypes in African music."[107]

The debate (outlined in some detail by D. K. Wilgus in his book *Anglo-American Folksong Scholarship Since 1898*) went on for decades, with European academics such as Erich von Hornbostel arguing that the essential character of African American music was European and Americans such as Melville Herskovitz insisting that it was African.[108] In 1943, George Pullen Jackson, an American scholar of southern hymnody, published *White and Negro Spirituals*, in which he demonstrated that many black spirituals were of white origin. Jackson maintained that virtually all the distinctive features of black spirituals were rooted in the British folk tradition. "I do not deny the possibility that there are . . . certain African hang-overs," he wrote. "I would merely state that I haven't found any yet."[109]

Still, American musicologists generally continued to believe that African American music contained African ingredients. In 1952, Richard Alan Waterman wrote that "Metronism [the keeping of a strictly regular pulse] . . . is present in all Negro sacred and secular styles, as is the importance of percussion . . . and the overlapping call-and-response pattern."[110]

Waterman, like most of his colleagues, thought that African Americans had preserved musical elements from the coast of West Africa rather than the interior. But in his 1970 book *Savannah Syncopators*, Paul Oliver claimed that the African roots of the blues could be found in the griot music of the western Sahel, a semi-arid region south of the Sahara stretching from Senegal and Gambia through Mali and Burkina Faso. This was the music that Alex Haley's *Roots* brought to the attention of the American public.

Around the time that *Roots* came out, Ali Farka Touré's first albums were released. Born near Timbuktu in 1939, Touré learned to play traditional music in his youth, although he was not a member of the griot caste of professional musicians. Hearing John Lee Hooker's records in the 1960s, he thought they sounded Malian; although he later denied that Hooker had influenced him, his music occasionally resembles Hooker's. Hailed as a living link between Africa and the blues after cutting his first internationally distributed album in 1987, Touré later recorded with such American bluesmen as Gatemouth Brown, Taj Mahal, and Corey Harris. His meeting with Harris in Mali, during which Touré opined that African American music came from Africa, was captured in the Martin Scorsese–directed video documentary "Feel Like Going Home," part of the PBS series *The Blues*.

In 1977, Alan Lomax interspliced a Senegalese harvesting song with a Mississippi field holler on the same album track to demonstrate the kinship of African music and blues.[111] Since Touré's emergence, a number of albums have made the same point by different means: juxtaposing American blues and African tracks, staging collaborations between African musicians and American bluesmen, recording African musicians who have been influenced by American blues, or simply compiling bluesy-sounding African songs.

No one imagines that the twelve-bar structure of the blues originated in Africa—in his book *In Griot Time: An American Guitarist in Mali,* Banning Eyre describes how even highly accomplished and versatile Malian musicians struggled to follow blues chord changes—but in its use of blues-like notes and scales, some African music sounds amazingly similar to the blues.[112] Even so, the Mali-to-Mississippi theory of blues origins is problematic, to say the least.

Blues-like music can be found not only in Mali but throughout the Sahel region, from Mauritania to Ethiopia, suggesting that a bluesy modality resulted when sub-Saharan Africans were exposed to the Islamic music of North African Arabs. Some of the bluesiest-sounding African music is made by the Tuareg, or Kel Tamashek, a nomadic people of the Sahara, related to the Berbers, whose caravans formerly transported West African slaves to North Africa. It was Tuareg music in particular that Ali Farka Touré reportedly identified as resembling John Lee Hooker's blues.[113]

But the bluesy feeling of Sahelian music may not come entirely from Islamic contact. While acknowledging the influence of Islamic music in the Sahel, the Austrian musicologist Gerhard Kubik identifies the use of pentatonic scales, similar to those found in Delta blues, as native to the region. In his book *Africa and the Blues,* Kubik writes that "Arabic-Islamic musical concepts were superimposed on a local pentatonic stratum that had flourished perhaps for several thousand years in the pearl millet-growing savanna cultures of West Africa."[114] Kubik's theory, based on his own field recordings in isolated villages in Nigeria and Cameroon, is plainly speculative, but pentatonic scales without obvious Arabic inflections can also be heard in the Wassoulou region of southern Mali, whose music has been popularized internationally by female singers such as Oumou Sangare.

Most of the slaves who were taken to the United States are thought to have come from areas near the West African coast, where the music is more percussive and less bluesy, but at least a few came from as far inland as Timbuktu.[115] It is possible, as Kubic asserts, that the musical style of even a small minority of the slaves could have come to be preferred by the majority. And in the United States, as he points out, the drum-dominated music of the coastal Africans was more harshly suppressed than the string-based styles of the savanna peoples.[116] But it is hard to explain why the blues-like savanna strain is virtually never heard in parts of the Caribbean or Latin America where African music survived in much purer form. The bluesy sound is absent even in former British colonies such as Jamaica or the Bahamas, where slaves were often brought before being shipped to the United States and where the folk music otherwise resembles that of African Americans.

Still harder to explain is the time lag between the end of the slave trade and the emergence of the blues. The United States outlawed the importation of slaves as of 1808, and though some slaves were brought in illegally until 1859, the blues did not appear until fifty years after that. According to Kubik, blues-like strains "were not reported . . . because they were among the most strikingly African . . . expressive forms that had survived in the United States. . . . They symbolized the core of everything that the established elements of society were deeply afraid of."[117] Yet white observers did not hesitate to describe African American songs and dances that they considered savage and barbaric, and those who first reported the blues seemed to find the music more curious than frightening.

Paradoxically, the blues songs published before 1920 sound less African than those recorded afterward. The pentatonic minor scale that gives the Delta blues of Charlie Patton and Son House its ancient, African feeling is not explicit in the vaudeville-style blues of Bessie Smith or Ma Rainey and is only vaguely suggested in earlier published blues. Even in Delta blues, the pentatonic minor scale—a natural minor scale with the second and sixth notes missing, or C, Eb, F, G, Bb in the key of C—is not heard in pure form, as it is in some African music.

Blues historians have assumed that the Delta style was created before the vaudeville style but not recorded until later, and that the Delta blues records of the 1920s and 1930s preserve the music as it was played in previous decades. But there is no evidence that the Delta blues originated earlier than about 1910, and though one musician who met Charlie Patton around 1907 claimed that "he's playin' the same kind of music [then] like he did when he put out them records [some twenty years later]," it is scarcely credible that the style emerged full-fledged and remained static thereafter.[118] Early country blues recordings show the influence of jazzy "classic" blues, and country bluesmen were quick to copy one another's records.

As the blues gained popularity, the pentatonic mode became more prominent, and flatted third and seventh notes were added to songs that predated the blues. On a 1928 recording, Louisiana bluesman Ramblin' Thomas transforms "Poor Boy, Long Ways from Home" into "Poor Boy Blues," a Delta-like lament with a melody similar to Blind Lemon Jefferson's 1926 "Jack O'Diamond Blues." Similarly, Charlie Patton's 1929 recording of "Frankie and Albert" is much bluesier than Mississippi John Hurt's 1928 version, titled "Frankie," not to mention earlier pop and jazz versions by 'Gene Greene, Al Bernard, Frank Crumit, Isham Jones, Fate Marable, and Ted Lewis, all titled "Frankie and Johnny."

Based on the 1899 murder of Allen Britt by Frankie Baker in St. Louis, the song was apparently in circulation as "Frankie and Albert" before being published as "Frankie and Johnny" in 1912, with words by the brothers Bert and Frank Leighton, a white vaudeville team, and music by Ren Shields. But the now-familiar melody, which Patton largely ignores, had already appeared in the Leightons' 1908 composition "Bill, You Done Me Wrong," an adaptation of Hughie Cannon's 1904 composition "He Done Me Wrong." That song was a follow-up to Cannon's 1902 smash "Bill Bailey, Won't You Please Come Home?" which in turn is based on John Queen and Walter Wilson's 1901 "Ain't Dat a Shame?"[119] But the African American St. Louis pianist and balladeer Bill Dooley apparently wrote the first version of the song, "Frankie Killed Allen," the day after the killing, including the enduring line "he was my man, but he done me wrong."[120]

As it happens, all the variations of "Frankie and Johnny" are wholly or partly in twelve-bar form. According to Peter Muir, the twelve-bar structure entered American commercial music with "The Bully Song" in 1895 and appeared in a number of popular coon songs, including several by Hughie Cannon, but was associated exclusively with the blues after 1912 (Muir either ignores the many twelve-bar verse-and-refrain hokum songs or lumps them in with the blues). Muir assumes that the "Frankie and Johnny" melody was adapted from folk sources, and the South African musicologist Peter van der Merwe traces the tune to the Scottish folk song "Tattie Jock."[121]

Besides "Frankie and Johnny," a number of folk songs that are regarded as precursors of the blues—among them "John Henry," "Ella Speed," "Stagolee," and "Joe Turner"—apparently derive from British ballads, at least in their music. The texts, however, are based on contemporary events: the construction around 1870 of the West Virginia tunnel where the legendary John Henry labored, the murder in 1894 of the New Orleans prostitute Ella Speed, the killing in 1895 of Billy Lyons by the flamboyant St. Louis pimp "Stack" Lee Shelton, and the transportation of convicts in the 1890s by the prison agent Joe Turney [sic], whose brother was the governor of Tennessee.

Abbe Niles cited "Joe Turner" as "perhaps the prototype of all blues."[122] In 1915, W. C. Handy adapted the song into his own "Joe Turner Blues," changing the story into one of unrequited love. Big Bill Broonzy, in his autobiography and in taped interviews, dated the song to around 1890 but identified Turner as a mysterious white benefactor who supplied food and other provisions to poor black sharecroppers.[123] Broonzy's recordings of the song, made near the end of his life, simply repeat the line "They tell me Joe Turner been here and gone," without the convict-related reference to "forty links of chain" that Handy recalled (but left out of his published song) and that Howard Odum reported in 1911 as part of a folk text.[124]

Peter van der Merwe observes that traditional British folk music shares certain characteristics with the blues, including the use of lowered third and seventh notes and occasionally even twelve-bar structures.[125] As early as 1907, the English musicologist Cecil Sharp observed that British folk singers used "neutral" thirds and sevenths, pitched between major and minor, as well as hexatonic, heptatonic, and other nondiatonic scales, with the pentatonic found mainly in Scotland.[126] George Pullen Jackson later described the use of neutral thirds and sevenths among both black and white folk singers in the American South.[127]

But neutral third and seventh notes are common in West Africa as well; as Gerhard Kubik points out, Erich von Hornbostel noted the African use of neutral thirds as far back as 1913.[128] African music also employs pentatonic, hexatonic, and heptatonic scales; in fact, the pentatonic, Islamic-inflected African music that sounds most like Delta blues bears less resemblance to British folk music than does the heptatonic music of the Manding griots. Manding music, descended from the court music of the medieval Kingdom of Mali, sounds strikingly similar to some Appalachian folk music and to the pre-blues material of African American songsters such as Mississippi John Hurt.

African slaves surely found familiar elements in the British-based folk songs they were exposed to in the United States, just as African musicians today find familiar elements in contemporary Celtic music. "I used to buy some tapes in England of Irish music," the Senegalese star Baaba Maal told the writer Don Palmer, "and when I listened to them, I could easily sing with them without changing anything of my melodies."[129] This musical affinity has even produced a successful world-music fusion band, the Afro Celt Sound System, made up of Irish and West African musicians.

Van der Merwe surmises that the similarities between West African and British folk music resulted from mutual contact with Islamic culture. The Arab conquests took in not only North Africa but parts of Europe as well, and Middle Eastern music and instruments were disseminated throughout Western Europe, their influence lingering longest in isolated areas such as Ireland and Scotland.[130] It's an intriguing theory, but it fails to explain the virtual absence of blues-like music in Spain or Portugal, which remained under Arab rule for centuries, or in Latin America, where African and Iberian musics blended.

Black and white musicians in the United States freely borrowed from one another, intermingling British- and African-based styles. "Before the Civil War there did not exist in America two distinct bodies of music, one white and one black," asserts the American musicologist Richard Nevins in his liner notes to the three-album compilation *Before the Blues*. "Both groups shared a common tradition and repertoire. Indeed, the divergence of white music and black music into two separate genres doesn't really become clear until the turn of this [the twentieth] century."[131]

Of the musical examples offered on *Before the Blues,* the two that most persuasively support Nevins's thesis are "Jack O'Diamond Blues," recorded in May 1926 by Blind Lemon Jefferson, and "Reuben Oh Reuben," recorded around 1931 by Emry Arthur, a Kentucky country singer best known for his 1928 recording of "Man of Constant Sorrow." The Texas folklorist W. H. Thomas published a text of "Jack of Diamonds" in his 1912 pamphlet *Some Current Folk-Songs of the Negro*, but the song, thought to derive from a British ballad, is more commonly found in white country music, often conflated with "Rye Whiskey."[132] Jefferson, however, sings it to the tune of "Reuben Oh Reuben," a variation of "Reuben's Train" often conflated with another train song, "Nine Hundred Miles." While not in blues form, Jefferson's version, his only recording with slide guitar, sounds much bluer than Arthur's.

The early development of country blues can be heard in the two dozen recordings of Henry "Ragtime Texas" Thomas, made between 1927 and 1929. An obscure figure in his own lifetime, Thomas eventually earned a footnote in rock history after his songs were revived by Bob Dylan, Canned Heat, the Lovin' Spoonful, and others. Born in East Texas in 1874, he was one of the oldest bluesmen to record, with a style that apparently dates back to the 1890s. Thomas's recorded repertoire comprises mostly "reels"—square dance tunes such as "Old Country Stomp," country breakdowns such as "Charmin' Betsy," folk ballads such as "Bob McKinney," and vaudeville songs such as "Honey, Won't You Allow Me One More Chance?"—along with a couple of gospel numbers and a few actual blues. Among the songs he interpolates are "Alabama Bound," "Liza Jane," "The Bully Song," and "Make Me a Pallet on the Floor."[133]

Thomas takes a somewhat archaic approach to the blues, singing conventional blues verses only on the first half of "Cottonfield Blues." Each stanza of "Bull Doze Blues" and "Texas Worried Blues" consists of the same line repeated three times (as on Gus Cannon's "Poor Boy, Long Ways from Home"), and every stanza of "Texas Easy Street Blues" ends with the same third line. But all of Thomas's blues are in twelve-bar form, with standard blues chord changes and conventionally placed blue notes, suggesting that he adopted the blues later in his career. His style reflects the musical milieu from which the country blues emerged, but he is not quite the missing link between blues and reels.

The blues does not appear to have been created by any single person or at any one place or time, nor did it emerge merely as the commercial appropriation of a folkloric idiom. The twelve-bar form first appeared in commercial coon songs in the 1890s; the flatted third and seventh notes that give the blues its melodic character were introduced by professional songwriters and vaudeville performers during the following decade. These blue notes had long been a fixture of African American folk music, a carryover from African tradition reinforced through contact with similarly inflected British-based ballads and hymns. As D. K. Wilgus puts it: "To America from Africa the Negro brought a song tradition differing from and yet in some respects resembling the European folk tradition. . . . From the songs of the whites, the Negro borrowed what was congenial to him, and the whites were debtors as well as creditors. The resulting hybrid is a folk music which sounds African in the Negro tradition and European in the white tradition."[134]

The structure of the blues gradually became fixed as the genre established itself. In a process analogous to the increased use of melisma in R&B singing in recent decades, the blue notes became more prominent, while other notes were omitted, producing modes resembling those found in Mali and other parts of West Africa. Like the story of Kunta Kinte in Alex Haley's *Roots,* the notion that the blues was transported directly from Africa to the antebellum South is a latter-day invention.

The widespread belief that the country blues preceded the vaudeville blues is understandable, even though the reverse seems to have been the case. Just as nineteenth-century minstrel songs written by northern whites had been presented as the authentic expression of southern blacks, the newfangled country blues of the 1920s were promoted from the start as folk music from the distant past. Blind Lemon Jefferson's first blues record, for example, was advertised as "a real, old-fashioned Blues by a real, old-fashioned Blues singer," although the two songs—called "old-time tunes" in the ad copy—are apparently original, and Jefferson was not yet thirty-five years old.[135]

If Jelly Roll Morton's account has any credibility, songs such as "Alabama Bound" and "Make Me a Pallet on the Floor"—the immediate precursors of the blues—were as familiar to the first generation of New Orleans jazz musicians as to the first generation of Mississippi bluesmen. From the inception of jazz, the blues was an integral part of it, and the earliest recordings of both white and black jazz bands include blues numbers. A few country-blues songs were taken up by jazz bands in the 1930s and 1940s, but jazz—besides preserving Handy's tunes and other early blues compositions—continued to generate its own blues material, and it was from this bluesy side of the jazz repertoire that rhythm-and-blues and rock 'n' roll ultimately derived. To the extent that black country blues found its way into rock 'n' roll at all, it may be as much through white country music as through R&B.

Chapter Four

The Rocks

THE WALKING BASS

Although the most typical early rock 'n' roll form is not the blues but the verse-and-refrain hokum song, the musical style that, more than any other, propelled rock 'n' roll into being is the boogie-woogie, a subspecies of the blues characterized by a "walking" ostinato bass line. Developed by African American pianists in the early years of the twentieth century, boogie-woogie emerged as a distinct genre in the late 1920s; a decade later it was taken up by left-wing intellectuals and popularized by swing bands. By the early 1940s, the boogie-woogie had become a national sensation, but it faded from mainstream pop after World War II, lingering on in rhythm-and-blues and country music.

The boogie-woogie bass line was a foundation of postwar R&B, powering such proto-rock songs as "Good Rockin' Tonight" and "Rocket 88." Boogie-woogie bass lines were also a staple of early rock 'n' roll and rockabilly, as on Elvis Presley's 1957 hit "All Shook Up." But boogie patterns in rock were not confined to the bass register. On Bill Haley's "Rock Around the Clock," the second line of each verse ("We'll have some fun when the clock strikes one," "If the band slows down we'll yell for more," etc.) has a boogie melody. On Larry Williams's 1957 rock 'n' roll classic "Bony Moronie," a saxophone and guitar play a typical boogie figure in response to Williams's vocal line.

In some cases, the difference between swing-era boogie-woogies and 1950s rock 'n' roll is merely a matter of instrumentation and lyrics. If the horns on Gene Krupa's "Drum Boogie" were replaced by guitars and the word "boogie" changed to "rock," the 1941 hit would hardly be distinguishable from a rock song. In fact, Danny and the Juniors' 1957 rock 'n' roll standard "At the Hop" rides practically the same bass line.

Many of the earlier piano boogies also have a rock feel. Big Joe Turner's 1938 debut record, "Roll 'Em Pete," with pianist Pete Johnson, rocks much harder than Turner's actual rock 'n' roll hits of the 1950s, with their relatively stiff combo arrangements. Romeo Nelson's "Gettin' Dirty Just Shakin' That Thing," from 1929, could easily be imagined as a rocker if the African American dialect were not so thick and the piano rhythms so sophisticated.

Piano boogie devotees disdained the pop boogies of the 1940s and had no use for rhythm-and-blues or rock 'n' roll. "Every dance band featured synthetic boogie, popular songs based on the idiom were soon common and some of them were worthy forebears of the moronic rock songs of the 1950's," wrote the British jazz critic Max Harrison in 1959.[1] Youthful rock fans, on the other hand, had no memory of the boogie era and only latched on to the word "boogie" in the late 1960s after the band Canned Heat revived the guitar boogies of John Lee Hooker, which were not really boogie-woogies at all.

Still, it's hard to understand how the resemblance between pop boogies and early rock 'n' roll could be so widely overlooked, except in terms of a cultural clash between a generation sobered by depression and war and the rebellious teens who came after them. To the rock pioneer Chuck Berry, the relationship is obvious. "The nature and backbone of my beat is boogie," he writes in his autobiography. "Call it what you may . . . it's still boogie as far as I'm connected with it."[2]

Like jazz and blues, the boogie-woogie, or at least the boogie bass line, can be traced back to the ragtime era. But the boogie-woogie did not attract scholarly interest until white listeners discovered it in the late 1930s. The New Orleans–based composer and musicologist William Russell published the first serious essay on boogie-woogie in 1939, consisting mainly of biographical sketches.[3] The German-born jazz critic Ernest Borneman researched the origins of boogie-woogie in the mid-1940s, while he was living in Canada, and published the results in 1957.[4]

Perhaps the first published example of a boogie bass line occurs just before the final chords of Antonín Dvořák's *New World* Symphony, written in 1893, during the composer's American sojourn. Already known for using Czech folk music in his work, Dvořák incorporated elements of African American spirituals into the *New World* Symphony, notably the famous "Goin' Home" theme of the second movement. But like the jazzy walking bass section in that movement—anticipating the innovations of Walter Page, Count Basie's bassist, by some four decades—the brief snatch of what sounds like boogie-woogie at the end of the fourth movement is apparently a fluke.

Since one type of boogie-woogie bass line is built on the habanera rhythm, Eubie Blake's recollection of Jesse Pickett playing "The Dream" in the late 1890s ranks among the earliest boogie citations. Blake also recalled an obese pianist in Baltimore named William Turk, who "had a left hand like God. . . . He could play the ragtime stride bass, but it bothered him because his stomach got in the way of his arm, so he used a walking bass instead. I can remember when I was thirteen—this was 1896—how Turk would play one note with his right hand and at the same time four with his left. We called it 'sixteen'—they call it boogie-woogie now."[5]

Reminiscing in the May 1949 issue of *The Record Changer* magazine, H. B. Kay claims that as a teenage newsboy in the racially mixed Tenderloin District of Manhattan, he heard young black pianists play boogie-woogie bass lines, which he calls "8-beats," in the late 1890s. "The 8-beat was known to that part of New York before the Spanish American War," he says. "The Alabama Negroes were the personification of syncopation in most everything they did, including their traditional 8-beat." Kay adds that the celebrated black vaudeville team of Bert Williams and George Walker used boogie rhythms in their revue at Koster and Bial's Music Hall during the fall and winter of 1898–1899, saying that "Walker, a nimble buck and wing dancer . . . did some entirely new steps to the 8-beat knocked out on three pianos."[6]

In 1939, Richard M. Jones, best known for his composition "Trouble in Mind," told *Down Beat* magazine's correspondent Onah L. Spencer how he'd heard a pianist called Stavin' Chain at Bully Reynolds' TP Saloon in Donaldsonville, Louisiana, between New Orleans and Baton Rouge. "Chain walked into that saloon one night—it was still 1904—and sat down at an old piano," said Jones. "I was a youngster but I remember him. He started rambling around on the keyboard, then he told some onlookers he was going to play a tune he called *Lazy Rags* which featured a lot of walking bass. I'm telling you, customers started coming into that saloon like gangbusters when they heard him go. 'Roll that walkin' bass, Papa Stavin' Chain. Roll it a week,' I remember them all shouting."[7]

In his 1938 Library of Congress interviews with Alan Lomax, Jelly Roll Morton demonstrates how Tony Jackson played "Michigan Water Blues," which he claimed (in a letter to Robert Ripley the same year) that Jackson had performed in 1905. "Then they'd do the single—single running bass," Morton adds, playing a boogie-woogie bass line. "Then they'd do what they call a double running bass there," he continues, playing a boogie-woogie bass line with each note repeated.[8]

In 1946, Leadbelly told the record producer Ross Russell that he'd heard boogie-woogie piano as a teenager in Shreveport, Louisiana, around 1906. "Boogie-woogie was called barrelhouse in those days," he said. "One of the best players was named Chee-Dee. He would go from one gin mill to the next on Fanning St. [actually Fannin Street]. He was coal black and one of the old-line players, and he boogied the blues." Leadbelly mentioned another pianist, Pine Top Williams, to the jazz critic Charles Edward Smith. "He played that boogie woogie," Leadbelly said. "That's where I got that bass—on Fannin' [sic] Street. And that's what I wanted to play on guitar, that piano bass."[9]

Ernest Borneman writes that Tony Catalano, a white cornet player, heard Charlie Mills, a black pianist, play boogie-woogie on riverboats near New Orleans in 1907. Borneman gives no attribution, but one of the principals of the Streckfus steamship company confirmed that Catalano did play in a band with Mills on the riverboat J.S. around that time.[10] Mills later recorded with ragtime bands but not in a boogie style.

In his autobiography, *Born with the Blues,* the black vaudeville performer Perry Bradford (best known for convincing OKeh Records to record Mamie Smith singing his composition "Crazy Blues") writes that "St. Louis, Memphis, Atlanta, Chicago, Cincinnati and Louisville had a gang of piano sharks. From these 'Hotspots' where ragtime piano men were making the natives hug and kiss each other and shouting for more and more; along with those piano fiends in Texas who only played the after-beat bass style (what was called the Texas roll); and Birmingham's Lost John, the man who came to Chicago in 1908 beating out nothing but lost chords; all this was the same stuff that Pete Johnson, Albert Ammons and Meade Lux Lewis laid on New Yorkers at Carnegie Hall, which the Broadway slickers nick-named Boogie-Woogie."[11]

Borneman writes, again without attribution, that "in 1909, W. C. Handy heard Seymour Abernathy, Benny French and Sonny Butts at the Monarch, on Beale Street, and at Mulcahey's saloon in Memphis, playing the blues with 'eight to the bar boogie-woogie pre-influence.'"[12] French was evidently the same pianist Jelly Roll Morton called Benny Frenchy, whom Morton said he'd encountered at the Monarch Saloon on Beale Street in Memphis around 1908. But when he demonstrates Frenchy's piano style on his Library of Congress recordings, Morton plays a striding ragtime bass line, without a hint of boogie-woogie feeling.[13]

Pianist James "Stump" Johnson said that that the boogie was created by a St. Louis pianist named Son Long. "He never had a chance to record but he was the originator of what they call the boogie woogie," Johnson told Paul Oliver. "He was born around and lived around 15th and Morgan at that time, and I used to hear him there. That was the coloured limelight."[14] Johnson, born in Clarksville, Tennessee, in 1902, could not have heard Long earlier than about 1909, when Johnson's family moved to St. Louis.[15]

Around this time, boogie-like bass lines began to appear in published ragtime compositions. The last section of Scott Joplin's "Pine Apple Rag," from 1908, contains an eight-note bass figure that's rhythmically identical and melodically similar to ones found in boogie-woogie. Joplin's "Solace," from 1909, makes substantial use of habanera rhythms, and the "Alabama Bound" section of Blind Boone's "Southern Rag Medley No. Two," also from 1909, features a vaguely boogie-ish walking bass.

A few measures of walking bass in the final part of Artie Matthews's "Pastime Rag No. 1," from 1913, barely hint at boogie-woogie. But the second part of Matthews's "Weary Blues," from 1915, features an unmistakable boogie-woogie bass line in the context of a twelve-bar blues chorus—the first passage of full-blown boogie in print. The trilled introduction foreshadows the opening of Pinetop Smith's "Pine Top's Boogie Woogie," while the melody over the walking bass anticipates Paul Williams's 1949 rhythm-and-blues hit "The Huckle-Buck." "Weary Blues" was extensively recorded from the 1920s through the 1950s, usually without the boogie bass line, by artists ranging from Clarence Williams, Jelly Roll Morton, and Louis Armstrong to Duke Ellington, Tommy Dorsey, and the McGuire Sisters. But that bass line, which has become the most common boogie-woogie pattern to this day, is what gives "Weary Blues" its enormous though virtually unrecognized influence.

The distinction of having written the first blues with a boogie-woogie bass line is usually given to George W. Thomas, who published his "New Orleans Hop Scop Blues" in 1916, with an ascending four-note bass figure rather than the more typical ascending and descending eight-note figure found in "Weary Blues." In 1923, Thomas sold "New Orleans Hop Scop Blues" to Clarence Williams, who recorded it in July of that year with singer Sara Martin and in October with his own Blue Five band. The Blue Five's instrumental version swings harder, and when the riffing horns—including Sidney Bechet's soprano saxophone—wail the blues over the vamping boogie figure, there's a faint but definite rock 'n' roll feeling. Williams later claimed that he'd first heard Thomas play "New Orleans Hop Scop Blues" at a theater in Houston in 1911. "At that time he called it the 'Hop Scop Blues,'" wrote Williams, "because of the rolling, hopping bass."[16]

In April 1917, Wilbur Sweatman recorded an original composition titled "Boogie Rag," but it bears no resemblance to the boogie-woogie. Also in 1917, Eubie Blake published and made a piano roll of "The Charleston Rag," featuring an un-boogie-like walking bass line that descends like the one in Artie Matthews's "Pastime Rag No. 1." Blake claimed to have composed the piece in 1899, before he learned how to write music. The famous African American violinist and composer Will Marion Cook heard him play the tune around 1905 and dubbed it "Sounds of Africa." He took Blake to a New York publisher, who offered buy it, but the deal fell through when the hot-tempered Cook took racial umbrage at an innocent remark, delaying the publication of "The Charleston Rag" for years.[17]

The first pop song to use a walking bass—though not a boogie-ish one—was "Dardanella," published in 1919, with music by Felix Bernard and Johnny S. Black and words by Fred Fisher, who was also the publisher. Bandleader Ben Selvin's instrumental recording of the tune was a huge hit in 1920. Soon afterward, Jerome Kern composed the Hawaiian-flavored "Ka-Lu-A," featuring a very similar repeating figure, and Fred Fisher sued for copyright infringement. In his 1924 decision, the eminent jurist Learned Hand ruled for the plaintiff, finding that "the defendants have been able to discover in earlier popular music neither this figure, nor even any 'ostinato' accompaniment whatever."[18]

"The Fives," composed by George W. Thomas and his brother Hersal Thomas, was copyrighted in 1921 and issued by George's publishing company in Chicago the following year. The lyrics, by George Thomas, are about a train, and the chugging rhythms prefigure those of later boogie-woogies. The music has a few frilly ragtime passages, with stride bass accompaniment, but it's dominated by boogie beats, with a variety of walking bass lines, among them a rising-and-falling eight-note pattern in a twelve-bar blues passage. Like the boogie figure in "Weary Blues," it's essentially an arpeggiated major sixth chord with each note played twice—what Jelly Roll Morton referred to as a "double running bass."

"The Rocks" was recorded for the OKeh label in February 1923 by a pianist using the name Clay Custer—thought to be George W. Thomas, who is credited on the label as the composer. Although it uses the blues form only intermittently and contains snatches of stride bass, it is generally regarded as the first boogie-woogie recording. Like "The Fives," it features a number of different walking bass lines, including habanera figures and the same sort of double running bass as on "Weary Blues" or "The Fives." The next month, Fletcher Henderson recorded "Chime Blues," a piano solo featuring chiming effects and a "Weary Blues"–style boogie-woogie bass line.

Hersal Thomas, more than twenty years younger than George, had followed his brother from Houston to New Orleans and then Chicago, where he made a piano roll of "The Fives" in 1924. He made two solo recordings in 1925, "Suitcase Blues" and "Hersal Blues," while recording more extensively as an accompanist to his sister, Sippie Wallace, and his niece, Hociel Thomas. Before his sudden death in July 1926, at the age of nineteen, Hersal Thomas was a popular entertainer at South Side rent parties and a prime influence on his Chicago-born peers Albert Ammons and Meade "Lux" Lewis, who would become standard-bearers of the boogie-woogie movement.[19]

William Russell wrote that "Hersal played all the favorite blues and was known especially for his own *Suitcase Blues.* In those days if a pianist didn't know the *Fives* and the *Rocks* he'd better not sit down at the piano at all. Whenever Hersal Thomas, who made a deep impression on young Ammons, came to a party, the other pianists were afraid to play; so he became unusually popular and got all the girls."[20]

Meade "Lux" Lewis mistakenly attributed "The Fives" to a pianist from St. Louis, although he was apparently referring to Hersal Thomas. "This man played *The Fives,*" Lewis said. "It was something new and it got Ammons and me all excited. (Sure wish I could remember his name.) The best way to describe his way of playin' is to say that the right hand played *The Fives* while the left hand didn't matter. You could play any kind of left hand—a rumble bass, a walkin' bass, and so on."[21]

In September 1923, pianist Eddie Heywood recorded "The Mixed Up Blues," featuring a prominent boogie-woogie bass line toward the end of the piece. Little is known about Heywood's background except that he played in Atlanta theaters and was a graduate of the Boston Conservatory of Music.[22]

Jimmy Blythe, a Kentucky-born pianist who moved to Chicago sometime between 1915 and 1918, cut "Chicago Stomp" in April 1924. Basically just a series of blues choruses accompanied by a walking bass, plus a short introduction and coda, it's considered to be the first pure boogie-woogie to be recorded. The melody on the first chorus is reminiscent of the "Huckle-Buck" theme in "Weary Blues," and all but the last two choruses use the "Weary Blues" boogie bass line. Many of the melodic figures from "Chicago Stomp" turn up in later boogie-woogies, and despite its plodding rhythms, the piece as a whole is clearly a rock 'n' roll ancestor.

The boogie-woogie may have reached its mature form in Chicago, but its geographical origins are uncertain. Boogie antecedents were reported in New York, Baltimore, New Orleans, Memphis, and Houston, among other places. Scott Joplin, born in Texas, was living in Sedalia, Missouri, when he wrote "Pine Apple Rag"; Blind Boone's "Southern Rag Medley No. Two" is subtitled "Strains from the Flat Branch," referring to a district of Columbia, Missouri; Artie Matthews, born in Illinois, published "Weary Blues" in St. Louis. Two of the most significant boogie pianists, Cow Cow Davenport and Pinetop Smith, hailed from Alabama.

The consensus among historians, however, is that the boogie-woogie first emerged in Texas or Louisiana. In 1939, E. Simms Campbell wrote that "Boogie Woogie piano playing originated in the lumber and turpentine camps of Texas and in the sporting houses of that state. . . . In Houston, Dallas and Galveston—all Negro piano players played that way."[23] But Campbell was a cartoonist—one of the first successful African American commercial artists—and not a musicologist. And he gave no attribution for his statement, which appears in the context of a highly subjective essay on the blues that was published in the same influential book, *Jazzmen,* as William Russell's essay on boogie-woogie.

Born in St. Louis, Campbell was educated in Chicago and made his career in New York, where he befriended jazz musicians and published a "Night-

Club Map of Harlem." For his blues essay he interviewed Clarence Williams, a Louisiana native who was a teenager performing in a vaudeville show in Houston when he met the older George W. Thomas. When he republished Thomas's "New Orleans Hop Scop Blues" in 1940, Williams commented in the annotation that "the 'Boogie Woogie' originated in Texas many years ago. It wasn't called the 'Boogie Woogie' then. George Thomas was the fellow who used this style and first wrote it down."[24]

In the same song folio, Williams recalls "playing piano for a boarding house maintained for turpentine workers in a little town called Oakdale, La., near the borderline of Texas."[25] He notes that Thomas played piano to accompany silent movie screenings in Houston, but he does not place Thomas at any lumber or turpentine camps. According to the blues scholar David Evans, Thomas was born in Little Rock, Arkansas, in 1883 but had moved to Houston by 1900.[26]

In his book *A Left Hand Like God: A History of Boogie-Woogie Piano,* Peter J. Silvester writes that "during the 1890s, large-scale lumbering operations started in the western Louisiana/eastern Texas area."[27] Silvester describes how the black workers used shacks built on railroad cars and furnished with pianos as rolling barrelhouses, which were moved along newly laid rails as the logging progressed further into the forest. But there seems to be no account of any early boogie-woogie pianist actually playing in such a shack.

The musician most often cited to substantiate the connection between lumber camps and boogie-woogie is Eurreal "Little Brother" Montgomery. Born in the sawmill town of Kentwood, Louisiana, in 1906, he began playing piano at the age of five. Many of the itinerant pianists who entertained at the nearby honky-tonk his father ran also played at the family's home; Montgomery later recalled the names of more than a dozen of them—most from Louisiana or Mississippi, all virtually unknown today except for Jelly Roll Morton. Montgomery's recordings of their material—such as "Crescent City Blues," which he adapted from "Loomis Gibson Blues"—contain occasional walking bass lines.[28]

"We were playing all those kind of basses down there, way before ever it came out on records," Montgomery maintained. "I used to only play a walking bass with one finger then, but after I got up around twelve, fourteen I could double up and play with all of my hand. We called it Dudlow Joe." At the age of eleven, he had run away from home to play piano professionally. "My first job was at a juke joint in Holton, Louisiana," he said. "I moved on to Plaquemine, Louisiana, where I played for five or six months for a fellow called Tom Kirby at a cabaret. . . . Then I left there and went to Ferriday, Louisiana, and played for Ed Henderson at Henderson's Royal Garden."[29]

For the next ten years, Montgomery played in what he called nightclubs or barrelhouses in small towns around Louisiana, Mississippi, and Arkansas, as well as in New Orleans. In recounting his early career, he doesn't mention performing at lumber or logging camps until the mid-1920s. The blues singer and guitarist Big Joe Williams remembered playing with Montgomery at a camp in Electric Mills, Mississippi, but Montgomery said he did not meet Williams until 1926.[30]

The backgrounds of many of the first boogie-woogie pianists are obscure, and though some of them might have played in lumber or turpentine camps before 1920, only Will Ezell is actually reported to have done so.[31] Born in Shreveport, Louisiana, in 1896, Ezell is said to have been the regular pianist in the sawmill town of Haslam, Texas, near the Lousiana border, around the time of World War I.[32] Speckled Red, born Rufus Perryman in Monroe, Louisiana, in 1892, was living in Detroit before he returned to the South in the late 1920s, when it is claimed that he played in sawmill camps.[33]

Of the few other known boogie pianists born before 1900—old enough to have made an impact before the publication of "Weary Blues" or "New Orleans Hop Scop Blues"—even fewer were from the rural South. Cripple Clarence Lofton was born in Kingsport, Tennessee, in 1887 and worked in tent shows before moving to Chicago around 1917. Cow Cow Davenport, born in Anniston, Alabama, in 1894, honed his craft in urban honky-tonks and traveling shows. Doug Suggs was born in St. Louis in 1894 but made his career in Chicago. Jimmy Yancey was born in Chicago in 1898 and didn't learn to play piano until he was about sixteen years old, by which time he had toured the United States and Europe as a vaudeville singer and tap dancer, even performing for the king and queen of England.

The Texas lumber camp theory of boogie origins probably started with E. Simms Campbell's interpretation of remarks by Clarence Williams. But the boogie-woogie, an offshoot of ragtime, more likely developed in the same urban areas where ragtime flourished, and was then disseminated into the hinterlands. By the late 1910s, walking bass lines were surely being played by pianists in lumber and turpentine camps, as well as levee camps, tent shows, taverns, brothels, and vaudeville theaters.

Although a few of the early boogie musicians had some musical education—Jimmy Blythe, for example, studied with the ragtime composer Clarence M. Jones in Chicago—most are thought to have had little or no formal training.[34] Cow Cow Davenport said that the boogie beat "was originated by uneducated pianists."[35] Jelly Roll Morton's friend Roy Carew concurred: "I would say that Boogie Woogie was the bad little boy of the rag family who wouldn't study. . . . More crude than Pine Top's efforts, such music never got played in the 'gilded palaces.'"[36] According to Eubie Blake, "The higher-class fellows who played things from the big shows looked down on this music. Nobody thought of writing it down. It was supposed to be the lower type of music, but now it is considered all right."[37]

By the late 1920s, most of the major and minor boogie-woogie pianists were living or had lived in Chicago, including Jimmy Yancey, Meade "Lux" Lewis, Albert Ammons, Hersal Thomas, Jimmy Blythe, Cripple Clarence Lofton, Doug Suggs, J. H. "Freddie" Shayne, Charles Avery, Montana Taylor, Romeo Nelson, Little Brother Montgomery, Cow Cow Davenport, Pinetop Smith, and possibly Turner Parrish, Will Ezell, and Charlie Spand. In 1927, Meade "Lux" Lewis made his first recording, the classic "Honky Tonk Train Blues," but it was not released for a couple of years. Also in 1927, Jimmy Blythe made a piano roll of "Boogie Woogie Blues," the first known use of the term "boogie woogie" in a song title.

Pinetop Smith arrived in Chicago in the summer of 1928. Born near Troy, Alabama, in 1904, he began his career in Birmingham; after moving to Pittsburgh in 1920, he toured the Midwest and South in vaudeville shows, singing and dancing as well as playing piano. According to William Russell, Smith lived in the same Chicago rooming house as Albert Ammons and Meade "Lux" Lewis, and the three shared Ammons's piano. Smith auditioned for Mayo Williams, possibly at Cow Cow Davenport's instigation, and in December 1928 recorded "Pine Top's Boogie Woogie," backed with "Pine Top's Blues," for Vocalion.

Much of "Pine Top's Boogie Woogie" consists of spoken instructions on how to dance the boogie-woogie: "Hold yourself, now! Stop! Shake that thing!" But nearly all of it rides an ascending walking bass pattern—four doubled notes, eight beats to the bar—similar to the one in "New Orleans Hop Scop Blues" (or, for that matter, to the one in Elvis Presley's "All Shook Up"). Smith borrowed the trilled opening of "Pine Top's Boogie Woogie" from Hersal Thomas's introduction on Sippie Wallace's 1926 recording of "Special Delivery Blues," which features Louis Armstrong on cornet. He took the main theme—a treble figure repeated over the walking bass—from a motif that appears near the end of Jimmy Blythe's 1925 recording of "Jimmie Blues." The same theme was published as part of a 1925 composition titled "Syncophonic No. 4" by Axel Christensen, a Danish-American pianist from Chicago who ran a nationwide chain of ragtime schools. Christensen took a different theme in "Syncophonic No. 4" from Blythe's 1924 piano roll of George W. Thomas's "Underworld Blues." In 1927, Christensen published Blythe's "Chicago Stomp" under his own name, crediting Blythe as his co-composer; soon afterward he republished it as "Walking Blues," and later as "Boogie Woogie Blues," without crediting Blythe at all.[38]

"Pine Top's Boogie Woogie" was a smash hit, and it lent its title to a whole musical genre. Among the many recordings it inspired are Roosevelt Sykes's "Boot That Thing," Romeo Nelson's "Head Rag Hop," Charles Avery's "Dearborn Street Breakdown," and Montana Taylor's "Detroit Rocks," all from 1929. But Pinetop Smith did not have long to enjoy his success; less than three months after his landmark recording, on the eve of his next studio date, he was accidentally shot to death at a dance. He was twenty-five years old and had cut a total of eight sides.[39]

A DASH OF HOKUM

This first boogie-woogie boom coincided with the hokum craze sparked by Tampa Red and Georgia Tom's October 1928 recording of "It's Tight Like That," one of the best-selling "race" records of the era. "It's Tight Like That" follows the twelve-bar verse-and-refrain model of Papa Charlie Jackson's "Shake That Thing," the same structure used on such prototypical rock songs as Bill Haley's "Rock Around the Clock," Little Richard's "She's Got It," and Chuck Berry's "Reelin' and Rockin'." Tampa Red's boogie guitar lines, partially duplicating the melody sung by Haley on "Rock Around the Clock," lend an indisputable rock 'n' roll flavor to risqué couplets such as "The gal I love, she's long and slim / When she whip it, it's too bad, Jim."

In December 1928, just days before Pinetop Smith's historic session, James "Stump" Johnson recorded "The Duck's Yas-Yas-Yas," another influential hit. Here Johnson plays stride piano, not boogie, but his lyrics are pure hokum, typified by the title verse: "Mama bought a rooster, she thought it was a duck. / She brought him to the table with his legs straight up. / In come the children with the cup and the glass, / To catch the liquor from his yas-yas-yas." The song was further popularized by Tampa Red and Georgia Tom, who recorded it in May 1929, and by the St. Louis cornetist Oliver Cobb, who recorded it with his jazz band, the Rhythm Kings, in August 1929.

In October 1929, Romeo Nelson recorded "Gettin' Dirty Just Shakin' That Thing," the flip side of "Head Rag Hop." Paraphrasing Stump Johnson's words over a driving boogie beat, Nelson sings, "Hey, mama killed a chicken and she thought he was a duck, / [Put him] on the table with his heels cocked up. / Old folk, run and get your glass, / Catch the juice from the two black bass." At the end, he displays the range of his influences, first singing, "Clap hands, here comes Nelson," a reference to the white "ukulele ace" Johnny Marvin's 1926 pop hit "Clap Hands! Here Comes Charley," and then, "Too tight, just won't right now," alluding not to "It's Tight Like That" but to Blind Blake's "Too Tight," also from 1926.

Another example of hokum-boogie fusion is Speckled Red's September 1929 recording of "The Dirty Dozen," an expurgated adaptation of an African American insult game. Like "Gettin' Dirty Just Shakin' That Thing," it uses boogie bass runs and—with the line "[If] you can't shake your shimmy, shake your yas-yas-yas"—makes explicit reference to Stump Johnson's song. But "The Dirty Dozen" was a much bigger hit than "Gettin' Dirty Just Shakin' That Thing," inspiring cover versions by artists ranging from Kokomo Arnold to Count Basie. In his Library of Congress interviews, Jelly Roll Morton claims that the song originated in Chicago, where he heard it "about 1908." But the obscene version he demonstrates bears little resemblance to Speckled Red's recording except for the tag line "Yo mammy don't wear no drawers," which Red renders as "Yo mama do the lordy lord."[40]

Intriguingly, one of Red's verses, "Yonder go yo mama goin' across the field, / Runnin' an' a-shakin' like an automobile. / I hollered at yo mama and I told her to wait. / She slipped away from me like a Cadillac eight," turns up on Bo Diddley's hard-pounding 1957 rocker "Hey! Bo Diddley" as "Saw my baby runnin' 'cross the field, / Slippin' an' slidin' like a automobile. / Hollered at my baby, done told her to wait. / Slipped out from me like a Cadillac eight."

In 1930, Speckled Red recorded a sequel, "The Dirty Dozen No. 2," with another hokum song, "The Right String, but the Wrong Yo Yo," on the flip side. That song is loosely based on Eddie Green's composition "You've Got the Right Key, but the Wrong Keyhole," recorded in 1924 by singer Virginia Liston with Clarence Williams and his Blue Five, featuring Louis Armstrong and Sidney Bechet. Adapting the lyrics to suit the yo-yo fad that had taken hold in 1929, Red changes Liston's line "Yesterday I went down to the hardware store / And put another lock on my front door" to "Passed yesterday by the hardware store. / Bought a brand new string to fit my yo-yo."

"You've Got the Right Key, but the Wrong Keyhole" is apparently based on "You're in the Right Church but the Wrong Pew," written by the African American lyricist Cecil Mack and composer Chris Smith for Bert Williams and George Walker's 1908 Broadway show *Bandanna Land.*[41] The song was recorded that year by Eddie Morton, a white vaudevillian who often covered Bert Williams's songs, and became a major hit in 1909 when it was recorded by Arthur Collins and Byron Harlan, the leading blackface duo of the day.

"The Right String, but the Wrong Yo-Yo" was revived in 1950 by Speckled Red's younger brother Piano Red (Willie Perryman) and became an R&B hit the following year, although it preserved much of the old-fashioned vaudeville feel of Speckled Red's original, with its primitive-sounding walking bass lines. In 1956, Carl Perkins recorded a rockabilly-style "Right String Baby, Wrong Yo-Yo," for Sun Records, which released it only as an album track in 1958. Under the name Dr. Feelgood and the Interns, Piano Red scored a minor pop hit when he recorded the song again, with a more modern sound, in 1962. Johnny Kidd and the Pirates, a British rock group that predated the Beatles, covered it in 1964, as did Gerry and the Pacemakers, another British group. In 1969, the Beatles made a rehearsal tape of "Right String, Wrong Yo-Yo," which was later bootlegged. Shortly before his death in 1985, at the age of seventy-three, Piano Red recorded the song once more, this time with country singer Danny Shirley, and it made *Billboard*'s country singles chart.

BIG BAND BOOGIE

With the onset of the Depression, record sales plummeted, and few boogies were recorded until the mid-1930s. A peculiar exception is the piano introduction to "Jam House Blues," recorded in December 1933 by Gene Austin, the leading white pop crooner of the 1920s. Charlie Segar, a black pianist born in Florida and based in Chicago, cut an altered version of "Pine Top's Boogie Woogie" for the Decca label in January 1935, titled simply "Boogie Woogie." But it was Cleo Brown's March 1935 rendition for the same label, also titled "Boogie Woogie," that catalyzed the genre's resurgence. Brown, born in Mississippi and based in Chicago, was a suave stylist, and she turned Smith's piece into a virtuoso vehicle, revving the piano part to warp speed (and changing the bass line to the ascending and descending "Weary Blues" figure) while delivering the recitation with silky-smooth insouciance.

John Hammond was producing records and writing magazine articles when he encountered Albert Ammons on a trip to Chicago in late 1935. "Ever since 1928, when I first heard Clarence 'Pinetop' Smith's original boogie-woogie piano, I had been fascinated by this eight-to-the-bar left-hand blues style, which had never been recognized by white audiences," Hammond wrote in his autobiography. "And when I heard a record of 'Honky Tonk Train Blues' in 1931 I knew I had found the ultimate practitioner in Meade Lux Lewis. But no matter where I looked, or whom I asked, I couldn't find him. Now years later in Chicago, I raised the question again while chewing the fat with Albert Ammons. 'Meade Lux?' said Albert. 'Why sure. He's working in a car wash around the corner.' And so he was!"[42]

In November 1935, Hammond had Lewis redo "Honky Tonk Train Blues"—his first solo recording since the 1927 original—for the Parlophone label, a British subsidiary of Columbia. On the heels of Cleo Brown's success, Decca released Lewis's record in the United States the following year. Like Brown's "Boogie Woogie," "Honky Tonk Train Blues" is a high-speed technical showpiece, but it's not a typical boogie. The bass line is just a rudimentary chugging riff, which Lewis's left hand maintains in a rigid tempo while his right hand plays a variety of figures in a contrasting rhythm.

In January 1936, Lewis made his next recording, "Yancey Special," for Decca. It features the kind of habanera bass line often used by Jimmy Yancey, one of Lewis's early models (Lewis had already recorded a Yancey-style bass line in 1930 as the accompanist on singer George Hannah's "Freakish Man Blues"). But while Yancey would vary the bass pattern from one measure to the next, Lewis repeats the same riff over and over. It was 1939 before Yancey made records, which were appreciated mainly by cognoscenti. By contrast, Lewis's "Yancey Special" was widely influential, especially in New Orleans, where its bass line became a rhythm-and-blues fixture, propelling such early rock 'n' roll hits as Fats Domino's "Ain't It a Shame" and "Blueberry Hill."

The provenance of the "Yancey Special" bass line became a legal issue after the Chicago pianist Sonny Thompson used it in his band's instrumental "Long Gone," a No. 1 R&B hit in 1948, and Lewis's publisher sued Thompson's record company for copyright infringement. Yancey testified that he and not Lewis had originated the bass line; Lewis contradicted himself, first denying and then admitting that he had named the tune after Yancey. Judge Michael L. Igoe did not conclude that Yancey was the composer but found for the defendant on a number of grounds, among them "that this bass is too simple to be copyrightable."[43]

Albert Ammons had played with several bands before making his first record with his own sextet for Decca in January 1936, two days after Meade "Lux" Lewis's "Yancey Special" session. On one side was "Nagasaki," a Tin Pan Alley song by Harry Warren and Mort Dixon that had already been recorded by Don Redman, Fletcher Henderson, the Mills Brothers, and Cab Calloway. On the other side was "Boogie Woogie Stomp," Ammons's version of "Pine Top's Boogie Woogie," on which he drops the recitation but stays close to the original piano part, playing it with considerably more flair and drive than Smith did. By William Russell's account, "a few days before he died Pine Top called Albert Ammons aside and said, 'Albert, I want you to learn my *Boogie Woogie*.'"[44]

Ammons was hardly the first to play boogie-woogie in a group setting. The Tampa Blue Jazz Band (a pseudonym for the Joseph Samuels Jazz Band, a white combo that accompanied the blues singer Mamie Smith in the late summer of 1921) had recorded George and Hersal Thomas's "The Fives" for OKeh in February 1923, the same month Clay Custer cut "The Rocks." The New Orleans Rhythm Kings, an influential white band, recorded Artie Matthews's "Weary Blues," complete with boogie bass line, the following month. In August 1923, Fletcher Henderson and His Orchestra recorded "Dicty Blues," an adaptation of "Chime Blues" featuring real chimes and a one-chorus boogie-woogie run played by the bass saxophonist Billy Fowler. Besides recording "New Orleans Hop Scop Blues" in 1923 with his Blue Five, Clarence Williams was part of the accompanying quartet on Bessie Smith's recording of the same song in 1930. King Oliver recorded a tune called "Boogie Woogie" with a big band in 1930, but it had no connection to the boogie-woogie other than the title.

Will Ezell cut "Pitchin' Boogie" in 1929 with Blind Roosevelt Graves on guitar, his brother Uaroy (or Aaron) Graves on tambourine, and Baby Jay (or James) on cornet; at the same session, the same group cut "Guitar Boogie" (not the same as Arthur Smith's country hit by the same title) and "Crazy about My Baby," which were issued under Roosevelt Graves's name. As the Mississippi Jook Band, the Graves brothers and pianist Cooney Vaughn recorded a number of boogie-driven tunes in July 1936, among them "Dangerous Woman" and "Barbecue Bust," which the critic Robert Palmer described as featuring "fully formed rock & roll guitar riffs and a stomping rock & roll beat."[45]

In early 1936, John Hammond, Benny Goodman, and Johnny Mercer went to a Chicago club where Meade "Lux" Lewis was playing with a trumpeter and drummer under the name Lux and His Chips. Goodman was so impressed that he arranged for Lewis to record "Honky Tonk Train Blues" again, for Victor. Hammond took Lewis to New York twice that year—first to perform in a star-studded show at the Imperial Theatre that was billed as the first swing concert and then to play an engagement at a Greenwich Village nightclub—but he was not well received.[46] Neither Ammons nor Lewis recorded between May 1936 and December 1938, but their reputation was growing, thanks largely to articles in *Down Beat* by Hammond and Sharon Pease, the magazine's new piano columnist.

Hammond had heard Count Basie's band on a radio broadcast around the end of 1935. Dazzled, he wrote about the band in *Down Beat* and traveled to Kansas City to sign Basie to a recording contract, only to discover that Dave Kapp of Decca Records had beat him to the punch. While the band was in Chicago in the autumn of 1936, on its way to its official studio debut in New York, Hammond arranged for Basie and several of his musicians, including the tenor saxophonist Lester Young and the blues singer Jimmy Rushing, to record a few numbers for Vocalion under the pseudonym Jones-Smith Incorporated.[47] Among them was "Boogie Woogie"—a combination of "Pine Top's Boogie Woogie" and Rushing's "I May Be Wrong." The arrangement transforms Pinetop's theme into a Basie-esque call-and-response riff for saxophone and trumpet, omitting the boogie bass line almost entirely.

Rushing is considered to be the first blues "shouter," a term that has come to be associated not only with vocal power but with the jazzy phrasing and intonation that Rushing brought to the blues. Born in Oklahoma City, he studied violin and piano, then traveled to California, where he sang with Jelly Roll Morton and other New Orleans jazz musicians. He preceded Count Basie in Walter Page's Oklahoma City Blue Devils and followed Basie into Bennie Moten's band, joining Basie's own band along with Page after Moten's death in 1935. Rushing's swinging, sophisticated style was the model for the following generation of rhythm-and-blues singers as well as for urbane bluesmen such as B. B. King.

Basie recorded "Boogie Woogie (I May Be Wrong)," again featuring Rushing, for Decca with his big band in March 1937, playing an extended piano solo that contains only a single boogie chorus. In November 1938, accompanied by just a rhythm section, Basie recorded "Boogie Woogie" once more, without Rushing's song, as part of a session that also included "The Dirty Dozens" and "The Fives." This time he plays the boogie bass part intermittently in his own deft, economical style, using it as much for decoration as propulsion. His introduction features a repeating figure like the one played two years later by Jess Stacy in Bob Crosby's "Cow Cow Blues" and by Sonny White in Benny Carter's "Boogie Woogie Sugar Blues," which may have inspired Freddie Slack's piano riff in "Cow Cow Boogie."

Benny Goodman's big band recorded a version of "Pine Top's Boogie Woogie," titled "Roll 'Em," in July 1937. Like Basie's "Boogie Woogie (I May Be Wrong)," it turns Pinetop Smith's tune into a swing vehicle, dispensing with the boogie bass line even on Jess Stacy's piano solo. At Hammond's behest, Goodman had solicited the chart from Mary Lou Williams, the pianist and arranger for Andy Kirk and His Twelve Clouds of Joy, a black band from Kansas City.[48] A boogie bass is conspicuous on Kirk's February 1938 recording of "Little Joe from Chicago," written by Williams and trombonist Henry Wells, but not on Williams's September 1938 piano trio recordings of "The Rocks" and Freddie Shayne's boogie-woogie standard "Mr. Freddie Blues."

Bob Crosby's big band recorded "Yancey Special" in March 1938 and "Honky Tonk Train Blues" that October. The arrangements are highly respectful—orchestrated transcriptions rather than creative adaptations—and Bob Zurke does an admirable job of duplicating Meade "Lux" Lewis's original piano parts, bass lines and all, though he can't equal Lewis's rhythmic intensity.

Cab Calloway sang on his big band's recording of "The Boogie-Woogie" in August 1938. As on the original "Pine Top's Boogie Woogie," the lyrics consist mainly of instructions on how to do "the boogie woogie dance," but there's no walking bass to speak of and only a brief allusion to Pinetop's melody. With its jive-talking introduction—"I'm gonna spiel to ya about a brand new dance that's gonna slide to your conk and kill ya"—the song is a forerunner of the pop boogies of the 1940s.

Tommy Dorsey's big band recorded "Boogie Woogie," another variation on Pinetop's anthem, in September 1938, featuring pianist Howard Smith. The arrangement, by saxophonist Deane Kincaide, is more-or-less faithful but so rhythmically staid as to be almost comically square by today's standards. Nevertheless, it was a hit when it was first released and a bigger one after it was reissued in 1943, during a recording ban imposed by the musicians' union. Reentering the pop charts in 1944 and 1945, it became the biggest-selling boogie-woogie instrumental of them all.

Woody Herman's big band recorded "Indian Boogie Woogie" on December 22, 1938, featuring Tommy Linehan's genuine if slightly wooden boogie piano. Blending mild exoticism with kitsch, it prefigures Will Bradley's less corny 1940 novelty tune "Strange Cargo," the inspiration for Henry Mancini's "Theme from Peter Gunn."

BOOGIE-WOOGIE FEVER

In 1936, John Hammond saw pianist Pete Johnson's combo, featuring the blues shouter Big Joe Turner, at nightclub in Kansas City, Johnson's and Turner's home town. Johnson had absorbed Fats Waller's stride piano style as well as Pinetop Smith's boogie-woogie, while Turner had been influenced by classic blues singers such as Bessie Smith, Mamie Smith, and Ethel Waters. Hammond persuaded them to come to New York that summer, where they played an engagement at the Famous Door on Fifty-second Street but were booed off the stage at the Apollo Theatre in Harlem. In the spring of 1938, they returned to New York, again at Hammond's request, to perform on *The Camel Caravan* radio show with Benny Goodman.

In December 1938, Hammond invited Johnson and Turner back to New York to appear at Carnegie Hall along with Albert Ammons and Meade "Lux" Lewis in the first "From Spirituals to Swing" concert. The program illustrated the development of African American music with performances by artists of Hammond's choosing, among them the gospel singer Sister Rosetta Tharpe, the bluesmen Sonny Terry and Big Bill Broonzy, and Count Basie, who led a quintet and sextet as well as his big band. It may have been the first presentation of country blues at Carnegie Hall, although W. C. Handy had staged a similarly themed concert there ten years earlier, featuring spirituals, minstrel songs, ragtime, jazz, and blues.

Sponsored by the Marxist magazine *New Masses,* Hammond's December 23 show drew a packed house (the second "From Spirituals to Swing" concert was held on Christmas Eve the following year). Ammons and Lewis each played a solo piece, Johnson accompanied Turner on two songs and Big Bill Broonzy on one, and all three pianists played together on two numbers, backed on one by Walter Page and Jo Jones, Basie's bassist and drummer. (Recordings of the concert were made but not released until 1959.)

This time the boogie-woogie pianists were a sensation, igniting a boogie craze that would last for a decade. The day after the concert, Alan Lomax recorded Ammons, Lewis, and Johnson for the Library of Congress. On December 30, the three pianists cut the two-sided "Boogie Woogie Prayer" for Vocalion; Lewis recorded "Bear Cat Crawl" on the same date, and Ammons recorded the flip side, "Shout for Joy," two days later. The December 30 session also yielded Turner and Johnson's first record, "Roll 'Em Pete," backed with "Goin' Away Blues."

"Roll 'Em Pete" was Johnson's signature tune at Kansas City clubs such as the Sunset Crystal Palace. "On a good night, I would play chorus after chorus, always keeping adding to them . . . sometimes for an hour or longer," he recounted.[49] Mary Lou Williams appropriated the title for the Benny Goodman arrangement she wrote. "Ben Webster would yell, 'Roll for me, roll 'em, Pete, make 'em jump,'" she recalled, "and then Pete would play boogie for us."[50] Johnson performed the song with Turner at Carnegie Hall under the title "It's All Right Baby" (with verses somewhat different than on their Vocalion disc) and recorded it the next day for Alan Lomax as an instrumental called "Roll 'Em." But the December 30 Vocalion recording, usually credited to Turner rather than Johnson, is considered definitive.

Predating "Good Rockin' Tonight" by nearly ten years, "Roll 'Em Pete" may well be regarded as the first rock 'n' roll record. Although earlier songs contain elements of rock 'n' roll, "Roll 'Em Pete" is a full-fledged rocker in all but instrumentation—similar in melody and structure to Turner's 1950s hits "Honey Hush" and "Shake, Rattle and Roll" but faster and more intense. Johnson's bass line is a simple Chuck Berry–like chug, and his furious right-hand embellishments anticipate Berry's entire guitar style. Some of Turner's verses are the stuff that rock is made of, such as the opening "I've got a gal, lives up on the hill. / Well, this woman tried to quit me, Lord, but I love her still." But others—such as "You so beautiful, but you gotta die some day. / All I want [is a] little lovin', babe, just before you pass away"—are too mature for teenage listeners. If anything, Turner's brilliant phrasing and Johnson's breathtaking keyboard technique are too sophisticated for rock 'n' roll: the music has yet to be formularized for mass consumption.

On January 6, 1939, Lewis and Ammons became the first artists to record for Blue Note, a record label founded by Alfred Lion, a jazz-loving refugee from Nazi Germany who had attended the Carnegie Hall concert. Johnson would likewise record for Blue Note in 1939, and all three pianists also recorded that year for Solo Art, another new label that catered to jazz purists.

Ammons and Lewis played "Roll 'Em" with Benny Goodman's band on *The Camel Caravan* on January 3 and April 11 of 1939; Johnson did the same on January 31. On February 1, at John Hammond's suggestion, Ammons and Johnson each recorded a couple of sides with trumpeter Harry James, who had just left Goodman's band.[51] Later that year, all three pianists were billed with James's own big band, featuring the yet-unknown Frank Sinatra, at the Hotel Sherman in Chicago.

The "From Spirituals to Swing" concert had coincided with the opening of Cafe Society, a Greenwich Village nightclub run by a politically engagé former shoe-store owner, Barney Josephson, whose financial backers included Hammond and Goodman. Ammons, Lewis, Johnson, and Turner were regulars at Cafe Society from its inception, using it as a home base between tours. Turner and Lewis departed in 1941, but Ammons and Johnson stayed on for several more years, appearing at the club's upscale Midtown Manhattan branch as well as its original location. Josephson's novel policy of racial integration, not to mention such performers as Billie Holiday and Lena Horne, attracted left-wing luminaries such as Eleanor Roosevelt and Paul Robeson, lending boogie-woogie an air of radical chic. Regular radio broadcasts from the club helped cement its reputation as the boogie-woogie mecca.

At this point, boogie-woogie was viewed both as folk art and commercial entertainment. Although they also performed and recorded ballads and slow blues, Ammons, Lewis, and Johnson were best known for fast boogies that showcased their pianistic prowess. They often played with one another in duos or as a trio, furthering the transformation of boogie-woogie from dance music into bravura display. But in 1939, Solo Art recorded Jimmy Yancey and Cripple Clarence Lofton, older boogie pianists who were more idiosyncratic and less virtuosic. Yancey went on to release some dozen sides for Victor, Vocalion, and Bluebird over the next year and a half, ironically surpassing the individual major-label output of Ammons, Lewis, or Johnson during the same period. Turner meanwhile recorded prolifically for various commercial labels (but not for Blue Note or Solo Art), accompanied by such pianists as Johnson, Willie "The Lion" Smith, Art Tatum, Sammy Price, and Freddie Slack, as well as by Benny Carter's band.

The earliest boogie-woogie albums mixed swing-band and piano boogies indiscriminately. Decca's *Boogie Woogie Music,* from 1940, features two new recordings by Johnson along with reissues going back to 1935, among them Ammons's "Boogie Woogie Stomp," Lewis's "Yancey Special," Cleo Brown's "Boogie Woogie," Mary Lou Williams's "Overhand," and band arrangements by Bob Crosby, Woody Herman, Teddy Powell, and Andy Kirk. Only two numbers besides Johnson's were recorded after the "From Spirituals to Swing" concert. Columbia's *Boogie Woogie,* from 1941, includes most of the Ammons, Lewis, Johnson, and Turner Vocalion recordings from December 1938 together with Basie's 1936 "Boogie Woogie" and one each of Ammons's and Johnson's 1939 sides with Harry James.

Few boogie recordings from before 1935 were reissued until much later. Several of the earlier boogie-woogie pianists—Yancey, Cow Cow Davenport, Montana Taylor, Freddie Shayne—were rediscovered and recorded in the 1940s, but their music appealed mainly to aficionados. The public's attention turned instead to a new, racially mixed generation of boogie players, mostly big-band pianists such as Ken Kersey, Bob Zurke, and Freddie Slack.

Big-band boogies proliferated after the Carnegie Hall show. Oddly enough, one of the earlier ones was by James P. Johnson, known as the father of stride piano, who recorded "Harlem Woogie" in March 1939 with a swing combo featuring singer Anna Robinson. Like Cab Calloway's "The Boogie-Woogie," it's a conventional pop song rather than a real boogie, announcing the arrival of a new dance over bouncing stride rhythms. The Basie-like "Teddy's Boogie Woogie," recorded in October 1939 by the briefly successful white bandleader Teddy Powell, is truer to the boogie form, with a brawny tenor saxophone solo by Pete Mondello that anticipates the "honking" style of postwar R&B. Harry James's bluesy "Back Beat Boogie," from November 1939, is another rock precursor: behind Jack Gardner's boogie piano, drummer Mickey Scrima sharply accents the second and fourth beats of each measure, a departure from the typically even 4/4 swing rhythm.

In February 1940, Earl Hines and his big band recorded "Boogie Woogie on the St. Louis Blues," a takeoff on W. C. Handy's classic that proved to be a substantial hit. Like Jelly Roll Morton and James P. Johnson, Hines was a jazz-piano pioneer, having played on Louis Armstrong's historic Hot Five and Hot Seven sessions before forming his own band in 1928. Although "Boogie Woogie on the St. Louis Blues" doesn't use walking bass lines throughout, Hines does play an authentic boogie solo in his own distinctive style. But not every jazz pianist jumped on the boogie bandwagon. Fats Waller, a protégé of James P. Johnson, so disliked the boogie-woogie that he stipulated in his performance contracts that he not be required to play it.[52]

In March 1940, Cab Calloway recorded "Boog It," a jiving update on "The Boogie-Woogie" with no connection to the boogie beyond the title phrase. The song was a pop hit for Glenn Miller, then at the peak of his fame, and for Gene Krupa, though not for Calloway; it was also covered by Harry James, Jimmy Dorsey, and Louis Armstrong with the Mills Brothers.

"Beat Me Daddy (Eight to the Bar)," later dismissed by the distinguished jazz historian Gunther Schuller as an "inane novelty tune," was the highest-charting boogie-woogie hit, a bestseller for Will Bradley, the Andrews Sisters, and Glenn Miller.[53] Bradley's version, produced for Columbia by John Hammond in May 1940, opens with Freddie Slack playing boogie piano with a bass line of his own invention, but the walking bass is heard only on Slack's solos.[54] The Andrews Sisters' snappy version, recorded in August 1940, is musically boogie-less except for a short piano solo featuring a Pinetop-style bass line. Glenn Miller's imaginative arrangement, recorded in September, contains occasional boogie patterns, mostly played on upright bass, and a couple of clever thematic references to "Pine Top's Boogie Woogie."

"Scrub Me, Mama, with a Boogie Beat," its melody borrowed from the familiar jig "The Irish Washerwoman," was nearly as big a hit for Bradley as "Beat Me Daddy (Eight to the Bar)," and his September 1940 recording makes greater use of boogie rhythms—not only Slack's original piano bass line but bassist Doc Goldberg's more typical "Weary Blues" pattern, which gives the band's riffing ensemble passages a Bill Haley–style rock feel. The Andrews Sisters' "Scrub Me, Mama, with a Boogie Beat," a lesser hit, features a walking bass variation that could easily fit a rock 'n' roll song.

Walter Lantz's 1941 cartoon "Scrub Me Mama with a Boogie Beat," part of his Swing Symphony series, displays the degree to which racism was still acceptable in mainstream American entertainment. While the song itself—depicting blacks as menials with a natural sense of rhythm—is offensive by today's standards, it's innocuous compared to the cartoon, which transplants the song's setting from Harlem to "Lazy Town," a ramshackle southern hamlet whose dark-skinned, blubber-lipped residents move in slow motion, when they're not sleeping, until a light-complexioned, fine-featured Lena Horne look-alike struts off a riverboat and galvanizes them into rhythmic action.

Three more boogie-themed songs made the pop charts in 1941: the Andrews Sisters' "Boogie Woogie Bugle Boy," about a jazz trumpeter swept up in America's first peacetime draft; Glenn Miller's "The Booglie Wooglie Piggy," based on the children's rhyme "This Little Piggy Went to Market"; and Gene Krupa's "Drum Boogie," whose title is a pun on the 1940 hit "Rhumboogie," which Krupa also recorded. Krupa's band is featured playing "Drum Boogie" in the Howard Hawks–directed screwball-comedy movie *Ball of Fire*, with Barbara Stanwyck, as the nightclub singer Sugarpuss O'Shea, performing the vocal part originally recorded by Irene Daye. Trumpeter Roy Eldridge, who was one of the first black musicians to become a full-time member of a white band and who cowrote "Drum Boogie" with Krupa, is seen playing a brief solo. Gary Cooper, in the role of a stuffy English professor researching an encyclopedia article on slang, hears the song and asks a waiter, "What does 'boogie' mean?" prompting the reply, "Are you kiddin'?"

The studio dates of the next two Top 10 boogie-woogie hits, Freddie Slack's and Ella Fitzgerald's respective versions of "Cow-Cow Boogie," straddle the recording ban imposed by the American Federation of Musicians in August 1942. The head of that union, James C. Petrillo, demanded that record companies compensate musicians for income supposedly lost when live music was replaced by recordings played on radio programs and jukeboxes. Fitzgerald's label, Decca, was the first of the majors to give in, two months before her "Cow-Cow Boogie" session in November 1943; RCA and Columbia held out until November 1944.

Because this first recording ban (Petrillo called a second one in 1948) coincided with a crucial phase in the gestation of the bebop movement, jazz historians have viewed it as a musical watershed dividing the swing and bebop eras. One might also regard the ban as marking off swing from rhythm-and-blues, but the transition between those two genres was so gradual that any temporal boundary is purely arbitrary. The stylistic difference between Slack's and Fitzgerald's "Cow-Cow Boogie" is minimal, but the two recordings do illustrate a significant shift: before the ban, the musicians who recorded pop boogies were mostly white; afterward—country artists excepted—they were mostly black.

Of course, black bandleaders recorded boogie tunes before 1942: besides Count Basie, Andy Kirk, Cab Calloway, Benny Carter, James P. Johnson, and Earl Hines, there was Franz Jackson ("Boogie Woogie Camp Meeting"), Louis Jordan ("Pinetop's Boogie Woogie"), Buddy Johnson ("Boogie Woogie's Mother-in-Law"), Red Allen ("K.K. Boogie"), and Jay McShann ("Vine Street Boogie"), among others. And white artists continued to record boogies after 1944: Freddie Slack, for example, had his biggest hit with "House of Blue Lights" in 1946.

After World War II, however, the boogie-woogie found more favor with white "sweet" bands—the decorous progenitors of what would come to be known as easy-listening music—than with white swing bands. In 1946, a year after the flashy pianist Carmen Cavallaro scored a Top 10 hit with a pop-styled "Chopin's Polonaise," his rival Frankie Carle recorded "Chopin's Polonaise in Boogie." Also in 1946, bandleader Freddy Martin had a Top 10 pop hit with "Bumble Boogie," an adaptation of Rimsky-Korsakov's "Flight of the Bumblebee" featuring pianist Jack Fina. In 1947, Cavallaro cut "Anitra's Boogie," based on "Anitra's Dance" by Grieg. And in 1948, Martin scored one of the last big pop-boogie hits with "Sabre Dance Boogie," based on Khachaturian's "Sabre Dance." Such classical adaptations date back at least to 1941, when bandleader Larry Clinton recorded "Bach to Boogie."

If a single breakthrough hit can be said to have established the boogie-woogie as a staple of postwar rhythm-and-blues, it is "Hamp's Boogie Woogie," recorded by Lionel Hampton's big band in March 1944. Unlike most pop boogies of the time, it's essentially a keyboard piece, and it uses different bass lines in a manner similar to "The Rocks" or "The Fives," but more propulsively. Pianist Milt Buckner opens with octave chords in his innovative "locked-hands" style before switching to a more orthodox, Albert Ammons–like pattern (Hampton recorded "Hamp's Boogie Woogie No. 2" in 1949, with Ammons himself replacing Buckner). Then Buckner shifts to a "Yancey Special" bass while Hampton plays a percussive piano solo with his index fingers, mimicking his mallet technique on vibraphone, his main instrument. Only near the end does the full band come in for the wailing climax.

"Hamp's Boogie Woogie" was a No. 1 hit on *Billboard*'s Harlem Hit Parade (a predecessor to the magazine's Rhythm & Blues chart) and also crossed over to the pop charts. Hampton was well known to white fans, having played alongside Gene Krupa and Teddy Wilson in Benny Goodman's quartet, one of the first integrated jazz groups. He'd also recorded pop hits under his own name, notably "After You've Gone," from 1937. But in his autobiography, referring to his music in the mid-1940s, he writes, "I stayed in the black groove. You'd know my band was black just from listening to it. The crossover to the white audience hadn't happened yet."[55]

Louis Jordan managed to cross over to the white audience at the same time that he dominated the rhythm-and-blues charts. A showman in the mold of Louis Armstrong, Fats Waller, and especially Cab Calloway, he was, like Hampton, an entertainer as much as a musician. Before forming his own combo in 1938, he spent two years playing saxophone and sometimes singing with Chick Webb's highly regarded swing band, which featured Ella Fitzgerald. "I loved playing jazz with a big band. Loved singing the blues," he reflected. "But . . . I wanted to play for the people, for millions, not just a few hep cats."[56]

Having acquired a pair of kettledrums, Jordan dubbed his band the Tympany Five, keeping the misspelled name even as the group expanded to six or seven members. From the beginning, he took a commercial approach, applying swing rhythms to comedy songs, Tin Pan Alley standards, country blues, even nursery rhymes, often using jive lyrics and stereotypically African American themes. At one point, he billed himself as "the modern Bert Williams."[57]

Jordan had recorded such numbers as "Saxa-Woogie" and "Boogie Woogie Came to Town" before cutting "G.I. Jive" in March 1944. That song, likening army jargon to hepster lingo, had already been recorded by its composer, Johnny Mercer, but it was a much bigger hit for Jordan, reaching the top spot on both the pop and rhythm-and-blues charts. Unlike Mercer's version, Jordan's is driven by a boogie-woogie bass line and a shuffling drumbeat that in parts give it an uncanny rock 'n' roll feel.

In January 1945, Jordan cut "Caldonia," circumventing his publishing contract by registering the song under his wife's maiden name, Fleecie Moore, so that he could film it as a Soundie.[58] By the time Decca released Jordan's record, cover versions of "Caldonia" by the white bandleader Woody Herman (sung by Herman himself) and the black bandleader Erskine Hawkins (sung by pianist Ace Harris) had already been issued, and both were big hits. But Jordan's rendition, with a more emphatic boogie bass and shuffle beat than "G.I. Jive," eclipsed all others. The screeching refrain—"Caldonia! Caldonia! What makes your big head so hard?"—is taken from "Old Man Ben," a Louis Armstrong–style comic blues recorded in 1938 by the trumpeter and singer Hot Lips Page. The Spirits of Rhythm had already used the phrase in their 1941 recording of "We've Got the Blues," but it became Jordan's trademark line.

Jordan used boogie bass patterns on such 1945 R&B hits as "Salt Pork, West Virginia" and "Reconversion Blues," but "Choo Choo Ch'Boogie," recorded in January 1946, also features a genuine boogie-woogie piano solo by Wild Bill Davis. That song became Jordan's biggest-selling single, although as a contemporary reviewer noted, the main theme was lifted directly from the piano part on "Hamp's Boogie Woogie."[59] The same session yielded another No. 1 R&B hit, "Ain't That Just Like a Woman," which likewise shuffles to a boogie beat and features a boogie piano solo by Davis, as well as the Carl Hogan guitar introduction that inspired "Johnny B. Goode." Chuck Berry made no bones about his stylistic debt to Jordan, saying, "I identify myself with Louis Jordan more than any other artist."[60]

During the next couple of years, boogie bass lines turned up on such Jordan hits as "Ain't Nobody Here but Us Chickens," "Reet, Petite and Gone," "Boogie Woogie Blue Plate," and "Barnyard Boogie." By this time the boogie-woogie had become a rhythm-and-blues fixture, a hit-making template for veterans and newcomers alike. Count Basie enjoyed success with "The Mad Boogie" in 1946 and "One O'Clock Boogie" in 1947, although they were boogies in little more than name. Albert Ammons made the R&B Top 10 in 1947 with his sprightly "Swanee River Boogie," which was resurrected as a pop hit in 1953 by a white big band, the Commanders.

For the rhythm-and-blues artists of the postwar era, boogie-woogie records were a little like calling cards. There was "Cecil Boogie" (Cecil Gant), "T-Bone Boogie" (T-Bone Walker), "Milton's Boogie" (Roy Milton), "Amos' Boogie" (Amos Milburn), "Wynonie's Boogie" (Wynonie Harris), "Camille's Boogie" (Camille Howard), "Tiny's Boogie Woogie" (Tiny Grimes), "Hazel's Boogie Woogie" (Hazel Scott), "Slim Gaillard's Boogie," "Roy Brown's Boogie," "Hadda's Boogie" (Hadda Brooks), "Little Joe's Boogie" (Joe Liggins), and "Bradshaw Boogie" (Tiny Bradshaw), just to name a few. Naturally, these represent only a small fraction of the R&B boogies of the period, many of which do not use the word "boogie" in the title. Conversely, some titular boogies—the Los Angeles blues shouter Duke Henderson's "18th and Vine Street Boogie," for example—are scarcely boogies at all.

White bandleaders were not alone when it came to boogying the classics. Pianist Hadda Brooks, billed as the Queen of the Boogie, recorded "Humoresque Boogie" and "Grieg's Concerto Boogie in A Minor." Camille Howard, the pianist in Roy Milton's band, cut "Song of India Boogie" and "Schubert's Serenade Boogie." But most R&B boogies of the late 1940s and early 1950s were bluesy, up-tempo numbers, the kind that became associated with the word "rock." Roy Brown's "Good Rocking Tonight" has a boogie bass line, as does Wild Bill Moore's "We're Gonna Rock," which also contains an extended piano boogie section. The boogie bass grew more pronounced on songs that followed Wynonie Harris's "Good Rockin' Tonight," such as Jimmy Preston's "Rock the Joint," Joe Lutcher's "Rockola," and Jackie Brenston's "Rocket 88." A few songs even combined the words "rock" and "boogie" in the same title, such as Lutcher's "Rockin' Boogie," Cecil Gant's "Rock the Boogie," and Jimmie Gordon's "Rock That Boogie."

Though hardly a typical boogie-woogie pianist, Alphonso "Sonny" Thompson was one of the most influential, if only because his hit "Long Gone" had a singular impact on the rhythm-and-blues scene. Born in Centerville, Mississippi, or Memphis, Tennessee, depending on which source can be believed, he moved to Chicago as a youth, studying music at a conservatory while listening to Earl Hines and Art Tatum.[61] He played in the band of violinist Erskine Tate, then formed his own group; he also worked as a solo pianist and filled in with the bands of Lonnie Simmons, Red Allen, and Stuff Smith. In 1945, following a wartime army stint, he was hired to replace Earl Hines at a prestigious South Side club, leading a big band. During the same period, he made his recorded debut with a sextet that backed singer June Richmond on Mercury.

In the spring of 1946, Thompson cut his first two sides as a leader for the small, Detroit-based Sultan label, which issued them on two different records with two different artists on the flip sides. "South Side Boogie" and "Sonny's Boogie" are both flashy pop boogies for solo piano, with "Sonny's Boogie" interpolating a few bars of "Anitra's Dance." In September 1946, Thompson began recording for the new Chicago label Miracle as a member of the tenor saxophonist Dick Davis's band, initially backing the torch singer Rudy Richardson. Thompson plays furiously proto-rocking boogie-woogie piano between bluesy saxophone solos on Davis's own "Screamin' Boogie," from early 1947, and sings the lead on "Sonny's Blues," from the same session. Later that year, he played—often together with an instrumental trio called the Sharps and Flats—on Miracle recordings by the blues shouter Piney Brown, the jazz singer Gladys Palmer, and the rhythm-and-blues crooner Browley Guy.[62]

Thompson recorded "Long Gone (Part I)" with the Sharps and Flats in November 1947, cutting "Long Gone (Part II)" later the same month with Eddie Chamblee added on tenor saxophone. Both sides of "Long Gone" ride a "Yancey Special" bass line played by guitarist Arvin Garrett, who also solos alternately with Thompson on "Part I"; Chamblee plays the lead throughout "Part II," with Thompson adding embellishments. One of the biggest rhythm-and-blues hits of 1948, "Long Gone" has a relaxed, bluesy groove and a melody that prefigures "The Huckle-Buck." Its bass line began showing up on other R&B records shortly afterward, with the octave-jumping second note sometimes omitted.

Thompson followed "Long Gone" with "Late Freight," again featuring Eddie Chamblee, and it, too, became a No. 1 R&B hit. Recorded in December 1947, before "Long Gone" was released, "Late Freight" has a chugging bass line played on piano, with Garrett's "Yancey Special" riff heard only momentarily. Thompson cut his next hit, the mellow "Blue Dreams," the same month; not until the spring of 1949 did he repeat the "Long Gone" formula on the two-part hit "Still Gone." He switched to King Records in January 1950, and though a United States District Court in Illinois found for Miracle shortly afterward in the "Yancey Special" copyright case, that label soon folded. But Thompson did not have another hit until 1952, after he recorded the two-part instrumental "Mellow Blues," largely a tenor saxophone vehicle for Robert Hadley with a "Yancey Special" bass line. Thompson had two more hits in 1952, both written by Henry Glover and both featuring the high-pitched singer Lula Reed, whom Thompson later married. One of them was "I'll Drown in My Tears," which Ray Charles covered as "Drown in My Own Tears" for a No. 1 R&B hit in 1956; the song, its melody based on Leroy Carr's "How Long, How Long Blues," has since been sung by everyone from Stevie Wonder and Aretha Franklin to Johnny Winter and Janis Joplin.

Although he recorded regularly for King into the mid-1950s, Thompson had no further hits. He also recorded in accompaniment to other King artists, including Wynonie Harris, Lucky Millinder, the Swallows, the Charms, the Royals (who became the Midnighters), and Lula Reed. He began recording for the former King producer Henry Stone's Miami-based Chart label in 1955 but returned to King in 1956. He toured nationally together with Lula Reed through the 1950s but then stopped performing, recording only infrequently. In 1959, he replaced Ralph Bass as King's A&R director in Chicago, where he produced hits for the bluesman Freddie King.[63] Thompson continued to do session work after King Records closed its Chicago office in 1964 and cut a pair of his own albums in France for the Black & Blue label in 1972. He died in 1989.

Jo Stafford's "Kissin' Bug Boogie," sporting a prominent boogie bass line, was a pop hit in 1951, and the white ragtime pianist Johnny Maddox charted with "Eight Beat Boogie" in 1953, but by the middle of the decade the boogie-woogie had practically vanished from the popular mainstream, just as boogie-based rock 'n' roll came in. An artifact of the transition is "Little Richard's Boogie," recorded with Johnny Otis's band for the Peacock label in 1953. Less frantic than Richard's classic Specialty hits, "Little Richard's Boogie" is nevertheless a manifest harbinger of things soon to come. Citing an unspecified 1990 interview, the website of the Rock and Roll Hall of Fame and Museum quotes Little Richard as declaring, "I would say that boogie-woogie and rhythm & blues mixed is rock and roll."[64]

Bill Haley recorded the mildly boogie-ish "Birth of the Boogie" in early 1955 and, on the heels of "Rock Around the Clock," scored a minor hit in late 1955 with "Rock-A-Beatin' Boogie," a song he'd written two years earlier. Big Joe Turner cut "Boogie Woogie Country Girl," featuring Vann "Piano Man" Walls, in November 1955; released as the flip side of the hit "Corrine Corrina," it inspired several rockabilly covers. Huey "Piano" Smith had a hit in 1957 with "Rockin' Pneumonia and the Boogie Woogie Flu," which was later covered by Johnny Rivers and by Dave Edmunds, among others; although it's not really a boogie, Smith's original features a habanera-like bass line and a recurring piano riff borrowed from "Pine Top's Boogie Woogie."

The boogie lingered through the 1950s in rockabilly music, itself an outgrowth of the postwar hillbilly-boogie movement that peaked with the crossover success of Red Foley's "Chattanoogie Shoe Shine Boy" in 1950 and Tennessee Ernie Ford's "The Shot Gun Boogie" in 1951. Joe Bennett and the Sparkletones' "Boppin' Rock Boogie" and Johnny Burnette's "Rock Billy Boogie," both from 1957, are boogies in name only. But Bobby Poe and the Poe Kats' feverish "Rock & Roll Boogie," from 1958, is the real thing, featuring a strong boogie bass throughout, plus the piano work of Big Al Dowling, one of the few black musicians on the country music scene of that era. And Boyd Bennett's "Boogie Bear," an authentically boogie-based number built around the Yogi Bear cartoon character from television's *The Huckleberry Hound Show*, was a minor pop hit in 1959.

The boogie-woogie made a last splash on the pop charts at the hands of B. Bumble and the Stingers, an offshoot of Ernie Fields's band of Los Angeles studio musicians that producer Kim Fowley enlisted to update Freddy Martin's 1946 pop hit "Bumble Boogie." On the Stingers' "Bumble Boogie," a 1961 pop hit, Ernie Freeman plays Rachmaninoff's theme on a what sounds like a toy piano—actually a piano with thumbtacks stuck in the hammers—over a surf-music rhythm rather than a boogie beat. The group's follow-up single, "Boogie Woogie," a rinky-dink version of the Pinetop Smith classic with a heavy boogie bass, barely cracked the Top 100. (Pianist Al Hazan replaced Freeman on the Stingers' final hit, "Nut Rocker," a tacky take on the "March" from Tchaikovsky's *Nutcracker Suite* that became a No. 1 smash in England in 1962. Although it lacks a boogie bass line, "Nut Rocker" seems to be based largely on the introduction to pianist Moon Mullican's 1951 country hit "Cherokee Boogie.")

The word "boogie" disappeared from pop music for most of the 1960s but made a comeback in 1968 with the release of the album *Boogie with Canned Heat*. The "boogies" of Canned Heat, a white rock group with a strong interest in older blues, were not based on the boogie-woogie, however, but on a guitar rhythm introduced on John Lee Hooker's "Boogie Chillen," a No. 1 R&B hit in 1949. Bernard Besman, who produced "Boogie Chillen" in Detroit for the Modern label, says he suggested that Hooker record a boogie-woogie. "I go up to the piano and play a few bars of a boogie," Besman recounted. "Todd Rhodes was still there, and he was a pianist, so I said, 'Todd, why don't you play some boogie for him and see what happens?' So he played, and I said to John, 'Do you think you can do that, some of that?' And he said, 'Oh yeah, sure.' That's why the word 'boogie' is in there. Nothing to do with the song, you know. 'Boogie Chillen''s not a boogie. That was just what he thought was a boogie, and so I called it 'Boogie Chillen.'"[65]

Hooker denied Besman's story but did take credit for creating a new kind of boogie, inspiring such knockoffs as Little Junior Parker's 1953 R&B hit "Feelin' Good." "A long time ago, they used to call it boogie-woogie, on an old piano," Hooker said. "But as the years went by, as the time went by into the modern day, they called it the boogie. It ain't the boogie-woogie anymore, it was the boogie. And I think I started all of that."[66]

By the mid-1970s, the word "boogie" had become a verb meaning "to dance" or simply "to move," as in Eddie Kendricks's song "Boogie Down" or Stevie Wonder's "Boogie On Reggae Woman." After a few more hits—

the Sylvers' "Boogie Fever," A Taste of Honey's "Boogie Oogie Oogie," K.C. and the Sunshine Band's "Boogie Shoes," Claudja Barry's "Boogie Woogie Dancin' Shoes"—the boogie made a nominal departure from the pop charts, although boogie-woogie bass lines still turn up occasionally on retro-rock tunes and advertising jingles.

CODA

Albert Ammons, Meade "Lux" Lewis, and Pete Johnson continued to perform and record through World War II, making radio broadcasts and appearing in films. Ammons and Johnson worked together as a duo, although they usually recorded separately, while Lewis went out on his own, moving to Los Angeles. After the war, Ammons returned to Chicago, where he recorded for the Mercury label and sometimes performed with Jimmy Yancey. In 1945, he made four records with Sippie Wallace; in 1947, he appeared with Pete Johnson at the Streets of Paris club in Hollywood. He played for the inauguration of President Harry Truman in January 1949 and cut seven sides with Lionel Hampton's band the following week. But in December 1949 he died, at the age of forty-two; Jimmy Yancey died two years later, at fifty-three.

Meade "Lux" Lewis performed in Hollywood clubs and appeared in the movies *It's a Wonderful Life* (with James Stewart) in 1946 and *New Orleans* (with Louis Armstrong and Billie Holiday) in 1947 but did not have the same postwar recording success as Ammons. In 1952, he toured with Pete Johnson, Art Tatum, and Erroll Garner and played a few dates with Johnson alone; in 1956, he appeared in the film noir *Nightmare* (with Edward G. Robinson). As the popularity of the boogie waned, he made a series of long-playing albums, whose titles—*Boogie Woogie Interpretations* (Atlantic, 1952), *Yancey's Last Ride* (Clef, 1954), *Cat House Piano* (Verve, 1955), *Barrel House Piano* (Tops, 1956), and *Out of the Roaring Twenties* (ABC-Paramount, 1956)—trace his turn toward Tin Pan Alley and Dixieland material. He cut two more albums in the early 1960s and made television appearances on the *Roaring 20's* series and *The Steve Allen Show*. But after a performance in suburban Minneapolis in June 1964, a speeding driver struck his car, killing Lewis instantly.

Pete Johnson's career suffered the most precipitous decline. After Ammons's death, Johnson moved to Buffalo, New York, where he worked at various day jobs while performing mostly in local clubs. In 1958, he and Big Joe Turner toured Europe with the Jazz at the Philharmonic package show and played the Newport Jazz Festival, but soon afterward, Johnson was incapacitated by a series of strokes. In January 1967, two months before he died, Johnson made a final appearance, playing piano with only his right hand while Turner sang "Roll 'Em Pete" at a latter-day "From Spirituals to Swing" concert produced by John Hammond at Carnegie Hall.

Of the four artists who presented the boogie-woogie at the original "From Spirituals to Swing" concert, only Big Joe Turner achieved long-term success. He had a rhythm-and-blues hit in 1945 with a cover of Saunders King's "S.K. Blues," accompanied by Pete Johnson's band, and another hit in 1946 with "My Gal's a Jockey," accompanied by Wild Bill Moore's combo. The latter song, a mid-tempo rocker a with prominent boogie bass line, marks the approximate stylistic halfway point between "Roll 'Em Pete" and "Shake, Rattle and Roll."

In the late 1940s, Turner recorded for such labels as National, Imperial, Aladdin, Modern, and MGM, with bands featuring pianists such as Pete Johnson, Bill Doggett, and Fats Domino. He did a cover version of Wynonie Harris's "Around the Clock" that rocked harder than the original and sang a duet with Harris himself on "Battle of the Blues." But Turner did not make the R&B charts again until the 1950s, when he cut a string of hits on the Atlantic label, among them the pop crossovers "Chains of Love," "Honey Hush," "Shake, Rattle and Roll," and "Corrine Corrina." His output declined in the 1960s, although he did record albums with Bill Haley in Mexico and with the Zagreb Jazz Quartet in Yugoslavia. By the 1970s, he was back in demand, as an old-time jazz and blues singer, and he remained active until his death in 1985, touring Europe and cutting albums for Pablo and other labels, including a couple with Count Basie. The sole swing-era survivor to become a recognized rock 'n' roll star, he was an outsize figure in more ways than one.

Besides Lewis and Johnson, few of the pianists associated with the boogie-woogie continued to perform after the 1950s. Little Brother Montgomery and Roosevelt Sykes kept working until their deaths in the 1980s, but both were considered bluesmen rather than boogie specialists. Jay McShann recorded through 2003, three years before his death, but he was regarded mainly as a jazz musician. Almost all of today's boogie pianists are white revivalists such as Erwin Helfer, from Chicago, and Axel Zwingenberger, from Germany. And while boogie bass lines are inescapably familiar to rock fans, the boogie-woogie per se has little more than nostalgic appeal outside collectors' circles.

A fascinating sidelight to the boogie-woogie phenomenon is the influence of the boogie in Jamaica. The island's upper crust embraced American swing music in the 1940s, and local big bands copied arrangements by the likes of Count Basie and Glenn Miller. Imported rhythm-and-blues swept the country after World War II; one of the biggest-selling records was Wynonie Harris's "Bloodshot Eyes," a 1951 cover of Hank Penny's 1950 country hit. The postwar R&B sound, with its boogie bass lines and shuffle drumbeats, gave way to rock 'n' roll in the United States but hung on in Jamaica, where bands made up mostly of jazz musicians fashioned their own "Jamaican boogie."

Produced by Chris Blackwell, Laurel Aitken's "Boogie in My Bones," with a shuffling boogie beat taken from Rosco Gordon's 1952 R&B hits "Booted" and "No More Doggin'," was a seminal Jamaican smash in 1959. Sometimes cited as the first ska record, Theophilus Beckford's "Easy Snappin'," produced by Clement "Coxsone" Dodd and released in 1959, has essentially the same rhythm, but Beckford plays an afterbeat on piano that gives the song a distinctive Jamaican cast. Another disc that's been identified as the first ska record, the Folkes Brothers' "Oh Carolina," produced by Prince Buster during the same period, features Afro-Jamaican drumming over a habanera bass line. The ska rhythm, with the afterbeat usually played on guitar, dominated Jamaican pop music through the mid-1960s before giving way to rocksteady and then reggae. It can thus be said that the boogie-woogie lies at the foundation of both rock 'n' roll and reggae, two of the most popular and influential musical genres of the twentieth century and beyond.

Chapter Five

The Jumpin' Jive

JUMP JAZZ

"They have a new expression along old Harlem way," proclaims Fats Waller in the opening line of his hit "The Joint Is Jumpin'," recorded with his sextet on October 7, 1937. "To say that things are jumpin' leaves not a single doubt," Waller continues, "that everything is in full swing when you hear someone shout."

Exactly three months earlier, Count Basie and his big band had cut their first hit, "One O'Clock Jump," which became Basie's theme song and was also recorded by Benny Goodman, Harry James, and Duke Ellington. The piece is essentially a pastiche of riffs, the most distinctive of which is taken from the introduction to "Six or Seven Times," a Fats Waller composition first recorded in 1929 by members of McKinney's Cotton Pickers—including Don Redman, Benny Carter, Coleman Hawkins, Rex Stewart, and Waller himself—under the name the Chocolate Dandies.

The term "jump," used as a synonym for "swing," was indeed a new expression. Under the headline "'Jitter-Bugs' Thrill at N.Y. Jam-Session," an anonymous *Down Beat* reviewer uses the words "ride," "sock," "jive," and "truckin'"—but not "jump"—to describe the music at a May 1936 show billed as the first swing concert.[1] In October 1938, Jimmy Mitchelle, a saxophonist in Erskine Hawkins's big band, sang on Hawkins's hit "Do You Wanna Jump, Children?" using "jump" interchangeably with "swing," "stomp," and "jive." Before the year was out, that song (whose writers include the white bandleader Al Donahue, the black bandleader Willie Bryant, and the white composer Jimmy Van Heusen) had been covered by the bands of Cab Calloway, Charlie Barnet, Count Basie, and Gene Krupa. But although both white and black artists were involved with jump music at the outset, the word "jump" was mainly used in an African American context and eventually became associated with the blues.

Beginning in 1938, there was a profusion of jazz tunes—mostly straight-ahead swing numbers—with "jump" in the title, among them Hot Lips Page's "Jumpin'," Mildred Bailey's "Jump Jump's Here," the Savoy Sultans' "Jump Steady," Slim and Slam's "Jump Session," Count Basie's "Jumpin' at the Woodside," and Andy Kirk's "Jump Jack Jump," not to mention Ollie Shepard's "This Place Is Leaping." A headline in the October 15, 1938, issue of the *New York Amsterdam News* ran, "Jump Band Will Record," heralding the studio debut of Louis Jordan's combo, whose blend of swing, blues, and boogie-woogie—with an occasional Caribbean tinge—would redefine jump music and set the parameters for rhythm-and-blues.[2]

Swing only came into vogue after August 1935, when Benny Goodman's hot arrangements caused a sensation at the Palomar Ballroom in Los Angeles, but the music itself had germinated a decade earlier. Jump music, loosely considered as the bluesier aspect of jazz, had an even longer gestation. The success of Mamie Smith's "Crazy Blues" in late 1920 sparked a demand not just for black female blues singers but for instrumental blues played by jazz bands in an ostensibly black style. Until then, the Original Dixieland Jazz Band had recorded mostly material by its own, white members, including a few blues. But in 1921, beginning with an instrumental version of "Crazy Blues," the group cut nothing but blues, the majority by black songwriters such as W. C. Handy, Clarence Williams, and Tom Delaney (although one, "Home Again Blues," was cowritten by Irving Berlin). Other white jazz bands made bluesy records under black-sounding pseudonyms, assuming different aliases for different labels: the New York–based Joseph Samuels Jazz Band recorded as the Tampa Blue Jazz Band and the Six Black Diamonds, while the Original Memphis Five, also from New York, recorded as Ladd's Black Aces, Jazz-Bo's Carolina Serenaders, and the Cotton Pickers.[3]

Naturally, the post–"Crazy Blues" blues craze—lasting roughly until 1924, when the Charleston craze set in—also drew black musicians into the studios. Fletcher Henderson, the most prolific black recording artist of the period, cut his first sessions as an accompanist to blues singers such as Alberta Hunter and Ethel Waters, beginning in 1921, and his instrumental records as a bandleader in 1923 and 1924 include many blues tunes, even though Henderson had a middle-class background and recorded for various labels' "general" series rather than the race series to which other black musicians were confined.[4]

The blues was a component of jazz from the beginning, and some of the earliest African American jazz recordings were of blues—or at least bluesy—tunes, going back as far as Ford Dabney's "The Jass—'Lazy Blues'" in 1917. The first jazz record by a black group from New Orleans, made by Kid

Ory's Original Creole Jazz Band in June or July of 1922, featured "Society Blues" as the B-side of "Ory's Creole Trombone." Fats Waller's first record, from October 1922, coupled "Muscle Shoals Blues," written by George W. Thomas, with "Birmingham Blues," cowritten by Artie Matthews. The pioneering New Orleans jazz musicians Jelly Roll Morton, Sidney Bechet, Freddie Keppard, King Oliver, and Louis Armstrong, as well as Bennie Moten's seminal Kansas City Orchestra, all made their first recordings in 1923, and each of their earliest sessions contained blues material.

Moten's group, along with other southwestern "territory" bands—Troy Floyd's Shadowland Orchestra from San Antonio, Walter Page's Blue Devils from Oklahoma City, Jesse Stone's Blues Serenaders from Kansas City, Alphonso Trent's Orchestra and Terrence Holder's Dark Clouds of Joy from Dallas—forged a bluesy, rhythmic, riff-driven style that ultimately became the dominant school of swing, as exemplified by Count Basie's "One O'Clock Jump." These ensembles also incubated many musicians who helped blaze the trail for rhythm-and-blues, including saxophonists Herschel Evans and Buddy Tate, trumpeter Hot Lips Page, pianist Lloyd Glenn, guitarist Eddie Durham, singer Jimmy Rushing, and bandleaders Count Basie and Andy Kirk. Kirk took over Holder's group in 1929, shortening its name to the Clouds of Joy and moving it to Kansas City. Jesse Stone went on to write R&B hits, notably Big Joe Turner's "Shake, Rattle and Roll," as a composer-arranger for Atlantic Records in the 1950s.

THE BACKBEAT AND THE JITTERBUG

A pair of 1920s recordings is sufficient to secure the Moten band's place in rock 'n' roll prehistory. On "Tulsa Blues," cut for OKeh in November 1924, ragged horns wail tragicomically over Moten's crude boogie piano vamp and drummer Willie Hall's backbeat, played on what sounds like a wood block. On "The New Tulsa Blues," cut for Victor in June 1927, the horns sound cleaner, drummer Willie McWashington's backbeat is more emphatic, and the melody of the final two choruses—not heard on the original "Tulsa Blues"—bears a remarkable resemblance to the tune of Fats Domino's rocking 1956 hit "I'm in Love Again."

Three more early examples of blues with a backbeat can be found on a Paramount session recorded in Chicago around June 1928 by the Dixie Four, consisting of pianists Buddy Burton and Jimmy Blythe, bassist Bill Johnson, and drummer Clifford "Snags" Jones. Jones, originally from New Orleans, puts a backbeat behind all four selections the group recorded; of the three blues tunes, the most extraordinary is "Kentucky Stomp" (titled after Burton's native state), where the backbeat combines with Johnson's boogie-woogie bass line to create a rock-like rhythm that's years ahead of its time. It would seem that the combination of a backbeat and a boogie bass line automatically produces the feel of early rock 'n' roll.

But backbeats are not widely found in either traditional or swing-era jazz, the usual swing rhythm consisting of four unaccented beats to the bar. A backbeat, strummed by banjo player Charlie Dixon, can be heard behind Louis Armstrong's solo on the Fletcher Henderson band's October 1924 recording of "Go 'Long Mule," from Armstrong's first session with Henderson. According to Henderson's biographer Jeffrey Magee, "We can hear that kind of accompaniment behind a few solos in the band's pre-Armstrong period, but once Armstrong came on board, it was reserved almost exclusively for him."[5] In his autobiography, cornetist Rex Stewart, who played in Henderson's and Duke Ellington's bands, writes that in New York around 1923, the clarinetist and saxophonist Happy Caldwell "started teaching me the Western 'get-off' style of playing, which had a heavy accented back beat on the second and fourth bars." Stewart claims that Caldwell, trombonist Jimmy Harrison, and trumpeter June Clark—all of whom had spent time in the Midwest—"were the only musicians in town playing 'Western' style" at that time.[6]

The white swing trumpeter Harry James strikingly foreshadowed rhythm-and-blues and rock 'n' roll with his "Back Beat Boogie" in 1939. The backbeat found its way into R&B as early as May 1944, when Lucky Millinder's band recorded "Who Threw the Whiskey in the Well" with singer Wynonie Harris, adding handclapped accents on the second and fourth beat of each measure on the choruses. Because the song parodies a church service, it might seem that the backbeat is borrowed from gospel music. But Millinder uses similar handclapped backbeats on such nonspiritual songs as "There's Good Blues Tonight" and "Shorty's Got to Go," both from February 1946. Harris's "Good Rockin' Tonight," recorded at the end of 1947, also features a handclapped backbeat, although Roy Brown's original July 1947 version does not.

But though backbeats are a fixture of gospel music today, they are not generally heard on early gospel recordings. The handclapped rhythms on recordings from the Georgia Sea Islands, thought to represent older African American traditions, are more complex and varied than the simple backbeats of modern gospel music. And gospel music since the 1920s has been strongly influenced by jazz, blues, and R&B. The exact derivation of the backbeat—the basic rhythm of rock 'n' roll (and of rhythm-and-blues, from its post–World War II inception through the hip-hop era)—remains unclear.

The derivation of the basic rock 'n' roll dance—the jitterbug—is better known, due in part to the contemporary revival of swing dancing. The jitterbug remained the most popular dance among young people for some three decades, a remarkable span. The term "jitter bug" was introduced in Cab Calloway's January 1934 recording by that title, referring to an alcoholic. In the 1939 edition of *Cab Calloway's Cat-ologue: A Hepster's Dictionary,* a "jitter bug" is defined as "a swing fan; formerly a person addicted to 'jitter sauce' (liquor)."[7] Over time, the word "jitterbug" was attached to the most popular swing-era dance, previously called the Lindy hop.

The Lindy hop had been named after Charles Lindbergh, who began his famous transatlantic flight on May 20, 1927. George "Shorty" Snowden claimed he came up with the tag while competing in a dance marathon in New York around the end of June 1928. When a newsreel reporter asked what he was doing with his feet, Snowden replied, "the Lindy."[8] But a "Lindbergh Hop" had already been recorded on May 25, 1927, by a group of musicians associated with banjo player Elmer Snowden and led for the occasion by trombonist Te Roy Williams. It's a semi-arranged jazz romp in the typical 2/4 rhythm of the period, better suited to the Charleston than to the Lindy hop as seen in later film clips. By comparison, Calloway's "Jitter Bug" is an up-tempo swing number in 4/4 time—exactly the kind of tune normally associated with the Lindy or jitterbug dance.

The Lindy hop had earlier antecedents, most importantly the Texas Tommy, an African American dance that had been introduced to white society in San Francisco around 1910 and brought to New York in the groundbreaking 1913 review *The Darktown Follies*. Described as similar to the Lindy hop, the Texas Tommy contained a step called the breakaway, where the dance partners pulled apart from each other and danced independently, in African style, instead of remaining together in the "closed" position of European ballroom tradition.[9] As a defining element of the Lindy/jitterbug, the breakaway became the principal basis for American popular dancing from the 1930s until the 1960s, when the twist and its successors separated the dancers completely. According to one observer, the Lindy hop "seemed to gobble up and incorporate every novelty that followed it."[10]

JUG BANDS AND HOKUM

In September 1928, the Memphis Jug Band recorded its own "Lindberg [sic] Hop," with a Charleston-esque melody and such verses as, "Now, Mama, how can it be? / You went way across the sea, / [To] keep from doin' that Lindyberg with me." Led by guitarist Will Shade, the group was the most popular and prolific of the jug bands that that enjoyed a brief heyday in the late 1920s, and it established Memphis as the jug-band capital, although Shade was inspired by the jug bands of Louisville, Kentucky, where the genre likely originated.[11]

The jug-band style was revived during the folk-music boom of the late 1950s and early 1960s; the Rooftop Singers had a No. 1 pop hit in 1963 when they resurrected "Walk Right In," originally recorded by Cannon's Jug

Stompers in 1929. Some of the revivalists went on to play in rock bands such as the Grateful Dead, the Lovin' Spoonful, Country Joe and the Fish, and the 13th Floor Elevators, popularizing such jug classics as "On the Road Again" and "Stealin'." But though some later rockers mirrored their mischievous spirit and ragged disposition, the jug bands made little direct contribution to early rock 'n' roll except through their predilection for hokum.

Southern skiffle bands using washboards, kazoos, and harmonicas, together with conventional instruments, are said to date back at least to the 1890s. In 1898, by one account, an itinerant black banjo player from Louisville named B. D. Tite encountered an elderly man in southwestern Virginia who played tuba-like bass lines by blowing over the mouth of a jug; adopting the instrument for himself, Tite became the first professional jug player.[12] It's better established that several jug bands were active in Louisville around the time of World War I, but none was recorded until a white skiffle trio from St. Louis, the Mound City Blue Blowers, had a big hit with "Arkansaw Blues."

Recorded in February 1924, "Arkansaw Blues" is a winningly clever interpretation of Spencer Williams's composition "Arkansas Blues," a hit for Lucille Hegamin in 1921. Historians David Jasen and Gene Jones describe the tune, with its walking bass line, as "a blues that wants to boogie," but the Blue Blowers, with Jack Bland on banjo, Dick Slevin on kazoo, and Red McKenzie humming through a paper-covered comb, reduce the rhythm to a steady strum.[13] Imitators soon tried to capitalize on the Blue Blowers' success, among them a white trio calling themselves Fred Ozark's Jug Blowers, who recorded a pair of sides in May 1924. That group comprised singer Cliff "Ukulele Ike" Edwards, banjo and kazoo player Vernon Dalhart, and kazoo player Dick Smalle, but had no jug player. (Later that year, Dalhart, a classically trained tenor who had recorded all sorts of material under dozens of pseudonyms, had a huge hit with "Wreck of the Old 97," backed with "The Prisoner's Song," establishing a mass market for country music.)

The first actual jug band to record consisted of musicians from two Louisville groups, the Louisville Jug Band and the Clifford Hayes Orchestra, who cut ten sides as Sara Martin's Jug Band in September 1924—eight in accompaniment to the classic blues singer Sara Martin, a Louisville native, and two on their own. Days later, Whistler's Jug Band, another Louisville group, recorded four titles, including "Jail House Blues," a song better known as "He's in the Jailhouse Now." Jug player Earl McDonald and violinist Clifford Hayes, the two bandleaders who'd backed Sara Martin, continued to collaborate on records through 1927 as the Old Southern Jug Band, Clifford's Louisville Jug Band, and the Dixieland Jug Blowers. On their December 11, 1926, session for the Victor label, the Dixieland Jug Blowers were joined by the great New Orleans clarinetist Johnny Dodds, a veteran of Kid

Ory's, King Oliver's, and Louis Armstrong's jazz bands and of several washboard bands led by Jimmy Blythe.

Jug bands are usually classified with blues groups, but though a few prominent blues artists, such as Sleepy John Estes and Memphis Minnie, performed in jug bands, jug-band music owes as much to ragtime and jazz as to blues. Beginning with the Original Dixieland Jazz Band's snorts and whinnies on "Livery Stable Blues," early jazz musicians recorded antic instrumental sounds similar to the ones that jug-band players produced on their kazoos and stovepipes. Essentially string ensembles at first, jug bands later added the occasional cornet or saxophone; drawing on Tin Pan Alley and medicine-show songs as well as blues, jazz, and old-time country music, they blurred the distinctions between genres. The Five Harmaniacs, one of the first white bands to record with a jug, wear cowboy costumes in publicity photographs, but one of their mid-1920s releases, "Carolina Bound," was listed in the Brunswick and Vocalion labels' otherwise all-black race catalogs.[14]

The rowdy, comical jug-band sound lent itself naturally to hokum material. Jug bands recorded variations on Georgia Tom and Tampa Red's "It's Tight Like That," and Georgia Tom and Tampa Red—the original Hokum Boys—worked with jug bands. In June 1928, four months before cutting "It's Tight Like That," Georgia Tom Dorsey joined the Tub Jug Washboard Band on several of their own records and in accompaniment to Ma Rainey. At the end of October, just days after "It's Tight Like That" was recorded, the Vocalion producer J. Mayo Williams had Dorsey and Tampa Red cut a couple of sides with members of the Tub Jug band, plus vocalist Frankie "Half-Pint" Jaxon, under the name Tampa Red's Hokum Jug Band.

The same group recorded three more numbers in early November, including a jug-band version of "It's Tight Like That." The flip side was a comic take on Leroy Carr's smash hit "How Long, How Long Blues," with Jaxon doing his female-impersonation routine. "How Long, How Long Blues"—Carr's first record, made for Vocalion in June 1928—is based on "How Long Daddy," which Ida Cox had recorded with Papa Charlie Jackson in 1925. But Carr's relaxed, introspective singing, accompanied by his own spare piano playing and by Scrapper Blackwell's piquant single-string guitar runs, give the bluesy eight-bar song a singular feel—earthy yet sophisticated. "How Long, How Long Blues" was covered by Count Basie, Big Joe Turner, Big Bill Broonzy, Ella Fitzgerald, and Ray Charles, among many others. Although his music deeply influenced country bluesmen such as Robert Johnson, Carr, who was born in Nashville and spent most of his short life in Indianapolis, is considered to be the forefather of the urban blues style.

The third song recorded by Tampa Red's Hokum Jug Band in November 1928 was "You Can't Come In," which singer-pianist Bert Mays had cut for Vocalion a month earlier and which evolved into Little Richard's 1957 rock 'n' roll classic "Keep A Knockin'." Singer and kazoo player James "Boodle It" Wiggins had recorded essentially the same song with pianist Bob Call for Paramount in February under the title "Keep a Knockin' an You Can't Get In," but with a somewhat different melody. Clarence Williams recorded a similar but slower song, "I'm Busy and You Can't Come In," twice in September 1928, first with Eva Taylor singing and then as an instrumental. Sylvester Weaver had recorded a solo guitar piece titled "I'm Busy and You Can't Come In" in 1924, but it bears little resemblance to the tune Williams played.

Bert Mays's record seems to have been the first to marry the melody of "Bucket's Got a Hole in It" to the lyrics of "You Can't Come In" (the same melody is also used for "Midnight Special"). "My Bucket's Got a Hole in It" was initially recorded as such in June 1927 by a white Minneapolis band led by saxophonist Tom Gates, but a black New Orleans band led by cornetist Louis Dumaine had recorded a jazzier version of the same tune in March of that year under the title "To-Wa-Bac-A-Wa."[15] A similar melody is heard on "She's Crying for Me," recorded twice in early 1925 by the New Orleans Rhythm Kings. J. Paul Wyer and H. Alf Kelley first published the "Bucket's Got a Hole in It" melody as part of their 1914 composition "The Long Lost Blues." But "Bucket's Got a Hole in It" has been attributed to Buddy Bolden, which if true would date it to before 1906.[16]

Accompanying himself on slide guitar, Kokomo Arnold recorded his adaptation of Wiggins's "Keep a Knockin' an You Can't Get In" in April 1935, calling it "Busy Bootin'." Lil Johnson recorded "Keep On Knocking" to the approximate tune of "Bucket's Got a Hole in It" in July 1935, with Black Bob Hudson on piano and Big Bill Broonzy on guitar. Hudson's introduction is based on the one Bob Call used with Wiggins, but on the second verse, Johnson sings "Kinda busy and you can't come in," indicating a familiarity with Eva Taylor's song, which Alura Mack had covered in 1929.[17] In 1937, Lil Johnson recorded "Bucket's Got a Hole in It" itself. But she was best known for double-entendre numbers such as "Get 'Em from the Peanut Man (Hot Nuts)," which decades later became the theme song of Doug Clark and the Hot Nuts, a long-lived rhythm-and-blues group that performs risqué shows at college fraternity parties.

Johnson was one of a number of 1930s blues singers, among them Lucille Bogan and Bo Carter, who specialized in ribald material. Both Bogan and Johnson came out of the "classic" blues tradition, both began recording in the 1920s (Bogan in 1923, Johnson in 1929), and both were accompanied on record by boogie-woogie pianists—Bogan by Eddie Heywood, Will Ezell, Cow Cow Davenport, and Charles Avery; Johnson by Avery and Montana Taylor. Bogan's approach became cruder as her career progressed: in March 1935 she updated "Shave 'Em Dry Blues," a verse-and-refrain hokum song recorded by Ma Rainey in 1924 with guitar accompaniment by the Pruitt twins; at the same 1935 session, Bogan cut an obscene version of "Shave 'Em Dry"—not released until many years later—that begins, "I got nipples on my titties big as the end of my thumb / I got somethin' between my legs'll make a dead man come." Lil Johnson recorded her own "New Shave 'Em Dry" the following year.

By contrast, Bo Carter, born Armenter Chatmon, was a rural guitarist who grew up with Charlie Patton near Bolton, Mississippi, just south of the Delta. Carter was a member of the musical Chatmon family, who performed mostly for white audiences, and he played occasionally with the Mississippi Sheiks, a recording duo consisting of violinist Lonnie Chatmon (Carter's brother) and guitarist Walter Vinson (or Vincson) that was popular among blacks and whites alike. Carter's first recording session, in 1928, produced "Corrine Corrina," a blues-country-pop song that's been covered by everyone from Tampa Red to Cab Calloway, Bob Wills, Art Tatum, Big Joe Turner, Dean Martin, Bill Haley, and Bob Dylan. But his output in the 1930s ran heavily to phallic blues such as "My Pencil Won't Write No More," "Banana in Your Fruit Basket," "Pin in Your Cushion," "Ram Rod Daddy," and "Please Warm My Weiner [sic]." Although their music had more of a white country flavor, the Mississippi Sheiks also recorded bawdy songs; "Bed Spring Poker," for example, sounds like hokum blues in slow motion.

Blues and hokum intertwined at least through the mid-1930s, when the hokum bands faded out. After Georgia Tom committed himself exclusively to religious music in 1932, Tampa Red continued to perform blues and hokum songs as a highly successful solo artist. Big Bill Broonzy recorded occasionally as a member of the Hokum Boys and the Famous Hokum Boys from 1930 until 1936. Even Leroy Carr dabbled in hokum, cutting such songs as "Papa's on the House Top" and "Don't Start That Stuff," although their lyrics are unusually clean. Less circumspect about alcohol, Carr turned Lucille Bogan's "Sloppy Drunk Blues" into a blues standard, anticipating the booze-drenched R&B of the late 1940s and early 1950s.

Hokum was also absorbed into the jazz tradition. "It's Tight Like That" was covered by such jazz players as Jimmie Noone, McKinney's Cotton Pickers, and a group featuring Jack Teagarden and Benny Goodman that recorded under the pseudonym Jimmy Bracken's Toe Ticklers. In December 1928, Louis Armstrong cut a sort of answer song, "Tight Like This," with an extended trumpet improvisation that transformed the nature of the jazz solo. In March 1929, Duke Ellington cut his own answer song, "Who Said 'It's Tight Like That'?"

Hokum jazz found its way into country music. Luis Russell, a Panamanian-born bandleader who helped make the transition from traditional New Orleans–style jazz to swing, recorded "It's Tight Like That" on January 1929. On the flip side was "The Call of the Freaks," an instrumental showcasing bluesy solos over weird-sounding harmonies. In September, Russell cut “The New Call of the Freaks,” adding a shimmering vibraphone (played by drummer Paul Barbarin) and a ragged trio singing, “Stick out your can, here comes the garbage man.” In April 1934, at his band’s first recording session, the pioneering western-swing singer Milton Brown cut “Garbage Man Blues,” discarding the eerie arrangement of “The New Call of the Freaks” while expanding on the vocal chorus (but spoiling the pun by changing “Stick out your can” to “Get out your can”). In March 1936, at his last session before his fatal auto accident, Brown recorded “Keep A Knockin’,” based on the Lil Johnson version and featuring Bob Dunn’s electrified steel guitar (Dunn had become the first musician to record with an electric instrument the previous year). In May 1938, Bob Wills, Milton Brown’s former band mate in the Light Crust Doughboys, recorded “Keep Knocking (but You Can’t Come In).”

SCAT, JIVE, AND HARMONY SINGING

With the rise of hokum came the popularity of jive talk, which proved to be a broader-reaching and longer-lasting trend. A blend of jazz musicians’ lingo and underworld argot, jive, unlike the mocking African American dialect of blackface minstrelsy, was perceived as raffishly urbane and sophisticated—in a word, “hep.”

Three prime movers of jive crossed paths in the review *Connie’s Hot Chocolates,* which opened at Connie’s Inn in Harlem in the spring of 1929 and by summer was running concurrently at the Hudson Theatre on Broadway. Featuring the hit “Ain’t Misbehavin’,” the show made Fats Waller’s reputation as a songwriter, established Louis Armstrong as a pop singer, and helped launch the career of Cab Calloway. Waller would not become known for his racy lyrics and spoken interjections until the mid-1930s. Armstrong is considered to be the first musician to popularize jive talking, as well as the related art of scat singing. But it was Calloway who made jive his specialty and established it—through records, films, and even animated cartoons—as a staple of mainstream American entertainment.

Like jive talking, scat singing—or at least the singing of nonsense syllables, à la the Edsels’ 1961 hit “Rama Lama Ding Dong”—made its way into rock ’n’ roll. Jelly Roll Morton claimed that “the first man that ever did a scat number in history of this country was a man from Vicksburg, Mississippi, by the name of Joe Sims, an old comedian. And from that, Tony Jackson and myself and several more grabbed it in New Orleans.”[18] A white vaudevillian, ’Gene Greene, sang nonsense syllables on his 1911 hit “King of the Bungaloos,” as did Al Jolson later the same year on his first recording, “That Haunting Melody.” In 1922, Cliff Edwards sang wordlessly on his first issued recording, “Virginia Blues,” with Ladd’s Black Aces, and on “Nobody

Lied" and "Homesick," with Bailey's Lucky Seven (both band names were pseudonyms for the Original Memphis Five). Don Redman did a scat-like vocal as a member of Fletcher Henderson's band on "My Papa Doesn't Two-Time No Time," from April 1924, and Louis Armstrong made his recorded vocal debut with a snatch of jivey speech at the end of Henderson's "Everybody Loves My Baby," from November of the same year.

But what was to become the dominant style of scat singing, represented most prominently by Ella Fitzgerald, can be traced to the February 1926 recording of "Heebie Jeebies" by Louis Armstrong and His Hot Five—Armstrong's recorded debut as a full-fledged singer. Armstrong later said that he "started to Scatting [sic]" after accidentally dropping the lyric sheet during the session, but the record itself, with its smoothly executed vocal, belies that account.[19] Accident or not, "Heebie Jeebies" was successful enough that, less than four months later, Armstrong cut "Skid-Dat-De-Dat," whose title virtually defined the new idiom. Armstrong may also have become the first artist to record a song with the word "jive" in the title when he cut the instrumental "Don't Jive Me" (written by his wife Lil Hardin) in June 1928, although it was not released until 1940. The following month, Cow Cow Davenport recorded "State Street Jive," a rehash of his "Cow Cow Blues" piano motifs with a running commentary—"Boot that thing, boy! You hear me talkin' to ya"—by Ivy Smith.

Cab Calloway first met Louis Armstrong in 1928 at Chicago's Sunset Café, where Armstrong was the star soloist with Carroll Dickerson's band and Calloway was the house singer. "I suppose that Louis was one of the main influences in my career," Calloway later reminisced. "Louis first got me freed up from straight lyrics to try scatting."[20] The following year, Armstrong moved to New York, leading what had been Dickerson's band at Connie's Inn while performing in *Hot Chocolates* on Broadway. Calloway took over the Alabamians, the group that replaced Dickerson's at the Sunset Café, and brought them to New York at the end of 1929. But after losing a battle of the bands to the Missourians, the house band at the famed Savoy Ballroom in Harlem, the Alabamians left town without Calloway, who joined the cast of *Hot Chocolates*.

Calloway's showmanship had made an impression at the Savoy: "I would run across the stage, directing the band, singing along with it into my megaphone, leading the guys in call and response, and the audience loved it," he recounted.[21] In March 1930, after *Hot Chocolates* closed, he took over the Missourians, a group originally from St. Louis that had been influenced by Bennie Moten's band. "In their rough, unsubtle way," writes Gunther Schuller, "the Missourians produced a brand of exciting, elemental jazz that few, if any, bands could match at that time."[22]

Although he had signed a management contract with Moe Gale, a co-owner of the Savoy, Calloway was scheduled to debut with the Missourians at Harlem's brand-new Plantation Club. The day before that club was to open, however, it was destroyed, presumably by the white mobsters who ran the rival Cotton Club, where Duke Ellington led the house band. When Ellington and his musicians went to Hollywood to appear in the 1930 Amos 'n' Andy movie *Check and Double Check* (starring the white radio stars Freeman Gosden and Charles Correll in blackface makeup), the same mobsters demanded that Calloway and the Missourians fill in for them, much to Calloway's delight.

With Ellington pursuing an increasingly hectic tour schedule, Cab Calloway and His Orchestra, as the Missourians were renamed, became the house band at the Cotton Club in early 1931. (Ironically, the Missourians had been the house band at the Cotton Club before Ellington took over in 1927.) The club was the most luxurious and prestigious in Harlem, with elaborate floor shows that featured singers, dancers, and comedians as well as musicians. Celebrities and journalists were often in attendance, and regular live network radio broadcasts brought the performers to national attention. But though all the entertainers were black, few blacks were allowed in the audience, and the shows were geared strictly toward whites. With his light complexion, straight hair, and polished enunciation, Calloway, born into a solidly middle-class African American family in Rochester, New York, and raised in Baltimore, was eminently qualified to bridge the racial divide.

Calloway dropped Moe Gale and signed with Ellington's manager, Irving Mills, a white singer and song plugger turned publisher, songwriter, bandleader, and all-around musical entrepreneur. The Calloway orchestra made its first record in July 1930 as the Jungle Band, the same pseudonym Mills had been using for some of Ellington's recordings. Even on this early date, the group sounds more refined than it had as the Missourians, reflecting Calloway's stern approach to discipline. And on the hopped-up rendition of "St. Louis Blues," Calloway already displays his over-the-top singing style, including a chorus of scat-like double talk.

After cutting some dozen other tunes, Calloway collaborated with Mills and lyricist Clarence Gaskill to write "Minnie the Moocher," which he recorded in March 1931. As Calloway later acknowledged, the song follows the minor-blues chord progression of "St. James Infirmary," which Louis Armstrong had recorded in December 1928 and Calloway had recorded in December 1930 (using a speedier version of the arrangement on the Missourians' February 1930 recording of "Prohibition Blues"). The title is adapted from "Minnie the Mermaid," a pop novelty that the white bandleader Bernie Cummins had recorded in 1930; the lyrics, as well as part of the melody, are based on "Willie the Weeper," which was written by Grant V. Rymal, Walter Melrose, and Marty Bloom in 1927 and recorded that year by King Oliver, Louis Armstrong, Frankie "Half-Pint" Jaxon, and Doc Cook (or Cooke).

The verses sung by Jaxon and by Cook's drummer Andrew Hilaire are taken from the Rymal-Melrose-Bloom composition (Oliver's and Armstrong's versions are instrumentals); but an earlier 1927 recording titled "Willie the Chimney Sweeper," by the white Atlanta journalist and radio broadcaster Ernest Rogers, is similar to folk texts of "Willie the Weeper" published in 1926 and 1927 by Sigmund Spaeth and in 1927 by Carl Sandburg.[23] The pop song is clearly of folk origin, but the folk song, describing the extravagant pipe dreams of an opium-addicted chimney sweep, has a vaudeville or medicine-show feel. The folk texts explicitly refer to Willie's "hop habit" or "dope habit," which Rymal, Melrose, and Bloom discreetly call a "dreamin' habit," although they do mention in one verse that Willie "smoked a little hop."

Calloway's "Minnie the Moocher" displays an awareness not only of the pop version of "Willie the Weeper" but of the folk song as well, particularly with the line, "She had a million dollars worth of nickels and dimes / And she sat around and counted them all a million times," which appears in the folk texts but not in the pop song. Another line, "He took her down to Chinatown / He showed her how to kick the gong around," uses underworld slang to veil its reference to opium smoking. But Calloway's best-remembered line is the nonsensical refrain "Ho de ho de ho / Hi de hi de hi," which he professed to have made up on the spot when he forgot the lyrics during a live radio broadcast. Like Louis Armstrong's "Heebie Jeebies" story, it's a dubious claim, especially since folk versions of "Willie the Weeper" also have a wordless refrain.

"Minnie the Moocher" was a huge pop hit; for the rest of Calloway's long career it was his theme song, and "hi-de-ho" was his signature phrase. In early 1932, Calloway made his film debut in the Betty Boop cartoon "Minnie the Moocher," which opens with footage of Calloway doing a sort of moonwalk dance in front of his band. Then it cuts to an amazing piece of animation that features a ghostly walrus "singing" a new recording of "Minnie the Moocher" where Calloway briefly scats in Armstrong's style. The walrus copies Calloway's dance moves perfectly, thanks to the rotoscope technique invented by Max Fleischer, the producer of the Betty Boop series, in which the drawings are traced frame by frame from filmed images.

Later that year, Calloway sang "Minnie the Moocher" with his band in *The Big Broadcast,* the first in a series of thinly plotted feature-length movies intended to give radio stars a visual showcase. The film established Bing Crosby as a screen idol and gave valuable exposure to Kate Smith, the Boswell Sisters, and the Mills Brothers, as well as Calloway. In 1933, Calloway made two more Betty Boop cartoons, "Snow-White," where he sings "St. James Infirmary" in the guise of Koko the Clown, and "The Old Man of the Mountain," where his Old Man character duets with Betty Boop on "You Gotta Ho-De-Ho (to Get Along with Me)." The same year, a tail-coated

Calloway appeared in the zany W. C. Fields comedy *International House,* singing, dancing, and conducting his band in a high-speed version of "Reefer Man."

Calloway was one of the few black artists, along with Louis Armstrong, Duke Ellington, Fletcher Henderson, and the Mills Brothers, to record steadily through the early years of the Great Depression, when record sales were at their nadir. He continued to appear in feature films and short subjects throughout the 1930s and afterward. He recruited top-flight musicians, and by the end of the decade his band was one of the finest in jazz. He scat-sang and made slangy references to drugs, but he did not make a habit of using jive talk in his lyrics until 1938, when he recorded "The Boogie-Woogie," with its jiving introduction, and "Jive (Page One of the Hepster's Dictionary)," a sort of advertisement for the pamphlet he originally published that year. And though he was always a sharp dresser, he did not wear his trademark zoot suits until the early 1940s, when they first came into fashion.

Among the most influential singers of the early 1930s, besides Calloway and Bing Crosby, were the Mills Brothers and the Boswell Sisters. Barbershop harmonies had fallen from fashion after World War I, but the jazzed-up stylings of the Mills and Boswell siblings brought harmony singing back into the mainstream and a set the stage for the pop and R&B vocal groups of future decades. The Mills Brothers recorded with Crosby, Ella Fitzgerald, Louis Armstrong, and Duke Ellington's band; in December 1932, they cut "Doin' the New Low Down" with Cab Calloway, accompanied by Don Redman's band. The Boswell Sisters often recorded with the Dorsey Brothers' band; in November 1932, they covered Calloway's hit "Minnie the Moocher's Wedding Day." Connie Boswell, who pursued a solo career after the sisters disbanded, recorded with Bing Crosby and with Bob Crosby's and Woody Herman's bands. In October 1931, the Boswell Sisters, the Mills Brothers, and Bing Crosby teamed up to record a medley of songs, including "Life Is Just a Bowl of Cherries," from that year's edition of *George White's "Scandals,"* the perennial Broadway revue.

A few male vocal groups had enjoyed success in the 1920s, notably the Revelers, a white quartet that began recording as the Shannon Four in 1917 and scored its biggest hit in 1926 with "Dinah," an even bigger hit that year for Ethel Waters. (The Revelers also inspired the ill-fated German sextet the Comedian Harmonists.) From 1927 to 1930, the Rhythm Boys—Bing Crosby, Al Rinker, and Harry Barris—recorded with Paul Whiteman's band and on their own, combining harmony, scat singing, and humor in a jazzy style that prefigured the Mills Brothers'. "Actually, some of our music came from listening to what they were doing," Donald Mills told Crosby's biographer Gary Giddins.[24] A number of white sister duos and trios—including the Brox Sisters, the Trix Sisters, the Ponce Sisters, the Duncan Sisters, and the Keller Sisters (who sang with their girlish-sounding brother Frank Lynch)—

achieved fame in vaudeville during the same decade. Most black vocal groups of the era specialized in spirituals, but some, such as the Four Harmony Kings and the Taskiana Four, also performed pop songs and appeared in Broadway reviews. One group recorded sacred music as the Norfolk Jubilee Quartette and secular music as the Norfolk Jazz Quartette. The Southern Quartet, another black group that sang both pop and spiritual songs, harmonized a prototypical doo-wop version of Trixie Smith's "My Man Rocks Me (with One Steady Roll)" in 1924, singing "my baby" instead of "my man."

Unusually for an African American quartet at that time, the Mills Brothers were squarely rooted in the barbershop tradition. John Mills Sr. was a barber in Piqua, Ohio, who sang in a barbershop quartet. His four sons, all born between 1910 and 1915, sang together from an early age, with the oldest, John Jr., providing accompaniment on guitar and the second youngest, Harry, playing kazoo. At one show, Harry lost his kazoo and, cupping his hands over his mouth, produced a kazoo imitation that sounded remarkably like a trumpet. The other brothers learned to imitate instruments as well, with John Jr. taking the bass parts and Herbert and Donald mimicking saxophones, trumpets, or trombones.

The Mills Brothers were not the first singing group to replicate instrumental sounds. An 1887 vocal performance of "General Grant's Funeral March" by gang of African American convicts in Norfolk, Virginia, was described as "absolutely startling in its likeness to a full brass band."[25] A black quartet was reported to have performed an "Imitation of Caliope" [sic] and "Imitation of Band" at a church function in Indianapolis in 1894.[26] The Revelers included a crude mock-instrumental break, featuring what sounds like a kazoo imitation, on their July 1925 recording of "Every Sunday Afternoon." The Taskiana Four did a growling trumpet imitation over a proto-doo-wop background on "Dixie Bo-Bo," from July 1927. (Adelaide Hall also did a growling trumpet imitation on Duke Ellington's "Creole Love Call," from October 1927.)

But no other group could equal the Mills Brothers' instrumental verisimilitude, mellifluous harmony, or glossy ease. In 1928, the brothers began singing on a radio station in Cincinnati; in September 1930, they went to New York and were hired by William Paley, the head of the CBS radio network. They made their first record, "Tiger Rag," for Brunswick in October 1931; combining barbershop harmonies with snappy jazz rhythms, fleet scat singing, and a faux-trumpet solo, it was a No. 1 hit. In December, they joined with Bing Crosby to record another No. 1 hit, "Dinah," with Crosby scatting stiffly over the brothers' nimble harmonies. A couple of months later Crosby and the Mills Brothers gave a similar treatment to "Shine," a 1910 coon song by Cecil Mack and Ford Dabney that Louis Armstrong had revived in March 1931.

The Mills Brothers turned out a steady stream of hits through the 1930s. They performed on Rudy Vallee's and Bing Crosby's popular radio programs and hosted their own CBS network show. They appeared in Hollywood musicals such as *Twenty Million Sweethearts* and *Broadway Gondolier*—both starring Dick Powell—and cartoons such as "I Ain't Got Nobody" and "Dinah," where Max Fleischer's patented "bouncing ball" prompts the audience to sing along. In 1942, the Mills Brothers recorded their all-time best-seller, "Paper Doll," a 1915 composition by Johnny S. Black; they continued to score occasional hits until the late 1960s, but their music became progressively less jazzy, and they gradually dispensed with their scat singing and instrumental effects.

The Mills Brothers' nascent influence on the doo-wop sound can be detected on their February 1932 recording of Don Redman's composition "I Heard" (which Redman himself talk-sings in the 1933 Betty Boop cartoon of the same title). Here, and on the group's September 1934 version of Hoagy Carmichael's "Rockin' Chair," John Mills Jr. uses a "talking bass" technique that the Ink Spots' Hoppy Jones later adopted and that eventually became a doo-wop staple. The Mills Brothers spawned a number of early imitators, among them the Three Keys (including George "Bon Bon" Tunnell), the Three Spades, the Four Blackbirds, the Four Southern Singers, the Five Jinks, the Five Jones Boys, the Mississippi Mud Mashers, and the Delta Rhythm Boys—plus the more gospel-oriented Charioteers and Golden Gate Quartet—but the Ink Spots were by far the most important, inspiring every rhythm-and-blues vocal group that came after them. The Mills Brothers made the R&B charts through the 1940s and had a direct effect on doo-wop through such covers as the Cadillacs' altered 1954 version of the brothers' 1948 recording of "Gloria."[27] In 1958, the Mills Brothers acknowledged their impact on rock 'n' roll with a successful cover of the Silhouettes' smash "Get a Job."

Because of their career longevity and the devotion of rhythm-and-blues enthusiasts, the Mills Brothers are relatively well-remembered as forerunners of doo-wop. But since the Boswell Sisters broke up in the mid-1930s and were emulated as an ensemble only by such white artists as the Andrews Sisters and the King Sisters (no black female vocal group made the pop charts until the Teen Queens did in 1956, followed by the Bobbettes and the Chantels in 1957), they have largely been consigned to the nostalgia category, although some jazz critics have recognized their brilliance. The paucity of public appreciation is especially unfortunate as the Boswell Sisters were one of the most innovative American vocal groups ever. While they made no more than an oblique impression on rock 'n' roll, they anticipated rock music by adopting jazz rhythms and African American vocal inflections with an authenticity that few other white artists could match. So genuine was their approach to jazz that Ella Fitzgerald modeled her style after Connie Boswell's. "I tried so hard to sound just like her," Fitzgerald said.[28]

Born between 1905 and 1911, Martha, Connie, and Helvetia "Vet" Boswell grew up in New Orleans, where they acquired a taste for jazz while studying classical music. Connie, who would become the lead singer, admired both Mamie Smith and Enrico Caruso; unable to walk due to a childhood injury or a bout with polio (the accounts differ), she performed while seated or concealed by a long gown. The sisters appeared on a New Orleans radio station, singing pop songs and playing classical pieces on piano, cello, and violin. In 1925, they recorded the vaudeville-style blues "I'm Gonna Cry (Cryin' Blues)," which was issued by the Victor label under Connie's name; in 1928 they performed in Chicago, then moved to Los Angeles, where they had a daily radio show. In 1930, they recorded a song with Jackie Taylor's band for Victor and several more on their own for OKeh, but except for "Heebie Jeebies," these are not particularly jazzy.

The Boswell Sisters made their breakthrough in 1931, moving to New York, signing with the CBS radio network, and recording the first of their dozens of records on the Brunswick label, all of which featured some variant of the Dorsey Brothers' band until September 1933. Their debut session, in March, yielded the hit "When I Take My Sugar to Tea," including such Boswell hallmarks as abrupt tempo changes, hot instrumental solos, and a transposition of the chorus into a minor key. The tempos shift even more frequently, and the sisters scat-sing in unison, on their next hit, "Roll On, Mississippi, Roll On," recorded in April. The Boswells sing close-harmony nonsense syllables at breakneck speed on "Everybody Loves My Baby," where Connie also scats and imitates a banjo, her horn-like contralto taking on a distinctly African American cast. On the accelerated version of "Heebie Jeebies" the group filmed for *The Big Broadcast,* the pulsing harmonies uncannily foreshadow those on Joe Bennett and the Sparkletones' 1957 rockabilly hit "Black Slacks."

Connie Boswell was mainly responsible for the group's arrangements, which departed radically from pop-singing tradition. Typically opening with a more-or-less straightforward rendition of a Tin Pan Alley standard, the sisters would segue effortlessly into what the musician and author Richard M. Sudhalter describes as a "wholesale reconstruction of melody, harmony, and lyrics." Some of the recorded arrangements would have been even more unconventional if Brunswick's manager, Jack Kapp, hadn't obliged the Boswells to tone them down.[29]

The Boswell Sisters made a series of hit records, along with frequent radio broadcasts and occasional movie appearances, until Martha and Vet retired in 1936, ostensibly to enjoy domestic life. Connie, who had been cutting her own records since 1931, pursued a solo career that lasted through the 1950s, changing the spelling of her name to "Connee." She continued to record hits, including a couple of best sellers with Bing Crosby—"Bob White (Whatcha Gonna Swing Tonight)," in 1937, and "Alexander's Ragtime Band," in 1938. She performed in movies and stage shows and on radio and television programs, seemingly unhindered by her physical disability. But while she left her stylistic imprint on Ella Fitzgerald, Kay Starr, and other jazz and pop singers, she could never fully recapture the magic of the Boswell Sisters' records.

Although he was not as popular as Cab Calloway, the Mills Brothers, or the Boswell Sisters, Leo "Scat" Watson was highly influential, bridging the gap between the scat-singing styles of Louis Armstrong and Ella Fitzgerald. A Kansas City native, Watson cut his first sides in 1932 with the Washboard Rhythm Kings, a hokum-jazz group whose shifting personnel performed material ranging from "Minnie the Moocher" to "Tiger Rag" to "Sloppy Drunk Blues" (the Kings' June 1931 "Call of the Freaks" was the immediate model for Milton Brown's "Garbage Man Blues"). In 1933, Watson recorded as a member of the Spirits of Rhythm, an African American string-band-cum-vocal-harmony-group that included three tiples—ukulele-like Latin American instruments—plus a guitar, a bass, and a suitcase used as a drum.

The Onyx Club, originally a speakeasy that catered to musicians, was the first jazz venue between Fifth and Sixth Avenues on New York's Fifty-second Street, a block that became known as Swing Street. The Spirits of Rhythm were regulars at the Onyx after it reopened as a legitimate nightclub in early 1934, following the repeal of Prohibition. Later that year, the group recorded on its own and with Red McKenzie, the white singer and comb player from the Mound City Blue Blowers. Soon afterward, the Spirits of Rhythm disbanded, only to re-form in 1941, when they recorded behind the Scottish singer Ella Logan. Meanwhile, Watson appeared at the Onyx Club with a group that soon became John Kirby's sextet; he recorded with Artie Shaw's and Gene Krupa's big bands, with a British band led by the jazz critic Leonard Feather, and with his own group.[30] He continued to perform and record through the mid-1940s, including a stint with Slim Gaillard, but his eccentric attitude, irascible temperament, and proclivity for alcohol and drugs undermined his career, and he drifted through a number of nonmusical jobs before dying of pneumonia in 1950.

Beginning as a growling Louis Armstrong imitator—on the Washboard Rhythm Kings' "Underneath the Harlem Moon," his fellow vocalist Wilbur Daniels calls him "Satchel" (short for Satchelmouth, Armstrong's nickname)—Watson developed a unique style that seamlessly combined words, nonsense syllables, trombone imitations, and musical quotations into a what Leonard Feather is said to have called a "vocal stream of consciousness."[31] Together with guitarist Teddy Bunn, Watson gave the Spirits of Rhythm an improvisatory feel, so that they sounded like a jazzier if less polished version of the Mills Brothers. But his greatest importance was as an inspiration to such late-1930s jive acts as Slim and Slam, the Cats and the Fiddle, and the King Cole Trio.

Stuff Smith's singing was only lightly seasoned with scat syllables and jive lyrics, but his bluesy, buoyant brand of swing helped set the tone for the jump music that followed. A violinist and singer from Ohio, Smith had switched from classical music to jazz after hearing Louis Armstrong. He toured with Alphonso Trent's band before forming his own combo with trumpeter Jonah Jones, adding drummer Cozy Cole after the group began an extended residency at the Onyx Club in February 1936. That month, he recorded his own novelty song "I's A Muggin'," which became a pop hit and was covered by Andy Kirk, Mezz Mezzrow, Django Reinhardt, and the Three T's (a group of musicians from Paul Whiteman's band that included Jack Teagarden on trombone, his brother Charlie Teagarden on trumpet, and Frankie Trumbauer on saxophone). Smith made a mark on the hepster scene the same year with the pot-smoking songs "You'se a Viper," sung by Jonah Jones, and "Here Comes the Man with the Jive."

But when the Ink Spots recorded "That Cat Is High" in 1938, they were referring to drunkenness. The group was formed in Ohio (though its members were from Indianapolis) in 1933 when Deek Watson and Hoppy Jones, formerly of the Four Riff Brothers, joined up with Charlie Fuqua and Jerry Daniels, who had been working together as a duo. All four founding Ink Spots played string instruments—guitar, tenor guitar (a small four-string guitar tuned like a mandolin), ukulele, tiple, even a cello that Hoppy Jones tuned like a bass—and they initially sounded more like the Spirits of Rhythm than the Mills Brothers. Following the Mills Brothers' path, they moved from Cincinnati to New York, where they came under Moe Gale's management. In the fall of 1934, they toured Britain with the English bandleader Jack Hylton, who had first intended to book the Spirits of Rhythm.[32]

In January 1935, they recorded four sides for Victor, including "Your Feet's Too Big," written by the Tin Pan Alley composer Fred Fisher with the lyricist Ada Benson. By the time the Ink Spots rerecorded the song for Decca in May 1936, Jerry Daniels had been replaced by Bill Kenny, who sang in a high tenor voice—inspired by the sentimental Irish American balladeer Morton Downey—but did not play an instrument.[33] Unlike the better-known hit recording of "Your Feet's Too Big" made by Fats Waller in 1939, both Ink Spots versions have a slight rock 'n' roll feel—not just a doo-wop flavor but hints of the sort of rhythmic phrasing later used by Elvis Presley or Jerry Lee Lewis. It is Waller's rendition, however, that forms the basis for Chubby Checker's "Your Feet's Too Big," recorded for his 1961 album *For Twisters Only*. And it was Checker's recording that prompted the Beatles to include "Your Feet's Too Big" in a performance later released on the album *Live! at the Star-Club in Hamburg, Germany; 1962*.

In 1938, the Ink Spots cut "Brown Gal," a wistful, racially charged ballad cowritten and first recorded by Lil Hardin Armstrong in 1936. In late 1949, Big Al Sears, a veteran swing saxophonist who turned to R&B, recorded the song as "Brown Boy" with a group called the Sparrows, featuring lead singer Clarence Palmer. Without Sears, the same group, now called the Jive Bombers, rerecorded "Brown Boy" in 1951. In 1956, the Jive Bombers recorded it as "Bad Boy," this time scoring a Top 10 R&B hit that crossed over to the pop charts. Quickly covered by several other doo-wop groups, "Bad Boy" was later recorded by such rock artists as Mink DeVille and Ringo Starr.

Although they had been regularly featured on NBC radio since 1935, the Ink Spots did not have a hit record until they cut "If I Didn't Care," by the white songwriter Jack Lawrence, in January 1939. An instant smash, it became the model for almost every Ink Spots record that followed, with its arpeggiated guitar introduction, followed by Bill Kenny's mawkishly romantic tenor over softly crooned background harmonies, then Hoppy Jones's "talking bass" on the bridge, and finally Kenny's falsetto climax. The group had used all these elements before, but not in combination. After "If I Didn't Care," they virtually ceased to sing scat, talk jive, play instruments (other than Charlie Fuqua's guitar), or alternate lead vocalists, as they had previously. Instead, they scored hit after formulaic, sentimental hit through the 1940s, a number of which were revived by doo-wop groups in the following decade. By far the most successful of these covers was the Platters' version of the Ink Spots' 1939 hit "My Prayer"—a No. 1 smash on both the pop and R&B charts in 1956 (the song had been adapted from the tango "Avant de Mourir," which the Romanian Gypsy violinist Georges Boulanger recorded in 1924). The Ink Spots survived a number of personnel changes but fragmented in the 1950s, with several groups claiming the Ink Spots name.

BIG BANDS AND SHUFFLE RHYTHMS

Cab Calloway's exuberant style left an impression on bands as well as singers. To exploit his popularity, along with Duke Ellington's, their manager, Irving Mills, took over drummer Willie Lynch's group in 1930 and renamed the it the Mills Blue Rhythm Band, although it included Mills in name only. The Blue Rhythm Band recorded material from Calloway's and Ellington's repertoires, much of it composed by Mills; in 1931, the group recorded three versions of "Minnie the Moocher" for three different labels. Mills also used the band to fill in between Calloway's or Ellington's sets or to substitute when they were unavailable.

Recording under different names with different leaders, arrangers, and singers, the Mills Blue Rhythm Band failed to establish a distinctive stylistic identity. But though none of its early members was especially well known, the group was always musically solid. After Lucky Millinder assumed the leadership in 1933, he recruited such notable players as trumpeter Henry "Red" Allen and alto saxophonist Tab Smith, and the band had several hit records before breaking up in 1938.

The Alabama-born, Chicago-bred Millinder, a conductor who seldom sang and never played an instrument, then took over a Philadelphia-based band led by pianist Bill Doggett but went bankrupt in 1939. Millinder organized his own big band the following year, including Doggett and the guitar-playing gospel singer Sister Rosetta Tharpe. That group often played straight-ahead swing arrangements and, before disbanding in 1952, featured a number of eminent jazz musicians, among them trumpeters Dizzy Gillespie and Freddie Webster, saxophonists Frank Wess and Eddie "Lockjaw" Davis, bassist George Duvivier, and drummer Panama Francis. But Millinder's band is remembered today mostly as a precursor of rhythm-and-blues.

Except for its big-band sonorities, Millinder's first hit, the bluesy "Big Fat Mama" (featuring a vocal by guitarist Trevor Bacon), is indistinguishable from postwar R&B. "Apollo Jump," from the same September 1941 session, features a honking tenor saxophone solo by Stafford Simon that precedes Illinois Jacquet's landmark solo on Lionel Hampton's "Flying Home" by nearly nine months. Tharpe plays a Chuck Berry–like electric guitar solo on her pop-gospel number "That's All," from November 1941, more than six months before T-Bone Walker, Berry's principal inspiration, cut "Mean Old World," the record that established his style. Tharpe's February 1942 recording of "I Want a Tall Skinny Papa," one of her few forays into secular music, is a sort of answer to "Big Fat Mama," with a similar proto-rock feel. But after rerecording the song in 1943 for the Armed Forces Radio Service, Tharpe left Millinder to pursue a strictly spiritual career. In 1944, she recorded "Strange Things Happening Every Day" with a combo including pianist Sammy Price, and it became a No. 2 rhythm-and-blues hit. With its chugging, boogie-like beat, it's been cited as a rock 'n' roll antecedent and an influence to Elvis Presley, Jerry Lee Lewis, Carl Perkins, and Johnny Cash.[34]

Wynonie Harris joined Millinder's band in March 1944, after Trevor Bacon left to join Tab Smith's new group. Originally from Omaha, Harris was a blues shouter who modeled his style after Big Joe Turner's. His first recording session, in May 1944, produced the minor pop hit "Hurry, Hurry," a slow blues that had already been a minor hit earlier that year for Benny Carter's band with singer Savannah Churchill. On the same date, Harris cut "Who Threw the Whiskey in the Well," which had been recorded for Bluebird two years earlier by Doc Wheeler and His Sunset Orchestra, including tenor saxophonist Sam "the Man" Taylor, who would later play with Millinder.[35] But Millinder's label, Decca, did not release his version with Harris until 1945, by which time Harris was no longer working with Millinder. Nonetheless, "Who Threw the Whiskey in the Well" became a No. 1 rhythm-

and-blues hit, prompting Bull Moose Jackson, the singing tenor saxophonist in Millinder's band, to record "I Know Who Threw the Whiskey in the Well."

After recording under his own name for the Philo, Apollo, Hamp-Tone, Bullet, and Aladdin labels, Harris cut Roy Brown's "Good Rockin' Tonight" for King on December 28, 1947. Brown had recorded the song himself only after offering it to Harris, who initially turned it down. Although Brown told writer John Broven, "I really don't know what the inspiration of the song was," he could have been influenced by the vaguely similar "There's Good Blues Tonight," published by the white husband-and-wife songwriting team of Abe and Edna Osser and inspired by the radio commentator Gabriel Heatter's catchphrase "There's good news tonight." Les Brown's band recorded "There's Good Blues Tonight" with singer Doris Day in February 1946, one day before Millinder cut it with singer Annisteen Allen, and Tommy Dorsey's band recorded it with singer Sy Oliver a few days later.[36] But the lyrics of "Good Rockin' Tonight" also include the stock characters Deacon Jones and Elder Brown, both mentioned in "Who Threw the Whiskey in the Well."

The transition between Lucky Millinder's takeover of the Mills Blue Rhythm Band and Wynonie Harris's recording of "Good Rockin' Tonight" nearly fifteen years later provides perhaps the clearest illustration of the transformation of big-band swing into rhythm-and-blues and rock 'n' roll. Bill Doggett, after switching from piano to organ, went on to earn his own place in rock 'n' roll history: in June 1956, less than two years after Elvis Presley recorded "Good Rockin' Tonight" for Sun, Doggett cut the instrumental "Honky Tonk (Parts 1 & 2)" for King with guitarist Billy Butler and saxophonist Clifford Scott. A No. 1 R&B hit, "Honky Tonk" failed to reach the top of the pop charts only because another double-sided smash, Presley's "Hound Dog," backed with "Don't Be Cruel," came out around the same time.

Irving Mills briefly managed yet another big band that helped lay the foundation for rhythm-and-blues. Jimmie Lunceford, born in Mississippi, was raised in Oklahoma City and then Denver, where he studied classical music with Wilberforce Whiteman, Paul Whiteman's father. After graduating from Fisk University in Nashville in 1926, Lunceford played in several New York jazz bands before taking a job as a high school music teacher in Memphis. He founded a student band, the Chickasaw Syncopaters, which turned professional in 1929 and eventually became the Jimmie Lunceford Orchestra, also known as the Harlem Express. The group struggled until 1934, when Mills took Lunceford under his wing, arranging for him to record for Victor and play a long engagement at the Cotton Club. Lunceford split with Mills after just a few months, but by then his name was made.

Lunceford's band was renowned for scrupulous precision, stylistic versatility, and choreographed stage moves. Lunceford employed a number of talented arrangers, notably Sy Oliver, who gave the ensemble a relaxed 2/4 rhythm—in contrast to the unaccented 4/4 of most swing bands—that became known as the "Lunceford bounce." Even before Benny Goodman touched off the swing craze in 1935, Lunceford's hot arrangements won him a following among white college students.[37] Some who heard Lunceford on stage insist that his was the greatest big band of the era, surpassing even Ellington's or Basie's.[38]

Beginning in late 1934, after he switched to the Decca label, Lunceford had a string of pop hits that ran through the mid-1940s, including "Rhythm Is Our Business," "Organ Grinder's Swing," and "Blues in the Night"—the last from the 1941 movie of the same title, in which Lunceford appeared. Band members sang on many of Lunceford's numbers, either singly or, as on "My Blue Heaven," in Mills Brothers–like harmony. Joe Thomas's burly, bluesy tenor saxophone influenced younger players such as Arnett Cobb, who, along with Illinois Jacquet, popularized the honking style.[39] And Eddie Durham, the trombonist, guitarist, and arranger, was the first musician to play electric guitar in a straight-ahead jazz band, performing with the instrument in Lunceford's ensemble but not recording with it until March 1938 as a member of the Kansas City Five, a group drawn from Count Basie's band.[40]

Like many other swing bands of period, both black and white, Lunceford's played sweet as well as hot material, often featuring the falsetto crooning of alto saxophonist Dan Grissom on the former. Together with the Ink Spots' Bill Kenny, Grissom and his rival Pha Terrell, the crooner with Andy Kirk's band (who had a big hit in 1936 with "Until the Real Thing Comes Along"), were the stylistic forebears of the silky doo-wop and R&B singers of subsequent decades.

For the first ten years after its inception in 1936, *Down Beat* magazine's readers' poll included both swing- and sweet-band categories, but the distinction was often blurred, with bands like Tommy Dorsey's or Glenn Miller's voted sweetest and Benny Goodman's or Duke Ellington's most swinging. Society orchestras such as Guy Lombardo's, which advertised "The Sweetest Music This Side of Heaven," were relegated to a separate "corn" list, although Lombardo could play hot when the occasion demanded, and Lunceford, with Grissom singing, covered Lombardo's 1927 smash "Charmaine!"

It was a sweet band that formally introduced the shuffle beat, one of the basic elements of early rhythm-and-blues and rock 'n' roll. The shuffle can be defined as a rhythm in 4/4 time in which each of the four beats consists of three eighth notes, with the first two tied together. In poetry, it would be called trochaic tetrameter. The shuffle is inherent in the "double running bass" variety of boogie-woogie that Artie Matthews included in his 1915 composition "Weary Blues." But even before swing bands adopted boogie bass lines, a sweet band led by trumpeter Henry Busse began playing a boogie-less shuffle beat.

Busse, who immigrated to the United States from Germany around the time of World War I, was a charter member of Paul Whiteman's band. He cowrote a couple of Whiteman's early hits, "Wang Wang Blues," from 1920, and "Hot Lips," from 1922, which became Busse's theme song. His muted trumpet solo on "When Day Is Done," from 1927, has been cited as a prototype for the sweet-jazz style. By 1928, Whiteman was paying Busse $350 a week, much more than he paid Bix Beiderbecke or Bing Crosby.[41] But Busse split from Whiteman that year to form his own band, which recorded for the Victor, Columbia, and Decca labels.

Busse's musicians came up with the shuffle rhythm either at the Sui Ren in Galveston in 1932, according to a 1938 article in *Down Beat*, or at the Forest Club in Miami in 1933, according to a 1970s interview with the band's pianist, Paul Sprosty.[42] By Sprosty's account, "One night I was trying to be cute so I played a *juggajuggajuggajugga* kind of fast beat on one of the tunes. Ted Tillman, the drummer, decided to prove he could sound just as ridiculous and answered with a *chooka/chooka/chooka/chook.* Suddenly the dancers speeded up . . . shuffling . . . jumping . . . getting all excited. Every time we played that way, the response was overwhelming. Within three weeks, Sandy Runyan [actually Runyon], one of our saxophonists, made the first of many arrangements known—as all of our arrangements were—as 'Henry Busse arrangements.'"

Jan Savitt claimed to have been born in St. Petersburg, Russia, in 1913, the son of a musician in the czar's imperial band. But he was probably born in the Jewish shtetl of Shumsk, in what is now Ukraine, in 1908.[43] Raised in Philadelphia, he was a violin prodigy who played in the Philadelphia Orchestra under Leopold Stokowski. In the mid-1930s, he became the musical director of a local radio station, then switched to another station and in 1937 formed a dance band, the Top Hatters. In 1938, five years after the debut of the *Lone Ranger* radio series, the group recorded its first hit, "Hi-Yo Silver," featuring singer Bon Bon Tunnell. (The song was also a hit that year for the cowboy star Roy Rogers; the title phrase would turn up on Big Joe Turner's 1953 hit "Honey Hush.") By that time, the Top Hatters had come up with their trademark beat, named in the title of their March 1937 recording "Shuffle Rhythm."

Savitt's rhythm was similar to Busse's but faster and subtler, with the triplet figure usually played only by the piano. In the February 1938 issue of *Down Beat,* Savitt is reported to have accused Busse of stealing his beat, saying that Busse "ought to be ashamed of himself." Busse responded: "I don't mind the guy's imitating my band so much, but that he should tell everybody that HE originated it and I should be ashamed to copy HIM! THAT IS TOO MUCH!"[44] In a letter published in the following month's issue, Savitt replied that he had never disparaged Busse and claimed that the shuffle rhythm had been used by Bach and Brahms as well as George Gershwin and many traditional New Orleans jazzmen. Savitt added that Busse's beat was in 6/8 time, while his own shuffle rhythm was "fundamentally a moving bass in four-four time and a push-beat treble consisting of a series of dotted eighth notes and a sixteenth note tied to an eighth with the ensuing syncopation assuming the character of four downbeats and four afterbeats to each bar."[45] Nevertheless, Busse began to use the term "shuffle rhythm" for his own beat.

Critics consigned Busse's music to the cornball category, but Gunther Schuller compares Savitt to Jimmie Lunceford and Count Basie, saying, "Savitt's band played with such consistently impeccable ensemble and propulsive swing that it kept even its famous shuffle rhythm . . . from becoming a stale cliché."[46] Still, the shuffle was generally regarded as a gimmick, and in the short run, few other bandleaders picked it up. In April 1939, Lionel Hampton recorded "Shufflin' at the Hollywood," with Cozy Cole playing a fast shuffle on the drums. In June 1940, the banjo player Lou Breese, whose band included a number of Busse's former sideman, updated the 1926 standard "Breezin' Along with the Breeze" with a prominent shuffle beat.

The musician most often credited with popularizing the shuffle was Louis Jordan. John Chilton, Jordan's biographer, writes: "It's unlikely that he was impressed by the Busse band's stilted phrasing, but he enjoyed the emphatic bouncy rhythm that enlivened their music. He tried to hear as many of their radio shows as he could, and he also liked the shuffle rhythms created by another white band . . . led by Jan Savitt."[47] Chilton's notion that Jordan got his shuffle rhythm from Busse and Savitt is intriguing but dubious. Chilton has the Arkansas-born Jordan listening to Busse and Savitt on the radio while living in Philadelphia, but Jordan left Philadelphia for New York in 1935, before Savitt began broadcasting with his band. Jordan did not adopt the shuffle rhythm until the early 1940s, and when he did it was in conjunction with a boogie-woogie bass line, as on "Pinetop's Boogie Woogie" or "Saxa-Woogie," both from 1941. In 1944, Jordan scored perhaps the biggest hit of his career with a boogied-up version of Johnny Mercer's "G.I. Jive," featuring a mid-tempo shuffle noticeably slower than Busse's or Savitt's beat. (Mercer's own rendition also topped *Billboard*'s R&B chart, but Jordan's topped both the R&B and pop lists.) He used a faster shuffle rhythm on his signature hits "Caldonia" and "Choo Choo Ch'Boogie."

Jordan's musical tastes may have been as broad as Chilton maintains, and he was surely familiar with Busse and Savitt, who were very successful at the time. Most likely, Jordan's shuffle represents a confluence between the Busse-Savitt rhythm and the boogie-woogie, both of which entered the pop-music mainstream in the mid-1930s, shortly before Jordan formed his Tympany Five.

Jordan's band can be seen as the model for the rhythm-and-blues combos that flourished after the postwar decline of the big bands, but small groups were not uncommon in the big-band era. One of the most popular was John Kirby's sextet, which followed Stuff Smith's band into the Onyx Club in 1937. Kirby had played bass with the hard-swinging bandleaders Fletcher Henderson and Chick Webb, but on his own he courted white audiences with politely swung versions of Tin Pan Alley standards ("Blue Skies"), folk chestnuts ("Loch Lomond"), and classical pieces ("Anitra's Dance)."

While copying Kirby's instrumentation, Jordan took a virtually opposite approach, managing to attract white listeners while drawing heavily on blues, boogie-woogies, and African American slang. It has been suggested that Jordan was influenced by the Harlem Hamfats, a band founded in 1936, two years before the Tympany Five, but it's probably more accurate to say that both Jordan and the Hamfats reflected the musical vision of Mayo Williams, who put together the Hamfats and produced Jordan's early records.

THE BLUES-JAZZ NEXUS

A star athlete at Brown University, Williams had been one of the first black players in the National Football League. As a talent scout and producer for the Paramount and Vocalion labels, he recorded Ma Rainey, Ida Cox, Papa Charlie Jackson, Blind Lemon Jefferson, Blind Blake, Tampa Red and Georgia Tom, Leroy Carr, Cow Cow Davenport, and Pinetop Smith, among many other blues artists. In 1934, Decca, a British label, hired Jack Kapp to run its newly established American branch; as the former manager of Brunswick, Vocalion's parent label, Kapp had already worked with Williams, whom he hired to oversee Decca's race division.

Mayo Williams had also recorded jazz musicians such as Clarence Williams, Fletcher Henderson, and Johnny Dodds, on their own and as accompanists to classic blues singers. At Decca, he began to use jazz players to back country bluesmen. The combination of horns and strings in rural or semi-rural African American music was not unprecedented: the Dixieland Jug Blowers' December 11, 1926, session included not only Johnny Dodds but the band's regular alto saxophonist, Lockwood Lewis, along with a violinist and three banjo players. In August 1934, Williams recorded a single side with the Tennessee-born, St. Louis–based singer-guitarist-pianist Peetie Wheatstraw and a nonce group, the Blue Blowers, that included a trombone and a clarinet. (Robert Johnson adopted Wheatstraw's falsetto whoops, which anticipated those of Little Richard.) In September 1935, Williams produced a session with the Georgia-born singer-guitarist Bumble Bee Slim and a similar group, the Rhythm Riffers, that featured two saxophones and a trumpet.

The husband-and-wife country-blues team of Lizzie Douglas and Joe McCoy, both singer-guitarists, first recorded for Columbia in 1929, billing themselves as Memphis Minnie and Kansas Joe in apparent emulation of Tampa Red and Georgia Tom. The following year, they began recording on Vocalion for Mayo Williams, who brought them to Decca in 1934. After the couple split up in 1935, Memphis Minnie left Decca, and Williams assembled a new band with Joe McCoy singing and playing guitar, his younger brother Charlie McCoy on mandolin, Herb Morand on trumpet, Odell Rand on clarinet, and Horace Malcolm on piano, plus a bassist and drummer. Although all the musicians were living in Chicago, Williams came up with the name Harlem Hamfats, "Harlem" having by then become synonymous with all things African American.

The McCoy brothers hailed from the Jackson, Mississippi, area. In the 1920s, Joe McCoy migrated to Memphis, where he hooked up with Memphis Minnie, while Charlie McCoy remained in Mississippi and recorded with the seminal Delta bluesmen Tommy Johnson and Ishmon Bracey, as well as with Bo Carter and Walter Vinson as the Jackson Blue Boys, Mississippi Hot Footers, and Mississippi Mud Steppers. Herb Morand, who co-led the Hamfats with Joe McCoy, was born in New Orleans, where he worked in trumpeter Chris Kelly's legendary jazz band. He toured the Southwest with Nat Towles's Creole Harmony Kings and joined Cliff Jackson's Krazy Kats in New York before moving to Chicago, where he played with Johnny Dodds in the Beale Street Washboard Band. Odell Rand, an Illinois native, played an E-flat clarinet in New Orleans style, and the Atlanta-born Horace Malcolm performed blues and jazz at house parties and nightclubs in Chicago.

The Harlem Hamfats' first recording session, in April 1936, produced the group's biggest hit, "Oh! Red," a snappy blues in 2/4 time with trumpet, piano, mandolin, and clarinet solos in between Joe McCoy's vocal choruses. It was popular enough to inspire several cover versions, including a sleekly harmonized vocal arrangement by the Ink Spots in 1938 (the flip side of "That Cat Is High") and an elegantly understated instrumental by Count Basie and his rhythm section in 1939. "Oh! Red" was recorded by Sammy Price in 1940 and by Howlin' Wolf in 1952; redone in New Orleans style as "Sick and Tired," it was an R&B hit for Chris Kenner in 1957 and a crossover pop hit for Fats Domino in 1958. The song entered the Jamaican tradition in the late 1960s and early 1970s via rocksteady and reggae renditions (titled "Sick and Tired" or "Oh Babe") by Ewan McDermott and Jerry Matthias, Ken Boothe and Delroy Wilson, Derrick Morgan, and Neville Grant.

"Oh! Red" had its greatest influence, however, as the basis for Chuck Berry's first hit, "Maybellene," in 1955. In his autobiography, Berry claims that he adapted "Maybellene" from "Ida Red," a white country song he'd heard as a teenager.[48] "Ida Red" had been recorded by a number of country artists from 1924 on, the best-known version being Bob Wills's from 1938. But "Maybellene" sounds practically nothing like "Ida Red"; instead, it closely follows the tune of "Oh! Red," which Berry, who was born in St.

Louis in 1926, would likely have heard as a youth. And Berry's refrain, "Maybellene, why can't you be true? / You done started back doin' the things you used to do," echoes the Hamfats' line, "Oh, Red, what'cha gonna do? / I'm sick and tired [of] chastisin' you."

The Harlem Hamfats continued to record for Decca until 1938, frequently recycling the "Oh! Red" theme under different titles. Among their other material was "Let's Get Drunk and Truck," a pop-style novelty first recorded for the Bluebird label on April 1, 1936—a couple of weeks before the Hamfats' debut session—by Tampa Red and the Chicago Five, featuring Arnett Nelson on clarinet and Black Bob Hudson on piano. In October 1936, the Hamfats cut a version of "The New Call of the Freaks" titled "The Garbage Man," with jazzy instrumental solos brasher than those on Luis Russell's original but without Russell's "freakish" harmonies. The flip side of that record was "Southern Blues," where Joe McCoy sings the line "the blues jumped a monkey and run him for a solid mile" in Louis Armstrong's growling style, following Herb Morand's Armstrong-like trumpet introduction. It's a mangled version of a line dating back at least as far as Blind Lemon Jefferson's December 1926 recording of "Rabbit Foot Blues"—more than a year before Jim Jackson cut "Old Dog Blue"—in which Jefferson wails, "Blue jumped a rabbit, run him one solid mile." The line would turn up again on Hot Lips Page's 1944 recording of "The Blues Jumped the Rabbit," which Wynonie Harris adapted in 1946, substituting "Mr. Blues"—Harris's nickname—for "The Blues."

The Hamfats are sometimes cited as the fathers of jump blues, but despite occasional boogie bass lines and other up-to-date touches, their style is a crude fusion of blues and hokum with New Orleans–style jazz rather than with swing, as the word "jump" would imply. Even "Hamfat Swing," an instrumental from November 1936, is firmly in the traditional mold. The writer James Lincoln Collier identifies the formation of the Harlem Hamfats with the beginning of rock 'n' roll; he quotes the jazz historian Paige Van Vorst as saying, "This group successfully combined New Orleans jazz and Mississippi Delta blues into one music, something that is the likely antecedent of rhythm-and-blues."[49] But that is an exaggeration: although their music was antecedent to rhythm-and-blues, the jazz and country-blues elements in the Hamfats' music are never fully integrated. With such exceptions as "Weed Smoker's Dream"—one of the group's most modern songs, which became a hit for Peggy Lee after Joe McCoy rewrote it for Lil Green as "Why Don't You Do Right?"—the Hamfats' sound made more of an impact on blues than on jazz or pop music, and their influence on rhythm-and-blues was mainly indirect.

Besides making their own records, the Harlem Hamfats recorded as accompanists to singers Johnnie Temple, Rosetta Howard, and Frankie "Half-Pint" Jaxon in 1937 and 1938. The sessions with Temple, a Mississippi-born singer-guitarist, suggest a jazzier take on the blues of Peetie Wheatstraw; those with Howard, a Chicago native, update the classic-blues sound of the previous decade (although her biggest seller was "If You're a Viper," a laid-back cover of Stuff Smith's "You'se a Viper").[50] The rollicking songs the Hamfats cut with Jaxon—an Alabama-born, Kansas City–bred former minstrel trouper—are as close as the band ever came to rock 'n' roll: with their verse-and-refrain hokum structures, "She Brings Me Down," "Wet It," "She Sends Me," and "She Loves So Good" form a link between vaudeville and rhythm-and-blues.

After their Decca contract expired in 1938, the Hamfats cut sixteen sides for Vocalion in 1939 before disbanding. During their brief career, the Hamfats functioned exclusively as a studio ensemble, never performing together on stage.

Other, even shorter-lived Chicago bands, some sharing the same core personnel, sprang up to copy the Hamfats' style. The State Street Swingers, with clarinetist Arnett Nelson and pianist Black Bob Hudson, made their first record for Vocalion in July 1936, following up in August with a cover of "Oh! Red" sung by Washboard Sam, Big Bill Broonzy's putative half-brother. In October 1936, Arnett Nelson and His Hot Four cut their only record—"Oh! Red," backed with "You Waited Too Long"—for the ARC label; the group included Hudson and probably Broonzy, with Casey Bill Weldon singing and playing slide guitar. Nelson and Hudson also accompanied Lil Johnson when she recorded "Let's Get Drunk and Truck" in August 1936, less than a week after the Hamfats cut the song.

Little is known about Arnett Nelson—he toured with Yankee Robinson's Circus in 1915, played in bands led by the Chicago trumpeter Jimmy Wade in the 1920s, and wrote the tune "Buddy's Habits"—or about Alfred Bell, a trumpeter who sometimes recorded with Big Bill Broonzy.[51] Equally obscure is Ollie Shepard, a blues singer and pianist who recorded more than fifty sides between 1937 and 1942, mostly for Decca, accompanied by various jazz combos. Like the Harlem Hamfats, these musicians have been overlooked by both jazz and blues historians because their styles fall between the two genres—too coarse for jazz lovers, too commercial for blues fans. Yet the jazz-blues fusion of the late 1930s, as clumsy and formulaic as it sometimes was, left its mark on rhythm-and-blues and western swing, brought country blues to a more mainstream audience, and paved the way for the electrified blues of the postwar years.[52]

On Louis Jordan's earliest recordings, beginning in December 1938, his band sounds like John Kirby's, only more exuberant, with Jordan adding comedy vocals such as the one on "Barnacle Bill the Sailor" (an expurgated take on a bawdy folk song published anonymously in 1927 as "Ballochy Bill the Sailor," then bowdlerized by the country singer-songwriters Carson Robison and Frank Luther and first recorded in 1930 by Hoagy Carmichael and

His Orchestra, including Bix Beiderbecke, Benny Goodman, Tommy Dorsey, Joe Venuti, Eddie Lang, and Gene Krupa).[53] At his second session, in March 1939, Jordan recorded a smooth swing arrangement of "Keep A-Knockin'," for which Perry Bradford claimed composer's credit, although the melody and lyrics were only slightly altered from previous versions. (Bradford was probably familiar with a 1921 recording of "You Can't Come In" by the African American blackface comedy team of Flournoy Miller and Aubrey Lyles, since OKeh Records issued it on the flip side of "Darktown Court Room," recorded by the black vaudevillian Shelton Brooks at a session set up by Bradford.) The middling success of Jordan's "Keep A-Knockin'" prompted other renditions by Jimmy Dorsey's big band with vocalist Helen O'Connell, by the classic blues singer Lizzie Miles, and by Nora and Delle, a black female duo whose jivey vocal harmonies anticipate both postwar R&B and rockabilly. But it was most likely Jordan's record that inspired Little Richard's rock 'n' roll smash.

Jordan recorded few blues until November 1941, when he cut his breakthrough hit, "I'm Gonna Move to the Outskirts of Town," which Casey Bill Weldon had originally recorded for Vocalion in September 1936. Substituting his suave saxophone and seductive croon for Weldon's twangy steel guitar and bluff wailing, Jordan thoroughly urbanizes the country blues. In the words of John Chilton, "It was the telling blend of vocal and instrumental feeling on 'I'm Gonna Move . . . ' that really launched Louis Jordan as a major recording star."[54] Berle Adams, Jordan's agent, said that Mayo Williams had brought Weldon's composition to Jordan, but Jordan himself said he'd first heard the song "on the tracks in Dallas, Texas."[55]

A mysterious figure, Weldon may have been born in Pine Bluff, Arkansas, as Big Bill Broonzy maintained. He is usually assumed to be the same singer-guitarist who recorded for Victor as a member of the Memphis Jug Band in 1927 and 1928 under the name Will Weldon, but this has been disputed, as has his supposed brief marriage to Memphis Minnie around the same time.[56] He is presumed to have sojourned in Kansas City before moving to Chicago (or perhaps he just adopted a pseudonym, like Kansas Joe McCoy), for in March 1935 he recorded four sides for Vocalion as Kansas City Bill Weldon, accompanied on piano by Peetie Wheatstraw; on some of the labels he is further identified as the Hawaiian Guitar Wizard. By October 1935, when he cut his next session as Casey Bill (signifying K. C. Bill), he seems to have appropriated Wheatstraw's whooping vocal style. What made his sound distinctive, lending some of his material the feel of western swing, was his slide guitar, which he played in the Hawaiian manner, holding the instrument horizontally across his lap. Weldon recorded quite successfully as a leader for the Bluebird and Vocalion labels through 1938 and as a sideman for such artists as Peetie Wheatstraw, Bumble Bee Slim, and Memphis Minnie. But in the early 1940s, he vanished and, aside from a couple of uncorroborated reports, was never heard from again.

At a July 1942 session produced by Milt Gabler, three months after Jimmie Lunceford cut his hit version of "I'm Gonna Move to the Outskirts of Town," Jordan recorded his own sequel, "I'm Gonna Leave You on the Outskirts of Town," as well as Ollie Shepard's "It's a Low Down Dirty Shame," a slow blues number that Shepard had recorded in October 1937. The two tracks were paired on the same disc, which rose to No. 3 on *Billboard*'s Harlem Hit Parade. On "I'm Gonna Leave You," Jordan simply fits new lyrics to the melody of "I'm Gonna Move," but on "It's a Low Down Dirty Shame," he polishes Shepard's rough-hewn original—already a better-integrated blend of blues and jazz than the Harlem Hamfats' material—into a proto-R&B gem. Shepard's recording, his first release, features just his own piano and vocal, Edgar Saucier's alto saxophone, and an unknown drummer, with Shepard playing a boogie-woogie bass line only on the final chorus, beneath Saucier's solo. Jordan, singing like Jimmy Rushing, uses a shuffling boogie beat throughout, giving the song a feel remarkably like that of postwar rhythm-and-blues.

At the same session, Jordan cut "Somebody Done Changed the Lock on My Door," which Casey Bill Weldon had recorded for Bluebird in 1935 and for Vocalion in 1936. But Jordan's initial version was not released; instead, Decca ultimately issued his January 1945 rerecording of the song as the flip side of "Caldonia," a No. 1 R&B hit that also made the pop Top 10. Here, as on "I'm Gonna Move to the Outskirts of Town," Jordan substitutes urbanity for rural grit, refining even Weldon's falsetto whoops. In August 1945, Wynonie Harris covered "Somebody Done Changed the Lock on My Door" in his own shouting style, accompanied by Jack McVea and His All-Stars; the track was released on the Apollo label as the flip side of "Wynonie's Blues," the first of Harris's records under his own name to make the Harlem Hit Parade.

If only because Jordan and Harris picked up his songs, Casey Bill Weldon can be regarded as a missing link between country blues and R&B.[57] In general, however, the blues made less of an impression on jazz than vice versa. "Lord, I wanna hear some swingin' music, I wanna hear Fats Waller's sound," sang Sonny Boy (John Lee) Williamson on his 1941 recording of "Ground Hog Blues"; but no prominent jazz singer seems to have expressed any such admiration for a blues artist.

One musician who did link country blues to R&B, biographically if not musically, was T-Bone Walker, who as a teenager in Dallas led Blind Lemon Jefferson around the speakeasies of the "Deep Ellum" district. Walker's stepfather, Marco Washington, played bass with the Dallas String Band, which recorded "Hokum Blues" in 1928. Walker played banjo in a medicine show and in accompaniment to Ida Cox in a traveling carnival; he cut his first record, for Columbia, in 1929, singing like Leroy Carr and playing guitar like Scrapper Blackwell. After touring Texas with Cab Calloway's band, he billed himself as the "Cab Calloway of the South." He played with a number of other bands, as well as with Ma Rainey, before moving to Los Angeles in the mid-1930s, where he took up the electric guitar and joined Les Hite's big band. When that group recorded in New York around June 1940, Walker sang "T-Bone Blues," with its "Yancey Special"–like bass line, but the steel guitarist heard on the record is Frank Pasley, who anticipates Chuck Berry's 1957 slide-guitar showpiece "Deep Feeling." Louis Jordan covered "T-Bone Blues" in January 1941, replacing the steel guitar with his saxophone but changing little else.

Not until July 1942, when Walker recorded "Mean Old World" and "I Got a Break, Baby" with Freddie Slack's trio in Los Angeles for the fledgling Capitol label, was his electric guitar captured on vinyl. On these sides, made two years before Cecil Gant's "I Wonder" initiated the surge of West Coast independent-label recordings that propelled the rhythm-and-blues revolution, the mature Walker style that inspired Chuck Berry, B. B. King, and a host of other guitarists appears fully formed. The musicians' union imposed its recording ban the following month, and Walker didn't cut his next session until March 1944, as a guitarist in Slack's big band. In October 1944, following a series of engagements at the Rhumboogie Cafe in Chicago, Walker recorded a half-dozen sides under his own name for the affiliated Rhumboogie label, accompanied by Marl Young's eight-piece band.[58] These include "Sail On Boogie," a jump-style adaptation of Bumble Bee Slim's 1934 country-blues classic "Sail On, Little Girl, Sail On," and "T-Bone Boogie," a medley of verses from Big Joe Turner's songs set to a speeded-up version of Count Basie's "Boogie Woogie" arrangement. With a frantic tenor-saxophone solo by Moses Gant and an insistent guitar break by Walker that one imagines Chuck Berry must have heard, "T-Bone Boogie" grounds rock 'n' roll solidly in the jump-blues tradition.

After a second Chicago session with Young's band, Walker switched to the Los Angeles–based Black & White label and in September 1946 recorded his biggest hit, "Bobby Sox Blues," backed by tenor saxophonist Jack McVea's quintet. Although it's a slow blues and not a rocker, the song, about an obsessed pop fan ("You've got a head full of nothin' but stage, screen, and radio"), prefigures the teen anthems of the 1950s. In September 1947, Walker cut his most famous song, "Call It Stormy Monday but Tuesday Is Just as Bad," which was originally released as the flip side of the now-forgotten "I Know Your Wig Is Gone." He had several more R&B hits through 1950, but his influence was far out of proportion to his record sales. Not only did other guitarists copy his jazzy chord progressions and slinky single-note runs, punctuated with percussive slides and bends, but his flamboyant stage antics, including picking the guitar behind his head while doing a full split, inspired players ranging from Chuck Berry to Jimi Hendrix.

FROM HOKUM TO RHYTHM-AND-BLUES

A lesser-known figure linking R&B to its antecedents is Sam Theard, a singer, songwriter, dancer, and comedian whose career stretched from southern vaudeville to Hollywood. Born in New Orleans, he is said to have left home in 1924 to tour with the elegant tap dancer Jack Wiggins, one of the first of the so-called class acts.[59] Theard began recording in 1929, accompanied by Cow Cow Davenport and Tampa Red, singing mostly double-entendre hokum songs in emulation of "It's Tight Like That." His early records were credited to Lovin' Sam from Down in 'Bam, after the title of Perry Bradford's song "Lovin' Sam from Alabam," which Mamie Smith recorded in 1921 and the tap-dancing team of Rufus Greenlee and Thaddeus Drayton, another class act, performed in the 1922 Broadway show *Liza*.[60]

Theard departed from the standard hokum formula on "You Rascal You," a comically baleful cuckold's complaint he recorded with Davenport in July 1929. The song took a couple of years to bubble up into the popular mainstream: the Louisville-based washboard and kazoo player Walter Taylor recorded the first cover version in February 1930, followed in June by the vaudeville veteran Socks Wilson, who usually performed under the name Kid Wilson with his wife, Coot Grant. Clarence Williams also cut the song in June 1930, and Tampa Red and Georgia Tom recorded it as a double-sided single in July. Later in July, the New Orleans–born, Chicago-based clarinetist Jimmie Noone, one of Benny Goodman's models, recorded a klezmer-like minor-key version, and in August, Tampa Red's Hokum Jug Band cut "You Rascal You" with Frankie "Half-Pint" Jaxon. In October, Andy Kirk recorded the song with the Seven Little Clouds of Joy, a smaller variation of his big band.

Louis Armstrong cut "I'll Be Glad When You're Dead, You Rascal You," the most enduring rendition of the song, in April 1931, but the version recorded in May by Red Nichols and His Five Pennies—a white nonet including Nichols on trumpet, Glenn Miller on trombone, Jimmy Dorsey on alto saxophone, and Ray McKinley on drums—was a bigger hit at the time. "You Rascal You" was also recorded in 1931 by the Mound City Blue Blowers, the Washboard Rhythm Kings, the Mills Brothers, and the big bands of Fletcher Henderson, Luis Russell, Cab Calloway, and Jack Teagarden, the last featuring Fats Waller. In 1932, Armstrong, wearing a leopard-skin tunic, performed the song with his band in the film short "A Rhapsody in Black and Blue" and, as the detached head of a spear-throwing African warrior, sang it in the Betty Boop cartoon "I'll Be Glad When You're Dead

You Rascal You." "You Rascal You" has since been recorded by everyone from Louis Prima to Serge Gainsbourg.

Theard continued to record in Chicago under the name Lovin' Sam through the 1930s, maintaining his prurient approach with songs such as "Rubbin' on That Darned Old Thing" as his style evolved from hokum to swing. He recorded for Vocalion with pianist John Oscar in 1930 and with Oscar and Kansas Joe McCoy in 1931. Switching to the Decca label, he recorded in 1934 with Banks' Chesterfield's Orchestra (led by drummer Louis Banks, with Albert Ammons on piano) and in 1936 with Oscar's Chicago Swingers (including Odell Rand on clarinet). In August 1937, leading his own Swing Rascals, Theard recorded "Spo-Dee-O-Dee" for Vocalion, defining the title with such lines as "The chickens wouldn't lay no eggs, wouldn't flap no wings / if that rooster didn't serve that thing." He changed the tune and made the lyrics jivier but less sexual when he recorded "Spo-De-O-Dee" [sic] for Decca in June 1940 with Tiny Parham's Four Aces, featuring Parham on electric organ. A year earlier, the song had been covered by the Four Clefs, a Chicago group whose members all sang and played instruments.

In 1947, the singer-guitarist Stick (or Sticks) McGhee, accompanied by his brother, the singer-guitarist Brownie McGhee (who was the longtime partner of the harmonica player Sonny Terry), cut "Drinkin' Wine Spo-Dee-O-Dee" for Mayo Williams's Harlem label, with new, oenophilic lyrics but the same basic melody as the one on Theard's first "Spo-Dee-O-Dee."[61] The record was not a big seller, but when McGhee rerecorded the song in February 1949 for Atlantic with a quintet that included his brother, pianist Wilbert "Big Chief" Ellis, and bassist Gene Ramey, it became a huge R&B hit, sparking a craze for drinking songs. The song was also a hit later that year for both Wynonie Harris and Lionel Hampton.

A white country band, Loy Gordon and His Pleasant Valley Boys, covered "Drinkin' Wine Spo-Dee-O-Dee" in August 1949 for Atlantic, and Malcolm Yelvington did a rockabilly rendition in October 1954 for Sun, which released it just after Elvis Presley's "Good Rockin' Tonight." Johnny Burnette's trio cut the song on July 2, 1956, the same day the group recorded "Train Kept A-Rollin'." Other rockabilly versions include one by Sid King and the Five Strings from 1955 ("Drinkin' Wine Spoli Oli") and another by Glenn Reeves from 1956, as well as Donny Baker and the Dimensionals' "Drinkin' Pop-Sodee Odee (Pop Pop)," from 1953. The fourteen-year-old Jerry Lee Lewis is said to have performed "Drinkin' Wine Spo-Dee-O-Dee" in 1949 at a promotional event for a car dealership—his first public show.[62] Lewis recorded the song for Sun in 1957 and again in 1958, but these takes went unreleased for decades; he cut the song for Smash in 1963, and it was issued as an album track in 1966. In 1973, an inebriated-sounding Lewis, accompanied by such British rockers as Peter Frampton and Rory Gallagher, recorded "Drinkin' Wine Spo-Dee-O-Dee" in London, and the resulting single made the American pop and country charts.

Sam Theard last recorded as Lovin' Sam on a March 1938 session for Bluebird with Burns Campbell's band; he makes heavy use of jive talk on swing numbers such as "You're Solid with Me" and "That's Chicago's South Side," singing, "I'm just beatin' up my chops, just to hip you that you're tops" and "If you want to get your solid kicks, truck on out south and dig them mellow chicks." In April 1941, he recorded as Spo-De-O Sam with Sammy Price's band on his own composition "Lead Me Daddy Straight to the Bar," a jiving takeoff on Will Bradley's "Beat Me Daddy (Eight to the Bar)."[63]

According to John Chilton, Louis Jordan met Theard while playing nightclubs in Chicago.[64] In November 1943, Jordan first recorded "You Can't Get That No More," Theard's humorously rueful composition about wartime rationing, on a V-Disc, exempt from the union recording ban then in force because it was intended for military listeners only. He rerecorded the song for Decca in March 1944, on the same date that he cut "G.I. Jive," and after almost a year's delay it followed "G.I. Jive" onto the R&B and pop charts. In June 1946, Jordan recorded Theard's "Let the Good Times Roll"; released on the flip side of "Ain't Nobody Here but Us Chickens," it was a major R&B hit. "Let the Good Times Roll" was a minor pop hit for Ray Charles in 1960 and was also recorded by Jerry Lee Lewis and by B. B. King and Bobby Bland, among others.

In March 1947, Tiny Bradshaw recorded a pair of songs credited to Theard and Henry Glover—"I've Been Around" and the proto-rocker "Take the Hands Off the Clock"—both melodically similar to "Let the Good Times Roll." In July 1947, Wynonie Harris cut another proto-rocker, "Hard Ridin' Mama," cowritten by Theard and the prolific R&B composer Rudy Toombs; the song was covered by Manhattan Paul (Paul Bascomb) with the Three Riffs in October 1948. Theard may have sung on Hot Lips Page's March 1949 recording of "The Egg or the Hen," a song that Theard may have cowritten.[65] In 1950, Hal Singer recorded "Rock Around the Clock"—written by Singer and Theard and a proto-rocker if ever there was one—with Theard, credited as Spoo-Dee-O-Dee, harshly growling the vocal part. In February 1951, Harris recorded Theard and Glover's composition "I'll Never Give Up."

In February 1950, Count Basie recorded the jump blues "If You See My Baby," cowritten by Theard and pianist Teddy Brannon, with a shouted vocal by Vernon Gardner, the lead singer of the Deep River Boys. In May 1950, Wynonie Harris cut "Stormy Night Blues," by Theard, Brannon, and Henry Glover. In March 1951, the alto saxophonist and blues singer Eddie "Cleanhead" Vinson recorded another Theard and Brannon composition, "Home Boy." In August of that year, trumpeter Roy Eldridge sang on his recording of Theard and Brannon's "Baby, What's the Matter with You?" Theard then faded from the music scene, only to reappear in the 1970s as an actor in Los Angeles, performing on the television shows *Sanford and Son* and *Little House on the Prairie* and in the movies *Norman . . . Is That You?* (with Redd Foxx and Pearl Bailey) and *Which Way Is Up?* (with Richard Pryor). He died in 1982, a virtually forgotten figure.

Sammy Price and Hot Lips Page can also be regarded as rhythm-and-blues progenitors. Both were born in 1908 and raised in Dallas, where they were exposed to the blues; both gained early experience in territory bands—Price as a dancer with Alphonso Trent's Orchestra, Page as a trumpeter with the Oklahoma City Blue Devils and Bennie Moten's Kansas City Orchestra. But while Page attained a measure of celebrity from the late 1930s until his death in 1954, Price was known primarily as an accompanist until the 1950s and achieved only minor recognition thereafter.

Price taught himself piano, modeling his style after that of Ida Cox's husband, Jesse Crump, and began touring on the Theatre Owners Booking Association vaudeville circuit in 1927.[66] In October 1929, he cut a single, Dixieland-style side with a quartet in Dallas for Mayo Williams on Brunswick. He moved to Kansas City, Chicago, and Detroit before arriving in New York, where Williams had him play on Cow Cow Davenport's Decca session, then hired him as the label's staff pianist. From 1938 until 1954, Price recorded behind such singers as Jimmie Gordon, Trixie Smith, Coot Grant and Kid Wilson, Blue Lu Barker, Johnnie Temple, Peetie Wheatstraw, Georgia White, Big Joe Turner, Nora Lee King, Helen Humes, Wee Bea Booze, Cousin Joe, and Sister Rosetta Tharpe.

Beginning in March 1940, Price also recorded for Decca with his own group, the Texas Blusicians, which usually included alto saxophonist Don Stovall and sometimes featured jazz luminaries such as trumpeter Freddie Webster or tenor saxophonist Lester Young. Price cut blues, boogies, ballads, and swing tunes—everything from "Sweet Lorraine" to "Do You Dig My Jive?"—singing himself on some numbers and using little-known vocalists such as Yack Taylor, Ruby Smith, and Jack Meredith on others. Most of his repertoire consisted of cover versions or thinly veiled rewrites of other artists' material; and while his music incorporated many of the elements that later coalesced into rhythm-and-blues, his style was thoroughly conventional, never jelling into a clear-cut semblance of postwar R&B. During the 1940s, Price played clubs on Fifty-second Street as well as Cafe Society in Greenwich Village. He made his first trip to Europe in 1948 and returned many times before his death in 1992, enjoying considerably greater acclaim there than at home.

Although he apparently got his nickname by practicing Henry Busse's "Hot Lips," Oran Page was regarded as a Louis Armstrong imitator, initially at least.[67] By his own account, he played behind Ma Rainey and Bessie

Smith early in his career; other sources have him working in a number of jazz bands before recording with the Blue Devils in 1929.[68] He spent the early 1930s with Bennie Moten, then joined Count Basie's band, where he was recognized as an exceptional trumpeter with a distinctive growling tone. But Page was quickly signed as a solo artist by Louis Armstrong's manager, Joe Glaser, and stayed behind in Kansas City when Basie left for New York in 1936. Page made his New York debut soon afterward and began recording with his own band in 1938. Over the next decade and a half, he led various large and small groups; he became a Fifty-second Street fixture and toured as a member of the white clarinetist Artie Shaw's big band in 1941, singing on Shaw's hit recording of "Blues in the Night."

Page's style lay somewhere between Louis Armstrong's and Louis Jordan's, with a particular emphasis on the blues, which Page shouted in a rasping voice that grew rougher with the passing years. While maintaining its bluesy essence, his music followed commercial trends, leaning toward swing in the 1930s, rhythm-and-blues in the 1940s, and mainstream pop in the 1950s. But Page also participated, together with Thelonious Monk, Charlie Christian, and other jazz experimenters, in the early-1940s Harlem jam sessions that spawned the bebop genre, and he made occasional use of Latin rhythms, as on the driving "Harlem Rhumbain' the Blues," from December 1940. Many prominent musicians passed through his bands, especially saxophonists, among them Don Byas, Lucky Thompson, Buddy Tate, Ike Quebec, Paul Quinichette, Ben Webster, Hal Singer, Earl Bostic, and Sam "the Man" Taylor.

"The Blues Jumped the Rabbit," from March 1944, is one of the most R&B-like of Page's earlier recordings. Like many country blues, it's a collection of unrelated verses, including Blind Lemon Jefferson's title line (Page also borrowed lines from Jefferson's "Dry Southern Blues" for his own "Uncle Sam's Blues" and "Old Man Ben"). After pianist Ace Harris plays the Basie-style "Pine Top's Boogie Woogie" introduction, Page sings, "When you lose your money, please don't lose your mind," a line from Jesse Crump's composition "'Fore Day Blues," which Ida Cox recorded in July 1927. (In November 1929, the country bluesman Blind Joe Reynolds recorded his adaptation of Crump's song, "Outside Woman Blues," which Eric Clapton sang on Cream's 1967 album *Disraeli Gears*.) On the final, instrumental chorus of "The Blues Jumped the Rabbit," the great jazz drummer Big Sid Catlett plays a slamming backbeat, nearly three months before Lucky Millinder's "Who Threw the Whiskey in the Well."

In late 1947, Page and his band toured with Wynonie Harris, and it was that group, including Hal Singer on tenor saxophone, that accompanied Harris on "Good Rockin' Tonight." On the same December 1947 series of sessions for King, just before the second musicians' union recording ban, Page's band backed Big Maybelle, who in 1955 would sing "Whole Lotta Shakin'

Goin' On," the original R&B version of Jerry Lee Lewis's first hit. In June 1949, Page and Pearl Bailey sang "Baby, It's Cold Outside," the Frank Loesser standard introduced that year in the movie *Neptune's Daughter*. Unlike several other versions of the song, their record was not a nationally charted hit, but it was successful enough that Page began recording more pop-oriented material with different female vocalists.

In May 1951, less than three months before Tiny Bradshaw cut "The Train Kept A-Rollin'," Page recorded a western-themed R&B romp, "I Want to Ride Like the Cowboys Do," complete with handclapped backbeats. During the same period, he also performed Dixieland material as part of the traditional-jazz revival movement. Page enjoyed increasing popularity in Europe, where he spent summers in the early 1950s, but he suffered a heart attack in October 1954 and died a month later.

The most celebrated rhythm-and-blues forerunner was Fats Waller, whose fame rivaled even Louis Armstrong's. Until the 1930s, the Harlem-born Waller was known primarily as an organist and theatrical songwriter, but after he signed an exclusive contract with the Victor label in 1934 and began recording mainly vocal material with his new sextet, the Rhythm, he became an international pop star, appearing in movies, touring Europe, even performing on an early BBC television broadcast in England. Although Waller's sound generally bears scant outward resemblance to R&B—he recorded few blues and practically no boogie-woogies—his leering, winking approach carried over into the suggestive humor of postwar black music.

Waller began to sing while performing on radio in early 1930s, after the Great Depression put his recording career on hold. His first regular program, *Paramount on Parade,* had only been on the CBS network for three months before Waller made his first vocal recordings, with Ted Lewis's band.[69] Eight days later, on March 13, 1931, with just his own piano accompaniment, he cut a more exuberant version of one of the songs he'd recorded with Lewis, "I'm Crazy 'Bout My Baby." Here, his mature singing style seems fully formed, lacking only some of its ultimate effervescence, as he delivers such typical asides as "Mercy! Oh, you slay me, you sweet thing" during his piano solo.

Waller's next recording session, three years later, produced "I Wish I Were Twins," the first in a steady series of pop hits that continued until his death in 1943. In August 1935, he recorded his first chart-topper, "Truckin'," a song about a Harlem dance craze that was written by Ted Koehler and Rube Bloom for a review at the Cotton Club that year. But with its striding rhythms, "Truckin'," aside from its subject matter and Waller's hearty shouts of "Yeah," has little in common with postwar rhythm-and-blues. Most of his material, including his original compositions, is even less R&B-like, and he makes sparing use of jive talk—as opposed to mere slang—even on his jivier songs, such as "The Joint Is Jumpin'" (which incidentally features a hard backbeat behind Waller's extemporized monologue).[70] An exception is "It's You Who Taught It to Me," from November 1939, where he sings "I can mug, cut the rug, tiptoe like a jitterbug." Just as a bluesman's slurred syllables may imply more than his lyrics denote, Waller's brashly insinuating voice, broadly satirical manner, and brilliant keyboard technique make relatively plain speech sound like hepster lingo.

About as close to rhythm-and-blues as Waller got was "Hold Tight (Want Some Sea Food Mama)," which he recorded in January 1939, just as the version the Andrews Sisters had cut with Jimmy Dorsey's band the previous November entered the pop charts. The sisters' record (released under Dorsey's name) was the bigger seller, but Waller's cartoonishly lecherous delivery seems better suited to such lines as "I like oysters, lobsters, too. I like my tasty butterfish. / When I come home late at night, I get my favorite dish." According to the radio section of the April 24, 1939, issue of *Time* magazine, "In Harlem *Hold Tight*'s fishy lyrics are considered no ordinary clambake stuff, but a reasonable duplication of the queer lingo some Harlem bucks use in one form of sex perversion."[71]

The magazine's anonymous reporter goes on to maintain that "*Hold Tight* was originally conjured up in Harlem's 'Congo' district where a black and elemental breed of cats drink cheap King Kong liquor, puff reefers and shout a frank and sexy jive talk all their own." In fact, just five days before the Andrews Sisters cut the song, it was recorded for the first time by the New Orleans clarinet and soprano saxophone master Sidney Bechet, at Bechet's first recording session as a bandleader. On "Hold Tight," his sextet, including the electric guitarist Leonard Ware, is joined by a vocal duo credited as the Two Fishmongers, said to be Willie Spottswood and Eddie Robinson.[72]

In a letter to the editor published in *Time*'s May 15 issue, Lou Levy, the Andrews Sisters' manager, tells how two white dancers, Jerry Brandow and Lenny Kent (whom Levy calls Larry), approached him with a snippet of a song they'd heard "in a New York or Philadelphia night club where a colored band was playing."[73] That band might have been Bechet's quartet, then working at Nick's Tavern in Greenwich Village, or Ware's trio, with Spottswood and Robinson on piano and bass. Kent, Patty Andrews (the sisters' lead singer), and Vic Schoen (their arranger) tweaked "Hold Tight" into final form, adding a new introduction, and after considerable dispute, composers' royalties were awarded to Brandow, Kent, Ware, Robinson, and Spottswood. But others continued to claim credit for at least parts of the song, among them Sy Oliver, Count Basie, Gene Krupa, singer Jerry Kruger, dancer and trumpeter Taps Miller, and Sidney Bechet, who explained that Clarence Williams had deemed the lyrics too lewd to publish in 1924.[74]

"Hold Tight" was clearly inspired by "Nagasaki," the tongue-twisting 1928 Warren-Dixon standard, "where the fellers chew tobaccy and the women wicky wacky woo." ("Nagasaki" in turn was likely inspired by Albert von

Tilzer, Stanley Murphy, and Charles McCarron's Hawaiian-themed 1916 composition "Oh, How She Could Yacki Hacki Wicki Wacki Woo," a big hit that year for Arthur Collins and Byron Harlan.) As Levy lets on, the Andrews Sisters' distinctive scat expression "foo-ra-de-ack-a-sa-ki" is adapted from the Bechet record's phrase "floogie Nagasaki," a confused cross between "Nagasaki," with its Fujiyama mama, and "The Flat Foot Floogie," Slim and Slam's landmark hit from February 1938. "Foo-ra-de-ack-a-sa-ki" was picked up by Fats Waller (who also referenced Bechet's "Hold Tight") and found its way into Leo Watson's "It's the Tune That Counts," from August 1939. Melodically, "Hold Tight" strongly resembles Count Basie's riff tune "Out the Window," from October 1937.

After "Hold Tight" was denounced as obscene by the influential newspaper columnist Walter Winchell, some radio stations stopped playing it. Nevertheless, it was a major hit for both Waller and the Andrews Sisters. "Winchell came out implying that it was a dirty song," Maxene Andrews commented. "So it was banned from the airwaves, which increased the sales of the records because people wanted to know what was terrible in the song."[75] Waller's version, where his band members serve as a responsive chorus, may have influenced Louis Jordan. More importantly, as a proto-R&B song that achieved mass popularity at the hands of both black and white artists in spite (or because) of its sexual connotations, "Hold Tight" was a harbinger of the rock 'n' roll revolution.

JIVE

"The Flat Foot Floogie" was probably the song that ignited the jive explosion, even though it contains no actual jive talk except for spoken interjections such as "Solid!" and "Man, that's a killer!" Instead, it consists mainly of the nonsense refrain "The flat feet floogie with a floy, floy / Floy joy, floy joy, floy joy, floy joy." A huge smash for its creators, singer-guitarist Slim Gaillard (who also played piano and vibraphone) and bassist Slam Stewart (whose specialty was to scat-sing in unison with his bowed solos), "The Flat Floot Floogie" was a lesser hit for Benny Goodman, for the white New Orleans trumpeter Wingy Manone, and for Louis Armstrong with the Mills Brothers; it was also recorded by Fats Waller, Count Basie, Woody Herman, and Django Reinhardt—all in 1938.

Gaillard, who modeled his singing style on Cab Calloway's, Louis Armstrong's, and especially Fats Waller's, went on to invent a hepster language all his own, which he called "vout" (rhymes with "shout"). "Slim Gaillard is a tall thin Negro with big sad eyes who's always saying, 'Right-orooni' and 'How 'bout a little bourbon-orooni,'" wrote Jack Kerouac in his ur-beatnik novel *On the Road*. "And then Slim goes mad and . . . yells crazy things in

Spanish, in Arabic, in Peruvian dialect, in Egyptian, in every language he knows, and he knows innumerable languages."[76]

Later in life, Gaillard would claim that he was born in Cuba and that when he was twelve, his father, a steward on an ocean liner, had accidentally left him on the island of Crete for six months. More likely, he was a native of Detroit, where he worked as a guitar-playing tap dancer before moving to New York around 1937. He cut his first two sides in April 1937, as the singer with a band led by trumpeter Frankie Newton, a Fifty-second Street regular. Discovered by the pioneering disc jockey Martin Block, a Swing Street habitué, Gaillard was already performing on radio station WNEW when he met Slam Stewart and invited him onto his program. The two clicked immediately, and Block became their manager, securing a recording contract with Vocalion.[77] In January 1938, Slim and Slam recorded "The Flat Foot Floozie," but Vocalion, objecting to the word "floozie," refused to release it, so the duo rerecorded the song the following month. With the help of Lou Levy, Gaillard had "The Flat Foot Floogie" published by the Green Brothers and Knight, one of whose principals, Bud Green, appropriated a share of the composers' credit.

The flip side of Slim and Slam's "The Flat Foot Floogie" was "Chinatown, My Chinatown," a Broadway standard from 1910 that Fletcher Henderson had revived as a jazz tune in 1930.[78] Gaillard first sings the chorus as Stewart scats responsively; then he engages Stewart in some jivey dialogue, borrowing the phrase "kicked the gong around" from Cab Calloway. In an interlude that's totally unacceptable by today's standards, Gaillard breaks into mock-Chinese gibberish, to which Stewart replies, "Chop chop chop chop chop." (Gaillard is no more respectful on "African Jive," from July 1941, where he intersperses faux-African nonsense chanting with phrases such as "scotch and soda" and "fried chicken.")

In June 1938, Slim and Slam recorded their second hit, "Tutti-Frutti," a song about ice cream that contains no jive talk besides the endless repetition of the title phrase. It remained for Little Richard to add the immortal "awop-bop-aloo-mop alop-bam-boom" to his September 1955 recording of "Tutti-Frutti" in New Orleans with members of trumpeter Dave Bartholomew's band—Richard's debut for the Specialty label and his first hit. According to Robert "Bumps" Blackwell, who produced the session, the singer had already cut several tracks that day in a more typical jump-blues style—similar to those he'd recorded two years earlier for the Peacock label in Houston—when, during a break, he began singing, "Awop-bop-a-loo-mop a-good Goddamn—tutti frutti, good booty." It was a number he'd been performing while touring the South with his own band.[79]

Blackwell had to coax Richard into singing the raunchy lyrics for Dorothy LaBostrie, a young songwriter who happened to be at the studio, so that she could clean them up. The recorded version, written on the spot, has nothing in common with Gaillard's text except for the title flavor, but though one swings while the other rocks, the two songs are similar enough in metrical structure and nonsensical concept to suggest that Little Richard's "Tutti"—which enshrined gibberish as a hallmark of rock 'n' roll—is based, however indirectly, on Slim and Slam's. It's also possible that Little Richard was influenced by the jiving 1939 swing anthem "Wham (Re-Bop-Boom-Bam)," which was written for Glenn Miller by Eddie Durham and Taps Miller and also recorded by Andy Kirk, Jimmie Lunceford, Teddy Wilson, Jack Teagarden, Roy Eldridge, Will Bradley, and Mildred Bailey, among others.

Jive talk, scat singing, foreign languages, and sheer nonsense were all conspicuous in the American pop-music mix from the late 1930s through the war years. In early 1938, the Andrews Sisters, who were not Jewish, scored their first No. 1 hit with "Bei Mir Bist Du Schoen," an English-language rewrite of a Yiddish theater song from 1932. The sisters followed with "Ti-Pi-Tin," "Pross Tchai," and "Say 'Si Si,'" songs of Mexican, Russian, and Cuban derivation, respectively. Slim and Slam parodied the ethnic trend in August 1938 with "Vol Vist Du Gaily Star," whose lyrics include such verses as "Vol vist du gaily star / I found my lucky star / Vol vist du gaily star / Lombello." The song ends with a dialogue where Gaillard asks, "What do you think 'Vol vist du gaily star' means?" Stewart responds, "Man, I don't know. What does it mean, man?" "Don't mean a thing," Gaillard answers. "Just a little jive talk, in the floogie language."

Slim and Slam had a few more hits before Stewart left to join the Spirits of Rhythm in 1939, reuniting with Gaillard for occasional performances and recordings, as well as appearances in the movies *Hellzapoppin'* and *Almost Married.* Gaillard continued to explore the comic possibilities of vout with his Flat Foot Floogie Boys, which at different times included tenor saxophonist Ben Webster, drummers Kenny Clarke and Chico Hamilton, and singer Leo Watson. After serving in the Army Air Corps, Gaillard resumed his career in Los Angeles, recording his final hit, the weirdly free-associative "Cement Mixer (Put-Ti-Put-Ti)," in December 1945 with drummer Zutty Singleton and bassist Bam Brown. Later the same month, he took part in a historic session with Charlie Parker and Dizzy Gillespie that included a bebop-tinged take on "Flat Foot Floogie."

Gaillard recorded prolifically for various labels through the early 1950s, reprising his hits on the fancifully titled medleys "Avocado Seed Soup Symphony" and "Opera in Vout." He dropped out of show business for a while in the 1960s, but by the following decade he was singing in nightclubs and acting on such television shows as *Along Came Bronson* and *Marcus Welby, M.D.* A part in the 1979 miniseries *Roots: The Next Generations* brought him wider attention, and in the early 1980s Dizzy Gillespie persuaded him to make an international comeback. Gaillard moved to London, where he recorded his final album in 1982, appeared in the movie *Absolute Beginners* in 1986, and was the subject of a BBC documentary in 1989. He died of cancer in 1991.

Before 1938, the word "jive" showed up in the titles of jazz instrumentals such as Duke Ellington's "Jive Stomp" (1933), Lionel Hampton's "Jivin' the Vibres" [sic] (1937), and Red Norvo's "Jiving the Jeep" (1937), as well as in blues songs such as Frankie "Half-Pint" Jaxon's "Jive Man Blues" (1929), Coot Grant and Kid Wilson's "Jive Lover" (1932), and Bumblebee Slim's "The Jive of Mine" (1936). But it was not generally used to refer to jitterbug jargon until Cab Calloway recorded "Jive (Page One of the Hepster's Dictionary)" in August 1938, at the same session where he cut "The Boogie-Woogie." A proliferation of jive songs followed, and jive talk enjoyed mainstream pop appeal through the mid-1940s, turning up in such incongruous settings as Alfred Hitchcock's grim 1944 war movie *Lifeboat,* in which William Bendix, as a Lindy-hopping merchant seaman whose wounded leg must be amputated, boasts, "I can outjive the rest of those hepcats even with a bum gam."

The concurrent emergence of jump music and jive talk led to their combination in songs such as the Four Clefs' "The Jive Is Jumpin'" and Cab Calloway's "(Hep-Hep!) The Jumpin' Jive," from June and July 1939, respectively. The former was a mere blip on the musical radar screen, while the latter was a massive hit, Calloway's biggest after "Minnie the Moocher." Although Calloway shares the composers' credit for the "The Jumpin' Jive" with the white songwriters Frank Froeba and Jack Palmer, the song was first recorded by Lionel Hampton, in June 1939. The white bandleaders Van Alexander and Jimmy Dorsey (with singer Helen O'Connell) also recorded it before Calloway, and the Andrews Sisters recorded it after him, while Benny Goodman and Glenn Miller performed it on radio broadcasts. But Calloway's version was the most popular by far.

"The Jumpin' Jive" has a couple of nonsense words in common with "Hold Tight"—the enigmatic "foo," for example—and Calloway cements the connection by using the phrase "de-boodle-de-ack-a-saki" in his introduction, which is not heard in the other versions. Calloway's combination of hepster lingo and mumbo jumbo ("Palomar, shalomar, Swanee shore / Let me dig that jive once more") set the tone for the jive songs of the era.

In late June 1939, between Lionel Hampton's and Cab Calloway's recordings of "The Jumpin' Jive," the Cats and the Fiddle made their studio debut. Formed in Chicago in 1937 in the mold of the Spirits of Rhythm, the group comprised lead singer Austin Powell, who played tenor guitar, bass singer Chuck Barksdale, who played bass fiddle, first tenor Jimmie Henderson, who played the tiple, and second tenor Ernie Price, who played both tiple and guitar. Even before their first recordings, they appeared in the 1938 movies *The Duke Is Tops*, a musical starring Lena Horne, and *Two-Gun Man from Harlem*, a western starring the black singing cowboy Herb Jeffries.

Signed to the Bluebird label by Lester Melrose, the Cats and the Fiddle cut both jive songs and harmony ballads, the latter closer in feel to 1950s doo-wop than anything the Ink Spots recorded. Their jive songs included "Gang Busters," "Public Jitterbug No. 1," "That's On Jack, That's On," and the marijuana paean "Killin' Jive" ("You will think you've blown your top / Oh, baby, you start laughin' and you can't stop")—all from 1939. They also perform "Killin' Jive" in *The Duke Is Tops*, twirling their instruments or playing them behind their backs but omitting the "Johnny B. Goode" opening riff that Ernie Price plays as part of his tiple solo on the "Killin' Jive" record.

Explicitly referencing Cab Calloway and Fats Waller, the Cats and the Fiddle raised jive to a new level with their clever lyrics, snappy scat singing, fluid harmonies, and solid musicianship. But the closest they ever came to a hit was "I Miss You So," a romantic ballad written by Jimmie Henderson and recorded in December 1939 at the group's second studio session, with Henderson singing the lead. Henderson never profited from his song's success, however; he died of meningitis in 1940 and was replaced by Herbie Miles. After the Cats rerecorded "I Miss You So" with Miles for the Regis label in 1946 (prompting Bluebird to reissue the original), it was covered in 1947 by the Charioteers, the King Cole Trio, and the Lionel Hampton Sextet (with vocals by Roland Burton and the Hamp-Tones). But it was the Orioles' 1950 version (released in 1951 and again in 1953) that made the song a pop/doo-wop standard, covered by Bill Kenny's brother Herb Kenny (1953), Chris Connor (1956), Fats Domino (1958), Steve Gibson and the Red Caps (1959), Paul Anka (1959), Lee Andrews (1960), the Mills Brothers (1960), Little Anthony and the Imperials (1965), and Charlie Rich (1968), among others.

With varying personnel, the Cats and the Fiddle continued to perform and record through the early 1950s. In late 1940, Herbie Miles was replaced by the Virginia-born guitarist Tiny Grimes, who left in 1942 and joined Slam Stewart in California; the following year, Grimes and Stewart formed a trio with the virtuoso jazz pianist Art Tatum. Returning to New York, Grimes recorded with such jazz greats as Coleman Hawkins, Charlie Parker, and Billie Holiday, meanwhile cutting rhythm-and-blues material with singers such as Gatemouth Moore, Walter Brown, and the Three Barons. He straddled the two genres on sessions with Hot Lips Page, Dud Bascomb, and Earl Bostic, as well as with his own bands, which often included tenor saxophonist Red Prysock and pianist Freddie Redd. Around 1950, he led a kilted R&B group called the Rocking Highlanders; a couple of years later, he played on singer Screamin' Jay Hawkins's first sides. On his quintet's November 1951 recording of "Tiny's Boogie Woogie" (or "Tiny's Boogie"), Grimes, playing his four-string electric guitar, sounds like a more sophisticated Chuck Berry.

But with the rise of rock 'n' roll, he went back to straight-ahead jazz, enjoying a long career before his death in 1989.

Like Tiny Grimes or Hot Lips Page, the clarinetist and alto saxophonist Skeets Tolbert blurred the line between jazz and R&B, leaning even further toward the latter. Raised in North Carolina, he attended college in Charlotte, where he joined Taylor's Dixie Serenaders. After moving to New York in 1934, he played in a short-lived band fronted by the Olympic sprinter Jesse Owens, then took over trombonist Snub Mosley's group, performing at clubs such as the Black Cat in Greenwich Village and the Cafe Creole in Midtown, where the ensemble was cited by Maurie Orodenker in *Billboard* as "one of the best on the street of the rock-and-rollers."[80] Signed to Decca with John Hammond's help, Tolbert cut jump-blues and jive songs with his Gentlemen of Swing between 1939 and 1942 but never recorded again after the first musicians' union ban, although he did make several Soundies.[81]

Most of his records feature vocals by band members or by singers such as Babe Wallace, whose "Fine Piece of Meat" contains the verse "Yes, I know you're just as hip as can be / Whenever you're near, you do things to me / You got mellow cheeks and the right size feet / Baby, you're a fine piece of meat." Tolbert also cut a couple of songs by Jesse Stone, including "Papa's in Bed with His Britches On," which was covered by Cab Calloway. But Tolbert's own composition "Hit That Jive, Jack," which he recorded in December 1940, is his most famous song, if only because the King Cole Trio covered it in October 1941.[82]

While Skeets Tolbert's name is scarcely mentioned in jazz reference books, Nat "King" Cole remains one of the best-loved figures in American pop-music history. But Cole is now recognized almost exclusively as a balladeer, his early career as a jazz pianist and jive singer nearly forgotten. Born in Montgomery, Alabama, he grew up in Chicago, where he absorbed Earl Hines's stride-piano style. He first recorded in 1936 with a band led by his brother Eddie Cole, a bassist. Later that year, the brothers went on tour with a revival production of the Sissle and Blake review *Shuffle Along*. Eddie soon quit, but Nat went west with the show, remaining in Los Angeles after the troupe ran out of money and disbanded in 1937.

With bassist Wesley Prince and guitarist Oscar Moore, he formed the King Cole Trio to work in West Coast nightclubs. Beginning in September 1938, the group cut a series of transcription discs—for radio play only—that were broadcast by stations around the country. The repertoire on these discs consists largely of jive songs, including such nursery-rhyme takeoffs as "Three Blind Mice" "Patty Cake, Patty Cake," and "Georgie Porgie." The material is stylistically similar to the trio's later records, but female vocalists are sometimes added. On the transcription take of Cole's jivey composition "I Like to Riff," recorded in April 1939, Prince and Moore sometimes sing in responsive harmony to Cole's vocal lead, imparting more of a rock 'n' roll flavor than on versions of the same song recorded for the Ammor label in November 1940 or for Decca in July 1941, where Prince and Moore scat-sing in unison with Cole rather than harmonizing.

It was at the November 1940 session that Cole, Moore, and Prince made their first retail records as the King Cole Trio. In May and July of that year, they had recorded eight sides with Lionel Hampton for Victor under Hampton's name, including two, "Dough-Ra-Me" and "Jivin' with Jarvis," that feature Hampton, Cole, and Moore singing together as the Hampton Rhythm Boys. "These were some of my biggest-selling hits that year," Hampton writes in his autobiography, "and they also helped Nat."[83]

In December 1940, the King Cole Trio cut the first of four sessions for Decca, recording a pair of standards ("Honeysuckle Rose" and "Sweet Lorraine"), an original instrumental ("This Side Up"), and a comic novelty ("Gone with the Draft"), but no real jive songs. With support from disc jockeys such as Al Jarvis (to whom "Jivin' with Jarvis" had been dedicated), the records were successful enough to launch the trio on a national tour. The group's second Decca session took place in Chicago in March 1941 but again produced no true jive songs, although "Scotchin' with the Soda," like "Gone with the Draft," is jive in all but vocabulary. Cole moved on to New York, performing at Nick's Tavern in Greenwich Village and then Kelly's Stable on Fifty-second Street. The trio recorded "I Like to Riff" at its third Decca session, in July 1941; its final, October session for the label, also in New York, yielded the jive classics "Are You Fer It?" and "Hit That Jive, Jack," as well as the similar-sounding but practically jiveless "Call the Police."

Cole's "Hit That Jive, Jack" is faster and more jittery but, surprisingly, less jivey than Skeets Tolbert's cucumber-cool original, substituting the phrase "goin' downtown to see a man," for example, for Tolbert's "goin' to the corner to dig the man." As the flip side of Cole's first big R&B hit, the bluesy "That Ain't Right," "Hit That Jive, Jack" reached a wide but still limited audience. Cole's first pop hit was the love song "All for You," an October 1942 recording for the tiny Excelsior label that Capitol rereleased the following year, during the recording ban.

Just before its studio debut for Capitol in November 1943, Cole's trio, with Johnny Miller now on bass, recorded four sides for the Premier label, which afterward changed its name to Atlas. Oscar Moore then arranged for his older brother, guitarist Johnny Moore, to record with his own trio for Atlas. The resulting records were the first for Johnny Moore's Three Blazers, with singer-pianist Charles Brown; that group had a landmark R&B hit, "Drifting Blues," in 1946, popularizing a cool approach to the blues that echoed the King Cole Trio's jazzier nonchalance. Two of the Three Blazers' Atlas sides feature Frankie Laine, a white singer whose Cole-like crooning on "Maureen" and "Melancholy Madeline" is at opposite poles from the intensely emotional style that would soon make him a pop star.

At its first Capitol session, the King Cole Trio recorded "Straighten Up and Fly Right," a Cole composition the group had already performed for the movie *Here Comes Elmer*. The song is a jived-up variation of an African American folk tale, a different version of which was recorded in 1947 by Willie Dixon's Big Three Trio as "Signifying Monkey." A bigger smash than "All for You," "Straighten Up and Fly Right" made Cole's name, but though he had hits in 1946 with the nonsense song "The Frim Fram Sauce" and the jive-like "(Get Your Kicks on) Route 66"—the latter covered by Bing Crosby and the Andrews Sisters, Louis Jordan, Perry Como, Chuck Berry, and the Rolling Stones, among others—his output on Capitol for the duration of his career consisted mainly of romantic ballads. Following a number of personnel changes, his trio broke up in 1951, and Cole reinvented himself as a standup singer, seldom seen playing piano.

Dimly remembered today, the King Cole Trio was highly influential, inspiring such jazz trios as Art Tatum's and Oscar Peterson's. Besides being a superb singer, Cole was one of the finest jazz pianists ever, combining propulsive rhythms with progressive harmonies that anticipated the bebop of Thelonious Monk and Bud Powell. Oscar Moore, elaborating on the electric innovations of his fellow Texas native Charlie Christian, paved the way for modern jazz guitarists such as Kenny Burrell and Grant Green. As for the group's jive songs, Gunther Schuller writes, "the taste and sheer skill with which the King Cole Trio handled such material was of such high order that they all but turned it into a new art form."[84]

Cole was a principal model for both Ray Charles and Chuck Berry. Charles, by his own admission, imitated Cole (as well as Charles Brown) in the early part of his career, making some of his first records with a guitar-bass-and-piano trio. He even cut a 1949 session for Swing Time with Johnny Miller and Oscar Moore, crooning like Cole's clone on the standard "I Wonder Who's Kissing Her Now." "He influenced me above all others," Charles writes of Cole in his autobiography. "Musically, I walked in his footsteps until I found a stride of my own."[85] Berry, too, was deeply indebted to Cole, less for his jive songs, ironically, than for his ballads. "Listening to my idol Nat Cole prompted me to sing sentimental songs with distinct diction," Berry writes.[86]

Perhaps the jivingest of the jive singers, possibly excepting the bebop vocalist Babs Gonzales, was Harry "the Hipster" Gibson, a white singer-pianist who combined jive with boogie-woogie in a frenzied act that prefigured 1950s rock 'n' roll. On the remarkably rock-like "4F Ferdinand, the Frantic Freak," from 1944, he pounds out a Pete Johnson–esque boogie while talk-singing couplets such as "He's got epileptic fits, a very bad rash / Now he's 4F Ferdinand in the draft." Watching the Soundies that Gibson made the same year, where he stands at the piano or crouches atop the bench, mugging and rolling his eyes as he attacks the keyboard, one is inescapably reminded—despite Gibson's superior technique—of Jerry Lee Lewis, if not Little Richard. "Everybody acted like a gentleman until I got into it," Gibson reminisced.[87]

Born into a musical family in the Bronx, Harry Raab began playing in a white jazz band at age thirteen; a couple of years later he joined a black band and was invited to the Rhythm Club, a musicians' hangout in Harlem. He picked up pointers from Harlem pianists and learned Fats Waller's style by listening to his records. He was filling in for the regular pianist at a Harlem nightclub in the late 1930s when he was discovered by Waller himself, who hired him to play during intermissions at his steady gig at the Yacht Club on Fifty-second Street.[88] Soon, Gibson—he'd taken the surname from a brand of gin—was a Swing Street institution, incorporating many of Waller's stage mannerisms but with boogie rhythms and a jivier vocabulary. He began writing his own material and in April 1944 recorded an album for the classical Musicraft label—*Boogie Woogie in Blue,* featuring Big Sid Catlett on drums and including a jive glossary on the inside cover.

The album included his self-referential song "Handsome Harry, the Hipster" ("He's frantic and fanatic / With jive he's an addict"), where he plays the "Johnny B. Goode" opening riff in his piano solo before breaking into a torrid boogie-woogie. Gibson claimed to have coined the word "hipster" after musicians started using the word "hip" to replace "hep." He even recorded a song called "It Ain't Hep," explaining the change with lines such as "Man, you ain't hip if you don't get hip to this 'hip' and 'hep' jive."

The success of *Boogie Woogie in Blue* landed Gibson a yearlong engagement at Billy Berg's club in Hollywood, where he was often billed together with Slim Gaillard; a number of the shows were recorded for broadcast by the Armed Forces Radio Service. In 1946, Gibson appeared in the teen movie *Junior Prom*, turning a classroom into a dance hall with a jiving performance of "Keep the Beat." The same year, he recorded his signature song, "Who Put the Benzedrine in Mrs. Murphy's Ovaltine?" for Musicraft, with Gaillard on guitar and Zutty Singleton on drums. In its March 25, 1946, issue, *Time* magazine reported that the Los Angeles radio station KMPC had banned both Gibson's and Gaillard's records on the grounds that "be-bop," as program director Ted Steele referred to their music, "tends to make degenerates out of our young listeners."[89]

After returning east with the touring company of the Mae West stage comedy *Come On Up*, Gibson worked nightclubs with the likes of Louis Armstrong, Stuff Smith, and the jive comedian Lord Buckley. In 1947, he recorded an album for the Diamond label and a half-dozen transcription discs for Armed Forces Radio. In 1953, perhaps inspired by Buckley, he recorded several jived-up fairy tales for Aladdin ("the little beanstalk said, 'Hey boy, lay a deuce on the man, take me to your pad, and stash me out in the back yard'"). In 1957, Gibson issued a single and an EP on his own Hip label, but he did not record again until 1974, when he cut a pair of singles in California. Two years later, he made the album *Harry the Hipster Digs Christmas,* including such spoofs as "Twas the Night Before Christmas Boogie." Embracing the role of hippie godfather, he recorded two more albums in the 1980s, the second not released until after his 1991 suicide.

Partly because of an association with drug abuse that musicians such as Gibson did little to dispel, jive fell from mainstream favor after World War II, lingering on among beboppers and beatniks, as well as rhythm-and-blues singers, who tended to celebrate alcohol rather than drugs. In other words, jive went underground, resurfacing briefly during the rock 'n' roll explosion of the mid-1950s, as when Little Richard sang, "Oh, big conniver, nothin' but a jiver / I done got hip to your jive" on his 1956 hit "Slippin' and Slidin' (Peepin' and Hidin')." Over time, jive talk faded from rock music, as the genre distanced itself from its African American roots; meanwhile, R&B artists updated their lyrics with newer slang.

BIG BAND JUMP

While jive songs were often associated with small groups, jump music, although sometimes performed by combos such as the Savoy Sultans, was largely the province of the big bands. Along with Count Basie's, Andy Kirk's, and Jimmie Lunceford's bands, those of Erskine Hawkins, Lionel Hampton, Buddy Johnson, and Jay McShann were part of the musical movement that led to the birth of rhythm-and-blues. All these bandleaders were originally from the Midwest, South, or Southwest; arriving in New York in the 1930s or early 1940s, they brought with them a bluesy sensibility lacking in such established Harlem bands as Claude Hopkins's, which could (and did) make a tune called "Swingin' and Jivin'" sound stiff and lame.

Born in Birmingham, Alabama, Erskine Hawkins took up the trumpet as a teenager, inspired by Louis Armstrong. At State Teachers College in Montgomery, he joined the 'Bama State Collegians, a student band that toured to raise money for the school. The Collegians were so well received at their 1934 Harlem debut that the group turned professional; two years later, they returned to New York and recorded for Vocalion, with Hawkins—already known for his flashy high-note playing—as their leader. Under Moe Gale's management, the band became the Erskine Hawkins Orchestra in 1938, recording for Bluebird and performing regularly at the Savoy Ballroom.

Mixing hot and sweet material, Hawkins patterned his ensemble sound after Jimmie Lunceford's, with rich, danceable arrangements by trumpeter Sammy Lowe, pianist Avery Parrish, and alto saxophonist Bill Johnson. The personnel roster was unusually stable, with several of the original 'Bama State Collegians remaining until Hawkins reduced his big band to a combo in

1953. Among the band's stalwarts were alto saxophonist Jimmy Mitchelle (who also sang the blues or crooned in the style of Dan Grissom or Pha Terrell), baritone saxophonist Haywood Henry, tenor saxophonist Paul Bascomb, and trumpeter Wilbur "Dud" Bascomb, Paul's younger brother.

Hawkins's biggest hit was "Tuxedo Junction," a catchy riff tune written by Hawkins with Bill Johnson and tenor saxophonist Julian Dash and recorded in July 1939. The tune was a No. 1 hit for Glenn Miller the following year and was also covered by Jan Savitt, Gene Krupa, Ella Fitzgerald, and the Andrews Sisters, to name a few. Among other noteworthy Hawkins recordings are the classic "After Hours," a mellow Avery Parrish piano boogie from June 1940, and "Tippin' In," an Ellington-esque swing tune from January 1945. Hawkins maintained his popularity after World War II, turning toward rhythm-and-blues with songs such as "Big Fat Sam," from December 1947, where Jimmy Mitchelle's singing about a Birmingham glutton is accompanied by a chorus of band members and a handclapped backbeat.

Paul and Dud Bascomb left Hawkins in 1944 and formed their own band in New York, performing at the Downbeat Club on Fifty-second Street.[90] Dud had played the famous trumpet solo on "Tuxedo Junction," often mistakenly credited to Hawkins. Paul's saxophone solo on "Big John's Special," from September 1936, may contain the first true example of R&B-style honking on record. In 1946, the brothers split up to lead separate groups, Dud's oriented more toward bebop and Paul's toward rhythm-and-blues. Drummer Albert Alston plays a pounding backbeat on Paul Bascomb's "Leap Frog Blues," recorded for the Alert label in 1946. Bascomb switched to the Manor label the following year and began singing under the name Manhattan Paul. His boisterous "Rock and Roll" (usually dated to 1947 but more likely recorded in 1948, after Wynonie Harris's "Good Rockin' Tonight") alternates verse-and-refrain and standard blues choruses, with a swing rather than rhythm-and-blues saxophone solo. While remaining jazzy, Bascomb's style becomes more R&B-like on the sides he cut for the States label in 1952. But the shuffling "Mumbles Blues," which he recorded for Mercury in August of that year, is outright rock 'n' roll, with a stuttering vocal that anticipates the Rivingtons' "Papa-Oom-Mow-Mow" and the Trashmen's "Surfin' Bird" by a decade.[91]

Julian Dash, a Hawkins sideman from 1938 until 1953, cut his own jazzy R&B records for Mercury, Vee-Jay, and other labels in the early 1950s. Bill Johnson formed his Musical Notes, a combo that set vocal harmonies to jump rhythms, in 1946. "Rock, rock, rock, everybody," Johnson shouts on "Elevator Boogie," recorded for RCA Victor in August 1947. Several of Johnson's recordings were later covered by such doo-wop groups as the Orioles ("Don't You Think I Ought to Know") and the Flamingos ("Dream of a Lifetime"). Haywood Henry played rock 'n' roll shows as a member of Alan Freed's mid-1950s stage band, along with Sam "the Man" Taylor and Big Al Sears.

And Sammy Lowe went on to arrange and conduct recording sessions for such rock and soul artists as the Platters ("My Prayer"), Sam Cooke ("Sad Mood"), the Tokens ("The Lion Sleeps Tonight"), and James Brown ("It's a Man's Man's Man's World"). Among the musicians on "It's a Man's Man's Man's World" are Dud Bascomb and Haywood Henry. Erskine Hawkins himself continued to perform into the 1980s, dying in 1993.

Lionel Hampton had perhaps the most enduringly successful career of any jazz musician. Born in Louisville, raised in Birmingham and Chicago, he learned to play drums in a youth band sponsored by the *Chicago Defender,* an African American newspaper. In high school, he played in a band led by an older teenager, Les Hite; after Hite moved to California, he got Hampton a job in Paul Howard's Los Angeles–based band, which Hite took over in 1930. "He wanted me because I had a different style on drums," Hampton recalled. "I was already playing with a heavy afterbeat, getting that rock-and-roll beat that wouldn't even get popular until the 1950s."[92] Backbeats can indeed be heard on many of the sides Hampton recorded with Howard for Victor in 1929 and 1930, but they are mostly supplied by banjo player Thomas Valentine.

Louis Armstrong, sojourning on the West Coast, fronted Hite's band from the summer of 1930 to the spring of 1931. On a recording session in October 1930, Hampton played a vibraphone that Armstrong had noticed in the studio, popularizing the xylophone-like device as a jazz instrument; it soon became his instrument of choice, although he continued to play drums and two-fingered piano. Hampton was leading his own band at a Los Angeles club in August 1936 when Benny Goodman dropped in; duly impressed, he hired Hampton to record with him in a quartet including Teddy Wilson on piano and Gene Krupa on drums. For the next four years, Hampton toured with Goodman's quartet, quintet, and sextet, racially integrated groups that performed between the shows of but not together on stage with Goodman's all-white big band. Meanwhile, Hampton recorded for Victor under his own name with various pickup bands, which, since they did not perform live, could include both black and white musicians. These recordings, featuring Johnny Hodges, Coleman Hawkins, Harry James, and other instrumental stars, are generally in a mainstream swing mold; with such exceptions as "The Jumpin' Jive," they scarcely hint at rhythm-and-blues.

Hampton formed his own, all-black big band in late 1940 and, after a couple of Victor sessions, began recording for Decca the following year. The band's studio output was quite conventional until May 1942, when Hampton cut "Flying Home," a tune he had previously recorded with Goodman's sextet (including Charlie Christian) in October 1939 and on his own in February 1940. Hampton always maintained that he'd come up with the melody himself but had to share the composer's credit with Goodman; John Hammond, however, attributed the theme to Charlie Christian.[93] Hampton's 1940 recording of "Flying Home," featuring a Budd Johnson tenor saxophone solo that was punctuated with several honks, had already been a hit. What made the 1942 recording stand out—besides Hampton's flag-waving arrangement—was the tenor saxophone solo by Illinois Jacquet, a nineteen-year-old from Houston who'd just switched from alto sax to join Hampton's band. "I experimented at the Apollo Theatre, and one day I played a solo similar to the one I did on the record, and the house stood," Jacquet recalled. "When we got ready to make the record, as I was walking to the mike, Marshall Royal, who was the straw boss in Hamp's band, said, 'Go for yourself, man,' because he knew I could do it. And I *heard* that."[94]

At first, Jacquet's solo follows the basic contours of Budd Johnson's, in a style grainier than but otherwise similar to that of Jacquet's idol, Herschel Evans, who'd played with both Hampton and Count Basie before dying in 1939, a month shy of his thirtieth birthday. But then, as trombones riff insistently behind him, Jacquet breaks into a series of irresistibly urgent cries—not honks—that he repeats before playing a final chorus. After the full band comes in, the number climaxes with a vibraphone figure that anticipates the "What makes your big head so hard?" rhythm in Louis Jordan's "Caldonia."

"Flying Home," in its 1942 incarnation, quickly became Hampton's theme song, an ideal vehicle for his energy—he'd been billed as "the World's Fastest Drummer"—and showmanship.[95] "I would come up with things like this at the Apollo," Hampton told writer Ted Fox. "I used to have this part in 'Flyin' Home' [sic] where the lights would go out and you'd see airplanes projected on the scrim behind the bandstand. You'd hear the motors humming and that's when the saxophone player, Illinois Jacquet . . . started playin'. . . . The band would be shouting down, and we used to have a lot of acrobatic stuff with the horns. . . . Everybody'd be rockin'. We were the originators of that." Malcolm X described one of Hampton's shows at the Savoy Ballroom: "The people kept shouting for Hamp's 'Flyin' Home,' and finally he did it. . . . I had never seen such fever-heat dancing."[96]

Jacquet left Hampton in 1943 and joined Cab Calloway's band, with which he appeared in the movie *Stormy Weather,* starring Bill "Bojangles" Robinson and Lena Horne. Although he made no commercial recordings with Calloway, some of the band's radio performances were captured on transcription discs, including "105 in the Shade," where Jacquet's horn leaps into an unusually high register. Jacquet left Calloway and formed a quintet in Los Angeles in 1944; in July of that year, he played together with Nat "King" Cole, guitarist Les Paul, and others in a benefit concert staged by the promoter Norman Granz at L.A.'s Philharmonic Auditorium. The performance was recorded for broadcast on Armed Forces Radio, and Granz had the recordings released commercially, first on Moses Asch's Disc label and then, after Disc went bankrupt, on Mercury. A ten-minute jam titled "Blues" was divided among three 78-rpm sides, with "Blues, Pt. 2" containing a saxophone solo where Jacquet, after working up a head of steam, breaks into prolonged, freakishly high shrieks.

The show became the basis for Jazz at the Philharmonic, the long-running concert series with which Jacquet toured and recorded into the 1950s. "Blues, Pt. 2," coming on the heels of "Flying Home," secured his reputation as a frantic saxophone howler, the object of popular adulation and critical scorn. Following a stint with Count Basie at the end of World War II, Jacquet divided his time between Jazz and the Philharmonic and his own groups. In August 1945, his band backed Wynonie Harris on "Wynonie's Blues" and "Here Comes the Blues." Through the end of the decade, he recorded for Aladdin, Apollo, Savoy, and Victor—fiery tunes that mixed swing, blues, and bebop as well as original ballads such as "Black Velvet" and "Robbin's Nest" that helped redeem him in critics' eyes. In the 1950s, he turned toward straight-ahead jazz, recording mostly for Norman Granz's Clef label; his 1952 hit "Port of Rico," with Count Basie playing organ, prefigured the soul-jazz of Jimmy Smith and others. He struggled through the 1960s and 1970s but made a comeback in the 1980s, leading a big band until his death in 2004. But his chief legacy is the fervid saxophone style that inspired a generation of R&B honkers, setting the feverish tone for the rock-guitar rhapsodies that followed.

Jacquet's replacement in Lionel Hampton's band was Arnett Cobb, also from Houston. On the same March 1944 date that the band cut "Hamp's Boogie Woogie," Cobb played a honking, wailing, huge-toned solo on the rearranged "Flying Home, No. 2." Cobb formed his own group in 1947, recording for Apollo, OKeh, and other labels through the 1950s in a swinging style only lightly tinged with R&B.

In August 1945, Helen Humes, who'd sung with Count Basie and others, recorded the bluesy "Be-Baba-Leba" with Bill Doggett's band, including Wild Bill Moore on tenor saxophone. Adapted from saxophonist Big Jim Wynn's "Ee-Bobaliba" and likewise shifting from a blues structure to twelve-bar verse-and-refrain, Humes's hit version is virtually pure R&B, with an intermittent backbeat and boogie bass line. In December 1945, Hampton sang on his own variation, "Hey! Ba-Ba-Re-Bop," which despite its clunky rhythm was a much bigger hit. Later the same month, Wynonie Harris covered "Hey! Ba-Ba-Re-Bop" with members of Hampton's band for Hampton's short-lived Hamp-Tone label. Louis Prima cut it with his big band in April 1946, but the best-selling version was the one recorded in May 1946 by Tex Beneke, the tenor saxophonist who assumed the leadership of Glenn Miller's band after Miller's death in 1944. The song's appeal proved broad enough that it was recorded by Leon McAuliffe, the western-swing steel guitarist; Natalino Otto, the pioneering Italian swing singer; and Ernest Léardée, a Martinican violinist and saxophonist who helped introduce the biguine to Paris. Humes reprised "Be-Baba-Leba" with Dizzy Gillespie's big band in the 1946 film *Jivin' in Be-Bop.* The rhythm-and-blues singer Thurston Harris revived the song in 1958, giving it an all-out rock 'n' roll treatment. The following year Chuck Berry recyled Harris's (and Humes's) opening line, "Oh well, oh well, I feel so fine today," on his "Back in the U.S.A.," changing "fine" back to Wynn's original "good."

Hampton's boisterous brand of jazz did not appeal to critics such as Gunther Schuller, who wrote in the 1980s that "Hampton foreshadowed the empty-minded hysteria of today's more outrageous rock singers. Nor is the distance between rock and Hampton's 1940s' early form of rhythm-and-blues all that great, certainly not in respect to its rhythmic, dynamic, and energy levels."[97] But with his populist approach, Hampton was able to maintain his big band well into the 1960s, long after most swing-era outfits had folded. In his autobiography, he complains that his style was misconstrued during a tour of England in 1956. "There we were giving concerts of music in a program I had worked out . . . a kind of history of jazz. Meanwhile, people think it's mostly rock and roll."[98] He had no apparent qualms, however, about performing alongside Chuck Berry, Little Richard, Screamin' Jay Hawkins, and other rockers in the 1957 Alan Freed movie *Mister Rock and Roll.* By the 1960s, Hampton's music had lost whatever allure it may have had for rock fans, but he continued to perform and record, mostly with small groups, almost up to his death in 2002, at the age of ninety-four.

No bandleader made the transition from swing to rhythm-and-blues more smoothly than Buddy Johnson. Even his earliest recording session, done for Decca in November 1939, has a strong R&B feel, thanks largely to the harmony vocals of the Mack Sisters. A song written by Johnson for that session, "Stop Pretending (So Hip You See)," was a hit for the Ink Spots in 1940 and was also covered that year by Fats Waller. His second session, in October 1940, featured his younger sister Ella singing on the eerily minor-ish "Please, Mr. Johnson," which Amos Milburn transformed into a Charles Brown–style blues in 1952. "Boogie Woogie's Mother-in-Law," a showcase for Leonard Ware's steel guitar recorded in April 1941 at Johnson's third session, was the basis for the Mississippi bluesman Elmore James's 1952 "Hawaiian Boogie." The hit ballad "Baby, Don't You Cry," crooned by Warren Evans on Johnson's November 1941 recording, was covered by Charles Brown in 1945; Ray Charles, setting the song to his bossa-like "new swingova rhythm," made it a hit again in 1964.

Trumpeter Chester Boone sings on Johnson's "I Ain't Mad with You," from January 1942, which Gatemouth Moore accelerated into "I Ain't Mad at You, Pretty Baby" in May 1945. A few days later, Count Basie segued between two songs on his V-Disc recording "High Tide/I Ain't Mad at You," featuring a raucous, scatting vocal by Taps Miller; Basie rerecorded the paired tunes for Columbia a few months later. Wynonie Harris borrowed the line "I ain't mad at you, don't be mad with me" for his August 1945 recording of "Wynonie's Blues." Jesse Price, a drummer and singer who'd played with Basie in Kansas City, cut an altered "I Ain't Mad at You" with an octet in October 1946 and with a quartet in April 1947. Basie scored a pop hit with his May 1947 recording of his peculiarly rising and falling "I Ain't Mad at You," again featuring Taps Miller. In August 1949, Jimmy "Baby Face" Lewis, a Harlem-based singer-guitarist, adapted the song as the hard-rocking "I'm So Good to You (Pretty Baby)." Huey "Piano" Smith used elements of Lewis's and Moore's versions to write the even harder-rocking "Roberta," which the white New Orleanian Frankie Ford, backed by Smith's band, sang on the flip side of his 1959 rock 'n' roll hit "Sea Cruise." The British rock group the Animals covered "Roberta" on the 1965 album *Animal Tracks*.

But though Johnson has been slighted by jazz historians and sometimes categorized as an R&B artist, he was steeped in swing. His November 1941 cover of Sam Theard's "I Wonder Who's Boogiein' My Woogie," which Theard recorded with Oscar's Chicago Swingers in May 1936, provides a good example. Melodically based on Speckled Red's "The Dirty Dozen," Theard's original is already jazzy, but in a traditional way, with striding rhythms and an Armstrong-like trumpet solo that quotes "Old Folks at Home." Johnson's riffing version, sung by Chester Boone, sounds more like a Lunceford or Basie arrangement, with a sleek tenor saxophone solo by the former Louis Jordan sideman Kenneth Hollon.

Having studied piano in his home town of Darlington, South Carolina, Johnson moved to New York in 1938. After touring Europe with the Tramp Band, a washboard group that performed in hobo costumes at the Cotton Club and Apollo Theatre, he began recording with his own combo, which he gradually expanded into a big band. Buddy himself sang on his first charted hit, "Let's Beat Out Some Love," from July 1942, but it was Ella Johnson's bluesy, ingenuous vocals that sparked Johnson's biggest sellers—"When My Man Comes Home," also from July 1942, and "That's the Stuff You Gotta Watch" from October 1944. Among the band's other singers were Arthur Prysock and Etta Jones.

Prysock's lush baritone is featured on the hit ballad "They All Say I'm the Biggest Fool," while Buddy sings on "Fine Brown Frame" (a 1948 R&B smash for Nellie Lutcher), both from the same date as "That's the Stuff You Gotta Watch." A November 1945 session yielded the gorgeous ballad "Since I Fell for You" and the strutting blues "Walk 'Em," both composed by Buddy Johnson: the former exposed Ella Johnson's vocal shortcomings but was revived as an R&B hit by Annie Laurie in 1947 and became a standard after Lenny Welch's 1963 recording crossed over to the pop charts; the latter, with its shuffling backbeat, defined the band's trademark postwar dance rhythm.

Like Lionel Hampton, Johnson was able to keep his big band together long after the swing era ended. Between residencies at the Savoy Ballroom, he maintained a tour schedule so hectic that he was nicknamed the King of the One-Nighters. Although he sometimes performed for whites and occasionally crossed over to the pop charts with hits such as "Did You See Jackie Robinson Hit That Ball?" from June 1949, he concentrated his efforts on southern black audiences. "They don't want the Ellington type of music in the halls where I play. . . . They come to dance and they want to hear that beat," he told the writer John S. Wilson in 1950. "We've set our style now and we can't change it to please New York because our bread and butter is in the south."[99]

Johnson's music veered even further toward rhythm-and-blues, complete with honking tenor saxophone solos by Purvis Henson, after he switched to the Mercury label in 1953. He recorded a pair of R&B hits that year, "Hittin' on Me" ("I don't want no man who always hittin' on me / The last man that hit me has been dead since '43") and "I'm Just Your Fool," both sung by Ella Johnson. Also in 1953, Buddy's band appeared in the "Biggest Rhythm and Blues Show," a package tour whose Cleveland concert was promoted by Alan Freed. The group also performed for Freed's first East Coast show, the "Mayday Moondog Coronation Ball" in Newark, New Jersey, in May 1954; for his first New York show, the "Rock 'n' Roll Jubilee Ball," in January 1955; and for his "Diddley Daddy" show (headlined by Bo Diddley) in Boston in May 1955, as well as for the "Rock 'n' Roll Revue" presented in New York in February 1957 by Freed's rival disc jockey Jocko Henderson.[100]

Some of Johnson's mid-1950s recordings are out-and-out rock 'n' roll, in big-band form. These include "Ain't Cha Got Me (Where You Want Me)," from July 1953; "So Good," from August 1955; and "They Don't Want Me to Rock No More," from June 1957—all sung by Ella Johnson. Buddy talk-sings on his final R&B hit, "Rock On!" from January 1957, which was backed with another rocker, "Oh! Baby Don't You Know." But though he tried to keep up with the times, Johnson, entering middle age, could no longer attract young audiences. After an album for Roulette and a single for the Old Town label, he retired in the early 1960s, just as his health began to fail. He died in 1977; Ella Johnson, who quit the music business in order to care for her brother, died in 2004.

Jay McShann led the last territory band to achieve national prominence. Born in Muskogee, Oklahoma, he taught himself piano behind the backs of his disapproving parents, inspired by James P. Johnson's accompaniment on Bessie Smith's "Back Water Blues," a record he found in his father's furniture-moving truck. Modeling his style after Earl Hines's, he played in a few bands before moving to Kansas City, where, after hearing Pete Johnson and Big Joe Turner, he added boogie-woogies and blues to his repertoire. He formed a combo in 1938 and expanded it to a big band, including the teenage Charlie Parker on alto saxophone. With the help of the journalist Dave Dexter, McShann obtained a recording contract with Decca, hiring the blues singer Walter Brown, a Dallas native, shortly before the first session.

On that April 1941 date, the band cut "Swingmatism," a state-of-the-art jazz arrangement, but at the insistence of producer Dave Kapp (the brother of Jack Kapp and the man who'd signed Count Basie to Decca), the remaining material consisted of blues and boogies, using only a rhythm section on three of the six sides. Kapp's judgment was vindicated when the initial release—"Confessin' the Blues," featuring Walter Brown singing with the rhythm section—became a big hit. (It was covered by the Chicago bluesman Little Walter in 1958 and by the Rolling Stones in 1964.) The flip side, "Hootie Blues," where Brown sings with the full band, caught the ears of forward-looking musicians around the country for its single-chorus solo by Charlie Parker, which hints at the bebop revolution Parker was about to launch.

Conceived as a Basie-style swing band, McShann's group was marketed as a jump-blues combo. Eager to repeat the success of "Confessin' the Blues," Dave Kapp omitted most of the brass and reed instruments throughout McShann's second session, in November 1941, with Walter Brown singing the blues on all but one tune. After touring the South and Midwest, McShann's ensemble made its triumphant New York debut at the Savoy Ballroom in February 1942, defeating Lucky Millinder's group in a battle of the bands. Critics who saw the full band in performance complained that the recordings didn't do it justice, so Kapp included all sixteen members on the group's July 1942 session, shortly before the union recording ban took effect.[101] Only two of the four numbers were blues, sung by Walter Brown; one was a ballad, marking the recorded debut of singer Al Hibbler, who would soon find fame with Duke Ellington's band; and one, "Sepian Bounce," was a swinging instrumental.

McShann's solo on "The Jumpin' Blues," from that date, contains the seeds of Nat "King" Cole's "(Get Your Kicks on) Route 66," or at least its distinctive Oscar Moore guitar riff, while Parker's solo opens with the same phrase as his 1946 bebop classic "Ornithology." A true jump blues in the original sense of the term, with Walter Brown singing "Forget your troubles and jump your blues away" as the band riffs propulsively in swing rhythm, "The Jumpin' Blues" illustrates the close connection between two nascent genres that would soon part company—bebop and rhythm-and-blues. "A lot of that stuff we were doin' was strictly on that bop kick," McShann acknowledged. "So I said, 'Wait a minute. We keep this shit up here, we ain't gonna be swingin'."[102]

When the recording ban ended, McShann did one more session for Decca, without Parker, before being drafted in 1944. Given a medical discharge after a few months, he re-formed his big band in New York but disbanded it in Los Angeles and formed a combo, replacing Walter Brown with the suave Arkansas-born shouter Jimmy Witherspoon. McShann recorded for several independent labels, cutting "Ain't Nobody's Business," a bluesy standard first popularized by Bessie Smith, for Supreme in November 1947. Released in 1949 under Witherspoon's name (since McShann was under contract to Mercury at the time), the record shot to the top of the rhythm-and-blues charts.[103] McShann had two more R&B hits under his own name around the same time with the blues instrumentals "Hot Biscuits" and "Buttermilk," both recorded for the Down Beat label in July 1948.

But in the early 1950s, McShann stopped touring and recording and settled in Kansas City, performing locally with a sextet. He returned to the studio in September 1955 to cut several tracks for Vee-Jay in Chicago, one of which, "Hands Off," written and sung by the Kansas City native Priscilla Bowman, quickly became a No. 1 R&B hit. The lyrics date back at least as far as Big Bill Broonzy's "Keep Your Hands Off Her," from October 1935, but McShann's arrangement is surprisingly modern, rhythmically similar to the one on the Cadillacs' doo-wop classic "Speedoo," recorded around the same time. (The opening bars of "Hands Off" have a strikingly reggae-like feel, and the song was reportedly popular in Jamaica.) "Hands Off" is the obvious basis for Ann Cole's "Got My Mo-Jo Working (but It Just Won't Work on You)," which Muddy Waters adopted as his theme song; Elvis Presley put the two songs together on a June 1970 studio jam that was released on the album *Love Letters from Elvis*.[104]

With the success of "Hands Off," McShann again took to the road, stopping in Chicago in January 1956 to record another Vee-Jay session with Bowman. In what may have been his closest brush with rock 'n' roll, McShann backed Bowman at Chicago's Regal Theater on an early-1957 bill that included Screamin' Jay Hawkins, Gene and Eunice, the El Dorados, and Big Joe Turner. Later that year, Bowman went off on her own, and McShann reunited with Jimmy Witherspoon to record the nostalgic album *Goin' to Kansas City Blues* for RCA Victor. His next recording, the 1966 album *McShann's Piano,* was made possible by Dave Dexter, who had become a powerful executive at Capitol, having signed the Beatles to the label.

In the 1960s, McShann began touring Europe, where he would perform frequently until the mid-1990s. From 1969 on, McShann recorded prolifically in the United States, Canada, and Europe, playing (and occasionally singing on) standards as well as his older material. Together with Count Basie, Big Joe Turner, and others, he appeared in the 1979 film *The Last of the Blue Devils,* documenting a 1974 reunion of Kansas City musicians that McShann later characterized as "a good drunk weekend."[105] He also appeared in the Clint Eastwood–directed "Piano Blues" segment of Martin Scorsese's 2003 PBS video series *The Blues*. He died in Kansas City in 2006, at the age of ninety, remembered more as a master of jazz, blues, and boogie-woogie than as the successful and influential R&B artist he had also been.

JUMP, JIVE, AN' WAIL

Louis Prima spanned the historical gamut from traditional New Orleans jazz to small-combo jive to big-band jump to rhythm-and-blues and rock 'n' roll, with Italian-accented novelty songs thrown in. Born into the large Italian-American community in New Orleans, Prima abandoned the violin, his first instrument, to follow in the footsteps of his cornet-playing older brother, Leon. In his early teens, he formed his first band, including clarinetist Irving Fazola; influenced primarily by Louis Armstrong, he played trumpet in a number of groups, including a theater orchestra with which he also sang and danced in costumed skits. He played with Red Nichols in Cleveland in 1932 and made a record for Bluebird with the Hotcha Trio (including pianist David Rose, the future composer of "Holiday for Strings" and "The Stripper") in Chicago in 1933, scat-singing like Armstrong on "Chinatown, My Chinatown" and "Dinah." He was back in New Orleans in 1934, performing at a nightclub owned by his brother, when he was discovered by Guy Lombardo, who persuaded him to move to New York.

Even with Lombardo's help, Prima was unable to land a Big Apple gig for months after his arrival. Beginning in September 1934, however, he made a series of recordings for Brunswick with a septet billed as His New Orleans Gang, although most of the musicians were not New Orleanians. Stylistically, the music falls between Dixieland and swing, with Prima singing on nearly every number in what one listener called "that hoarse, horny voice of his."[106] Finally booked for the opening week of the Famous Door on Fifty-second Street in March 1935, he was an overnight sensation, packing the house with musicians, adoring women, wide-eyed teenagers, and journalists.[107] Soon Prima was being featured on a nationally broadcast CBS radio show called *Swing It*.[108]

Reporting in the December 28, 1935, issue of *The Billboard* (as *Billboard* magazine was then called), Jerry Franken identified the Famous Door as the spawning ground for the white combos he termed jam bands and cited Prima's group, with Pee Wee Russell on clarinet, as the spearhead of this new trend. "The music of a jam band is the music of a hot Negro orchestra made more compact, even hotter," Franken wrote. "That may explain why people like it—because it is savagely rhythmic, almost primitive in its qualities."[109] Prima's "jam band" style—a crude update of Louis Armstrong's Hot Five and Hot Seven sound, with more singing—is displayed on the critically respected pop hits he recorded for Brunswick between April and June of 1935. For example, on his de-Latinized "The Lady in Red," a song introduced that year by Xavier Cugat, he intertwines improvised licks with Russell, then sings in a style that colors Armstrong's rhythmic growl with Fats Waller's sense of parody and a foretaste of Harry "the Hipster" Gibson's frenzy.

In the fall of 1935, at the height of his early success, Prima moved to Los Angeles with his combo and opened his own Famous Door club, not affiliated with the original one. Before long, he was appearing in movies—short subjects showcasing his band, such as *Swing It,* as well as feature films such as *Rhythm on the Range, The Champ's a Chump, You Can't Have Everything,* and *Manhattan Merry-Go-Round,* where he played small parts as a musician or bandleader, often himself. In February 1936, he recorded his own composition "Sing, Sing, Sing" for Brunswick; the following year, Benny Goodman cut a double-sided version for Victor, driven by Gene Krupa's pounding drums, that became the best-known anthem of the swing era.

Later in 1936, Prima expanded his group to twelve pieces and played a heavily publicized engagement in Chicago, where he also recorded four sides for Vocalion. But the big band was poorly received, and in late 1937 Prima returned to the Famous Door in New York for an extended engagement with a new combo. In 1938, he took his group on the road, touring mostly around the East Coast, meanwhile recording for Decca and appearing in more movies. He formed another big band, featuring singer Lily Ann Carol, which he called the Gleeby Rhythm Orchestra on his 1940 recordings for Varsity. Turning increasingly to pop and novelty material, he alienated critics while drawing overflow crowds to large theaters around the country.[110]

Besides major downtown venues, Prima's big band regularly played black theaters such as the Royal in Baltimore, the Howard in Washington, D.C., the Regal in Chicago, the Paradise in Detroit, and the Apollo in Harlem. After attending a performance at the Howard in January 1942, Eleanor Roosevelt invited Prima to the White House, where, he later claimed, he greeted the president in hepster fashion, saying "Hello, Daddy!"[111] With his olive complexion, wavy hair, and broad features, Prima looked as though he might be of mixed race, and his gritty, New Orleans–accented singing sounded passably black. Three of his 1944 recordings for the Hit label—"I'll Walk Alone," "Robin Hood," and "The White Cliffs of Dover"—made the Harlem Hit Parade, and he became one of the first white artists to cover an R&B song when he cut "Who Threw the Whiskey in the Well?" [sic] for Majestic in 1945.

Around the end of World War II, Prima was approached by the songwriter Barbara Belle, whom he hired as his personal manager. Prima wrote (or at least took credit for writing) a song with Belle, Anita Leonard, and Stan Rhodes called "A Sunday Kind of Love," which he first cut for Majestic in February 1946. But the label did not release that or Prima's second, September recording of the song, finally issuing his third recording, from January 1947. By then, bandleader Claude Thornhill had already recorded "A Sunday Kind of Love" with singer Fran Warren, and it was Thornhill's version, along with Jo Stafford's, that made the charts. The song became a pop standard, covered by Ella Fitzgerald, Billy Eckstine, Dinah Washington,

Frankie Laine, and Kay Starr, and, beginning with the Harptones' 1953 rendition, a doo-wop favorite, recorded by the Marcels, Regents, Mystics, Earls, and Devotions. Yet none of these versions, possibly excepting the Harptones', rivals Prima's wistfully rasping original.

In April 1944, Prima recorded "Angelina," a song about a pizzeria waitress that mixes Italian phrases (*"Ti voglio bene"*) with references to minestrone, spumoni, lasagna, and the like ("What's the story with the chicken cacciatore?"). It was a hit, and Prima followed with "Please No Squeeza da Banana," "Felicia No Capicia," and "Baciagaloop (Makes Love on the Stoop)." Italian immigrants had been caricatured in song as far back as the 1880s, when Frank Dumont published "The Dagoe Banana Peddler," with verses such as "Plenty garlic and nice maccaroni [sic], / For my dinner I want ev'ry day, / In de winter I buy me a monkey, / And in front of your house I will play."[112] Irving Berlin's earliest songs include at least a dozen Italian-dialect numbers, among them "Sweet Italian Love" (1910), "Dat's-a My Gal" (1911), and "Hey Wop" (1914). Songs about Irish, German, Jewish, and other immigrants were also popular, but the vogue for Italian-themed material lasted longest, continuing into the 1950s and 1960s with hits such as Rosemary Clooney's "Botch-A-Me," Dean Martin's "That's Amore," and Jay and the Americans' "Cara, Mia."

Besides Italian novelties, Prima's repertoire included everything from Louis Jordan's "Caldonia" to the calypso "Rum and Coca-Cola," the 1917 minstrel song "It Takes a Long, Tall Brown-Skin Gal to Make a Preacher Lay His Bible Down," the country-flavored "Mary Lou" (with the Riders of the Purple Sage), the Yiddish-inflected "(You've Got to Have a Little) Mahzel," and the purely nonsensical "Hitsum-Kitsum-Bumpity-Itsum." One of the trademark hits that he continued to perform for the rest of his working life, along with "Angelina," was "Robin Hood," apparently inspired by the 1938 Errol Flynn swashbuckler.

Ever the entertainer, Prima had been disparaged by critics for his off-color comic stage antics since his early days on Fifty-second Street. In 1937, he made the "corn trumpet" list in the *Down Beat* readers' poll; by 1945, he was being dismissed in *Metronome* magazine as a "buffoon" whose act "consists solely of repeating the same questionable Italian jokes, wild-arm-and-leg waving, and screeching of idiotic lyrics."[113] Nevertheless, Prima's career flourished during the immediate postwar years. Like Lionel Hampton and Buddy Johnson, he was able to maintain his big band after others had foundered, and he scored two of his biggest hits with "Bell Bottom Trousers" in 1945 and "Civilization (Bongo, Bongo, Bongo)" in 1947. (The former, a cleaned-up version of a bawdy British sea chantey, was also a hit for Tony Pastor, Kay Kyser, Guy Lombardo, and Jerry Colonna, while the latter also charted for Ray McKinley, Woody Herman, Jack Smith, and the Andrews Sisters with Danny Kaye.)

In 1948, while on tour in Virginia, Prima auditioned and immediately hired a sixteen-year-old local singer named Dorothy Jacqueline Keely Smith. As Keely Smith, she would be Prima's musical partner for the next dozen years, humorously contrasting his brash exuberance with her deadpan insouciance. But Prima soon had to break up his big band; his career hit bottom in the early 1950s and did not rebound until he moved to Las Vegas and formed a new combo, the Witnesses, with tenor saxophonist Sam Butera in 1955, two years after he married Smith. For the rest of the decade, Prima was a late-night fixture at the Casbar Lounge of the Sahara Hotel—one the first of the lounge acts that came to typify the Las Vegas entertainment scene.

Reviewing a 1957 Prima performance at the Mocambo club in Hollywood, the *Down Beat* critic John Tynan wrote, "No, this isn't jazz. Often, in fact, it's downright rock 'n' roll."[114] Playing more to adult audiences than teenagers, he gave vintage material a modern feel, making new hits out of chestnuts such as "That Old Black Magic" and "I've Got You Under My Skin." On his 1956 album *The Wildest,* the first of several Capitol LPs seeking to capture the excitement of his Las Vegas shows, he segues together a pair of songs he first recorded as two sides of a 1945 V-Disc—"Just a Gigolo" (originally from the late 1920s) and "I Ain't Got Nobody" (originally from the mid-1910s)—adding a shuffling backbeat, a boogie-ish bass line, a pop-style vocal chorus, and Butera's honking saxophone. On the same album, he introduces his own composition "Jump, Jive, an' Wail," styled loosely after Big Joe Turner's "Shake, Rattle and Roll."

By the end of the 1950s, Prima was riding a wave of popularity, appearing in movies and on television shows and cutting a string of albums and singles for the Dot label. But after Smith divorced him in 1961, his career went cold. He replaced her with a younger singer, Gia Maione (whom he also married), and played long engagements in Las Vegas and Lake Tahoe with Sam Butera and the Witnesses, recording for his own Pr1ma [sic] label. In 1967, he supplied the voice for King Louie, the jive-talking orangutan in the animated Walt Disney movie *The Jungle Book,* based on Rudyard Kipling's stories. But in 1975, he underwent surgery for a benign brain tumor and lapsed into a coma, dying three years later.

In 1985, just before he split from the rock band Van Halen, singer David Lee Roth had a hit with his high-energy take on "Just a Gigolo/I Ain't Got Nobody." In 1998, the Brian Setzer Orchestra made the charts with a cover of "Jump, Jive, an' Wail," just as Prima's original was being heard on a television commercial for the clothing chain the Gap. Prima's *Jungle Book* song "I Wan'na Be Like You" was covered by Los Lobos on their 1993 album *Just Another Band from East L.A.*, by Big Bad Voodoo Daddy on the soundtrack album (but not the actual soundtrack) of the 1996 movie *Swingers,* and by Smash Mouth on the soundtrack of the 2003 sequel *The Jungle Book 2*. Prima's own recordings have been featured on dozens of movie soundtracks and his compositions on dozens more. Revered by today's swing and lounge-music revivalists, Prima ranks higher in critical esteem now than he ever did during his lifetime.

Prima was an anomaly, an artist who transcended musical eras by fitting swing tunes to a rock beat. For the most part, jump and jive music gave way to bebop and rhythm-and-blues shortly after World War II. But at its height, the swing craze united society in much the same superficial way that disco did in the 1970s, bringing people of different racial, ethnic, and social backgrounds together under the same musical umbrella. Enlisted to boost wartime morale, swing acquired the additional impetus of patriotic fervor. A number of movies served as big-screen USO shows, with flimsy plots to underpin the musical and comedic performances. Among these films was *Thousands Cheer* from 1943, starring Gene Kelly as a circus aerialist turned army private and Kathryn Grayson as a colonel's daughter who stages a variety show for the troops. The featured bands include Kay Kyser's, Bob Crosby's, and Benny Carter's; the musical numbers include Liszt's Hungarian Rhapsody no. 2 (played by José Iturbi), "Pine Top's Boogie Woogie" (danced by Eleanor Powell), and "Honeysuckle Rose" (sung by Lena Horne).

Toward the end of the movie, just before Kelly's climactic trapeze act, Judy Garland sings "The Joint Is Really Jumpin' Down at Carnegie Hall," accompanied by Iturbi, a classical pianist with a flair for showmanship. Iturbi begins with a series of classical flourishes, and Garland delivers the decorous introduction: "Millions have heard you play Chopin, the critics applaud and approve, / But millions more would simply adore to hear you get in the groove." Iturbi then plays a boogie bass line, an offscreen orchestra chimes in, and Garland sings verses that echo the Andrews Sisters' "Boogie Woogie Bugle Boy" while anticipating Chuck Berry's "Roll Over Beethoven": "They're playing deetlee-yada, deetlee-yada with Shostakovich, / Deetlee-yada, deetlee-yada, Mozart and Bach, / Deetlee-yada, deetlee-yada, and they don't know which, / 'Cause anything can happen when they start to rock."

In the same way that Walter Murphy and the Big Apple Band's "A Fifth of Beethoven" marked the peak of disco fever, "The Joint Is Really Jumpin' Down at Carnegie Hall" represents the point at which swing achieved its broadest acceptance, when jive talk and boogie rhythms extended from African American ghettos to the lily-white enclaves of the cultural elite. In the postwar years, jump and jive would fade, but not entirely disappear, from the musical mainstream, as the big bands broke up and pop singers came to the forefront. But just as disco morphed into "dance" music, swing evolved into rhythm-and-blues, which, along with country music, kept the spirit of jump alive until it could reemerge under the banner of rock 'n' roll.

Chapter Six

Get With It

COUNTRY ORIGINS

Although it's often said that rock 'n' roll originated as a fusion of country music and rhythm-and-blues, the styles of black and white musicians in the American South have intertwined at least since the days of blackface minstrelsy. Country music absorbed the influences of ragtime, blues, jazz, boogie-woogie, and rhythm-and-blues in turn; but whereas white southerners such as Jimmie Rodgers and Bob Wills achieved country-music stardom in the 1920s and 1930s by incorporating African American styles, country-rooted rockers of the 1950s such as Bill Haley and Elvis Presley used black music to conquer the pop charts.

The traditional view of country music history was that the genre stemmed mainly from British ballads and hymns. Interest in American folk music was awakened by the publication of the Harvard University professor Francis J. Child's multivolume compilations *English and Scottish Ballads* (in the late 1850s) and *The English and Scottish Popular Ballads* (in the 1880s and 1890s), which Child culled from centuries-old British manuscripts. Included were such well-known songs as "Barbara Allen" and "The Maid Freed from the Gallows," the latter recorded by Leadbelly in 1939 as "The Gallis Pole" and by Led Zeppelin in 1970 as "Gallows Pole." The American Folklore Society was established in 1888, with Child as its first president.

Child's protégé George Lyman Kittredge was a mentor to John A. Lomax when Lomax, a teacher at Texas A&M University, pursued graduate studies at Harvard. At Kittredge's suggestion, Lomax helped found the Texas Folklore Society in 1909. The following year, Lomax published his anthology *Cowboy Songs and Other Frontier Ballads.* "Out in the wild, far-away places of the big and still unpeopled West," Lomax writes, "yet survives the Anglo-

Saxon ballad spirit that was active in secluded districts in England and Scotland."[1] Another collector, N. Howard Thorp, had already published some of the same song texts in his 1908 book *Songs of the Cowboy,* but Lomax's volume, perhaps the first published collection of white American folk songs to include both words and music, had a much greater impact.

The London-born scholar Cecil Sharp began collecting English folk songs and dances in the early 1900s. During World War I, he took a number of trips to the United States to lecture and teach. In 1915, while visiting Massachusetts, he met Olive Dame Campbell, one of several American collectors who had been gathering folk songs directly from local singers in the southern Appalachians.[2] Sharp was impressed enough to spend nine weeks the following year collecting folk songs in North Carolina, Tennessee, and Virginia with his assistant, Maud Karpeles, who transcribed the texts while Sharp notated the music.[3] Putting this material together with Campbell's, he published *English Folk Songs from the Southern Appalachians* in 1917 under both their names. Included are Child ballads such as "The False Knight upon the Road" as well as American songs such as "Poor Omie," based on an 1807 murder in North Carolina but modeled after a British broadside ballad.

"It is fairly safe, I think, to conclude that the present-day residents of this section of the mountains are the descendants of those who left the shores of Britain some time in the eighteenth century," writes Sharp. "Their language, wisdom, manners, and the many graces of life that are theirs, are merely racial attributes which have been gradually acquired and accumulated in past centuries and handed down generation by generation, each generation adding its quotum to that which it received." While acknowledging that a "modern street-song" such as "John Hardy," based on an 1893 murder in West Virginia, might occasionally worm its way into the traditional canon, Sharp insists that for the average mountaineer, "the only secular music, that he hears and has, therefore, any opportunity of learning is that which his British forefathers brought with them from their native country and has since survived by oral tradition."[4]

The idea that American country music was primarily of Anglo-Saxon or Celtic origin appealed to both right-wing nativists and left-wing cosmopolitanists, who shared an aversion to anything that smacked of commercialism. But recent researchers have taken a broader approach, stressing the importance of religious as well as secular music, the prevalence of commercial as well as folkloric material, and the contributions of African Americans and immigrants from Continental Europe. "I must point out," writes the folklorist Norm Cohen, "that hillbilly music had important antecedents other than traditional Anglo-Irish-American folk music—namely the commercial musical traditions of the late nineteenth and early twentieth centuries: minstrel shows, vaudeville, ragtime, blues, jazz, Tin Pan Alley sentimental balladry, and hymnody and gospel music, both black and white."[5]

The country-music historian Bill C. Malone notes that the square-dance caller's "do-si-do" came from the French dance instructor's "dos-à-dos" and that the first southern hymnal was published entirely in German. He adds that some popular ballads and fiddle tunes were brought to the United States by professional British entertainers after the American Revolution and that "by the end of the eighteenth century . . . puppet shows, circuses, animal acts, medicine shows, equestrian shows, and . . . formal dramatic and musical concert troupes traveled from town to town along the Atlantic Seaboard."[6] The fiddle tune "Ricketts' Hornpipe," a bluegrass staple to this day, was popularized by John Bill Ricketts, a British equestrian who opened the first American circus in Philadelphia in 1793, astonishing audiences by dancing a hornpipe on the back of a galloping horse.

Typical of the minstrel material that entered the country repertoire is "Listen to the Mockingbird," published as "a sentimental Ethiopian ballad" in Philadelphia in 1855 by Septimus Winner, who took the melody from an African American youth, "Whistling Dick" Milburn. Sentimental songs swept the South after the Civil War but enjoyed wide popularity even earlier; for example, "Home, Sweet Home," with lyrics by the American actor and playwright John Howard Payne and music by the British composer Henry Bishop, became an immediate favorite with the public when it was introduced in the operetta *Clari, or The Maid of Milan* in London in 1823. A number of early recording artists cut "Home, Sweet Home," among them John Yorke Atlee (1891), Emma Albani (1904), Richard Jose (1906), Alma Gluck (1912), and Alice Nielsen (1915).

In May 1927, Frank Jenkins, a North Carolina fiddler and banjo player, recorded "Home, Sweet Home" as a banjo solo. The banjo, originally made from a gourd, was probably introduced to the southern Appalachians by African Americans before the Civil War, but the modern instrument, with its wooden or metal shell, is the product of blackface minstrelsy. Minstrel shows—along with commercial sheet music and, later, phonograph records—made their way into remote mountain communities as well as the cow towns and mining camps of the Old West. A white Virginian named Joel Walker Sweeney, who was playing the banjo on stage in the 1830s, even before the debut of Dan Emmett's minstrel troupe, is said to have popularized the clawhammer technique used by later "hillbilly" stylists. Country players were also influenced by ragtime banjo virtuosos such as Vess Ossman and Fred Van Eps, who began recording in the 1890s.

In 1908, Fleta Jan Brown, a white woman songwriter from Iowa, published "The Party That Wrote 'Home Sweet Home' Never Was a Married Man," a humorous response to John Howard Payne, who in fact never married. In June of that year, the song was recorded by the white vaudevillian Eddie Morton, who recites comic stage patter between the verses. In November 1927, Mack Woolbright, a blind North Carolina banjo player, recorded

"The Man Who Wrote 'Home Sweet Home' Never Was a Married Man" with guitarist Charlie Parker, playing "Home, Sweet Home" between the verses in place of Morton's recitation. The resemblance to bluegrass is no coincidence: Woolbright was an early influence on Earl Scruggs, whose three-fingered picking defined the bluegrass banjo style.[7] In 1961, the New Lost City Ramblers, a folk-music revival group, covered Parker and Woolbright's version, and in 1963, before he helped found the Grateful Dead, Jerry Garcia performed the song with his first wife at a San Francisco Bay Area folk club.

Eddie Morton also recorded ethnic dialect numbers ("Mariuch—Mak-a-the Hootch-a-ma Kootch Down at Coney Isle") and coon songs. In 1909, he cut "You Ain't Talking to Me," a Bert Williams–style song composed that year by Shelton Brooks, with lyrics by Mat Marshall. "You Ain't Talking to Me" is apparently based on "I May Be Crazy but I Ain't No Fool," which was written for Bert Williams in 1904 by another black songwriter, Alex Rogers. In July 1927, the white North Carolina singer and banjo player Charlie Poole recorded "You Ain't Talkin' to Me" with fiddler Posey Rorer and guitarist Roy Harvey. Poole's first recording session, in July 1925, had produced "Don't Let Your Deal Go Down Blues," a seminal string-band hit.

Poole and his North Carolina Ramblers cut a number of coon songs, including "Good-Bye Booze," written in 1901 by the future silent-comedy screenwriter Jean Havez; "Monkey on a String," a "laughing song" originally recorded by the white vaudeville comedian Cal Stewart in 1906; "Coon from Tennessee," written in 1901 by the black vaudevillian Shepard Edmonds as "I'm Goin' to Live Anyhow, 'till I Die" and sung by the black minstrel Ernest Hogan and the white minstrel Eddie Leonard, among others; "It's Movin' Day," written by the Tin Pan Alley team of Andrew Sterling and Harry von Tilzer and recorded in 1906 by Arthur Collins; "He Rambled," adapted from the British folk song "The Derby Ram" by the black songwriters James Weldon Johnson, John Rosamond Johnson, and Bob Cole in 1902 as "Oh! Didn't He Ramble"; "Good-Bye Sweet Liza Jane," written by Sterling and von Tilzer in 1903 and recorded by the Peerless Quartet in 1912; and "Just Keep Waiting till the Good Time Comes," written by George Christie and Louis Weslyn as "Baby Rose" in 1911 and recorded that year by the vaudeville star Billy Murray.

Some of Poole's coon-song covers, such as "It's Movin' Day" or "Monkey on a String," are reasonably faithful to the vaudeville versions, with string-band instead of brass-band backing, while others are thorough deconstructions. Poole's "Coon from Tennessee," recorded in July 1927, may have been influenced by a garbled and truncated rendition recorded by the Georgia Crackers four months earlier. Like the Crackers, Poole interpolates another old coon song, "I'm Going to Start a Little Graveyard of My Own," which the black bluesman Jim Jackson recorded in January 1928. But Poole, while mangling the lyrics even more than the Crackers do, includes a couple of lines from "Graveyard" that the Crackers leave out. On "You Ain't Talkin' to Me," Poole sticks closer to the original text while altering the melody, his drawling, nasal tenor and twangy instrumental accompaniment turning vaudeville into country. But it's his deadpan delivery that transforms the song from a comedy routine to a haunting, seemingly callous declaration of indifference. Woolbright and Parker's sardonic harmony singing and smoothly meshed string picking likewise transmute "The Man Who Wrote 'Home Sweet Home' Never Was a Married Man."

EARLY COUNTRY RECORDINGS

Rural white southern performers may have adapted material from the vaudeville stage, but the hillbilly style evolved independently and was well established by the time the earliest country recordings were made. What is generally considered to be the first country record was cut in June and July of 1922 by two fiddlers, A. C. "Eck" Robertson from Texas and Henry Gilliland from Oklahoma, who traveled to New York to audition for the Victor label after playing for a reunion of Confederate veterans in Virginia. The resulting disc, not issued until the following April, combined the familiar mid-nineteenth-century tune "Arkansaw Traveler," done as a fiddle duet without the usual comic recitation, with "Sallie Gooden," a Celtic-sounding number of similar vintage played brilliantly by Robertson as a solo.

In March 1922, Fiddlin' John Carson appeared on the pioneering Atlanta station WSB, becoming the first country musician to make a radio broadcast. Carson had an earlier brush with fame in 1913 when he performed his ballad "Little Mary Phagan" outside the Atlanta courthouse where the Jewish factory manager Leo Frank was being tried for Phagan's murder; Carson also showed up with his fiddle two years later at the scene of Frank's lynching.[8] In June 1923, he cut "The Little Old Log Cabin in the Lane," backed with "The Old Hen Cackled and the Rooster's Going to Crow," for the OKeh Records producer Ralph Peer, who had brought portable recording equipment to Atlanta. Unlike Eck Robertson's debut disc, Carson's was vigorously promoted—though only after initial sales proved unexpectedly strong—and it is often considered to represent the beginning the of the commercial country-music recording business.

"The Little Old Cabin in the Lane" [sic] was written in 1871—within a few years of Carson's birth—by Will S. Hays, a prolific composer of minstrel songs. It was cut around 1901 by the early recording star Len Spencer and in 1909 by the classically trained baritone Carroll Clark, one of the first African Americans to make records; both Spencer's and Clark's renditions were accompanied by Vess Ossman. Another version was recorded by the classical soprano Alma Gluck around 1913. Hays's minstrel dialect—"De darkies am all gone, / I'll nebber hear dem singing in de cane"—fades through the successive versions; Carson barely hints at it, giving the lyrics a kind of backwoods vaudeville delivery.

Carson's success prompted record companies to seek out comparable performers—Ernest Stoneman, Uncle Dave Macon, Gid Tanner, Charlie Poole, and others—whose music was initially labeled "old time" or "old familiar." At his July 1924 debut session, Macon cut "Hill Billie Blues," an adaptation of a folk-song adaptation that had been published in 1915 by three white songwriters from St. Louis as "Hesitation Blues" and by W. C. Handy as "Hesitating Blues." At a recording session in January 1925, Ralph Peer christened a nameless band led by the singer-pianist Al Hopkins as the Hill Billies. Before long, the word "hillbilly," although offensive to many southerners, was applied generically to what would later be called country music.

Some of the early hillbilly recording artists had hardscrabble backgrounds—Charlie Poole was an itinerant textile-mill worker and moonshiner who drank himself to death at the age of thirty-nine—while others were respectably middle-class—Al Hopkins, the son of a North Carolina legislator, managed his brother's medical practice. Yet most shared a similarly rough-hewn musical style. A notable exception was Vernon Dalhart, who grew up on a Texas ranch as Marion Try Slaughter before studying voice in Dallas. He moved to New York before 1910 to pursue an operatic career, taking his stage name from the Texas towns of Vernon and Dalhart; in 1916, he began to make records, singing everything from arias to Hawaiian numbers and coon songs.

Henry Whitter, one of the first country singers to record, cut "The Wreck on the Southern Old 97" for OKeh in December 1923, based on the actual wreck of a mail train in Virginia in 1903. Modeled after the railroad ballad "Casey Jones" (based on an actual wreck in 1900) and set to the tune of Henry Clay Work's 1865 sentimental song "The Ship That Never Returned," "The Wreck on the Southern Old 97" was probably written by Charles Noell, a North Carolina resident, though others also claimed authorship.[9] Whitter, a Virginian, sang it in a pinched nasal drawl, accompanying himself on guitar and harmonica.

Whitter's record was first covered by the blind Tennessee street musician George Reneau, who cut "The Wreck on the Southern 97" for Vocalion on April 18, 1924; Reneau played guitar and harmonica at the session, but since Vocalion's A&R man Cliff Hess reportedly didn't care for his voice, the Texas-born crooner Gene Austin, soon to become famous for such pop hits as "Yes Sir! That's My Baby," "Bye Bye, Blackbird," and "My Blue Heaven," was brought in to sing. On April 26, the blind North Carolina street musician Ernest Thompson recorded "The Wreck of the Southern Old 97" for Columbia, accompanying his own singing with guitar and harmonica.

Vernon Dalhart cut "The Wreck on the Southern Old 97" for the Edison label in May 1924, accompanied by his own harmonica and by the Hawaiian guitarist Frank Ferera. In August 1924, Dalhart rerecorded the song for Victor as "Wreck of the Old 97," with the singer and songwriter Carson Robison on guitar. On both the Edison and Victor recordings, Dalhart follows Whitter's version fairly closely, although he calls the engineer "Pete" instead of "Steve"; but while he sings with a southern accent (not noticeable on his earlier records), his voice is much fuller and more refined than Whitter's.

As what he later called a "filler-in" for the flip side of the Victor disc, Dalhart suggested a song he'd heard his cousin Guy Massey sing; Massey had gotten it from his brother Robert, who'd heard his fellow inmates sing it in a Texas or Louisiana prison.[10] The song seems to be at least partly based on the sentimental ballad "Meet Me by Moonlight," published in 1826 by the British composer J. Augustine Wade. Accompanied by Robison on guitar and, at the behest of producer Nat Shilkret, Lou Raderman on viola, Dalhart's rendition of "The Prisoner's Song" is as maudlin as could be. Nevertheless (or for that very reason), it was a spectacular hit that sold millions of copies across the nation and overseas, demonstrating the appeal of country music—albeit in watered-down form—beyond the South.

Uncle Dave Macon, a Tennessee teamster who did not become a professional musician until he was middle-aged, represented the more traditional side of country music. Macon was born in 1870 on a farm between Nashville and Chattanooga; in his early teens he moved to Nashville, where his family operated a hotel that catered to vaudevillians. Inspired by a circus musician named Joel Davidson, Macon took up the banjo, performing as an amateur for more than thirty years. Around 1920, as motor vehicles took freight-hauling business away from his mule-drawn wagon, he turned to vaudeville, touring as far north as Boston with the Loew's company. In July 1924, he made his studio debut for Vocalion in New York, first recording solo and then with his vaudeville partner, fiddler Sid Harkreader; on later sessions he was often accompanied by the brothers Sam and Kirk McGee. In December 1925, Macon made his first appearance on Nashville radio's *WSM Barn Dance*, which in 1927 became the *Grand Ole Opry*. He would be an *Opry* regular until his death in 1952, revered as much for his rustic humor and showmanship as for his music.

Besides British-derived ballads and reels ("My Daughter Wished to Marry," "Soldier's Joy"), American folk songs ("Death of John Henry"), Tin Pan Alley weepers ("Save My Mother's Picture from the Sale"), and nineteenth-century hymns ("Shall We Gather at the River"), Macon's repertoire included many minstrel and coon songs ("The Little Old Log Cabin in the Lane," "New Coon in Town," "Eli Green's Cake Walk," "The Coon That Had the Razor"). By his own account, his exposure to African American music was not limited to blackface minstrelsy. "Raised in the South among the colored folk, and working the fields of corn with 'em all the days of my life, I will sing them good old southern songs," he says, introducing "Run, Nigger, Run!"

A text of the song "Sail Away, Ladies" was published in the 1922 book *Negro Folk Rhymes: Wise and Otherwise* by Thomas W. Talley, a Fisk University chemistry professor who was one of the first African American folk-song collectors. The white Tennessee fiddler Uncle Bunt Stephens recorded an instrumental version in March 1926, but Macon's May 1927 recording was the first to feature lyrics, including the chorus "Don't she rock, die-dee-o." In 1956, the London-based Vipers Skiffle Group recorded the song as "Don't You Rock Me Daddy-O," which was quickly covered by the British skiffle star Lonnie Donegan. The song was then taken up by the Quarrymen, a schoolboy skiffle band from Liverpool that included the future Beatles John Lennon, Paul McCartney, and George Harrison.

Another hillbilly traditionalist was fiddler Gid Tanner, whose March 7, 1924, recording session with the blind guitarist Riley Puckett yielded the Columbia label's first country disc. Born in northern Georgia around 1885, Tanner, who made his living as a chicken farmer, regularly competed with Fiddlin' John Carson during the 1910s at the annual Georgia Old-Time Fiddlers' Convention. In 1926, he began to record with Puckett, fiddler Clayton McMichen, and banjo player Fate Norris—all from northern Georgia—in a group called the Skillet Lickers. Until they disbanded in 1931 (they reformed in 1934 with altered personnel), the Skillet Lickers were one of the most popular country recording acts. Similar to Uncle Dave Macon's, their repertoire contained many minstrel and coon songs; Tanner and Norris even performed minstrel-style comedy routines with Norris in blackface makeup.[11]

According to Norm Cohen, "The Skillet Lickers are important not only because of their unusually rich traditional repertoire, but also because of their many attempts at recording 'popular' music and jazz."[12] In truth, only Clayton McMichen was much inclined toward jazz, and Columbia's A&R man Frank Walker discouraged the Skillet Lickers from recording nontraditional material, leaving McMichen, some fifteen years younger than Gid Tanner, to cut more modern music under his own name. From 1925 through the 1930s, he recorded with McMichen's Home Town Band, McMichen's Melody Men, the McMichen-Layne String Orchestra, McMichen's Harmony Boys, and Clayton McMichen's Georgia Wildcats, as his style evolved from pop to swing. Under the pseudonym Bob Nichols, he cut the sentimental waltz-time ballad "My Carolina Home" in April 1926, singing in harmony with Riley Puckett; it became a pop hit, as did Vernon Dalhart's May 1927 cover version, with Carson Robison singing the harmony part.

McMichen's Melody Men included a clarinetist as early as 1926, two years before Jimmie Rodgers first used the clarinet on a record. McMichen himself recorded with Rodgers in 1932, his fiddle echoing Rodgers's yodel on McMichen's composition "Peach Pickin' Time in Georgia." By the late 1930s, when his Georgia Wildcats recorded for Decca, McMichen was playing full-blown western swing, a genre he'd anticipated a decade earlier. The Wildcats' "Farewell Blues," from July 1937, reworks a version of the New Orleans Rhythm Kings' 1922 original that was recorded in 1931 by Joe Venuti and Eddie Lang's All-Star Orchestra, featuring Jack Teagarden and Benny Goodman. In August 1938, McMichen and the Wildcats cut "I'm Gonna Learn to Swing," with such lines as, "I don't give a heck about corny fiddling, / It's driving me insane. / I ain't no mule, I don't like corn. / I'm a swinger, man, with a brand new horn."

BLUES AND HOKUM

Hillbilly music was not an exclusively white preserve. Blacks were the first to play the banjo, of course, but there are also reports of black fiddlers in the American South dating back as far as the 1690s.[13] In the eighteenth and nineteenth centuries, the fiddle was the most common African American instrument; in the 1920s, black fiddlers were recorded playing not only jazz, blues, and hokum but hillbilly music as well. Andrew and Jim Baxter, a black father-and-son fiddle-and-guitar duo from northwest Georgia, sound something like the Skillet Lickers on their August 1927 Victor recording of "The Moore Girl"; Andrew Baxter also recorded with a white string band, the Georgia Yellow Hammers. Similarly, the black Kentucky fiddler Jim Booker recorded with his own Booker Orchestra and with a white band, Taylor's Kentucky Boys.

The flip side of Henry Whitter's "The Wreck on the Southern Old 97" was "Lonesome Road Blues," which was covered in April 1924 by George Reneau and Gene Austin and—under the title "The Worried Blues," with somewhat different lyrics—by Samantha Bumgarner, the first female country recording artist. The song, also known as "Goin' Down the Road Feelin' Bad," became a folk and bluegrass standard, recorded by everyone from Fiddlin' John Carson to the Skillet Lickers, Bill Monroe, Flatt & Scruggs, Woody Guthrie, and Burl Ives. Although it's in a major pentatonic scale rather than a minor one and follows a sixteen-bar rather than a twelve-bar pattern, it resembles the blues in that the first line of each verse repeats—three times rather than twice, as in standard blues—before the second, responsive line comes in.

An even bluesier old country song is "Pretty Polly," which was recorded for Brunswick in March 1927 at the debut session of the Virginia singer and banjo player Dock Boggs and for Victor in July 1927 at the only session of the Kentucky singer and banjo player B. F. Shelton. "Pretty Polly" is based on an eighteenth-century British murder ballad called "The Cruel Ship's Carpenter" or "The Gosport Tragedy," many versions of which were collected by Cecil Sharp in the Appalachians. Nearly half of these, like the early British broadside versions, are in sixteen-bar form, with four lines to each stanza. The rest have only two lines per stanza, with some repeating the first line of each verse three times, as in "Lonesome Road Blues," and others repeating the first line twice, resulting in a twelve-bar structure, as in Boggs's and Shelton's "Pretty Polly."[14] Various modes are used in British and American versions of "The Cruel Ship's Carpenter," but both Boggs's and Shelton's "Pretty Polly" are in a pentatonic minor scale, making the blues connection palpable.

Both Boggs's and Shelton's "Pretty Polly," especially Boggs's, have a bone-chilling intensity reminiscent of the Delta blues. Boggs's banjo technique was influenced by local black musicians he heard as a youth, and he acquired some of his material from records by classic blues singers such as Clara Smith, whose July 1923 recording of "Down South Blues" is the probable basis for Boggs's March 1927 version. Shelton's "Pretty Polly," while also blues-like, is sufficiently dissimilar to Boggs's (including a number of different verses) to indicate that he did not simply learn the song from Boggs's record. It's possible, as Peter van der Merwe suggests, that "Pretty Polly" was "Africanized" though adoption by blacks and then reappropriated by whites.[15] An example of what's been termed a "blues ballad," the song, aside from its text, could never be confused for its British ancestor (unlike some hillbilly fiddle tunes), yet it may nonetheless represent a British source of the blues.[16]

Many early country recordings have the then-voguish word "blues" in the title, but few are actual blues songs. One exception is the passably black-sounding instrumental "Bristol Tennessee Blues," recorded in October 1926 by two members of Al Hopkins's band—fiddler Fred Roe and his brother, guitarist Henry Roe—and issued on Vocalion under the Hill Billies' name (and also on Brunswick, Vocalion's sister label, as by Al Hopkins and His Buckle Busters). Another is Frank Hutchison's September 1926 debut recording for OKeh, "Worried Blues," a disjointed collection of twelve-bar verses accompanied by Hutchison's stirring Hawaiian-style slide guitar. But it was "Train That Carried the Girl from Town," the flip side of "Worried Blues," that became a country standard.

A West Virginian who, like Dock Boggs, worked as a coal miner, Hutchison took up guitar as a boy after seeing a black railroad worker play the instrument with a slide; he learned much of his material from another black musician named Bill Hunt. But though he cut blues-like songs such as "Stackalee" and "Coney Isle," Hutchison recorded only a few real blues, including "Worried Blues," "The Miner's Blues," and a July 1929 rewording of "Worried Blues" titled "Cannon Ball Blues" (not the same as the "Cannon

Ball Blues" recorded in August 1928 by the Memphis bluesman Furry Lewis, although both feature slide guitar). In May 1929, another West Virginia singer-guitarist, Dick Justice, recorded a faithful cover of the Virginia bluesman Luke Jordan's "Cocaine Blues," as well as his own remarkably black-sounding "Brown Skin Blues."

Boggs, while recording many songs titled "blues," generaliy avoided the twelve-bar form, using it, ironically enough, only for "Pretty Polly." His take on "Down South Blues"—originally a standard blues composed by Fletcher Henderson, who plays piano on Alberta Hunter's and Rosa Henderson's 1923 versions, as well as Clara Smith's—features eight-bar stanzas, without the repetition of the first line. Yet his deeply felt music, with its floating verses, pentatonic modes, and hard-luck themes, often suggests the blues.

The Chattanooga-based Allen Brothers—singer and banjo player Austin and singer, guitarist, and kazoo player Lee—likewise recorded many blues-titled songs, but their sound is more hokum than blues. Their first disc—from April 1927, a year and a half before Tampa Red and Georgia Tom cut "It's Tight Like That"—pairs a revision of Papa Charlie Jackson's "Salty Dog Blues" with another verse-and-refrain hokum song, "Bow Wow Blues" (not the 1921 Tin Pan Alley song recorded by the Original Dixieland Jazz Band and others). Their follow-up record, from November 1927, features two more-or-less genuine blues, "Chattanooga Blues," tricked out with antic kazoo solos, and "Laughin' and Cryin' Blues," a descendent of "The Laughing Song," an 1890 hit by the first black recording artist, George W. Johnson. "Laughin' and Cryin' Blues" opens with the line "Blue jumped a rabbit, run him for a solid mile," which Blind Lemon Jefferson had recorded the previous year.

After the contretemps over their listing in Columbia's race catalog, the Allens switched to Victor, where they continued to record hokum-style material, including topical songs such as "Jake Walk Blues," about the impaired gait brought on by drinking an adulterated Jamaica-ginger tonic known as Jake during Prohibition. Although they were among the most successful hillbilly acts, the Allen Brothers could not sustain their recording career past 1934, but they laid the groundwork for other hokum-influenced country performers such as Jimmie Davis and Cliff Carlisle.

Like the Allens, the duo of Tom Darby and Jimmie Tarlton began recording for Columbia in Atlanta in April 1927. Tarlton was born in South Carolina but traveled widely; he learned slide guitar from black musicians in the Carolinas and Georgia, later picking up pointers from Frank Ferera in California. Darby, by contrast, played standard guitar and seldom strayed from his home town of Columbus, Georgia, where the two met. Their second studio session, in November 1927, produced the country classics "Columbus Stockade Blues" and "Birmingham Jail," with harmony vocals that inspired duos such as the Dixon Brothers and the Delmore Brothers. Tarlton's slide guitar gives the music a bluesy cast, although he plays with more of a Hawaiian feel than most black bluesmen; the duo did record a number of authentic blues, including "Slow Wicked Blues," "Sweet Sarah Blues," and "Rising Sun Blues," although they took liberties with the meter. After 1927, their music reflected the influence of Jimmie Rodgers and the Carter Family, with both Darby and Tarlton sometimes yodeling like Rodgers. After leaving Columbia in 1930, the two split up and recorded separately, reuniting for joint sessions in 1932 and 1933 before retiring from the music business.

At the end of July 1927, Ralph Peer, having left OKeh, traveled to Bristol, Tennessee, on the Virginia border, to audition new talent for the Victor label. Among the artists he recorded were B. F. Shelton, the Carter Family, and Jimmie Rodgers; the last two would soon become the biggest stars of country music. The Carter Family were essentially traditionalists who embellished folkloric material with churchy vocal harmonies and Maybelle Carter's propulsive guitar playing. Rodgers, on the other hand, was a modernist whose style formed the main model for the next generation of country singers.

At his Bristol audition, Rodgers recorded a yodeling version of "Sleep, Baby, Sleep," which Riley Puckett had cut for Columbia in September 1924 with a similar yodel.[17] At his next Victor session, in November 1927, Rodgers recorded "Blue Yodel," the first of the yodeling blues that became his stylistic trademark. Its famous opening line, "T for Texas, T for Tennessee," is also found in "Jim Jackson's Kansas City Blues," recorded the previous month. "Blue Yodel," backed with "Way Out on the Mountain" (written but never recorded by the hillbilly singer Kelly Harrell), was a huge seller, bringing Rodgers to national and even international attention. W. C. Handy's white associate Abbe Niles praised Rodgers's "engaging, melodious and bloodthirsty 'Blue Yodel'" in the July 1928 issue of *The Bookman,* a New York literary magazine. Two months later, Niles noted, under the heading "White man singing black songs," that it had "started the whole epidemic of yodeling blues that now rages." Two months after that he characterized Rodgers as a "White man gone black."[18]

Rodgers, born in Meridian, Mississippi, in 1897, left home at thirteen to sing with a traveling medicine show; his father, a railroad worker, retrieved him and got him a job on the railroad. He worked at various railroad and other jobs, but legend has enshrined him as the Singing Brakeman. Meanwhile, he performed as a banjo- and guitar-playing singer, favoring pop over hillbilly material, at events ranging from picnics to tent shows. He worked solo and in bands, occasionally doing blackface routines. He contracted tuberculosis in 1924 but, contrary to myth, did not become a full-time entertainer until after signing with Victor.

It has been speculated that Rodgers learned the blues from black railroad workers, but he "was fascinated by shows and show people," according to his second wife, Connie. "As long as he could possibly scare up a dollar that wasn't busy he would spend it for shows—of any kind—[and] for phonograph records," she writes. "He bought phonograph records by the ton" and "would play those records over and over."[19]

Although it's not a blues number, Rodgers's "In the Jailhouse Now," recorded for Victor in February 1928, is adapted from Jim Jackson's "He's in the Jailhouse Now," recorded for Vocalion in January 1928, some three weeks earlier. Jackson's song is in turn adapted from Blind Blake's version, recorded for Paramount in November 1927. Blake's song is adapted from "She's in the Graveyard Now," recorded for Columbia by Earl McDonald's Original Louisville Jug Band in March 1927. And McDonald's song is adapted from "Jail House Blues," recorded for Gennett in September 1924 by Whistler's Jug Band.[20]

The version by Whistler (Buford Threlkeld) is redolent of vaudeville, with a raucous accompaniment that suggests a circus band. McDonald stays fairly close to Whistler's rendition but sings more clearly, omitting some of Whistler's racial references ("Remember the last election / When the white folks was in action"). Blake's singing sounds surprisingly like Rodgers's, although his guitar playing is more sophisticated. Jackson's guitar playing is cruder than Rodgers's, and he substitutes verses about gambling for the original ones about ballot fraud. Adding yodels, Rodgers roughly follows Jackson's lyrics but shuffles some of the lines, leaving out the ones about the woman whose pickpocketing attempt has fatal consequences.

Rodgers's pick-and-strum guitar technique was shared not only by white country and black blues players of the era (Blind Lemon Jefferson, for one) but by jazz guitarists as well, as illustrated by Johnny St. Cyr's solo with Louis Armstrong's Hot Seven on "Willie the Weeper," from May 1927. Rodgers's yodeling, his most distinctive musical trait, clearly reflects Alpine models, however indirectly. Beginning the 1830s, Alpine yodeling and harmony singing were popularized in the United States by touring acts such as the Tyrolese Minstrels, a family group from Austria. Imitators such as the Hutchinson Family, from New Hampshire, brought yodeling and harmony singing into the American mainstream, and both were incorporated into blackface minstrelsy. White and black vaudevillians alike yodeled in the Alpine manner; Charles Anderson, the cross-dressing "colored mammy" who recorded "Baby Seals Blues" in 1923, also recorded several yodeling songs the same year, including "Sleep, Baby, Sleep."

Rodgers's yodeling is sometimes said to be derived from black blues, work songs, or field hollers, but the influence would seem to run more in the opposite direction. Tommy Johnson's falsetto on such recordings as "Cool Drink of Water Blues," from February 1928, has been cited as the sort of blues voicing that may have inspired Rodgers, but a recently discovered Paramount test pressing of Johnson's "I Want Someone to Love Me," from December 1929, suggests that Rodgers may have inspired him. The Mississippi Sheiks' June 1930 recording of "Yodeling Fiddling Blues," where Lonnie Chatmon's fiddle echoes Walter Vinson's yodels, is an obvious Rodgers knock-off. Howlin' Wolf acknowledged that his falsetto whoops were based on Rodgers's yodels. "I couldn't do no yodelin' so I turned to howlin'," he said.[21] And according to Robert Johnson's erstwhile partner Johnny Shines, "Robert used to play a hell of a lot of [Rodgers's] tunes."[22] Peetie Wheatstraw, the most influential blues whooper, began recording in 1930, but whether he owed a stylistic debt to Rodgers remains moot.

In October 1928, Rodgers recorded two sessions with a white jazz quintet—clarinet, cornet, guitar, steel guitar, and string bass—that he'd come across in Atlanta. The sessions yielded one of Rodgers's classic records, "Blue Yodel No. 4 (California Blues)," backed with "Waiting for a Train." In June 1930, he recorded the poppy "My Blue-Eyed Jane" with a jazz band led by pianist Bob Sawyer; the following month, he cut "Blue Yodel No. 9 (Standin' on the Corner)," accompanied by Louis Armstrong on trumpet and his wife, Lil Hardin Armstrong, on piano. In June 1931, he recorded "My Good Gal's Gone Blues" with the Louisville Jug Band, an all-black group that included a couple of the same musicians who'd cut "She's in the Graveyard Now."

Rodgers was the first country-music superstar, selling millions of records before dying of tuberculosis in 1933, at the age of thirty-five. His fame was greatest in the South—especially Texas, where he moved in 1929—but his popularity extended as far as Australia and South Africa. His impact on country music is unparalleled. He anticipated western swing in his use of jazz instrumentation, and many of his songs were later covered by western swing bands. Although he didn't wear cowboy clothes on stage, he paved the way for the singing movie cowboys with songs such as "Yodeling Cowboy," "When the Cactus Is in Bloom," and "Prairie Lullaby." The yodeling craze he touched off had practically died out by 1940, but his bluesy singing formed the basis for the honky-tonk style that would dominate modern country music. Although he was one of the first artists inducted into the Rock and Roll Hall of Fame and an early model for Jerry Lee Lewis, his biggest influence on rock was probably that he helped popularize the guitar.

A number of country stars began as Jimmie Rodgers imitators, including Jimmie Davis, Cliff Carlisle, and Gene Autry. Davis, born into a sharecropping family in northern Louisiana, sang in glee clubs and quartets while attending college and graduate school. He performed on and, in the summer of 1928, made his first recordings for the Shreveport radio station KWKH, crooning pop songs (except for "Way Out on the Mountain") with piano accompaniment. In September 1929, he began recording for Victor, singing and yodeling like Rodgers to the accompaniment of guitars.

Among the least Rodgers-like of Davis's early sides is "She's a Hum Dum Dinger," from May 1930, one of more than a dozen recordings where he's backed by guitarists Oscar "Buddy" Woods and Ed "Dizzy Head" Schaffer, an African American duo who recorded on their own as the Shreveport Home Wreckers. Adapted from the white bandleader Phil Baxter's jazzy 1928 composition "I'm a Ding Dong Daddy," a 1930 hit for Louis Armstrong, "She's a Hum Dum Dinger" is a twelve-bar verse-and-refrain hokum song with a strummed backbeat. With lines such as "I took her to church in my home town / The preacher got hot and throwed his bible down" and "[He] overtook her way uptown / She got warm and turned his damper down," its verbal rhythms unmistakably foreshadow those of Chuck Berry's "Maybellene."[23] (Berry's memory of having adapted "Maybellene" from a country song may not be entirely inaccurate.)

While he closely followed Rodgers's musical model, Davis's singing was even bluesier, with raunchier lyrics. In November 1932, he recorded "Tom Cat and Pussy Blues" and "Organ-Grinder Blues," both featuring double entendres that were scandalous by the country-music standards of the day; for example, "Rooster got up in the tip-top, pussy crawled out on the limb / Rooster said to that pussy, 'When you comin' up again?'" and "I was an organ grinder up and down the Santa Fe / Now I have about decided, my organ's done failed on me."

Davis gradually shifted from bawdy blues to chaste sentimental and western-themed songs, scoring his first real hit with "Nobody's Darlin' but Mine" after switching to the Decca label in 1934. In February 1940, he cut his best-known song, "You Are My Sunshine," which had been recorded the previous year by the Pine Ridge Boys and the Rice Brothers Gang. Davis (together with his frequent accompanist, steel guitarist Charles Mitchell) claimed authorship of the song, but he'd actually bought the copyright from Paul Rice, one of the Rice brothers.[24] "You Are My Sunshine" was a hit for Wayne King, Gene Autry, and Bing Crosby in 1941 and has since been recorded by Johnny Cash, Ray Charles, Doris Day, Erroll Garner, Bill Haley, Joni James, B. B. King, Jerry Lee Lewis, the Mills Brothers, Ricky Nelson, Willie Nelson, Ike and Tina Turner, Gene Vincent, and Brian Ferry, among many others.

Not one to quit his day job, Davis worked as a city court clerk in Shreveport through most of the 1930s. He was elected city commissioner of public safety in 1938 and public service commissioner for northern Louisiana in 1942, in which capacities he put a number of musicians on the public payroll. In 1944, he ran for governor as a Democrat and won, having sung "You Are My Sunshine" throughout his campaign. He cut some of his biggest-selling records in the mid-1940s, including the No. 1 country hit "There's a New Moon over My Shoulder." He appeared in several Hollywood movies between 1942 and 1944, mostly B-westerns starring Charles Starrett; in 1947, he played himself in the biographical *Louisiana,* singing a number of his songs.

After completing his first term as governor, Davis devoted himself to music full-time, with an increasing emphasis on sacred songs. Returning to politics, he was reelected to the Louisiana governorship in 1960, running on a segregationist platform. In 1962, Davis had his final hit, "Where the Old Red River Flows," which he'd first recorded with Ed Schaffer and Oscar Woods in 1930 and which has become a country standard, with the words "old folks," "voices," or even "hippies" substituted for Davis's "darkies" in the original line "You can hear those darkies singin' soft and low." Davis continued to perform and record mainly religious material into the 1990s, dying in 2000 at the reported age of 101.

Cliff Carlisle, born near Louisville, Kentucky, took up slide guitar as a youth, inspired by such Hawaiian musicians as Frank Ferera. He began performing around 1920 and a few years later formed a duet with guitarist Wilbur Ball. By February 1930, when he and Ball first recorded, Carlisle had adopted Jimmie Rodgers's style whole hog, outyodeling his model, in the opinion of some critics. Rodgers himself was impressed enough, at least with their guitar playing, to have Carlisle and Ball accompany him on a couple of June 1931 sessions in Louisville. In October 1931, Carlisle cut "Shanghai Rooster Yodel," the first in a series of ribald records that included "Tom Cat Blues" (September 1932), "Mouse's Ear Blues" (July 1933), and "That Nasty Swing" (June 1936), the last two featuring Carlisle's younger brother Bill on guitar. In June 1936, Cliff also recorded a Rodgers-like yodeling blues titled "My Rockin' Mama." Carlisle's double entendres are generally more risqué than Jimmie Davis's; for example, "My little mama, she's got a mouse's ear / But she gonna lose it when I shift my gear" and "Wind my motor, honey, I've got a double spring / Place the needle in that hole, and do that nasty swing."

Besides accompanying his brother, Bill Carlisle recorded on his own, cutting his first hit, "Rattlesnake Daddy," at his debut session in July 1933. Playing standard guitar instead of slide, he sang and yodeled like Cliff, with a similarly racy repertoire. In 1938 and 1939, the Carlisles recorded together for Decca under each of their names. After World War II, they signed with King and, as the Carlisle Brothers, had a Top 10 country hit in 1946 with "Rainbow at Midnight." Bill worked solo when Cliff briefly retired; when Cliff returned in 1951, he and Bill formed a new group, the Carlisles, including the gospel singer Martha Carson. Between 1951 and 1954, the Carlisles, with Chet Atkins on guitar, had a string of rollicking, mostly humorous country hits on Mercury, including the No. 1 smash "No Help Wanted" in 1953 and a remarkably faithful cover of the Drifters' R&B chart-topper "Honey Love" in 1954. Among the group's other recordings from this period are the hillbilly boogie "Busy Body Boogie," a rockabilly-ish take on "Rattlesnake Daddy," and a version of the old gospel song "Leave That Liar

Alone," which Ray Charles would transform into the soul classic "Leave My Woman Alone" in 1956.

The Carlisles joined the *Grand Ole Opry* in 1953, but Cliff retired permanently not long afterward. Bill continued to record through the 1960s, fully embracing the rockabilly sound on sides such as "Uncle Bud" (RCA-Victor, 1957) and "Air Brakes" (Columbia, 1960). He had his last hit in 1965 with "What Kinda Deal Is This," on Hickory. One of the few artists to make the transition from old-time country music to rock 'n' roll, Bill Carlisle continued to perform with the *Grand Ole Opry* until his death in 2003.

Gene Autry, born in North Texas and raised in Texas and Oklahoma, originally aspired to be a pop crooner like Gene Austin or Rudy Vallee. In 1928, he took time off from his railroad job to audition for the Victor label in New York, where he met the Oklahoma-born Frankie Marvin, the younger brother of the ukulele-playing crooner Johnny Marvin. One of the first singers to record cover versions of Jimmie Rodgers's hits, Frankie encouraged Autry to do likewise.[25] Soon Autry was yodeling the blues for various budget labels under a number of different names, including his own. In April 1931, he recorded "Do Right Daddy Blues," with such lines as "You can feel-a my legs and you can feel-a my thighs / But if you feel-a my legs, you got to ride me high." In October, he recorded the sentimental "That Silver Haired Daddy of Mine," a duet with his railroad colleague Johnny Long that became a belated hit in 1935.

Moving to Chicago, Autry became a regular on the WLS radio station, known for its weekly *National Barn Dance* show. Billed as the Oklahoma Yodeling Cowboy, he cultivated a western image, exchanging his business suits for cowboy outfits. In early 1933, just before contracting exclusively with the ARC conglomerate of record labels, Autry abandoned his occasionally risqué blue yodels and instead recorded such wholesome western ballads as "The Little Ranch House on the Old Circle B," "Cowboy's Heaven," and "The Yellow Rose of Texas" (although the last originated as a minstrel song about a woman described as a "rose of color"). Later that year he cut his first hit, "The Last Round-Up," already a bigger hit for, among others, Guy Lombardo, Bing Crosby, and bandleader George Olsen, who introduced it. Written by Billy Hill, a classically trained violinist from Boston who'd gone west to find his vocation, the song was a breakthrough for western-themed pop music.

In 1934, Autry was invited to Hollywood to perform in the movie *In Old Santa Fe,* starring Ken Maynard, a silent-western hero who, with the advent of the talkies, had become the screen's first singing cowboy. Autry then appeared in Maynard's twelve-part serial *Mystery Mountain*; the hard-drinking, highly demanding Maynard so offended the producer that he dropped him from his next serial, *The Phantom Empire,* and cast Autry in the leading role instead. *The Phantom Empire,* from 1935, is a bizarre conflation of western musical and science-fiction adventure, with Autry playing himself as a singing radio cowboy who runs a dude ranch located above a futuristic subterranean civilization. Despite its absurd plot, *The Phantom Empire* was a signal success, inspiring such serials as *Flash Gordon*, from 1936, and launching Autry as a movie star. By the end of 1935, the fledgling Republic Pictures Corporation had released four more Autry vehicles—*Tumbling Tumbleweeds, Melody Trail, Sagebrush Troubadour,* and *The Singing Vagabond*—establishing Autry's affable screen persona and solidifying the singing cowboy trend.

Sticking to a formula that featured a protagonist named Gene Autry; his horse, Champion; his sidekick, Smiley Burnette (later replaced by Pat Buttram); a modern rather than Old West setting; and an emphasis on action over romance so as not to put off pre-teen boys, Autry became the leading western-movie box-office attraction, cranking out nearly a hundred films through the mid-1950s. Dozens of other singing cowboys followed his cinematic trail, including some, such as Jimmy Wakely and Autry's arch rival, Roy Rogers, who gained early experience working with Autry.

Autry's late-1930s songs, while often western-themed, tended increasingly toward Tin Pan Alley pop, with arrangements by Carl Cotner, who also played fiddle with Clayton McMichen's Georgia Wildcats. By the early 1940s, Autry was sharing material with the likes of Bing Crosby and Glenn Miller. In August 1940, he recorded "Blueberry Hill," a No. 1 hit for Miller; the following year, Autry sang it in his movie *The Singing Hill.* He recorded "You Are My Sunshine" in June 1941, three weeks before Bing Crosby cut it; Crosby had already covered Autry's 1935 recording of "Mexicali Rose."

Autry's records were popular in Latin America, and with such movies as *South of the Border* (1939) and *Down Mexico Way* (1941), he helped spur the development of the *charro* film, the Mexican equivalent of the singing-cowboy western, whose stars included Jorge Negrete, Pedro Infante, Javier Solis, and Vicente Fernández. As the *charro* film did for *ranchera* music in Mexico, the singing cowboy movie brought country music, however diluted, into the American pop mainstream.

From 1940 to 1956, Autry hosted a weekly CBS radio show, *Melody Ranch*; from 1950 to 1956, he starred on CBS television's *Gene Autry Show.* From 1949 to 1950, his horse had his own Mutual Broadcasting System radio serial, *The Adventures of Champion,* which was made into a CBS television show in 1955. Autry scored his biggest hits with Christmas songs, beginning with "Here Comes Santa Claus (Down Santa Claus Lane)" in 1947; his "Rudolph, the Red-Nosed Reindeer," first released in 1948, became a perennial smash. A shrewd businessman, Autry ran his own rodeo and museum and owned television and radio stations, a record label, a music-publishing company, hotels, oil wells, a cattle ranch, and the baseball team now known as the Los Angeles Angels of Anaheim. He died in 1998, at the age of ninety-one.

Because his music was so widely exposed, especially to younger listeners, Autry was extremely influential, inspiring artists ranging from the rock 'n' roll pioneers Bill Haley and Jerry Lee Lewis to the soul singers Aaron Neville and Solomon Burke. Although Fats Domino adapted his classic 1956 rock 'n' roll hit "Blueberry Hill" from Louis Armstrong's 1949 version, the song, written by three Tin Pan Alley tunesmiths, is still associated with Autry.[26]

WESTERN SWING

When Jimmie Rodgers blended country music with jazz and cloaked it in cowboy imagery, he was embracing two tendencies that combined in the 1930s in a genre that became known a decade later as western swing. But western swing began to evolve independently of Rodgers. A November 1927 recording of "Hesitation Blues" by the blackface singer Al Bernard, accompanied by a white jazz band, the Goofus Five, has been cited as a western-swing precursor, although Bernard first cut the song in 1919 in a similar style. In December 1927, the East Texas Serenaders, a string band led by the fiddler Daniel Huggins Williams, recorded "Combination Rag," a mildly jazzy hoedown; the group cut the same sort of material over the next few years, changing little by the time of its final session in 1937, when western swing was in full flower.

In March 1928, Prince Albert Hunt's Texas Ramblers, a Dallas-area fiddle-and-guitar duo, recorded "Blues in a Bottle," featuring Hunt's remarkably gritty, authentically bluesy singing and fiddling. Like some other white country bluesmen, Hunt assumes an African American identity in the lyrics, singing "Asked my baby, could she stand to see me cry / [She] said, 'Whoa, black daddy, I can stand to see you die.'" Hunt died a blues legend's death, shot outside a Dallas dance hall by a jealous husband at the age of thirty. "Blues in a Bottle" was revived in 1964 by the Holy Modal Rounders, a folk duo, as the waggish "Blues in the Bottle," which was popularized in 1965 by the Lovin' Spoonful, a folk-rock band. Another early fiddle-and-guitar duo, the Humphries Brothers, from central Texas, recorded vintage ragtime pieces such as "Black and White Rag" and "St. Louis Tickle" in June 1930.

But it is commonly agreed that western swing was born in Fort Worth in 1930 when singer Milton Brown and his guitar-playing younger brother Derwood joined the Wills Fiddle Band, previously consisting of fiddler Bob Wills and guitarist Herman Arnspiger. Playing on radio shows for different sponsors, the group became the Aladdin Laddies and then the Light Crust Doughboys. Frustrated by the restrictive policies of W. Lee "Pappy"

O'Daniel, who managed the sponsoring Burrus Mill and Elevator Company, Milton Brown left the Doughboys to form his own band in September 1932, and Wills followed in August 1933. O'Daniel himself left Burrus in 1935 to found his own Hillbilly Flour company and Hillbilly Boys band, setting a precedent for Jimmie Davis when he used the band in his victorious 1938 campaign for the Texas governorship. (O'Daniel won a U.S. Senate seat in 1941, handing Lyndon Johnson his only electoral defeat. A character in the 2000 movie *O Brother, Where Art Thou?* is loosely based on him.) The Light Crust Doughboys, featuring such musicians as pianist Knocky Parker, enjoyed continuing success as a radio and recording group until World War II. The group re-formed after the war and still exists today.

Bob Wills, the son of a traditional fiddler, grew up mostly in the southern Texas Panhandle, picking cotton alongside black workers. He acquired an early taste for the blues, once riding fifty miles on horseback to see Bessie Smith.[27] He took up the fiddle as a boy, playing with his father at country dances. In 1929, he moved to Fort Worth, where he was performing in blackface as a fiddler and comedian with a medicine show when he met Herman Arnspiger. The two cut a couple of numbers for Brunswick that November, "Wills Breakdown" and the 1923 Bessie Smith hit "Gulf Coast Blues," but no record was released. In February 1932, the Light Crust Doughboys—Wills, Milton and Derwood Brown, and Clifton "Sleepy" Johnson, who had replaced Arnspiger—recorded a pair of sides for Victor, "Sunbonnet Sue" and "Nancy Jane," the latter a verse-and-refrain hokum song that had been recorded in April 1930 by the Famous Hokum Boys—Big Bill Broonzy, Georgia Tom Dorsey, and guitarist Frank Brasswell. On this earliest Doughboys record, the jazzy 2/4 beat that would characterize western swing is already in evidence.

The popularity of the original Light Crust Doughboys drew other string bands onto the Fort Worth airwaves, among them the Southern Melody Boys (not related to the Kentucky hillbilly band of the same name). Featuring two classically trained fiddlers, Kenneth Pitts and Cecil Brower, the Melody Boys favored pop and jazz over country material, with Brower improvising his solos in the manner of the jazz violinist Joe Venuti.[28]

By April 1934, when Milton Brown and His Musical Brownies made their first recordings, Brower had become a member, joining Derwood Brown, banjo player Ocie Stockard, string bassist Wanna Coffman, and pianist Fred "Papa" Calhoun; the band would later include steel guitarist Bob Dunn and fiddler Cliff Bruner. It was Coffman who introduced to country music the slap-bass technique that later became a rockabilly hallmark (New Orleans jazz bassists such as Bill Johnson, Steve Brown, and Pops Foster had been the first to snap the strings against the fingerboard). Dunn's studio debut with Brown in January 1935 produced what are considered to be the first commercial recordings with an electrified string instrument—Dunn's guitar, to which he'd attached a homemade pickup. Dunn, who was also a trombonist, patterned his steel-guitar phrasing after Jack Teagarden's jazz trombone solos. Calhoun, originally a drummer in a jazz band, got his nickname because he idolized pianist Earl "Fatha" Hines.

By the time Bob Wills and His Texas Playboys made their first recordings, Brown had already cut over fifty sides, establishing the basic style, instrumentation, and repertoire of western swing. A fiddler's son who'd moved to Fort Worth as a teenager from nearby Stephenville, Texas, Brown was an unusually eclectic singer, at home with pop, jazz, blues, and country material. Among the songs on the Brownies' 1934 sessions for the Bluebird label were countrified takes on Sophie Tucker's "Hula Lou," Jimmie Noone's "Four or Five Times," Bo Carter's "Corrine Corrina," Memphis Minnie and Kansas Joe's "I'm Talking about You," and the Mississippi Sheiks' "Sitting on Top of the World." Their Decca output over the following two years included "Sweet Georgia Brown," "Chinatown, My Chinatown," "You Rascal You," "The Darktown Strutters' Ball," and "When I Take My Sugar to Tea," as well as "The Yellow Rose of Texas" and the popular *ranchera* "Allá en el Rancho Grande." Fond of hokum, Brown brought a rollicking if not rocking feel to his versions of the Hokum Boys' "Somebody's Been Using That Thing," the Hokum Trio's "You're Bound to Look Like a Monkey When You Get Old," and the Famous Hokum Boys' "Eagle Riding Papa," the last having previously been adapted into the Light Crust Doughboys' radio theme song.[29]

One of the few major country singers of his era who was not particularly influenced by Jimmie Rodgers, Brown has been compared to Al Jolson, Bing Crosby, Fred Astaire, Cab Calloway, and the talk-singing white clarinetist and bandleader Ted Lewis (from whom he borrowed more than a few numbers), but his vocal style was unique.[30] Brown could deliver sentimental ballads but never plumbed the depths of pathos, seeming more comfortable on lighthearted material. Bob Wills's spoken interjections—"Ah-ha! Take it away, Leon!"—were a western swing trademark, but Brown preceded him, at least on record, with such exhortations as "Aw, take it away!" "Beat it out, Freddy!" "Yeah, pick it out, Derwood!" and "Swing it!"

In April 1936, at the height of his popularity, Milton Brown was severely injured in a car crash near Fort Worth, dying a few days later at the age of thirty-two. Derwood Brown maintained the band for another year, recording a final session in February 1937 that featured a pair of vocal performances by Jimmie Davis, including "Honky Tonk Blues," a likely ancestor of the 1952 Hank Williams hit by the same title and the 1969 Rolling Stones chart-topper "Honky Tonk Women." The Brownies' "Honky Tonk Blues" (not the same song as Al Dexter's earlier recording by the same title) is based on the melody of "Deep Elem Blues," first recorded by the Lone Star Cowboys in August 1933 and based in turn on the Georgia Crackers' March 1927 recording of "The Georgia Black Bottom," which Gene Autry covered as "Black Bottom Blues" in June 1932.

Although he never enjoyed more than regional fame during his lifetime, it was Milton Brown, more than any other single figure, who set the western swing movement in motion. His connection to rock 'n' roll, indirect at best, can be heard on "Keep A Knockin'," "St. Louis Blues," with its rockabilly-like vocal harmonies on the last chorus, and "Who's Sorry Now," a 1923 Tin Pan Alley song that became a rock-era hit for Connie Francis in 1958.

Even before the Brownies broke up, members began leaving to join other groups or form their own. Cliff Bruner moved to Houston and organized the Texas Wanderers, while Cecil Brower and Bob Dunn played with various western swing bands. After the Brownies dissolved, Ocie Stockard formed his own Wanderers band. Meanwhile, other western swing groups proliferated not only in the Southwest but as far east as Kentucky (the Prairie Ramblers), Tennessee (the Tennessee Ramblers), and Alabama (Hank Penny and His Radio Cowboys).[31]

The standard-bearer for western swing, however, was Bob Wills, whose name has become virtually synonymous with the genre. Essentially an old-fashioned hoedown fiddler, Wills could never improvise like Cecil Brower, but he filled his band with musicians who could play jazz, adding trumpets, saxophones, and drums—besides a piano and bass—to the traditional string lineup.

When Wills left the Light Crust Doughboys—fired because of his heavy drinking—Tommy Duncan, who had replaced Milton Brown as the band's singer, went with him.[32] Duncan, like Wills, admired both Jimmie Rodgers and the blackface singer Emmett Miller. Duncan had auditioned for the Doughboys in 1932 by singing "I Ain't Got Nobody," which Miller had recorded at the same June 1928 session where he cut "Lovesick Blues."[33] Duncan recorded "I Ain't Got Nobody" at the Texas Playboys' first session in September 1935, copying Miller's yodeling version closely.

Following a trail of radio stations, Wills took his original string band to Waco, Texas, where the group was first called the Playboys; then to Oklahoma City, where the name became the Texas Playboys; and finally, in 1934, to Tulsa, where Wills would hold forth nightly on WVOO until World War II. Before recording, Wills hired Leon McAuliffe, who would popularize the electric steel guitar; Al Stricklin, an Earl Hines–influenced pianist; and William "Smokey" Dacus, a jazz drummer whose 2/4 dance beat would anchor the ensemble. He also hired horn players, whom the English-born ARC Records producer Art Satherley (also Gene Autry's producer) was initially reluctant to record.[34] Wills's studio debut yielded "Get With It," with a melody based on "Has Anybody Seen My Gal?" and lyrics that celebrate "red-hot rhythm" while nodding to Cab Calloway and Betty Boop (or to Helen Kane, the real-life singer Betty Boop was modeled on); the song prefigures Johnny Cash's 1956 rockabilly hit "Get Rhythm," a paean to rock 'n' roll.

The Texas Playboys returned to the studio a year later, in September 1936, and again in June 1937, May 1938, and November 1938. While not excluding traditional country songs and fiddle tunes, Wills's early recorded repertoire leans heavily on jazz, blues, and hokum, including Henry Busse's "Wang Wang Blues," Earl Hines's "Rosetta," Bessie Smith's "Empty Bed Blues," Big Bill Broonzy's "I Can't Be Satisfied," and Memphis Minnie's "What's the Matter with the Mill." Wills cut some of the same numbers as Milton Brown, among them "Four or Five Times," "Mexicali Rose," "Sittin' on Top of the World," "Corrine Corrina," and "Keep Knocking (but You Can't Come In)." He also covered several Jimmie Rodgers records, favoring Rodgers's jazzy or bluesy material over his strictly country songs.

As the band's fame grew, Wills added more horn players (as well as the electric guitarist Elton Shamblin, whose jazzy style may have influenced Charlie Christian) and turned toward Tin Pan Alley, shifting from traditional jazz to swing.[35] A November 1938 recording of Wills's wordless composition "San Antonio Rose" became the Texas Playboys' first crossover hit, popular enough that Irving Berlin's company in New York expressed interest in publishing it, if only Wills would provide lyrics. After winning a dispute with Berlin's firm, which tried to alter the lyrics he submitted, Wills recorded "New San Antonio Rose" in April 1940, accompanying Tommy Duncan's vocal with reeds and brass, minus the usual fiddles, banjo, and steel guitar. The record, sounding more like sweet-band pop than country music, became Wills's best seller, winning him a national audience.

Bing Crosby's version of "New San Antonio Rose," recorded in December 1940 with Bob Crosby's band, was an even bigger hit. Bing had starred in the 1936 singing-cowboy movie *Rhythm on the Range* and had cut several western-themed hits, including "Home on the Range," "My Little Buckaroo," and "Along the Santa Fe Trail." "Crosby was one of the main fellas in those days and if he sang a song and it was a halfway decent song, it became a hit," said Roy Rogers, who appeared in *Rhythm on the Range* as a member of the Sons of the Pioneers vocal group. "And what we would do, we'd take those big top hit songs and build a story around them and use them to name our pictures."[36] *San Antonio Rose,* the movie, was released in June 1941, starring the B-actor Robert Paige and featuring Shemp Howard, Lon Chaney Jr., and the Merry Macs, who sing the title song.

"New San Antonio Rose" was registered with the American Society of Authors, Composers and Publishers, an organization cofounded by Irving Berlin in 1914 that collected licensing fees from radio stations. But at the end of 1940, after the radio networks formed their own licensing agency—Broadcast Music, Incorporated—ASCAP went on strike, barring its members' compositions from the airwaves. BMI scrambled to acquire the rights to songs not controlled by ASCAP, which represented mainly the established Tin Pan Alley composers. As a consequence, Latin, rhythm-and-blues, and especially country music (as well as older, public-domain material) received unprecedented radio exposure, a trend that continued even after the strike was settled in late 1941.

Wills and members of the Texas Playboys appeared in four Hollywood westerns, beginning with *Take Me Back to Oklahoma* in 1940, before he broke up his band and joined the army in late 1942. Discharged the following year, he moved to California, re-formed the band, and began making movies again. From then until the end of the decade, Wills enjoyed his greatest success, recording a string of pop and country hits and touring nationwide. Like Cab Calloway or Louis Jordan, he was a showman as much as a musician, maintaining a stream of wisecracking stage patter not only between but throughout the songs. From mid-1945 through 1947, he made a series of transcription discs for the Tiffany Music Company that were distributed to radio stations around the country. Keeping up with the times, he cut hits such as "Bob Wills Boogie" (in September 1946) and "Ida Red Likes the Boogie" (in May 1949) that clearly anticipate the rockabilly sound. Listening to Wills's "Brain Cloudy Blues" (from September 1946), "Rock-A-Bye Baby Blues" (from April 1950), and "Cadillac in Model 'A'" (from March 1954), one hears a progression from country-accented R&B to country-accented rock 'n' roll.

Although Tommy Duncan quit the band in September 1948, Wills continued to score hits for a couple of years longer. Struggling with drinking and money problems, he moved to Oklahoma, then back and forth between Texas and California. At the end of 1957, he returned to Oklahoma, where he expressed his appreciation of rock music in an interview for the *Tulsa Tribune*. "Rock and roll? Why, man, that's the same kind of music we've been playin' since 1928!" he said. "We didn't call it 'rock and roll' back when we introduced it as our style in 1928, and we don't call it rock and roll the way we play it now. But it's just basic rhythm and has gone by a lot of different names in my time."[37]

By the early 1960s, Wills was entertaining regularly in Las Vegas, but after two heart attacks, he had to break up his band for good. He continued to perform and record occasionally even after suffering a paralytic stroke in 1969, lingering on until his death from pneumonia in 1975. Although later country artists would tone down the jazzier elements of his style, they could not escape his influence, which filtered through the dominant honky-tonk school. No aspect of his sound had a greater impact than the beat; as the first country bandleader to incorporate drums, Wills brought the music into the dance hall and paved the way for rockers such as Bill Haley.

The popularity of western swing spread within and beyond Texas and Oklahoma. Cliff Bruner's Texas Wanderers became the most successful group along the Gulf Coast, with a string-and-piano format similar to Milton Brown's and a repertoire that included some of the same numbers—"Corrine Corrina," "Four or Five Times," "Oh! You Pretty Woman," "Sunbonnet Sue," "San Antonio Rose"—as Brown's or Bob Wills's. Like Wills, Bruner covered Kokomo Arnold's "Milk Cow Blues," but he also covered Ollie Shepard's "She Walks Like a Kangaroo" and Lonnie Johnson's "New Falling Rain Blues"—urban rather than rural blues. Perhaps his biggest hits were "It Makes No Difference Now," written by Floyd Tillman and recorded in September 1938, which Bing Crosby sang on the flip side of "New San Antonio Rose," and "Truck Driver's Blues," written by Ted Daffan and recorded in August 1939, which is often cited as the daddy of all country truck-driving songs.

Among Bruner's sometime sidemen were Bob Dunn and Aubrey "Moon" Mullican, a bluesier pianist than Fred Calhoun or Al Stricklin (and a bluesier singer than he was a pianist). Before joining Bruner, Mullican had already recorded with another Houston band, the Blue Ridge Playboys, led by fiddler Leon "Pappy" Selph and at times including Floyd Tillman on guitar, Ted Daffan on steel guitar, and Mancel Tierney on piano. Tillman became an influential singer-songwriter in the honky-tonk mold; Daffan formed his own western swing band, the Texans, and wrote such enduring songs as "I'm a Fool to Care," a hit for Les Paul and Mary Ford in 1954 and, in a prototypical swamp-pop arrangement, for Joe Barry in 1961. Mullican played and sang with Bruner on and off through the war years before forming his own group, the Showboys, and recording for the King label in a hillbilly-boogie style that strongly influenced Jerry Lee Lewis.

In 1939, the Texas Wanderers went to Hollywood to perform in the movie musical *Village Barn Dance*; back in Houston the following year, singer-guitarist Dickie McBride left the Wanderers to form the Village Boys, a swing-style combo that included Floyd Tillman. In April 1941, the Village Boys, without Tillman, recorded what is considered to be the first hillbilly boogie—"Boogie Woogie in the Village," a sophisticated variation of "Pine Top's Boogie Woogie" featuring Mancel Tierney. Singer-guitarist Johnny Barfield, a veteran of the Skillet Lickers and the Georgia Wildcats, had cut "Boogie-Woogie" in August 1939, but rather than a real boogie-woogie, that song is a reworded adaptation of Rex Griffin's 1936 recording "Everybody's Tryin' to Be My Baby," which Barfield covered on the flip side of "Boogie-Woogie." ("Everybody's Tryin' to Be My Baby" was also covered by Roy Newman in 1938, by Glen Thompson and by Jimmy Short in 1951, by Carl Perkins in 1956, and by the York Brothers in 1957, but the song was not well known beyond country circles until the Beatles covered Perkins's version in 1964.)

Singer-guitarist Buddy Jones, born in North Carolina, traveled to Louisiana in tent shows together with his brother, steel guitarist Buster Jones.[38] In

Shreveport, Buddy met Jimmie Davis, whom he accompanied on several of Davis's 1931 recordings for Victor. In 1935 and 1936, he sang harmony duets with Davis on such Decca sides as "Red River Blues" and "I Ain't Gonna Let Ol' Satan Turn Me 'Round." By 1937, Jones was recording for Decca under his own name, accompanied by his brother; beginning in 1939, he recorded with members of Cliff Bruner's band, including Bob Dunn, Dickie McBride, and Bruner himself. His repertoire ran heavily to blues and the sort of risqué songs that Jimmie Davis had abandoned, such as "Easy Rollin' Sue" and "She's Selling What She Used to Give Away." An August 1939 session with Buster Jones on steel guitar and Moon Mullican on piano yielded "Settle Down Blues," which Buddy delivers in convincing African American style, and "Rockin' Rollin' Mama," where he sings, "Rockin' rollin' mama, I love the way you rock and roll," to the tune of "Deep Elem Blues." In April 1941, with Mullican on piano and Bruner playing an amplified tenor guitar, Jones cut "Red Wagon," a rock 'n' roll ancestor if only for its melodic resemblance to "Rock Around the Clock."

Other early western swing bands included Bill Boyd and His Cowboy Ramblers, from Dallas; Jimmie Revard's misleadingly named Oklahoma Playboys, from San Antonio; and the Swift Jewel Cowboys, who moved to Memphis from Houston. The Swift Jewel Cowboys leaned more toward jazz, the Cowboy Ramblers and Oklahoma Playboys more toward country, but like most western swing outfits, they shared a similar style and repertoire based on those of Bob Wills and Milton Brown, blending country, pop, jazz, blues, and hokum.

One of the jazziest western swing bands was Roy Newman and His Boys, from Dallas. Newman, a studio pianist for a local radio station, formed the group in 1933, recruiting members of the disbanded Rhythm Aces, led by Bill Boyd's brother, guitarist Jim Boyd (who played the first recorded electric standard guitar solos with Newman's band in September 1935). Although the Boys shared musicians with the Cowboy Ramblers, their approach was hotter, with material such as "Garbage Man Blues," "Mississippi Mud," "Kansas City Blues," "Corrine Corrina," and "Nagasaki." Guitarist Earl Brown's singing sounds nearly black on "Match Box Blues" and "My Baby Rocks Me (with One Steady Roll)," both from December 1938, but the veteran jazz clarinetist Holly Horton outdoes him on "Tin Roof Blues," from June 1935, croaking, "I smell yo' bread a-boinin', baby / Go toin yo' damper down."

Bob and Joe Attlesey formed the Lone Star Cowboys with guitarist Leon Chappelear in East Texas in 1929. Moving to Shreveport, they met Jimmie Davis, who had the trio back him on a pair of Victor sessions in Chicago in August 1933. The Cowboys made their own recordings on the same dates, including two classics, the original "Deep Elem Blues" (spelled "Elm") and "Just Because," a song originally recorded in 1929 by a group called Nelstone's Hawaiians. In 1934, the Attlesey brothers adopted the surname Shelton; the following year, they began recording as a duo, reprising "Deep Elem Blues" and "Just Because" for Decca. Ultimately settling in Dallas, the Shelton Brothers achieved greater popularity than the western swingers there by cultivating an acoustic style and a hillbilly image. But though their repertoire was long on traditional country material, it also included songs such as "Four or Five Times," "Match Box Blues," and "I'm Sitting on Top of the World." Chappelear, who turned fully to western swing, continued to lead the Lone Star Cowboys until 1938, reemerging in the 1950s as a honky-tonk singer under the name Leon Chappel.

Country-jazz bands also flourished in the Southeast, sometimes directly influenced by western swing and sometimes not, as in the case of Clayton McMichen's Georgia Wildcats. Hank Penny and His Radio Cowboys, perhaps the best-known such group, was certainly inspired by Milton Brown and Bob Wills, whom the Alabama-born Penny first heard in New Orleans. Returning to his native Birmingham, Penny, a singer and guitarist, formed the Radio Cowboys in 1937 and cut his first records, for Art Satherley, in November 1938, including the rockabilly precursor "Flamin' Mamie." By his next session, in July 1939, Penny had hired a second fiddler, Boudleaux Bryant, who would go on—together with his wife, Felice—to write such rock 'n' roll hits as the Everly Brothers' "Bye Bye Love" and "Wake Up Little Susie." The July date produced a jazzed-up version of the traditional fiddle breakdown "Black Eyed Susie," with the musicians chorusing "I want seafood, mama," a line from the Andrews Sisters' "Hold Tight." At the same session, Penny crooned "Tonight You Belong to Me," a 1927 Gene Austin hit that had been recorded in 1937 by Cliff Bruner and that would be revived in 1952 by Frankie Laine and again in 1956 by the youthful sister duo Patience and Prudence. The Radio Cowboys broke up during World War II, and Penny moved to the West Coast, where he experienced his greatest success.

Another eastern band that assumed a western air was the Prairie Ramblers, originally the Kentucky Ramblers, who began to record in 1933 after affiliating with radio station WLS in Chicago and adding singer Patsy Montana (née Ruby Blevins). In 1935, Montana and the Ramblers cut "I Wanna Be a Cowboy's Sweetheart," a crossover pop hit and the first major country hit sung—and yodeled—by a woman. The Ramblers recorded bawdy songs, such as "There's a Man Who Comes to Our House" ("There's a man who comes to our house every single day / Papa comes home and the man goes away"), under the pseudonym the Sweet Violet Boys, adding a clarinetist to disguise their sound.

Other, lesser-known eastern bands also played country jazz. The Hi Neighbor Boys, from South Carolina, featured guitarist Eddie Grishaw, who would record hillbilly boogies in the 1940s and 1950s under the name Zeb

Turner. The Swing Billies, from North Carolina, featured singer Charlie Poole Jr., whose tongue-twisting harmonies recall the Boswell Sisters on "Leavin' Home," the Billies' jazzed-up take on "Frankie and Johnny."

The group perhaps most responsible for propagating the western image was the Sons of the Pioneers, country music's answer to the Mills Brothers. Roy Rogers, then known as Leonard Slye, had migrated to California from his native Ohio in 1930; after singing, yodeling, and playing guitar in several Los Angeles groups, Slye formed the Pioneer Trio in 1933 with the Canadian-born singer-bassist Bob Nolan and the Missouri-born singer Tim Spencer. The trio's name was changed when a radio announcer introduced them as the Sons of the Pioneers. The Texas-born fiddler and bass singer Hugh Farr joined in 1934; his brother Karl, a guitarist, followed a year later. The Farr brothers' instrumental virtuosity, reflecting the jazzy influence of Joe Venuti and Eddie Lang, richly complemented the group's progressive vocal harmonies.

Signed to Decca Records, the Sons of the Pioneers recorded Nolan's composition "Tumbling Tumbleweeds" at their debut session in August 1934. One of the group's least jazzy songs, it was one of their most successful, covered by Gene Autry in 1935 (also lending its title to an Autry movie that year) and by Bing Crosby in 1940. Besides harmonizing closely, the singers sometimes yodeled in unison; while performing a variety of country and pop material, they gave heavy emphasis to western themes. "Reelin', rockin', rollin' covered wagon / Over the prairie we roam," they sing on "Westward Ho," recorded in October 1935. Their showpiece arrangement of "I'm an Old Cowhand (from the Rio Grande)," the tongue-in-cheek Johnny Mercer composition that Bing Crosby sang in *Rhythm on the Range* ("I know all the songs that the cowboys know . . . / 'Cause I learned them all on the radio"), is considerably more sophisticated than Crosby's version.

Beginning with *The Old Homestead* in 1935, the Sons of the Pioneers appeared in dozens of western movies, many starring Charles Starrett. A couple of their early films starred Gene Autry, but in 1938, when Autry disputed his contract with Republic Pictures, Leonard Slye replaced him in the movie *Under Western Stars,* leaving the Sons of the Pioneers and changing his name to Roy Rogers. While Rogers went on to singing-cowboy superstardom, the Sons of the Pioneers persevered into the 1990s through a succession of personnel changes, record labels, and film studios, their sound growing gradually more conventional. In 1941, they scored a pop hit with "Cool Water," another Nolan composition, and made the first in a series of movies where they were reunited with Rogers. One of their dozen or so country hits, the comic "Cigareetes, Whusky, and Wild, Wild Women," from 1947 (a pop hit for the former Spike Jones sideman Red Ingle in 1948), corresponds to similarly themed R&B songs of the period (and was covered by Willie Dixon's Big Three Trio), though it's performed in an exaggerated hillbilly style. Their last hit was "Ride Concrete Cowboy, Ride," from the 1980 movie *Smokey and the Bandit II,* starring Burt Reynolds and Jackie Gleason. A number of other groups modeled themselves after the Sons of the Pioneers, most notably Foy Willing and the Riders of the Purple Sage.

The Hoosier Hot Shots represented a parodic midwestern parallel to western swing. Formed in 1930 by members of a disbanded Indiana group, Ezra Buzzington's All Rube Band, the Hot Shots comprised Paul "Hezzie" Trietsch, who played washboard and slide whistle; his older brother Ken Trietsch, who sang and played guitar; Charles "Gabe" Ward, who sang and played clarinet; and string bassist Frank Kettering. After broadcasting from Fort Wayne, Indiana, the Hot Shots moved to Chicago in 1933 and joined the WLS *National Barn Dance*, where their tenure lasted until 1946. Beginning in 1934, they recorded for the ARC labels, switching to Decca after the wartime recording ban. In 1939, they made their first film appearance, in Gene Autry's *In Old Monterey*; they would perform in a dozen other Hollywood westerns through the 1940s, as well as the 1944 movie *National Barn Dance*.

The Hoosier Hot Shots were heirs to a tradition of rustic satire that included "Toby" shows—tent shows featuring a red-haired, freckle-faced bumpkin character named Toby that toured the Midwest and South in the early twentieth century. The Hot Shots mixed cornball and hip, giving cleverly risible treatments to pop standards and jazz songs—everything from "Ain't She Sweet" to "The Flat Foot Floogie"—as well as novelties such as "I Like Bananas Because They Have No Bones," "I've Got a Bimbo Down on Bamboo Isle," and "From the Indies to the Andies in His Undies." "What we had to sell," Gabe Ward reflected, "was a product called stupid."[39]

Many of the Hot Shots' records begin with Ken Trietsch shouting, "Are you ready, Hezzie?" Hezzie was the band's chief humorist, interjecting virtuosic comedy effects on whistle and washboard while the other musicians played relatively straight-ahead traditional jazz arrangements or sang in barbershop harmony. While a few of their songs had country themes—"I Like Mountain Music," "You Said Something When You Said Dixie," "Them Hill-Billies Are Mountain Williams Now," and the Latin-country hybrid "He's a Hillbilly Gaucho"—the Hot Shots made no attempt to sound southern. But they did record some of the same material as Milton Brown—"Ida Sweet as Apple Cider," "Who's Sorry Now," "The Darktown Strutters' Ball," "The Sheik of Araby," "Down by the O-Hi-O," "Avalon," and "St. Louis Blues." The Hot Shots inspired a number of other bands, including one from Texas, Bob Skyles and His Skyrockets, who recorded a song called "We're Not the Hoosier Hotshots." The best-known Hot Shots disciple was Spike Jones, who contrarily called his band the City Slickers.

World War II brought country music to new heights of popularity. The ironic result of the ASCAP strike was to break Tin Pan Alley's hold over the music-publishing industry. In 1942, the pop-turned-country songwriter Fred Rose and the country singer Roy Acuff founded the Acuff-Rose Music publishing company in Nashville, affiliated with BMI. Together with the growing ascendancy of the *Grand Ole Opry* over such rivals as the *National Barn Dance*, the rise of Acuff-Rose signaled the emergence of Nashville as the hub of the country music business. The musicians' union recording ban, directed at the major labels, encouraged the formation of independent record companies such as King, founded as a country label in Cincinnati in 1943, during the ban. The urban audience for country music expanded, as rural southerners moved to cities in both the North and South to take jobs in the defense industry. Meanwhile, country musicians were moving to the West Coast, following a wave of migration from the southwestern states that began with the Dust Bowl of the 1930s.

One of the biggest wartime country hits was Al Dexter's "Pistol Packin' Mama," recorded in Los Angeles for OKeh in March 1942. Born in East Texas, Dexter began singing with an all-black band in the early 1930s.[40] His recorded debut—for ARC, in November 1936, with a white trio—produced "Honky Tonk Blues," the first song with the term "honky-tonk" in the title. The flip side of that record was "New Jelly Roll Blues," where Dexter sets the black Georgia bluesman Peg Leg Howell's 1927 hokum song "New Jelly Roll Blues" to the tune of "Deep Elem Blues." In June 1939, Dexter cut "Diddy, Wah, Diddy with a Blah! Blah!" combining Blind Blake's 1929 hokum song "Diddie Wah Diddie" with "The Flat Foot Floogie." Ten years later, he would update it as "Diddy Wah Boogie."

Dexter claimed to have conceived "Pistol Packin' Mama," with the line "Lay your pistol down, babe," after a woman he knew was chased through the Texas fields by her lover's gun-toting wife; he adapted the title from Jimmie Rodgers's "Pistol Packin' Papa" and the melody from Bob Wills's "Take Me Back to Tulsa."[41] Released in 1943, during the recording ban, "Pistol Packin' Mama" became a No. 1 pop smash and even made the Harlem Hit Parade; re-released in 1944, it topped *Billboard*'s new country chart, called Most Played Juke Box Folk Records. One of Decca's first postban recordings was of Bing Crosby and the Andrews Sisters' version of the song, also a pop, country, and R&B hit. "Pistol Packin' Mama" was ultimately covered by artists ranging from the Pied Pipers (a white vocal group featuring Jo Stafford) to the Hurricanes (a black doo-wop group) to Gene Vincent, whose rockabilly rendition, recorded in London, was arranged by Eddie Cochran. A movie called *Pistol Packin' Mama* was produced in 1943, set mostly in New York and featuring the King Cole Trio.

"Hillbillies Owe Rise to Jukes" ran the headline of an article in the August 28, 1943, issue of *The Billboard,* which attributed country music's penetration of the previously impervious Philadelphia market to the introduction of Dexter's "Pistol Packin' Mama" on local jukeboxes. The phenomenon began, claimed the magazine, after a jukebox operator was urged to add the record by his brother, a soldier stationed in the South. "On the strength of the *Pistol Packin'* click," the article continued, "the music operators placed other hillbilly sides in the machines. And the repetitious playing of the records in the machines . . . created a major market for the retail shops." Radio play followed, with *"Pistol Packin' Mama* . . . getting more requests on the air than the Frank Sinatra sides."[42]

"The dominant popular music of the U.S. today is hillbilly," proclaimed an article in the October 4, 1943, issue of *Time*. Citing the triumph of "Pistol Packin' Mama," which it described as "a homely earful of the purest Texas corn"—as well as the crossover success of Gene Autry, Bob Wills, Jimmie Davis, and others—the magazine announced "the biggest revolution in U.S. popular musical taste since the 'swing' craze began in the middle '30s."[43]

Bob Wills energized the country music scene on the West Coast when he settled there in 1943, but the artist most closely associated with the rise of California as a country music center was Donnell Clyde "Spade" Cooley, who popularized the term "western swing." Cooley was born into a poor but musically talented farming family in Oklahoma; raised in Oregon, he studied classical cello at an Indian school (he was one-quarter Cherokee) while playing fiddle at barn dances. His family moved to California's San Joaquin Valley, north of Bakersfield, where Cooley harvested crops together with the southwestern and midwestern Dust Bowl refugees known generically as "Okies." He fiddled in several West Coast bands, including the Purple Sage Riders (not the same as the Riders of the Purple Sage), a group patterned after the Sons of the Pioneers.

In 1938, just after Roy Rogers became a movie star, Cooley approached him and was hired as Rogers's stand-in. He began to play bit parts, mostly as a musician, in Rogers's and other westerns, meanwhile fiddling with a number of Los Angeles–area bands. The Jimmy Wakely Trio, having traveled to Hollywood from Oklahoma at Gene Autry's suggestion, appeared in movies and backed Autry on his *Melody Ranch* radio show. Augmented by several other musicians, including Cooley, Wakely's group also played at the ballroom barn dances the disc jockey Bert "Foreman" Phillips began promoting on the Venice Pier in June 1942. (Phillips would operate some half-dozen country dance halls in the Los Angeles area during the war, presenting such artists as Al Dexter, Ted Daffan, and Hank Penny.) Soon afterward, Cooley re-formed the house band at the Venice Ballroom, and Wakely left to pursue a successful career as a country-pop singer and B-western star.

Cooley's ensemble was unusually configured, with three fiddles, three guitars (one steel), accordion, piano, bass, and drums, plus singer Tex Williams. Unlike other western swing outfits, Cooley's played written arrangements (by the Cleveland-bred accordionist Larry "Pedro" DePaul), lending it a sweet-band feel. Cooley engaged Bob Wills in a battle of the bands at the Venice Ballroom in late 1943; after the audience voted Cooley the winner, he billed himself as the King of Western Swing, giving the genre its name. After eighteen months on the Venice Pier, Cooley took over another of Foreman Phillips's venues, the Riverside Rancho. In December 1944, Cooley's group made its first recordings, for Columbia/OKeh, among them the No. 1 country smash "Shame on You."

Over the next couple of years, Cooley cut a few more hits and appeared in Soundies and movies, including the short subject "Spade Cooley: King of Western Swing." His style tended toward pop rather than jazz, with harp glissandos and other uncommon touches, even on up-tempo instrumentals such as "Oklahoma Stomp." After Tex Williams signed a solo contract with Capitol Records in 1946 and departed with most of the band members, Cooley rebuilt his group, enlarging it with horn players from sweet and jazz bands to create a sophisticated blend of country, pop, and swing.

In 1946, Cooley began hosting a radio show from the Santa Monica Ballroom. The following year, he launched a comedy-variety program, the *Hoffman Hayride,* on the pioneering Los Angeles television station KTLA. Featuring regular performers such as Hank Penny, in the role of a singing comic hayseed, and guests such as Frank Sinatra and Bob Hope, it was one of the highest-rated television shows in the country. But by the mid-1950s, Cooley's career was on the skids; his final recording, the 1959 album *Fidoodlin',* contained a tune called "Rockin' the Square Dance," a lame attempt to ride the rock 'n' roll bandwagon. In 1961, Cooley, suspecting that his wife had had an affair with Roy Rogers, beat her to death in a drunken rage in front of their teenage daughter. Convicted and sentenced to life in prison, he was granted a furlough to perform at a benefit concert in November 1969, three months before his scheduled parole. Just after the show, he suffered a heart attack and died.

Cooley's accordion-flavored sound was echoed by Tex Williams and His Western Caravan, whose March 1947 recording of "Smoke! Smoke! Smoke! (That Cigarette)" was a No. 1 hit on both the country and pop charts. Written for Williams by the influential guitarist Merle Travis, the song draws on the spoken form originated by the South Carolinian Chris Bouchillon on his November 1926 recording "Talking Blues." Unlike Bouchillon, Williams recites only the verses ("I don't reckon they hinder your health / I've smoked 'em all my life and I ain't dead yet"), singing on the choral refrain. The talking-blues style was later revived by Bob Dylan, who learned it from Woody Guthrie, but it was also used in a series of car-racing songs that began with Arkie Shibley's "Hot Rod Race" in 1950 and extended through Charlie Ryan's "Hot Rod Lincoln" in 1955 and Chuck Berry's "Jaguar and Thunderbird" in 1960.

Arriving in California, Hank Penny also adopted the Cooley sound, hiring an accordionist for his new band even before joining Cooley's TV show.

Though not as successful as Tex Williams, he had a few country hits, the last being "Bloodshot Eyes" in 1950, which Wynonie Harris, Penny's label-mate at King, transformed into an R&B hit the following year. Penny recorded the jazzy "Hillbilly Jump" in 1947 and the not-quite-bopping "Hillbilly Be-bop" in 1949; in 1948, Tex Williams recorded the more sophisticated "Artistry in Western Swing," based on Stan Kenton's progressive-jazz anthem "Artistry in Rhythm."

The postwar decline of western swing mirrored that of big-band jazz, with smaller combos replacing large ensembles. Instead of rhythm-and-blues, bebop, or mainstream pop music, however, western swing gave way mainly to the honky-tonk sound, whose prime exemplar was Hank Williams. Like other honky-tonkers, the Alabama-born Williams had little use for jazz but still showed the influence of western swing, especially in the steel-guitar-and-fiddle blend of his backing band, the Drifting Cowboys. A few of his early recordings, such as the twelve-bar verse-and-refrain songs "Move It On Over" and "Rootie Tootie," have a distinct rock 'n' roll flavor, though not a rock 'n' roll beat.

HILLBILLY BOOGIE

Another postwar trend in country music, embraced by honky-tonkers and western swingers alike, was the hillbilly boogie, which formed the basis for the rockabilly style of the 1950s. Around January 1944, the Rhythm Boys—a California–based trio comprising the Missouri-born guitarists Porky Freeman and Red Murrell plus the bassist Al Barker—recorded "Porky's Boogie Woogie on Strings" in Hollywood for the Morris Lee label. Though it was only a regional hit, it's a remarkable record, with Murrell repeating a four-chord motif that anticipates Red Garland's piano vamp on Miles Davis's "Milestones" while Freeman, who was influenced by the jazz guitarists Oscar and Johnny Moore and who worked with Roy Newman's and Bill Boyd's western swing bands in Texas before moving to the West Coast, plays a varied series of bluesy or jazzy twelve-bar riff choruses.[44] Only the first chorus features a boogie figure, played with the kind of thick, twanging tone later popularized by Duane Eddy; the second chorus prefigures the opening theme of "The Huckle-Buck." Suggesting rhythm-and-blues as much as country music, the piece as a whole is years ahead of its time. Around March 1946, Murrell would record "Git Fiddle Boogie" with his own band, the Ozark Playboys, seemingly appropriating a snatch of Charlie Parker's classic November 1945 bebop recording "Now's the Time" more than three years before it turned up as the second theme of "The Huckle-Buck."

But it was "Guitar Boogie," recorded for New York's Super Disc label around October 1945 by the Rambler Trio featuring Arthur Smith, that touched off the hillbilly-boogie boom. Smith, a South Carolina guitarist, began his career in his father's jazz band, but "Guitar Boogie" is more country than "Porky's Boogie Woogie on Strings," which it otherwise resembles. Like "Porky's Boogie Woogie," it's a succession of twelve-bar guitar choruses, the first one following a boogie-woogie pattern; here, the second chorus looks forward to the blues guitarist Freddie King's 1961 R&B instrumental hit "Hide Away." "I guess I picked that up from Tommy Dorsey's 'Boogie Woogie,' 'cause I didn't listen to country or blues, I listened to big band in those days," Smith later said.[45] Rereleased on MGM in 1948, Smith's "Guitar Boogie" made both the country and pop charts. It was covered in 1953 under the title "New Guitar Boogie Shuffle" by an obscure group called the Super-Sonics and in 1958 as "Guitar Boogie Shuffle" by a white Philadelphia rock band, the Virtues, whose version made both the pop Top 10 and the R&B Top 40 in 1959.

A couple of other country boogies were recorded in 1945: "Streamliner Boogie," by Jimmie O'Neal and the Colorado Hillbillies, and "Zeb's Mountain Boogie," by Brad Brady and his Tennesseans. Little is known about O'Neal's group (they recorded for the same Los Angeles label, Coast, as Walt Shrum and His Colorado Hillbillies, who performed in several western movies), but "Streamliner Boogie" is cutting-edge country, combining talking railroad blues ("Hiya folks, I'm a porter, and I work on the king of the road") and authentic boogie piano (quoting the "Habanera" from Bizet's *Carmen*), with wild steel-guitar runs thrown in. Brad Brady was actually Owen Bradley, a pianist who would go on to become an important record producer, and "Zeb's Mountain Boogie" is a brassy, Basie-style take on "Pine Top's Boogie Woogie," with solos on trumpet, clarinet, and fiddle as well as Zeb Turner's electric guitar.

In January 1946, the Delmore Brothers recorded "Hillbilly Boogie," the song that gave the style its name and established the most common template for subsequent country boogies. Alton Delmore and his brother Rabon, eight years younger, were born into a gospel-singing farm family in northern Alabama. They developed a brand of close-harmony singing (and even yodeling) that was softer and suppler than those of earlier country vocal duos, inspiring the Blue Sky Boys, the Louvin Brothers, and the Everly Brothers, among others. Their instrumental technique was highly refined, interweaving complex lines on standard and tenor guitars. Although much of their repertoire, whether folkloric or original, was in a traditional vein, they remained open to modern influences throughout their quarter-century career.

Encouraged by the Allen Brothers, the Delmores auditioned for Columbia in 1931, but their first record sold poorly. The following year, they joined the *Grand Ole Opry* in Nashville, where they would remain until 1938. In 1933, they began recording for Bluebird; their first session produced their first hit, "Brown's Ferry Blues," a slightly risqué song ("Two old maids playing in the sand / Each one wishin' that the other'n' was a man") that formed the model for such country-hokum numbers as Bob Wills's "Oozlin' Daddy Blues." By the late 1930s, they were one of the most successful country acts, touring with Uncle Dave Macon and Roy Acuff. Recording with Fiddlin' Arthur Smith (not Arthur "Guitar Boogie" Smith), they popularized the classic "There's More Pretty Girls Than One."

After leaving the *Grand Ole Opry,* the Delmore Brothers switched to the Decca label, moving from city to city to perform on different radio stations. They were broadcasting on WLW in Cincinnati in 1943, along with Merle Travis, when they met Syd Nathan, who began recording them on his new King label in January 1944. Two years later, on their third King session, they cut "Hillbilly Boogie," adding Travis and Louis Innis on guitars. The song intermittently features the same "Weary Blues" boogie-woogie guitar line as "Guitar Boogie," as well as harmonized lyrics by the Delmores ("It's just the hillbilly boogie, in the lowdown way"), but there are no overt jazz references; the boogie is wholly subsumed in the country idiom.

Following "Hillbilly Boogie," the brothers scored their first hit on *Billboard*'s country chart, "Freight Train Boogie," with railroad mimicry by guitarist Homer Haynes, mandolin player Jethro Burns (the duo known as Homer and Jethro), and harmonica player Wayne Raney. The boogie-woogie guitar line is similar to the ascending "New Orleans Hop Scop Blues" type of figure heard on "Porky's Boogie Woogie on Strings"; on the last pair of boogie choruses, the guitar shifts into an octave-jumping line that's pure rockabilly. The Delmores continued to cut propulsive songs such as "Boogie Woogie Baby," "Mobile Boogie," "Stop That Boogie," "Barnyard Boogie," "Down Home Boogie," "Peach Tree Street Boogie," and their final hit, "Pan American Boogie," while also recording more traditionally styled material. They had their biggest hit in 1949 with "Blues Stay Away from Me," which King's A&R man Henry Glover had adapted from the first theme of "The Huckle-Buck," adding a "Yancey Special" bass line (played by Zeb Turner's brother Zeke) that he lifted from Sonny Thompson's rhythm-and-blues smash "Long Gone." In a reverse crossover attempt, King then had Lonnie Johnson record "Blues Stay Away from Me" for the R&B market. The Delmore Brothers cut the R&B-flavored "Good Time Saturday Night" in 1951, but Rabon died of cancer the following year, bringing the act to an end.

In February 1946, Merl Lindsay and His Oklahoma Night Riders recorded their first single, "Shimmy Shakin' Daddy," for the 4 Star label in Hollywood. Although the instrumentation, featuring fiddles and steel guitar, is typical of western swing, and the walking bass does not follow a boogie pattern, the song as a whole has a strong proto-rockabilly feel, with a 4/4 rather than 2/4 meter, a twelve-bar verse-and-refrain structure, and a tune resembling "Rock Around the Clock" (Lindsay's next single was the melodically similar "Gotta Little Red Wagon"). During Jimmy Pruett's piano solo,

Lindsay says, "Hoy hoy," a rhythm-and-blues shibboleth introduced on Cab Calloway's 1938 song of that title and popularized by Joe Liggins's 1945 smash "The Honeydripper" (Lindsay would later cover Liggins's 1950 hit "Pink Champagne").

Spade Cooley recorded the richly orchestrated, accordion-powered "Three Way Boogie" for Columbia in May 1946, but perhaps the first boogie-woogie to make the national country charts was "Oakie Boogie," recorded for Capitol in October 1946 by Jack Guthrie, with Porky Freeman and Red Murrell on guitars. Barely hinting at a boogie-woogie guitar line, it's a boogie in name only, but it has a drummed backbeat, a verse-and-refrain structure, and a melody like "Rock Around the Clock." Guthrie, an Oklahoman, was Woody Guthrie's cousin; the two performed together on the radio in California in 1937, and Jack had a No. 1 country hit in 1945 with Woody's composition "Oklahoma Hills," Jack's debut recording for Capitol. He sang "Oakie Boogie" in the 1947 movie *Hollywood Barn Dance,* but by then he'd been diagnosed with tuberculosis, to which he succumbed the following year. Ella Mae Morse's 1952 recording of "Oakie Boogie," arranged by Nelson Riddle, was a minor pop hit.

By 1947, the hillbilly boogie craze was well under way, although many of that year's recordings were not released until 1948. Some artists, such as the Milo Twins, followed the Delmore Brothers' formula; others, such as Johnny Tyler (who wrote "Oakie Boogie"), gave a western twist to the piano-driven boogie stylings of jazz bands such as Will Bradley's or Freddie Slack's. Boogie patterns, if present at all, were often played on guitar rather than bass or piano, or sung as part of the melody, as in "Rock Around the Clock." Even on recordings made before Wynonie Harris's "Good Rockin' Tonight," the guitar solos, blending jazz and blues with country music, frequently have a rock 'n' roll feel. Like "blues," the word "boogie" was used loosely in the country field, and some nominal boogies—Arthur Smith's snappy "Country Boogie," for example—have no musical boogie-woogie content whatsoever.

One of the first country artists after Jack Guthrie to place a boogie on the national charts was Merle Travis, who cut the hits "Merle's Boogie Woogie" and "Crazy Boogie" in 1947. Born in the coal-mining region of western Kentucky, Travis learned the local fingerpicking guitar style from musicians such as Ike Everly, the father of the Everly Brothers, ultimately developing a virtuoso technique that influenced Chet Atkins and others. He began playing with Clayton McMichen's Georgia Wildcats in 1937 and broadcasting on Cincinnati's WLW the following year. In 1943, he and his radio colleagues Grandpa Jones and the Delmore Brothers formed one of the greatest-ever white gospel harmony quartets, the Brown's Ferry Four, in which Travis sang bass. Unusually for that time, the group's repertoire included songs by African American composers, such as Cleavant Derricks's "Just a Little Talk with Jesus," which became a country-gospel standard.

"Me and Grandpa found a source for songs," Travis told the folklorist William Lightfoot. "Down on Central Avenue, there in the black section of Cincinnati, was a little, used record shop run by a little, short Jewish man with real thick glasses. He had asthma and a scratchy voice and his name was Syd Nathan. We got acquainted with him and we'd go down to Syd's used record shop and find all these great records by the black spiritual quartets. We'd learn the songs and sing them on the air as the Brown's Ferry Four."[46]

In 1943, at Nathan's instigation, Travis and Grandpa Jones made the King label's very first recording, under the name the Sheppard Brothers. But in 1944, Travis moved to Los Angeles, where he played Foreman Phillips's ballrooms as a member of the singing movie cowboy Ray Whitley's band, recorded under his own name and as a sideman (he was a member of the Porky Freeman Trio when they remade "Boogie Woogie on Strings"), and appeared in movies and Soundies. In 1946, he signed with Capitol Records and immediately scored a double-sided hit with "Cincinnati Lou"/"No Vacancy," where his guitar is overshadowed by a pop-flavored band including an accordion and trumpet. Similar hits followed, including the country chart-toppers "Divorce Me C.O.D." and "So Round, So Firm, So Fully Packed."

Also in 1946, Travis recorded the album *Folk Songs of the Hills,* an initially unsuccessful attempt to tap the emerging folk-music market with traditional songs plus such Travis originals as the coal-mining laments "Dark as a Dungeon" and "Sixteen Tons." The former would become a country classic, while the latter was resurrected as a No. 1 pop and country hit in 1955 by Tennessee Ernie Ford. On "Merle's Boogie Woogie," Travis used the same kind of overdubbing and half-speed recording techniques that Les Paul was then experimenting with. During the same period, Travis designed a solid-body electric guitar that inspired Leo Fender to build his revolutionary Telecaster model. By the 1950s, his hit-making streak had ended, but Travis continued to record for Capitol (on his own and as a guitarist with Hank Thompson and His Brazos Valley Boys), perform on radio, and appear in movies (including the multiple Oscar winner *From Here to Eternity,* where he sang "Reenlistment Blues"). His career got a boost during the folk revival of the 1960s, and he remained active until suffering a fatal heart attack in 1983.

The hillbilly boogie made its way into religious music via the Homeland Harmony Quartet's 1948 recording of "Gospel Boogie," a landmark gospel hit. Founded in the mid-1930s, the group had included Doyle Blackwood and Hovie Lister, who went on to become respective stalwarts of the Blackwood Brothers and the Statesmen, two of Elvis Presley's favorite gospel quartets. Lee Roy Abernathy, who joined the Homeland Harmony Quartet in the mid-1940s, brought a commercial sensibility to white gospel music; his composition "Everybody's Gonna Have a Wonderful Time Up There," also known as "Gospel Boogie," alternates between a sung boogie-woogie bass line and a talking-blues-style recitation. Though condemned by some church leaders, the song was popular among both whites and blacks, covered by Red Foley, Sister Rosetta Tharpe, the Oak Ridge Boys, the Pilgrim Travelers, and Pat Boone, who had a Top 5 pop hit with it in 1958.

Among the better-known country artists to embrace the boogie were Al Dexter, who featured piano-driven pop-jazz arrangements on "New Broom Boogie" and the instrumental "Saturday Night Boogie," and Hawkshaw Hawkins, who made the country Top 10 with the guitar-powered "Doghouse Boogie," his second release on King. Cowboy Copas, who would die in the same 1963 plane crash as Hawkins and Patsy Cline, cut "Hangman Boogie," a novelty song about the spasmodic "dance" of an executed criminal that includes only a brief boogie guitar break. Even less of a boogie connection can be heard on Hank Snow's "Rhumba Boogie," a No. 1 country hit in 1951 that sets the tune of Snow's first No. 1 hit, "I'm Movin' On," to a Cuban clave beat. (Snow, a Canadian who'd been inspired by Jimmie Rodgers, was to play a key role in advancing Elvis Presley's career. "I'm Movin' On" was covered by Ray Charles in 1959 and by the Rolling Stones in 1965.) By contrast, Chet Atkins's "Boogie Man Boogie," featuring Homer and Jethro, is underpinned by a boogie-woogie bass line throughout, as is "Mean Mama Boogie" by Johnny Bond, a former member of the Jimmy Wakely Trio who enjoyed a successful solo career as an actor, singer, and songwriter.

Two rising honky-tonk stars from Louisiana, Webb Pierce and Faron Young, sang on hillbilly-boogie recordings made under the name of the bass player Tillman Franks, who performed on Shreveport's *Louisiana Hayride* radio show. On "Hayride Boogie," from early 1951, Pierce sings, "Every Saturday night around eight o'clock / this old place begins to reel and rock." Featuring an intermittent guitar vamp adapted from Glenn Miller's "In the Mood" rather than a boogie-woogie bass line, the song could easily be classified as rockabilly or rock 'n' roll, and Pierce rerecorded it for Decca in 1956 as "Teenage Boogie." On Franks's "Hot Rod-Shotgun Boogie No. 2," recorded later in 1951, Faron Young alludes to Arkie Shibley's "Hot Rod Race" and Bill Nettles's "Hadacol Boogie," with an emphasis on the Hadacol, an alcoholic tonic introduced in the mid-1940s by the Louisiana politician Dudley LeBlanc and peddled on a celebrity-studded touring medicine show called the Hadacol Caravan (only the song's title alludes to Tennessee Ernie Ford's "The Shot Gun Boogie").

Red Foley and Tennessee Ernie Ford cut the biggest-selling hillbilly boogies, "Chattanoogie Shoe Shine Boy" and "The Shot Gun Boogie"—both No. 1 country hits that crossed over to the pop charts. Foley, born in Kentucky, sang and played harmonica and guitar from an early age; he was studying music at a local college when a talent scout recruited him to join the WLS *National Barn Dance* in Chicago. He recorded for the ARC labels with members of the *Barn Dance* troupe and on his own before signing with

Decca, for whom he cut his breakthrough hit, the fierce war anthem "Smoke on the Water," in 1944. Lawrence Welk's sweet band accompanied him on his second No. 1 country hit, a 1945 cover of Spade Cooley's "Shame on You." In 1946, he replaced Roy Acuff as the star of the *Prince Albert Show,* the NBC network portion of WSM's *Grand Ole Opry.* He formed a new band, the Cumberland Valley Boys, including guitarists Zeke Turner and Louis Innis, steel guitarist Jerry Byrd, and fiddler Tommy Jackson, who became some of the first regular studio musicians in Nashville.

The smooth-singing Foley performed all sorts of material, but a number of his biggest hits were boogies. He had his first boogie hit in 1947 with a cover of the Delmore Brothers' "Freight Train Boogie" and a No. 1 smash in 1948 with "Tennessee Saturday Night," a country adaptation of such pop boogies as "Down the Road a Piece" that features a classic proto-rockabilly guitar riff by Zeke Turner. Foley reached the top of both the country and pop charts in 1950 with "Chattanoogie Shoe Shine Boy," a countrified pop boogie that simulates the rhythmic snapping of a bootblack's "boogie-woogie rag" over a bass vamp similar to the piano riff on Freddie Slack's "Cow-Cow Boogie." Ostensibly written by two members of the WSM staff, "Chattanoogie Shoe Shine Boy" was covered by Bing Crosby and Frank Sinatra, among others.[47] Foley's next country chart-topper was his cover of Hardrock Gunter's boogie-driven "Birmingham Bounce," and he continued to score such hits as "Hobo Boogie" and "Milk Bucket Boogie" through the early 1950s. (The guitarist on both "Chattanoogie Shoe Shine Boy" and "Birmingham Bounce" is Grady Martin, who went on to play studio sessions with Johnny Burnette, Elvis Presley, Buddy Holly, Roy Orbison, and many others.) In 1954, accompanied by the Anita Kerr Singers, Foley covered the Charms' doo-wop smash "Hearts of Stone." His record sales declined after the mid-1950s, but Foley continued to perform until his death in 1968.

While Foley flirted with pop music, Tennessee Ernie Ford became a full-fledged pop star, hosting network television shows after his success with "Sixteen Tons." Born in Bristol, Tennessee, Ford started his career as a radio announcer; after World War II, he settled in San Bernardino, California, and began working as a disc jockey under the name Tennessee Ernie. He met the California-born country musician and radio host Cliffie Stone, who hired Ford as a singer for his *Hometown Jamboree* show and got him a contract with Capitol Records. With his clear, penetrating baritone, Ford was an instant success as a recording artist. "Smokey Mountain Boogie," his third single (and third hit), is a countrified pop boogie in the Will Bradley mold, with guitar and steel guitar solos by Merle Travis and Speedy West. His next two country hits, "Mule Train" and "The Cry of the Wild Goose" (from late 1949 and early 1950), were covers of western-flavored No. 1 pop hits by Frankie Laine; Ford's versions crossed over to the pop charts as well.

In June 1950, Ford, together with Kay Starr, recorded "I'll Never Be Free," a torchy ballad by the interracial songwriting team of Bennie Benjamin and George David Weiss. The singer Savannah Churchill was probably the first to record it; versions by Paul Gayten and Annie Laurie, Dinah Washington, and Ella Fitzgerald with Louis Jordan all made the R&B charts in 1950 (Lucky Millinder followed in early 1951). Ford and Starr's record, the biggest hit, reached the Top 5 on both the country and pop charts, but its arrangement, steel guitar notwithstanding, smacks of rhythm-and-blues, with a "Yancey Special" bass line not heard on other versions. In later years, the song would be recorded by everyone from Pat Boone to Aretha Franklin.

In July 1950, Ford cut "The Shot Gun Boogie," similar to "Smokey Mountain Boogie" but with more-countrified lyrics ("Shotgun boogie, I done saw your track / Look out, Mr. Rabbit, when I cock my hammer back") and less of a boogie bass line. "The Shot Gun Boogie" topped *Billboard*'s country chart in late 1950 and entered the pop chart early the next year. Ford followed with similar songs such as "Blackberry Boogie" in 1952 and "Catfish Boogie" in 1953. He also recorded duets with pop singers such as Helen O'Connell, Ella Mae Morse, and Betty Hutton. He was joined by the Dinning Sisters, a pop-country trio, on the musically though not lyrically R&B-ish "Rock City Boogie," from August 1951. His series of crossover pop hits peaked in 1955 with "The Ballad of Davy Crockett," from the Walt Disney television series, and "Sixteen Tons," originally released as the flip side of "You Don't Have to Be a Baby to Cry," a 1950 hit for Ernest Tubb. With its slick arrangement, Ford's "Sixteen Tons" was received more as a pop novelty than a country protest song, and it shot to the top of the charts. From 1956 to 1961, Ford had his own prime-time variety show on NBC television; later, he hosted a daytime talk show on ABC. He turned toward gospel music in the 1950s and recorded mostly religious songs in the decades before his death in 1991.

Another boogie-associated country act to achieve prominence was the Maddox Brothers and Rose, a family group at home with both traditional and modern material. In 1933, the Maddoxes trekked from northern Alabama to California, where they worked as migrant harvesters. In 1937, Fred, Cliff, and Cal Maddox formed a quartet with their eleven-year-old sister, Rose, and began performing on a radio station in Modesto. The band broke up when Fred and Cal were drafted but re-formed after World War II, adding two more brothers plus a pair of unrelated instrumentalists, while Cliff drifted away. The Maddox Brothers and Rose began recording for the 4 Star label in 1947, switching to Columbia in 1952; although their records did not sell especially well, they were widely known for their elaborate stage shows, which blended broad comedy with old-time, honky-tonk, boogie, and gospel music, all performed with a strong backwoods flavor. They also became known for their gaudy western outfits, designed by Nathan Turk, the tailor who dressed Gene Autry and Roy Rogers. Although she traded the lead vocal role with her brothers, Rose Maddox was the band's cynosure, a powerful and expressive singer who could be funny or poignant as the material demanded.

Some of the early Maddox Brothers and Rose recordings have a rock 'n' roll feel, featuring antic screams (along with laughter and dialogue), rockabilly-like guitar solos, and Fred Maddox's slapped bass. "Mean and Wicked Boogie" is a twelve-bar verse-and-refrain song with a melody like "Rock Around the Clock," as is the group's cover of Hank Williams's "Move It On Over." Their cover of Merl Lindsay's "Shimmy Shakin' Daddy" also has a hokum structure, as does the rollicking "Hangover Blues." Like "Mean and Wicked Boogie," "George's Playhouse Boogie"—adapted from "The House of Blue Lights"—lacks a repeating boogie figure; but "Water Baby Boogie," a revved-up version of Lindsay's instrumental "Water Baby Blues," has a boogie-ish guitar vamp, and the group's cover of "No Help Wanted" adds a boogie riff (on mandolin) not present on the Carlisles' original. The Maddoxes also recorded Kokomo Arnold's "Milk Cow Blues" and Blind Boy Fuller's boogie-driven hokum song "Step It Up and Go."

The group's sound veered sharply toward rock after they shared the bill with Elvis Presley on the *Louisiana Hayride* in late 1954 (Presley's bass player, Bill Black, reportedly idolized Fred Maddox).[48] In February 1955, Rose Maddox, recording under her own name, covered Ruth Brown's uptempo 1953 R&B hit "Wild Wild Young Men" ("Well, they can romp and stomp / Well, they can rock 'n' roll"), living up to the original with an exuberant vocal performance set amid strings instead of horns but similarly propelled by a pounding backbeat. In December 1955, she cut "Hey Little Dreamboat," a driving rockabilly number featuring Merle Travis on guitar. In August 1956, the Maddox Brothers and Rose recorded "The Death of Rock and Roll," a hard-rocking, bass-slapping parody of Elvis Presley's cover of Ray Charles's "I've Got a Woman." Rather than adopting rock 'n' roll whole hog, the Maddoxes often put a rocking beat behind traditional-style country material, but they did cover Mickey and Sylvia's "Love Is Strange," a No. 1 hit on both the R&B and pop charts in early 1957.

The family band broke up in the late 1950s, and Rose went solo, scoring a string of hits on the Capitol label that outsold anything she'd recorded with her brothers. She cut the rockabilly gem "My Little Baby" in 1959, but it did not sell as well as her honky-tonk records, which included several duets with Buck Owens. She also made the album *Rose Maddox Sings Bluegrass* with Bill Monroe. Her recording career foundered in the mid-1960s, but she continued to perform, turning to the folk circuit in the 1970s; by the 1980s, she'd been embraced by rockabilly revivalists. She remained active even after suffering a series of heart attacks, dying of kidney failure in 1998.

Moon Mullican spent his early career as a sideman, not recording under his own name until he signed with King in 1946. Born in East Texas, he learned to play organ as a boy, drawing influences from a black guitarist who worked on the Mullican family farm. Set on music as a profession, he left for Houston, polishing his piano technique in honky-tonks and bordellos before joining the Blue Ridge Playboys. He sang on a few of the Playboys' recordings in 1936 but didn't display his bent for the blues until joining Cliff Bruner's Texas Wanderers, with whom he cut "Old Joe Turner Blues" and "Kangaroo Blues" in 1938. In 1940, after Bruner left the Wanderers, Mullican sang on their recording of his composition "Pipeliner Blues," an authentic-sounding blues he would record several more times. In the early 1940s, Mullican recorded for Decca, OKeh, Columbia, and Bluebird with musicians linked to Jimmie Davis, including Bruner, Charles Mitchell, Buddy Jones, Slim Harbert, and the Shelton Brothers, as well as Davis himself.

Mullican's first King session, in September or October 1946, produced the country hit "New Pretty Blonde (New Jole Blon)," a variation of Harry Choates's hit version of the Cajun standard "Jolie Blonde" on which Mullican substitutes Slim Gaillard–like double talk ("horse and buggy," "rice and gravy," "possum up a gum stump") for the original French lyrics. At the same session, Mullican cut "New Milk Cow Blues" and "Let Me Rock You Baby," the latter a bawdy twelve-bar verse-and-refrain hokum number ("Now my rockin' chair is easy and I'm feelin' mighty fine / I got two, three more gals standin' in line") that would certainly have been a candidate for first rock 'n' roll record if only King had released it.

Mullican plays outstanding blues piano on "Let Me Rock You Baby" and on "Wait a Minute," from December 1947, where he briefly adds a boogie-woogie bass line. The blues, however, was only a part of his repertoire: two of his biggest hits were the bluegrass weeper "Sweeter Than the Flowers" and the honky-tonk classic "I'll Sail My Ship Alone," which was later covered by Jerry Lee Lewis, among many others. Mullican also scored a double-sided hit covering Nat "King" Cole's pop smash "Mona Lisa" and the Weavers' chart-topping adaptation of Leadbelly's "Goodnight, Irene." At the probable instigation of producer Henry Glover, he recorded a country version of Tiny Bradshaw's "Well Oh Well," with steel guitar and fiddle solos over a snappy backbeat. But Mullican established his reputation as a boogie artist with his 1951 hit "Cherokee Boogie (Eh-Oh-Aleena)," where he plays some genuine boogie piano between Indian-themed verses.

Mullican is said to have cowritten the country classic "Jambalaya (On the Bayou)" with Hank Williams in 1952, adapting it from the Cajun standard "Grand Texas." In 1953, he adopted an R&B shouting style to cover Roy Brown's "Grandpa Stole My Baby," accompanied by the black tenor saxophonist Rufus Gore; on the same date, he cut "Rocket to the Moon," a full-blown rocker seemingly based on Kay Starr's "Kay's Lament." In early

1956, at his final King session, he shouted "Seven Nights to Rock," backed by Boyd Bennett and his Rockets; the same session yielded "I'm Mad with You," "Rock and Roll Mr. Bullfrog," and "Honolulu Rock-A Roll-A." In 1958, he recorded the even harder-rocking "Moon's Rock" for Coral. But the middle-aged Mullican had little appeal for youthful rockabilly fans and did not make the charts between 1951 and 1961, when he cut his last hit, the honky-tonker "Ragged but Right." Nevertheless, he continued to record rock, pop, and country songs—including rocked-up versions of earlier material such as "Pipeliner Blues"—for various labels until suffering a fatal heart attack at the end of 1966.

Following closely on Mullican's heels were the midwestern boogie pianists Merrill Moore and Chuck Miller. Moore, born in Iowa, discovered Freddie Slack at about the same time that he discovered Frankie Carle and Bob Wills. After serving in the navy during World War II, he settled in California and, around 1950, began leading his own band, the Saddle, Rock and Rhythm Boys, in San Diego. From 1952 until 1958, he recorded for Capitol Records, singing and playing virtuosic piano-boogie solos on steel-guitar-tinged arrangements. His biggest sellers were the car-racing song "Red Light" (released in 1953), "The House of Blue Lights" (1953), and "Down the Road a Piece" (1956), but none of his records made the national charts. Moore appeared on radio and television and worked as a studio musician in Los Angeles through the 1950s, then moved back to San Diego and played nightclubs into the 1990s, dying in 2000.

A year younger than Moore, Chuck Miller, born in Kansas, moved to Los Angeles and by the late 1940s was leading his own trio. He befriended the saxophonist Dave Cavanaugh, who became an A&R man and producer for Capitol Records and signed Miller to the label in 1953. Backed by Cavanaugh's band, Miller first recorded pop material, but in 1954 he covered Wade Ray's boogie-flavored country truck-driving song "Idaho Red" ("Idaho Red, wheelin' an' a-dealin' / Idaho Red, watch him reel and rock"). The following year, he switched to Mercury Records and cut a jivey arrangement of "The House of Blue Lights," featuring a scatting chorus as well as Miller's boogie piano. The record became a Top 10 pop hit, prompting *Time* magazine to ask, "Does it herald the decline of rock 'n' roll?"[49] Miller followed with boogie-rock versions of Bobby Lord's "Hawk-Eye," Gene Krupa's "Boogie Blues," George Gobel's "Bright Red Convertible," and Bob Temple's "Vim Vam Vamoose," but his only record to chart besides "The House of Blue Lights" was his cover of Leroy Van Dyke's crossover country hit "Auctioneer." Miller also cut "Down the Road a Piece," "Cow-Cow Boogie," and the Everly Brothers' "Bye Bye Love" for Mercury before switching to the Imperial label for one album in 1959. Fading into obscurity, he moved to Idaho, Alaska, and finally Hawaii, where he died at age seventy-five in 2000.

Many hillbilly boogies were recorded by artists who never made the *Billboard* charts, generally following the same models—the Delmore Brothers or the big bands of Will Bradley and Freddie Slack—as those who did. Some hillbilly-boogie artists also covered rhythm-and-blues songs; but with such exceptions as Rocky Rauch and His Western Serenaders' "Colorado Boogie," with its wailing saxophone introduction, R&B had relatively little direct influence on the hillbilly boogie itself, which developed mainly through variations on the same basic patterns. The music gradually evolved into rockabilly, with no sharp demarcation between the genres, but a turning point seems to have been reached around 1950 or 1951, when jiving lyrics and shuffling backbeats came to prominence. As early as October 1947, drummer Melvin Mountjoy played a crisp backbeat on Johnny Tyler's "Old McDonald's Boogie." Shuffle rhythms can be heard on Billy Briggs's "Pretty Baby Boogie" and Roy Hall's "Dirty Boogie," both from 1949. Buz Butler's "The Rubber Ball Bounce," from around 1949, features a boogie-woogie bass line and a shuffling backbeat. Hillbilly boogies are often sprinkled with jive talk, but "Be Bop Boogie," recorded in 1950 by the veteran comedy duo Mustard and Gravy (Frank Rice and Ernest L. Stokes), is virtually all jive; the song was covered in pure rockabilly style by Don Hager and the Hot Tots in 1957, by which time the term "bebop"—disconnected from any association with jazz—had become a rockabilly trademark.

By 1951, shuffling backbeats had become commonplace, helping to give a rock 'n' roll feel to songs such as "No Shoes Boogie" by Charlie Harris with R. D. Hendon's Western Jamboree Cowboys. "There's a new kind of rhythm to the hillbilly band," Hardrock Gunter explains on his "Dixieland Boogie." "It's an old-time boogie with a solid beat / With a Dixieland drag to make you shuffle your feet." A backbeat shuffle propels Bill Haley's "Green Tree Boogie," Zeb Turner's "Traveling Boogie," Vance Morris's "Crazy about the Boogie," and Texas Bill Strength's "Paper Boy Boogie," all from 1951. By early 1952, when Haley cut "Sundown Boogie," a twelve-bar verse-and-refrain song with a shuffling backbeat, the stage was set for the mature emergence of rockabilly.

COUNTRY AND R&B

Although rhythm-and-blues made only an oblique impact on the hillbilly boogie, country music and R&B did intermingle. In 1946, Henry "Red" Allen, a New Orleans–bred jazz trumpeter who, like Hot Lips Page, dabbled in rhythm-and-blues, recorded his own composition "Get the Mop," spelling out "M-O-P-P" to a frantic beat. In 1949, Johnnie Lee Wills, Bob's younger brother, recorded the country hit "Rag Mop," an extended, decelerated take on "Get the Mop" for which a steel guitarist from Texas, Deacon Anderson, claimed songwriting credit. "Rag Mop" was quickly covered by more than a dozen artists, including the Ames Brothers, a white vocal quartet whose rendition, featuring a rock-style guitar solo, became a No. 1 pop hit in early 1950; versions by Lionel Hampton, Jimmy Dorsey, Ralph Flanagan, the Starlighters, and Eddy Howard, not to mention Johnnie Lee Wills, also made the pop charts. Hampton's "Rag Mop" was an R&B hit as well, as were versions by Joe Liggins and a group called Doc Sausage and His Mad Lads.

A television clip from the mid-1950s shows the Treniers, an R&B combo that included several singing brothers named Trenier, performing "Rag Mop" in exuberant rock 'n' roll style, briefly doing what looks like Chuck Berry's duck walk. In 1956, the Teen Queens, an R&B sister duo, cut an adaptation titled "Rock Everybody," spelling out "rock" and "roll" instead of "ragg" and "mopp." "Rag Mop" was recorded by many other artists, from Banda da Lua, a Brazilian group that accompanied Carmen Miranda, to the Chipmunks, and was parodied as "Rat Fink" by Allan Sherman.

Crossovers between country music and rhythm-and-blues ran in both directions, but artists generally maintained their own country or R&B style even when borrowing material from the other genre. In 1949, Link Davis, a former singer, fiddler, and saxophonist with Cliff Bruner's Texas Wanderers, covered Wynonie Harris's "Good Rockin' Tonight" under the title "Have You Heard the News." In 1950, Bruner covered Roy Brown's "Hard Luck Blues," and Melvin Price and the Santa Fe Rangers covered Larry Darnell's "For You My Love," both No. 1 R&B hits. Around the same time, the York Brothers, recording for King, covered Tiny Bradshaw's "Gravy Train," written by Henry Glover; the brothers also covered the Dominoes' "Sixty Minute Man." In 1951, Hawkshaw Hawkins covered Ruth Brown's No 1. R&B hit "Teardrops from My Eyes." In 1953, Little Jimmy Dickens covered Piano Red's R&B hit "Rockin' with Red," and Red Foley covered Faye Adams's R&B chart-topper "Shake a Hand." In 1954, Johnnie and Jack charted country with "Goodnight, Sweetheart, Goodnight," a cover of the Spaniels' No. 1 R&B hit.

Singer-saxophonist Bull Moose Jackson, one of the first black artists signed to King, had a No. 2 R&B hit in 1949 with his cover of Wayne Raney's No. 1 country hit "Why Don't You Haul Off and Love Me," also on King; in 1951, Jackson covered Moon Mullican's "Cherokee Boogie." (Country singer Jimmy Ballard covered Jackson's "I Want a Bowlegged Woman" for King in 1952.) In yet another intra-label King crossover, Wynonie Harris covered Mullican's "Triflin' Woman Blues" in 1949, but the record was not released; King did release Harris's 1950 cover of Louis Innis's "Good Morning Judge," which Innis had recorded for Mercury earlier that year. Cab Calloway, Eddie Mack with Cootie Williams's band, and Cecil Gant all covered Tennessee Ernie Ford's "The Shot Gun Boogie." And the Crows cut a doo-wop version of the Carlisles' "No Help Wanted" in 1953.

Also in 1953, Darrell Glenn, a teenage singer from Texas, scored a pop and country hit with his father's gospel composition "Crying in the Chapel." A rendition by the singing movie cowboy Rex Allen also made both pop and country charts, while one by the pioneering doo-wop group the Orioles topped the R&B list and also charted pop. June Valli's pure-pop version was the biggest seller, but recordings by Ella Fitzgerald and the former big-band singer Art Lund also made the pop charts. Elvis Presley's "Crying in the Chapel" was recorded in 1960 but not released until 1965, when it reached the Top 5 in the United States and the No. 1 spot in England. Presley's is the best-remembered version, but the Orioles' "Crying in the Chapel" is also an enduring classic.

In August 1952, Willie Mae "Big Mama" Thornton recorded "Hound Dog" for the Houston-based Peacock label. Born in Alabama, Thornton turned from gospel to blues singing, touring the South as a teenager with the Hot Harlem Revue before settling in Houston and signing with Peacock. She went west with Johnny Otis's touring show, cutting "Hound Dog" in Los Angeles with members of Otis's band. Two young, white songwriters, Jerry Leiber and Mike Stoller, had brought "Hound Dog" to Otis, who helped rewrite it.[50] The song, a blues, expresses a woman's rejection of a man—the metaphorical dog in the title—and Thornton bawls the lyrics with grainy scorn, urging guitarist Pete Lewis on during his long solo. Issued in March 1953, Thornton's "Hound Dog" was a No. 1 R&B hit, prompting such thinly disguised covers as Rufus Thomas's "Bear Cat" on Sun and John Brim's "Rattlesnake" on Chess's Checker subsidiary. "Bear Cat," identified on the label as "The Answer to Hound Dog," became Sun's first hit, reaching No. 3 on *Billboard*'s R&B chart, but Peacock's owner, Don Robey, successfully sued Sun's Sam Phillips for copyright infringement, whereupon Chess withdrew "Rattlesnake."[51] Another answer song was Jimmie Wilson's "Call Me a Hound Dog" on the Big Town label, which also released trumpeter Frank Motley's frenetic "New Hound Dog," featuring singer Curley Bridges.

Additionally, within a month or so of its release, "Hound Dog" was covered by half a dozen white country singers. Billy Starr's rawboned rendition tries to copy the Latin-like rhythm of Thornton's version, while Eddie Hazelwood's two-steps in honky-tonk style. Jack Turner sings smoothly to a handclapped backbeat, accompanied on guitar by (possibly) Chet Atkins; Cleve Jackson, who later recorded as Jackson Toombs, sings nonchalantly to a snappy drumbeat, accompanied by bluesy guitar and honky-tonk piano. Tommy Duncan, the former singer with Bob Wills's Texas Playboys, takes a jazzy approach, backed by a growling trumpet and a steel guitar.[52] Betsy Gay, a Connecticut-born Hollywood child actress turned country singer, shouts the blues with bit of a yodel, accompanied by guitarists Merle Travis and Joe Maphis. Charlie Gore sings and Louis Innis plays guitar over a heavy backbeat on their "(You Ain't Nothin' but a Female) Hound Dog," reversing the original song's distaff point of view.

In 1955, Freddie Bell and the Bellboys, a white band from Philadelphia, recorded a version of "Hound Dog" for Bernie Lowe's Teen label. At Lowe's suggestion, Bell rewrote the lyrics to make them more pop-friendly, changing "been snoopin' 'round my door" to "cryin' all the time" and "you can wag your tail, but I ain't gonna feed you no more" to "you never caught a rabbit so you ain't no friend of mine," so that the song was now literally about a dog. The group was appearing at the Sands Hotel in Las Vegas in the spring of 1956 when Elvis Presley made his Las Vegas debut with a two-week engagement at the nearby New Frontier. "Elvis got his lyrics from those guys," said Scotty Moore. "He knew the original lyrics, but he didn't use them."[53] Presley performed "Hound Dog" on the nationally televised *Milton Berle Show* and *Steve Allen Show* before recording it for RCA Victor in July 1956. Backed with "Don't Be Cruel," it became his all-time best selling single—not just a signature smash but an emblem of the rock 'n' roll revolution.

Although Presley adapted some of his music directly from rhythm-and-blues and claimed that genre as the source of his style, it's clear from his recording of "Milkcow Blues Boogie" that he was acquainted with western swing, and it's hardly credible that he was less familiar with the hillbilly boogie.[54] Bill Haley's roots in western swing and hillbilly boogie are well documented, and the melody of "Rock Around the Clock," originally published by the African American bandleader Richard M. Jones, can be heard in a number of 1940s country songs. By the early 1950s, if not sooner, country artists were recording in an idiom recognizable as rockabilly or rock 'n' roll, terms that would not be used to characterize the music until a few years later. While rock 'n' roll was first performed by black artists under the rubric of rhythm-and-blues, early white rock 'n' roll was not simply a countrified version of R&B but an inventive adaptation that incorporated hillbilly-boogie innovations such as the transfer of the boogie-woogie bass line to the treble register. Swept up in the wave of youthful enthusiasm that accompanied rock 'n' roll's breakthrough into the popular mainstream, Haley and Presley were hailed as musical pioneers, but they were following a well-worn stylistic path.

Chapter Seven

Good Rockin' Tonight

R&B IS BORN

It is well if not widely understood that rhythm-and-blues, inspired by bands such as Louis Jordan's and Lucky Millinder's, arose out of swing music around the end of World War II. But jazz historians have generally dismissed R&B, in contrast to bebop, as an artistic dead end. "It was . . . a totally commercial music which permitted no fundamental stylistic deviations or advances," writes Gunther Schuller. "And as such it played no further role creatively in jazz, although it provided often desperately needed employment for many otherwise idealistically motivated musicians."[1]

The evolution of rhythm-and-blues—apart from doo-wop, which has it own loyal following—has consequently been given short shrift. As much attention has been paid to the means by which postwar R&B was disseminated—independent record labels, jukeboxes, disc jockeys, high-powered radio stations—as to the music itself. The only book devoted to the early development of rhythm-and-blues is *Honkers and Shouters* (1978) by Arnold Shaw, a former music-publishing executive who locates the roots of R&B more in blues than jazz. (The British writer Hugh Gregory covers some of the same ground in his 1998 book *The Real Rhythm and Blues,* a compendium of biographical sketches.)

The birth of rhythm-and-blues is associated with the breakdown of the big bands and the rise of small combos, but big jazz bands—including those of Duke Ellington, Count Basie, Cab Calloway, Jimmie Lunceford, Andy Kirk, Erskine Hawkins, Lionel Hampton, Lucky Millinder, and Buddy Johnson—continued to have R&B hits in the immediate postwar years. Basie's version of Jack McVea's "Open the Door Richard!" became a No. 1 pop smash in 1947; failing to displace Louis Jordan's "Ain't Nobody Here but Us Chickens," it topped out at No. 2 on *Billboard*'s Most-Played Juke Box Race Records chart, which had replaced the Harlem Hit Parade in 1945. But of the big bands, only Buddy Johnson's extended its streak of hits beyond the beginning of the 1950s.

The genesis of R&B is also linked to the establishment of independent labels such as Specialty, Aladdin, and Modern on the West Coast at the end of the war. But East Coast and midwestern independents such as Savoy, King, and Apollo were founded at the same time or earlier, and many of the West Coast labels' recordings were made in the East, Midwest, or South. It is true, however, that—like their western swing counterparts—some of the leading figures in the development of rhythm-and-blues were based in California and that many of them were originally from Texas or Oklahoma.

Arnold Shaw identifies Cecil Gant's "I Wonder," a No. 1 R&B hit in 1945 that briefly crossed over to the pop charts, as the song that "ignited the postwar blues explosion." Although "I Wonder" is a wistful ballad rather than a blues, Shaw claims that its success on the white-owned Gilt-Edge label "fired the imagination of other would-be 'indies' and promoted the rapid rise of small record companies on the west coast." Joe Bihari, explaining the 1945 founding of the Modern label in Los Angeles, told Shaw, "My brother Jules operated jukeboxes in all-black locations, and it was difficult to get R&B records at that time. His feeling of frustration was crystallized by the shortage of one particular record, Cecil Gant's 'I Wonder'. . . . Finally, one day he said, 'Let's make records ourselves.'"[2] Relying on Bihari's account, Shaw may have exaggerated the impact of "I Wonder."

Shaw writes that the Nashville-born Gant, then an army private, was playing piano at a war-bond rally in Los Angeles when he was discovered by Cliff McDonald, a Gilt-Edge associate. But according to Herb Abramson, who cofounded Atlantic Records, it was Gilt-Edge's owner, Richard Nelson, who made the discovery.[3] Not until 1995 did it come out that Gant had originally cut "I Wonder," his own composition, for a tiny black-owned Los Angeles label, Bronze, which had been founded around 1939 and taken over shortly afterward by Leroy Hurte.[4] According to Hurte, he produced the record after Gant, wearing his army khakis, walked unannounced into the Bronze studio in 1944 and auditioned.[5] The Bronze and Gilt-Edge versions of "I Wonder" were marketed simultaneously, but the Gilt-Edge disc, credited to "Pvt. Cecil Gant, the G.I. Sing-Sation," was better distributed and outsold the Bronze record by far.

As Maurie Orodenker noted in *Billboard*, it was "the song itself rather than this sepia lad's groaning" that made "I Wonder" a hit.[6] At a time when war kept many couples apart, lines such as "Will you think of me every day / Though I may be a million miles away?" had a special resonance. "I Wonder" was quickly covered by Louis Armstrong, Roosevelt Sykes, Woody Herman, and others, while Gant toured the country, performing in uniform.

The flip side of Gant's Gilt-Edge "I Wonder," "Cecil Boogie," a straightforward piano boogie with no vocal, was also a hit (an earlier version of the piece was recorded by Bronze and released later as "Original Cecil's Boogie"). Gant's subsequent R&B hits—two more on Gilt-Edge in 1945 and three others on Bullet and 4 Star in 1948 and 1949—were all ballads, but none approached the popularity of "I Wonder." Gant moved from Los Angeles to Nashville and back again, recording for such labels as Swing Time, Dot, and Imperial. His style was based on Leroy Carr's, though his voice was harsher and he performed more modern material—blues, boogies, ballads, and jive songs. In 1950, he cut a crudely hard-rocking version of Wild Bill Moore's "We're Gonna Rock" for Decca under the name Gunter Lee Carr. Among his last-recorded singles was a cover of Tennessee Ernie Ford's "The Shot Gun Boogie," backed with the proto-rocker "Rock Little Baby." As his career declined, he drank heavily, and he died in February 1951, at the age of thirty-seven.

Another seminal R&B smash, Joe Liggins's "The Honeydripper," was also cut for Bronze before being rerecorded for a different independent label. Liggins, born in Oklahoma, moved to San Diego as a teenager before settling in Los Angeles in 1939; he was playing piano with a band called the California Rhythm Rascals when he wrote "The Honeydripper" around 1942. Liggins later played in a band led by the trumpeter Sammy Franklin and tried to get Franklin to record the song, to no avail.[7] So Liggins put together his own combo and cut "The Honeydripper" as a two-sided single, first for Bronze, which never got around to releasing it, and then, in March 1945, for another black-owned Los Angeles label, Exclusive.

Exclusive had recently been founded by Leon René, whose brother Otis ran Exclusive's sister label, Excelsior. Originally from Covington, Louisiana, across Lake Pontchartrain from New Orleans, the René brothers had moved to Los Angeles in the early 1920s. Otis became a pharmacist, while Leon, a pianist, formed his own band, with which Otis sometimes sang. The brothers also wrote songs together, enjoying their first success in 1931 with "When It's Sleepy Time Down South," which became Louis Armstrong's anthem. Leon went on to write "When the Swallows Come Back to Capistrano," a 1940 hit for the Ink Spots and for Glenn Miller. He produced the King Cole Trio's first records for the Ammor label before launching Exclusive.

On "The Honeydripper," over a two-note piano vamp reminiscent of "Shortnin' Bread," Liggins sings the jiving lyrics in a staccato cadence: "That cat can jam a riff or swing a hot lick / Boy, he sure does jump for joy / He's a killer, a Harlem thriller / Hoy, hoy, hoy, hoy, hoy, hoy, hoy, hoy." A series of instrumental solos follows, including James Jackson's Illinois Jacquet–like tenor sax spot and Liggins's Count Basie–style piano break. The song is plainly rooted in swing, but the sheer simplicity and insistent repetitiousness of the rhythmic piano figure give it a novel character, especially on the opening vocal section. Although it's nearly as difficult to pin down the first rhythm-and-blues record as it is the first rock 'n' roll record, "The Honeydripper," which topped *Billboard*'s R&B chart for a record-setting eighteen weeks and crossed over to the pop list, is a good a choice as any.

Liggins had several more R&B hits on Exclusive, including one, "Got a Right to Cry," that also made the pop charts, but all were more conventionally jazzy than "The Honeydripper." Switching to Specialty, where his younger brother Jimmy was already established, he had a hit in early 1950 with "Rag Mop," using practically the same arrangement as on Lionel Hampton's version, only thinner, slower, and cruder-sounding. Later that year, he had a No. 1 R&B smash with "Pink Champagne," a drinking song (one of many following the 1949 success of Stick McGhee's "Drinkin' Wine Spo-Dee-O-Dee") that rides the same piano vamp as Freddie Slack's "Cow-Cow Boogie." But Liggins would have only two more hits, "Little Joe's Boogie" and "Frankie Lee," both in early 1951: "Frankie Lee" is melodically similar to "Pink Champagne," while "Little Joe's Boogie" culminates a series of shuffle tunes that Liggins recorded, among them "Walkin'," from 1946, and "Groovy Groove," from 1947. (In October 1951, Liggins recorded what could be considered the definitive boogie shuffle, "Shuffle Boogie Blues," but Specialty did not release it.)

Joe Liggins and his band, the Honeydrippers, continued to cut records for Specialty until 1954, including drinking songs, numbers featuring singer Candy Rivers, and remakes of his Exclusive hits. Meanwhile, he toured the country with such R&B luminaries as Amos Milburn, Roy Brown, and Bull Moose Jackson. He recorded for Mercury and Aladdin in the mid-1950s, but like other rhythm-and-blues veterans, he faced diminishing sales with the rise of rock 'n' roll. He made an album for Mercury and a few singles for smaller labels before fading into obscurity, only to be rediscovered before his death in 1987. His song "Going Back to New Orleans," which he recorded in 1952, was revived as the title track of a 1992 album by Dr. John.

After stints as a disc jockey and boxer, Jimmy Liggins became a chauffeur for his brother's band, whereupon he began writing songs, learned to play guitar, and organized his own group, the Drops of Joy. He signed with Specialty in 1947, but his first single—the up-tempo boogie shuffle "I Can't Stop It," backed with the stomping "Troubles Goodbye"—failed to make the charts. His second single, "Teardrop Blues," was an R&B hit in 1948; the flip side, "Cadillac Boogie," formed the basis for Jackie Brenston's "Rocket 88." Liggins had two more jump-blues hits in 1949, "Careful Love" and "Don't Put Me Down," but an accidental shooting that year left him temporarily incapacitated. By 1950, he'd returned to the studio, cutting rollicking boogie shuffles such as "Saturday Night Boogie Woogie Man" and "Shuffle Shuck," but he did not have another national hit until 1953, when he recorded his all-time best seller, the "Spo-Dee-O-Dee" knockoff "Drunk."

In 1954, Liggins left Specialty and recorded four sides for Aladdin, including "Boogie Woogie King," a thumping backbeat shuffle that easily qualifies as rock 'n' roll. He produced his and other artists' records for his own Duplex label over the next couple of decades, remaining active in various aspects of the music business until his death in 1983. His sound, more raucously aggressive and less jazzy than his brother's, typified the rhythm-and-blues of the postwar era and helped pave the way for the rock revolution.

Another key figure in the advent of postwar R&B was Roy Milton, whose 1946 hit "R.M. Blues" made Specialty Records a going concern. Part Native American, Milton spent his early childhood on the Chickasaw reservation in Oklahoma before moving to Tulsa, where he sang with a band led by trombonist Ernie Fields (who would have a Top 5 pop hit in 1959 with a rocked-up version of Glenn Miller's "In the Mood"). When the group's drummer was arrested during a tour, Milton took his place; from then on, Milton sang from behind a drum kit. After leaving Fields in 1933, Milton moved to Los Angeles and formed his own band, playing local nightclubs and in 1944 filming three Soundies with singer June Richmond. In September 1945, Milton made his first recordings, for Lionel Hampton's Hamp-Tone label.

In December 1945, Milton and his band, now known as the Solid Senders, cut a pair of records, "Milton's Boogie" and "R.M. Blues," that were released on the new Juke Box label. (Milton also released the same two titles, with different flip sides, on his own Roy Milton label, illustrated with cartoon drawings.) Juke Box was run by Art Rupe, who'd grown up as Arthur Goldberg in a largely black neighborhood of Pittsburgh. After attending college in Ohio, he enrolled at the University of California at Los Angeles in the hope of breaking into the movie business and changed his name to Rupe. His cinematic ambitions stymied, he invested in Robert Scherman's Atlas Records, the first label to record Johnny Moore's Three Blazers, but the company quickly foundered, and Rupe, with a different partner, founded Juke Box.

Rupe admired the big bands: "I remember being impressed by Lucky Millinder," he told Arnold Shaw. "I was looking for the same sound with a smaller group. I couldn't afford eighteen pieces, so I ended with two small acts. The first was only three pieces. . . . I called them the Sepia Tones. The other act consisted of six instruments—it was Roy Milton's combo. And he succeeded in getting a sound which was as good, and even better than, Lucky Millinder's. It was an uncomplicated sound, and yet it had the full harmonic range."[8]

Sparked by Camille Howard's florid piano, Hosea Sapp's wailing trumpet, and Buddy Floyd's moaning tenor saxophone, "R.M. Blues" spent nearly six months on *Billboard*'s R&B chart, kept out of the No. 1 spot only by Lionel Hampton's "Hey! Ba-Ba-Re-Bop." Released just before "R.M. Blues," "Milton's Boogie" charted afterward; it's essentially a retitled version of Jimmy Rushing's "I May Be Wrong," adding percussive horn riffs and shuffling drums, with Howard giving the boogie bass line more emphasis than Count Basie had. An influential hit, it makes a plausible candidate for first rock record.

Following the success of "R.M. Blues," Rupe split with his partner and founded Specialty Records. Besides Milton and the Liggins brothers, Specialty recorded such R&B artists as Percy Mayfield, Lloyd Price, Marvin and Johnny, Guitar Slim, and Chuck Higgins; signing Little Richard, Don and Dewey, and Larry Williams in the mid-1950s, Specialty became a force in early rock 'n' roll.

Roy Milton remained with Specialty until 1953, cutting nearly twenty R&B hits, many in a similar shuffling blues or boogie style, with prominent piano accompaniment, burly saxophone solos, and—increasingly as time went on—electric guitar breaks. His 1948 hit "Hop, Skip, and Jump" was covered by the Chicago blues pianist Little Johnny Jones in 1953 as "Hoy, Hoy"; the rockabilly singer Clyde Stacy covered "Hoy, Hoy" in 1957, and the Collins Kids, a teenage rockabilly brother-and-sister duo, followed suit (the Collins Kids also recorded a different song titled "Hop, Skip and Jump" in 1957). Milton, too, covered other artists' hits, among them Paul Williams's 1949 instrumental R&B smash "The Huckle-Buck," to which Milton added lyrics, and Louis Prima's 1950 pop hit "Oh, Babe!" a proto-rocking Prima composition also recorded that year by Kay Starr, the Ames Brothers, Benny Goodman, Ralph Flanagan, Lionel Hampton, Wynonie Harris, Jimmy Preston, and Larry Darnell.

Milton toured the country, appearing with the likes of Eddie "Cleanhead" Vinson, Johnny Ace, and Big Mama Thornton. Reviewing a 1952 show in Portland, Oregon, for *Down Beat,* Ted Hallock described Milton as "one squeal shy of Louis Jordan and a beat away from Lionel Hampton. . . . Mostly it's frantic riffing, fair drums from Milton, heavy and repetitive ensemble behind screaming (or whistling) soloists. The excitement is engendered by nothing more than a beat."[9] Later that year, Milton became one of the first rhythm-and-blues artists to tour Europe.

In 1955, Milton cut a session for DooTone, including the all-out rocker "You Got Me Reeling and Rocking"; the next year, he recorded the Little Richard–styled "One Zippy Zam" for King. He added singer Mickey Champion to his band, dueting with her on a cover of Huey "Piano" Smith's 1957 hit "Rockin' Pneumonia and the Boogie Woogie Flu." But like others of his generation, Milton could not compete with the younger rock 'n' roll artists; his last two hits, both in 1961, were a rerecording of "Red Light" and a reissue of "Baby You Don't Know," both jump blues he'd originally cut years earlier. Milton recorded sporadically for small West Coast labels through the 1960s. He continued to make appearances in the United States and Europe before his death in 1983, recording a final album in France in 1977.

An outstanding blues and boogie pianist, Camille Howard moved to Los Angeles from Galveston, Texas. Though already a member of Milton's Solid Senders, she cut "Try Try Again," backed with "Widow Jenkins Blues," with James Clifford's band for the Pan-American label in 1946. The following year, Milton featured her piano on "Camille's Boogie" and her voice on "Thrill Me," a blues hit that prompted Art Rupe to record her under her own name in December 1947. The resulting "X-Temporaneous Boogie," a vocal-less piano showcase, was also a hit, as was the flip side, "You Don't Love Me," where Howard sings an energized version of Paul Gayten's languid 1947 ballad hit "True." Her next release was "Barcarolle Boogie," the first of several classical adaptations. But she would only have two more national hits, the faux-Latin "Fiesta in Old Mexico," in 1949, and the swaggering "Money Blues," in 1951. She left Milton in early 1950, touring and recording with her own trio, but rejoined his band before the year was out, remaining until the mid-1950s. She made a couple of records for the Federal label in 1953 and one more—"Business Woman," backed with "Rock 'n Roll Mama"—for Vee-Jay in 1956, before devoting herself to gospel music. She died in 1993.

The emergence of new stars such as Cecil Gant, Joe Liggins, and Roy Milton around 1945 makes it convenient to date the dawning of rhythm-and-blues from that year. But other R&B luminaries began their careers earlier, and not just in big bands. Easily the most popular postwar rhythm-and-blues artist was Louis Jordan, who placed nearly fifty records on *Billboard*'s R&B chart between 1945 and 1951, fifteen of them in the No. 1 position. These hits included not only shuffle blues and boogies such as "Buzz Me" and "Boogie Woogie Blue Plate" but also jive songs such as "Reet, Petite and Gone," ballads such as "Don't Let the Sun Catch You Crying" (revived in 1964 by the British rock group Gerry and the Pacemakers), songs about barnyard animals such as "Don't Worry 'bout That Mule," and comic recitations such as "Beware." Jordan was also one of the first to bring calypso into the rhythm-and-blues arena with hits such as "Stone Cold Dead in the Market (He Had It Coming)," with Ella Fitzgerald, in 1946 and "Run, Joe" in 1948.

"Run, Joe" was composed by a doctor from the island of St. Vincent, Walter Merrick, who happened to be Jordan's personal physician; the lyrics were by a Trinidadian immigrant, Joe Willoughby. "Stone Cold Dead in the Market," about a woman who kills her husband, had been recorded as "He Had It Coming" in 1939 by its composer, the Trinidadian calypso singer Wilmoth Houdini. After the Jordan-Fitzgerald recording of "Stone Cold Dead in the Market," *Time* magazine proclaimed the song to be "the biggest Calypso hit since *Rum & Coca-Cola*."[10] Calypsos had been popularized in the United States after Roaring Lion and Atilla the Hun [sic] came to New

York from Trinidad in 1934 for a recording session that produced Atilla's "Graf Zeppelin" and Lion's "Marry an Ugly Woman" (which became a No. 1 pop and R&B hit in 1963 after Jimmy Soul redid it as "If You Wanna Be Happy"). But the calypso craze really took off when the Andrews Sisters scored a No. 1 pop hit with "Rum and Coca-Cola" in 1945.[11]

Jordan kept touring and recording almost until his death in 1975 but never had a charted hit after 1951. One problem was that he formed a short-lived big band in 1951, just as established big bands were folding. More importantly, although his sound was the chief model for the R&B combo style, as well as the rock 'n' roll of Bill Haley and Chuck Berry, his music—rustic lyrics notwithstanding—was too jazzy and sophisticated to suit the progressively coarsening tastes of rhythm-and-blues fans. Jordan's arrangements were tight and swinging, his bluesy alto saxophone was sleekly expressive, and his voice exuded personality and charm, while his epigones sang or played roughly over ragged charts. Although many of his records crossed over to the pop market, Jordan—unlike Nat "King" Cole, another R&B hit maker who dabbled in Caribbean music—could not remake himself into a pop singer. By the time he jumped on the rock bandwagon with records such as "Rock 'n' Roll Call" (RCA, 1955) and "Rock, Doc!" (Mercury, 1957), his time had passed.

Along with Nat "King" Cole and T-Bone Walker, Saunders King was one of the first West Coast rhythm-and-blues artists to record for an independent label. Born in Louisiana, King moved to Los Angeles as a child and was living in northern California by the mid-1930s, when he began singing with the Southern Harmony Four on the NBC-owned San Francisco radio station KPO. He took up guitar in 1938 and soon fell under the influence of Charlie Christian, who won fame with the Benny Goodman Sextet in 1939. King made his studio debut with his own sextet for Dave Rosenbaum's Rhythm Records in June 1942, cutting the double-sided "S.K. Blues," a groundbreaking record that failed to make the Harlem Hit Parade only because *Billboard* did not initiate that chart until October 1942. The song did make the magazine's Most-Played Juke Box Race Records list in 1945 after Big Joe Turner covered it; it was Turner's first charted hit.

King's singing on the original "S.K. Blues" shows the influence of Turner, while his band plays in pure swing style. King's music grew less jazzy after the war, when he recorded for such labels as Aladdin and Modern, as well as Rhythm. He scored a pair of hits in 1949, "Empty Bedroom Blues" and "Stay Gone Blues," but faded in the 1950s and retired the following decade, dedicating himself to religion. In 1979, he sang and played guitar on a track of his son-in-law Carlos Santana's album *Oneness*. He suffered a stroke in 1999 and died in 2000, at the age of ninety-one. His reputation rests almost entirely on "S.K. Blues," whose impact was based less on its laid-back sound than on lines such as, "Come here, pretty baby, and put your fine, mellow body on my knee" and "Give me back that wig I bought you, baby, and let your head go bald."

THE DOOR OPENS

The laid-back blues sound—harking back to Avery Parrish's "After Hours"—was popularized primarily by Charles Brown, the singer-pianist with Johnny Moore's Three Blazers. Born in Texas City, Texas, between Houston and Galveston, Brown studied classical piano and sang in a church choir, meanwhile listening to the blues behind his disapproving grandmother's back. He was in his teens, he later claimed, when he wrote "Drifting Blues," which would become his signature song. His pianistic models included Art Tatum, Fats Waller, and Earl Hines; his main vocal influences were Pha Terrell, the crooner in Andy Kirk's band, and Helen O'Connell, who sang with Jimmy Dorsey's band. Brown majored in chemistry in college, but after briefly working at a federal arsenal in Arkansas, he moved to California, settling in Los Angeles in 1943. Johnny Moore was in the audience when he won an amateur contest at the Lincoln Theatre on Central Avenue; soon afterward he asked Brown to join his trio, with Eddie Williams on bass. By late 1944, the group was entertaining Hollywood stars at a whites-only Beverly Hills nightclub, performing mostly ballads in a style similar to the King Cole Trio's. "We always kept 'Drifting Blues' as what they called our 'race number,'" Brown told writer Chip Deffaa, "but we didn't play many blues because Hollywood was kind of sophisticated."[12]

In September 1945, Johnny Moore's Three Blazers, plus Johnny Otis on drums, recorded "Drifting Blues" for Eddie and Leo Mesner's new Philo label (soon renamed Aladdin), and it became a major R&B hit. Brown's relaxed, Cole-like singing is far removed from the dominant blues-shouting style of the period, expressing despondency with a world-weary sense of resignation. The rhythmic keyboard triplets with which he accompanies himself became a rock and pop fixture after first being adopted by piano-playing rhythm-and-blues singers such as Amos Milburn, Little Willie Littlefield, and Fats Domino. Early in his career, Ray Charles incorporated elements of Brown's style. "I made many a dollar doing an imitation of his 'Drifting Blues,'" Charles would recount.[13] Charles's first R&B hit, "Confession Blues," recorded with a trio in Seattle in December 1948 for the Los Angeles–based Down Beat label, clearly shows Brown's influence.

Brown had a few more laid-back but not necessarily bluesy hits with Moore's Blazers on the Exclusive and Modern labels, including "Merry Christmas, Baby," which would become a holiday perennial, covered by everyone from Chuck Berry and Elvis Presley to Otis Redding, B. B. King, and Bruce Springsteen. But though Brown was the Blazers' main attraction, it was Moore's name that appeared on record labels and theater marquees. In 1948, following a financial dispute with Moore, Brown signed a solo contract with Aladdin and cut the ballad hit "Get Yourself Another Fool," perhaps a veiled message to Moore. In 1949, he reverted to the "Drifting Blues" format, complete with piano triplets, and topped the R&B charts with "Trouble Blues." His next hit, evincing the source of his sound, was an update of Leroy Carr's 1935 recording "When the Sun Goes Down." Brown's last R&B chart-topper came in 1951 with "Black Night," another bluesy dirge featuring triplet figures, this time played on guitar. He had his final hit for Aladdin in 1952 with the Leiber-Stoller composition "Hard Times," after which he sued the label over royalties.[14]

Johnny Moore's reconstituted Blazers recorded R&B hits on a variety of labels through the mid-1950s with a series of Charles Brown sound-alikes—Lee Barnes, Billy Valentine, Floyd Dixon, and Frankie Ervin. Brown, a chitlin circuit headliner during the late 1940s and early 1950s, kept touring until 1958 as his career wound down. In 1959, he recorded a duet with Amos Milburn, "I Want to Go Home," that Sam Cooke transformed into the soul classic "Bring It On Home to Me" in 1961. In 1960, Brown had another holiday hit, "Please Come Home for Christmas," which crossed over to the pop charts and was ultimately covered by Johnny and Edgar Winter, the Eagles, Willie Nelson, Aaron Neville, James Brown, Bon Jovi, Mariah Carey, and many others. He continued to perform and record but attracted little notice until 1979, when he began appearing at the New York nightclub Tramps. His 1986 album *One More for the Road* won rave reviews, as did his 1990 album *All My Life,* and his comeback flourished until his death in 1999.

Even before cutting "Drifting Blues," Johnny Moore's Three Blazers had backed Ivory Joe Hunter on the similar-sounding "Blues at Sunrise," which was recorded for Hunter's own Ivory label and became a national R&B hit in late 1945, after it was picked up by Exclusive. Born in East Texas and christened Ivory Joe, Hunter learned to play classical, gospel, and jazz piano, modeling himself after Duke Ellington and Fats Waller. He made his first recording for John Lomax in 1933, singing and playing "Stackolee" for the Library of Congress. He hosted a radio show in Beaumont and led a band in Houston before moving to California, where he met the Three Blazers while performing at a nightclub.

After "Blues at Sunrise," Hunter started another label, Pacific (which leased some of its titles to 4 Star), recording blues and boogies with a combo that briefly included guitarist Pee Wee Crayton, soon to emerge as a blues star in his own right. In 1948, Hunter had a No. 1 R&B hit with "Pretty Mama Blues," his soaring tenor complemented by his piano and Ernie Royal's muted trumpet. By the time it charted, Hunter was recording for King with members of Duke Ellington's band, crooning ballads such as the 1949 hit "Guess Who"; also in 1949, he foreshadowed his future direction with a cover of Tex Ritter's country hit "Jealous Heart."

Shifting to the MGM label, Hunter recorded the balladic blues "I Almost Lost My Mind" and the ballad "I Need You So"—both No. 1 R&B hits in 1950—followed shortly by a successful cover of Eddy Arnold's 1947 country chart-topper "It's a Sin." But Hunter would not have another hit until he switched to Atlantic in the mid-1950s. In 1956, Pat Boone, imitating Hunter's peculiar lilt but not his blue notes, covered "I Almost Lost My Mind" for a No. 1 pop hit. In response, Hunter recorded the similar "Since I Met You Baby" (backed with "You Can't Stop This Rocking and Rolling") and scored his final No. 1 R&B hit, this time crossing over to the pop charts. Hunter had a few more crossover hits before the end of the decade, the last a cover of Ray Price's country smash "City Lights." He recorded through the 1960s, with little success, for such labels as Capitol, Vee-Jay, and Stax. After Sonny James had a No. 1 country hit in 1969 with "Since I Met You Baby," Hunter performed on the *Grand Ole Opry* and, before his death in 1974, recorded the album *I've Always Been Country*.

Hunter wrote many songs, a number of which—besides "I Almost Lost My Mind" and "Since I Met You Baby"—became hits for white artists. The McGuire Sisters charted with "It May Sound Silly" in 1955, Eddie Fisher with "No Other One" in 1956, Teresa Brewer with "A Tear Fell" in 1956 and "Empty Arms" in 1957, and Elvis Presley with "My Wish Came True" in 1959 and "Ain't That Loving You Baby" in 1964. Although Hunter also recorded driving boogies and outright rock songs, he is remembered mainly for his blues-tinged ballads—melodic conflations of R&B, country, and mainstream pop that helped define the mellower side of the rock 'n' roll era.

At his first recording session, in September 1946, Amos Milburn echoed "Drifting Blues," piano triplets and all, on his own "After Midnight." At the same session, Milburn cut his propulsive take on "Down the Road a Piece," as well as the equally hard-rocking "Amos' Boogie." Five years younger than Charles Brown, thirteen years younger than Ivory Joe Hunter, and twenty years younger than Roy Milton, Milburn played with a heavier touch and a bluesier feel than any of them, although he, too, was grounded in swing. He continued to record Charles Brown–style blues and up-tempo numbers, but his reputation rests on his boogies and drinking songs.

Born into a large, poor family in Houston, Milburn taught himself piano as a child and, after a wartime hitch in the navy, led his own band in Houston and San Antonio. He was discovered by Lola Anne Cullum, a dentist's wife and aspiring talent agent who took him to Los Angeles, where he was rejected at Modern—"They offered me so little money 'til she [Cullum] refused it," Milburn told the German writer Norbert Hess—but signed by Aladdin.[15] (Milburn claimed to have discovered Lightnin' Hopkins, who made his recorded debut for Aladdin in November 1946 after Cullum brought him to Los Angeles from Houston.)[16]

Milburn cut over a dozen sides for Aladdin, several arranged by the tenor saxophonist Maxwell Davis, before hitting pay dirt with "Chicken Shack Boogie," where he recites lyrics similar to those of "Down the Road a Piece" to a more relaxed beat. Recorded in November 1947, it hit the *Billboard* R&B chart a year later, rising to the No. 1 spot. Before the end of 1948, Milburn charted with what would become his second No. 1 hit, a melodically altered version of Tommy Dorsey's 1938 ballad hit "Bewildered." (The song, also a No. 1 R&B hit in 1948 for an obscure singer named Red Miller, would chart again in 1949 for Billy Eckstine and in 1961 for James Brown.)

Milburn was the top rhythm-and-blues artist of 1949, with nine hits on the *Billboard* chart. He generally stuck with familiar formulas, emulating Charles Brown on "Empty Arms Blues" and "Let's Make Christmas Merry, Baby" and reworking the "Down the Road a Piece" pattern on the No. 1 hit "Roomin' House Boogie," where he talk-sings a line—"We gonna send down to the corner and get another fifth / And everybody else in the house is gonna take a little nip"—that would turn up two years later, slightly modified, on "Rocket 88." On "A and M Blues," Milburn appropriates the "Yancey Special" bass line of Sonny Thompson's 1948 hit "Long Gone"; on "In the Middle of the Night," he combines "Drifting Blues" with Lonnie Johnson's 1948 hit "Tomorrow Night."

At the end of 1950, Milburn scored his final No. 1 hit, "Bad, Bad Whiskey," the first in a series of drinking songs that included "Just One More Drink," "Thinking and Drinking," "Let Me Go Home, Whiskey," "One Scotch, One Bourbon, One Beer" (later revived by John Lee Hooker as "One Bourbon, One Scotch, One Beer"), "Vicious, Vicious Vodka," and "Juice, Juice, Juice." He last made the charts with "Good, Good Whiskey" in 1954, fading thereafter partly because he lived the life he sang about. "I was a heavy drinker," he told Nick Tosches. "I loved that Scotch."[17]

Milburn's 1952 recording of "Rock, Rock, Rock," featuring Maxwell Davis's wailing saxophone, anticipated the sound of classic rock 'n' roll (unlike his easygoing 1951 hit "Let's Rock a While"), but though he performed with the likes of Fats Domino and Bo Diddley on a number of mid-1950s package shows, his music did not appeal to the growing teenage market. He cut a single with Charles Brown for the Ace label in 1959 and kept recording through the following decade for such labels as King and Motown, with little success. After a pair of strokes left him disabled, he cut a final album, released in 1977 as *Volume 10* in Johnny Otis's *Great Rhythm & Blues Oldies* series, on which Otis played the left-hand piano parts. Milburn died in 1980.

Born in El Campo, Texas, near Houston, Little Willie Littlefield took up piano as a child, inspired first by Albert Ammons and later by Charles Brown and Amos Milburn. In 1948, at age sixteen, he cut his first single, the breakneck keyboard showpiece "Little Willie's Boogie," for Eddie's Records in Houston, following it with the similar "Littlefield's Boogie" on the rival Freedom label. Discovered at a Houston nightclub by Jules Bihari of Modern Records, he moved to Los Angeles and in October 1949 recorded "It's Midnight (No Place to Go)," a substantial R&B hit. With its piano triplets and habanera horn vamp, that song forms the obvious model for Fats Domino's 1950 hit "Every Night About This Time," the first of many Domino recordings in the same basic mold, including "Ain't It a Shame," "Blueberry Hill," "Blue Monday," and "Walking to New Orleans."

Littlefield had only two more national hits, the bluesy ballad "Farewell," in late 1949, and a balladic duet with Little Lora Wiggins, "I've Been Lost," in 1951. He also recorded the up-tempo rocker "Rockin' Chair Mama," where he pounds the piano like Jerry Lee Lewis, but it didn't chart. In 1952, he signed with the Federal label and recorded the Leiber-Stoller composition "Kansas City" for producer Ralph Bass, who changed the title to "K.C. Loving." A hit around Los Angeles, the song didn't make the national charts until 1959, when Wilbert Harrison redid it under the original title, scoring a No. 1 pop and R&B hit that was covered by Bill Haley, Little Richard, the Beatles, and James Brown, among many others. Although Harrison's version—with its assured vocal, ska-like shuffle-boogie beat and nearly psychedelic Wild Jimmy Spruill blues guitar break—is plainly superior, Littlefield's halfheartedly sung original, with its oddly popping backbeat and greasily suave Maxwell Davis saxophone solo, has its own shuffling charm.

Littlefield was backed by an R&B vocal-harmony group called the Mondellos on the doo-wop-flavored "Ruby-Ruby," one of several sides he cut for the revived Rhythm label in 1957 and 1958. He played San Francisco Bay Area clubs in the 1960s but did not record again until the following decade, when his comeback began. He toured and recorded in Europe through the 1980s and 1990s, then retired in the Netherlands, returning to the stage in 2006.

As a musician, bandleader, talent scout, producer, disc jockey, and record label owner, Johnny Otis played a key role in the propagation of West Coast rhythm-and-blues. Born in Vallejo, California, to Greek immigrant parents, he was raised in nearby Berkeley, where his father ran a grocery store in a mostly black neighborhood. From an early age, he embraced African American culture; although white in appearance, he managed to pass as black, marrying a black woman and changing his surname from Veliotes. He first played drums professionally with an Oakland-based combo led by the white trumpeter and trombonist Willard Marsh, but around 1940, he began drumming in a jump band led by the black boogie and blues pianist Count Otis Matthews.

Hitting the road, Otis played with the black territory bands of George Morrison in Denver and Lloyd Hunter in Omaha, formed a short-lived band in Omaha with the alto saxophonist Preston Love, and then joined Harlan Leonard's Rockets at the Club Alabam on Central Avenue in Los Angeles, after Leonard moved to L.A. from Kansas City in late 1942. Following a stint with Bardu Ali's group at the Lincoln Theatre, Otis organized his own big band—with pianist Bill Doggett, saxophonist Paul Quinichette, and bassist Curtis Counce—which served as the house ensemble at the Alabam. He modeled his sound on Count Basie's, using some of Basie's charts, as well as Lucky Millinder's.[18]

Otis and his band made their first records in September 1945, for Otis René's Excelsior label, with Jimmy Rushing singing on the risqué "My Baby's Business" and on a cover of Wynonie Harris's "Around the Clock," which Harris had cut that July with a combo led by Otis. But the most successful recording of the session was a jazzy instrumental, "Harlem Nocturne," which the white trombonist Earle Hagan had written in 1939 as a tribute to Duke Ellington's alto saxophonist Johnny Hodges. Otis's slowed-down rendition, featuring the white alto saxophonist Rene Bloch, brought out the tune's exoticism and inspired numerous covers, notably the 1953 version by Herbie Fields, a white saxophonist with a bent for rhythm-and-blues, and the 1959 version by Viscounts, a white rock group with a penchant for guitar tremolo.[19]

On the strength of "Harlem Nocturne," Otis performed across the country in 1946, opening for Louis Jordan in Detroit and New York; early the next year, he toured with the Ink Spots. But soon afterward, he had to replace his big band with a combo, including tenor saxophonist Big Jay McNeely and guitarist Pete Lewis; McNeely went solo after recording his hit "The Deacon's Hop" in late 1948, but Lewis—a T-Bone Walker disciple who prefigured Chuck Berry's style—would remain in Otis's band until 1957. "I used two saxes, trumpet and trombone, and piano/bass/drums/guitar. This became like the standard rhythm-and-blues ensemble," Otis told Arnold Shaw. "It surely wasn't big band; it wasn't swing; it wasn't country blues. It was . . . a hybrid form that became an art in itself. It was the foundation of rock 'n' roll."[20]

In late 1947 or 1948, Otis and Bardu Ali opened their own nightclub, the Barrelhouse, in the Watts neighborhood of Los Angeles; while there, Otis discovered Little Esther Phillips, Mel Walker, and the Robins, who would sing on many of his records. (In 1955, the Coasters split off from the Robins.) In 1948, Otis scored his first nationally charted hit backing the obscure singer Joe Swift on "That's Your Last Boogie," an adaptation of "Your Red Wagon" that rocks to a Cuban beat. After Ralph Bass signed him to Savoy Records, Otis had a No. 1 R&B hit in early 1950 with "Double Crossing Blues," an urbane blues tinged with doo-wop that features the Robins harmonizing behind Little Esther while Otis plays vibraphone with a quintet. Otis followed with nine more R&B hits that year, all featuring Little Esther and/or Mel Walker, most in a similar downbeat vein, with such proto-rocking exceptions as "Cupid's Boogie" and "Wedding Boogie."

Also in 1950, Otis put together one of the first touring R&B package shows, known at various times as the Savoy Barrelhouse Caravan, the California Rhythm & Blues Caravan, and the Johnny Otis Show. He continued to score hits through 1952, including the Latin-flavored "Mambo Boogie" and the hard-rocking "All Night Long." He switched to Mercury in late 1951 but had only one hit for the label, a Charles Brown–style cover of Floyd Dixon's "Call Operator 210"; he then signed with Peacock, where he produced and played on Big Mama Thornton's "Hound Dog" and Johnny Ace's posthumous R&B ballad smash "Pledging My Love" (on Peacock's affiliated Duke label), as well as a 1953 session with Little Richard, but had no hits of his own.

At a talent show in Detroit in 1951 or 1952, Otis discovered Jackie Wilson, Little Willie John, and a vocal group called the Royals; Otis wrote the rhythmic ballad "Every Beat of My Heart" for Wilson, but the Royals recorded it instead.[21] The song was not a hit until Gladys Knight covered it in 1961, but the Royals, after adding lead singer Hank Ballard and changing their name to the Midnighters, had a No. 1 smash in 1954 with "Work with Me Annie," whose raunchy lyrics—"Annie please don't cheat / Give me all my meat"—stirred considerable controversy. There followed a string of sequels—"Annie Had a Baby," "Annie's Aunt Fannie"—and answer songs—Hazel McCollum and the El Dorados' "Annie's Answer," the Midnights' "Annie Pulled a Hum-Bug," Danny Taylor's "I'm the Father of Annie's Baby," Linda Hayes and the Platters' "My Name Ain't Annie," and the Nu-Tones' "Annie Kicked the Bucket," among others. In November 1958, Ballard and the Midnighters would record "The Twist," which Chubby Checker turned into a trendsetting pop smash in 1960.

In 1954, Otis discovered the teenage Etta James in San Francisco and took her to Los Angeles, where she recorded "Roll with Me Henry"—her answer to "Work with Me Annie"—as a duet with Richard Berry, the future composer of "Louie Louie." Released on the Modern label under the more seemly title "The Wallflower," James's record was a No. 1 R&B hit in early 1955, but it was quickly eclipsed by the white singer Georgia Gibbs's adaptation "Dance with Me Henry (Wallflower)," which soared to the top of the pop charts. Too square to pass for rock 'n' roll, despite a hard backbeat and such lyrics as "Roll, roll, roll / rock, rock, rock," Gibbs's hit cleared the path for Bill Haley's breakthrough with "Rock Around the Clock" just weeks later. "Rock 'n' roll was a direct outgrowth of R&B," Otis told Shaw. "It took over all the things that made R&B different from big band swing: the afterbeat on a steady four; the influence of boogie; the triplets on piano;

eight-to-the-bar on the top-hat cymbal; and the shuffle pattern of dotted eighth and sixteenth notes."[22]

In the mid-1950s, Otis acquired his own Dig record label and began working as a disc jockey on the Los Angeles radio station KFOX, which soon led to a television show on KTTV. He signed with Capitol Records in 1957 and the following year sang on "Willie and the Hand Jive," drawing its shave-and-a-haircut rhythm from Bo Diddley's namesake 1955 hit, which is based in turn on Red Saunders's 1952 recording of "Hambone." Otis's record crossed over to the pop charts, prompting him to cut several commercially oriented songs with a Bo Diddley beat—to his later regret, as they diminished his credibility among R&B fans.[23] Still, they were potent rockers, and one of them, the hoodoo-themed "Castin' My Spell," was popular among British groups of the mid-1960s.

Otis recorded for King in the early 1960s, without success, then turned to politics, working as an aide to the Trinidadian-born California legislator Mervyn Dymally. He returned to the studio in 1968 to record *Cold Shot!* for the Kent label, the first of many albums featuring his son Shuggie on guitar. Signing with Epic, he cut a live double album at the 1970 Monterey Jazz Festival with a lineup of former rhythm-and-blues stars including Joe Turner, Roy Milton, Roy Brown, Pee Wee Crayton, Eddie "Cleanhead" Vinson, and Ivory Joe Hunter. He toured internationally with his R&B revue and produced the *Great Rhythm & Blues Oldies* series of albums on his own Blues Spectrum label, each showcasing a different R&B veteran backed by Otis's band. He also founded the nondenominational Landmark Community Church in Los Angeles, which he served as pastor.

Otis cut *The New Johnny Otis Show* for Alligator in 1981 and toured afterward with his revue; he recorded an album of swing standards, *Spirit of the Black Territory Bands,* for Arhoolie in 1990. In the 1990s, he bought a farm north of San Francisco, where he ran a natural-food market and blues club. He also taught at the University of California, Berkeley, broadcast on the Berkeley-based radio station KPFA, started a new record label, founded a new church, and published a couple of semi-autobiographical, semi-political books, plus a cookbook and a book of his own paintings and sculptures. He was inducted into the Rock and Roll Hall of Fame, as a nonperformer, and the Blues Hall of Fame, as a performer. He died in 2012, at the age of ninety.

Otis spent his career trying to popularize rhythm-and-blues, but it was another California native, the saxophonist Jack McVea, who was responsible for early R&B's greatest crossover success. As the February 10, 1947, issue of *Time* magazine reported: "Every radio blared *Open the Door, Richard!* Five record versions were on sale, and 13 more (by Louis Jordan, Dick Haymes, the Pied Pipers, etc.) were being rushed to market. A quartet known as The Yokels sang it in Yiddish. Bing Crosby . . . Bob Hope, Fred Allen and

Bea Lillie had only to mention the word Richard on the air to put their studio audiences in stitches."[24]

Born in Los Angeles, McVea made his professional debut in a band led by his father, the banjo player Satchel McVea. He played under a succession of local bandleaders—Dootsie Williams, Charlie Echols, Lorenzo Flennoy, Claude Kennedy, Cee Pee Johnson, and Eddie Barefield—through the 1930s before joining Lionel Hampton's band in 1940.[25] He led his own combos from 1944, recording as a leader and in accompaniment to T-Bone Walker and Wynonie Harris. He appeared at the first Jazz at the Philharmonic concert in July 1944, playing alongside the shrieking Illinois Jacquet on "Blues." Together with Dizzy Gillespie and Charlie Parker, he backed Slim Gaillard on a December 1945 session for the short-lived Bel-Tone label; just before Gaillard introduces McVea's Coleman Hawkins–like tenor-sax solo on "Slim's Jam," drummer Zutty Singleton plays a knocking beat and says, "Open up the door, Richard!"

During McVea's tenure with Lionel Hampton, Hampton often worked with the black vaudeville comedian Dusty Fletcher, who, pretending to come home drunk without his house key, would climb a ladder on stage and shout, "Open the door, Richard!"[26] McVea may also have seen Pigmeat Markham, another old-time black comedian who worked in blackface, do a similar act at the Club Alabam or Lincoln Theatre.[27] Louis Jordan alludes to the routine on his March 1944 V-Disc recording of "How High Am I?" yelling, "Hey, Richard, come on down here, boy, and open this door!" McVea set Fletcher's line to music and around September 1946 recorded "Open the Door Richard!" with producer Ralph Bass for the Black & White label. The record takes the form of a casual conversation among McVea and his sidemen over a relaxed beat, interrupted by sung choruses. The song fades out at the end, a significant innovation; Ralph Bass later explained that the skit simply ran too long.[28]

By early 1947, "Open the Door Richard!" had swept the nation. McVea's version crossed over to the pop charts, as did those of Count Basie, the Three Flames, Dusty Fletcher, the Charioteers, and Louis Jordan. The song was also recorded by white artists ranging from Hank Penny to the Merry Macs, but only the Pied Pipers charted. Dusty Fletcher's stereotypical portrayal of a drunken, shiftless black man outraged civil rights advocates even as "Open the door, Richard!" became a catch phrase for opponents of segregation.[29]

The song's success provoked lawsuits by Fletcher and another vaudevillian, John "Spider Bruce" Mason; both claimed to have written the original sketch, and each was awarded a share of the composer's credit. But in the end, "Open the Door Richard!" turned out to be the creation of Bob Russell, a black vaudeville producer and performer whose career dated back to the 1890s. Pigmeat Markham, who'd worked with him toward the end of Russell's life, said Russell had written the piece for a show called *Mr. Rareback,* where it was performed by John Mason. Mason said he'd performed the routine as early as 1919, reprising it a decade later in the Broadway revue *Bamboola,* which also featured Dusty Fletcher.[30]

The "Open the Door Richard!" fad ended as quickly as it had begun. McVea recorded a sequel, "The Key's in the Mailbox," which flopped, as did several answer songs. Black & White Records soon folded, but McVea continued to record for a series of labels through the 1950s, never scoring another hit. From the mid-1960s until his retirement in the 1980s, he played clarinet in a Dixieland band at Disneyland. He died in 2000.

HORN HONKERS

Instrumentalists, especially saxophonists, played a prominent role in postwar rhythm-and-blues, including some who also sang, such as the alto saxophonist Eddie "Cleanhead" Vinson. A Houston native, Vinson played alongside Illinois Jacquet and Arnett Cobb in territory bands led by Chester Boone, Milton Larkins, and Floyd Ray. Inspired by Big Joe Turner, he began to shout the blues during intermissions. He picked up songs from Big Bill Broonzy, with whom he toured the South accompanying singer Lil Green. After Jay McShann's band had a hit with Walter Brown singing "Confessin' the Blues" in 1941, trumpeter Cootie Williams, having left Duke Ellington, recruited Vinson to sing the blues with his own newly formed big band.

In January 1944, Williams's band, with Bud Powell on piano, Eddie "Lockjaw" Davis on tenor saxophone, and Vinson playing alto sax and singing, cut "Cherry Red Blues," which Big Joe Turner had recorded in June 1939 with a combo including Pete Johnson and Hot Lips Page. On lines such as "Rock me, mama, till my face turns cherry red," Vinson's voice leaps into a creaky falsetto, giving him a distinctive yodel-like sound and helping make the record a major R&B hit that crossed over to the pop charts. Vinson cut two more R&B hits with Williams's band in August 1944, singing without the falsetto creak on a cover of Louis Jordan's "Is You Is or Is You Ain't (Ma' Baby)" and with it on a chart-topping adaptation of Casey Bill Weldon's 1936 recording "Somebody's Got to Go," which Big Joe Turner had adapted somewhat differently in 1941.

Vinson toured the country with Williams on a bill with Ella Fitzgerald and the Ink Spots, then formed his own big band and in 1945 signed with the new Mercury label. He reduced his band to a septet before recording his only Mercury hit, the double-sided 1947 smash "Old Maid Boogie"/"Kidney Stew Blues," where Vinson keeps his vocal creak under greater control. Switching to King, he had has last hit in 1949 with "Somebody Done Stole My Cherry Red." By this time, he was known as "Cleanhead," having shaved his scalp after a botched hair-straightening attempt.

A first-rate jazz musician who jammed with Charlie Parker, hired John Coltrane for his band, and wrote a pair of tunes ("Tune Up" and "Four") that Miles Davis recorded, Vinson was promoted primarily as a blues singer. When he did play saxophone, he was compelled to follow the histrionic conventions of the R&B honkers, strutting down theater aisles or atop tavern counters. "You had to blow and jump up and down," he acknowledged, "but I never did like it."[31] His rhythm-and-blues career faded even before the emergence of Elvis Presley, and he returned to jazz, briefly rejoining Cootie Williams and later recording with saxophonist Cannonball Adderley and with members of Count Basie's band. But his fortunes did not revive until the late 1960s, when he began to tour Europe and hooked up with Johnny Otis's revue in Los Angeles. He performed at festivals and recorded for Norman Granz's Pablo Records and other labels, both playing jazz and singing the blues until his death in 1988.

Like Vinson, Benjamin "Bull Moose" Jackson started off as a saxophonist but became better known for his singing. Born in Cleveland, he sang in church and studied violin as a child; after switching to saxophone in high school, he joined a band led by trumpeter Freddie Webster. Jackson moved to Buffalo, New York, around 1942, then returned to Cleveland, where he was discovered by Lucky Millinder while playing in the house band at the Cedar Gardens club. He had to be coaxed into singing with Millinder's band when Wynonie Harris failed to perform at gig in Lubbock, Texas, but "after I got out there, I loved it," he recalled.[32]

Jackson first recorded with Millinder for Decca in June 1945, playing tenor saxophone; soon afterward, when the band performed in Cincinnati, Syd Nathan approached Millinder and his trumpeter/arranger Henry Glover about recording for him. Millinder was under contract to Decca but agreed to let several band members record for Nathan under Jackson's name. Cut in August 1945, the resulting four sides, with Jackson singing on "Bull Moose Jackson Blues," were the first to be issued on King Records' short-lived Queen rhythm-and-blues subsidiary. The session also marked the beginning of Glover's association with King.

Jackson continued to play and record for Decca with Millinder's band while recording for Queen with Millinder's musicians under the name Bull Moose Jackson and His Buffalo Bearcats. "I Know Who Threw the Whiskey in the Well," cut in December 1945, was Jackson's—and Queen's—first hit. Unlike Wynonie Harris, Jackson could croon as well as shout, and after doing a session for Irvin Feld's Super Disc label, he recorded the syrupy ballad "I Love You, Yes I Do" for King in August 1947. It became a No. 1 R&B hit and crossed over to the pop charts, establishing Jackson as a star and King as a force to be reckoned with in the rhythm-and-blues market. "I Love You, Yes I Do" was credited to Glover and Sally Nix, but their authorship was successfully challenged in court by the songwriters Guy B. Wood, Sol

Marcus, and Eddie Seiler, who in 1944 had copyrighted a similar ballad, "Tonight He Sailed Again," which Millinder, with Glover and Jackson in the band (but with Paul Breckenridge singing), recorded in October 1947.[33]

Jackson had a string of hits in 1948, including "Sneaky Pete," "I Want a Bowlegged Woman," and his all-time best seller, the ballad "I Can't Go On without You." He also sang "I Love You, Yes I Do" with Lucky Millinder's band that year in the movie *Boarding House Blues,* starring Dusty Fletcher and Moms Mabley. He charted in 1949 with the ballads "Little Girl Don't Cry" and "Don't Ask Me Why," as well as the country cover "Why Don't You Haul Off and Love Me," but he did not have a national hit after that until 1961, when he rerecorded "I Love You, Yes I Do" for the 7 Arts label. Although they were not big sellers at the time, Jackson is remembered today for such raunchy proto-rockers as "Nosey Joe" (written by Leiber and Stoller) and "Big Ten Inch Record," both from 1952. By then, Jackson no longer played saxophone on his own recordings; the honking solos on "Nosey Joe" are by Big John Greer, while those on "Big Ten Inch Record" are by Red Prysock and/or Rufus Gore.

Jackson performed together with such artists as Joe Liggins, Buddy Johnson, Larry Darnell, and Chuck Berry, plus the doo-wop groups the Clovers, the Drifters, the Orioles, and the Ravens. He recorded for King into 1955, then cut an unreleased session for Chess, followed by records for the independent Encino and Warwick labels, but after 1958 he made his living primarily in the catering business. He moved to Washington, D.C., working for a caterer while playing occasional gigs until he was rediscovered in 1983 by Carl Grefenstette, the leader of the Pittsburgh-based R&B revival band the Flashcats. In 1985, Jackson cut his final album (with the Flashcats), played Carnegie Hall, and toured Europe with Johnny Otis. He kept performing until shortly before his death in 1988.

One of the first honking-saxophone hits was Wild Bill Moore's "We're Gonna Rock," which charted briefly in July 1948. Born in Houston, Moore grew up in Detroit, where he boxed and played saxophone, switching from alto to tenor. He first recorded in 1944 with pianist Christine Chatman, the wife of blues pianist Memphis Slim, on a Decca session that also marked the studio debut of singer Big Maybelle. By 1945, he was in Los Angeles, where he recorded with Helen Humes (playing the jazzy tenor-sax solo on "Be-Baba-Leba"), Slim Gaillard, and Big Joe Turner. His signature record, "Wild Bill," was excerpted on Ralph Bass's short-lived Bop! label from a historic July 1947 concert showcasing Moore's band alongside such rising modern-jazz stars as Dexter Gordon, Wardell Gray, and Sonny Criss at the Elks Auditorium on Central Avenue. Moore himself played the blues with an occasional bebop tinge.

Moore moved back to Detroit later in 1947 and in December recorded "We're Gonna Rock" for Savoy with a sextet including the baritone saxophonist Paul Williams (the label credits "Bill Moore, featuring Paul Williams – Bar. Sax"). After Moore's brief tenor-sax introduction, T. J. Fowler plays boogie piano as Moore growls, "Ah, get it, Mr. Piano Player"; the musicians then shout in chorus, "We're gonna rock, we're gonna roll." For the rest of the number, Moore blows a honking, wailing solo over a boogie bass line, with Williams barely heard except possibly for a few honks toward the end. In 1948, Moore cut "Rock and Roll" for Modern—a similar saxophone vehicle with a more elaborate vocal part sung by (probably) Scatman Crothers. Moore's "Rock and Roll" was reportedly one of the first records played by Alan Freed on his Cleveland rhythm-and-blues radio show.[34]

Before the 1940s ended, Moore turned toward straight-ahead jazz, recording through the mid-1950s for Regal, King, and other labels with such sideman as trumpeter Jonah Jones, saxophonist Paul Quinichette, bassist Doug Watkins, and pianists Walter Bishop and Barry Harris. In the early 1960s, he made soul-jazz albums with pianist Junior Mance and organist Johnny "Hammond" Smith. He played on Marvin Gaye's 1971 album *What's Going On,* taking a long solo on the smash single "Mercy Mercy Me (the Ecology)." Moore eventually returned to Los Angeles, where he died in 1983.

Like "Open the Door Richard!" Paul Williams's "The Huckle-Buck" helped bring rhythm-and-blues into the popular mainstream, but with a longer-lasting impact. Born in Tennessee, Williams spent his childhood in Kentucky and his teenage years in Detroit, where he began playing alto saxophone. He formed his first band with a high school friend, performing for white audiences at the Morris Café; by the end of World War II, he was working in trumpeter Clarence Dorsey's band, playing for black audiences at the Sensation Club. He made his first recordings with a band led by trumpeter James Poe under the name King Porter, with whom Wild Bill Moore also recorded. After checking out Porter's group at a Detroit nightclub, Herman Lubinsky, the owner of Savoy Records, sent for producer Teddy Reig; more impressed by Williams than by the rest of the band, Reig urged him to play baritone saxophone instead of alto and to simplify his style. "He kept telling me not to play a whole lot of notes. He kept saying, 'Honk! Honk! Honk!'" Williams related. "I had come up in the swing tradition listening to Jimmie Lunceford, Andy Kirk and Duke Ellington. . . . And here's this guy telling me to honk!"[35]

Nevertheless, Williams played alto sax on the first recordings he made for Savoy under his own name in September 1947. He played baritone the following month on his first R&B hit, the bluesy instrumental "Thirty-Five Thirty," which is loosely based on "Red Top," a 1947 hit for saxophonist Gene Ammons that saxophonist Ben Kynard had written for the Lionel Hampton band a couple of years earlier. Blowing over a boogie-woogie bass line, Williams builds momentum on "Thirty-Five Thirty" without doing much honking, but he honks up a storm on his second hit, "The Twister," recorded in March 1948 with a band including Wild Bill Moore. After two jazzier hits, "Waxie Maxie" and "Walkin' Around," both featuring Moore, Williams had a No. 1 R&B smash with "The Huckle-Buck," recorded without Moore in December 1948. It literally made his name: from then on, he was billed as Paul "Hucklebuck" Williams.

Earlier in 1948, at a rehearsal for a show with Lucky Millinder's band, Williams had heard Millinder perform "D' Natural Blues" and decided to play it with his own group. Written by the jazz composer Andy Gibson, the tune incorporated the theme from one of the more straightforward of Charlie Parker's bebop anthems, "Now's the Time," which Teddy Reig had produced for Savoy in 1945. (Gibson's composition has been confused with the "'D' Natural Blues" recorded in 1928 by Fletcher Henderson's band, but those two numbers have little in common besides the punned title.) At his band's next engagement, Williams later recalled, "The place was packed; it looked like an ocean of people—a wave of dancers. I decided to try the new tune, and the people started doing a dance I had never seen. . . . I called out, 'What is that dance?' 'This is "The Hucklebuck,"' they answered. So that's what we called it."[36]

Millinder did not record "D' Natural Blues" for RCA Victor until January 1949, a couple of weeks after Williams cut "The Huckle-Buck" for Savoy, with both records crediting Andy Gibson as composer. Both made *Billboard*'s R&B chart, but though Millinder's version, with its "Yancey Special" bass line and exciting Slim Henderson tenor-sax solo, is livelier than Williams's, with its "Weary Blues" bass line and tepid baritone-sax and trumpet solos, "The Huckle-Buck" was a much bigger hit, holding the No. 1 position for fourteen weeks, while "D' Natural Blues" only reached No. 4. After lyrics were added—"Wiggle like a snake, waddle like a duck / That's the way you do it when you do the hucklebuck"—the song became a 1949 rhythm-and-blues hit for Lionel Hampton (sung by Betty Carter) and Roy Milton and a pop hit the same year for Tommy Dorsey (sung by Charlie Shavers) and Frank Sinatra.

"The Hucklebuck" (as it is usually spelled) has since been recorded by everyone from Pearl Bailey with Hot Lips Page to Homer and Jethro with June Carter to Freddie Bell and the Bellboys, Georgia Gibbs, Chubby Checker (his next hit after "The Twist"), Annette Funicello, King Curtis, Bo Diddley, the Royal Showband (a No. 1 hit in Ireland), and Otis Redding. As sung by Kay Starr, it features prominently in the classic 1956 episode of *The Honeymooners* where Art Carney shows Jackie Gleason how to dance. That the song is partly based on a Charlie Parker tune was appreciated only by bebop aficionados; that it was popularized by a reluctant honker who idolized the pre-bop alto saxophonists Johnny Hodges and Benny Carter is an irony lost on the boppers as well.

Williams had three more hits in 1949 but never again approached the success of "The Huckle-Buck." He was the only artist scheduled for Alan Freed's first big concert, the "Moondog Coronation Ball" at the Cleveland Arena in March 1952, who managed to perform before a near riot prompted the authorities to abort the oversold show. His band accompanied the headliners in films such as *Rhythm and Blues Revue* in 1955 and on package tours such as "The Biggest Show of Stars for '57." After leaving Savoy, Williams recorded for various labels into the 1960s, then worked as a studio musician. In 1968, he opened a booking agency in New York, seldom performing before his death in 2002.

Around June 1948, tenor saxophonist Hal Singer made what is perhaps the definitive honking record, "Corn Bread," for Savoy. While "We're Gonna Rock" is basically a compendium of bluesy riffs, punctuated by deep honks, "Corn Bread" is largely a collection of percussive honks and wails, interrupted by simple bluesy riffs. Among the most conspicuous of these riffs is one suggestive of Bill Haley's "Rock Around the Clock" that's apparently lifted from the white bandleader Charlie Barnet's 1942 recording "The Victory Walk." Performed by a quintet including pianist Wynton Kelly, a future Miles Davis sideman, "Corn Bread" was a No. 1 R&B hit, and the saxophonist was known thereafter as Hal "Cornbread" Singer.

Born in Tulsa, Oklahoma, Singer studied violin before taking up clarinet and saxophone. He played in the bands of Terrence Holder, Geechie Smith, Ed Christian, Ernie Fields, and Nat Towles before traveling to Kansas City with Lloyd Hunter's band and joining the bands of Tommy Douglas and Jay McShann there. Settling in New York in the early 1940s, he played with Willie "the Lion" Smith, Chris Columbus, Earl Bostic, Roy Eldridge, Big Sid Catlett, Don Byas, Trummy Young, and Henry "Red" Allen, recording with Eldridge and Byas.[37] In late 1947, he played alongside the tenor saxophonist Tom Archia in Hot Lips Page's band, taking the saxophone solo on Wynonie Harris's "Good Rockin' Tonight." Just as the solo begins, Harris shouts, "Rock, Oklahoma, rock!" referring to Singer by his pre-Cornbread nickname.

In the spring of 1948, Singer backed Brownie McGhee on "My Fault" for Savoy, his mellow saxophone lending the Leroy Carr–style blues a sophisticated feel that helped make it a major R&B hit. His first Savoy session as a leader yielded "Corn Bread," which he followed with other food-themed instrumentals—"Rice and Red Beans," "Jiblets," "Neck Bones," "Hot Bread," "Buttermilk and Beans"—but only "Beef Stew," from December 1948, made the national charts. Meanwhile, Singer passed through Lucky Millinder's, Bull Moose Jackson's, and Duke Ellington's bands, leaving Ellington to tour with his own group after the success of "Corn Bread."[38]

In early 1949, Singer's band accompanied the vocalist Chicago Carl Davis on two proto-rocking sides of the same Savoy single, "Travelin' Shoes" and "I Feel So Good," the latter melodically similar to Bill Haley's "Rock Around the Clock." In 1950, Singer cut his own "Rock Around the Clock" for Mercury, switching to the Coral label the following year and returning to Savoy the year after. In 1955, he recorded the frantically rocking instrumental "Hot Rod," singing on the flip side, an adaptation of "Rag Mop" titled "Rock and Roll." He toured nationally, often performing on rhythm-and-blues and rock 'n' roll package shows, until 1958, when he joined the all-star Dixieland band at New York's Metropole Cafe. After a European tour with Earl Hines's band in the mid-1960s, Singer settled in France, recording a string of albums and touring as far as Asia and Africa. Although he mainly played jazz, he returned to rhythm-and-blues with the British R&B revival band Rocket 88 and on a 1991 album, *Royal Blue,* with the American boogie pianist Al Copley. He also appeared in the critically acclaimed 1990 Russian movie *Taxi Blues*. He has remained active into the 2000s.

Jimmy Forrest played tenor saxophone in Duke Ellington's band for some months—longer than Hal Singer did—and the experience left a deeper impression on his style. Born in St. Louis, Forrest worked with Fate Marable, Jay McShann, and Andy Kirk before joining Ellington in 1949. He then formed his own combo in St. Louis, including the conga and bongo player Percy James, and in November 1951 recorded "Night Train" for the newly launched, black-owned, Chicago-based United label. "Night Train" combines the main melody from Johnny Hodges's 1940 recording of "That's the Blues Old Man" (accompanied by members of the Ellington band, including Ellington) and the shuffling theme from Ellington's 1946 composition "Happy Go Lucky Local" (the fourth movement of Ellington's *Deep South Suite*), with Forrest adding a few honks of his own. Forrest's record was a No. 1 R&B hit in 1952; a cover version by the white trombonist and bandleader Buddy Morrow made the pop charts. Subsequent versions were recorded by Louis Prima, Chet Atkins, James Brown, and many others.

Forrest had another hit in late 1952 with the Latin-flavored "Hey Mrs. Jones," featuring a vocal chorus by the band members as well as Forrest's jazzy saxophone solo. He never made the national charts again, but unlike most other honkers, he was able to reclaim his jazz credentials, performing in the former Count Basie trumpeter Harry "Sweets" Edison's quintet from 1958 to 1963 and in Basie's big band from 1972 to 1977. Meanwhile, he recorded his own albums, displaying a talent for bebop in addition to blues and swing. Before Forrest's death in 1980, he co-led a band with the former Basie trombonist Al Grey.

The most flamboyant saxophone honker was Big Jay McNeely, whose unabashed showmanship overshadowed his fervid musicianship. Born Cecil McNeely in the Watts district of Los Angeles, he began playing an older brother's saxophone while in high school; one of his early mentors was Jack McVea. He formed a band with a pair of schoolmates who went on to careers as bebop musicians—saxophonist Sonny Criss and pianist Hampton Hawes—and befriended Charlie Parker during Parker's postwar sojourn in California. Soon afterward, however, he turned to rhythm-and-blues. "I started playing jazz," he allowed, "but then I started thinking I wanted to make some money."[39] His primary inspiration was Illinois Jacquet's impassioned 1942 solo on Lionel Hampton's "Flying Home." "Every saxophone player back then was trying to redo that solo on 'Flying Home,'" he said. "Every time we picked up our horns we were just elaborating on that, trying to make it bigger, wilder, give it more swing, more kick."[40]

After winning an amateur contest at Johnny Otis's club, the Barrelhouse, McNeely joined Otis's band but recorded only one session with that group before Ralph Bass recruited him for Savoy. It was Savoy's proprietor, Herman Lubinsky, who dubbed the saxophonist "Big Jay," although he was of no more than medium height and build. At McNeely's second Savoy session, in December 1948, he cut "The Deacon's Hop," a raunchy adaptation of Count Basie's 1940 swinger "Broadway" that features McNeely's yelping, growling, honking tenor sax. "The Deacon's Hop" spent a week atop *Billboard*'s R&B chart before being displaced by Paul Williams's "The Huckle-Buck." "Wild Wig," from McNeely's first Savoy session, followed "The Deacon's Hop" onto the charts, but McNeely abruptly left Savoy and signed with Exclusive. He went on to record for Aladdin, Imperial, Federal, Vee-Jay, and other labels but did not have another national hit until 1959, after he cut the mellow blues "There Is Something on Your Mind" with singer Little Sonny Warner for the Swingin' label. Some of McNeely's recordings—such as "Real Crazy Cool," made for Aladdin in January 1950 but not released until 1954—achieve an ecstatic frenzy that anticipates not so much rock 'n' roll as the ululant free jazz of the 1960s.

McNeely was able to sustain his career through live performances rather than record sales, attracting growing numbers of white and Chicano listeners. Sometimes he would duel with saxophone rivals such as Joe Houston, who copied McNeely's style. "When I heard 'Deacon's Hop,' that just blew my wig wide open," Houston confessed.[41] Other honkers also marched along bar tops, through audiences, and into the streets, but none was as ostentatious as McNeely, who would climax his shows by blowing feverishly while writhing on his back. Big Jim Wynn, the veteran Los Angeles saxophonist whose composition "Ee-Bobaliba" formed the basis for Helen Humes's "Be-Baba-Leba" and Lionel Hampton's "Hey! Ba-Ba-Re-Bop," claimed to have inspired McNeely's stage act. "I was the first sax man in L.A. to lay on his back and play the horn," Wynn told the British writer Bill Millar. "Jay McNeely was a little kid when he used to come in and watch me play at weekends. Two or three years later, he was laying on his back and playing."[42] As McNeely remembered it: "I started walking, I guess, after I had my first hit recording in '49. . . . I had a great band then, but nobody was responding. . . . I got on my knees; nothing happened. I lay on the floor and that did it. . . . And that's how come I started lying on the floor."[43]

In the mid-1950s, McNeely began painting his horn so that it glowed in the dark under ultraviolet light; he also used a strobe light and a static-electricity generator in his act. But though he toured with a doo-wop group, the Penguins, and in a 1956 package show with Little Richard, Big Joe Turner, Bill Doggett, and other rock 'n' roll stars, his career faded, as saxophonists were relegated to sideman roles behind singers. His version of "There Is Something on Your Mind" was eclipsed by Bobby Marchan's, a No. 1 R&B hit in 1960, and his live album, released on Warner Bros. in 1963, was indifferently promoted. He did make a lasting impression on the teenage Jimi Hendrix, however, at a Seattle show around 1959. In their Hendrix biography, Harry Shapiro and Caesar Glebbeek write that "McNeely's act was a blueprint for the game plan that Jimmy [sic] himself would use later on. Jimmy was also impressed by the power of the horn itself, . . . and he incorporated horn sounds into the matrix of his own style and technique."[44]

By the end of the 1960s, McNeely had retired from music and taken a job as a mailman. In the early 1980s, he began his comeback; before long he was touring Europe, Australia, and Japan and cutting albums for British, German, Austrian, and Australian labels, as well as his own Big J imprint. His latest recording, the EP *Mac's Back,* was released in 2011.

Other saxophonists considered honkers included Frank "Floorshow" Culley, Willis "Gator Tail" Jackson, Chuck Higgins, Sam "the Man" Taylor, and Big Al Sears. The Maryland-born, Virginia-bred Culley played alto sax alongside Hal Singer's tenor on a December 1948 Wynonie Harris session for King. In January 1949, having signed with Atlantic, Culley cut "Cole Slaw," a honking tenor-sax adaptation of Jimmy Dorsey's 1942 hit "Sorghum Switch"; his next release was "Floor Show," which interpolates the main theme of Glenn Miller's "In the Mood." Jesse Stone, who'd originally written "Sorghum Switch" for Doc Wheeler's Sunset Orchestra in 1941, arranged "Cole Slaw" for Culley, adding a new bass line. "I designed a bass-pattern, and it sort of became identified with rock 'n' roll—doo, da-*doo, dum;* doo, da-*doo, dum*—that thing," Stone recalled. "The first record we used it on was 'Cole Slaw' by Frank Culley, the sax player."[45] Culley also played what is perhaps the first tenor saxophone solo on a doo-wop record when he was featured on the Clovers' first hit, "Don't You Know I Love You," in 1951. On subsequent sessions, the Clovers were accompanied by Willis Jackson or Sam Taylor.

Jackson, a Florida native, made his name and reputation with the two-sided "Gator Tail," a jazzy Jacquet-style honking tune that he cut for Mercury in 1949 as a member of Cootie Williams's band. On his own, he recorded for Apollo, Atlantic, and DeLuxe; a 1952 Atlantic side, "Rock, Rock, Rock," anticipates not rock 'n' roll but the organ-driven soul jazz that Jackson would soon embrace. Jackson also played on some Atlantic recordings of Ruth Brown, with whom he was romantically involved. From 1959 to 1964, he recorded soul-jazz albums for the Prestige label, often with organists such as Jack McDuff or Johnny "Hammond" Smith, guitarists such as Kenny Burrell or Pat Martino, and Latin percussionists such as Ray Barretto or Candido Camero. Although jazz critics generally ignored him, he continued to record albums for such labels as Verve, Cotillion, and Muse through the 1970s, remaining active until his death in 1987.

Chuck Higgins is remembered mainly for his first record, "Pachuko Hop," one of the cruder examples of saxophone honking, which he cut for the fledgling Combo label in 1952. Higgins had switched to saxophone from trumpet after moving to Los Angeles from Gary, Indiana. His quavering, squealing instrumental—originally intended as the B-side of "Motorhead Baby," sung by pianist John Watson (who would later reemerge as Johnny "Guitar" Watson)—became a local hit and an enduring favorite among Mexican-Americans, although it has no Mexican content other than the misspelled title reference to zoot-suited Chicano hipsters. Higgins kept recording for Combo, Aladdin, Specialty, and other labels but never made the national charts. He stopped performing in the 1960s but made a comeback the following decade and toured Europe in the 1980s before retiring in the 1990s.

Sam "the Man" Taylor, from Tennessee, took up the saxophone while attending Alabama's State Teachers College. He joined Scatman Crothers's band in the Midwest, then moved to New York, where he played for Doc Wheeler, Cootie Williams, Lucky Millinder, and Cab Calloway in the 1940s. In the 1950s, he worked as a studio musician, backing rhythm-and-blues singers ranging from Ray Charles to Louis Jordan to LaVern Baker for the Atlantic, Savoy, Apollo, Mercury, and Decca labels, as well as MGM, for which he also recorded under his own name. In August 1953, he recorded the swaggering tenor-sax solo on Clyde McPhatter and the Drifters' first hit, "Money Honey." In February 1954, he took a rollicking break on Big Joe Turner's "Shake, Rattle and Roll"; a month later, he played the steamy solo on the Chords' "Sh-Boom."

Taylor played the tortuous lead part on "Cloudburst," recorded for MGM in late 1954 by the guitarist Leroy Kirkland's band under the name Claude Cloud and His Thunderclaps. Alan Freed spun the record on his radio program and featured Taylor, along with saxophonists Red Prysock and Big Al Sears and guitarist Mickey Baker, on his "Rock 'n Roll Easter Jubilee" show at the Brooklyn Paramount Theatre in April 1955. Afterward, Taylor replaced Count Basie as the leader of Freed's house band, performing on Freed's radio programs, stage shows, and recordings for the Coral label. Singer Jon Hendricks set lyrics to Taylor's "Cloudburst" solo and recorded the song with Dave Lambert in 1955, laying the foundation for the "vocalese" jazz group Lambert, Hendricks and Ross. Taylor's solo also anticipated John Coltrane's modal-jazz classic "Giant Steps."

While continuing to play rock 'n' roll for Freed through the late 1950s, Taylor took a more mature direction on his own albums, recording with string orchestras or jazz combos. Although his big tone and expressive phrasing made him a standout among honkers, Taylor's solo career never really took off. He performed and recorded in Japan in the 1970s, then faded into obscurity, dying in 1990.

Big Al Sears boasted one of the most extensive jazz résumés of any saxophone honker. Originally from Macomb, Illinois, he began playing professionally in Buffalo, New York, then moved to New York City in 1928 and replaced Johnny Hodges in Chick Webb's band. After touring with the Fats Waller–James P. Johnson revue *Keep Shufflin',* he led his own groups and played in the bands of Elmer Snowden, Andy Kirk, Lionel Hampton, Duke Ellington, and others, even jamming with Thelonious Monk at Minton's Playhouse in Harlem. When Johnny Hodges left Ellington to form his own band, Sears joined him, playing the lead on Hodges's March 1951 recording of "Castle Rock." On this most sophisticated of honking vehicles, Sears alternates wailing passages with soft, subtle lines, set off by a sleek modern-jazz arrangement. Hodges's "Castle Rock" made both the R&B and pop charts, and with lyrics added by the white songwriters Ervin Drake and Jimmy Shirl, the song was a pop hit for Frank Sinatra and for the Fontane Sisters.

Sears had recorded a single under his own name in 1945; he cut two more singles for the Coral label in 1949 with a vocal/instrumental group called the Sparrows. After the success of "Castle Rock," he recorded eight sides for King, adopting a more exuberant honking style than before. He switched to RCA Victor in 1952, turning toward mainstream pop, but though he continued to record as a leader for such labels as Herald, Baton, Groove, and Jubilee through the mid-1950s, he had little success as a solo artist. Instead, he acquired a formidable reputation as an accompanist on recording sessions and stage shows. In January 1955, he played the understated tenor-sax solo on Big Joe Turner's "Flip Flop and Fly," a follow-up to "Shake, Rattle and Roll"; soon afterward, he began an association with Alan Freed that lasted through the late 1950s. In 1960, he returned to jazz with the album *Swing's the Thing,* also recording the first of three Dixieland albums with the Swingville All-Stars. After briefly participating in the rock 'n' roll revival a decade later, he retired, dying at the age of eighty in 1990.

Three nonhonking alto saxophonists, Joe Lutcher, Tab Smith, and Earl Bostic, also made the rhythm-and-blues charts. Lutcher was born into a large musical family in Lake Charles, Louisiana, but moved to Los Angeles before World War II, following his older sister Nellie. After wartime service in the navy, he led his own band in Los Angeles; discovered by Art Rupe, he began recording for Specialty in 1947. But he quickly switched to Capitol, for which Nellie Lutcher was already recording, and that label released his first hit, "Shuffle Woogie," before Specialty issued his previously recorded second hit, "Rockin' Boogie." ("Shuffle Woogie" was credited to Joe Lutcher's Jump Band and "Rockin' Boogie" to Joe Lutcher and His Society Cats, though the musicians on both discs are mostly the same.) While Lutcher sings on many of his other recordings, his first two hits are almost entirely instrumental—up-tempo boogie shuffles played in a jazzy jump-blues style and featuring Lutcher's sleek alto sax. On "Rockin' Boogie," Lutcher sings a single blues verse: "We're playin' this boogie, and we're playin' it because it rocks (2×) / Yes, we're playin' this boogie, and we're playing it for the bobby sox."

Despite the success of "Shuffle Woogie," Lutcher left Capitol in 1948, during the second musicians-union recording ban. In 1949, he signed with Modern, singing on his final hit, "Mardi Gras," which forms the basis for Professor Longhair's anthem "Mardis Gras in New Orleans," first recorded by Longhair later in 1949 and covered by Fats Domino in 1952. Lutcher subsequently cut singles for Peacock, London, and other labels, but after 1953 he turned to religion, recording gospel music for his own Jordan label and giving spiritual counsel to Little Richard. He died in 2006.

Tab Smith, a North Carolina native, found his way to St. Louis, where he played in Eddie Johnson's Crackerjacks and Fate Marable's riverboat band; moving to New York, he worked in the Mills Blue Rhythm Band and the Count Basie and Lucky Millinder Orchestras. The smooth-toned Smith formed his own group in the 1940s, scoring his first hit in 1945 with the treacly ballad "I'll Live True to You," sung by guitarist Trevor Bacon. Smith backed Wynonie Harris on a November 1946 session but retreated from the music scene after a car crash in which Bacon died. He came back in 1951 with an instrumental version of the ballad "Because of You," a 1940 Tin Pan Alley composition that was revived in the 1951 movie *I Was an American Spy* and became a No. 1 pop smash later that year for Tony Bennett. Smith's record was a No. 1 R&B hit that crossed over to the pop charts, but despite dozens of subsequent singles on the United label and others on Atlantic, Premium, King, and Chess—plus tours with the gospel-flavored rhythm-and-blues group the "5" Royales and performances on R&B package shows—Smith never had another national hit, leaving the music business in the 1960s to become a real estate agent.

Smith's more successful rival, Earl Bostic, played with a guttural tone but otherwise took a similar approach, refashioning old standards for the rhythm-and-blues market. Born in Tulsa, Oklahoma, he attended Xavier University in New Orleans, then worked in various territory bands before coming to New York, where he played in Edgar Hayes's, Don Redmond's, and other groups, making his recorded debut with Lionel Hampton. He led a combo in the early 1940s, meanwhile composing and arranging for Louis Prima, among others, and jamming with the nascent beboppers in Harlem. After another stint in Hampton's band, he played briefly with Hot Lips Page and began recording on his own, first in late 1945 with a big band and afterward with smaller groups. He had a national hit in 1948 with an instrumental version of "Temptation," a song introduced by Bing Crosby in the 1933 movie *Going Hollywood* that would be a hit again for the Everly Brothers in 1961.

Bostic's biggest hits were cut for the King label in 1951: "Sleep," from 1921, had been the theme song of Fred Waring's Pennsylvanians; "Flamingo," an R&B chart-topper, had been a pop hit for Duke Ellington in 1941, as sung by Herb Jeffries. Bostic's huge, vibrant tone made his alto sax sound like a tenor, and his brilliant technique gave the instrument a vocal-like expressiveness. A number of outstanding jazz musicians passed through his band, including the tenor saxophonists Stanley Turrentine, Benny Golson, Teddy Edwards, and John Coltrane. "He showed me a lot of things on my horn," Coltrane later said.[46] Bostic performed and recorded through the mid-1960s, turning from singles to albums after recovering from a heart attack in 1956. He attracted a considerable following among whites while maintaining an approach summarized by the title of his 1958 King album *Bostic Rocks Hits from the Swing Age*. But in 1965, while appearing in Rochester, New York, he suffered a second heart attack and died, at the age of fifty-two.

Tenor saxophonist Sil Austin cut his first hits in a honking style, then switched to syrupy ballads. A Florida native, he moved to New York as a teenager and worked with Roy Eldridge, Cootie Williams, and Tiny Bradshaw. After forming his own band, Austin began recording for Mercury in 1956, scoring a hit that year with "Slow Walk," an adaptation of Bill Doggett's "Honky Tonk" that crossed over from the R&B to the pop charts. His follow-up, "Birthday Party," in a similar honking mode, became a pop but not an R&B hit in early 1957. Afterward, Austin recorded another album's worth of honking material, but no hits resulted; so in 1959, accompanied by a string orchestra and chorus, he cut *Sil Austin Plays Pretty for the People*, an album of ballads that included such chestnuts as "Summertime," "Stardust," and what would be his final hit, "Danny Boy." Taking a cue from Earl Bostic, Austin wrung the last drop of emotion from sentimental songs by using the same exaggerated vibrato and bluesy embellishments that he applied to up-tempo jump tunes. He continued to cut albums for Mercury through the mid-1960s, then moved to Atlanta and recorded for Shelby Singleton's SSS International label. He died in 2001.

The last of the honkers, in a sense, was Curtis Ousley, known as King Curtis. He did not literally honk, unless one considers his rough bursts of notes honking, and other bawling tenor saxophonists came after him—most notably Junior Walker, who was actually three years older—but Curtis was the saxophonist who led the transition from rock 'n' roll to the more emotive soul music of the 1960s. Born in Ft. Worth, Texas, he played in the same high school band as the pioneering free-jazz saxophonist Ornette Coleman. At seventeen, he recorded four tunes for the Waco-based Humming Bird label, but they were not released. At eighteen, he traveled to New York and won the Wednesday-night amateur contest at the Apollo Theatre. Returning to Ft. Worth, he joined Lionel Hampton's touring band, which took him back to New York before breaking up, whereupon Curtis again went back to Ft. Worth, returning to New York to stay around 1954. Beginning in 1952, Curtis recorded as a leader and sideman, performing jazz as well as R&B; he worked with the jazz pianist Horace Silver for a time and later played in Alan Freed's rock 'n' roll band.

Curtis did studio work for a number of labels but made his reputation on Atlantic, backing Chuck Willis, Big Joe Turner, Ruth Brown, LaVern Baker, and the Coasters, among others. Curtis was evidently influenced by Gene Barge's gospel-edged tenor-sax solos on such Atlantic singles as Chuck Willis's "C.C. Rider." According to Barge, "the style that you hear King playing later is the style that he came up with after he heard my stuff."[47] A March 1958 session with the Coasters yielded the R&B and pop chart-topper "Yakety Yak," a comic Leiber-Stoller song featuring a stuttering solo by Curtis that gave rise to a riant style called "Yakety Sax" (after the title of a Curtis-inspired 1958 record by the country saxophonist Boots Randolph that became a pop hit in 1963 after Randolph rerecorded it). Later in 1958, Curtis played on a pair of Buddy Holly tracks, "Reminiscing" and "Come Back Baby." Having already recorded under his own name with little success, Curtis scored a No. 1 R&B and Top 20 pop hit in 1962 on producer Bobby Robinson's Enjoy label with "Soul Twist," where he uses the "Yakety Sax" technique intermittently but blows mainly in the soulful Gene Barge style.

While continuing to record prolifically as a sideman, Curtis had more hits on his own, including "Serenade" on Capitol in 1964 (with Curtis on soprano sax), "Memphis Soul Stew" on Atlantic's Atco subsidiary in 1967 (with Curtis verbally introducing the instruments as each comes in), and instrumental covers of rock or soul hits such as Buffalo Springfield's "For What It's Worth," Stevie Wonder's "I Was Made to Love Her," Otis Redding's "(Sittin' on) the Dock of the Bay," and Led Zeppelin's "Whole Lotta Love." Curtis hired Jimi Hendrix as his guitarist in 1966, led Aretha Franklin's band through the late 1960s, and recorded on a couple of tracks for John Lennon's *Imagine* album. But in August 1971, at the age of thirty-seven, he was stabbed to death outside a building he owned in New York City.

STRING SLINGERS

T-Bone Walker's bluesy electric guitar emerged around the same time as Illinois Jacquet's honking saxophone, but though the two instrumental styles developed in parallel, the saxophone remained more popular through the 1940s, with the guitar coming to the forefront in the 1950s. However inspirational Jacquet may have been for saxophonists, Walker was even more influential on guitarists, who often copied his licks note for note. Because Walker was Chuck Berry's principal model, the playing of Walker's earlier disciples resembles Berry's, but whether Berry listened to any of them or just emulated Walker directly is moot.

One of the first of Walker's followers to make the R&B charts was Pee Wee Crayton. Raised in Austin, Texas, Crayton moved to Los Angeles in 1935, settling in Oakland after World War II broke out. He was more than thirty years old when he took up the guitar, inspired by Charlie Christian's records. When T-Bone Walker toured the San Francisco Bay Area, Crayton befriended him; he picked up pointers from Walker and from John Collins, who would later become Nat "King" Cole's guitarist. In 1945, Crayton began playing with a trio in Oakland that included pianist David Lee Johnson. He made his first recordings accompanying Ivory Joe Hunter in 1946 and the following year cut the up-tempo "After Hours Boogie" under his own name for the 4 Star label, alluding more to Buddy Johnson's "I Ain't Mad with You" than to Avery Parrish's "After Hours."

"After Hours Boogie" was not a big seller, but Crayton's next release, "Blues After Hours," on Modern, topped the R&B charts in 1948. Here, Crayton stays closer to Parrish's laid-back formula while replicating Walker's sound, including the distinctive opening vamp from "T-Bone Blues." Later the same year, he recorded another instrumental hit for Modern, "Texas Hop," which rocks to a shuffle beat and a boogie bass line and features Buddy Floyd's honking tenor saxophone along with Crayton's Walker-like guitar. In 1949, he had his final hit, also on Modern, singing the ballad "I Love You So," where he plays only a short guitar solo. On the strength of his Modern hits, he toured the country, playing the Savoy Ballroom in New York along with Buddy Johnson's band.[48]

A 1950 session with the former Count Basie trumpeter Harry "Sweets" Edison's band produced "Rockin' the Blues," an aggressive adaptation of Walker's 1949 hit "T-Bone Shuffle." In 1951, after Crayton left Modern, he recorded the Walker-ish slow blues "When It Rains It Pours" for Aladdin with Maxwell Davis's band. His next studio date came in 1954, when he cut a pair of singles—reflecting the influence of Charles Brown and Nat "King" Cole as well as Walker—for the Los Angeles record-store owner John Dolphin's label Recorded in Hollywood. Later in 1954 and in 1955, he recorded in New Orleans with Dave Bartholomew's band for Imperial Records, adopting a rock 'n' roll sound on such sides as "Do unto Others," "I Need Your Love," and "You Know, Yeah." Around 1955, the rhythm-and-blues singer Billy "the Kid" Emerson took Elvis Presley to see Crayton perform at a club in Memphis. "He thought that was somethin'!" Emerson recounted. "He'd never seen him, and Pee Wee was *good!*"[49]

In 1956, Crayton moved to Detroit, where he engaged T-Bone Walker in a "Battle of the Guitars." Crayton traveled to Chicago in September of that year to record "The Telephone Is Ringing" for Vee-Jay, sounding less like T-Bone Walker than like the Chicago blues guitarist Otis Rush, who that summer had recorded his only national hit, "I Can't Quit You Baby" (covered on Led Zeppelin's 1969 debut album). Crayton's "I Found My Peace of Mind," recorded for Vee-Jay in February 1957 with a doo-wop vocal chorus, is loosely based on Ray Charles's "I've Got a Woman." By this time, Crayton had stepped out of T-Bone Walker's shadow with a more intense style of his own. But he couldn't score a hit, drifting from one small label to another through the early 1960s, when he moved back to Los Angeles and took a job as a truck driver.

Crayton began a modest comeback in 1970 with an album for Vanguard and a performance with Johnny Otis at the Monterey Jazz Festival. He recorded an LP in Otis's *Great Rhythm & Blues Oldies* series and accompanied Big Joe Turner on album sessions for the Pablo label. He visited Europe in 1980 but performed mostly around Los Angeles, often with the white blues harmonica player and singer Rod Piazza, with whom he cut his final pair of albums in the early 1980s for the small Murray Brothers label. He suffered a fatal heart attack in Los Angeles in 1985, just after returning from appearances at the Chicago Blues Festival and the Austin, Texas, blues club Antone's.

Ironically, the most successful postwar West Coast blues guitarist owed relatively little to T-Bone Walker. Of partial Native American ancestry, Lowell Fulson grew up in Oklahoma among the Choctaw Freedmen, descendants of black slaves held by Indians. Four years younger than Pee Wee Crayton, he began playing earlier, inspired by records of Blind Lemon Jefferson, Blind Boy Fuller, Peetie Wheatstraw, and Memphis Minnie. In 1938, he moved to Ada, Oklahoma, and joined a large string band led by the banjo player Dan Wright, playing mostly country music for white audiences. Around 1940, he traveled around western Oklahoma and West Texas accompanying the blues singer Texas Alexander; afterward he moved to Gainesville, Texas, north of Dallas, and became a short-order cook. Drafted into the navy in 1943, he was stationed in the San Francisco Bay Area, where he met Bob Geddins, who would produce Fulson's first records after the war. Sent to the South Pacific as a steward, he spent less time cooking than performing, entertaining both servicemen and islanders.

Discharged in Oklahoma, Fulson moved to the Bay Area and renewed his acquaintance with Geddins, who recorded him for his Big Town label in 1946. Singing to the accompaniment of piano and bass on these sides, Fulson plays single-note runs on electric guitar but with more of a country-blues feel than T-Bone Walker. He soon adopted a more sophisticated approach, however, influenced by singers such as Jimmy Rushing and guitarists such as Walker and Pee Wee Crayton.[50] He had his first national R&B hit in 1948 with his own composition "Three O'Clock Blues" on Geddins's Down Town label, featuring Fulson's brother Martin on second guitar; the song would become a No. 1 rhythm-and-blues smash for B. B. King in 1951—King's first hit.

Fulson scored his next hit in 1949 with a reworking of Walter Davis's 1940 release "Come Back Baby," itself a variation of Leroy Carr's "How Long, How Long Blues." Fulson's record was issued on Jack Lauderdale's Los Angeles–based Down Beat label, which soon changed its name to Swing Time; like Bob Geddins, Lauderdale was an African American record producer born in Texas. In late 1954, Ray Charles would redo Fulson's "Come Back Baby" as "Come Back," the flip side of "I've Got a Woman" and a Top 5 R&B hit in its own right.

Fulson had a Top 5 R&B hit on Swing Time in 1950 with "Everyday I Have the Blues," based on Memphis Slim's 1947 recording "Nobody Loves Me," which is based in turn on Aaron Sharp's 1935 recording "Every Day I Have the Blues." The song was a hit for the jazz singer Joe Williams with King Kolax's band in 1952 and for Count Basie's band with Williams singing in 1955. It was also a 1955 hit for B. B. King and was covered by Jimmy Rushing, James Brown, Ray Charles, Billy Stewart, Eric Clapton, and many others. Fulson's record was his first with the Texas-born, Los Angeles–based pianist Lloyd Glenn, a territory-band veteran who had accompanied T-Bone Walker on "Call It Stormy Monday." Glenn would perform on and arrange many of Fulson's records, including Fulson's biggest hit, "Blue Shadows," and the double-sided hits "Lonesome Christmas" and "I'm a Night Owl"—all from 1950 or 1951. Meanwhile, Glenn cut his own instrumental hits, "Old Time Shuffle Blues" and the chart-topping "Chica Boo," on Swing Time with the same band. But Glenn refused to travel, so Jack Lauderdale, who produced Ray Charles's first records, had Charles play piano in Fulson's touring band, which also included tenor saxophonist Stanley Turrentine.

Fulson's later Swing Time sessions produced no hits, nor did his single Aladdin session in New Orleans in 1953. But his first session for the Checker label, done in Dallas in September 1954, yielded the classic "Reconsider Baby," a distinctive Fulson composition that anticipates the soul blues of Bobby Bland and Little Milton. Here, Fulson sings convincingly and plays a pair of fierce, modern guitar solos over a boogie bass line and shuffling backbeat, buoyed by the rich saxophone harmonies of David "Fathead" Newman and Leroy "Hog" Cooper, who would later play together in Ray Charles's band. Elvis Presley recorded a rockabilly version of "Reconsider Baby" in 1960, with a tenor saxophone solo by Boots Randolph.

Fulson continued to record for Checker through the early 1960s, often with Lloyd Glenn, but had only one more national hit on that label, "Loving You (Is All I Crave)," in 1955. He toured with such artists as Big Joe Turner, Big Maybelle, and the Coasters, but his style did not appeal beyond the rhythm-and-blues market. Singing at the top of his range on "Tollin' Bells," from February 1956, he sounds like James Brown, who cut his first single, "Please, Please, Please," the same month. Fulson moved to Los Angeles in the mid-1960s and began recording for Kent, a label established by the Bihari brothers after Modern Records went bankrupt. He had a hit in 1967 with "Tramp," where he recites the verses, singing only on the refrain; the song, which Fulson wrote with the California-based blues singer and pianist Jimmy McCracklin, was a crossover hit the same year for Otis Redding and Carla Thomas, with Thomas handling the recitation.

Fulson had two minor hits on Kent in 1967 and a final hit on the Granite label in 1975—"Do You Love Me," in an arrangement that owes much to Isaac Hayes's "Theme from Shaft." Before his death in 1999, he made albums for such labels as Jewel, Rounder, and Bullseye Blues, sticking mostly to the blues while recording such oddities as the Beatles' "Why Don't We Do It in the Road?" He was well received in Europe, where he began touring at the end of the 1960s, but never achieved the stateside recognition of Chicago blues guitarists such as Buddy Guy, at least among white listeners. But unlike those artists, he retained a measure of popularity among blacks, who regarded him as a soul singer as much as a bluesman.

Clarence "Gatemouth" Brown resisted categorization as a blues musician even more emphatically than Lowell Fulson. Born in southwestern Louisiana, he grew up in Orange, Texas, just across the Louisiana border. He took up guitar to accompany his father, a fiddler who played country and Cajun music; he also learned to play fiddle and drums. Despite his small-town southern background, he was attracted to big-band swing rather than country blues. "I heard the music of Blind Lemon Jefferson and the other backwards bluesmen, but I just didn't like that caliber of music," he told the writer Jas Obrecht. "I was influenced by people like Count Basie, Duke Ellington, Lionel Hampton, and Woody Herman."[51]

Around 1940, Brown joined a local band called the Gay Swingsters, then toured with a troupe called the Brownskin Models.[52] After a wartime stint in the military, he performed at the Creole trumpeter and bandleader Don Albert's club in San Antonio, billed as "the Singing Drummer."[53] As Brown told it, he was invited to Houston in 1947 by Don Robey, the owner of the Bronze Peacock Dinner Club; when T-Bone Walker, the featured performer at the club, took ill, Brown picked up Walker's guitar and improvised "Gatemouth Boogie" on stage, to the audience's acclaim and Walker's chagrin. But according to Evelyn Johnson, who booked the club for Robey, it was the stricken Walker who recommended that Brown be brought in from San Antonio to fill out his engagement.[54]

In any case, Robey signed Brown to a management contract and took him to Los Angeles in August 1947 to record four sides for Aladdin with Maxwell Davis's band. On "Gatemouth Boogie," after playing the guitar vamp from the Delmore Brothers' "Hillbilly Boogie," Brown sings, "My name is Gatemouth Brown, I just got in your town / [If] you don't like my style, I will not hang around," in a Jimmy Rushing– or Big Joe Turner–like shouting style. He plays a T-Bone Walker–style single-string guitar solo, followed by a different hillbilly-boogie vamp, then shouts the final verses as the band plays Count Basie's "Boogie Woogie." The other three Aladdin sides are in a similar jump-blues vein but more laid-back and without the country tinge—pre-rock rather than proto-rock, as they lack a backbeat or boogie-woogie bass line.

Frustrated when Aladdin delayed the release of Brown's second single, Robey founded Peacock Records, with Brown as the label's first artist.[55] In January 1949, Brown cut six sides for Peacock with Jack McVea's band, the first four of which Robey released on three different discs, repeating "Didn't Reach My Goal" and "Mercy on Me" on two discs each. He coupled the remaining two songs, "My Time Is Expensive" and "Mary Is Fine," on a fourth disc, which became Brown's only nationally charted hit. These early Peacock sides are fairly conventional jump blues, except for the frantic instrumental "Atomic Energy" and the up-tempo proto-rocker "Mary Is Fine," the latter sporting a shuffling backbeat and boogie bass line. Brown's hot guitar playing—his scorching solo on "Mercy on Me," for example—draws from T-Bone Walker while pointing the way toward Chuck Berry and beyond.

Brown moves closer to rock 'n' roll on his next Peacock session in late 1949, shouting the blues over a shuffling backbeat and boogie bass line on "I Live My Life," "2 O'Clock in the Morning," "Boogie Rambler," "It Can Never Be That Way," and "Just Got Lucky." On "I've Been Mistreated," one of two slow blues from the same session, Brown anticipates Eddie Boyd's 1952 Chicago blues classic "Five Long Years" with the opening line "Have you ever been mistreated? / Then you know just how I feel" (Boyd sings, "If you ever been mistreated, / you know just what I'm talkin' about"). Brown fully embraces proto-rock in 1951 and 1952 on such jumping numbers as "She Walk Right In," "Too Late Baby," "Baby Take It Easy," "She Winked Her Eye," and "Pale Dry Boogie."

With Jimmy McCracklin on piano at a 1953 session, Brown rocks on "You Got Money" and plays wild guitar on "Dirty Work at the Crossroads." Recording with trombonist Al Grey's band later in 1953, Brown sizzles on the instrumentals "Boogie Uproar" and "Gate Walks to Board" (the latter composed by Brown and tenor saxophonist Johnny Board). The arrangements on a second session with Grey's band in 1954 have even more of a rock 'n' roll flavor. "Okie Dokie Stomp," an instrumental recorded later in 1954 with trombonist Pluma Davis's band, rocks hard, as does "Rock My Blues Away" from 1956, which refers to Deacon Jones and Elder Brown from Wynonie Harris's "Good Rockin' Tonight." Yet despite aural evidence to the contrary, Brown later said, "I didn't actually ever get into rock and roll. I refused getting into it, because to me it's not the kind of music that is tasteful."[56]

Whether or not Brown truly disdained rock 'n' roll, white rock fans had little chance to hear him, as he performed mainly in segregated venues in the South and Southwest, at least until the 1960s, when he began playing country-western clubs. In 1959, after a three-year recording hiatus, he cut the instrumental blues "Just Before Dawn," displaying the same sort of flashy technique on fiddle as he previously had on guitar. He also fiddles on his final Peacock single, "Slop Time," in 1961. He made a few more singles for the obscure Houston labels Cue and Cinderella in 1964 and 1965, then covered Little Jimmy Dickens's 1965 country smash "May the Bird of Paradise Fly up Your Nose" for the Hermitage label in Nashville. Hermitage's owner, the white rhythm-and-blues disc jockey Bill "Hoss" Allen, featured Brown regularly on his short-lived 1966 television show, *The !!!! Beat*.

By the early 1970s, Brown was working as a deputy sheriff in Aztec, New Mexico. Rediscovered in France, he made his first European tour in 1971, appearing at the Montreux Jazz Festival and recording the first of several albums for the French Barclay and Black & Blue labels. He performed with Canned Heat at the 1973 Montreux festival and played on Professor Longhair's 1974 album *Rock 'n' Roll Gumbo*. In 1976, he took a State Department–sponsored tour of East Africa; the following year, he released the album *Blackjack* on the American label Music Is Medicine, playing fiddle, guitar, harmonica, mandolin, and viola while mingling blues and jazz with Cajun, country, western swing, and bluegrass. In 1978, he recorded the album *Makin' Music* with the country star Roy Clark; afterward, he made a few appearances on *Hee Haw,* the long-running country-music television show that Clark cohosted.

Over the next two decades, Brown toured worldwide and received numerous honors; he cut a string of albums for Rounder, Alligator, and Verve, winning a 1982 Grammy award for *Alright Again!* on Rounder. He continued to perform even after being diagnosed with lung cancer in 2004; the following year, he evacuated his house in Slidell, Louisiana, just before Hurricane Katrina destroyed it, dying of heart failure days later. To the end, he refused to be labeled. "I'm not a blues player," he told Jas Obrecht. "I'm a musician."[57]

Mickey Baker was the most prolific studio guitarist of the early rock 'n' roll era, a presence—if not always a prominent one—on dozens of rock and R&B hits. Born in Louisville, Kentucky, he was caught stealing at age eleven and sent to an orphanage, from which he repeatedly ran away. By the early 1940s, he had made his way to New York, a teenage hustler with dreams of becoming a jazz trumpeter. But he could only afford a guitar, and after lessons with guitarists such as Rector Bailey (who would record with Big Joe Turner in 1952), he joined a band led by pianist Jimmy Neely and traveled to the San Francisco Bay Area, where he saw Pee Wee Crayton perform. Impressed as much by Crayton's wealth as by his style, he decided to switch from jazz to the blues. "I was starving to death and the blues was just a financial thing for me then," he reflected.[58]

Returning to New York, Baker began recording as a sideman and bandleader. He displays the greasy, trebly, Latin-flavored post-Walker style he would later characterize as "slip and slide guitar" on his first record as a leader—"Guitar Mambo," backed with "Riverboat"—cut for Savoy in August 1952 with a band including Hal "Cornbread" Singer.[59] Singing and strumming on his next record, "Love You Baby," from November 1952, he anticipates Elvis Presley or Carl Perkins. But Baker made his reputation almost entirely by accompanying others: from 1952 to 1956, he backed Ruth Brown, Ray Charles, Amos Milburn, LaVern Baker, Little Willie John, Little Esther, Wynonie Harris, Sil Austin, Earl Bostic, Louis Jordan, Screamin' Jay Hawkins, and many others for such labels as Savoy, King, Mercury, and Atlantic. Among the proto-rock classics on which he plays are Clyde McPhatter and the Drifters' "Money Honey," Big Joe Turner's "Shake, Rattle and Roll," and Big Maybelle's "Whole Lotta Shakin' Goin' On," although his guitar can barely be heard on any of them.

As Big Red McHouston (his given name was McHouston Baker), he recorded the full-blown rocker "I'm Tired" with Sam "the Man" Taylor and singer Larry Dale for RCA's Groove subsidiary in 1954. As Mickey "Guitar" Baker, he cut rock, jazz, and Latin instrumentals for Rainbow in 1955; he also played in several of Alan Freed's New York stage shows that year.

Baker had accompanied "Little" Sylvia Vanderpool, to whom he'd previously given guitar lessons, on a 1953 single for Atlantic's short-lived Cat subsidiary. Still a teenager, Vanderpool had been recording since 1950, when she sang bluesy duets with Hot Lips Page for Columbia. Seeking to replicate the success of Les Paul and Mary Ford, a white singing and guitar-playing duo, Baker enlisted Vanderpool to form Mickey and Sylvia. The two began recording together for Rainbow in 1955, then switched to Groove and in October 1956 cut the Caribbean-flavored "Love Is Strange," which became a No. 1 R&B hit and nearly made the pop Top 10.

Baker claims to have taken "Love Is Strange" from Bo Diddley, who never recorded it, after Mickey and Sylvia toured with him.[60] But guitarist

Jody Williams, who played in Bo Diddley's band at the time, maintains that it was adapted from his composition "Billy's Blues," which he'd recorded with singer Billy Stewart earlier in 1956.[61] Stewart's publisher, Arc Music, filed suit, but despite the obvious resemblance between Williams's guitar riff on "Billy's Blues" and Baker's on "Love Is Strange," the court ruled in Baker's favor. The influence of "Love Is Strange" can be heard on such hits as Billy and Lillie's "La Dee Dah," from 1957, and Ike and Tina Turner's "It's Gonna Work Out Fine," from 1961, for which Baker is said to have recorded the spoken parts attributed to Ike Turner.

Mickey and Sylvia had several lesser hits through 1961, more of them on the pop than the R&B charts. In 1962, the pair split up and Baker moved to Paris, where he worked as a studio musician, producer, and performer, reinventing himself as a traditional country bluesman. Still active today, he is best known for his jazz-guitar method books, the first of which he wrote in 1950 and had published in 1955. Sylvia Vanderpool recorded a string of disco-era hits under the name Sylvia, beginning with "Pillow Talk" in 1973. She and her husband, Joe Robinson, founded Sugar Hill Records and in 1979, at Sylvia Robinson's instigation, released "Rapper's Delight" by the Sugar Hill Gang, the first rap hit.

Goree Carter never had a national hit, but the rediscovery of his 1949 recording "Rock Awhile," with its Chuck Berry–like guitar part, brought him posthumous recognition as a rock 'n' roll forefather. Born in Houston, Carter took up the guitar at thirteen, inspired by T-Bone Walker's records. He was playing at a Houston club in a band led by the alto saxophonist Conrad Johnson five years later when he was signed to Freedom Records, a local label run by Solomon Kahal. Before recording for Freedom, Carter may have already cut a pair of Walker-style sides for Roy Milton's Miltone label under the name Little T-Bone. Kahal urged him to continue in the same vein. "He just wanted me to sound mostly like T-Bone," Carter recalled.[62]

Carter did just that on his first side for Freedom, "Sweet Ole Woman's Blues," which was coupled on the same disc with Little Willie Littlefield's "Littlefield's Boogie." Carter's next release was "Rock Awhile," where he's backed by Conrad Johnson's band recording as the Hepcats. The opening guitar riff of "Rock Awhile" resembles the one on Chuck Berry's "Carol," while the mid-song solo suggests the one on "Roll Over Beethoven," but it's doubtful that Berry ever heard Carter's record. Carter continued to record through 1954 for Freedom, Bayou, Imperial, Sittin' In With, Modern, Jade, Coral, and Peacock, cutting proto-rockers such as the raucous "Let's Rock," from 1950 but never straying far from Walker's shadow. After being drafted into the army, he quit playing music, working at various jobs until his death in 1990.

A similar foreshadowing of Berry's style can be heard on Johnny Otis's "Good Ole Blues" and "Boogie Guitar," both from 1949 and both featuring guitarist Pete Lewis, whom Berry is more likely to have heard than Goree Carter. On "Good Ole Blues," Lewis plays the same introductory part and later adds some of the same T-Bone Walker licks that Berry uses on "Johnny B. Goode." Lewis stays in a Berry-ish groove on "Boogie Guitar," accompanied by two other guitarists. Lewis performed on most of Otis's records through the mid-1950s and recorded a few sides of his own for Federal as Pete "Guitar" Lewis in 1952 and 1953, singing the blues and playing Berry-like instrumentals such as "Louisiana Hop" and "Scratchin'." He cut his last single in 1953 for Peacock, the label for which he also accompanied Big Mama Thornton and Johnny Ace. Almost nothing is known about Lewis's life; he is said to have been born in Louisiana and to have died in the 1960s or 1970s. His replacement in Otis's band was Jimmy Nolen, an Oklahoma-born, T-Bone Walker–inspired guitarist who went on to play the "chicken scratch" guitar parts in James Brown's late-1960s band.

Although he was raised in Mississippi and based his career in New Orleans, Guitar Slim played Texas-style guitar, inspired mainly by Gatemouth Brown. Born Eddie Jones in Greenwood, Mississippi, he grew up in Hollandale, in the heart of the Delta, where his exuberant dancing attracted attention at a local club. After Jones left Hollandale in 1948, the blues guitarist Willie D. Warren hired him to dance with his band, later letting him sing with the group and teaching him to play guitar. In 1950, Jones moved to New Orleans, where he became friendly with a teenage pianist named Huey Smith and began calling himself Guitar Slim. Soon he was appearing at nightclubs such as the Dew Drop Inn, where his performance led the African American newspaper *Louisiana Weekly* to describe him as "an exact copy of Gatemouth Brown."[63]

With Smith on piano, Slim cut four blues sides for Imperial in 1951; he recorded the gospel-tinged ballad "Feelin' Sad," soon to be covered by Ray Charles, for Nashville's J-B label in 1952. He was recruited the following year by Johnny Vincent, a white Mississippian (born John Vincent Imbragulio) whom Art Rupe had hired to run the Specialty label's New Orleans operation. Vincent had Ray Charles play piano and arrange for the October 1953 session that produced "The Things That I Used to Do," where Charles lays triplet piano rhythms over a habanera horn vamp and Slim plays distinctively spiky guitar lines while ardently singing the poignant lyrics. Despite Rupe's initial misgivings, the song, which Slim would claim had come to him in a dream, became a No. 1 hit, the biggest R&B seller of 1954.

Slim's next single, "The Story of My Life," recorded at the same New Orleans session, features a piercing guitar solo that influenced later rock guitarists such as Frank Zappa. But though Slim continued to record for Specialty through 1955, mostly in Los Angeles, and cut a few singles for Atco between 1956 and 1958, often recycling the "Things That I Used to Do" formula, the intensity of his guitar playing was never again captured in the studio, and he never had another national hit. Nevertheless, his flamboyant stage act made him a popular live attraction: he would dye his hair to match his brightly colored suits and shoes and, using a long guitar cord, would walk along bar tops and out into the streets like a saxophone honker. His trebly, overamplified guitar left a lasting impression on musicians such as the New Orleans singer-guitarist Earl King, who claimed that "Slim was gettin' a fuzztone distortion way before anyone else."[64] His heavy drinking impaired his health, however, and he died while on tour in upstate New York in early 1959.

An even more extravagant stylist was Johnny "Guitar" Watson, who was well ahead of his time when he first emerged in the 1950s, anticipating both psychedelic music and rap before reemerging as a funk star in the 1970s. Born in Houston, he began playing piano, then took up guitar. "I inherited my first guitar from my grandfather, who was a spiritualist preacher," he said. "My grandmother told me *not* to play any blues on it, and that was the first thing I taught myself to play."[65] He modeled himself after Gatemouth Brown and T-Bone Walker, performing in Houston clubs despite being underage. At fifteen, he moved to Los Angeles, where he successfully competed in amateur contests sponsored by Johnny Otis; he met Chuck Higgins at one such contest, leading to the 1952 recording session where he played piano and sang on "Motorhead Baby." He rerecorded that song for Federal at a much slower tempo on his first session as a leader in January 1953, credited as Young John Watson. He played piano on three of the four sides he cut that day but played guitar on "Highway 60," rapping the verses before singing the chorus to the tune of Amos Milburn's "Bad, Bad Whiskey."

After a later 1953 studio date where he played only piano, Watson came into his own as a guitarist on the February 1954 session where he recorded the instrumental "Space Guitar." While still rooted in the blues of Gatemouth Brown and T-Bone Walker, "Space Guitar" is a harbinger of Jimi Hendrix, but with its furious bursts of notes, talking-guitar effects, jangling chords, jarring starts and stops, and wrenching blasts of echo and reverb, it was too freakishly futuristic to sell in its own day. After switching to Modern Records' RPM subsidiary, Watson made his chart debut in 1955 with a fairly faithful cover of Earl King's New Orleans–style hit "Those Lonely, Lonely Nights," credited as Johnny "Guitar" Watson after the title of the 1954 Joan Crawford–Sterling Hayden western *Johnny Guitar*. But the clever originals he recorded for the label, where his slashing guitar is accompanied by Maxwell Davis's band, were not big sellers, and RPM dropped him in 1956.

In November 1957, Watson recorded "Gangster of Love" for the new Keen label, revamping an unreleased recording he'd cut for RPM the previous year under the title "Love Bandit." Following a pattern he'd used on earlier songs, he sings the choruses but raps such verses as "The sheriff said, 'Is your name Johnny "Guitar" Watson?' in a very deep voice / I said, 'Yes, brother sheriff, and that's your wife on the back of my horse.'" Not a hit, the song was revived by the white blues-rocker Steve Miller in 1968.

After unsuccessful sessions for several other labels, Watson had a hit on King in 1962 with the bluesy ballad "Cuttin' In," where he's accompanied by a violin section. In the mid-1960s, he collaborated with the New Orleans singer Larry Williams, who'd had the rock 'n' roll hits "Short Fat Fannie" and "Bony Moronie" in 1957. The two toured England and formed their own production company and record labels but had their biggest hit on OKeh with "Mercy, Mercy, Mercy" in 1967. Written in 1966 as an instrumental by Joe Zawinul, then the keyboard player for the jazz saxophone star Cannonball Adderley, the tune was a surprise hit for Adderley. With lyrics added by Watson and Williams, the song was a hit not only for them but for the rhythm-and-blues singer Marlena Shaw and the white rock band the Buckinghams, whose version was the biggest seller by far.

In 1968, Williams and Watson had another hit, "Nobody," backed by the psychedelic folk-rock band Kaleidoscope, with Solomon Feldthouse on sitar. But Watson did not return to the charts until the mid-1970s, after recording unsuccessfully again for several more labels. Signing with Fantasy Records, he scored a breakout hit in 1975 with the funky "I Don't Want to Be a Lone Ranger," sleekly produced, with minimal guitar, by Watson himself. A string of funk hits on the British DJM label followed, culminating in "A Real Mother for Ya" in 1977, as Watson assumed a broad-brimmed, bell-bottomed Superfly image to go with his new musical style. Following albums for A&M and Valley Vue in the early 1980s, Watson withdrew from the music scene until 1994, when he cut the album *Bow Wow* for Al Bell's Bellmark label. He resumed touring but suffered a fatal heart attack during a 1996 performance in Yokohama, Japan.

None of T-Bone Walker's other stylistic progeny—not even his indirect disciple Mickey Baker—had nearly the influence on rock music that Chuck Berry did. Making his recorded debut in May 1955 with "Maybellene," Berry caught the first wave of the rock 'n' roll tsunami and rode it into the genre's pantheon, leaving his mark on virtually every guitar rocker who came after him. So great was his impact that other rhythm-and-blues guitarists came to be regarded as his precursors rather than as fellow Walker followers. Nonetheless, it is Walker rather than Berry who should be seen as the father of rock 'n' roll—as well as modern blues—guitar.

SHOUTERS

The postwar trend for singers to take the spotlight from bandleaders was less pronounced in rhythm-and-blues than in pop music, and male R&B singers were more likely than their pop counterparts to play instruments. Two of the most prominent male R&B singers who did not play instruments or lead their own bands were the blues shouters Big Joe Turner and Wynonie Harris, who performed and recorded for various labels with pickup groups. Ironically, Turner, who was Harris's idol, did not have a national hit between 1946 and 1950, only to experience his greatest success after signing with Atlantic Records in 1951, while Harris enjoyed his heyday in the late 1940s and early 1950s, scoring his final hit in 1952.

Harris had moved to Los Angeles around 1940 from his native Omaha, where he'd taken up blues singing after starting as a dancer. He made a name for himself at the Club Alabam with his brash personality and raunchy material; he also worked other clubs in Los Angeles and the San Francisco Bay Area, sometimes engaging T-Bone Walker or Big Joe Turner in a "Battle of the Blues."[66] He spent some six months with Lucky Millinder's band in 1944, impressing the young Roy Brown when the band played Houston. "During my high school days I'd go and hear him and I'd always say if ever I was going to be a blues singer I'd like to be like that guy," Brown said.[67]

After leaving Millinder, Harris recorded jump blues in a shouting style like Turner's, only more intense, backed by groups led by Johnny Otis, Illinois Jacquet, Jack McVea, and the influential modern-jazz bassist Oscar Pettiford; he scored hits with "Wynonie's Blues" and "Playful Baby." Moving to New York in late 1946, he continued to record with various groups for King. "Lollipop Mama," cut at the same session as "Good Rockin' Tonight," followed it onto the R&B charts (the song had been the flip side of Roy Brown's original "Good Rocking Tonight"). But due to the second recording ban imposed by the American Federation of Musicians, Harris did not reenter the studio until December 1948, when he cut the double-sided hit "Grandma Plays the Numbers"/"I Feel That Old Age Coming On."

His next session, recorded in April 1949 with the trumpeter Joe Morris's band (including the jazz legends Johnny Griffin and Elmo Hope on tenor saxophone and piano), yielded the hit "Drinkin' Wine Spo-Dee-O-Dee" and the No. 1 R&B smash "All She Wants To Do Is Rock," Harris's all-time best seller. With Harris singing to a backbeat as he had on "Good Rockin' Tonight," "All She Wants To Do Is Rock" can be regarded as the belated sequel to that song. Harris gives the word "rock" a more specifically sexual meaning, with a refrain that repeats the title line three times, followed by the hollered "rock and roll all night long."

But Harris did not consistently pursue the rocking sound that inspired other artists and brought him his greatest success. His next hit, recorded prior to "All She Wants To Do Is Rock," was "I Want My Fanny Brown," a cover of Roy Brown's "Miss Fanny Brown"; his next two hits after that were the risqué "Sittin' on It All the Time" and "I Like My Baby's Pudding," both written by Henry Glover. Harris was being only partly facetious when he sang, "Gonna stop this rockin'," on his May 1950 recording of "Rock Mr.

Blues." Among the few other rockers he cut during this period were "Bad News Baby (There'll Be No Rockin' Tonight)," a takeoff on "Good Rockin' Tonight," and "Lovin' Machine," his last national hit.

On the strength of his fifteen charted R&B hits (sixteen if one counts "Who Threw the Whiskey in the Well"), Harris toured widely, playing nightclub and theater dates on his own and in package shows, occasionally vying with Roy Brown in blues battles. His lyrical focus drifted from sex to alcohol, but as blues shouters gave way to vocal-harmony groups, his popularity diminished, and in 1954—shortly after he tried to jump onto a new bandwagon with the songs "All She Wants To Do Is Mambo" and "Good Mambo Tonight"—King dropped him. His abrasive personality and vulgar stage antics had alienated promoters, musicians, and audiences alike, and by 1955 he was nearly broke.[68]

Harris recorded a single on the Atco label in 1956, angling for the teenage market with an up-to-date arrangement of the Leiber-Stoller song "Destination Love." King brought him back for two more singles the following year, but Harris, now in his forties, could no longer attract young fans. His voice gradually darkening, he continued to perform, revamping several of his earlier hits for Roulette in 1960, but he worked mostly outside the music business. After moving back to Los Angeles, he recorded his final session, for Chess, in 1964, but it was not released until 1971. In 1967, he appeared at the Apollo Theatre in Harlem, along with Big Joe Turner, T-Bone Walker, Jimmy Witherspoon, and others; his last performance, in Santa Monica, came shortly afterward. He was diagnosed with esophageal cancer in 1968 and died in 1969 before revivalists could rediscover him.

Harris inspired a number of imitators, notably Robert "H-Bomb" Ferguson, who "worshipped Wynonie and did his best to copy everything about him," according to the record producer Bobby Robinson.[69] The son of a South Carolina minister, Ferguson learned to play gospel music on piano, turning to the blues against his father's wishes. Still in his teens, he joined Joe Liggins's Honeydrippers as they toured the South, then moved to New York, where, as Bob Ferguson, he made his first two singles for the Derby label in 1950. On "Wine Head" and its proto-rocking flip side, "Hard Lovin' Woman," he shouts the blues smoothly, suggesting Eddie Vinson as much as Wynonie Harris. By 1951, when he cut the blatantly rocking "Rock H-Bomb Rock" for Atlas, the rechristened H-Bomb Ferguson had perfected his gritty Harris impersonation.

After a one-off single for Prestige, Ferguson recorded four singles for Savoy in 1952, each pairing an up-tempo rocker—complete with backbeat and boogie bass line—with a slower jump blues. None made the national charts, but Harris was able to tour the South on package shows. He recorded one single each for Specialty and Sunset in 1953 and one side of a single for Decca with Andy Kirk's big band in 1954. He moved to Cincinnati and between 1957 and 1961 cut a handful of singles for Finch, A.R.C., Big Bang, and Federal, among them such novelties as "No-Sackie-Sack," from 1958, lamenting the vogue for loose-fitting sack dresses. He retired from music in the early 1970s but returned in the mid-1980s, wearing an assortment of outrageous wigs. He recorded several singles and albums, including *Wiggin' Out* for the Chicago-based Earwig label in 1993. The last surviving blues shouter, he performed at music festivals in the United States and Europe nearly up to his death in 2006, the year that also saw the release of the documentary film *The Life and Times of H-Bomb Ferguson*.

As the careers of other shouters—Wynonie Harris, Jimmy Rushing, Eddie Vinson, Jimmy Witherspoon, Roy Brown—wound down, Big Joe Turner's took off. Rushing briefly retired when Count Basie broke up his big band in 1950; when Basie re-formed the band for a show at the Apollo Theatre, Turner took Rushing's place. The performance was not a success, and Basie cut back to a smaller combo, but Ahmet Ertegun of Atlantic Records had been in the Apollo audience and signed Turner to a contract. Turner's first Atlantic single, recorded with a band led by Vann "Piano Man" Walls, was "Chains of Love," a slow blues composed by Ertegun. It was an R&B smash in 1951 that crossed over to the pop charts (and would be a Top 10 pop hit for Pat Boone in 1956), initiating a series of Turner hits on the label.

Although he recorded the hard-rocking "Bump Miss Suzie" at the same session as "Chains of Love," Turner's first four Atlantic hits were slow or mid-tempo blues (including "Sweet Sixteen," later revived by B. B. King). Not until May 1953 did he cut the up-tempo "Honey Hush," a No. 1 R&B hit that crossed over to the pop charts and became a rock 'n' roll classic, covered by Johnny Burnette, Jerry Lee Lewis, Fleetwood Mac, Elvis Costello, and others. Written by Turner himself and recorded in New Orleans with Pluma Davis's band, "Honey Hush" rocks from start to finish, propelled by a thumping backbeat, a boogie-ish bass line, and a rollicking piano. Davis's trombone broadly counterpoints Turner as he sings, "Come in this house, stop all that yakety yak / Come fix my supper, don't want no talkin' back." The melody and misogynistic attitude are similar to those of "Adam Bit the Apple," a Turner original recorded in December 1949 with a Houston band including Goree Carter. The repeating chant of "hi-yo Silver" with which Turner closes "Honey Hush" is taken not from the 1938 number by that title sung by Roy Rogers and others but from a different "Hi-Yo Silver" that was cut by the Chicago R&B singer Harold Burrage in 1950 and covered by the Treniers in 1952.

Recorded in October 1953, Turner's next hit, the mid-tempo blues "TV Mama," features Elmore James on slide guitar; directly connecting the jazzy southwestern shouting tradition to the blues of the Mississippi Delta, it prefigures modern electric blues rather than rock 'n' roll. Four months later came "Shake, Rattle and Roll," an offshoot of "Honey Hush" that became one of the defining rock 'n' roll songs. The personnel—Jesse Stone on piano, Wilbur DeParis on trombone, Sam "the Man" Taylor on tenor sax, Haywood Henry on baritone sax, Mickey Baker on guitar, Lloyd Trotman on bass, and Connie Kay on drums—were all steeped in jazz; but except for DeParis, who led a traditional band called the New New Orleans Jazz, and Kay, the long-time drummer for the Modern Jazz Quartet, all became better known for their work on rhythm-and-blues and rock 'n' roll sessions.

Turner's next four R&B hits, "Well All Right," "Flip Flop & Fly," "Hide and Seek," and "The Chicken and the Hawk"—the first three recorded with Jesse Stone—followed the formula of "Shake, Rattle and Roll." But at a time when rock 'n' roll was conquering the pop charts, none of Turner's records crossed over until he recorded a pop-style rock 'n' roll arrangement of "Corrine Corrina" in 1956. Similar pop-rock arrangements were used on his last three R&B hits, "Lipstick, Powder and Paint," "Love Roller Coaster," and "Jump for Joy"—the last an update of "Roll 'Em Pete"—but none of them made the pop charts.

Having plied the R&B circuit in the early 1950s, Turner made the rock 'n' roll scene with mid-1950s performances in Alan Freed's "Moondog Birthday Ball," "Rock 'n' Roll Jubilee Ball," and "Rock N Roll Second Anniversary" shows. He also appeared, along with Fats Domino, in the 1956 movie *Shake, Rattle and Rock!* singing "Feeling Happy," which interpolates the chorus from Erskine Hawkins's "Do You Wanna Jump, Children?" Hedging its bets, Atlantic also recorded Turner performing some of his older material with a band including his former partner Pete Johnson for the 1956 album *The Boss of the Blues*. In 1958, Turner and Johnson toured Europe and played the Newport Jazz Festival. In September 1959, Turner cut his last album for Atlantic, *Big Joe Rides Again,* a collection of standards featuring such mainstream jazz musicians as tenor saxophonist Coleman Hawkins and guitarist Jim Hall. Later the same month, Turner, with an ensemble including King Curtis plus a string section, rerecorded "Chains of Love" and "Honey Hush," the latter reaching the lower echelons of the pop but not the R&B charts. It would be Turner's final hit, and Atlantic dropped him in 1961, the year he turned fifty.

By the 1960s, Turner's rootsy, rough-and-tumble rock 'n' roll was passé; while striving for a contemporary sound on singles for the Coral, Ronn, and Kent labels, he mostly reverted to old-school jazz and blues, appearing at the Monterey Jazz Festival, performing in England with the trumpeter Humphrey Lyttelton's band, and touring Europe with the American Folk Blues Festival. Toward the end of the decade, he made albums for producer Bob Thiele on the BluesWay and BluesTime labels; in 1970, he recorded with Johnny Otis's revue at the Monterey Jazz Festival. He cut a series of albums on Norman Granz's Pablo label through the 1970s, some featuring jazz and blues stars such as Count Basie, Dizzy Gillespie, Milt Jackson, Jimmy Witherspoon, Eddie "Cleanhead" Vinson, and Pee Wee Crayton. In 1983, Turner recorded *Blues Train* for Muse, backed by the jump-revivalist band Roomful of Blues. Despite failing health, he kept performing almost until his death in 1985.

RHYTHM-AND-BLUES WOMEN

Although some female rhythm-and-blues singers bellowed, squealed, or growled, blues shouting had no real parallel among women. Jazzy vocalists such as Dinah Washington and Etta James extended their careers into the rock era by embracing pop and even country material, while bluesier singers such as Big Mama Thornton and Big Maybelle faded. Ruth Brown, the most successful postwar female R&B singer except for Washington, started her career as a romantic balladeer and had to be coaxed into recording the up-tempo songs that made her a star.[70]

Hadda Brooks, a Los Angeles native, was the first artist to record for the Modern label, scoring a regional hit in 1945 with her piano instrumental "Swingin' the Boogie." She recorded a string of blues and boogie instrumentals, including such classical adaptations as "Polonaise Boogie" and "Minuet in G Boogie." But after making her vocal debut on the bluesy "You Won't Let Me Go," she scored her first national hit in 1947 singing "That's My Desire," which had been Frankie Laine's first hit earlier that year.

In the 1947 movie comedy *Out of the Blue,* Brooks sang the torchy title song, which made the R&B charts the following year, followed shortly by another ballad, "What Have I Done?" She sang the standards "I Hadn't Anyone Till You" and "Temptation" respectively in the Nicholas Ray–directed 1950 film noir *In a Lonely Place* (starring Humphrey Bogart) and the Vincente Minnelli–directed 1952 melodrama *The Bad and the Beautiful* (starring Lana Turner and Kirk Douglas). She also filmed several Soundies, including "Queen of the Boogie," and briefly hosted her own West Coast television show.

Brooks left Modern in 1950, recording for London in 1950 and OKeh in 1952 and 1954 before returning to Modern in 1956, but had no other national hits. She toured Europe, sojourned in Hawaii, and spent the 1960s in Australia, retiring in Los Angeles in 1971. She began her comeback in 1987; her nightclub performances won her new fans in Hollywood, and she appeared in the Sean Penn–directed 1995 thriller *The Crossing Guard* (starring Jack Nicholson), as well as the 1999 science-fiction mystery *The Thirteenth Floor* and the 2001 family drama *John John in the Sky*. She released a new album on DRG Records in 1994 and another on Virgin in 1996, followed by a 1999 double album on Virgin that combined old and new recordings. She remained active as a performer until her death in 2002.

Born Ruth Jones in Tuscaloosa, Alabama, Dinah Washington was raised in Chicago, where she sang and played piano in local churches, meanwhile idolizing Billie Holiday. Hired at age sixteen by the pioneering gospel singer Sallie Martin, she accompanied Martin on piano and sang with her group. After a couple of years, she quit to sing jazz in nightclubs and was discovered by Lionel Hampton when his band performed in Chicago in late 1942. Taking the name Dinah Washington, she toured with Hampton and, in December 1943, recorded four Leonard Feather compositions for the independent Keynote label with a Hampton-led septet including pianist Milt Buckner and saxophonist Arnett Cobb. Even on this debut session, Washington's smoky voice is wholly distinctive; though not previously known as a blues singer, she shows an effortless feel for the idiom on "Salty Papa Blues" and "Evil Gal Blues," her first hits.

Although she stayed with Hampton's band until 1945, she sang on only one hit recorded under his name—"Blow-Top Blues," where she invests Feather's outré lyrics with more dignity than they deserve. In December 1945, after leaving Hampton, she recorded three sessions with Lucky Thompson's All Stars for the Apollo label; the material, all blues, includes a pair of Slim Gaillard–inspired novelty songs, "My Voot Is Really Vout" and "No Voot, No Boot." But despite Washington's brilliant singing and the band's sumptuously jazzy arrangements, the sessions produced no national hits. She began recording for Mercury in January 1946, mixing twelve-bar numbers such as "Postman Blues" with balladic standards such as "Embraceable You" and jiving novelty songs such as "A Slick Chick (on the Mellow Side)."

Her first Mercury hit, cut in November 1947, was "Ain't Misbehavin'," the Fats Waller classic. Around the same time, she recorded her first R&B chart-topper, "Am I Asking Too Much," a ballad written by R. Dean Taylor and Deke Richards, two white men who would later affiliate with Motown Records. The flip side was "I Sold My Heart to the Junkman"; written by Leon and Otis René and first recorded in 1946 by the Basin Street Boys, that song would in 1962 become the first hit credited to the Blue-Belles (afterward known as Patti LaBelle and the Bluebelles), although a different group, the Starlets, is actually heard on the record. Washington cut her second No. 1 hit, the bluesy "Baby Get Lost," in March 1949; the flip side, a hit in its own right, was the raunchy "Long John Blues" ("You thrill me when you drill me," she tells her dentist), recorded a year or two earlier.

Although she was called the Queen of the Blues, Mercury used Washington through most of the 1950s mainly—and quite successfully—to cover pop and country hits for the rhythm-and-blues market. From 1950 to 1955, her versions of recent hits by Sammy Kaye ("It Isn't Fair," "Harbor Lights"), the Andrews Sisters ("I Wanna Be Loved"), Kay Starr and Tennessee Ernie Ford ("I'll Never Be Free"), Guy Mitchell ("My Heart Cries for You"), Tony

Bennett ("I Won't Cry Anymore"), Hank Williams ("Cold, Cold Heart"), Hank Snow ("I Don't Hurt Anymore"), the Four Aces ("Tell Me Why"), the DeCastro Sisters ("Teach Me Tonight"), and Jaye P. Morgan ("That's All I Want from You") all made the R&B charts; of these, only "I Wanna Be Loved" and "Teach Me Tonight" charted pop. In early 1959, Arnold Shaw, then creative director of the Edward B. Marks Music Company, brought the ballad "What a Diff'rence a Day Makes" (written in 1934 by the Mexican-born composer María Grever as "Cuando Vuelva a Tu Lado") to Mercury's A&R director Clyde Otis as a possible crossover vehicle for Washington. Backed by a string orchestra, her rendition became a Top 10 pop hit, even though Mercury did not promote it to white audiences.[71]

From then until her death from an overdose of sleeping pills in 1963, Washington had more pop than R&B hits. Like "What a Diff'rence a Day Makes," her versions of Nat "King" Cole's 1951 hit "Unforgettable," Clyde Otis's composition "This Bitter Earth," and the standards "Love Walked In" and "September in the Rain" made both charts, as did her rocking duets with Brook Benton, "Baby (You've Got What It Takes)" and "A Rockin' Good Way (to Mess Around and Fall in Love)." Switching from Mercury to Roulette in 1961, Washington continued to record with orchestral accompaniments. Although she excelled in a number of styles, including rock 'n' roll, she is remembered almost exclusively for her ballads and blues.

The singer and pianist Julia Lee made a successful transition from jazz to rhythm-and-blues. Born in Boonville, Missouri, she grew up in Kansas City, where she joined her brother George E. Lee's band, a principal rival to Bennie Moten's group. In 1923, she sang on the first recordings of Kansas City jazz, but the two sides were never issued. In 1927, she recorded two more sides with her brother for the short-lived Meritt label, singing a duet with him on one and playing a piano solo on the other. In 1929, she sang on another two sides with George's group for Brunswick, "He's Tall, Dark and Handsome" and the mildly risqué "Won't You Come Over to My House." She stayed with her brother's band after it merged with Moten's in 1933, going solo when the partnership dissolved at the end of 1934. She played a long engagement at Milton's, a popular Kansas City nightclub, singing racy songs such as "Two Old Maids in a Folding Bed." But she did not record again until 1944, when she redid "Won't You Come Over to My House" with an all-star band assembled by the Capitol Records producer Dave Dexter; transforming the song from traditional jazz into streamlined swing, "Come On Over to My House," credited to Jay McShann's Kansas City Stompers featuring Julia Lee, did not make the *Billboard* charts but sold well enough to secure Lee a Capitol contract.[72]

After a 1945 session for the St. Louis–based Premier label (not the same Premier that changed its name to Atlas), Lee cut her first two charted hits for Capitol in August 1946. The second one, "I'll Get Along Somehow," is a ballad, but the proto-rocking "Gotta Gimme Whatcha Got" is a twelve-bar verse-and-refrain hokum song done in jazzy style, with stop-time verses, a boogie piano bass, and a light backbeat. In June 1947, Lee recorded the No. 1 R&B smash "(Opportunity Knocks but Once) Snatch and Grab It," structured like "Gotta Gimme Whatcha Got" but even jazzier, with smooth trumpet, saxophone, piano, and guitar solos. In November 1947, she cut another No. 1 hit, "King Size Papa," again in twelve-bar verse-and-refrain form, but like "Gotta Gimme Whatcha Got" and "Snatch and Grab It," it's less suggestive than its title would indicate.

"That's What I Like," a lesser hit from the same session as "King Size Papa," follows a similar verse-and-refrain formula, with Lee playing a strong boogie-woogie piano solo. Recorded two days later, her next hit, "Tell Me, Daddy," while also suggestive, is a shuffling jump blues. Lee had a minor holiday hit in late 1948 with the mournful blues "Christmas Spirits" and a bigger hit in 1949 with "I Didn't Like It the First Time (the Spinach Song)," from the same November 1947 session; the latter song hints broadly at sex or—as Lee's two recordings of "Lotus Blossom," also known as "Sweet Marijuana," would imply—drugs. She returns to the verse-and-refrain format on her last two hits, "Tonight's the Night" and "You Ain't Got It No More," both recorded in April 1949. But Lee would not leave Kansas City to promote her hits, having survived a car crash while touring with her brother's band. On one of her few trips away from home, she entertained President Harry Truman in Washington, D.C. She continued to record, albeit at a reduced rate, for Capitol and a couple of independent labels nearly until her death in 1958. Two of her songs are featured on the soundtrack of the 1957 movie *The Delinquents*, Robert Altman's first feature film as director.[73]

Nellie Lutcher took Lee's jazzy style to a jivier, more modern level with expressive singing and scatting as well as swinging piano that stopped just short of bebop. The eldest daughter out of fifteen children, Lutcher played piano with the Imperial Jazz Band in her early teens; later she toured with another band, the Southern Rhythm Boys. In 1935, she moved from Louisiana to Los Angeles, where she performed at Central Avenue clubs and befriended Nat "King" Cole. But she was not signed to Capitol Records until 1947, when she recorded her first hit, "Hurry On Down," a jazzed-up adaptation of Julia Lee's "Come On Over to My House." Her next session, also in April 1947, yielded the still jazzier "He's a Real Gone Guy," her biggest hit. Her following, double-sided hit, "Do You or Don't You Love Me?" backed with Irving Berlin's "The Song Is Ended (but the Melody Lingers On)," is so jazzy, in terms both of Lutcher's vocal styling and her piano playing, that it hardly sounds like rhythm-and-blues at all. But her next hit after that, "Fine Brown Frame," while much jazzier than Buddy Johnson's 1944 original, fits neatly into the R&B mold.

"Come On and Get It, Honey," another 1948 Lutcher hit, follows the mildly risqué verse-and-refrain pattern of Julie Lee's songs. Lutcher's second double-sided hit that year coupled a jazzy interpretation of the Sons of the Pioneers' "Cool Water" with the sprightly keyboard showcase "Lake Charles Boogie." Her seventh and last song to make the R&B charts in 1948 was a cleverly humorous, semi-scatted update of "Alexander's Ragtime Band." Her popularity fell as quickly as it had risen, however, and her only hit in 1949 was "Wish I Was in Walla Walla," written by the *Down Beat* columnist Sharon Pease, who also wrote several songs for Julia Lee. Lutcher had her final hit in 1950, a duet with Nat "King" Cole on a cover of Larry Darnell's 1949 smash "For You My Love."

Lutcher remained in demand as a live performer, playing theaters and nightclubs across the United States and Canada. In 1950 and 1951, she toured England to great acclaim; in 1951 and 1952, she recorded singles with Billy May's and Harold Mooney's orchestras. But then Capitol dropped her and she signed with Columbia, cutting a single for the subsidiary OKeh label in 1952 and a ten-inch LP that was released on the Epic subsidiary in 1955. She also recorded for Decca, Liberty, and Imperial into 1957 and for the drummer Lee Young's Melic label in 1963. Cutting back her performance schedule, she served on the board of directors of the Los Angeles local of the musicians' union. She enjoyed a late-career comeback, playing engagements at the Cookery in New York in 1973 and 1980, but had retired by the 1990s and died in 2007.

Ruth Brown, born Ruth Weston in Portsmouth, Virginia, was exposed to white pop and country music before discovering such artists as Hadda Brooks and Una Mae Carlisle, a Fats Waller protégée who enjoyed her greatest popularity in the late 1930s and early 1940s.[74] Weston sang gospel music in church and jazz at local military bases; after winning an Amateur Night contest at Apollo Theatre in New York, she formed a duo with the singer-trumpeter Jimmy Earle Brown and took his surname. When they split up, she joined Lucky Millinder's band, but after just a month she was fired and left stranded in Washington, D.C., where Blanche Calloway, Cab Calloway's sister, hired her to sing at the nightclub she ran and became her personal manager. Ahmet Ertegun and his partner in the recently founded Atlantic label, Herb Abramson, saw her at Calloway's club and agreed to record her; but on her way to an engagement at the Apollo in late 1948, Brown was badly injured in a car crash and did not enter the studio until April 1949.

Her second session, recorded in May 1949—a month before *Billboard* substituted the term "rhythm & blues" for "race" on its black-music charts—yielded her first hit, "So Long," a 1940 ballad by the white bandleader, trombonist, and singer Russ Morgan that had been a pop hit that year for the Charioteers, a black vocal group. Brown's version, with a white band led by the guitarist Eddie Condon, was closely modeled after the one recorded in

1946 by Little Miss Cornshucks, a Chicago-based rhythm-and-blues singer whom Ahmet Ertegun greatly admired.[75] But none of Brown's next few releases charted. "The problem," she later admitted, "was my resistance to singing anything but my first love, ballads."[76]

To change her sound, Atlantic enlisted the tap dancer and actor turned songwriter Rudy Toombs, who composed the up-tempo torch song "Teardrops from My Eyes." Recorded by Brown in September 1950, it was a long-running R&B chart-topper, covered by Louis Jordan, Wynonie Harris, Louis Prima, the pop singers June Hutton and Helen O'Connell, the country singers Rex Allen, Hawkshaw Hawkins, and Billy Jack Wills, and the duo of June Stafford and Gene Autry, among others. The innovative arrangement of Brown's original version, with its honking saxophone solo, riffing horns, boogie-ish bass line, and heavy backbeat, resembles the rock 'n' roll of the later 1950s more than the usual rhythm-and-blues of its own day. The record not only jump-started the careers of Brown and Toombs but helped establish the Atlantic label, which, in a play on the nickname of Yankee Stadium, became known as "the house that Ruth built."

Brown followed with a succession of similar Toombs-composed R&B hits—"I'll Wait for You," "I Know," "Daddy Daddy," and the chart-topping "5-10-15 Hours," which had originally been titled "5-10-15 Minutes (Of Your Love)" after the Dominoes' "Sixty-Minute Man." In December 1952, she recorded her best-remembered song, "(Mama) He Treats Your Daughter Mean," a No. 1 R&B hit that crossed over to the pop charts. In April 1953, she cut the frantically rocking "Wild Wild Young Men." Other female rhythm-and-blues singers recorded in a rocking vein during this period; for example, Eunice Davis cut "Rock Little Daddy," based on Cecil Gant's "Rock Little Baby," with Freddy Mitchell's band in 1951. But Brown's rhythmic ballad style, spiced with a vocal squeal that Little Richard would later imitate, broke new ground, and she became the biggest-selling female R&B artist of the 1950s.[77]

Her next No. 1 hit, written by the R&B singer Chuck Willis and recorded in May 1954, was "Oh What a Dream," a slow ballad featuring a soulful tenor sax solo by Arnett Cobb and a "Yancey Special" bass line sung by a doo-wop group. She followed in August 1954 with the faux-Latin "Mambo Baby," another No. 1 hit. Although Brown would never top the charts again, she continued to score hits—six in 1955 alone, after which her records gradually lost popularity, although their arrangements reflect the commercial sounds of the late 1950s. The Leiber-Stoller composition "Lucky Lips," a hit for Brown in 1957, borrows its melody from Rosemary Clooney's No. 1 pop hit "This Ole House," itself a cover of Stuart Hamblen's country original, while Brown's up-tempo 1958 hit "This Little Girl's Gone Rockin'," co-written by Bobby Darin, sports a yakety-sax solo by King Curtis. Several of Brown's later hits crossed over to the pop charts, but she complained that white cover versions such as Patti Page's "What a Dream," Georgia Gibbs's "Mambo Baby," and Gale Storm's "Lucky Lips" hurt her sales.[78]

In the 1960s, after her string of R&B hits ended and her Atlantic contract expired, Brown recorded for Philips, Decca, Mainstream, and other labels, but by the middle of the decade she'd been reduced to working as a domestic. She cut occasional albums for various independent labels through the 1970s, including one with the Thad Jones–Mel Lewis Orchestra and another produced by the soul singer Swamp Dogg. Her comeback began in 1975, when the comedian Redd Foxx gave her cameo roles on his *Sanford and Son* television show and had her cast as Mahalia Jackson in *Selma,* a musical theater production about Martin Luther King. In 1980, after a label in Sweden reissued some of her early recordings, she performed and cut a new album there. During the following decade, she worked nightclubs in Los Angeles, Las Vegas, and New York and appeared on television programs such as *The Jeffersons,* in movies such as *Hairspray*, and in stage shows such as the Broadway revue *Black and Blue*, for which she won a Tony Award. She also took legal action against Atlantic for nonpayment of royalties, leading to a landmark settlement that helped compensate rhythm-and-blues veterans.

Brown kept recording through the 1990s. In 1993, she was inducted into the Rock and Roll Hall of Fame. She suffered a stroke in 2000 but continued to perform until another stroke ended her life in 2006.

LaVern Baker was the niece of Merline Johnson, a blues singer who specialized in drinking songs. Born in Chicago, Baker started singing at the prestigious Club DeLisa as a teenager, then moved with her family to Detroit. There she performed under the name Little Miss Sharecropper (a rival to Little Miss Cornshucks, whose career had taken off in Chicago slightly earlier) at the Flame Show Bar, whose manager, Al Green, also managed her career. She began recording as Little Miss Sharecropper around 1948, releasing a pair of jump-style blues on RCA Victor in 1949. In 1950 or 1951, she cut four sides for the National label—three blues and the steamy twelve-bar verse-and-refrain song "I Want to Rock." Under the name Bea Baker, she cut three more sides with Maurice King and the Wolverines, the house band at the Flame Show Bar, for Columbia and OKeh—two shouted blues and the mercenary "I Want a Lavender Cadillac." As Lavern Baker, she cut four sides for King in 1952 with the Detroit-based pianist Todd Rhodes's band—three ballads and the up-tempo novelty "Pig Latin Blues."

In 1953, she signed with Atlantic and, as LaVerne Baker, recorded the gospel-flavored "Soul on Fire," where her rough-edged voice, at once earthy and refined, presages the soul singing of the following decade. Her second, similarly soulful Atlantic single, "I Can't Hold Out Any Longer," from 1954 (where her name is finally spelled LaVern Baker), likewise failed to chart, but her third single for the label, the pop-oriented, Latin-tinged "Tweedlee

Dee," was a Top 20 pop and Top 5 rhythm-and-blues hit in early 1955. It might have been a bigger hit had Georgia Gibbs not covered it for a No. 2 pop hit, sounding whiter than Baker but otherwise imitating her version closely. Baker was so incensed that she tried unsuccessfully to have Congress ban the unauthorized copying of arrangements.[79] Winfield Scott, who wrote "Tweedlee Dee," was a member of Atlantic's in-house vocal backing group, the Cues (called the Gliders on Baker's records); later he would write or cowrite songs for Elvis Presley, who recorded "Tweedlee Dee" live in 1955.

Baker followed "Tweedlee Dee" with the double-sided R&B hit "Bop-Ting-A-Ling"/"That's All I Need"; another Scott composition, "Bop-Ting-A-Ling" anticipates later rock songs with lines such as "Great day in the mornin', I'm givin' you warnin'" and "Doo wah diddy, you walk so pretty." But none of her next few R&B hits—not the soulful "Play It Fair" or the "Tweedlee"-like "Get Up, Get Up (You Sleepy Head)"—crossed over until "Jim Dandy," an R&B chart-topper, made the pop Top 20 in early 1957. With its strong rhythm-and-blues feel and inane lyrics centering around the line "Jim Dandy to the rescue," the song is a rock 'n' roll landmark but attracted few covers (among those few was Black Oak Arkansas's minor hit version in 1974). However, the flip side, "Tra La La," another "Tweedlee Dee" knockoff, was quickly covered for a pop hit by Georgia Gibbs. Baker's next single, "Jim Dandy Got Married," milked the same "Jim Dandy" formula but with much less success.

Baker performed in Alan Freed's concerts and appeared with Freed in the movies *Rock, Rock, Rock!* (1956) and *Mister Rock and Roll* (1957). "Humpty Dumpty Heart," from *Mister Rock and Roll,* its melody drawn from the English folk song "Frog Went A-Courtin'," made *Billboard*'s pop but not its R&B chart in 1957, while the scatted "It's So Fine" charted R&B but not pop in 1958. At the end of 1958, Baker entered both charts with the country-tinged "I Cried a Tear," perhaps her all-time best seller. The same year, she released the album *Lavern Baker Sings Bessie Smith,* pointing up her resemblances to as well as her differences from the classic blues singer. She also recorded the hard-rocking, Phil Spector–produced "Voodoo Voodoo" in 1958, but it was not released until 1961, as the B-side of "Hey Memphis," Baker's answer to Elvis Presley's "Little Sister."

A string of minor hits followed, extending into the early 1960s. One was the Jesse Stone–arranged "Bumble Bee" (1960), which the English pop idol Billy Fury covered in 1963 and the English rock band the Searchers covered in 1965. Another was the duet "You're the Boss" (1961), a Leiber-Stoller composition that Baker performed with Jimmy Ricks and that was recorded by Elvis Presley and Ann-Margaret for (but not included in) the 1964 movie *Viva Las Vegas*. There was also the gospel-rocker "Saved" in 1961 and an update of "See See Rider" in late 1962. But though she'd paved the way for the soul music of the 1960s, Baker could not capitalize on the soul phenomenon. Her last Atlantic hit was the standard "Fly Me to the Moon" in 1965; the following year, she had her last national hit with "Think Twice," a duet with Jackie Wilson on Brunswick.

On a trip to Vietnam to entertain American troops, she fell ill; remaining in Asia after her recovery, she operated a nightclub near the American naval base at Subic Bay in the Philippines for some twenty years. On her return in 1988, she performed in the gala concert at Madison Square Garden to commemorate the fortieth anniversary of Atlantic Records. In 1990, she replaced Ruth Brown in the musical *Black and Blue* and recorded "Slow Rollin' Mama" for the soundtrack of the movie *Dick Tracy*. Inducted into the Rock and Roll Hall of Fame in 1991, she kept performing even after suffering strokes and having her legs amputated due to diabetes. She died in 1997.

Varetta Dillard, a Harlem native, was singing on Amateur Night at the Apollo in 1951 when she was discovered by Lee Magid, then a producer for Savoy. Dillard's voice could suggest either Dinah Washington or Ruth Brown, and she scored her first R&B hit in a distinctly Brownian vein in 1952 with "Easy, Easy Baby," a mid-tempo Rudy Toombs composition set to a heavy backbeat. The song was covered the same year by Eileen Barton, a white pop singer best known for her 1950 smash "If I Knew You Were Comin' I'd've Baked a Cake." Dillard appropriated Brown's squeal as well as her beat on her next hit, "Mercy, Mr. Percy," in 1953. Her final hit came in 1955 with "Johnny Has Gone," a ballad mourning the rhythm-and-blues singer Johnny Ace, who accidentally shot himself to death at the age of twenty-five.

In 1956, Dillard switched from Savoy to Groove, for which she cut doo-wop-tinged rockers such as "Skinny Jimmy" as well as the James Dean tribute "I Miss You Jimmy." When RCA folded Groove, she was picked up by the parent label, briefly working with Jerry Leiber and Mike Stoller. But although Dillard, like Ruth Brown, embraced the pop-rock formulas of the day, she had no further national hits. She recorded for the Triumph and Cub labels into 1961, then joined her husband's gospel group. In her heyday, she toured with the likes of Wynonie Harris and performed in such shows as Alan Freed's "Rock 'n' Roll Jubilee Ball," but by the time of her death in 1993, she was all but forgotten.

"Hound Dog" was Big Mama Thornton's only hit. Her first two sessions for Peacock in 1951 were in a more conventional jump-blues style, as were most of the other recordings she made at the 1952 session that produced "Hound Dog"—the sole track from that date to omit the horn section. "They Call Me Big Mama," from the same session, is a brassy jump blues, more jazz than rock, but Thornton wails, "I can rock, baby, I can roll / I can rock and I can roll and I can really go to town." After "Hound Dog," however, her Peacock sides often featured bluesy guitar and guttural vocais. In the early

1960s, she moved to the San Francisco Bay Area and recorded for several independent labels; in 1965, she toured Europe with the American Folk Blues Festival and cut an album in England for Arhoolie Records. The following year she recorded another Arhoolie album with Muddy Waters's band.

In 1967, Janis Joplin burst upon the national rock scene with a performance of Thornton's composition "Ball and Chain" at the Monterey Pop Festival; Thornton did not record the song until 1968. Thornton cut a pair of albums for Mercury in 1969 and 1970, an album each for Backbeat and Pentagram in 1970 and 1971, and another pair for Vanguard in 1975. She toured Europe and North America, playing festivals and nightclubs, often dressed in men's clothing. Heavy drinking caused her health to decline in the 1980s, and she died in 1984; her final album, *Quit Snoopin' Round My Door* (on Ace), was released posthumously.

Like Thornton, Big Maybelle began recording in a jazzy jump-blues vein before adopting a grittier style. Born Mabel Smith in Jackson, Tennessee, she sang in church as a child. Discovered by the promoter Dave Clark, she toured with the all-female International Sweethearts of Rhythm. In 1944, with Christine Chatman's band, she cut "Hurry, Hurry!" a cover of singer Savannah Churchill's swinging blues hit with Benny Carter's band. Afterward, she toured with Tiny Bradshaw's band, which accompanied her on her first recordings for King (as Mabel Smith) in November 1947; she was backed by Hot Lips Page's band on her next session the following month. But the records did not do well, and her career languished until Fred Mendelsohn saw her perform in Cincinnati and signed her to OKeh, dubbing her Big Maybelle.

Maybelle's material was bluesier and her voice raspier on OKeh than on King. Her first two OKeh sessions, both of them in October 1952 with a band led by guitarist Leroy Kirkland, produced her first three hits. On the grinding "Gabbin' Blues," Rose Marie McCoy, who cowrote the song with Kirkland, supplies sarcastic spoken commentary. "My Country Man" rocks to a shuffling backbeat and boogie bass, while "Way Back Home" sways slowly to the same bass line that Huey "Piano" Smith sped to mid-tempo on his 1958 New Orleans rocker "Don't You Just Know It."

Although she toured widely and appeared on R&B package shows, Big Maybelle had no other hits on OKeh, but a couple of her records for the label had an indirect impact. Her "One Monkey Don't Stop No Show," cowritten by Rose Marie McCoy and recorded in September 1954, was among the first of several songs by that title (preceded in 1950 by Stick McGhee's "One Monkey Don't Stop the Show"), including a 1965 hit by Joe Tex that was covered by the Animals and Bette Midler. Her "Whole Lotta Shakin' Goin' On," from March 1955, formed the basis for Jerry Lee Lewis's 1957 smash, though Lewis may not have heard Maybelle's original.

On Big Maybelle's recording of "Whole Lotta Shakin' Goin' On," the composer's credit is given solely to Dave Williams, also known as Curly or Curlee Williams, an African American songwriter from Kentucky. But the white hillbilly-boogie pianist Roy Hall claimed to have cowritten the song, although only Williams is credited on the label of Hall's own September 1955 Decca recording. While substituting guitar for horns and dispensing with the heavy backbeat of Maybelle's version, Hall repeats all but her most incomprehensible lyrics, including the introductory line "Twenty-one drums and an old bass horn / Somebody beatin' on a ding dong," but his melody sounds more like Lewis's. ("Beatin' on the Ding Dong" is the title of a 1954 country record by Jim Reeves.) "Whole Lotta Shakin' Goin' On" was recorded soon afterward by the white singer Doris Fredericks, who gives it a mainstream pop treatment, and by the Commodores, a white vocal group whose style might be described as rockabilly doo-wop (Darrell Glenn, their lead singer, had recorded the original "Crying in the Chapel").

Jerry Lee Lewis briefly played piano at a Nashville club owned by Roy Hall, but by the time he heard Hall's "Whole Lotta Shakin' Goin' On," he was working in a band led by the disc jockey Johnny Littlejohn at a club outside Natchez, Mississippi, across the Mississippi River from Lewis's home town of Ferriday, Louisiana.[80] In late 1956, he left Littlejohn's band and traveled to Memphis to audition for Sun Records. The audition resulted in Lewis's first record, a rocking adaptation of Ray Price's country smash "Crazy Arms." Afterward, he worked as a sideman on a number of Sun recordings, among them Billy Lee Riley's rockabilly classics "Flyin' Saucers Rock & Roll" and "Red Hot." In February or March 1957, Lewis cut his second Sun single, "Whole Lot of Shakin' Going On," with guitarist Roland Janes and drummer Jimmy Van Eaton from Riley's band, crediting Hall, under the pseudonym Sunny David, along with Williams as composers.

Lewis's rendition, propelled by his driving boogie piano and Van Eaton's pounding backbeat, brings the song fully into the rock 'n' roll idiom, eliminating the corny introduction, streamlining the lyrics, and adding a lasciviously spoken interlude near the end. Some radio stations banned the record because of its supposed salaciousness, although there is nothing explicitly lewd about it; other stations refused to play it because they thought Lewis was black.[81] Nonetheless, Lewis's "Whole Lot of Shakin'" became a No. 1 hit on both *Billboard*'s country and R&B charts, rising to No. 3 on the magazine's pop chart.

Big Maybelle's "Whole Lotta Shakin'" session was her last for OKeh. When the label failed to renew her contract, Fred Mendelsohn took her to Savoy and in 1956 produced her version of "Candy," which had been a No. 1 pop hit in 1945 for Johnny Mercer (who did not write it) with Jo Stafford and the Pied Pipers. Backed by a lushly arranged big band, Maybelle sang the ballad like a growling Dinah Washington, scoring a substantial R&B hit that reinvigorated her career. She kept recording for Savoy until 1959, cutting rock songs, blues, and ballads, but had no other hits on the label. Her boisterous performance of "I Ain't Mad at You" at the 1958 Newport Jazz Festival was captured in the documentary film *Jazz on a Summer's Day*.

Big Maybelle cut albums and singles for such labels as Brunswick, Scepter, Chess, and Rojac through the 1960s, scoring minor hits with her 1966 recordings of "Don't Pass Me By" and "96 Tears." But her performances became infrequent as her health deteriorated due to heroin addiction, and she died in 1972 after falling into a diabetic coma.

DOO-WOP

The decline of the blues shouters coincided with the rise of male harmony groups. The Mills Brothers and Ink Spots enjoyed their greatest success around time of World War II, as did lesser-known groups such as the 5 Red Caps, the Delta Rhythm Boys, and the Charioteers.

Founded in 1930 as the Harmony Four by a professor at Wilberforce University in Ohio, the Charioteers renamed themselves after the spiritual "Swing Low, Sweet Chariot." Adding secular songs to their sacred repertoire, the group performed on the same Cincinnati radio station that gave the Mills Brothers their start, then began broadcasting in New York. Between 1935 and 1939, they recorded for Decca, Brunswick, Vocalion, and Columbia, on their own and in accompaniment to such artists as pianist Eddie Duchin and singer Mildred Bailey. The Charioteers had their first hit with "So Long" in 1940; they would not have another hit until after the war, but in the meantime they appeared in the Broadway revue *Hellzapoppin* and the Hollywood comedy *Road Show*, backed Bing Crosby on his *Kraft Music Hall* radio show, recorded V-Discs for the armed forces, and cut four sides with Frank Sinatra, including the 1945 hit "Don't Forget Tonight Tomorrow."

In late 1947, the Charioteers recorded with Pearl Bailey on the rhythmic ballad "Don't Ever Leave Me" and with the white pop singer Buddy Clark on the pseudo-world-music hit "Now Is the Hour (Maori Farewell Song)."[82] From 1946 to 1949, they had half a dozen pop hits of their own, among them "Open the Door, Richard" and a cover of Perry Como's Italian novelty smash "Chi-Baba, Chi-Baba (My Bambina Go to Sleep)." In a reversal of the usual situation, only one of their hits, the ballad "A Kiss and a Rose," made the R&B charts. But while the group appealed to white pop fans, their smooth harmonies also anticipated the mellower sounds of the doo-wop era.

By 1950, the Charioteers' lead tenor, Billy Williams, had left to form his own quartet, which appeared on Sid Caesar and Imogene Coca's television program *Your Show of Shows*. Ending their dozen-year association with Columbia and acquiring a new lead singer, the Charioteers recorded for several labels through 1957 but had no further hits. Williams, recording for MGM, Mercury, and Coral, covered everything from Doris Day's pop hit "(Why Did I Tell You I Was Going To) Shanghai" to Eddie Arnold's country smash "Cattle Call" to the Chords' "Sh-Boom" but had only minor success until 1957, when he made both the pop and R&B Top 10 covering Fats Waller's 1935 hit "I'm Gonna Sit Right Down and Write Myself a Letter." In August 1957, he appeared on the first national broadcast of Dick Clark's *American Bandstand* show. Williams had a few more minor pop hits but stopped performing in the 1960s and died alone and penniless in 1972.[83]

Like the Charioteers, the Delta Rhythm Boys started off as a student quartet at a historically black college, in this case Langston University in Oklahoma. In 1936, two years after forming, the group transferred to Dillard University in New Orleans, but after a successful South American tour, they dropped out of school and moved to New York, performing in Broadway shows and on radio before signing with Decca in 1940. Jazzier than the Charioteers, the Delta Rhythm Boys recorded jive songs such as "Gimme Some Skin" as well as standards such as "Stardust" and spirituals such as "Dry Bones," which became their signature song. In 1945, they recorded their only hit, "Just A-Sittin' and A-Rockin'," for which the group's bass singer, Lee Gaines, had set his own lyrics to Duke Ellington and Billy Strayhorn's subtly swinging (but not rocking) 1941 tune. Gaines sang the lead on "Just A-Sittin' and A-Rockin'," setting a precedent for other vocal-group basses, notably Jimmy Ricks of the Ravens.

Despite their paucity of hits, the Delta Rhythm Boys maintained a relatively high profile. They recorded with such jazz musicians as Jimmie Lunceford, Charlie Barnet, and Les Paul and as accompanists to such singers as Mildred Bailey, Fred Astaire, Ella Fitzgerald, and Ruth Brown. They gave radio performances on *Amos 'n' Andy* and *The Abbott and Costello Show* and appeared in some dozen movies and as many Soundies. They first toured Europe in 1949, proving so popular in Sweden that they later cut an album's worth of material in Swedish. They recorded for Decca, RCA Victor, Atlantic, and Mercury through the mid-1950s, then moved to France and recorded for Barclay and Vega. The group remained in Europe for the next three decades, finally dissolving after the death of Lee Gaines in 1987.

Unlike most other vocal-harmony groups, the 5 Red Caps supplied their own instrumental accompaniment. They formed around 1940 as the Four Toppers, comprising the "top" members of three other Los Angeles–based groups, all of which made movie appearances. From the Basin Street Boys (not the same Basin Street Boys who recorded "I Sold My Heart to the Junkman") came the bass singer and guitarist Steve Gibson; from the Five Jones Boys, the lead tenor and drummer Jimmy Springs; from the Four Blackbirds, the baritone and bassist Richard Davis and the second tenor and bassist-guitarist David Patillo. The Four Toppers appeared in a few movies and recorded with the bandleader Larry Breese for the Ammor label. In 1942, they moved to New York, replacing Richard Davis with the bassist Doles Dickens and adding the baritone and pianist Romaine Brown. In 1943, they changed their name to the 5 Red Caps, referring to the headgear worn by railroad porters, virtually all of whom were African American.

The name change may have been an attempt to get around the musicians' union recording ban; in any case, the 5 Red Caps, all instrumentalists and thus union members, began recording for Beacon and other labels run by the independent record producer Joe Davis in 1943, during the ban.[84] Taking an almost entirely secular approach and dividing the vocal leads among the different singers, they sounded more like a 1950s doo-wop group than the Charioteers or Delta Rhythm Boys did. Although they recorded jive songs such as "Boogie Woogie on a Saturday Night" and "Mary Had a Little Jam," they had greater success with ballads such as the Joe Davis composition "I Learned a Lesson, I'll Never Forget," their first and biggest hit. Favorably reviewing that record in the January 22, 1944, issue of *Billboard,* Maurie Orodenker describes the Red Caps as a "carbon copy" of the Ink Spots, noting Jimmy Springs's high tenor lead and Steve Gibson's talking bass.[85]

Of the Red Caps' four R&B hits, all charting in 1944, three were sentimental ballads. Their only up-tempo hit was "Boogie Woogie Ball," which begins with a "Down the Road a Piece"–style dialogue over Romaine Brown's boogie piano, then continues in stride rhythm except during Brown's stomping boogie piano break. In October 1944, Romaine Brown, Steve Gibson, and Doles Dickens, inspired by the King Cole Trio, recorded such jive songs as "Get Off of That Kick" for the Joe Davis label as the Red Caps Trio. (The trio also backed George "Bon Bon" Tunnell on a number of recordings.) The full Red Caps group cut four sides for Savoy as the Toppers in December 1944 but returned to Davis's fold after he took legal action. They began recording for Mercury in 1946 as Steve Gibson and the Red Caps, scoring a pop (but not R&B) hit in 1948 with a hip version of "Wedding Bells Are Breaking Up (That Old Gang of Mine)." A Tin Pan Alley standard introduced in 1929 by Gene Austin, the song would be revived in 1954 by the white harmony quartet the Four Aces and again in 1956 by Gene Vincent and His Blue Caps. Gibson and the Red Caps also cut "Blueberry Hill" for Mercury in 1949, the same year Louis Armstrong recorded it.

In 1950, the Red Caps signed with RCA Victor; the following year, Damita Jo joined the group as featured singer. In 1952, she sang the lead on the Red Caps' recording of Jessie Mae Robinson's waltz-time composition "I Went to Your Wedding," a pop hit that was eclipsed by Patti Page's chart-topping cover version (not to mention Hank Snow's country rendition). A verse from the song, "You came down the aisle, wearing a smile, a vision of loveliness / I uttered a sigh, then whispered goodbye, goodbye to my happiness," prefigures one from the Penguins' landmark 1954 doo-wop smash "Earth Angel"—"I fell for you and I knew the vision of your loveliness / I hope and pray that someday I'll be the vision of your happiness." In 1954, Gibson and Damita Jo were married.

The 5 Red Caps played theaters and nightclubs nationwide, performing for white as well as black audiences, and appeared in movies and on television. Although they had no more hits after 1952, the group recorded for RCA Victor through the mid-1950s, then switched to ABC-Paramount, for which they cut "Rock 'n' Roll Stomp" in 1956. Sounding almost like a parody of rock 'n' roll, the song shows how out of touch with the teenage market the Red Caps had become. Still, they remained a popular live act and continued to record through the end of the decade for independent labels run by Al Browne, who sold some of the group's recordings to ABC-Paramount.

In 1961, the Red Caps split into two groups: one, led by Steve Gibson, stopped recording in 1962 but kept performing until 1968; the other, called the Modern Red Caps, recorded until 1967 and then disbanded.

Although only one of their records made the *Billboard* charts, the Treniers, having participated in the transition from swing to rock 'n' roll, helped introduce rock to a wider public through nightclub, movie, and television appearances. The identical twins Claude and Cliff Trenier grew up in a musical family in Mobile, Alabama. Both enrolled at State Teachers College, the same school Erskine Hawkins and Sam "the Man" Taylor attended, but left to pursue musical careers. Claude joined Jimmie Lunceford's band as a singer, making his recorded debut in February 1944. Then Cliff joined the band, and the two sang together on Lunceford's February 1945 recording of "Buzz Buzz Buzz," featuring a bawling tenor saxophone solo by Joe Thomas, but the record was not issued until 1949. Later in 1945, Claude recorded "Buzz Buzz Buzz" with Big Jim Wynn's band for the 4 Star label; he also sang on Wynn's recording of "Ee-Bobaliba," by which time Helen Humes had already cut her hit adaptation, "Be-Baba-Leba." In December 1945, Claude recorded "Young Man's Blues" with the Lamplighter All Stars, including clarinetist Barney Bigard, bassist Red Callender, and drummer Zutty Singleton. In January 1946, he sang on three progressive-jazz sides with bassist Charles Mingus's band for the Exelsior label, among them the disquieting "Weird Nightmare"; in April, he sang on two more sides with Mingus for 4 Star.

With a band including two other State Teachers College alumni, pianist Gene Gilbeaux and alto saxophonist Don Hill, Claude and Cliff Trenier recorded "Buzz Buzz Buzz" for Mercury in February 1947, credited on the label as the Trenier Twins and Gene Gilbeaux's Orchestra. (The song would be adapted into a pop and R&B hit in 1957 by the Hollywood Flames, a rhythm-and-blues vocal group that included Bobby "Rock-in Robin" Day; the Flames' "Buzz Buzz Buzz" would in turn be covered by Frankie Lymon and the Teenagers, Rusty Draper, the Cadillacs, Shakin' Stevens and the Sunsets, Jonathan Richman and the Modern Lovers, the Blasters, Huey Lewis and the News, and Doug Sahm, as well as the early British rocker Vince Eager.) By the end of 1947, the Trenier Twins had cut five records for Mercury, in a jazzy vein often leavened with jiving humor.

But they did not record again until January 1950, when they cut "Everybody Get Together," backed with "Why Did You Get So High, Shorty?" for the London label. In the meantime, they had established a reputation for high-spirited live performances in Los Angeles clubs and theaters, as the *Billboard* review of their London single indicates. "On wax, their antics lose something," the reviewer comments, noting that the "lack of sight factor detracts."[86] On their first, May 1951 session for OKeh, the Treniers, as the label credits them, recorded their lone hit, the hard-rocking "Go! Go! Go!" featuring Don Hill's saxophone. They followed in August with the slower "It Rocks! It Rolls! It Swings!" where the twins chant "It rocks, it rolls, it swings, it jumps" while Hill wails on sax over a boogie-woogie bass line and a shuffling backbeat. In January 1952, they recorded the similar "Rockin' on Sunday Night," with a more emphatic backbeat; in October, they cut "Rockin' Is Our Bizness," a reworded take on Jimmie Lunceford's 1935 smash "Rhythm Is Our Business" fitted with a backbeat and boogie bass line, plus a squealing saxophone solo in the manner of Illinois Jacquet on "Blues, Pt. 2." Having crossed paths with Bill Haley while playing a gig in Wildwood, New Jersey, they cut his composition "Rock-a-Beatin' Boogie" in September 1953, two years before Haley recorded it.

During the same period, the Treniers recorded "Hadacole [sic] That's All" and "Poon-Tang!" skirting the censors with the sung explanation, "Poon is a hug, tang is a kiss." Ironically, it was the flip side of "Poon-Tang!" that had to be dropped when The Lone Ranger, Inc., claimed a copyright violation for the song "Hi-Yo Silver!" which was then replaced by "The Moondog," a tribute to Alan Freed.[87]

The twins' younger brother Milt, who'd already cut a few singles of his own as a singer, joined the group around 1954, just as the act made its television breakthrough. As early as 1949, the Trenier Twins had appeared on *Cavalcade of Stars,* the predecessor of *The Jackie Gleason Show*, but in 1954, the Treniers appeared on *The Jackie Gleason Show,* the *Colgate Comedy Hour* with Dean Martin and Jerry Lewis, and Ed Sullivan's *Toast of the Town*; they would subsequently perform on television shows hosted by Frankie Laine, Perry Como, Steve Allen, Patti Page, and Dean Martin, among others. The Treniers also appeared in four movies, *The Girl Can't Help It* (1956), *Don't Knock the Rock* (1956), *Calypso Heat Wave* (1957), and *Juke Box Rhythm* (1959). By the time they made *Calypso Heat Wave*, an older brother, Buddy Trenier, had joined the group as its fourth singer.

Movie and television clips display the Treniers doing choreographed routines involving all the band members (though the twins are most prominent), with rubber-legged dancing, comic voicings, and histrionic gestures. The dynamism of their live shows made them a fixture in Las Vegas, where they first performed in the late 1940s. Ultimately, they would play nearly all the lounges and showrooms on the city's legendary Strip, enduring segregation policies that weren't abandoned until 1960.

Despite the popularity of their stage act, the Treniers' records were not strong sellers, not even such seemingly sure things as "Say Hey (The Willie Mays Song)," recorded for Epic in July 1954 with a spoken part for the New York Giants' star center fielder and a band directed by Quincy Jones. A final Epic session in December 1955 yielded "Rock 'n' Roll Call"; written by Jack Hammer (who went on to cowrite "Great Balls of Fire" with Otis Blackwell for Jerry Lee Lewis) and Rudy Toombs in an apparent effort to capitalize on the rock 'n' roll craze, it does not sound much different from the Treniers' earlier proto-rock songs. The Treniers went on to record for Vik, Brunswick, Hermitage, Dot, Ronn, Dom, Steel City, Mobile, TT, and other labels into the 1970s. They toured worldwide and performed regularly in Las Vegas, Atlantic City, and other resort areas into the 2000s. After Cliff died in 1983, a nephew, Skip Trenier, took his place as Claude's stage partner until Claude's death in 2003. Milt Trenier left the group in the 1960s to pursue a solo career and later ran a Chicago nightclub, Milt Trenier's Lounge.

Although similar in style to the Delta Rhythm Boys, the Ravens are generally considered the first true R&B vocal group, if only because their rise coincided with the inauguration of *Billboard*'s "rhythm & blues" chart. More certainly, they started the fashion for avian group names (Cardinals, Falcons, Flamingos, Hawks, Larks, Penguins, Robins, Sparrows, Swallows, Wrens, et al.), their own name neatly making the transition from racially oriented designations. Blacker-sounding than most of the African American harmony groups that preceded them, they influenced many that followed, but their style remained unique, due mainly to the presence of Jimmy Ricks, whose extraordinarily deep, rich bass could not be duplicated.

The Georgia-born, Florida-bred Ricks formed the Ravens in New York in 1946 with the baritone Warren Suttles and the tenors Leonard Puzey and Ollie Jones. They recorded their first six sides in June 1946 for the Hub label (owned by their manager, Ben Bart), with Ricks singing the lead on two numbers (including "Bye Bye Baby Blues," the only song with more of an R&B than a pop feel) and sharing the lead on a third. The following year, the Ravens signed with National Records, whose A&R director was Herb Abramson; by that time, Ollie Jones had been replaced by Maithe Marshall, whose high tenor would be featured on many of the group's ballads. Their first release on National was "Mahzel (Means Good Luck)," a Yiddish-based novelty song that's since been recorded by everyone from Benny Goodman and Louis Prima to the avant-garde guitarist Gary Lucas and the *Late Night with Conan O'Brien* television puppet Triumph the Insult Comic Dog.

Recorded in September 1947 with Ricks singing the lead, "Write Me a Letter" was the Ravens' first nationally charted hit. The Ravens established their sound with their next hit, "Ol' Man River," which they had recorded and released before "Write Me a Letter." Written by Jerome Kern and Oscar Hammerstein II for the 1927 musical *Showboat*, "Ol' Man River" is best known from Paul Robeson's performance in the 1936 movie version. The Ravens jazzed the song up, with Ricks delivering a more sonorous bass than the renowned Robeson.

Although they recorded a number of other standard ballads during the same period—"Summertime," "Until the Real Thing Comes Along," "September Song," Irving Berlin's "Always"—the Ravens' next hit, "Send for Me If You Need Me," was, like "Write Me a Letter," an original jump blues. It was followed on *Billboard*'s R&B chart by the similar "Bye Bye Baby Blues," which King Records had purchased from Hub and reissued. Next to chart was the Ravens' cover of the Orioles' "It's Too Soon to Know"; the bluesy flip side, "Be on Your Merry Way," was also a hit. The holiday pairing of "Silent Night" and "White Christmas" completed the Ravens' octet of 1948 R&B hits.

In January 1949, the group appeared on Ed Sullivan's new *Toast of the Town* television show; that November, they were featured on the cover of *Billboard*. They continued to record such standards as "Deep Purple," "Tea for Two," "Without a Song," and "Moonglow," but the only hit they would have in 1949 was "Rickey's Blues," another original jump song. The following year saw their final hit on National, "I Don't Have to Ride No More," again in a jump-blues vein. In March 1950, they recorded the ballad "Count Every Star," a pop hit that year for the white middle-of-the-roaders Hugo Winterhalter, Ray Anthony, and Dick Haymes. Although it did not chart, the Ravens' version was highly influential. "It is no overstatement to say that 'Count Every Star' is the recording which set in stone the basic black vocal group style for the next forty years," writes the music historian Billy Vera.[88]

In September 1950, as their National contract neared expiration, the Ravens signed with Columbia.[89] The next month, Jimmy Ricks sang the first half of the Benny Goodman Sextet's bebop-tinged version of "Oh, Babe!"; the white singer Nancy Reed sang the second half, duetting with Ricks at the end. But after a hitless year with Columbia and its OKeh rhythm-and-blues subsidiary, often recording with jazzy accompaniment, the Ravens disbanded. Ricks put together a new Ravens quartet, which began recording for Mercury in October 1951 and scored the Ravens' final hit in 1952 with "Rock Me All Night Long," a generally overlooked but not unreasonable candidate for first rock record, with its twelve-bar verse-and-refrain structure, stop-time breaks, shuffling backbeat, and boogie-woogie bass line.

The Ravens recorded for Mercury into 1953, but Ricks left the group in 1954, returning in time for their first sessions for the Jubilee label in early 1955. Ricks left for good a year later, recording on his own for some dozen labels through the 1960s without much success, then singing with Count Basie's band before his death in 1974. A re-formed Ravens—of whom only Joe Van Loan, Maithe Marshall's replacement, had previously been in the group—cut several singles for Chess's Argo subsidiary in 1956 and 1957. They gave their final performance at the Apollo Theatre in December 1958, but the Top Rank label issued a pair of singles by a different group under the Ravens name in 1959.

The Ravens were the model for many later doo-wop groups, which assimilated both Jimmy Ricks's cavernous bass and Maithe Marshall's falsetto tenor. The Ravens are also said to be the first vocal group to incorporate dance steps into their stage act, launching a trend that culminated in Cholly Atkins's choreography for the Miracles and Temptations in the 1960s. Although most of the Ravens' hits were up-tempo and bluesy, it is mainly their ballads that inspire the devotion of today's collectors.

Many R&B vocal groups had spiritual roots, but the Orioles had less of a gospel background than even the Ravens, as Jimmy Ricks had sung in a church choir as a teenager. Nonetheless, the Orioles injected their material with enough gospel flavor to appeal to African American listeners. The group's charismatic lead tenor, Sonny Til, sang with a trio in a Baltimore high school and then in USO shows while in the army. In 1946, he began competing in amateur shows at a Baltimore nightclub, the Avenue Cafe, where he met the other future Orioles. In 1948, inspired by the Mills Brothers, the Ink Spots, Johnny Moore's Three Blazers, the King Cole Trio, and the Cats and the Fiddle, Til formed a quintet called the Vibra-Naires, who acquired Deborah Chessler, an eighteen-year-old white songwriter, as their manager. Chessler arranged for the group to appear on *Arthur Godfrey's Talent Scouts,* a nationally broadcast prime-time television and radio contest, where they lost to the blind English jazz pianist George Shearing but proved popular enough to be invited back to New York to perform on the *Arthur Godfrey Time* morning show, which was also broadcast simultaneously on television and radio.[90]

Returning to New York once more, Chessler played the group's demos for Jerry Blaine of Jubilee Records, making such an impression that the label set up the It's a Natural subsidiary just for them. Before their first session, the Vibra-Naires renamed themselves the Orioles, after Maryland's state bird. In July 1948, they recorded Chessler's composition "It's Too Soon to Know," their first and only release on It's a Natural; subsequent Orioles records were issued on Jubilee. Animated by Til's dreamy tenor, the languorous ballad was a No. 1 R&B hit that crossed over to the pop charts. The song was quickly covered by Dinah Washington, Ella Fitzgerald, the Charioteers, and the Deep River Boys, as well as the Ravens; it would later be recorded by Johnny Otis, Pat Boone (for a Top 5 pop hit in 1958), Etta James, Irma Thomas, Little Esther Phillips, and Roy Orbison, among others.

The Orioles had their second hit later that year with the ballad "(It's Gonna Be a) Lonely Christmas," followed in the spring of 1949 by the chart-topping "Tell Me So," a Chessler ballad that Savannah Churchill and Dinah Washington had already recorded. The Orioles scored four more hits in 1949, all ballads: "A Kiss and a Rose," a cover of the Charioteers' hit; "I Challenge Your Kiss," released around the same time by the Four Jacks; "Forgive and Forget," another Chessler composition; and "What Are You Doing New Year's Eve," the 1947 Frank Loesser standard, which the Orioles first popularized. The group had an unusual predilection for the slow and sentimental; according to the rhythm-and-blues historian Marv Goldberg, "of the Orioles' first twenty records, only four sides were uptempo."[91]

The Orioles established a much-imitated formula, more amateurish-sounding than previous groups' styles, that featured Til's romantic tenor, occasionally relieved by George Nelson's rougher baritone rather than Johnny Reed's bass, with Alexander Sharp singing wordless falsetto counterpoint. At once passionate and nonchalant, Til's slightly stilted crooning drove young female fans to screaming, crying, fainting hysteria, as Frank Sinatra's voice had and Elvis Presley's would.

In February 1950, the Orioles became one of the first rhythm-and-blues groups to record with a string orchestra. They toured widely that year, but in November a car crash in Baltimore killed the group's guitarist and second tenor, Tommy Gaither, and injured George Nelson and Johnny Reed.[92] The surviving members quickly returned to the stage and studio but did not record another hit until September 1951, when they cut a harmonized adaptation of Big Joe Williams's 1935 blues classic "Baby Please Don't Go"—a singular transformation of Mississippi blues into doo-wop. Williams's song would later be recorded by Muddy Waters, Billy Lee Riley, Them, AC/DC, and Aerosmith, among many others, but it was the Orioles version that probably inspired James Brown's "Please, Please, Please."

George Nelson left the Orioles shortly before they recorded "Crying in the Chapel"—their all-time best seller—in June 1953. The group had an R&B hit in a similar vein later that year with the wistful ballad "In the Mission of St. Augustine," a pop hit for Sammy Kaye. They tried to mine the same lode with songs such as "In the Chapel in the Moonlight," a 1936 Billy Hill composition that was revived in 1954 by the white pop singer Kitty Kallen, but scored no further hits. The Orioles disbanded in 1955, but Til recruited another harmony group, the Regals, to perform with him under the Orioles' name. In 1956, the Orioles switched from Jubilee to Vee-Jay, but though they adopted a more modern, pop-oriented sound, their records no longer sold. Til recorded for Roulette as a solo artist in 1958 and rerecorded a few of the

Orioles early hits for Jubilee in 1959. The second Orioles group broke up at the end of 1959, but Til cut a few more sides for Jubilee on his own.

In 1961, Til put together a third Orioles, who performed as an oldies act and recorded mostly remakes of earlier material. Til formed a fourth Orioles in 1966; in the late 1960s and early 1970s, he recorded for RCA under his own name. By 1978, Til was singing in a group that billed itself as the Orioles or the Ink Spots, as the occasion demanded. In the late 1970s, he assembled yet another Orioles group, which recorded an album of pop standards. Although his health was failing, Til continued to perform until 1981, when he suffered a fatal heart attack.

One reason for the decline in the Orioles' popularity was the rise of the Dominoes and their stratospherically pitched lead singer, Clyde McPhatter, who replaced Sonny Til as the foremost black teen idol. The group was put together by Billy Ward, who was born Robert Williams in Savannah, Georgia, and raised in Philadelphia. The son of a minister, he sang and played organ in church as a child; later, he studied music at the Juilliard School in New York. In the late 1940s, he changed his name to Billy Ward and got a job as a pianist for Rose Marks, a white songwriter and Broadway talent agent. At Marks's urging, Ward formed a racially mixed vocal group called the Dominoes, which was unsuccessful and disbanded in early 1950. Ward then formed an all-black group called the Ques, which also disbanded quickly. Around September 1950, Ward formed a second Ques, comprising the lead tenor Clyde McPhatter, the second tenor Charlie White, the baritone William Joseph Lamon, and the bass Bill Brown—all of whom had performed in gospel groups—plus Ward himself, who played piano and sometimes sang. Ward and Marks jointly managed the group and wrote many of their songs.[93]

After winning on Amateur Night at the Apollo Theatre and on *Arthur Godfrey's Talent Scouts,* the Ques changed their name to the Dominoes and signed with King Records' new Federal subsidiary. Ralph Bass, who ran Federal, later said that when he first heard them, "Billy Ward was writing pop music, not R&B. They didn't sound like a black group to me."[94] Bass would assert that he was the one who steered them in a new direction; according to Clyde McPhatter, however, "We had patterned ourselves after the Ink Spots because I had such a high voice, but I just didn't believe in trying to sound like Bill Kenney [actually Kenny], and that's how we started the gospel stuff."[95] In any case, the Dominoes' first recordings, from November 1950, have a strong gospel flavor, especially "Do Something for Me," their first hit, which features McPhatter's melismatic singing. Although other artists—Sister Rosetta Tharpe, for one—had injected gospel music into rhythm-and-blues—the Dominoes can be credited for giving doo-wop a pronounced gospel feel.

In December 1950, the Dominoes recorded "Sixty-Minute Man," with Bill Brown singing the lead. Released in March 1951, it became that year's best-selling rhythm-and-blues record, topping *Billboard*'s R&B chart for fourteen weeks and crossing over to the pop list, even though radio stations refused to play it. It was not, as is sometimes claimed, the first rhythm-and-blues crossover record, but it may have been the first with such an overtly sexual theme. "Looka here, girls, I'm tellin' you now, they call me Lovin' Dan," sings Brown. "I rock 'em, roll 'em all night long, I'm a sixty-minute man." Dispelling any doubt about his meaning, Brown adds, "There'll be fifteen minutes of kissin', then you'll holler, 'Please don't stop!' / There'll be fifteen minutes of teasin', and fifteen minutes of squeezin', and fifteen minutes of blowin' my top."

The reference to "Lovin' Dan" roots the song in an older tradition. In December 1936, the blues singer Georgia White had recorded "Dan the Back Door Man," a song covered in March 1936 by a black vocal-harmony group, the Four Southerners. In July 1930, Bessie Smith had cut "Hustlin' Dan," singing, "Talk about your lovers, he could more than satisfy me." In December 1923, the Black Dominoes (probably a pseudonym for the all-white Original Memphis Five) had recorded the Dixieland instrumental "Dancin' Dan." And in 1921, Albert von Tilzer and Lew Brown had published "Dapper-Dan the Ladies Man from Dixie Land," indicating on the sheet-music cover that Eddie Cantor (pictured in blackface) had introduced the song that year in the show *Midnight Rounders*.[96]

Although it was hardly the first salacious rhythm-and-blues song, "Sixty-Minute Man" certainly pushed the envelope, launching a wave of increasingly licentious material that would prompt a music-industry backlash in 1954. It also demonstrated that there was a white market for R&B, which King vainly tried to exploit with cover versions by the York Brothers, a country duo, and the Elliot Lawrence Orchestra, a swing band. There were also covers by Clarence Palmer and the Jive Bombers and by Hardrock Gunter and Roberta Lee. "Sixty-Minute Man" spawned a number of spinoffs, among them the Swallows' "It Ain't the Meat" (from 1951), the Du Droppers' "Can't Do Sixty No More" (from 1952), the Checkers' "Don't Stop Dan" (from 1954), the Robins' "The Hatchet Man" (from 1954), and the Cadets' "Dancin' Dan" (from 1956).

For all its broad popularity, "Sixty-Minute Man" has been disparaged by rock historians. "'Sixty-Minute Man' met with unprecedented white acceptance for two reasons," writes John A. Jackson. "First, it reinforced the white stereotype of a slow-witted, sexually obsessed black man. Second, and more important, the song, with Brown's sexual braggadocio blatantly overstated, was not taken very seriously by most whites. To them, Brown posed no more of a threat than did 'Amos 'n' Andy.'"[97] Jim Dawson and Steve Propes concur: "Despite its national popularity, 'Sixty Minute Man' didn't break down the barriers between R&B and pop in 1951. When all was said and done, the song was a novelty, a throwback to minstrel songs like 'Open the Door, Richard,' in which black performers winked and rolled their eyes. Brown's delivery was more humorous than sincere or threatening, more in the 'coon-shout' tradition of years earlier than the soulful R&B tradition that was to follow."[98]

But while "Sixty-Minute Man" may have been old-fashioned in conception, it was cutting-edge in execution, with its hard backbeat, spiky guitar, bass lead vocal, and wordless falsetto background singing à la the Orioles' Alexander Sharp. Unlike "Open the Door Richard!" it cannot accurately be described as a throwback to minstrelsy, and its sexual braggadocio was no less threatening in its day than the sexual braggadocio of "Rapper's Delight" was nearly thirty years later. In its beat, its bold sexuality, and its use of the words "rock" and "roll," "Sixty-Minute Man" was a signal smash that helped light the fuse for the rock 'n' roll explosion soon to come.

In May 1951, the Dominoes cut "I Am with You," a hit ballad featuring Clyde McPhatter's emotive tenor and Bill Brown's talking bass. Recorded at the same session, the rocking "That's What You're Doing to Me"—with McPhatter wailing, "I'm gonna rock, I'm gonna roll"—did not chart until April 1952. "Have Mercy Baby," recorded in January 1952, closely followed "That's What You're Doing to Me" onto *Billboard*'s R&B chart, spending a couple of months in the No. 1 spot. Although it follows the twelve-bar blues form and features a honking saxophone solo, "Have Mercy Baby" is essentially a call-and-response gospel shout, with McPhatter repenting his ways—"I've been a good-for-nothin' / I've lied and cheated, too"—while improvising churchy melodic embellishments.

Ahmet Ertegun would adapt the song into "What'cha Gonna Do" (not the same song as Bill Haley's "Whatcha Gonna Do"), which McPhatter recorded with the Drifters and which formed the basis for Hank Ballard and the Midnighters' "The Twist." (Ballard first used the "What'cha Gonna Do" melody on the Midnighters' "Is Your Love for Real," a year before "The Twist.") "Have Mercy Baby" also inspired Little Richard's "True, Fine Mama." But as one of the first heavily gospel-inflected R&B hits, it had a more pervasive impact, influencing everyone from the "5" Royales to James Brown (who recorded "Have Mercy Baby" in 1964) and laying the groundwork for the soul music of the 1960s.

After "Have Mercy Baby," the group's records were credited to Billy Ward and His Dominoes. Their next hit, "I'd Be Satisfied," though less urgent than "Have Mercy Baby," was also in a gospel groove, with McPhatter singing, "Heavenly Father up above / Send me a bigger share of love." As he had at the end of "Have Mercy Baby," McPhatter sobs hysterically on "The Bells," a funereal 1953 hit; the flip side, a variation of "Sixty-Minute Man" titled "Pedal Pushin' Papa," also charted. The Dominoes' update of the

1936 standard "These Foolish Things (Remind Me of You)" was their final hit with McPhatter. In the spring of 1953, fed up with the domineering Ward, who went so far as to bill him as "Clyde Ward," his younger brother, McPhatter quit (or, by one account, was fired) and was quickly signed to Atlantic by Ahmet Ertegun.[99] The other members of the group also left and were replaced during the same period.

McPhatter's replacement, the powerhouse tenor Jackie Wilson, turned out to be another rhythm-and-blues legend. A Detroit native, Wilson sang in church as a youth and briefly pursued a boxing career, returning to music while still in his teens. After King Records declined Johnny Otis's recommendation to sign him, he cut his first record, as Sonny Wilson, for Dizzy Gillespie's short-lived Dee Gee label in 1952—a florid version of "Danny Boy," a song he performed throughout his career, backed with the feverish "Rainy Day Blues." When the Dominoes played Detroit the following year, Billy Ward auditioned Wilson, who joined the group shortly before McPhatter departed. In June 1953, Wilson and the other new Dominoes cut the gospelly hit "You Can't Keep a Good Man Down"; later in 1953, Wilson's soaring lead propelled the group's cover (on King rather than Federal) of Tony Bennett's pop smash "Rags to Riches" to the No. 2 spot on the R&B charts. Subsequently, however, there would be no further hits on King, Federal, or Jubilee, for which the Dominoes cut two singles.

At Ward's instigation, the group turned increasingly toward mainstream pop, performing in Las Vegas and signing with Decca. Recorded in April 1956, "St. Therese of the Roses," featuring Wilson accompanied by an orchestra and chorus, charted pop but not R&B. By this time, the Dominoes had already made their mark on rock 'n' roll, having been on the bill of Alan Freed's abortive "Moondog Coronation Ball" in 1952 and having actually performed at the "Moondog Maytime Ball" later that year, at the "Second Annual Moondog Birthday Party" in 1953, and at the "Moondog Jubilee of Stars under the Stars" in 1954.

Elvis Presley saw the Dominoes' show in Las Vegas around November 1956. Describing Wilson's performance to his companions Carl Perkins, Jerry Lee Lewis, and Johnny Cash at the December 1956 jam session dubbed the "Million Dollar Quartet," Presley says, "There's a guy out there who's done a takeoff of me, 'Don't Be Cruel.' He tried so hard until he got much better, boy, much better than that record of mine." Elvis then mimics Wilson singing "Don't Be Cruel." "I went back four nights straight and heard that guy do that," he adds. "Man, he sung the hell out of that song."

But in early 1957, Wilson quit the Dominoes to pursue a solo career. With Gene Mumford, formerly of the Larks, singing lead, the Dominoes recorded the Hoagy Carmichael–Mitchell Parish classic "Star Dust" (adding a "Yancey Special"–like bass line) for Liberty Records in March 1957. It proved to be their all-time best seller, making both the pop and R&B charts; the group's last two hits—the standard "Deep Purple" and a cover of the kooky 1958 novelty hit "Jennie Lee" (by Jan & Arnie, the predecessor of the surf-music duo Jan & Dean)—only charted pop.

Billy Ward and His Dominoes stayed with Liberty until the end of the 1950s, recording mostly pop and religious songs while continuing to change personnel. In 1960, they recorded four sides for ABC-Paramount, but these sold poorly, and by the middle of the decade the group was moribund. In 1965, Ward reformed the Dominoes, who cut four last sides for King before finally disbanding.

After leaving the Dominoes, Jackie Wilson sang at the Flame Show Bar in Detroit and came under the management of Al Green, who had also managed the careers of LaVern Baker and Johnnie Ray. Green arranged for Wilson to record for Decca, but just as the contract was about to be signed, Green died, and his assistant Nat Tarnopol became Wilson's manager. Decca assigned Wilson to its Brunswick subsidiary, which Tarnopol eventually took over. Wilson's first release, "Reet Petite," was cowritten by Berry Gordy, who went on to found Motown Records. Recorded in July 1957, it was a minor pop hit (and a Top 10 pop hit in England) but did not make the R&B charts. Nevertheless, with its whooping, trilling, bawling vocal, brassy horn arrangement, and boogie-woogie bass line, "Reet Petite" was a historic record that bridged the gap between rock 'n' roll and soul music.

Wilson's next release, the soaring ballad "To Be Loved" (also cowritten by Gordy), made both the pop and R&B charts in the spring of 1958. By early 1959, his gospel-flavored "Lonely Teardrops" (again cowritten by Gordy) had topped *Billboard*'s R&B chart and made the pop Top 10. "Lonely Teardrops" clearly inspired the Isley Brothers' first hit, "Shout," released later in 1959, and the song's Latin-like beat, plucked on muffled guitar strings, was widely imitated.

From that point until the mid-1970s, Wilson had some fifty pop and R&B hits, including five more R&B chart-toppers. Several of his songs, among them the hits "Night," "Alone at Last," and "My Empty Arms," are based on classical melodies, the better to display his operatic power. Perhaps his best remembered hit is "(Your Love Keeps Lifting Me) Higher and Higher," from 1967, which, as its title implies, showcases Wilson's remarkable range. Wilson toured the country, playing to screaming, largely female audiences, and appeared in movies and on television. Years of drinking, drug abuse, and womanizing took their toll, however, and in September 1975, Wilson collapsed on stage while touring with Dick Clark's "Good Ol' Rock 'n' Roll Revue." He remained comatose until his death in January 1984.[100]

Having left the Dominoes, Clyde McPhatter formed his first Drifters group in May 1953. McPhatter had a gospel background: his father was a minister and his mother a church organist. Growing up in North Carolina, he'd sung in a church choir; after his family moved to Harlem, he joined the

Mount Lebanon Singers, from which he later drew three of the original Drifters. In June 1953, the Drifters recorded four songs at their first session for Atlantic, only one of which, the doo-wop blues "Lucille," was ultimately released. Dissatisfied with the sound, Atlantic prompted McPhatter to replace the other singers, so he recruited three different gospel veterans, plus a bass singer, and in August 1953 cut five numbers—three remakes of songs recorded at the first session and two new ones. The new ones, "Money Honey" and "The Way I Feel," were coupled on the group's first single, credited to Clyde McPhatter and the Drifters; "Money Honey" written by Jesse Stone, shot to the top of the R&B charts. (One of the remakes, the hard-rocking "Let the Boogie Woogie Roll," is apparently the first issued recording to actually feature the vocable "doo-wop," but it was not released until 1960.)

"Money Honey" is certainly a rock 'n' roll song, or at any rate it became one when Elvis Presley covered it at his first recording date for RCA in January 1956. Hank Ballard and the Midnighters had already adopted the Drifters' chant of "ah-ooh, ah-ooh" for their "Work with Me Annie" in January 1954. The melody of "Money Honey" is similar to the one on Roy Orbison's first Sun record, "Ooby Dooby," from March 1956; the resemblance is even more obvious on the slower "Ooby Dooby" recorded previously by Orbison's band, the Teen Kings. The chorus of "Money Honey" is similar to the one on Gene Vincent's "Be-Bop-A-Lula," from May 1956, and the verse is similar to the one on Tommy James and the Shondells' "Hanky Panky," recorded in 1964 but not discovered by the public until 1966. The mercenary theme of "Money Honey" would later be taken up on other songs, notably Barrett Strong's 1959 hit "Money (That's What I Want)," which the Beatles covered in 1963.

Recorded in November 1953, "Such a Night," with a Latin-ish bass line taken from Eddie Heywood Jr.'s 1944 version of "Begin the Beguine," was the Drifters' next hit, backed with "Lucille," from their first session. Although there is nothing sexually explicit about "Such a Night," at least one radio station banned it, characterizing the song as "suggestive trash."[101] After that came another R&B chart-topper, the calypso-flavored "Honey Love" (recorded in February 1954), which crossed over to the pop charts. Meanwhile, McPhatter was drafted into the army, but as he was stationed in Buffalo, New York, he could still record and perform with the group while on leave. By this time, however, he had already cut what would be his last three hits with the Drifters—the suggestive rocker "Bip Bam," a Ravens-style "White Christmas," and the group's third version of "What'cha Gonna Do," a song they'd recorded at both their first two sessions.

In 1955, McPhatter split from the Drifters, although he still occasionally performed with them. He continued to record for Atlantic as a solo artist (and in duets with Ruth Brown), scoring some dozen pop and rhythm-and-blues hits, including three R&B chart-toppers: the ballads "Treasure of Love" and

"Long Lonely Nights" and the more rhythmic "A Lover's Question." In 1959, he switched to the MGM label and scored a few minor pop hits; the following year, he moved on to Mercury, scoring several more hits, the biggest being "Lover Please," which made the pop Top 10 in 1962 but did not chart R&B. By the mid-1960s, McPhatter's career was on the rocks; he recorded without success for the Amy label, moved to England and cut two singles for Deram, then returned and cut two more for Decca. Embittered, he turned to drink, dying in 1972 at the age of thirty-nine. Although he'd been nearly forgotten, McPhatter left his mark on a generation of rhythm-and-blues singers.

The Drifters carried on, replacing McPhatter first with David Baughan and then with Johnny Moore (not the guitarist/leader of the Three Blazers). Moore sang the lead on such R&B hits as "Adorable," a cover of the Colts' original, and "Ruby Baby," a Leiber-Stoller composition that became a pop hit for Dion in 1963. He also sang the lead on Leiber and Stoller's "Fools Fall in Love," a 1957 Drifters hit that Elvis Presley covered in 1966. But Moore had been drafted and replaced by Bobby Hendricks by April 1958, when the group recorded Leiber and Stoller's "Drip Drop," which, like "Ruby Baby," would be a much bigger hit for Dion than for the Drifters.

In June 1958, the Drifters' manager, George Treadwell, fired all the singers and hired a different vocal group, the Crowns, to assume the Drifters' name. The new lead singer, Ben E. King, wrote the song "There Goes My Baby," which became a No. 1 R&B and No. 2 pop hit in 1959 after Jerry Leiber and Mike Stoller produced it for Atlantic using a string section and a Brazilian beat. The recording served as a template not only for subsequent Drifters hits—including "Dance with Me," "This Magic Moment," and the No. 1 pop smash "Save the Last Dance for Me"—but for a host of elaborate 1960s soul productions for other artists. One producer who adopted the new approach was Phil Spector, whom Atlantic hired as an assistant to Leiber and Stoller in 1960 and who cowrote Ben E. King's first solo hit, "Spanish Harlem," with Leiber that year after King left the Drifters.

The Drifters cut a steady stream of hits through the mid-1960s, among them "Up on the Roof," "On Broadway," and "Under the Boardwalk, with Rudy Lewis or the returning Johnny Moore singing lead. With material furnished by such Brill Building songwriters as Doc Pomus and Mort Shuman, Gerry Goffin and Carol King, Cynthia Weill and Barry Mann, Bert Berns, and Burt Bacharach, the group dispensed with gospel inflections and took a pure pop stance, recording such rock-era gems as "Please Stay," "Sweets for My Sweet," "When My Little Girl Is Smiling," and "At the Club." They kept recording for Atlantic, their sound growing increasingly formulaic, until 1970, when they disbanded, after which several groups featuring former members continued to perform as the Drifters. Virtually the only group to survive the transition from doo-wop to soul music (although they survived in name only), the Drifters made a significant impact in both eras.

The most popular rhythm-and-blues vocal group of the early 1950s, however, may well have been the Clovers, who had twenty R&B hits between 1951 and 1956.[102] Formed around 1946 by high school classmates in Washington, D.C., the group was influenced by the Charioteers, Ravens, and Orioles, among others. Discovered in 1950, they recorded the standard "Yes Sir! That's My Baby" for Rainbow Records in an Ink Spots–like style. Ahmet Ertegun heard them in Washington but didn't care for their pop-ish repertoire, so he wrote them the bluesy "Don't You Know I Love You," which they recorded at their first Atlantic session in February 1951. With its habanera bass line and the added novelty of Frank Culley's saxophone, the song became a No. 1 R&B hit. At their second session in July 1951, the Clovers cut the blues "Fool, Fool, Fool," another chart-topping Ertegun composition. Kay Starr had a pop hit with her cover of "Fool, Fool, Fool" in 1952, and Elvis Presley made an unreleased acetate recording of the song at a radio station in Lubbock, Texas, while on tour in early 1955. Curiously, Presley uses the same bland substitution as Starr for the Clovers' risqué line "There goes my meat."

In December 1951, the Clovers recorded "One Mint Julep," a comical Rudy Toombs composition about the perils of alcohol that Vann Walls invigorates with a descending piano vamp. A No. 2 R&B hit for the Clovers, the song was covered in 1952 by Louis Prima and by Buddy Morrow, who had a minor pop hit with it. Chet Atkins's 1959 instrumental version was also a minor pop hit, while Ray Charles's 1960 instrumental version (with Charles playing organ) made the pop Top 10 and topped the R&B chart. Various rock, pop, jazz, soul, country, and Latin versions followed, including many instrumentals—ironically enough, since the original depends heavily on vocal harmonies and amusing lyrics.

The group's next hit, the chart-topping "Ting-A-Ling," from March 1952, typifies the original Clovers sound—mid-tempo and bluesy, with spare instrumental accompaniment and rhythmic accents on just the second beat of each measure. The up-tempo "Hey, Miss Fannie," a No. 2 R&B hit recorded in August 1952, is a true rocker, complete with backbeat and boogie-woogie bass line. Both "Ting-A-Ling" and "Hey, Miss Fannie" were written by Ertegun, and as with "One Mint Julep," the flip sides also charted. Buddy Bailey sang the lead on all the Clovers' early hits, but after the session that produced "Hey, Miss Fannie" and the group's following hit, the Rudy Toombs drinking song "Crawlin'," Bailey was drafted and replaced by Charlie White, formerly of the Dominoes. With White singing lead on the rocking hits "Good Lovin'," "Little Mama," and "Lovey Dovey" (the last covered for a pop hit by Bunny Paul in 1954, by Clyde McPhatter in 1958, and by Buddy Knox in 1960), Bailey was hardly missed.

But White had personal problems and was fired not long after cutting "Lovey Dovey" and "Little Mama" in September 1953. His replacement, Billy Mitchell, sang the lead on Jesse Stone's clever composition "Your Cash Ain't Nothin' but Trash" in April 1954; an R&B hit for the Clovers, the song made the pop charts in 1974 when it was redone by the white blues-rocker Steve Miller. Mitchell remained with the group even after Buddy Bailey returned in May 1954, following his army discharge. Bailey sang lead on the Clovers' next hit, a cover of Tony Bennett's 1951 ballad hit "Blue Velvet," which Bobby Vinton would revive for a pop chart-topper in 1963. He also sang lead on Rudy Toombs' 1955 soft-drinking song "Nip Sip" ("I go for soda and root beer, too") and the pop-oriented "Devil or Angel," an R&B hit in 1956 that Bobby Vee covered for a pop hit in 1960. Recorded with an added vocal chorus in March 1956, the saccharine "Love, Love, Love" was even more pop-oriented, and it became the first Clovers release to cross over to the pop charts. Both "Nip Sip" and "Love, Love, Love" were covered by the Diamonds, a white Canadian doo-wop group that would have its biggest success in 1957 with a cover of the Gladiolas' "Little Darlin'."

At the Clovers' final Atlantic session in July 1957, they rerecorded "Down in the Alley," which they had originally cut, but not released, in 1953. For this composition, Jesse Stone set up-to-date lyrics—"Just rockin' and reelin', we'll get that feelin'"—to the tune of Leroy Carr's "How Long, How Long Blues." But though "Down in the Alley" became something of a cult classic, it never charted. Even before the Clovers' Atlantic contract expired, their manager, Lou Krefetz, had established his own Poplar label, hiring Jesse Stone as musical director. In 1958, Poplar released two Clovers singles and an album, *The Clovers in Clover,* consisting largely of pop standards. In 1959, Krefetz sold the Poplar catalog to the new United Artists label, for which he became national sales manager.

Produced by Leiber and Stoller, the Clovers' first United Artists session, in June 1959, yielded the R&B and pop hit "Love Potion No. 9," a humorous Leiber-Stoller composition similar to ones the pair were writing for the Coasters. The song became a bigger hit in 1964 when it was covered by the Searchers. In 1961, the Clovers left United Artists and cut a single for Winley Records, owned by the brother of their bass singer, Harold Winley, but it was not successful, and the group broke up. Former members then put together various Clovers groups, which continued to record through the 1980s and perform on the oldies circuit into the 2000s. Although blacker-sounding than most doo-wop groups, at least until the mid-1950s, the Clovers appeared on a number of Alan Freed's early rock 'n' roll shows and made a significant impact on the nascent rock scene.

Another important doo-wop group, the Charms, made a practice of covering other artists' records and were covered themselves in turn. Formed in Cincinnati around 1952, the group was soon joined by the sixteen-year-old

Otis Williams (not the Temptations' founder), who became the lead singer. In 1953, the Charms cut their first single, the sour-noted original ballad "Heaven Only Knows," for Henry Stone's Rockin' label. Stone soon became partners with King's Syd Nathan in DeLuxe, an established independent rhythm-and-blues label that Nathan had acquired; the revived label absorbed the Rockin' catalog and reissued "Heaven Only Knows" as its first release. Four more unsuccessful singles followed before the Charms, at Nathan's behest, recorded a cover of the Jewels' "Hearts of Stone" in September 1954. The Charms' version has an amateurish feel, but it almost completely eclipsed the Jewels' even cruder original, rising to the top of *Billboard*'s R&B chart and crossing over to the pop Top 20. Notwithstanding the strong rhythm-and-blues flavor of the Jewels' and Charms' renditions, a square-sounding cover by the Fontane Sisters, Perry Como's backup singers, became a No. 1 pop smash, and Red Foley's cover made the country Top 5. Other white covers included those by the singer Vicki Young and the comic group the Goofers. Elvis Presley sang "Hearts of Stone" on the *Louisiana Hayride* in January 1955; an acetate recording of the performance was first issued on the 1999 double CD *Sunrise*.

In November 1954, again at Nathan's urging, the Charms recorded a cover of the Five Keys' "Ling, Ting, Tong," which plays on the supposed resemblance of the song's nonsensical refrain to Chinese. "I went to Chinatown / way back in old Hong Kong / to get some egg foo young / and then I heard a gong," goes the first verse. This time the Charms' version, while still an R&B and pop hit, sold no better than the original; the flip side, a cover of "(Bazoom) I Need Your Lovin'"—a Leiber-Stoller composition that was originally a pop hit for the white group the Cheers—also made the R&B charts. "Ling Ting Tong" was covered for a minor pop hit by Buddy Knox in 1961.

The Charms' next release paired a cover of Gene and Eunice's late-1954 recording "Ko Ko Mo" with a cover of the Robins' "Whadaya Want?" (another Leiber-Stoller song); but amid "Ko Ko Mo" covers by Perry Como, Louis Armstrong and Gary Crosby, the Crew-Cuts, the Flamingos, Marvin and Johnny, Bill Darnel and Betty Clooney (Rosemary's sister), the Hutton Sisters (Betty and Marion), the Dooley Sisters, Hawkshaw Hawkins and Rita Robbins, Goldie Hill and Red Sovine, Jack Cardwell, Tito Rodríguez, and Andy Griffith (the actor), the Charms' version was lost in the shuffle. (Although it was released and covered by pop, rhythm-and-blues, country, and Latin artists before Bill Haley's or Elvis Presley's breakthrough, Gene and Eunice's "Ko Ko Mo," with its habanera bass line and Caribbean lilt, has somehow been overlooked as a possible first rock 'n' roll record. The Los Angeles–based duo of Gene Forrest [born Forest Gene Wilson] and Eunice Levy deserves recognition not only for their epochal debut single but for later recordings such as "Bom Bom Lulu" that were popular in Jamaica and influenced the development of reggae.)

The Charms' poppy original composition "Two Hearts" had been recorded in September 1954 and issued that November, but it did not chart until March 1955, whereupon it was covered by Frank Sinatra, Doris Day, Gisèle MacKenzie, the Crew-Cuts, the Lancers, the 5 De Marco Sisters, and Pat Boone, becoming Boone's first hit, just before "Ain't That a Shame." But at the height of the Charms' success, the other singers left Otis Williams and legally challenged his right to use the Charms name; Williams recruited new members for what would be credited on the label of his next DeLuxe release, the Rudy Toombs composition "Gum Drop," as His New Group. Meanwhile, Henry Stone split with Syd Nathan and began issuing records by the departed Charms on his own new Chart label. The dispute was resolved in Williams's favor, and his next hit, the Rudy Toombs song "That's Your Mistake," was first credited to Otis Williams and His New Group and then relabeled as by Otis Williams and His Charms.

In February 1956, Williams and His Charms covered the white pop singer Cathy Carr's hit ballad "Ivory Tower" (also covered by Gale Storm) and the black female harmony trio the Cookies' R&B hit "In Paradise." The two songs were issued on the same single, and "Ivory Tower" made both the R&B and pop charts. Williams's group scored their last R&B hit in 1957 with a cover of the Love Notes' doo-wop ballad "United." After shifting from DeLuxe to the parent King label, they barely made the pop Hot 100 with "Little Turtle Dove" and "Panic" in 1961. Williams made his final recordings for King in 1963; turning to soul music, he cut four singles for OKeh in 1965 and 1966. Williams then worked as a barber in Cincinnati until 1969, when he took a job as a booking agent and talent scout in Nashville. The steel guitarist Pete Drake persuaded Williams to record pair of LPs for his Stop label—*The Greatest Hits Of Otis Williams* in 1970 and the country album *Otis Williams and the Midnight Cowboys* in 1971. Williams later ran his own First Note Cafe in Cincinnati. He re-formed the Charms in the 1990s, touring internationally, and continued to perform into the 2000s.

Two of the most influential doo-wop records were the only hits for the New York groups that cut them. The Crows "Gee" and the Chords "Sh-Boom" were both B-sides that became No. 2 rhythm-and-blues hits while crossing over to the pop charts. Each has been proposed as the first rock 'n' roll record or inaccurately cited as the first R&B crossover hit, but because each charted in 1954, the year Elvis Presley cut "That's All Right" and Bill Haley cut "Rock Around the Clock," both were harbingers of the rock 'n' roll revolution.

The Crows formed in Harlem around 1951; in 1952, after seeing them win the Amateur Night competition at the Apollo, the talent agent Cliff Martinez got them recording sessions on Jubilee backing the singer-trumpeter Frank "Fat Man" Humphries and the singer-pianist Viola Watkins. In 1953, Martinez took Watkins and the Crows to Rama, a new rhythm-and-blues label established by George Goldner, whose Tico label recorded such Latin artists as Tito Puente. Two singles were cut at an April 1953 session: the Crows accompanied Watkins on the first one, a cover of Georgia Gibbs's country-flavored pop hit "Seven Lonely Days" that was backed with the Crows' cover of the Carlisles' country smash "No Help Wanted"; Watkins played piano behind the Crows on the second single, the ballad "I Love You So," which was backed with "Gee."

At first, "I Love You So" was the more popular side, but by the end of 1953, "Gee" had begun to take off, with help from the white disc jockey Dick "Huggy Boy" Hugg, who broadcast from the window of the Dolphin's of Hollywood record shop in South Central Los Angeles. Written in a matter of minutes by the Crows' baritone, Bill Davis, "Gee" could hardly have been simpler or less controversial, with the chorus "Oh-ho-ho-ho gee, my oh-oh gee, well oh-ho gee, why I love that girl." The sole touch of sophistication is the jazzy guitar solo, probably by Tiny Grimes, who briefly quotes the familiar Scottish air "The Campbells Are Coming." The ending of "Gee" would be copied on Frankie Lymon and the Teenagers' 1956 doo-wop smash "Why Do Fools Fall in Love," released on Goldner's Gee label. "Gee" was covered in 1954 by the white pop singer June Hutton, on Capitol; by another Harlem doo-wop group, the Skylarks, on OKeh; and (as an instrumental) by the Latin pianist Joe Loco, on Tico. None of these charted, but Jan & Dean's surprisingly faithful 1960 rendition did make the low end of *Billboard*'s Hot 100, as did the Pixies Three's 1964 take; the Hollywood Flames' 1961 version made the R&B list.

The Chords were formed around 1951 by members of three other vocal groups in the Morrisania section of the Bronx. With influences that included such white groups as the Four Freshmen, the Chords leaned toward mainstream pop. In 1953, they wrote "Sh-Boom," filled with nonsense syllables, and auditioned for Bobby Robinson's Red Robin label, but Robinson turned them down. The following year, they came to the attention of the Atlantic producer Jerry Wexler, who was looking for someone to cover Patti Page's hit "Cross Over the Bridge." In March 1954, the Chords recorded four songs for Atlantic's new Cat subsidiary, including "Cross Over the Bridge" and "Sh-Boom," which were paired on the same single, with "Cross Over the Bridge" as the A-side. It soon became evident, however, that "Sh-Boom" was the breakout side, helped along, as "Gee" had been, by "Huggy Boy" Hugg. By the time "Sh-Boom" charted in July, Atlantic was pressing it with a different flip side in order to avoid paying publishing royalties for "Cross Over the Bridge."[103]

"Sh-Boom" launched a wave of R&B nonsense songs that included the Platters' "Voo Vee Ah Bee," the Harptones' "Oobidee-Oobidee-Oo," Arthur

Lee Maye and the Crowns ' "Oochie Pachie" ("When the clock strikes three, we're gonna have a ball / We're gonna rock 'n' roll and that ain't all"), and the Jac-O-Lacs' "Sha-Ba-Da-Ba-Doo." "Sh-Boom" was covered by the Billy Williams Quartet and by the country artists Bobby Williamson and Leon McAuliffe; Stan Freberg's parody, mocking the Chords' supposedly unintelligible lyrics, was a hit in its own right. But the cover version by the Crew-Cuts, a white Canadian quartet, became a long-running No. 1 pop hit, far outselling the Chords' original. With its pop-style horn arrangement (by Mercury Records' musical director, David Carroll), clean-cut harmonies, and crisply enunciated lyrics, the Crew-Cuts' "Sh-Boom" scarcely suggests rock 'n' roll at all, but it certainly raised public awareness of doo-wop, in Britain as well the United States. The Chords' version is cruder but hardly less pop-oriented; the blackest thing about it is Sam "the Man" Taylor's saxophone solo. The Crows' "Gee" is blacker-sounding, but only slightly.

After "Gee," the Crows had several other releases on Rama and other Goldner labels, but none was successful, and the group disbanded in 1955. The Chords were threatened with legal action by a preexisting group with the same name and by the end of 1954 were calling themselves the Chordcats; in 1955, they became the Sh-Booms. With no further hits on Cat, the group, after some personnel changes, released a single on RCA's Vik subsidiary, then broke up. The original quintet reunited to cut a single for Atlantic in 1960.

Two other noteworthy doo-wop songs were recorded around September 1954, the Moonglows' "Sincerely" and the Penguins' "Earth Angel." The Moonglows were formed in Cleveland around 1951 by Harvey Fuqua; at first, they called themselves the Crazy Sounds and performed vocalese, a jazz style where singers set lyrics to instrumental jazz solos. Hearing them sing doo-wop, not vocalese, Alan Freed was so impressed that he became their manager and started his own Champagne label to record them, renaming them the Moonglows. After cutting a one-off single for Freed, who claimed composer's credit for the two songs they'd written, and appearing on Freed's "Big Rhythm and Blues Show" in the summer of 1953, the Moonglows signed with the Chicago-based Chance label.[104] In September 1953 and January 1954, they recorded five singles for Chance, including a pair of Christmas songs, a cover of Doris Day's smash "Secret Love," the proto-rocking "Ooh Rockin' Daddy," and the bluesy "219 Train." The melody on the verses of "Real Gone Mama," the flip side of "Secret Love," anticipates that of Little Richard's "Tutti-Frutti," and one line, "Hey, Miss Blue, yes, she knows just what to do," prefigures Richard's "I got a girl named Sue, she knows just what to do." On these sides, Freed took only partial composer's credit for the original material. But despite heavy airplay on his radio show, none of the records charted nationally.

By the time Chance folded in late 1954, the Moonglows, still under Freed's management, had switched to Chess Records. Their first Chess release, recorded in September or October, was "Sincerely," a ballad composed by Fuqua (with a bridge lifted from the Dominoes' "That's What You're Doing to Me") for which Freed claimed half credit. Released in October or November, "Sincerely" became a No. 1 R&B hit, displacing "Earth Angel," and crossed over to the pop charts. It might have been a bigger pop hit if not for the McGuire Sisters' chart-topping cover version. Unlike the Moonglows, who set off Bobby Lester's tenor lead with innovative background harmonies, the three McGuire Sisters harmonize the melody together, leaving instruments to play the background parts; the effect is to turn doo-wop into vocal vanilla.

At the height of the rock 'n' roll craze, the Moonglows performed on Freed's and other package shows and appeared in the movie *Rock, Rock, Rock!* along with Chuck Berry, the Flamingos, Jimmy Cavallo and His House Rockers, the Johnny Burnette Trio, LaVern Baker, Frankie Lymon and the Teenagers, and Alan Freed. Their mid-1950s recordings virtually defined the classic doo-wop sound. They had another R&B hit with the ballad "Most of All" in 1955 and three more in 1956, including the teen-oriented "We Go Together," a minor pop hit for Jan & Dean in 1960, and "See Saw," which crossed over to the pop chart and, like "Most of All," was covered by the veteran white pop singer Don Cornell; Harvey Fuqua's chants of "whoa-oh-oh" on "See Saw" anticipate Sam Cooke's on Cooke's first hit, "You Send Me." In 1957, the Moonglows' cover of Percy Mayfield's 1950 R&B chart-topper "Please Send Me Someone to Love" made the R&B Top 5 and the lower ranks of the pop charts. In 1958, the group, under the name Harvey and the Moonglows, scored their last hit, "Ten Commandments of Love," with guitarist Billy Johnson reciting the commandments after Fuqua sings them. Though it made the R&B Top 10 and crossed over to the pop charts, "Ten Commandments of Love" was hardly the Moonglows' biggest seller, but it may be their best-remembered record after "Sincerely."

In 1959, Fuqua replaced the other Moonglows with a group from Washington, D.C., that included the young Marvin Gaye, adding the bass singer Chuck Barksdale. But the new Moonglows soon disbanded, and Fuqua moved to Detroit, becoming a producer and A&R man for Motown. Bobby Lester re-formed the Moonglows in 1970; two years later, with Fuqua on board, RCA Victor released the album *The Return of the Moonglows*. Lester revived the group again, without Fuqua, from 1978 until his death in 1980; Fuqua led a Moonglows group at the 1983 Grammy Awards and a 1986 show at Radio City Music Hall. The last surviving original member, Fuqua died in 2010.

The Penguins were formed in Los Angeles in 1953 by Curtis Williams and Cleveland "Cleve" Duncan. By that time, Williams, who had recently left the Hollywood Flames, was already working on "Earth Angel" with his former Flames colleague Gaynel Hodge. The melody resembles that of Jesse and Marvin's 1953 R&B hit "Dream Girl," written by Jesse Belvin, a mentor to Williams and Hodge, while the bridge is adapted from "I Went to Your Wedding," which the Hollywood Flames had recorded as demo for its composer, Jessie Mae Robinson. The piano introduction is taken from the Flames' 1953 recording of "I Know," and the chord structure reflects that of the 1934 Rodgers and Hart standard "Blue Moon."[105]

Duncan's uncle Ted Brinson, a former big-band musician, ran his own recording studio, which Dootsie Williams used for his DooTone label. The Penguins recorded a demo for DooTone, which the label issued as their first single. They recorded a second demo, coupling the rhythmic "Hey Senorita" with the balladic "Earth Angel (Will You Be Mine)." Again DooTone released the rough demo as a finished product, with "Hey Senorita" as the A-side, but it was "Earth Angel" that took off, topping *Billboard*'s R&B chart and making the pop Top 10. A number of white artists quickly covered it, including Gloria Mann, Pat O'Day, and Les Baxter, but the Crew-Cuts' version was the most successful, reaching the pop Top 5. Like their "Sh-Boom," the Crew-Cuts' "Earth Angel" lacks rhythm-and-blues or rock 'n' roll feeling.

After a dispute with Dootsie Williams over royalties, the Penguins engaged the white songwriter and musician Buck Ram as their manager. Ram got them a contract with Mercury, the Crew-Cuts' label, while insisting that Mercury also sign the Platters, another group that Ram managed. The Platters first single for the label, Ram's composition "Only You (and You Alone)," was a No. 1 R&B and Top 5 pop hit, after which Mercury and Ram gave the Penguins short shrift. With no hits on Mercury, the Penguins switched to Atlantic, scoring an R&B hit with "Pledge of Love" in 1957, but the group soon split with both Atlantic and Ram and returned to DooTone. They reorganized when Curtis Williams departed but left DooTone in 1960, cutting a final single for the Sun State label in 1962 before disbanding. Cleve Duncan put a new Penguins group together and cut a pair of mid-1960s singles for Original Sound, one of which, "Memories of El Monte," was written by Frank Zappa and the future Mothers of Invention singer Ray Collins. Duncan continues to lead a Penguins group, sometimes billed as the Fabulous Penguins, as of 2010.

The relationship of doo-wop to rock 'n' roll is problematic. Some doo-wop records of the 1940s and 1950s feature backbeats, boogie-woogie bass lines, and other typical rock characteristics, but others are simply harmonized pop songs, including many slow ballads. Perhaps this is why white pop artists were more likely to cover doo-wop hits than jump blues. Nonetheless, doo-wop was received as an integral part of the rock 'n' roll phenomenon before fading in the 1960s, represented by such genre-defining hits as the

Cadillacs' "Speedoo," the Platters' "The Great Pretender," Frankie Lymon and the Teenagers' "Why Do Fools Fall in Love," and the Diamonds' "Little Darlin'" (the last being one of the few white covers to improve on the black original). Doo-wop groups appeared on rhythm-and-blues and rock 'n' roll shows alongside the honkers and shouters. Elvis Presley cut at least half a dozen doo-wop songs, including "Earth Angel" (informally recorded during his army hitch in Germany) and the Clovers' "Down in the Alley." Presley was just one of the solo rock singers who recorded ballads as well as up-tempo songs, but it was largely the doo-woppers who made slower material a staple of the early rock 'n' roll repertoire.

New York and Los Angeles may have been the most important doo-wop centers, but New Orleans contributed at least one influential group, the Spiders, who began around 1947 as a gospel quintet called the Zion City Harmonizers (not to be confused with the Zion Harmonizers). After changing their name to the Delta Southernaires, they were discovered by Phyllis Boone, who worked for Cosimo Matassa's J&M Recording Service and offered them an audition there. They performed gospel songs for Matassa, but he was looking for rhythm-and-blues, so they returned to the studio with two songs written by the singer and guitarist Adolph Smith—a member of another New Orleans group known first as the Mellow Drops and then as the Monitors—and landed a contract with Imperial Records.

Renamed for secular purposes, the Spiders recorded Smith's "I Didn't Want to Do It" and "You're the One" with Dave Bartholomew's band in December 1953, and both sides of the single made the R&B Top 10. "You're the One" is a straightforward ballad, while "I Didn't Want to Do It" is a bluesy rocker, complete with backbeat and "Yancey Special" bass pattern. The first line, "Fine little mama came knockin', knockin' on my front door," anticipates the El Dorados' 1955 doo-wop smash "At My Front Door," which opens with "Crazy little mama come knockin', knockin' at my front door"; another line refers to "rockin' and a-rollin' all around the clock," four months before Bill Haley cut "Rock Around the Clock."

The Spiders continued to sing gospel music as the Delta Southernaires until a local disc jockey exposed them, whereupon they were banned from performing at their church. Recorded in April 1954, their next hit, the Dave Bartholomew composition "I'm Slippin' In," has a strong gospel feel, although the jiving lyrics are about a man coming home drunk late at night. Lew Chudd, the owner of Imperial Records, tried to persuade the Spiders' lead singer, Chuck Carbo, to go solo, causing bad blood within the group even though Carbo declined. Chuck Carbo did leave the Spiders soon afterward, and his brother Chick Carbo sang the lead on the group's next hit, "21," an update of Jewel King's Bartholomew-composed 1950 hit "3×7=21." But after three subsequent Spiders releases failed to chart, Chuck Carbo returned and in August 1955 cut the hit "Witchcraft" with the group. Written by Dave Bartholomew and Earl King, the song has a melody on the verses that mirrors the habanera bass line beneath it. Elvis Presley had a pop hit with "Witchcraft" in 1963.

The Spiders toured from coast to coast, recording through 1956, though on some sessions Chuck Carbo sang most of the lead and harmony parts himself. The group then disbanded, reuniting to cut a final single in 1960. Chuck Carbo pursued a solo career, recording a pair of singles for Imperial before moving on to Rex and Ace, while Chick Carbo recorded on his own for Atlantic, Vee-Jay, and Instant. Chuck recorded sporadically in the 1970s and 1980s, making a comeback with two mid-1990s albums on Rounder, *Drawers Trouble* and *The Barber's Blues*.

THE CRESCENT CITY

Rhythm-and-blues may have first emerged in Los Angeles, but New Orleans R&B played a crucial part in the development of rock 'n' roll. In January 1947, just as Jack McVea's "Open the Door Richard!" was making its initial breakthrough, Paul Gayten recorded "True," an update of Don Albert's 1936 ballad "You Don't Love Me" that is now generally recognized as the first national R&B hit by a New Orleans artist. (Recorded in New Orleans a few months afterward, Annie Laurie's "Since I Fell for You," with Gayten on piano, charted slightly earlier, but Laurie was not a native New Orleanian.) The brothers David and Jules Braun, who formed the DeLuxe label in Linden, New Jersey, in 1944, had discovered Gayten and Laurie on a scouting trip to New Orleans that also resulted in the first recordings by Dave Bartholomew and Smiley Lewis. Gayten kept recording for DeLuxe and Regal (the label the Braun brothers started with Fred Mendelsohn after selling DeLuxe to Syd Nathan) but only had three more R&B hits, two featuring Laurie. Besides ballads, Gayten also sang blues, up-tempo proto-rockers such as Louis Prima's "Yeah! Yeah! Yeah!" and Latin-tinged New Orleans–style numbers such as "Hey, Little Girl," which Professor Longhair later appropriated.

Born in New Orleans, Gayten began playing piano in Kentwood, Louisiana, the birthplace of Little Brother Montgomery, his uncle.[106] After moving to Jackson, Mississippi, at age fourteen, he toured with a local band and with a carnival and a tent show before forming his own jazz sextet, including the future bebop saxophonist Teddy Edwards. He led an army band during World War II, then moved back to New Orleans and began recording for DeLuxe. In 1949, he wrote the jump blues "For You My Love" for Larry Darnell, a young singer who'd moved to New Orleans from Columbus, Ohio; Darnell recorded the song for Regal with Gayten's band, and it became a No.

1 R&B hit. Gayten also accompanied Chubby Newsome on her signature hit "Hip Shakin' Mama."

Gayten toured the country through the early 1950s, together with Laurie, Darnell, Newsome, and Little Jimmy Scott. In 1951, he began recording in New York for OKeh, but by 1953 he was back in New Orleans leading a new band that featured the Denver-bred tenor saxophonist Lee Allen at a club called the Brass Rail. "It Ain't Nothing Happening," recorded in May 1953 for OKeh, finds Gayten in a rocking groove, with Allen playing a fierce solo. Gayten's version of "Cow Cow Blues," cut the same month, sounds like the model for Ray Charles's "Mess Around," recorded a few days later.

In 1954, Gayten began working for Chess as a producer and A&R man, recording Bobby Charles's "Later Alligator" and Clarence "Frogman" Henry's "Ain't Got No Home." He also cut his own records for Chess's Checker and Argo subsidiaries into the late 1950s with bands that included such New Orleans studio stalwarts as saxophonists Lee Allen and Red Tyler, guitarists Ernest McLean and Edgar Blanchard, drummers Earl Palmer and Charles "Hungry" Williams, and bassist Frank Fields. He had a minor pop hit in 1957 with the rock 'n' roll instrumental "Nervous Boogie" and another in 1958 with "Windy," a cover of "Tom Hark," a hit in England for the South African *kwela* band Elias and His Zig-Zag Jive Flutes. Gayten's last hit, recorded for the Chess-distributed Anna label in Detroit in 1959, was a cover of Bobby Peterson's funky instrumental "The Hunch." Moving to Los Angeles, he ran Chess's West Coast operations through the 1960s, then started his own Pzazz label, which had little success. Retiring from the music business, Gayten remained in California until his death in 1991.

A New Orleans native, Roy Brown was raised in Eunice, Louisiana, where he sang in church. He began writing his own songs, influenced by the spirituals he heard his fellow field workers sing as he harvested cotton, rice, and sugar cane. After attending high school in Houston, he moved to Los Angeles and boxed professionally, then won an amateur singing contest, crooning in the style of his idol, Bing Crosby. In 1945, he returned to Houston, where a nightclub owner heard him and, intrigued by the idea of a black singer who sounded white, booked him for what turned out to be a long engagement in Shreveport. He went on to Galveston, performing with his own combo on a local radio station; he wrote "Good Rocking Tonight" but, since he sang only ballads, had trumpeter Wilbert Brown sing it on the air. One night, Wilbert took sick, so Roy sang the song himself, shouting instead of crooning.[107]

Back in New Orleans, he offered "Good Rocking Tonight" to Wynonie Harris, who brusquely turned him away. The same night, he took the song to Cecil Gant, who had him sing it over the telephone to Jules Braun of DeLuxe Records. When Braun came to New Orleans for a Paul Gayten session at the J&M Recording Service in the early summer of 1947, he cut Brown singing

"Good Rocking Tonight" with drummer Bob Ogden's combo. The record was an immediate local hit. "It seemed like Roy Brown's 'Good Rockin' [sic] Tonight' was the first instance where New Orleans felt there was such a thing as black music," said Vernon "Dr. Daddy-O" Winslow, the city's first African American radio disc jockey. But it did not make the national R&B charts until the middle of 1948, after Wynonie Harris's version charted.[108] Brown's original doesn't rock as hard as Harris's cover: although it sports a shuffle rhythm and a boogie bass line, it lacks a backbeat; tenor saxophonist Earl Barnes leans closer to jazz than to rhythm-and-blues; and Brown's high-pitched, smoothly melodic shouting is carefully enunciated.

Recorded in December 1947, Brown's next hit, "'Long About Midnight," topped *Billboard*'s R&B chart in the fall of 1948 and established Brown's trademark vocal style, a gospel-tinged, intensely emotional way of crying the blues that was closely copied by black singers such as Larry Darnell and partially assimilated by white ones such as Johnnie Ray and Elvis Presley. According to the rock historian Charlie Gillett, Brown's singing also influenced B. B. King, Bobby Bland, Little Richard, Jackie Wilson, and James Brown, among others.[109] Between 1949 and 1951, Brown had a dozen national hits, all roughly in the mold of either the rollicking "Good Rocking Tonight" or the plaintive "'Long About Midnight." Over this period, his accompaniment became noticeably more modern, manifested in part by the increasing presence of backbeats and guitars. The hardest-rocking of these hits is "Boogie at Midnight," from 1949, but the biggest seller was the wailing "Hard Luck Blues," a No. 1 R&B hit in 1950.

From late 1949 through 1955, Brown did most of his recording in Cincinnati, where King Records was headquartered, but the company did not shift him from its DeLuxe subsidiary to the parent label until 1953. Although he toured the country through the mid-1950s, he claimed he was blackballed by the music industry because of a 1951 dispute over royalty payments, and he did not have another hit until 1957, after he was dropped by King and signed by Imperial.[110] Brown's last two hits—"Party Doll," a cover of Buddy Knox's rockabilly smash, and "Let the Four Winds Blow," which became a rock 'n' roll classic after Fats Domino recorded it in 1961—both crossed over to the pop charts.

Although he wrote what is arguably the first rock 'n' roll song in 1946 and sang in an authentically hard-rocking style as early as December 1952, when he recorded the frantic "Hurry Hurry Baby," Brown was yet another casualty of the rock revolution. He returned to the King label for a couple of sessions in 1959 and recorded for a number of small labels through the 1960s but was reduced to selling encyclopedias door to door to make a living. After appearing with Johnny Otis at the 1970 Monterey Jazz Festival, he cut a pair of singles for Mercury and an album for ABC-BluesWay but gained little career traction until the end of the decade, when he performed in Europe following an LP reissue of some of his King material. He died of a heart attack in May 1981, shortly after headlining at the New Orleans Jazz and Heritage Festival.

Smiley Lewis sang in a style bluesier than but otherwise comparable to Fats Domino's yet never enjoyed anything close to Domino's success. Born Overton Amos Lemons in DeQuincy, Louisiana (near the Texas border), in 1913, he moved to New Orleans as a youth and learned to play guitar.[111] He was in his twenties when he sang and played in a band led by trumpeter Thomas Jefferson that included pianist Isidore "Tuts" Washington and bazooka player Edward "Noon" Johnson (the bazooka, invented and popularized by the white comedian Bob Burns, was a kazoo-like novelty horn that gave its name to the World War II antitank weapon).[112] During the war, Lewis worked in a band with Washington and clarinetist Kid Ernest Moliere in Bunkie, Louisiana; after the war, he worked with Washington and drummer Herman Seale in New Orleans.

Lewis's powerful singing, in a Big Joe Turner–like shouting style, attracted a following, and in September 1947, Dave Braun recorded him for DeLuxe, accompanied by Washington's boogie piano; but of the two singles listed in the label's catalog, only one seems to have been issued. Lewis did not record again until March 1950, when Dave Bartholomew produced four sides for Imperial with Lewis's group, augmented by Bartholomew himself on trumpet and two saxophone players from his band. The first release, "Tee Nah Nah," borrows the melody of Fats Domino's first hit, "The Fat Man," with lyrics supplied by Washington. "That's a song that the boys used to sing up in the penitentiary," Washington claimed.[113] It became a regional hit, with help from the disc jockey Dr. Daddy-O, and has since become New Orleans standard.

Imperial and its Colony subsidiary released five more bluesy Lewis singles, replacing his musicians with Bartholomew's until only Washington remained, before scoring a hit in 1952 with "The Bells Are Ringing," a reworded adaptation of Lloyd Price's "Lawdy Miss Clawdy." Washington then departed, irked that Lewis had become "big headed."[114] After that, Lewis's guitar was deemphasized, and his recorded repertoire, once confined almost entirely to blues, grew more varied, often resembling Fats Domino's material. A case in point is "Blue Monday," a Bartholomew composition that Lewis cut with Domino on piano in December 1953 and that Domino covered in March 1955 for a smash hit when it was finally released in 1957.

But Lewis did not have another hit until 1955, when he recorded "I Hear You Knocking," a song written by Bartholomew and Earl King (under the name Pearl King) that sets the slightly altered refrain from the various "Keep A-Knockin'" songs to a different, slower melody (not unlike the tune of "Bucket's Got a Hole in It" or of Fats Domino's "Ain't It a Shame," recorded some two months earlier) and adds new verses. Like many of Lewis's records, it features piano triplets (played by Huey Smith) and a "Yancey Special" bass line. It rose to No. 2 on *Billboard*'s R&B chart but never crossed over, eclipsed by Gale Storm's mannered cover version. Many other versions followed, including Fats Domino's, but the biggest seller was the one recorded in 1970 by the Welsh singer-guitarist Dave Edmunds, which reached the pop Top 5.

Lewis's next R&B hit, "One Night," also written by Bartholomew and King, met a similar fate when Elvis Presley's version made the pop Top 5 in late 1958, more than two and a half years after the original charted. Presley had cut a reasonably faithful but unreleased cover of "One Night" in January 1957, a month before recording the reworded version that was ultimately issued, where he sings "One night with you / is what I'm now praying for" instead of Lewis's "One night of sin / is what I'm now paying for" and climaxes with the stop-time verse "Now I know that life without you / has been too lonely too long" instead of "Now I know that bad and wild life / will cause me nothin' but harm."

Although Lewis's following Imperial releases contained strong material, well performed and produced, Lewis would have only one more hit, "Please Listen to Me," from 1956—a sweet tune propelled by piano triplets and a "Yancey Special" bass line. Even the driving rocker "Shame, Shame, Shame," featured on the soundtrack of the 1956 movie *Baby Doll,* failed to chart, though it may just have been ahead of its time. Aerosmith's rendition, on the group's 2004 album *Honkin' on Bobo,* replaces horns with guitars but is otherwise surprisingly similar to Lewis's, if somewhat stiffer. Lewis's output declined after 1957, and Imperial dropped him at the end of 1960. He continued to perform in the New Orleans area, recording for the OKeh, Dot, and Loma labels into the mid-1960s, when he was diagnosed with stomach cancer. He died in 1966.

Virtually alone among postwar rhythm-and-blues artists, Antoine "Fats" Domino successfully made the transition to rock 'n' roll and maintained his popularity through the rock era without altering the basic character of his music. A lifelong New Orleans resident, he was influenced as much by the sounds he heard on the radio, the record player, and the jukebox as by the storied musicians of his home town. He learned to play piano with the help of an older brother-in-law, guitarist Harrison Verrett; his keyboard models included Albert Ammons, Pete Johnson, Meade "Lux" Lewis, Charles Brown, and especially Amos Milburn. Invited to sit in at a Paul Gayten concert in 1947, shortly after forming his first band, he played Ammons's "Swanee River Boogie," one of the first pieces he'd mastered.[115] He then joined a combo led by the bass player Billy Diamond, who gave the short, chubby pianist the nickname "Fats."

Domino formed another band and was performing at a Ninth Ward club called the Hideaway in late 1949 when Lew Chudd stopped in. Chudd had started Crown Records in New York in 1945, then moved to Los Angeles and founded Imperial, recording Mexican artists at first; soon he was recording rhythm-and-blues, country-western, and an assortment of ethnic music. On a trip to Houston in 1947, he saw Dave Bartholomew's band perform at the Bronze Peacock Dinner Club; Don Robey had booked Bartholomew after seeing him in New Orleans. When Chudd, on the recommendation of the white New Orleans R&B disc jockey Duke "Poppa Stoppa" Thiele, went to see Domino at the Hideaway, he brought Bartholomew along.

Domino had previously sat in with Bartholomew's band but left Bartholomew unimpressed.[116] A trumpeter who'd cut his teeth on traditional jazz, Bartholomew formed his own jump-style combo in 1946. By September 1947, when he made his recorded debut for DeLuxe, his group included bassist Frank Fields and drummer Earl Palmer—the consummate New Orleans R&B rhythm duo. His next and last DeLuxe session, in April 1949, yielded his biggest hit, "Country Boy," featuring the habanera horn vamp that would become a Crescent City rhythm-and-blues trademark.

Bartholomew recorded his first session for Imperial at the J&M studio in November 1949, backing the New Orleans blues shouter Tommy Ridgley and the Texas-born singer Jewel King. In December, Bartholomew's band—including Earl Palmer, Frank Fields, guitarist Ernest McLean, and saxophonists Herb Hardesty and Red Tyler—played on Fats Domino's debut session, which produced the hit "The Fat Man." At the Hideaway, Domino had performed "Junker Blues," which the New Orleans–born blues singer and pianist Champion Jack Dupree recorded in 1941, having learned it from his early idol Willie "Drive 'em Down" Hall. On "The Fat Man," Bartholomew's rewrite of "Junker Blues," Domino refines and accelerates Dupree's crudely pounding piano style while singing Bartholomew's lyrics, substituting "They call me the fat man, 'cause I weigh two hundred pounds" for Dupree's druggy "They call me a junker, 'cause I'm loaded all the time." In place of Dupree's piano solo, Domino does a falsetto-voice trumpet imitation. The song's melody would show up again on Smiley Lewis's "Tee Nah Nah," with Dupree's first model, Tuts Washington, on piano; Lloyd Price's "Lawdy Miss Clawdy," with Domino on piano; and Professor Longhair's "Tipitina."[117]

Following the success of "The Fat Man," Domino toured the western states with Bartholomew's band, forming a new band of his own after returning to New Orleans. Domino cut the hit "Every Night About This Time" with Bartholomew in September 1950 and toured with his band again before the trumpeter left Imperial. With his own band, Domino recorded his next hit, the chugging blues "Rockin' Chair," in April 1951 and his first R&B chart-topper, "Goin' Home," that November. With its prominent habanera horn line, "Goin' Home" inspired Guitar Slim's "The Things That I Used to Do"; its flip side was "Reeling and Rocking," a mid-tempo, triplet-driven lament whose title refers to the singer's despondency since "my baby went away and left me."

Domino had two more hits in 1952, "Poor Poor Me" and "How Long," the latter featuring a guitar solo by Harrison Verrett. Both songs are emotionally downbeat, paving the way for a bigger hit the next year, the suicidal blues "Going to the River," which was successfully covered by the Atlanta-born rhythm-and-blues singer Chuck Willis. Domino sang "woo woo woo" through much of his next hit, the rollicking "Please Don't Leave Me," which rose nearly as high on the R&B charts in 1953 as "Going to the River." Revived at the height of the rock 'n' roll craze, "Please Don't Leave Me" was recorded in 1956 by Johnny Otis, the Fontane Sisters, Johnny Burnette, and the Four Lovers, the doo-wop group that evolved into the Four Seasons.

Another of Domino's 1953 hits, "Rose Mary," looks back to "Lawdy Miss Clawdy," while "Something's Wrong" anticipates "Ain't It a Shame" with piano triplets, a "Yancey Special" bass line, and the phrase "ain't that a shame" in the lyrics. His next three hits—"You Done Me Wrong," "Thinking of You," and "Don't You Know"—recycle the keyboard triplets, habanera vamps, and shuffling backbeats of his earlier songs; "You Done Me Wrong" even reprises the wordless singing of "Please Don't Leave Me." By 1955, when the term "rock 'n' roll" came into vogue, Domino's style was fully formed. Domino performed at Alan Freed's "Rock 'n' Roll Jubilee Ball" at the beginning of that year, but there is no essential difference between his subsequent rock 'n' roll hits and the rhythm-and-blues hits that preceded them.

In March 1955 in Los Angeles, Domino recorded "Ain't It a Shame," his breakthrough smash. "Goin' Home" and "Going to the River" had already crossed over to the pop charts, but "Ain't It a Shame," a long-running No. 1 R&B hit, made the pop Top 10, with help from disc jockeys such as Bill Randle, who spun Domino's singles on his pop-oriented Cleveland radio show. It was Randle who passed an advance copy of "Ain't It a Shame" to Randy Wood of Dot Records, who had Pat Boone cover it with the title "Ain't That a Shame"; Boone's version entered *Billboard*'s pop chart a week before Domino's and rose to No. 1, both competing with and drawing attention to the original.[118] Although his "Ain't That a Shame" sounds hopelessly square today—he'd first tried to sing "isn't that a shame"—it made the R&B charts, and Boone would later claim that before he began appearing on national television, "a lot of disc jockeys and record fans around the country thought I was black."[119]

Written by Domino, "Ain't It a Shame" was arranged by Dave Bartholomew, who had returned to Imperial in 1952 and would continue to collaborate with Domino for decades. The song's "Yancey Special" riff, as played by guitarist Walter "Papoose" Nelson, has an up-to-date feel, as does the jaunty tenor saxophone solo by Herb Hardesty, but the most strikingly contemporary touch is Domino's stop-time phrasing at the beginning of each verse. At the same session, Domino modernized Big Bill Broonzy's "All by Myself" with a bouncy New Orleans second-line rhythm that he would use again on such songs as "I'm in Love Again," a Top 5 pop and No. 1 R&B hit in 1956, and the ska-like "My Girl Josephine," from 1960.

With "Ain't It a Shame," Domino became the first black rock 'n' roll artist to connect with a mass white audience, preceding Chuck Berry and Little Richard. In the fall of 1955, he recorded two songs with a distinct country-western sound: "I Can't Go On," a takeoff on Berry's "Maybellene," was an R&B hit, while "Bo Weevil," featuring a mandolin-like guitar solo by Ernest McLean, crossed over to the pop charts and was covered by the white pop singer Teresa Brewer. Adding a second-line beat to a pair of to a pair of old standards, Domino crossed over again in 1956 with "My Blue Heaven," a 1928 smash for Gene Austin, and "When My Dreamboat Comes Home," a 1937 hit for Guy Lombardo that Kay Starr revived in 1953.

Together with Ruth Brown, Little Richard, the Cadillacs, the Clovers, and Little Willie John, Domino performed for mostly black audiences on the touring "Rhythm and Blues Show of 1956"; later the same year, he performed for mostly white audiences on Alan Freed's nine-day "Rock N Roll Second Anniversary" show at the Brooklyn Paramount, along with Big Joe Turner, Frankie Lymon and the Teenagers, the Cleftones, the Harptones, the Moonglows, and the Penguins. Also in 1956, he appeared on the televised *Steve Allen Show* and *Ed Sullivan Show* and in the movies *Shake, Rattle and Rock!* and *The Girl Can't Help It*.

In June 1956, Domino cut "Blueberry Hill," which had been recorded in 1940 by Sammy Kaye, Gene Krupa, Glenn Miller, Kay Kyser, Russ Morgan, Gene Autry, Connee Boswell, and Jimmy Dorsey and in 1949 by Louis Armstrong with the white bandleader Gordon Jenkins. Domino's keyboard introduction has the sort of slicked-up country flavor that pianist Floyd Cramer would soon make part of the Nashville sound; the rest of the song is propelled by a sharp backbeat and a strong "Yancey Special" vamp, played in octaves on guitar and bass, with rhythmic triplets played together on piano and cymbal. It's a masterly arrangement by Dave Bartholomew, who excelled at varying the instrumentation of the same few basic motifs so that similar songs sounded slightly different. But Bartholomew did not think much of the recording, and "Blueberry Hill," slapped together out of unfinished takes, was released as the B-side of "Honey Chile."[120] It turned out to be Domino's biggest hit, covered by Elvis Presley, Bill Haley, Little Richard, and many others.

The year 1957 was a high point for Domino. He made television appearances on *The Perry Como Show* and Dick Clark's new *American Bandstand,* filmed a performance for the movie *The Big Beat,* and toured North America twice with Irvin Feld's "The Biggest Show of Stars"—first in the spring with an all-black program featuring Bill Doggett, LaVern Baker, Clyde McPhatter, and Chuck Berry and then in the fall on an integrated bill that included Buddy Holly and the Crickets, the Everly Brothers, Eddie Cochran, and Paul Anka. Domino also played Alan Freed's "Christmas Jubilee of Stars," along with Jerry Lee Lewis, Buddy Holly, the Everly Brothers, and a dozen other top rock acts; over Lewis's objections, Domino closed the show.[121]

Domino scored nearly a dozen pop and rhythm-and-blues hits in 1957 (mostly but not all the same ones on both charts). Sporting a habanera horn line and piano triplets, "Blue Monday" became a No. 1 R&B hit after being featured in *The Girl Can't Help It*; cut almost two years later, "I'm Walkin'," with Earl Palmer drumming a furious parade-ground backbeat, was also a 1957 R&B chart-topper. Ricky Nelson made his musical debut singing "I'm Walkin'" on his family's TV show, *The Adventures of Ozzie and Harriet,* and the record that followed was his first hit. Nelson made a much more credible rocker than Pat Boone, but his "I'm Walkin'" couldn't rival the intensity of Domino's original. A June 1957 *Time* magazine article on Domino reported that "his reputation rivals that of Elvis Presley with rock 'n' roll fans," but Lew Chudd, taking note of Presley's visual allure, signed Nelson, a handsome white teenager, to Imperial in August.[122]

Domino's career began to wind down in 1958, as Chudd pressured him to record more pop-oriented material, but he still had a half-dozen R&B and pop hits, including the timeless rocker "Whole Lotta Loving." In 1959, with Elvis Presley in the army, Buddy Holly killed in a plane crash, and Alan Freed caught up in a payola scandal, Domino continued to score hits, including a pair of old standards, "When the Saints Go Marching In" and "Margie," that made the pop but not R&B charts, as well as the rock 'n' roll classics "I'm Ready," "I Want to Walk You Home," and "I'm Gonna Be a Wheel Some Day," the last a rhythm-and-blues chart-topper.

Accompanied only by a rhythm section, Domino celebrates rock 'n' roll to a torrid second-line beat on "I'm Ready" ("I'm ready, I'm willin', and I'm able to rock 'n' roll all night"), with handclapped rhythms counterpointing the drums in Afro-Caribbean style. The lyrics ("Don't send me no letter 'cause I can't read") underscore the music's visceral impact, at opposite poles from the intellectual rock that would emerge in the 1960s.[123] "I Want to Walk You Home," a rudimentary tune with a relatively orthodox boogie bass line in place of Domino's customary habanera vamp, was his final No. 1 R&B hit. The flip side, "I'm Gonna Be a Wheel Some Day," had been submitted by the Louisiana songwriter Roy Hayes to Dave Bartholomew, who first produced it in 1957 for Imperial with the New Orleans R&B singer Bobby Mitchell and his band, the Toppers.

The contrast between Mitchell's stiff reading and Domino's easy delivery—as well as the much livelier rhythms of Domino's studio band—helps explain Domino's enduring appeal. In a sense, he was the anti-Elvis, with his unimpressive appearance, unassuming personality, and unaffected musicianship, yet his artless singing and piano playing conveys the spirit of rock 'n' roll with a deep-dyed authenticity few others could match. Although fights and even riots had broken out at his shows almost from the beginning of his career, he was seen as nonthreatening, an artist who won audiences over with his musical ingenuousness rather than personal charisma.

In the 1960s, Domino had more than twice as many pop as R&B hits, including covers of old standards and country songs. He made the pop Top 10 for the last time in 1960 when Bartholomew added strings to his production of Bobby Charles's ruefully nostalgic composition "Walking to New Orleans." Domino reached the No. 2 spot on *Billboard*'s R&B chart in 1961 with "Let the Four Winds Blow," which he'd written with Bartholomew but which Bartholomew had first recorded under his own name as "Four Winds" in 1955; Bartholomew also produced Roy Brown's hit version in 1957. Roy Montrell's clipped guitar chords give Domino's "Let the Four Winds Blow" the feeling of second-line ska.

Domino switched to the ABC-Paramount label in 1963, scoring several minor hits through 1964. After a stint on Mercury, he had one more hit in 1968 with a cover of the Beatles' "Lady Madonna," a song originally inspired by Domino.[124] Although his heyday was over, he never fell from fame, and he continued to tour and record, maintaining a tight band as younger players gradually replaced the veterans. He headlined rock 'n' roll revival shows, played Las Vegas, performed in Europe and Japan (he was especially popular in England), and cut albums for Mercury, Reprise, Atlantic, United Artists, and other labels. In 1980 he appeared in the movie *Any Which Way You Can,* starring Clint Eastwood; Domino had his final hit when his soundtrack recording of "Whiskey Heaven" was released as a single and made the country charts.

Domino pared down his touring and recording schedule in the 1980s and 1990s, spending more and more time at home in New Orleans. One of the few early R&B artists who retained his royalty rights, he was able to live comfortably on the proceeds from his many reissue albums. When he did perform, however, he was still able to summon up the old magic, his rhythmic grooves and New Orleans drawl as irresistible as ever. He was in the first group of artists inducted into the Rock and Roll Hall of Fame in 1986, and he was awarded a Grammy Lifetime Achievement Award in 1987, although he'd never been nominated for a regular Grammy. In 1993, he released a rare major-label album, *Christmas Is a Special Day,* on EMI. Fears that he'd perished during Hurricane Katrina in 2005, followed by news of his rescue, brought Domino more attention than he'd had in decades. Showered with additional honors, he rebounded with the 2006 album *Alive and Kickin',* recorded mostly before the hurricane, and with a 2007 performance at Tipitina's in New Orleans.

Lloyd Price is another New Orleanian who made a successful transition from rhythm-and-blues to rock 'n' roll. Born in the suburb of Kenner, Louisiana, he sang along with the records of Louis Jordan, Charles Brown, Amos Milburn, and Rosco Gordon on the jukebox of his parents' shop, then formed a band in high school. According to Lew Chudd, the teenage Price was singing at the Hideaway in New Orleans, accompanied by Fats Domino, when he visited in 1949, but Chudd was only interested in Domino.[125] Three years later, Dave Bartholomew heard Price singing a song he'd made up, based on a catchphrase used by the local radio disc jockey James "Okey Dokey" Smith, and invited Price to audition for Art Rupe, who was making his first trip to New Orleans in search of new talent. By Rupe's account, Price began to cry when told that Rupe only had time to listen to one song, but Rupe was so impressed by Price's "Lawdy Miss Clawdy" that he canceled his flight to Los Angeles and stayed in New Orleans to record it.[126] By Price's account, Rupe returned to New Orleans some weeks later for the recording.[127]

In March 1952, Price cut "Lawdy Miss Clawdy" with Dave Bartholomew's band at Cosimo Matassa's studio. Sitting in on piano, Fats Domino plays the distinctive introduction, after which Price shouts essentially the same melody as on Domino's "The Fat Man," with drummer Earl Palmer playing a heavy, shuffling backbeat. The record was a long-running No. 1 R&B hit, and though it never made the pop charts, it is said to have sold unusually well to whites.[128] Elvis Presley recorded "Lawdy Miss Clawdy" in 1956, and it was issued on the flip side of his "Shake, Rattle and Roll." Roy Orbison's Teen Kings group and Frankie Valli's Four Lovers group also cut "Lawdy Miss Clawdy" in 1956, and Price's cousin Larry Williams included it on his 1959 album *Here's Larry Williams*. Many others covered the song in the ensuing years, among them Little Richard, the Beatles (in a medley from the 1970 film *Let It Be*), Led Zeppelin (in concert, 1970–1972), Fats Domino, and Bill Haley.

Recording again with Bartholomew's band, Price reused the "Lawdy Miss Clawdy" melody on his 1952 hit "Restless Heart," which was outsold by its flip side, "Oooh-Oooh-Oooh." Price had another double-sided hit for Specialty in 1953 with the remarkably percussive "Tell Me Pretty Baby" (from the same session that yielded "Oooh-Oooh-Oooh"), backed with "Ain't It a Shame," which despite its New Orleans–style piano triplets and "Yancey Special" bass line was recorded in Los Angeles. But then Price was drafted and spent two years in the army, mostly in Korea and Japan, his career on hold. He returned in late 1955, just as Little Richard's first hit, "Tutti-Frutti," entered *Billboard*'s R&B chart. Ironically, it was Price who was responsible for putting Richard in touch with Art Rupe, but after a few new singles failed to chart, Price and Specialty parted company.[129]

Price then founded his own KRC (Kent Record Company) label in Washington, D.C., which in January 1957 issued its first single, Price's "Just Because." Price later admitted to have borrowed the melody from the New Orleans rhythm-and-blues duo Shirley & Lee, evidently from their 1956 Aladdin release "A Little Word," which is based on the famous aria "Caro nome" from Verdi's 1851 opera *Rigoletto*.[130] As Price tells it, Larry Williams, who got his start as Price's chauffeur and valet, took "Just Because" to Art Rupe in Los Angeles, claiming to have written it, and recorded it for Specialty. But according to the Specialty producer Bumps Blackwell, Williams covered the song at Rupe's instigation.[131] Unable to compete with the larger label, Price leased his record to ABC-Paramount, whose rerelease of "Just Because" made both the R&B and pop charts, outselling Williams's Specialty disc, which only charted R&B.

Rupe quickly pressed Williams into service as a less flamboyant Little Richard imitator. Williams had already cut the rock 'n' roll hits "Short Fat Fannie" and "Bony Moronie"—as well as "Slow Down," later popularized by the Beatles—by the fall of 1957, when Richard renounced rock 'n' roll to pursue religion. Williams had one more hit the following year, "Dizzy, Miss Lizzy," which was also covered by the Beatles; the two sides of another 1958 Williams single, "Bad Boy" and "She Said Yeah," were covered respectively by the Beatles and the Rolling Stones. But though he continued to record for a number of labels after Specialty dropped him following a narcotics arrest in 1959, he would not have another hit until 1967, when his collaboration with Johnny "Guitar" Watson on "Mercy, Mercy, Mercy" charted. As the West Coast producer for the OKeh label, Williams fashioned a couple of albums for Little Richard, who had returned to secular music. From the late 1960s to the late 1970s, he withdrew from the music scene, involving himself in drugs and prostitution, but did act in a few movies. Around 1977, he threatened to shoot Little Richard over a drug debt.[132] In 1978, he released a poorly received funk album on Fantasy, with songs such as "Bony Moronie (Disco Queen)." In 1980, he was found dead of a gunshot wound to the head at his Los Angeles home.

After "Just Because," Lloyd Price reorganized his KRC label, signing a distribution deal with Atlantic's Atco subsidiary; he cut several singles, but none was successful, so in 1958 he agreed to record directly for ABC-Paramount. Late that year, he released his "Stagger Lee," a slick arrangement of the folk song "Stagolee" featuring the Ray Charles Singers, a white chorus that chants "Go, Stagger Lee!" Both lyrics and melody are similar to those on the New Orleans pianist Archibald's 1950 R&B hit "Stack-A'Lee," and Archibald ultimately succeeded in winning a share of the composer's credit, along with Price and his manager, Harold Logan—a valuable acknowledgement, as the record, originally intended as the B-side of "You Need Love," was a No. 1 smash on both the pop and R&B charts.

Price next charted in 1959 with "Where Were You (on Our Wedding Day)?" which was covered by Billy Joel for the soundtrack of the 1999 movie *Runaway Bride*. He followed with the even more mainstream-oriented "Personality" and "I'm Gonna Get Married," both arranged by Don Costa (who would win recognition as an arranger for Frank Sinatra) and featuring the Ray Charles Singers; both were No. 1 R&B and Top 5 pop hits, but "Personality" is much better remembered and became Price's signature song. A string of lesser hits in the same poppy mold followed, but though some dozen of his ABC-Paramount sides made the charts between 1958 and 1960, none did subsequently. After another couple of years, Price formed his own Double-L label, scoring a pair of hits in late 1963 and early 1964 with an oddly phrased version of the jazz standard "Misty" and an adaptation of "Bill Bailey, Won't You Please Come Home?" titled "Billie Baby." But Price had no further hits on Double-L, which folded in the mid-1960s, nor on Monument, Reprise, Hurd, Ludix, or JAD, for which he also recorded during that decade.

In the late 1960s, Price opened his own Midtown Manhattan nightclub and formed another record label, both called Lloyd Price's Turntable. In 1969, he had a minor hit on Turntable, "Bad Conditions," recorded in Jamaica in a psychedelic-soul style inspired by the Temptations' "Cloud Nine." But then Harold Logan was murdered, and Price, who'd previously traveled to Ghana on business, began spending time in Africa. During this period, Price met Don King, with whom he would promote the "Rumble in the Jungle" championship boxing match between George Foreman and Muhammad Ali in the Congo in 1974; Price also produced the Zaire 74 music festival, which was documented in the 2008 film *Soul Power*. He recorded for a number of labels in the 1970s, then moved to Lagos, Nigeria, returning to the United States in 1984. In 1993, he toured Europe with Jerry Lee Lewis, Little Richard, and Gary U.S. Bonds; in the 2000s, he performed in the "Four Kings of Rhythm and Blues" tour with Jerry Butler, Gene Chandler, and Ben E. King. He published a biography written by his associate William "Dollar Bill" Waller, *Lawdy Miss Clawdy: The True King of the 50's, The Lloyd Price Story,* in 2010 and planned to stage a musical based on the book.

Eddie and Leo Mesner of Aladdin Records made their first trip to New Orleans in the fall of 1951, ahead of Art Rupe. In 1952, Cosimo Matassa played Eddie a demo tape that a group of teenage singers had paid him two dollars to record. Mesner recruited the lead singers, Shirley Goodman and Leonard Lee, to redo their song, "I'm Gone," for Aladdin that June with Dave Bartholomew's band.[133] Riding a distinctive "Yancey Special"–like bass line that Bo Diddley would reuse on his 1959 hit "I'm Sorry," "I'm Gone" alternates Lee's down-to-earth tenor with Goodman's shrill soprano, creating a sort of lovers' dialogue—an approach later copied on Jamaican ska and reggae records. "I'm Gone" was a No. 2 R&B hit for Shirley & Lee, as the duo was credited. Although their real-life relationship was strictly platonic, they were billed as the Sweethearts of the Blues, and they continued their lyrical courtship on songs such as "Shirley Come Back to Me," "Shirley's Back," and "The Proposal," all with similar bass lines. But they didn't chart again until 1955, when they cut the No. 2 R&B hit "Feel So Good," which extends the romantic theme and responsive format of the preceding singles but with a different, descending bass line and in a more exultant mood. The white singer Johnny Preston had a pop hit in 1960 with a cover version titled "Feel So Fine."

"Feel So Good" set the stage for Shirley & Lee's "Let the Good Times Roll," a No. 1 R&B smash that crossed over to the pop charts in 1956. "Let the Good Times Roll" borrows the introductory riff from "Feel So Good" but uses it more extensively, along with a more conventional boogie bass line. With its rollicking Lee Allen saxophone solo, the record has a strong New Orleans feel, but the song has become more than just a Crescent City anthem, covered by everyone from Conway Twitty to Barbra Streisand to the Animals; the Philadelphia singer/producer Bunny Sigler had a pop and R&B hit in 1967 with "Let the Good Times Roll & Feel So Good." Shirley & Lee's next hit, "I Feel Good," crossed over from R&B to pop later in 1956, but their popularity diminished thereafter, and they released their last Aladdin single in 1959. They had a few minor hits for the short-lived Warwick label, including a 1960 remake of "Let the Good Times Roll," and cut several records for Imperial, but by 1963 they had broken up.

Shirley Goodman moved to Los Angeles, where she sang on sessions for Dr. John, the Rolling Stones, and others. She recorded with Jessie Hill as Shirley & Jessie and with Brenton Wood as Shirley and Alfred, again alternating rather than harmonizing with her male partner. Leonard Lee remained in New Orleans, recording for such labels as Broadmoor and Trumpet. In 1972, the two reunited for an oldies concert at Madison Square Garden. In 1974, Sylvia Robinson invited Goodman to record for Robinson's Vibration label; the result was "Shame, Shame, Shame," credited to Shirley (And Company)—a No. 1 R&B hit in 1975 that crossed over to the pop charts and spurred the nascent disco craze. After another minor hit or two, Goodman moved back to New Orleans and withdrew from the music scene. Lee, who'd become a social worker, died of a heart attack in 1976, at the age of forty. Goodman engaged Lee's survivors in a long legal battle over the composer's royalties for "Let the Good Times Roll"; having suffered a stroke, she moved to California, dying some ten years later in 2005.

Although he grew up in Macon, Georgia, Little Richard recorded most of his classic rock 'n' roll hits at Cosimo Matassa's studio in New Orleans, accompanied by musicians from Dave Bartholomew's band. Born Richard Penniman, he sang gospel songs as a youth; his favorite singer was Sister Rosetta Tharpe, but he took his falsetto whoops from another gospel diva,

Marion Williams. As a teenager, he began singing in traveling minstrel and medicine shows, sometimes dressed as a woman. At a theater in Atlanta, he met Billy Wright, a local blues shouter who had several national R&B hits between 1949 and 1951. By Richard's admission, he was heavily influenced by Wright, who wailed the blues like Roy Brown and wore makeup, loud clothing, and a high-piled hairdo.[134]

Around the same time, Richard also met a flamboyant singer, Esquerita (né S. Q. Reeder), who taught him to play piano. Wright put him in touch with the white Atlanta rhythm-and-blues disc jockey Zenas "Daddy" Sears, who got him a contract with RCA Victor. Little Richard cut four sides for the label at an Atlanta radio studio in October 1951, backed by the trumpeter Roy "Willie" Mays's band; one of them, "Every Hour," became a regional hit, helped by airplay from Sears. The flip side, "Taxi Blues," contains an eight-bar couplet on the bridge—"I can't stand to see my gal tonight / When I beat her up, she's an awful sight"—that's set to the same melody as the verses of "Blue Suede Shoes." On these tracks, Richard copies Wright's style; Wright reciprocated by covering "Every Hour," altering the lyrics and changing the title to "Every Evenin'."

Little Richard did a second RCA session in the same jump-blues vein in January 1952, but it produced no hits, so he returned to Macon and performed in clubs. After his father was killed, he took a day job washing dishes but soon became the lead tenor in a vocal-harmony quartet called the Tempo Toppers, who were accompanied on trumpet, organ, and drums by a married couple calling themselves the Duces of Rhythm. Booked around the South by the Macon promoter and club owner Clint Brantley (or Brantly), the Tempo Toppers sojourned in New Orleans, where Richard absorbed the influence of Earl King, then moved on to Houston, where Don Robey signed them to Peacock, possibly at Lloyd Price's instigation.[135] In February 1953, the Tempo Toppers recorded four sides, backed by the Duces of Rhythm and Roy Montrell's band. Blending blues with gospel music and doo-wop, songs such as the Dominoes-influenced "Fool at the Wheel" ("Slippin' and slidin' all over the road / because he's drivin' a brand new Ford"), while not full-fledged rock 'n' roll, certainly qualify as proto-rock. But Little Richard's mature style, if one can call it that, is hardly in evidence.

Richard had a rocky relationship with Don Robey, who once beat him so badly he later need a hernia operation.[136] Still, Robey afforded him another studio session in October 1953, where he recorded his last four sides for Peacock with Johnny Otis's band and without the Tempo Toppers. Not released until 1956, after his breakthrough with "Tutti-Frutti" on Specialty, "Little Richard's Boogie" is more jump-blues than boogie-woogie, with a boogie bass line that's mostly tacit. The flip side, Richard's composition "Directly from My Heart to You," has the same melody as his classic 1957 hit "Lucille," only slower. The shuffling blues "I Love My Baby," backed with the ballad "Maybe I'm Right," was not released until 1957, by which time Richard had already rerecorded "Maybe I'm Right" and "Directly from My Heart to You" for Specialty.

Parting with Peacock, Little Richard formed his own band, the Upsetters, and toured the South for Clint Brantley performing songs by Roy Brown, Fats Domino, B. B. King, Little Walter, and Billy Wright, plus such originals as "Tutti-Frutti."[137] In 1954, Richard and the Upsetters accompanied the Nashville singer Christine Kittrell on a pair of driving rhythm-and-blues sides for the Republic label, "Lord Have Mercy (I'm So Lonely)" and "Call His Name." After meeting Lloyd Price, Richard made a demo tape of the gospelly ballads "Wonderin'" and "She's My Star" (or "He's My Star") and sent it to Specialty, where the Seattle-born African American producer Bumps Blackwell heard it and urged Art Rupe to sign Richard. "The songs were not out-and-out gospel, but I could tell by the tone of his voice and all those churchy turns that he was a gospel singer who could sing the blues," Blackwell remembered. "And that's what Art Rupe had told me to find."[138]

Although Little Richard was based in Macon and Specialty in Los Angeles, the label decided to record him in New Orleans with a studio band including Lee Allen and Red Tyler on saxophones, Justin Adams on guitar, Frank Fields on Bass, and Earl Palmer on drums. "They were Fats Domino's session men," said Bumps Blackwell.[139] On his first two Specialty dates, September 13 and 14 of 1955, Richard began by cutting gospelly material such as "Wonderin'" and the Dorothy LaBostrie composition "I'm Just a Lonely Guy" and blues such as Leiber and Stoller's "Kansas City" and Richard's own "All Night Long." Here his voice sounds rougher and more emphatic than on his Peacock or RCA records, but except on the shuffling "Kansas City," complete with falsetto whoops, the sound is more soul than rock 'n' roll.

As Blackwell tells it, "Tutti-Frutti" was the last song recorded at the September sessions, since LaBostrie needed time to rewrite the lyrics.[140] The original words, "Tutti frutti, good booty / If it don't fit, don't force it / You can grease it, make it easy," apparently refer to anal sex, although they may derive from Barrel House Annie's "If It Don't Fit (Don't Force It)," which avoids anal insinuations but was still too raunchy to release when it was recorded in 1937. LaBostrie, however, claimed she came up with the song on her own. "Little Richard didn't write none of 'Tutti Fruitti' [sic]," she told the writer Jeff Hannusch.[141] But Phil Walden, who co-founded Capricorn Records, recalled seeing Richard perform "Tutti-Frutti," with the refrain "Tutti frutti, good booty," at a show in Macon around 1953.[142] "Tutti-Frutti" was the only song from Richard's September 1955 sessions where he played piano; the others featured Huey Smith.

Facing tough competition from the Platters' "The Great Pretender" and the Cadillacs' "Speedoo," Little Richard's "Tutti-Frutti" topped out at No. 2

on *Billboard*'s rhythm-and-blues chart. It also made the pop Top 20 but was quickly eclipsed by Pat Boone's cover version, for which the British-born songwriter Joe Lubin was hired to further scrub the already cleaned-up lyrics. For example, Lubin replaced "She knows how to love me, yes indeed / Boy, you don't know what she do to me" with "She's a real gone cookie, yessiree / Pretty little Susie is the gal for me." The beat behind Boone is much stiffer than on the original, but ultimately it's his foursquare singing that gives his version its flat-footed feel. Elvis Presley, singing LaBostrie's lyrics, is much more convincing on his version of "Tutti-Frutti," released in March 1956 on his first album, *Elvis Presley*. Yet even Elvis can't match Little Richard's vocal richness or effortless fervor—Richard's, after all, was the voice that inspired Otis Redding and James Brown.

Arriving before Carl Perkins's "Blue Suede Shoes" or Presley's "Hound Dog," "Tutti-Frutti" helped define the rock 'n' roll sound, raising the bar for rock intensity—what seemed at the time to be mere wildness, although every note is firmly controlled. It also transformed Little Richard from gospel-blues shouter to rock 'n' roller, setting the frantic tone for his ensuing hits. His next hit, recorded in February 1956 with Edgar Blanchard replacing Justin Adams on guitar, was the even more frenetic "Long Tall Sally," which Blackwell had Richard accelerate in order to keep the likes of Pat Boone from covering it—unsuccessfully, as it turned out. According to Blackwell, a teenage girl from Mississippi named Enortis Johnson had written crude lyrics—"Saw Uncle John with Long Tall Sally / They saw Aunt Mary comin' / So they ducked back in the alley"—to which Blackwell and Richard added additional words and a melody.[143]

"Long Tall Sally" was Little Richard's all-time best seller, topping the R&B charts and making the pop Top 10. With its twelve-bar verse-and-refrain structure, suggesting a hopped-up hokum song, and its chugging beat, similar to the guitar rhythm Chuck Berry would use on such songs as "Sweet Little Sixteen" and "Johnny B. Goode," "Long Tall Sally" typifies rock 'n' roll even more than "Tutti-Frutti" does. Like "Tutti-Frutti," it was covered by both Pat Boone and Elvis Presley: Boone's rendition, again with bowdlerized lyrics, is even lamer than his "Tutti-Frutti," and this time Richard outsold him; Presley's version, released on his second album, *Elvis,* is much livelier than Boone's but more strained and less energetic than Richard's. The Beatles cut "Long Tall Sally" in 1964, with Paul McCartney imitating Richard's falsetto wail. Others who covered the song include Wanda Jackson, the Kinks, Led Zeppelin, Eddie Cochran, Gene Vincent, and Jerry Lee Lewis.

The flip side of "Long Tall Sally" was "Slippin' and Slidin' (Peepin' and Hidin')," recorded at the same February 1956 session. Little Richard may have adapted "Slippin' and Slidin'" from "I'm Wise," recorded for the Apollo label the same month by singer-pianist Eddie Bo and for Imperial's subsidiary Post label in January by singer Ruth Durand. Jivier but less nonsensical than "Slippin' and Slidin'," "I'm Wise" more explicitly rebukes a cheating lover. Bo and Durand both sing, "Oh, you big conniver, two-timin' jiver"; Bo follows with, "Been told a long time ago," Durand with, "Been told that a long time ago." Richard sings, "Oh, big conniver, nothin' but a jiver / I done got hip to your jive." The melody for "I'm Wise" was taken from Al Collins's 1955 single "I Got the Blues for You," the very first release on Johnny Vincent's Ace label, on which Eddie Bo plays piano. But Little Richard also recorded three rough takes of "Slippin' and Slidin'" in November 1955 that were not issued until many years later.

All the "Slippin' and Slidin'" variations, from Collins's to Richard's, were recorded in New Orleans, all ride habanera bass lines, and all feature similarly shuffling, Latin-like second-line drumbeats, with the backbeat becoming more pronounced on successive versions. Earl Palmer said that "the only reason I started playing what they come to call a rock-and-roll beat came from trying to match Richard's right hand [on piano]. . . . Little Richard moved from a shuffle to that straight eighth-note feeling."[144] Palmer claimed to have played a shuffle on "Tutti-Frutti" and then switched to a "rock beat" on subsequent Little Richard sessions. But "Long Tall Sally" and "Slippin' and Slidin'" clearly exhibit shuffle rhythms, while Palmer's alleged shuffle on "Tutti-Frutti" is difficult to discern.

The same session that produced "Long Tall Sally" and "Slippin' and Slidin'" also yielded the relatively relaxed "Miss Ann," where Earl Palmer plays a backbeat over what he calls Richard's "straight eighth-note" piano, as well as the raucous "Rip It Up," with wilder lyrics ("Well, it's Saturday night and I just got paid / Fool about my money, don't try to save") than music. Richard's next session, in May, produced "Ready Teddy," faster than "Rip It Up" but similar in melody and lyrics. Both songs were composed by songwriter John Marascalco (with Bumps Blackwell also credited), both feature stop-time sections and Lee Allen saxophone solos, and both were released on the same single, with "Rip It Up" topping *Billboard*'s R&B chart, "Ready Teddy" making the Top 10, and both crossing over to the pop chart. "Rip It Up" was covered by Bill Haley and Elvis Presley in 1956, by the Everly Brothers in 1958, and by Chuck Berry in 1961, but only Haley's version charted. Curiously, only the Everly Brothers alter Richard's line "I'm gonna rock it up, and ball tonight," changing it to "I'm gonna rock it up, have a ball tonight." "Ready Teddy" was covered by Presley in 1956, by Buddy Holly in 1957, by Gene Vincent in 1958, and by the British rock idol Cliff Richard in 1959.

At end of July 1956, Little Richard returned to the J&M studio and recorded the frantic "Heebie-Jeebies," with Lee Allen soloing over Richard's percussive eighth-note piano. The song, written by John Marascalco and Maybelle Mae Jackson, is derived from "Tutti-Frutti, as evidenced by an alternate take where Richard sings, "wop-bop-a-leema-lama-wop-bobbaloo." In September, Richard cut "She's Got It," a version of his own previously recorded (but subsequently released) composition "I Got It," a sort of street-vendor's song that Marascalco reworded for Richard to perform in *The Girl Can't Help It,* along with "Ready Teddy" and the title track. The movie has Jayne Mansfield sashaying past a nightclub owner she's trying to impress just as Richard, on stage with his band, sings the inaccurate description "big blue eyes, long black hair." At Richard's insistence, "She's Got It" was recorded in Los Angeles with his touring group, the re-formed Upsetters. "I told Art Rupe that my band was . . . better than those studio musicians from New Orleans," he said. "I didn't see why the Upsetters couldn't back me on my records the same way as they did on the stage."[145] Still, the New Orleans studio band on "I Got It"—Edgar Blanchard, Frank Fields, Lee Allen, Red Tyler, and Earl Palmer—rocks considerably harder than the Upsetters on "She's Got It." Richard's voice is the primary instrument on both tracks, carrying not only the melody but much of the rhythm, most noticeably on the stop-time sections. "She's Got It" is one of the clearest examples of the twelve-bar verse-and-refrain structure in Little Richard's repertoire, with Richard singing the melody of a boogie-woogie bass line in the third and fourth measures of each verse. It was issued on the same single as "Heebie-Jeebies," and both sides made the R&B Top 10.

Little Richard's next session, in New Orleans in October 1956, yielded three rock 'n' roll classics. The first to be released was "The Girl Can't Help It," heard over the opening credits of the movie; written by Bobby Troup, who also wrote "(Get Your Kicks on) Route 66," and recorded with the vocal group the Robins in addition to the usual New Orleans musicians, it made the R&B Top 10 and the pop Top 50 in early 1957. "Jenny, Jenny," paired on a single with "Miss Ann" (with both songs credited to Little Richard and Enortis Johnson), was released in May 1957 and made the R&B and pop Top 10. "Good Golly, Miss Molly," credited to Maralasco and Blackwell but with a piano introduction inspired by Jackie Brenston's "Rocket 88," was not released until February 1958 (after an accelerated, Blackwell-produced version by the Valiants, a black vocal quartet, was issued on the Keen label) and also made both charts' Top 10. All three songs would be repeatedly covered, "The Girl Can't Help It" by Conway Twitty, Bobby Vee with the Crickets, the Animals, Wayne Fontana, and others; "Jenny, Jenny" by Carl Perkins, Jerry Lee Lewis, the Sonics, and, as part of "Jenny Take a Ride," by Mitch Ryder and the Detroit Wheels; and "Good Golly, Miss Molly" by Jerry Lee Lewis, the Astronauts, the Swinging Blue Jeans, Gene Vincent, the Everly Brothers, Creedence Clearwater Revival, and, adapted into Spanish as "La Plaga" ("The Plague"), by the pioneering Mexican rock band Los Teen Tops.

"Lucille," recorded with the Upsetters in January 1957 but released before "Jenny, Jenny," was a No. 1 R&B hit, though it didn't quite make the pop Top 20. Based on Little Richard's composition "Directly from My Heart to You," "Lucille" is credited to Richard and Al Collins, who provided the melody for "Slippin' and Slidin'." "Keep A Knockin'," recorded at the same session as "Lucille" and released a few months after "Jenny, Jenny," reached the No. 2 spot on the R&B chart and made the pop Top 10. The song was originally credited to Little Richard alone, but shares of the composer's credit were later given to Bert Mays and to J. Mayo Williams, who produced Mays's "You Can't Come In" for Vocalion in 1928. Nevertheless, Richard almost certainly got the idea for "Keep A Knockin'" from Louis Jordan's 1939 version. Unlike other early versions, Jordan's contains the verse "I hear you knockin' but you can't come in / I know you been drinkin' gin"; according to Richard's biographer Charles White, "one verse with the words 'I'm drinkin' gin and you can't come in' was . . . deleted from [Richard's] final release." White also says that the original track, less than a minute long, was repeated more than once to create the record as issued.[146] In any case, Richard's stripped-down, speeded-up "Keep A Knockin'," sung in a hoarse shriek to a tune distinct from that of any previous version, is the one best remembered today.

Little Richard had his heyday in 1956 and 1957, when he recorded some sixteen pop and R&B hits, performed in three movies (*The Girl Can't Help It, Don't Knock the Rock,* and *Mister Rock and Roll*), and headlined rock 'n' roll package shows. His concerts brought black and white fans together, whipping them into a screaming frenzy. In an era when even a performer as obviously gay as Liberace could deny his homosexuality and get away with it, Richard's perceived threat to social mores was mainly his sexual appeal to teenage white girls. "We decided that my image should be crazy and way-out," he said, "so that adults would think I was harmless."[147]

But at the height of his fame, while touring Australia in October 1957, Little Richard abruptly abandoned rock 'n' roll to become a preacher. On his return to the United States, he cut one more session for Specialty with the Upsetters, which produced the fiery hit "Ooh! My Soul." After a farewell concert at the Apollo Theatre, he enrolled at a religious college, toured the U.S. as an evangelist together with Joe Lutcher, and recorded gospel songs for several labels. Although he had stopped performing secular music, he had three hits in 1958, "Good Golly, Miss Molly," "Ooh! My Soul," and "Baby Face," the last a second-line version of the 1926 standard recorded at the same session as "The Girl Can't Help It," "Jenny, Jenny," and "Good Golly, Miss Molly."

Booked for what he thought would be a gospel-singing tour of England in October 1962, Little Richard was prevailed upon to sing his rock 'n' roll hits, to the overwhelming approbation of the audience. He finished the tour with the up-and-coming Beatles as his opening act, then spent a month playing clubs in Hamburg, Germany, with the four Liverpudlians who idolized him. He recorded a single secular track for Specialty, keeping open the option of returning to gospel music, before returning to Britain in October 1963, where he toured with the still-little-known Rolling Stones. "I couldn't believe the power of Little Richard on stage," said Mick Jagger. "He was amazing."[148] At the end of the tour, Richard filmed the performance documentary *It's Little Richard* for Granada Television.

Back in Los Angeles, Little Richard recorded his final Specialty session in April 1964 with a hornless band including Don "Sugarcane" Harris on bass and violin, Harris's duo partner Dewey Terry on guitar, and Earl Palmer on drums. The label released the single "Bama Lama Bama Loo," patterned after Richard's 1950s hits, but it peaked disappointingly at No. 82 on the Hot 100 chart (*Billboard* did not publish an R&B chart in 1964). Nevertheless, Richard put a new band together, including the unknown Jimi Hendrix on guitar, and toured the country performing rock 'n' roll. Signing with Vee-Jay Records, he mostly rerecorded his own and other artists' old rock hits, but in 1965 he cut the soul-style "I Don't Know What You've Got but It's Got Me—Part 1," written by Don Covay. Released not long before Vee-Jay went bankrupt, it was a pop and R&B hit.

Little Richard then recorded a pair of albums for Modern, mostly reprising earlier hits, and another pair for OKeh—one of contemporary material, the other of old hits, both produced by Larry Williams and featuring Johnny "Guitar" Watson. The contemporary album, *The Explosive Little Richard,* yielded the minor 1966 R&B hit "Poor Dog (Who Can't Wag His Own Tail)," propelled by a distinctive bass line midway between Motown and funk. In 1967, Richard cut three soul-style singles for Brunswick, but none was successful. He did not record again until 1970, but he maintained a hectic performance schedule, touring throughout North America. Meanwhile, he led an orgiastic lifestyle, drinking heavily and growing increasingly dependent on cocaine.

In 1970, Little Richard cut a swamp-rock album for Reprise, *The Rill Thing,* which generated two minor hits, "Freedom Blues" and "Greenwood Mississippi." He also appeared on many television shows that year. In 1971 and 1972, he recorded two more Reprise albums, *King of Rock and Roll,* including covers of songs by the likes of Hank Williams, Martha and the Vandellas, and the Rolling Stones, and *The Second Coming,* flavored with New Orleans funk. Without another hit, Richard moved on to the United label, cranking out the quickie soul album *Right Now!* in 1973. He cut singles for the Greene Mountain, Manticore, and Mainstream labels before recording another new album of his old hits for the "as seen on TV" company K-tel in 1976. Although many of his post-Specialty recordings were in a contemporary rhythm-and-blues vein, his audience, once predominantly black, had become overwhelmingly white.

His paranoia fueled by drug and alcohol abuse, Little Richard returned to religion in 1977 after several people close to him died. Renouncing sex, drugs, and rock 'n' roll, he traveled the country as an evangelist and bible salesman. In 1979, he recorded a gospel album, *God's Beautiful City,* for the World label. Setting spiritual lyrics to a rock 'n' roll beat, he cowrote the quasi-religious song "Great Gosh A'Mighty! (It's a Matter of Time)" with organist Billy Preston; featured in the 1986 movie *Down and Out in Beverley Hills,* it was Richard's final hit.[149] In 1989, he sang "Lucille" at an AIDS benefit hosted by Cher, marking his return to rock.

In the 1990s, Little Richard cut a children's album for Walt Disney Records and appeared in movies, television shows, and music videos. He remained active through the following decade, performing live, making television appearances (including commercials), and recording album tracks. In 2009, he underwent hip surgery. Although he sings rock 'n' roll, he has put debauchery behind him and still sometimes functions as a minister.

His long career notwithstanding, Little Richard's reputation rests almost entirely on the records he made for Specialty between 1955 and 1957. Together with Fats Domino's hits, these gave early rock 'n' roll a distinct New Orleans tinge. But Richard's gritty, pitch-perfect voice, conveying rhythm as much as melody, trumps his instrumental accompaniment and transcends geography.

No one, not even Elvis Presley, had a greater impact on the sound of rock 'n' roll than Little Richard, whose songs were covered by Bill Haley, Carl Perkins, Eddie Cochran, Buddy Holly, the Everly Brothers, Gene Vincent, and Jerry Lee Lewis, as well as Presley and Pat Boone. Among the better-known black artists who imitated Richard, besides Larry Williams, were Etta James, whose "Tough Lover" was issued in 1956; Marvin Phillips of the duo Marvin and Johnny, who released "Have Mercy Miss Percy" under the name Long Tall Marvin in 1956; Richard Berry, who recorded "Yama Yama Pretty Mama" in 1956; Lowell Fulson, who recorded "Rock This Morning" in late 1957; Dee Clark, who did "24 Boy Friends" in 1957 and "Oh, Little Girl" (accompanied by the Upsetters) in 1958; Joe Tex, whose "You Little Baby Face Thing" came out in 1958; Don Covay, who joined Richard's entourage in 1957 and released "Rockin' the Mule" as Pretty Boy in 1958; Otis Redding, who did "Fat Girl" around 1961; and Ike and Tina Turner, whose "This Man's Crazy" came out in 1963. Lesser-known imitators included Big Danny Oliver, Big Al Downing, Little Ike, Ronnie Molleen, Ba Ba Thomas, Wild Child Gibson, Earl Wade, Rockin' Bradley, Cledus Harrison, Tommy Louis (aka Kid Thomas), Ricky Ricardo, and Bunker Hill—the last a former gospel singer (born David Walker) whose 1962 recording of "The Girl Can't Dance" (backed by Link Wray and the Raymen) is so raucous that, in the words of one listener, "This guy makes Little Richard sound like Pat Boone."[150] (Screamin' Jay Hawkins cut what sounds like a Little Richard imitation, which wasn't released for decades, but in fact his recording of "What That Is" dates from January 1955, eight months before Richard's

"Tutti-Frutti" and twenty months before Hawkins's breakthrough hit, "I Put a Spell on You.")

Unlike Fats Domino, whose brand of rhythm-and-blues was simply reclassified as rock 'n' roll when that term gained currency, Little Richard abruptly switched from jump blues to rock 'n' roll when he recorded "Tutti-Frutti." By then, Bill Haley, Domino, and Chuck Berry had already broken through with "Rock Around the Clock," "Ain't It a Shame," and "Maybellene"; Elvis Presley's first national hit, "Baby Let's Play House," had already made the country charts, although his first national pop hit, "Heartbreak Hotel," had yet to be released. But Richard's "Tutti-Frutti" sounded wilder than any previous rock song. Pat Boone's toned-down version helped raise awareness of Richard's original, even as it cut into Richard's sales. Presley, the King of Rock 'n' Roll, gave the song his royal imprimatur by covering it after Richard's and Boone's records had already been released. But Presley could not eclipse Richard as he had Big Boy Crudup or Big Mama Thornton.

Contrary to the opinion of Little Richard's biographer David Kirby, Richard did not give birth to rock 'n' roll, though he did raise its energy level to a degree seldom, if ever, equaled since.[151] Following World War II, rhythm-and-blues songs with verse-and-refrain hokum structures, backbeats, shuffle rhythms, boogie-woogie bass lines, and other characteristics of early rock 'n' roll became prevalent; after Wynonie Harris's "Good Rockin' Tonight," songs with the word "rock" in the title and/or lyrics proliferated. By the early 1950s, the sound that would soon be known as rock 'n' roll was solidly established.

When rock 'n' roll made its bombshell impact on the white pop market in 1955, the music's rudimentary phase as a form of rhythm-and-blues ended. Rock songs, by white as well as black artists, attracted black listeners for a few more years; for example, Elvis Presley's "(Let Me Be Your) Teddy Bear" and "Jailhouse Rock," Jerry Lee Lewis's "Whole Lot of Shakin' Going On," Paul Anka's "Diana," Jimmie Rodgers's "Honeycomb," and the Everly Brothers' "Wake Up Little Susie" were all No. 1 R&B hits in 1957. But with the rise of soul music in the 1960s, rock songs and white artists practically vanished from the R&B charts.

The black rock 'n' roll era, beginning at least half a dozen years before the white one, lasted little more than a decade, divided almost evenly between pre- and post-Elvis periods. The black rock artists who, like Chuck Berry, Bo Diddley, or the Coasters, emerged after Presley, or who, like Fats Domino and Little Richard, continued to have hits after Presley's rise, remain well-known today. Those whose peak years preceded Presley, such as Joe and Jimmy Liggins, Amos Milburn, Wynonie Harris, and the Orioles, have been largely forgotten. Yet it was during the pre-Elvis years that the foundations of rock 'n' roll were laid, and a good deal of the superstructure erected. While not all postwar rhythm-and-blues qualifies as rock 'n' roll, much of it is rock in all but name. The distinction between the two genres—at that time, at least—seems mainly racial.

Chapter Eight

Rock Love

BLUE-EYED R&B

The rock 'n' roll revolution is usually thought to have begun with the emergence of artists such as Bill Haley and Elvis Presley, both of whom could be considered country singers who crossed over to the pop market. But before them had come black-influenced white pop singers such as Ella Mae Morse, Frankie Laine, Kay Starr, and Johnnie Ray, who covered rhythm-and-blues records or simply sang with an African American feeling. White artists had sung with an African American feeling long before that, of course, and had covered R&B records at least since Louis Prima's "Who Threw the Whiskey in the Well?" in 1945. But by the early 1950s, it was not uncommon for record companies such as Capitol, who had both Starr and Morse under contract, to have pop singers cover rhythm-and-blues as well as country-western records.

Morse's father was a dance-band drummer from England and her mother a singer and pianist from Texas; as a young girl in Paris, Texas, Ella Mae befriended and sang along with a black blues guitarist. Although her records sold well enough in her heyday, she never became as famous as her contemporaries Doris Day, Rosemary Clooney, and Patti Page, perhaps because of her black-tinged style. Although she didn't sound as black as most rhythm-and-blues singers or as southern as most country singers, she seemed as natural in those two idioms as she did singing pop or jazz. As one of the only white artists to have multiple No. 1 rhythm-and-blues hits, she may have alienated some white listeners while attracting others. It's been said that Elvis Presley told her he learned to sing by listening to her records.[1] But she was largely forgotten after her recording career ended and has only recently gained recognition as a foremother of rock 'n' roll.

Shortly after "Cow-Cow Boogie," Morse recorded two more hits with Freddie Slack's band. The jiving "Mr. Five by Five," written by Gene DePaul and Don Raye in ostensible tribute to Count Basie's rotund singer Jimmy Rushing, had been introduced by Grace McDonald in the 1942 Ritz Brothers movie *Behind the Eight Ball*. The song was a No. 1 pop hit for Harry James's band with singer Helen Forrest and a lesser hit for the Andrews Sisters, but in a reverse crossover, Morse's version reached the No. 1 spot on the Harlem Hit Parade, as well as the pop Top 10. Morse made the pop Top 20 with "Get on Board, Little Chillun," adapted by DePaul and Raye from an African American spiritual and first performed by the Delta Rhythm Boys in the 1943 movie *Crazy House*.

Morse's next four hits, all recorded in October 1943 with Dick Walters's band, were also borrowed from Hollywood. The Andrews Sisters had a No. 1 pop hit with "Shoo-Shoo Baby," which they sang in the movie *Follow the Boys*; Morse sang it in the movie *South of Dixie* and once more topped the Harlem Hit Parade, also making the pop Top 5. The flip side, "No Love, No Nothin'," which Alice Faye had sung in the 1943 musical *The Gang's All Here,* made the pop Top 5 as well. In 1944, Dinah Shore sang "Tess's Torch Song (I Had a Man)" in the musical comedy *Up in Arms,* and Nancy Walker sang "Milkman, Keep Those Bottles Quiet," another DePaul-Raye composition, in the musical *Broadway Rhythm*; Morse covered both songs on the same single for a second double-sided pop hit.

Morse continued to chart with "The Patty Cake Man," a jived-up nursery rhyme, in late 1944; "Captain Kidd," a send-up of the Charles Laughton movie of the same title, in 1945; and "Buzz Me," a No. 2 R&B hit cover version of a No. 1 R&B hit by Louis Jordan, in early 1946—the last two with Billy May's band. Later in 1946, she scored with "The House of Blue Lights," accompanied by Freddie Slack's combo. She recorded similar pop boogies with different groups through 1947, then retired to raise a family but came back in 1951, recording for Capitol with Nelson Riddle's band. Turning from the bluesy or jivey style of her earlier recordings, she took more of a middle-of-the-road approach and, on her first Riddle session, found a new direction with a cover of Red Foley's country smash "Tennessee Saturday Night." Her second session with Riddle produced "The Blacksmith Blues," a country-tinged pop song that rose to No. 3 on the *Billboard* chart—Morse's biggest hit without Slack.

Morse's next Riddle session, in February 1952, yielded covers of two country hits, Jack Guthrie's "Okie Boogie" and Little Jimmy Dickens's "A-Sleeping at the Foot of the Bed." In May, accompanied by Joe Lippman's band, she covered two rhythm-and-blues songs, Amos Milburn's propulsive "Greyhound" and Hadda Brooks's calypso-tinged "Jump Back, Honey, Jump Back"; Gene Vincent would record the latter in rockabilly style in 1956. After cutting another pop song with Riddle, Morse duetted with Tennessee

Ernie Ford on Ford's composition "I'm Hog-Tied Over You" and the Delmore Brothers' "False Hearted Girl." Accompanied by Riddle again, Morse covered Hank Snow's "The Gal Who Invented Kissin'" as "The Guy Who Invented Kissin'" and, singing in French and English, covered Link Davis's "Big Mamou," a version of the Cajun classic "Le Grand Mamou."

Morse's final hit came in 1953 with a pop cover of singer-guitarist Danny Overbea's rhythm-and-blues record "40 Cups of Coffee," accompanied by Dave Cavanaugh's band; the song, with its twelve-bar verse-and-refrain structure and stop-time breaks, would be covered as a rocker by Bill Haley in 1957. Also in 1953, she recorded a series of R&B covers with Cavanaugh's band that included the Dominoes' "Have Mercy Baby," the Drifters' "Money Honey," the Ravens' "Rock Me All Night Long," Bull Moose Jackson's "I Love You, Yes I Do," LaVern Baker's "How Can You Leave a Man Like This?" and Ruth Brown's "Daddy Daddy," "5-10-15 Hours," and "Teardrops from My Eyes"—all released on Morse's 1954 album *Barrelhouse, Boogie, and the Blues*.

Morse kept covering rhythm-and-blues and rock 'n' roll songs through the mid-1950s, among them the Clovers' "Lovey Dovey," the Spaniels' "Goodnite Sweetheart, Goodnite," Jesse Stone's "Smack Dab in the Middle" (recorded by Stone under the name Charlie Calhoun and also covered by the Deep River Boys, the Du Droppers, the Jacks, Joe Williams with Count Basie's band, and, a decade later, by Ray Charles), Bill Haley's "Razzle-Dazzle," Fats Domino's "Ain't It a Shame," Nappy Brown's "Piddily Patter Patter," Boyd Bennett's "Seventeen," and the Coasters' "Down in Mexico." In addition, she was the first to record several songs by black rhythm-and-blues songwriters. But her last Capitol sessions, for the 1957 album *The Morse Code,* featured mainstream pop standards such as "My Funny Valentine," "I Can't Get Started," and "You Go to My Head." Morse made no further studio recordings after parting with Capitol, but she did continue to tour, with decreasing frequency, well into the 1980s. She died in 1999, at the age of seventy-five.

Frankie Laine's muscular belting marked a sharp departure from the crooning style that had been dominant among male pop singers at least since the rise of Bing Crosby. According to the author Jonny Whiteside, "Laine's intense style owed nothing to Crosby, Sinatra or Dick Haymes. Instead he drew from Billy Eckstine, Joe Turner, Jimmy Rushing, and with it Laine had sown the seeds from which an entire new perception and audience would grow."[2] Although he did not sound particularly black (and does not credit Eckstine, Turner, or Rushing as influences in his autobiography), Laine successfully impersonated Nat "King" Cole on a couple of his earliest recordings and was assumed to be black by many listeners when they first heard his 1947 breakthrough record, "That's My Desire."[3]

Born Francesco LoVecchio to Sicilian immigrant parents in Chicago, he discovered Bessie Smith's "Bleeding Hearted Blues" amid his family's collection of opera and Italian-pop records. "The first time I laid the needle down on that record I felt cold chills and an indescribable excitement," he remembered.[4] He began singing in his elementary school choir and later sang for the Depression-era dance marathons at Chicago's Merry Garden Ballroom. In 1937, at Perry Como's instigation, he briefly joined Freddie Carlone's band in Cleveland; the following year, he was hired to sing at a New York radio station and changed his name to Frankie Laine. He struggled for the next few years, working day jobs as well as singing, before moving to Los Angeles in 1943.

Laine cut his first record for the Beltone label in 1944, then signed with Atlas, which had him imitate Nat "King" Cole on two songs and let him be himself on a number of others. Hoagy Carmichael heard Laine at Billy Berg's Hollywood club and got him a contract with Mercury, for which he initially cut the 1929 standard "I May Be Wrong (but I Think You're Wonderful)" as the B-side of a single whose A-side featured the comedian Artie "Mr. Kitzel" Auerbach singing "Pickle in the Middle with the Mustard on Top." The disc jockey Al Jarvis, whom Laine had befriended, played "I May Be Wrong" on the radio, and Laine's career began to take off.

It was at Billy Berg's that Laine introduced what he announced as "a brand new song"—actually a 1931 Tin Pan Alley composition, "That's My Desire," that Laine had heard during his stay in Cleveland.[5] The song was rapturously received by the clubgoers, and Laine recorded it for Mercury in August 1946 with a band led by trumpeter Manny Klein. Laine's record made the Top 5 on both the pop and R&B charts in 1947 but was outsold by the sweet-band leader Sammy Kaye's version with singer Don Cornell. "That's My Desire" was also covered that year by Hadda Brooks, Ella Fitzgerald, Louis Armstrong, Martha Tilton, Art Mooney, and Woody Herman; it has since been recorded by Pat Boone, Gogi Grant, the Four Freshmen, the Channels, the Flamingos, Jerry Lee Lewis, Buddy Holly, Dion and the Belmonts, Patsy Cline, Jim Reeves, Cliff Richard, the Hollies, Chris Isaak, and James Brown, among others—with all renditions based on Laine's rather than any earlier recording.

Laine scored eight more pop hits through the end of 1949, including one, "You're All I Want for Christmas," that also charted R&B. Most of his early hits are in a richly arranged pop or jazz vein, with Laine convincingly delivering not only Nat "King" Cole's bluesy "That Ain't Right" (retitled "Baby, That Ain't Right") but also Fats Waller's "Black and Blue" and the older "Shine," both clearly intended for a black singer. Charting in the spring of 1948, "Baby, That Ain't Right" may have been the first white cover of a rhythm-and-blues song to make *Billboard*'s pop list.

During the second musicians' union recording ban, which lasted throughout 1948, Laine began working with Mercury's new A&R director, Mitch Miller. A classical oboist with a distinctive Vandyke beard, Miller initiated new production techniques that would influence the way rock music was recorded, notwithstanding his reputation for making bland pop music and his professed distaste for rock 'n' roll. Detecting a "universal quality" in Laine's voice, Miller sought to broaden his stylistic range, and in June 1949 Laine recorded "That Lucky Old Sun," a Tin Pan Alley pseudo-folk song that, in Laine's opinion, had a "Western flavor."[6] Similar in theme to "Ol' Man River," the song became a No. 1 hit for Laine and also charted in 1949 for Vaughn Monroe, Sarah Vaughan, Frank Sinatra, Louis Armstrong, and Bob Houston. It would later be covered by LaVern Baker, Jerry Lee Lewis, Sam Cooke, Bobby Darin, Dean Martin, the Isley Brothers, Aretha Franklin, Ray Charles, Jackie Wilson, Willie Nelson, James Brown, Tom Jones, Jerry Garcia, Johnny Cash, and Brian Wilson, among others. Recorded in Russian by the Ukrainian-born singer Mark Bernes, "That Lucky Old Sun" was performed in the Soviet Union as an anticapitalist anthem.

Laine had previously recorded his next hit, the Frank Loesser ballad "Now That I Need You" (from the 1949 movie *Red, Hot and Blue*), also a hit for Doris Day. At Miller's urging, he followed with "Mule Train," a Tin Pan Alley cowboy song that has Laine describing the goods he's peddling—"There's a plug of chaw tobaccy for a rancher in Corona / a gee-tar for a cowboy way out in Arizona"—while driving his mule team to the accompaniment of whip cracks. The gimmicky production became Laine's second No. 1 smash, quickly covered by Bing Crosby, Tennessee Ernie Ford, Vaughn Monroe, and Gordon MacRae. "Mule Train" has been cited for its precedent-setting use of sound effects, and the author Will Friedwald has described Miller, disparagingly, as "the inventor of rock 'n' roll mentality."[7]

According to Friedwald: "Miller established the primacy of the producer, proving that even more than the artist, the accompaniment, or the material, it was the responsibility of the man in the recording booth whether a record flew or flopped. Miller also conceived of the idea of the pop record 'sound' per se: not so much an arrangement or a tune, but an aural texture (usually replete with extramusical gimmicks) that could be created in the studio and then replicated in live performance, instead of the other way around. Miller was hardly a rock 'n' roller, yet without these ideas there could never have been rock 'n' roll. 'Mule Train,' Miller's first major hit (for Frankie Laine) and the foundation of his career, set the pattern for virtually the entire first decade of rock. The similarities between it and, say, 'Leader of the Pack,' need hardly be outlined here."[8]

In early 1950, "The Cry of the Wild Goose," a histrionic western-tinged three-minute melodrama—"My heart knows what the wild goose knows / and I must go where the wild goose goes"—became Laine's third and final chart-topper. His eight subsequent Mercury hits are in a more conventional jazz-pop mold, except for "The Metro Polka," the "Wild Goose"–like "Swamp Girl," and a version of Sousa's "Stars and Stripes Forever" with lyrics added. Miller moved to Columbia Records in 1950 and Laine followed in 1951, combining the devil-as-woman theme of his Mercury hit "Satan Wears a Satin Gown" with mock-flamenco rhythms on the No. 2 smash "Jezebel."

By the end of 1953, Laine had charted twenty-seven more hits, including the flip side of "Jezebel," eight duets with Jo Stafford, two duets with the juvenile singer Jimmy Boyd (best known for "I Saw Mommy Kissing Santa Claus"), and one duet with Doris Day. Of these hits, only "Tonight You Belong to Me" and "Way Down Yonder in New Orleans," both composed in the 1920s, have the jazzy flavor of Laine's earlier records. Instead, he turned toward pure pop, with such exceptions as the rhythmic African American chant "Hambone," the South African folk-song adaptation "Chow, Willy," the Hank Williams hits "Hey, Good Lookin'," "Settin' the Woods on Fire" (retitled "Tonight We're Setting the Woods on Fire"), and "Your Cheatin' Heart," and the Carl Smith country hit "Hey Joe!"—all but the last two featuring Stafford.

Laine's "High Noon (Do Not Forsake Me)" outsold Tex Ritter's soundtrack version from the 1952 western *High Noon*, leading Laine to record the actual soundtrack themes for the westerns *Blowing Wild* (1953), *Man Without a Star* (1955), *Strange Lady in Town* (1955), *3:10 to Yuma* (1957), *Gunfight at the O.K. Corral* (1957), *Bullwhip* (1958), and *Blazing Saddles* (1974), as well as the television series *Rawhide* (1959–1966), *Gunslinger* (1961), and *Rango* (1967). Laine, who appears on several album covers wearing cowboy outfits, recorded additional western songs such as "Cool Water," "Along the Navajo Trail," and "(Ghost) Riders in the Sky," not to mention "Champion the Wonder Horse," a cover of the theme to the mid-1950s TV western *The Adventures of Champion*.

Laine acted or played himself in the movies *Make Believe Ballroom* (1949), *When You're Smiling* (1950), *Sunny Side of the Street* (1951), *Rainbow 'Round My Shoulder* (1952), *Bring Your Smile Along* (1955), *He Laughed Last* (1956), and *Meet Me in Las Vegas* (1956). He hosted his own TV variety shows and made many other television appearances, singing and occasionally acting.

Laine had his first religious hits, "I Believe" and "Answer Me, Lord Above," in 1953. With the line, "She was mine yesterday / I believed that love was here to stay," "Answer Me, Lord Above," adapted from a German song, is the apparent inspiration for the Beatles' "Yesterday," although Paul McCartney probably heard the British tenor David Whitfield's version along with Laine's, the two having topped the *New Musical Express*'s UK Singles Chart simultaneously in late 1953.[9] After recording the black-gospel-style hit single "Rain, Rain, Rain" with the white harmony group the Four Lads in 1954, Laine released the similarly styled album *Frankie Laine and the Four Lads* in 1956. Also in 1956, he duetted with Johnnie Ray on a remarkably exuberant cover of Sister Rosetta Tharpe and Marie Knight's gospel hit "Up Above My Head, I Hear Music in the Air."

Laine had Top 10 hits with the western-flavored "Moonlight Gambler" in 1956 and the folkish "Love Is a Golden Ring" in 1957 but did not make the national charts between 1957 and 1963. He released a string of Columbia albums into the early 1960s, including jazz-, folk-, and western-themed LPs as well as collaborations with the French composer-arranger Michel Legrand. He left Columbia in 1964 and spent two hitless years with Capitol before returning to the lower ranks of the charts with ABC, for which he adopted more of an easy-listening sound. He had his last hits in 1969, one of which, "You Gave Me a Mountain," was written by the country singer Marty Robbins and later performed by Elvis Presley. He cut a pair of rock-tinged albums for the small Amos label in 1970 and 1971, then launched his own Score label. He continued to record into the 2000s and gave his last performance in 2005, dying of heart failure in 2007 at the age of ninety-three.

Born Katherine Starks in Dougherty, Oklahoma, and raised in Dallas, Texas, and Memphis, Tennessee, Kay Starr sang country, pop, and western swing on the radio from an early age. In her mid-teens, she joined Joe Venuti's band, with which she performed intermittently into the 1940s. In 1939, she briefly worked in Bob Crosby's and Glenn Miller's bands, making her recording debut with Miller. Venuti's band broke up when the United States entered World War II, and Starr went on to Wingy Manone's and Charlie Barnet's bands, remaining with Barnet for a couple of years. She made a few recordings with Barnet, including two eloquent 1944 readings of the Dust Bowl lament "Share Croppin' Blues," one on a V-Disc and the other for Decca. But in 1944, she temporarily lost her voice and left the band.

Having settled in Los Angeles, Starr recorded jazzy songs for several small labels with various groups in 1945 and 1946; at Dave Dexter's request, she also cut two numbers with an all-star group for Capitol Records, one of which, "If I Could Be with You," was released on the 1945 album *The History of Jazz, Vol. 3: Then Came Swing*. In 1947, she signed with Capitol, which steered her in a less jazzy direction, but with Peggy Lee, Ella Mae Morse, Jo Stafford, and Margaret Whiting already under contract, the label could not find enough new material for Starr.[10] Her first Capitol release, "I'm the Lonesomest Gal in Town," was a 1912 composition; her first four hits for the label were covers of recent hits by the sweet-band leaders Blue Barron and Russ Morgan and the pop singers Connie Haines and Perry Como.

In 1950, Starr covered Pee Wee King's country hit "Bonaparte's Retreat," which King had adapted from a traditional fiddle tune. Her brass-accompanied version made the pop Top 5, and she followed with a hit cover of Red

Foley's "M-I-S-S-I-S-S-I-P-P-I" and a pair of double-sided hit duets with Tennessee Ernie Ford, separated by a hit cover of Louis Prima's "Oh, Babe!" Her next two hits were a cover of Rosemary Clooney's 1951 smash "Come On-A My House" and a revival of the 1925 composition "Angry."

"Wheel of Fortune," written by Bennie Benjamin and George David Weiss (the same interracial team responsible for Starr and Ford's hit "I'll Never Be Free"), had already been recorded by the jazz singer Johnny Hartman, the Baltimore doo-wop group the Cardinals, the Billy Williams Quartet, Dinah Washington, and the white singer Sunny Gale with the black Eddie Wilcox Orchestra by the time Starr covered it in January 1952, taking most closely after the Gale/Wilcox rendition. The Cardinals' and Washington's versions made the R&B charts, those by the singer Bobby Wayne and the youthful Bell Sisters duo charted pop, and the Gale/Wilcox record made both charts, but Starr's version, a No. 1 pop smash, outsold them all. Washington's delivery may be more poignant and world-weary, but Starr makes the song wholly her own, belting the lyrics with stirring conviction. Although it's a ballad without a backbeat or boogie-woogie bass line—"a cartoonish melodramatic song," in the words of Will Friedwald—parts of it, especially the bridge, where Starr overdubs her own backing harmonies, have a slow-motion rock 'n' roll feel.[11]

Starr recorded her next hit, the Donald O'Connor–composed ballad "I Waited a Little Too Long," with the Lancers, the same harmony group featured on her following, double-sided hit, "Kay's Lament"/"Fool, Fool, Fool." For jazz-oriented critics such as Friedwald, this venture into rhythm-and-blues represents Starr's descent into campy commercialism. "Behind Starr's intense statement," he writes of "Kay's Lament," "you get a hodgepodge of trends corny enough in themselves that acquire the sheen of absolute awfulness when alloyed: bongo drums, electric guitar, and six [actually four] idiots chanting 'Sing it, Sister Katie!'"[12]

Starr's subsequent Capitol hits—including Cole Porter's "Allez-Vous En," Edith Piaf's "If You Love Me (Really Love Me)" (translated from "Hymne à l'amour"), and the 1927 standard "Side by Side"—are in a mainstream pop mold. She stuck to the middle of the road after switching to RCA Victor in 1955, following the Top 20 hit "Good and Lonesome" with the chart-topping "Rock and Roll Waltz," a huge seller in 1956 even though it's in 3/4 time and doesn't try to appeal to teenagers. She scored eight more pop hits with RCA, but only two made the Top 40 and just one, "My Heart Reminds Me," reached the Top 10. She had three last hits in the early 1960s after returning to Capitol—two covers of country hits by Buck Owens and Jim Reeves and a solo rerecording of "I'll Never Be Free."

The bluesy cast that distinguishes Starr's early recordings can hardly be heard on her later hits, but she did return to jazzy form on albums such as RCA's *Rockin' with Kay* (1958) and Capitol's *Movin'* (1959), *Jazz Singer*

(1960), and *I Cry by Night* (1962). Her final RCA album, *I Hear the Word* (1959), consists of traditional African American spirituals such as "Sometimes I Feel Like a Motherless Child," "Rock-a-My Soul," and "Go Down, Moses," sung persuasively by Starr with a white chorus. After parting with Capitol for the second time, in 1966, she toured the U.S. and England and played hotels in Las Vegas and Reno, Nevada. She continued to record jazz albums such as *How About This* with Count Basie's band (ABC-Paramount, 1969) and *Back to the Roots* (GNP Crescendo, 1975), as well as the album *Country* (GNP Crescendo, 1974).

In the 1980s, Starr toured with a shifting group that included Rosemary Clooney, Helen O'Connell, Martha Raye, Margaret Whiting, and Kay Ballard in the revue *4 Girls 4*. In 1993, she performed in Britain with Pat Boone's "April Love Tour"; introducing a medley of "I'm Walkin'," "Great Balls of Fire," and "Rock Around the Clock" at the Glasgow Royal Concert Hall, she says over a hard drumbeat, "Sometime along about '55 / rock 'n' roll took over from jive / Everybody sayin' it was new as could be / Sure sounded awfully familiar to me."[13] In 2001, she cut "Blue and Sentimental" (a Count Basie tune she'd first recorded in 1957) with Tony Bennett for *Playin' with My Friends: Bennett Sings the Blues,* a star-studded album of duets. As of this writing, she continues to perform occasionally. Acclaimed as an outstanding jazz singer with an extraordinary facility for the blues as well as a flair for country music, she has also been recognized as a rock 'n' roll forebear.

ROCK STARS

As an up-and-coming young singer, Johnnie Ray idolized Kay Starr, along with Billie Holiday. Born in rural Oregon, Ray grew up listening to country, gospel, pop, and jazz; he sang in church and played boogie-woogie piano. But when he was thirteen years old, an accident caused the loss of hearing in his left ear; undeterred, he sang with a hearing aid. After graduating from high school, he performed in dives in Portland, Los Angeles, and Cleveland, enjoying little success until he was engaged by the Flame Show Bar in Detroit, a club that featured black artists. There he signed a management contract with Al Green, befriended LaVern Baker, and absorbed rhythm-and-blues material into his repertoire.

In 1951, Columbia Records revived the OKeh label as an R&B imprint. On a trip to Detroit, Danny Kessler, the label's A&R director, discovered Ray and put him in touch with Bernie Lang, who became his new manager. In May, Ray recorded for OKeh with Maurice King and His Wolverines, an all-black band, and the resulting single was marketed to an African American audience. His mature style appears fully formed on the thumping "Whiskey and Gin," backed with the ballad "Tell the Lady I Said Goodbye"—both written by Ray. His high tenor resembled a woman's contralto, leading some early listeners to believe he was female. Like Frankie Laine, he belted rather than crooned, but his phrasing was more idiosyncratic. He stretched words and syllables and fell out of time with his accompanists, possibly because he couldn't hear them; most distinctively, a catch in his voice made it seem that he was about to break into sobs. His impassioned delivery was accentuated by his stage act, in which he kicked over the piano bench and stood at the keyboard or took the microphone from its stand and roamed the stage. He would tear at the curtains, throw his arms forward, fall to his knees, and roll on the floor. In his exaggerated display of abandon, as well as his appropriation of rhythm-and-blues elements, he was a rock 'n' roll prototype.[14]

Mitch Miller heard Ray in New York and was impressed enough to propose that he record "Cry," a song written by a black night watchman in Pittsburgh named Churchill Kohlman and first recorded for New York's small Cadillac label by the white singer Ruth Casey. At Miller's suggestion, Ray was accompanied on the October 1951 session by the Four Lads, a gospel-oriented white harmony quartet from Canada. For the flip side of "Cry," Miller let Ray record his own maudlin composition "The Little White Cloud That Cried." The lachrymose pairing was not merely Ray's first national hit but a tremendous double-sided pop and R&B smash, with "Cry" topping both charts. With its extended wails and broken rhythms, "Cry" would remain Ray's best-known and perhaps most characteristic song, earning him such sobriquets as the Nabob of Sob and inspiring a Stan Freberg parody, "Try," that was a Top 20 hit in its own right.

In early 1952, Ray moved from OKeh to the parent Columbia label and scored his second double-sided Top 10 hit, "Please, Mr. Sun," backed with "Here Am I—Broken Hearted," both produced by Mitch Miller and featuring the Four Lads. With lines such as "Babble to her, Mr. Brook / Kiss her for me, Miss Raindrop," the mawkish "Please, Mr. Sun," a 1951 Tin Pan Alley composition, is right up Ray's alley, and he gives it a much more emotional reading than the black pop singer Tommy Edwards or the phlegmatic Perry Como, both of whom also had hits with the song. Ray's quavering rendition of "Here Am I—Broken Hearted" is likewise more ardent than any of the hit versions from 1927, when the song was introduced. The Four Lads are prominent in the mix, giving the recording the feel of a rock 'n' roll ballad from the later 1950s. Underscoring the connection, Tommy Edwards revived his own wistful 1951 pop hit "It's All in the Game" for a No. 1 pop and R&B hit in 1958 using a new arrangement similar to the one on Ray's "Here Am I—Broken Hearted." Ironically, Ray used an older-style big-band arrangement when he recorded "It's All in the Game" for his 1959 British album *A Sinner Am I*.[15]

Ray broke from the tearful formula on his next two hits, the tongue-in-cheek, Middle Eastern–flavored "What's the Use" (cowritten by Ross Bagdasarian, who would later record the speeded-up voices of Alvin and the Chipmunks under the name David Seville) and an update of the 1930 standard "Walkin' My Baby Back Home." But he was back in histrionic form on the double-sided hit "All of Me," a throbbingly jazzy version of the 1931 standard, backed with Ray's own semi-confessional composition "A Sinner Am I," which hints at his bisexual orientation with lines such as "a love like this was never made for man's imagination." His following hit "Love Me (Baby Can't You Love Me)," cowritten by the pop-classical composer Alec Wilder, was given a sort of doo-wop arrangement with help from the Four Lads.

Ray's final 1952 hit was the double-sided "A Full-Time Job"/"Ma Says, Pa Says," a pair of steel-guitar-flavored duets with Doris Day. "A Full-Time Job" is a cover of Eddie Arnold's country smash, while "Ma Says, Pa Says" is an adaptation of a South African folk song by Josef Marais, the same white South African émigré responsible for the original version of Frankie Laine's "Chow, Willy." Ray's biographer Jonny Whiteside speculates that Mitch Miller produced the record at least in part to dispel Ray's image as a rhythm-and-blues-influenced singer. He quotes Miller as saying, "I didn't want Johnnie to be noted just for his black-inspired singing."[16]

Ray's string of hits continued in 1953, beginning with a cover of the white gospel singer Martha Carson's rocking "I'm Gonna Walk and Talk with My Lord" that features the Four Lads.[17] His remaining 1953 hits were the old standards "Somebody Stole My Gal," "All I Do Is Dream of You," and "Please Don't Talk about Me When I'm Gone"; a lightweight duet with Doris Day on the country songwriter Fred Rose's "Candy Lips"; and a fervent treatment of "With These Hands," a Tin Pan Alley ballad that the British pop singer Lee Lawrence had introduced in 1951 and that Ray gives much more of a rock 'n' roll flavor than Eddie Fisher does on his more successful version.

Ray had nearly as many hits in 1954, including an update of Irving Berlin's 1919 composition "You'd Be Surprised," which Marilyn Monroe also recorded in 1954; the double-sided "Hey There"/"Hernando's Hideaway," both from the Broadway musical *The Pajama Game*; and the syrupy "To Ev'ry Girl—To Ev'ry Boy (The Meaning of Love)," cowritten by Jerry Samuels, who, under the name Napoleon XIV, would have a novelty hit in 1966 with "They're Coming to Take Me Away, Ha-Haaa!" Turning away from Miller's template, Ray also charted with a cover the Drifters' "Such a Night"; his singing, accompanied by the Four Lads, can't really compare to Clyde McPhatter's with the Drifters, but one hears in McPhatter's rendition some of the same vocal manipulations that Ray based his style on. Elvis Presley's 1960 recording of "Such a Night" became a hit in 1964.

Ray had his heyday in the early 1950s, performing at top nightclubs such as the Copacabana in New York and Ciro's in Los Angeles, touring Britain and Australia, making frequent television appearances, and acting as well as singing in the movie *There's No Business Like Show Business*. Occasionally he appeared on the same bill with rhythm-and-blues artists such as Big Jay McNeely, Tiny Bradshaw, or the Dominoes. Ray was popular enough among African Americans that in March 1953 *Ebony* magazine published an interview with him under the headline "Negroes Taught Me to Sing." On the strength of a brief but well-publicized marriage, followed by a torrid affair with the influential newspaper columnist Dorothy Kilgallen, he was able to survive scandalous rumors about his sexuality and even the revelation that he'd been arrested a few months before recording "Cry" for soliciting sex from an undercover policeman.

He also survived the onset of rock 'n' roll. In 1955, he covered Big Joe Turner's "Flip Flop and Fly," but it was not a hit, with Ray sounding stiff and unconvincing compared to Turner (though not to Pat Boone, who recorded the song in late 1956) on lines such as "I'm like a Mississippi bullfrog sittin' on a hollow stump." In July 1956, at Mitch Miller's insistence, Ray recorded "Just Walking in the Rain," a song that had been written by an African American inmate at the Tennessee State Prison, Johnny Bragg, and recorded for the Sun label in 1953 by the Prisonaires, a vocal harmony group consisting of Bragg and four fellow inmates. According to Peter Guralnick, "It was the song that put Sun Records on the map . . . and, very likely [a July 15, 1953, newspaper article about the Prisonaires in the *Memphis Press-Scimitar* was], the item that captured the attention of Elvis Presley as he read about the studio, the label, and . . . Sam Phillips."[18] Although it features Ray Conniff's orchestra and chorus, as well as a professional whistler, Ray's straightforward rendition is much more of an individual showcase than the Prisonaires' Ink Spots–style original, and it was a major hit, kept out of the No. 1 spot by Elvis Presley's "Don't Be Cruel." (The song's bridge section bears a suspicious melodic resemblance to the one on the Silhouettes' 1958 smash "Get a Job.")

Ray followed with the double-sided hit "You Don't Owe Me a Thing"/ "Look Homeward, Angel." Like "Just Walking in the Rain," "You Don't Owe Me a Thing," recorded in November 1956, opens with whistling, after which Ray gives a teen-pop reading—Jonny Whiteside calls it "bubblegum jazz"—to Marty Robbins's country composition.[19] The earlier session that produced "Just Walking in the Rain" also yielded "Look Homeward, Angel" (first recorded in 1956 by the white harmony group the Four Esquires), which anticipates Roy Orbison's 1961 hit "Running Scared" with strummed rhythms reminiscent of Ravel's *Boléro* and a climactic finale. As if to validate Ray's teen-anthem approach, two white pop groups—the Fortunes, from Birmingham, England, and the Monarchs, from Louisville, Kentucky—released versions of "Look Homeward, Angel" in 1964, and Cliff Richard included the song on a 1965 album.

Also in November 1956, Ray recorded *The Big Beat,* an album mostly of rhythm-and-blues covers, among them Faye Adams's "Shake a Hand," Julia Lee's "Lotus Blossom," Savannah Churchill's "I Want to Be Loved (but Only by You)," and Ruth Brown's "So Long." Included as well were the Cats and the Fiddle's "I Miss You So" and four songs that Count Basie had recorded: "Sent for You Yesterday (and Here You Come Today)," "I'm Gonna Move to the Outskirts of Town," "Everyday I Have the Blues," and "How Long, How Long Blues." Rounding out the album were "Trouble in Mind," "I'll Never Be Free," and "Pretty Eyed Baby," the last a Mary Lou Williams and/or Snub Mosely composition that Frankie Laine had recorded with Jo Stafford in 1951.[20] Listening to *The Big Beat,* it's hard to believe that rock 'n' roll had just exploded onto the national scene. While Ray had a better feel for black music than most white artists of the era, he remained more of a pop singer interpreting rhythm-and-blues than a genuine rocker, and the recording sounds as if it had been made before rather than after Elvis Presley's arrival.

Ray's next two hit singles were both chirpy pop-rockers, complete with backbeats. "Yes Tonight, Josephine," with the chorus "Yip yip way bop de boom ditty boom," was followed by "Build Your Love (on a Strong Foundation)," which sounds like a trial run for Mitch Miller's early-1960s television show *Sing Along with Mitch.* Ray's next two albums, however, showed little rock influence. *In Las Vegas,* recorded at the Desert Inn in October 1957, mixes his hits with old standards such as "Ain't Misbehavin'," "As Time Goes By," and "Yesterdays," but even "Yes Tonight, Josephine," without the chorus and with its backbeat muted, is drained of rock 'n' roll feeling. *'Til Morning,* recorded with the jazz pianist Billy Taylor's trio in March 1958, consists entirely of standards, the oldest, "It All Depends on You," dating from 1926 and the newest, "Teach Me Tonight," from 1953.

Nonetheless, Ray was quickly recognized as a rock 'n' roll forerunner. "Indeed, there are times when his tunestering shows lines indicating that he fathered the rock 'n' roll movement, with the latter breed of singers expanding on an original and clean model propounded by Ray," wrote a reviewer in the December 11, 1957, issue of *Variety.*[21] But his rock-style 1957 single "Pink Sweater Angel"/"Texas Tambourine" was a flop, and he would have only two more hits, Otis Blackwell's gospel-toned composition "Up Until Now" in 1958 and his own purely pop "I'll Never Fall in Love Again" in 1959. He cut a single with Duke Ellington's band and an album of western songs and again toured England and Australia, but surgery to restore his hearing damaged it still further, and he was arrested once more (although this time acquitted) for soliciting sex from a policeman.

In February 1960, Ray recorded "I'll Make You Mine," a pop-rocker in a style suaver than but otherwise similar to Freddy "Boom Boom" Cannon's. The record sold poorly, however, and the session proved to be Ray's last for Columbia. He then recorded for a succession of labels—Decca, Cadence, Liberty, and others—but without success; he cut four duets with the soulful white singer Timi Yuro, but the two sides that were released also failed to sell. After recovering from tuberculosis and then cirrhosis of the liver, the latter brought on by years of heavy drinking, he continued to tour, frequently visiting England and Australia. But his popularity steadily faded, perhaps because his style was simply too sophisticated for listeners raised on rock 'n' roll, even though Ray was one its pioneers. He died of liver failure in Los Angeles in 1990, at the age of sixty-three.

Pat Boone was one of the most popular singers of the 1950s, selling more records than anyone but Elvis Presley. With his wholesome good looks and squeaky-clean persona, Boone helped broaden the acceptance of rock 'n' roll among more conventionally minded listeners. Supposedly descended from the frontiersman Daniel Boone, he was born in Jacksonville, Florida, but raised outside Nashville, Tennessee, where his family attended the Church of Christ. He began singing in church, then competed in talent shows and performed for fraternal lodges, crooning pop songs in the manner of his favorite singers, Bing Crosby and Perry Como. By his senior year in high school he was hosting his own radio show, for which he also sang.

He was still in high school when he met his future wife, a daughter of Red Foley. Through her, Boone met the country star Eddie Arnold, who introduced him to the owner of the Nashville-based Republic label. In May 1953, just before his high school graduation, Boone made his first record, the Latin-flavored "Until You Tell Me So," backed with the tango-tempoed "My Heart Belongs to You," singing both in pure pop style. Later that year, he would cut four more sides for Republic, crooning pop ballads without the Latin tinge. In July 1953, he entered a talent contest and won a trip to New York to audition for *Ted Mack and the Original Amateur Hour,* where he beat the competition three weeks in a row. In the summer of 1954, having married and moved to Texas, he returned to New York for a runoff among previous *Amateur Hour* winners; but while awaiting the results of the finals competition, he entered and won the *Arthur Godfrey's Talent Scouts* contest and, having thereby become a professional, was disqualified from the *Amateur Hour*. He went on to become a regular on Godfrey's shows.

On the way back to Texas, Boone stopped in Tennessee to meet Randy Wood, the head of Dot Records, who'd seen him on the *Amateur Hour* and *Talent Scouts* programs. He didn't hear from Wood again until 1955, when Wood proposed that he cover the Charms' "Two Hearts." For the flip side, Wood chose "Tra-La-La"—not the same song as LaVern Baker's "Tra La La" but a Dave Bartholomew composition that Bartholomew had recorded with the New Orleans singer Tommy Ridgely in May 1951 and that the Griffin Brothers, a jump band from Norfolk, Virginia, had covered on Dot the same year for a Top 10 R&B hit. Despite competing versions by everyone from Frank Sinatra to the Crew-Cuts, Boone's March 1955 recording of "Two Hearts"—a fair approximation of the original, with Boone striving to copy Otis Williams's vocal leaps—was the one that made the pop charts, thanks in part to Boone's hectic promotion. The personnel at some of the radio stations he visited, however, were reluctant to believe he was Pat Boone. "I captured enough of the flavor of the real rock 'n' roll or the real rhythm-and-blues that they assumed the recording artist was black," he reflected.[22]

In May 1955, Boone recorded his pop-chart-topping cover of Fats Domino's "Ain't It a Shame" (backed with a cover of Red Foley's "Tennessee Saturday Night"), catapulting him to a prominence that would include movie stardom and his own television show. He followed with a string of hit covers of R&B songs, including the El Dorados' "At My Front Door," the Five Keys' "Gee Whittakers!" the Flamingos' "I'll Be Home," Little Richard's "Tutti-Frutti" and "Long Tall Sally," and Ivory Joe Hunter's "I Almost Lost My Mind." After that came a double-sided hit combining the title song from the soundtrack of the movie *Friendly Persuasion* with a cover of Big Joe Turner's "Chains of Love," where Boone brings out the melodic resemblance to "I Almost Lost My Mind." In late 1956, he had a No. 1 hit with "Don't Forbid Me" by the black songwriter Charlie Singleton, which Elvis Presley recorded at his "Million Dollar Quartet" session. "Have you heard Pat Boone's new record?" Presley asks his illustrious associates. "It was written for me, and it was sent to me, and it stayed over in my house for ages. Man, I never did even see it."

Boone next charted with "Why Baby Why"—not the George Jones country hit by that title but a rocking number written by two black songwriters, Luther Dixon and Larry Harrison—backed with a cover of Lucky Millinder's 1951 R&B hit "I'm Waiting Just for You." But beginning with his next, double-sided hit, the chart-topping "Love Letters in the Sand" (a 1931 composition based on an 1881 composition), backed with "Bernadine"—both from the soundtrack of the 1957 movie *Bernadine*, which starred Boone—he recorded mostly pop songs, although some were embellished with rock effects such as backbeats or habanera bass lines. Nevertheless, "Love Letters in the Sand," like Boone's "Ain't That a Shame," "Don't Forbid Me," and "At My Front Door," crossed over to the R&B charts.

Written by the Tin Pan Alley stalwart Sammy Fain and his longtime collaborator Paul Francis Webster, the pop ballad "April Love," from Boone's 1957 movie by the same title, was his third No. 1 hit, backed with Leon René's "When the Swallows Come Back to Capistrano." But Boone's 1950s hits also included "A Wonderful Time Up There," his version of

"Gospel Boogie"; the Orioles' "It's Too Soon to Know"; a rocked-up take on Eddie Arnold's 1946 country smash "That's How Much I Love You," which Frank Sinatra had covered in 1947; the gospelly Otis Blackwell–Bobby Stevenson rocker "For My Good Fortune"; Wynonie Harris's "Good Rockin' Tonight"; the goofy faux-Latin "Wang Dang Taffy-Apple Tango (Mambo Cha Cha Cha)"; and the 1936 hymn "Beyond the Sunset," a country hit for the Three Suns with Rosalie Allen and Elton Britt in 1950.

None of Boone's 1960s hits was an R&B cover, although a few were covers of country hits such as Ernest Tubb's "Walking the Floor over You," Jean Shepard and Ferlin Husky's "A Dear John Letter," and Cowboy Copas's "Alabam." Boone's only real rock hit in the 1960s was a cover of David Dante's 1961 comic novelty "Speedy Gonzalez," although his "Beach Girl," produced by Terry Melcher in Beach Boys style, rocks after a fashion. He had his last No. 1 hit in 1961 with a cover of Chase Webster's morbidly catchy "Moody River." He also had hits with a cover of the Bahamian singer (not the bluesman) Blind Blake's version of the American murder ballad "Delia Gone"; the movie theme "The Exodus Song (This Land Is Mine)," for which Boone wrote the lyrics; the Italian pop song "Quando Quando Quando (Tell Me When)"; the Antonio Carlos Jobim bossa nova "Meditation (Meditação)"; and the sarcastic pro–Vietnam War song "Wish You Were Here, Buddy," which Boone composed himself. He made *Billboard*'s Hot 100 singles chart, just barely, for the last time in 1969 with a cover of the former Kingston Trio member John Stewart's "July, You're a Woman," including such out-of-character verses as "I can't hold it on the road / When you're sittin' right beside me / And I'm drunk out of my mind / Merely from the fact that you are here."

In the 1970s, as his fame diminished, Boone turned heavily to gospel music, along with country. He published a steady stream of inspirational books, which eventually outnumbered his movie appearances. In 1997, he spoofed his strait-laced image with *In a Metal Mood: No More Mr. Nice Guy*, an album featuring brassy pop arrangements of well-known heavy-metal songs. In 2006, he released *R&B Classics: We Are Family*, featuring modern arrangements of hits by James Brown, the Four Tops, Sister Sledge, and the like. As of this writing, he continues to perform and to participate in philanthropic and conservative political activities.

Boone has been ridiculed for his bloodless interpretations of rhythm-and-blues, but while he couldn't hold a candle to Fats Domino or Little Richard, he was a decent singer whose versions of songs such as "Gee Whittakers!" and even "I Almost Lost My Mind" compare favorably to the originals. And his clean-cut appearance and upstanding manner made him palatable to those who saw Elvis Presley, to say nothing of Little Richard, as unacceptably rough and wild, providing a bridge to rock 'n' roll and rhythm-and-blues for the musically faint of heart. "Who among us has a soul so pure that he never liked Pat Boone?" wrote Ellen Willis, the first pop critic for *The New Yorker* magazine. "I tended to prefer the tame, white versions of rhythm-and-blues records to the black originals. . . . I was one of the white teen-aged reasons the music was being watered down.[23]

MYSTERY WOMEN

The trend for white singers to record rhythm-and-blues material accelerated toward the mid-1950s, drawing in even such staunch middle-of-the-roaders as Perry Como ("Ko Ko Mo"), Eddie Fisher ("Song of the Dreamer"), and Doris Day ("Two Hearts"). Many of these singers were women, and many of their records were issued on major labels. Although much of their output consisted of pop ballads, they also recorded up-tempo rock songs.

Sunny Gale, born Selma Sega in New Jersey and raised in Philadelphia, sang with the bands of Jules Helzner and Hal McIntyre before pursuing a solo career. Her version of "Wheel of Fortune" on the independent Derby label reached No. 2 on *Billboard*'s R&B chart in February 1952; reviewing a May 1952 performance at New York's Paramount Theatre, a *Billboard* reviewer commented that "much of her phrasing was almost a carbon of Johnnie Ray."[24] She scored a Top 20 pop hit in 1953 when she covered Ruth Brown's "Teardrops from My Eyes" for RCA Victor under the title "Teardrops on My Pillow." Later in 1953, she recorded two sides, "Mama's Gone, Goodbye" and "The Note in the Bottle," with a black doo-wop group, the Du Droppers. She made the pop charts again in 1954 with her cover of the Spaniels' "Goodnite Sweetheart, Goodnite."

In 1955, she covered another doo-wop record, the Four Fellows' "Soldier Boy," which Elvis Presley would record in 1960. She last made the national charts in 1956 with a half-baked attempt to ride the rock bandwagon, "Rock and Roll Wedding," backed with a cover of the Platters' "Winner Take All." She left RCA Victor for Decca that year, covering the Coasters' "One Kiss Led to Another" and recording the semi-rocking Don Raye composition "Hot Dog! That Made Him Mad," which the white singer-actress Betty Hutton had recorded in 1953 and which Wanda Jackson cut in rockabilly style around the same time that Gale did it. In 1957, Gale covered "Come Go with Me," originally by the racially mixed doo-wop group the Dell-Vikings, and cut the mid-tempo rocker "Let's Be Friendly" and the pop-rocker "A Meeting of the Eyes." She recorded another pop-rocker in 1958, "Three O'Clock," where she acts the part of a schoolgirl, but in 1959 Decca dropped her. In 1960, Gale covered the Willows' "Church Bells May Ring" for Warwick, but after releasing a few more records, she faded from view and has since been nearly forgotten.[25]

Like Sunny Gale, Bunny Paul did not sound black but nevertheless made the transition from swing-era pop to rhythm-and-blues, covering R&B hits and recording with a black vocal group. She sang with various bands in her native Detroit in the 1940s, making her first record with Don Pablo's sweet band around 1948; by 1950, she was hosting a local television show. In 1953, she recorded her first hit, "Magic Guitar," on the Dot label; in 1954, she switched to Essex, Bill Haley's label at the time, and with Sy Oliver as her musical director recorded a cover of the Drifters' "Such a Night" that preceded Johnnie Ray's version onto the pop charts. She charted again in 1954 with a cover of the Clovers' "Lovey Dovey," which Oliver's arrangement gives even more of a doo-wop feel. The same year, she covered the Drifters' "Honey Love" with accompaniment by the Harptones, on loan to Essex from the Bruce label; the flip side was Paul's cover of the Harptones' own "I'll Never Tell." The Harptones give Paul's "Honey Love" a more authentic sound than the white singer Vicki Young's rival version, but it was Young's record, not Paul's, that made the pop charts.

In 1955, Paul signed with Capitol Records and covered Linda Hayes and the Platters' rhythm-and-blues recording "Please Have Mercy," but neither Paul's nor Hayes's disc charted. Next, Paul covered Billy Brooks's R&B ballad "Song of the Dreamer," which Johnnie Ray and Eddie Fisher also recorded, but after a few more releases, Capitol let her go. In 1956, she covered Faye Adams's waltz-time "Teen-Age Heart" for Detroit's independent Dash label, backed with Paul's own hard-rocking composition "Baby Sitter's Blues." Later the same year, she cut "History," backed with "Sweet Talk," both in classic rockabilly style and both composed by Paul, for RKO's subsidiary Point label. She cut one more single in 1956, the rocking "That's Love," backed with the doo-wop-flavored "The Gypsy," for the small Dynamic label. At year's end, she performed at the Fox Theatre in Detroit along with Ivory Joe Hunter, Della Reese, and Bo Diddley.

In 1957, Paul cut two singles for Brunswick: the first coupled the rocker "Buzz Me" with the calypso "Poor Joe" (the latter written by Joe Willoughby, the lyricist of Louis Jordan's "Run, Joe"); the second paired the pop-rocker "Beedle-Lump-Bump" with the ballad "The One You Love." She also cut two singles for Roulette, the sugary "Love Birds"/"We Wanted to Marry" in 1958 and a rerecording of "Such a Night," backed with a cover of Brook Benton's rhythmic ballad "A Million Miles from Nowhere," in 1959. Diagnosed with a brain tumor in 1960, she was left partially paralyzed after surgery, but in 1963 she recorded a final single for the Motown-affiliated Gordy label, a cover of the Marvelettes' "I'm Hooked," backed with "We're Only Young Once," for which Paul composed the music. Both songs are arranged in Motown style, with Martha Reeves, of Martha and the Vandellas, contributing as a background singer. Unlike Johnnie Ray, who maintained his distinctive approach no matter what genre he tackled, Paul was a musical chameleon whose records closely mirrored prevailing trends. But her later records did not sell, and Paul retired from music, neither performing nor recording again.[26]

Born Wanda Stegall in Oklahoma, Vicki Young sang and played banjo in her family's band as a child. She continued with the band as a teenager when the family moved to Southern California, later striking out on her own. After performing in nightclubs and on Spade Cooley's television show, she signed with Capitol Records in 1953. She made the pop charts that year with the 1928 Tin Pan Alley standard "I Love You So Much" and again in 1954 with her cover of "Honey Love," which was backed with a cover of the Robins' raucous "Riot in Cell Block #9." In 1955, she covered LaVern Baker's "Tweedlee Dee" and the Charms' "Hearts of Stone," but neither charted, nor did the other pop and country songs she recorded through 1958 for Capitol and then Brunswick. Her 1956 recording of her own ballad composition "Let There Be You," however, was covered for a minor pop hit in 1957 by the black doo-wop group the Five Keys. After one of her sons was killed by an automobile, she quit the music business. She died in 2007 and remains virtually unknown today.[27]

Little is known about the Philadelphia-born singer Gloria Mann. In the mid-1940s, she sang with the Don Renaldo Quartet (whose leader, born Vincent Pignotti, later directed the string sections for Kenny Gamble and Leon Huff's Philadelphia International rhythm-and-blues record label). In 1954, she covered "Goodnite Sweetheart, Goodnite" on both the S-L-S and Jubilee labels, accompanied by the Carter Rays, another name for the Eddie Carter Quartet, a black Philadelphia doo-wop group. A *Billboard* reviewer noted that she "sounds a lot like Sunny Gale."[28] The same year, again with the Carter Rays, she cut "The Waltz You Saved for Me," backed with "I'm Living My Life for You," for the Philadelphia-based Sound label, but the record didn't chart. She had her first pop hit, on Sound, in 1955 with a cover of the Penguins' "Earth Angel" and her second at the end of the year with "A Teenage Prayer," the latter less successful than the version by the white singer-actress Gale Storm but more successful than the one by the black jazz singer Kitty White. She had her third hit, on Decca, in 1956 with a cover of Frankie Lymon and the Teenagers' "Why Do Fools Fall in Love," again less successful than the version by Gale Storm. She kept recording teen-oriented pop-rockers for Decca and, in 1957, for ABC-Paramount, but none made the charts.

Unrelated to Betty Hutton, June Hutton, like her older half-sister, the bandleader Ina Ray Hutton, was of partial African American ancestry but passed as white throughout her career. In the late 1930s, she sang in Ina Ray's band under the name Elaine Merritt. In 1941, she joined the vocal harmony group associated with Charlie Spivak's big band, the Stardusters, with whom she sang on a couple of hit records and appeared in the 1944

Betty Grable movie *Pin Up Girl*. Later in 1944, Hutton replaced Jo Stafford in the Pied Pipers, a vocal group that often accompanied Frank Sinatra. She recorded several hits with the Pipers, including their 1945 chart-topper "Dream." She went solo in 1950, recording a cover of Lefty Frizzell's country smash "If You've Got the Money I've Got the Time" for Decca, backed with a cover of Ruth Brown's "Teardrops from My Eyes." In 1951, she married Tommy Dorsey's former arranger Axel Stordahl, who led the bands on her records for Capitol, including her perky 1954 cover of the Crows' "Gee."

Born Frieda Lipschitz in Massachusetts, Georgia Gibbs sang in vaudeville shows and toured as a teenager with the Hudson-DeLange swing band, with whom she cut two sides under the name Fredda Gibson. In the 1940s, she performed and recorded with such bands as Tommy Dorsey's and Artie Shaw's and appeared on such radio programs as *The Camel Caravan*, often working with comedians. After cutting V-Discs with several bands during World War II, she began recording on her own in 1946 but did not have a hit until 1950, when she charted with "If I Knew You Were Comin' I'd've Baked a Cake" (on Coral), a bigger hit for Eileen Barton. Her subsequent string of hits (most on Mercury) continued through the mid-1950s, including the 1952 smash "Kiss of Fire," adapted from the classic Argentine tango "El Choclo." She sang mostly straightforward pop ballads but covered everything from country (Bonnie Lou's "Seven Lonely Days") to faux-Latin (Ruth Brown's "Mambo Baby") to faux-calypso (Eartha Kitt's "Somebody Bad Stole de Wedding Bell").

Gibbs is remembered today, however, mainly for her R&B covers "Tweedle [sic] Dee" and "Dance with Me Henry (Wallflower)," which respectively reached the No. 2 and No. 1 spots on *Billboard*'s pop chart in early 1955, leaving both LaVern Baker and Etta James furious. "My version went underground . . . while Georgia's whitewash went through the roof," James later wrote. "I was enraged to see Georgia singing the song on *The Ed Sullivan Show* while I was singing it in some funky dive in Watts."[29]

Gibbs had four more hits in 1955: "Sweet and Gentle," an adaptation of the Cuban cha-cha-chá "Me Lo Dijo Adela"; "I Want You to Be My Baby," a cover of the white singer Lillian Briggs's hard-rocking cover of Louis Jordan's 1953 original, itself adapted by Jon Hendricks from "Rag Mop"; the much-recorded English-language adaptation of the Italian song "Arrivederci Roma"; and its flip side, "24 Hours a Day," modeled after "Sixty-Minute Man." She had another four hits in 1956, including the mid-tempo rocker "Rock Right" and a cover of LaVern Baker's "Tra La La." The following year brought her final Mercury hit, the country-flavored "Silent Lips," and her only RCA Victor hit, a cover of Ernest Tubb's 1941 country classic "Walking the Floor over You." She also covered Jerry Lee Lewis's "Great Balls of Fire" in 1957, but her version, while reasonably convincing, didn't chart. The same year, she hosted her own short-lived *Georgia Gibbs and Her Million Record Show* on NBC television. She last made the pop charts in 1958 with "The Hula Hoop Song" (on Roulette), also a novelty hit for Teresa Brewer. She kept recording into the mid-1960s, then retired, dying in 2006.

Easily the best known of the white women who covered rhythm-and-blues songs was Gale Storm, who'd been acting in movies and television shows for fifteen years by the time she made her first record. Born Josephine Cottle in Texas, she acted in high school; at seventeen, she entered a radio talent contest, *Gateway to Hollywood,* and won a contract with RKO Radio Pictures. Renamed Gale Storm, she debuted in the 1940 movie *Tom Brown's School Days* but made only one more film with RKO. She soon signed with Monogram Pictures, winning fame in B-movies that ranged from *Freckles Comes Home* to *Revenge of the Zombies*. She also sang on a few Soundies. In the 1950s, she switched to television, starring in the situation comedies *My Little Margie* (1952–55) and *The Gale Storm Show* (1956–60).

Randy Wood heard Storm sing on the televised *Colgate Comedy Hour* in 1954 and offered her a contract with Dot. "I Hear You Knocking," her first release, "was a cover of something someone named Smiley Louis [sic], the rhythm-and-blues man, had done," she writes in her autobiography.[30] Storm's singing on "I Hear You Knocking" is more affected than Smiley Lewis's; her accompaniment features the same piano introduction but not the subsequent keyboard triplets, and it omits the octave jump from the "Yancey Special" bass line. Nonetheless, Storm's version was a No. 2 pop and No. 15 R&B hit in late 1955, far outselling the original.

She followed with a double-sided hit, a cover of Gloria Mann's "A Teen-age Prayer" backed with a cover of Dean Martin's "Memories Are Made of This." She charted in 1956 with a doo-wop cover of "Why Do Fools Fall in Love," followed by a cover of Cathy Carr's "Ivory Tower," the latter recorded by pop, rock, R&B, and country artists alike. Her next hit was a cover of Marie Knight's moving rhythm-and-blues ballad "Tell Me Why," a song—written by the R&B singer Titus Turner to the approximate tune of the spiritual "Just a Closer Walk with Thee"—that was also covered by the Crew-Cuts and by Elvis Presley (although Presley's early-1957 recording was not released until late 1965). Storm's "Tell Me Why," featuring one of her better vocal performances, keeps the piano triplets from Knight's original but omits the habanera bass line that helped make it a local hit in New Orleans. The Crew-Cuts omit the triplets but keep the bass line, while Presley, in masterly form, dispenses with both.

Storm's final 1956 hit was the double-sided "Now Is the Hour"/"A Heart without a Sweetheart," the first side being a reprise of the New Zealand song that charted for more than half a dozen American artists in 1948, the second a double-tracked original ballad. She had another double-sided hit in 1957, an update of Tommy Dorsey's 1935 smash "On Treasure Island" backed with a cutesy version of Ruth Brown's crossover R&B hit "Lucky Lips." She last made the charts later in 1957 with a cover of Bonnie Guitar's crossover country hit "Dark Moon." She quit recording soon afterward, although Dot continued to release her records through 1960. Storm's career wound down after *The Gale Storm Show* ended, although she continued to make occasional television appearances. She battled alcoholism the 1970s, then turned to religion, dying in 2009.

VOCAL GROUPS

White vocal groups also played a part in the development of rock 'n' roll. Beginning in the 1930s, ensembles such as the Merry Macs, the Modernaires, and the Pied Pipers jazzed up traditional barbershop harmonies, appearing in movies and on television. The Merry Macs were formed in Minneapolis by the three McMichael brothers, who sang harmony while their mother sang melody. In the mid-1920, they performed on local radio and toured with Joe Haymes's band, billed as the Mystery Trio and then the Personality Boys; in 1930, Cheri McKay was hired to sing melody, and the group was renamed the Merry Macs. In 1933, they performed on network radio and made their recorded debut with "In a Little White Church on the Hill," backed with "Hiawatha's Lullaby," which Victor released on its country series. They became radio favorites and performed with many top big bands; meanwhile, Helen Carroll replaced Cheri McKay.

In 1938, the Merry Macs made their first Decca recording, "Pop Goes the Weasel"; the following year, Mary Lou Cook replaced Helen Carroll, and the group scored its first national hit with "Hawaiian War Chant (Ta-Hu-Wa-Hu-Wa-I)," adapted from a nineteenth-century Hawaiian love song. In 1940, they made their feature-film debut in the Jack Benny–Fred Allen comedy *Love Thy Neighbor*. In 1941, they charted with "The Hut-Hut Song," a mock-Swedish novelty that was also a hit for Freddy Martin, Horace Heidt, and the King Sisters. After they filmed *Ride 'Em Cowboy* that summer, Marjory Garland replaced Mary Lou Cook, and the group cut the western-themed hits "Deep in the Heart of Texas" and "Jingle, Jangle, Jingle." The Merry Macs had their best seller in 1944 with the chart-topping "Mairzy Doats," another tongue-twisting novelty. They seem to have had a penchant for nonsense songs, even covering Slim and Slam's "Vol Vist Du Gaily Star."

The group continued to score hits into 1946, all on Decca, including collaborations with Bing Crosby and Judy Garland. In 1946 and 1947, they recorded seven singles for the Majestic label, among them a version of "Open the Door Richard!" They recorded several singles for Era in 1955 and 1956, released an album on Capitol in 1957, and cut the "The Christmas Cha

Cha" for Portrait in 1961. They disbanded in 1964, reuniting for a concert at the Hollywood Bowl in 1968.

Inspired by Bing Crosby's Rhythm Boys, the Modernaires were formed in Buffalo, New York, in 1935 as a high school trio, the Three Weary Willies. After appearing with Ted Fio Rito's band, the trio moved to New York City, where they sang with the bands of George Hall and Ozzie Nelson under the names Don Juan Two and Three and the Three Wizards of Ozzie. Adding a fourth member and renaming themselves the Modernaires, they performed with Fred Waring's and Charlie Barnet's bands, recording the radio anthem "Make Believe Ballroom" with Barnet in 1936. They were featured on Paul Whiteman's radio show and sang with Ray Noble's band before joining Glenn Miller's band, with whom they recorded "Make Believe Ballroom Time," an update of "Make Believe Ballroom," in 1940. Soon afterward, Paula Kelly, one of the Miller band's singers, became the fifth Modernaire, giving the group a sound similar to the Merry Macs'. They had a number of hits with Miller (some recorded before but released after he joined the Army Air Forces in 1942), including "Perfidia (Tonight)," "The Booglie Wooglie Piggy," "Chattanooga Choo Choo," "Delilah," "Elmer's Tune," "Don't Sit under the Apple Tree (with Anyone Else but Me)" "(I've Got a Gal in) Kalamazoo," "Juke Box Saturday Night," "That Old Black Magic," and "It Must Be Jelly ('Cause Jam Don't Shake Like That)," the last crossing over to the Harlem Hit Parade. They also appeared in a few movies.

After Miller's plane disappeared over the English Channel in late 1944, the Modernaires began recording on their own, scoring hits on Columbia through 1947, including the medley "Salute to Glenn Miller." They backed Doris Day on the 1948 hit "Thoughtless" and Frank Sinatra on the 1950 hits "The Old Master Painter" and "Sorry." Signing with Coral, they had three more hits of their own: "New Jukebox Saturday Night," a different "Salute to Glenn Miller," and "April in Paris," the last in 1956. They also cut a 1953 cover of the Davis Sisters' hillbilly boogie "Rock-A-Bye Boogie" and a 1956 cover of the El Dorados' R&B hit "At My Front Door," backed with a rock-tinged version of "Alright, Okay, You Win." They appeared in a few other movies, including *The Glenn Miller Story,* and performed on several television shows.

The Modernaires covered the Platters' "Only You (and You Alone)" and "The Great Pretender" for Alan Freed's 1956 album *Rock n' Roll Dance Party*. Together with Freed, his fellow disc jockey Al "Jazzbo" Collins, and the television personality Steve Allen, they recorded the 1956 single "The Space Man" in emulation of Buchanan and Goodman's comic novelty record "The Flying Saucer," which interspersed a fictional news broadcast with clips of current rock 'n' roll hits; for "The Space Man," the Modernaires faked the rock clips. The group cut a few more singles for United Artists in the early 1960s and toured the country in a 1964 show called "Music Made

Famous by Glenn Miller." Today, a quartet including two daughters of Paula Kelly and her husband Hal Dickinson, an original group member, continues to perform under the Modernaires' name.

The Pied Pipers formed as an octet in Los Angeles after members of three different harmony groups—the Four Esquires, the Three Rhythm Kings, and the Stafford Sisters—sang together while waiting to audition for the 1938 movie *Alexander's Ragtime Band.* Hired to perform on radio with Tommy Dorsey's band, they were soon dismissed, reportedly because a sponsor objected to such songs as "Hold Tight (Want Some Sea Food Mama)."[31] In 1939, they recorded four sides for Victor. Reduced to a quartet comprising three men and Jo Stafford, the Pipers were rehired by Dorsey around the same time the bandleader hired Frank Sinatra. The Pipers backed Sinatra on the huge 1940 hit "I'll Never Smile Again" and on thirteen more hits with Dorsey through 1942; they sang without Sinatra on three other Dorsey hits.

Near the end of 1942, the Pied Pipers left Dorsey and signed with Capitol. They had their first hit on their own with "Mairzy Doats" in 1944, a couple of months after the Merry Macs' version charted, followed by "The Trolley Song," an even bigger hit. But Capital began recording Jo Stafford as a solo artist, leading to her replacement by June Hutton, who sang on Johnny Mercer's composition "Dream," the Pipers' only No. 1 hit. The group accompanied Mercer on many of his mid-1940s hits, including "Ac-Cent-Tchu-Ate the Positive," "Candy," "On the Atchison, Topeka and Santa Fe," and "Personality." The Pipers also recorded nine more hits of their own through 1948, including a version of "Open the Door Richard!" that's not as funky as Jack McVea's but not as corny as one might expect. Their last hit was "My Happiness," one of the two songs Elvis Presley first recorded at Sam Phillips's studio.

The Pied Pipers appeared in about ten feature films between 1939 and 1950, later performing on television. From 1945 to 1947, they toured and sang on radio with Frank Sinatra. In 1950, June Hutton was replaced by Sue Allen, who was later replaced by Virginia Marcy. As of this writing, a group continues to perform under the Pied Pipers' name.

The Four Freshmen had perhaps a greater influence on later rock 'n' roll than any other white vocal group, if only because they were the principal harmonic model for the Beach Boys. "Months at a time. Days on end. He'd listen to Four Freshmen records," said the Beach Boy Carl Wilson of his older brother Brian, the group's leader.[32] In 1948, conservatory students in Indianapolis formed a barbershop quartet, Hal's Harmonizers, who then adopted a jazzier repertoire and became the Toppers, playing instruments as well as singing. Influenced by the Modernaires and Pied Pipers as well as other harmony groups such as Mel Tormé and the Mel-Tones and the Stan Kenton band's Pastels, they developed unusual chord voicings that made the quartet sound like a quintet.[33] Renamed the Four Freshman, they toured the

Midwest until Stan Kenton discovered them and recommended them to Capitol Records.

In October 1950, the Four Freshmen made their studio debut with "Mr. B's Blues," which Billy "Mr. B" Eckstine had recorded at the end of 1947. Uncharacteristically, the group's rendition features no harmonizing whatsoever; instead, the lead singer shouts the blues in a style cruder and more raucous than the smooth-voiced Eckstine's. Afterward, the Freshmen showed little rhythm-and-blues influence, except on such recordings as the similarly unharmonized "Stormy Weather," from 1952, and the gospelly "Crazy Bones," from 1954. The group appeared in the 1951 movie *Rich, Young and Pretty,* but Capitol was reluctant to release the two sides they recorded that year—a complex, wordless arrangement of "Tuxedo Junction" and a richly harmonized version of "It's a Blue World," the latter originally a hit for Tony Martin after he sang it in the 1940 movie *Music in My Heart.* Finally issued in 1952, "It's a Blue World," backed with "Tuxedo Junction," became the Freshmen's first hit. They charted again in 1953 with "It Happened Once Before," in 1954 with the Duke Ellington standard "Mood Indigo," in 1955 with a mambo-flavored version of the 1946 Frank Sinatra hit "Day by Day" and a tango-tempoed take on the 1927 Guy Lombardo smash "Charmaine!" and in 1956 with "Graduation Day" (also a hit for the Canadian vocal group the Rover Boys), which the Beach Boys covered on a live recording in 1964 and a studio recording in 1965.

The Beach Boys used the Freshmen's sumptuous a cappella arrangement of Bobby Troup's composition "Their Hearts Were Full of Spring," from the 1961 album *The Freshman Year,* on their 1963 album *Little Deuce Coupe*, rewording the song into the James Dean tribute "A Young Man Is Gone." The Beach Boys closely copied "Their Hearts Were Full of Spring" itself on the televised *Andy Williams Show* in 1965 and included that song on their British album *Live in London* (released in the United States as *Beach Boys '69*). The Four Freshmen recorded for Capitol until 1965, then cut a few more sides for Decca and Liberty before succumbing to the British Invasion, although they kept on recording sporadically, ultimately releasing nearly as many albums as singles. Although the last original member retired in 1992, a changing roster of Freshmen has continued to perform to this day. Besides the Beach Boys, the Four Freshman influenced such vocal groups as the Harptones, the Lettermen, and the Manhattan Transfer.

Like the Four Freshmen, the Four Lads displayed only a limited affinity for black music. Having met as students at the St. Michael's Choir School in Toronto, they began performing in area clubs. They were discovered when they sang for the Golden Gate Quartet, a black gospel group whom they idolized, backstage at a local theater where the quartet was appearing; a Golden Gate member recommended the Lads to the quartet's manager, who invited them to New York.[34] Following their success on Johnnie Ray's

"Cry," the Four Lads recorded for Mitch Miller on their own, beginning in 1952 with "The Mocking Bird," an original song, seemingly based on the "Goin' Home" theme from Dvořák's *New World* Symphony, that turns into a takeoff on the African American spiritual "Children, Go Where I Send Thee." Like "Cry," it was released on Columbia's OKeh rhythm-and-blues label. The group's subsequent Columbia hits included another African American spiritual, "Down by the Riverside," in 1953, and the Zimbabwean song "Skokiaan," in 1954. But when they ventured into rock 'n' roll on the 1955 Percy Faith–Carl Sigman composition "Too much! Baby, Baby!" the results were distressingly square.

Most of the Four Lads' hits were upbeat pop songs such as "Istanbul (Not Constantinople)" and "Gilly Gilly Ossenfeffer Katzenellen Bogen by the Sea." Ironically, their biggest hits, "Moments to Remember," "No, Not Much," and "Standing on the Corner"—all strictly pop—coincided with the rock 'n' roll explosion of the mid-1950s. They continued to score hits through 1959, including both a reissue and a re-recording of "The Mocking Bird," but afterward the group gradually disbanded before ultimately re-forming. Today, a Four Lads group including only one original member still performs.

Products of the same Toronto choir school that the Four Lads attended, the Crew-Cuts formed in 1952, performing as the Jordonaires [sic], the Otnorots, the Four Tones, and the Canadaires. A television appearance in Cleveland around the end of 1953 led to their meeting the disc jockey Bill Randle, who renamed them the Crew-Cuts and got them a contract with Mercury Records. Their first release, "Crazy 'Bout You Baby," was a Top 10 hit in 1954; if anything, the up-tempo song, written by two of the group's members, rocks harder than their next hit, the landmark "Sh-Boom."

The Crew-Cuts followed "Sh-Boom" with a string of pop hits in 1954 and 1955, mostly covers of rhythm-and-blues records such as Shirley Gunter and the Queens' "Oop Shoop," the Penguins' "Earth Angel," Gene and Eunice's "Ko Ko Mo," Nappy Brown's "Don't Be Angry," the Danderliers' "Chop Chop Boom," the Nutmegs' "A Story Untold," and Otis Williams's "Gum Drop." *Billboard* noted that "the boys were among the first pop artists to make it big with r.&b. ditties."[35] But their popularity declined when they stopped covering R&B songs, and they scored their last hit in 1957 with a cover of "Young Love," a No. 1 pop smash for both the country singer Sonny James and the movie star Tab Hunter. Beginning in 1958, they recorded eight singles for RCA, but none charted; in the 1960s, they recorded for Warwick, Vee-Jay, Camay, ABC-Paramount, Chess, Firebird, and other labels. After disbanding, they reunited for a 1977 concert in Nashville, performing occasionally for a few years longer.

White female vocal groups such as the Fontane Sisters, the McGuire Sisters, and the Chordettes were at least as likely as their male or mixed-sex counterparts to tackle rhythm-and-blues material. The Fontane Sisters, actually surnamed Rosse, began as church singers in their native New Jersey. Performing as the Ross [sic] Trio, the two older sisters and their guitar-playing brother Frank were hired by NBC in New York and dispatched to Cleveland to do radio work. But in 1944, Frank was drafted and sent into combat, where he died. A younger Rosse sister took his place, and the all-female trio adopted a shortened version of their great-grandmother's name, Fontaine.

In 1948, the Fontane Sisters replaced the Satisfiers as Perry Como's back-up group on his radio show, *The Chesterfield Supper Club*. They started accompanying Como on his RCA-Victor sessions and, beginning in 1949, recorded for the label on their own. One of their early sides was an update of Paul Whiteman's 1928 hit "Mississippi Mud" that omits the word "darkies." Their first hit, in 1951, was a cover of Patti Page's huge smash "Tennessee Waltz," itself a cover of Pee Wee King's 1948 country hit, which was also successfully covered by several other pop and country artists. The Fontanes collaborated with the Sons of the Pioneers on "Handsome Stranger"/"Grass-hopper Heart (and a Butterfly Brain)," then scored their second hit, "Let Me In," in collaboration with the country singer Texas Jim Robertson. Their next hit, a lyricized version of Johnny Hodges's instrumental "Castle Rock," charted just after Frank Sinatra's bigger-selling rendition did. Their fourth and final 1951 hit was a cover of Hank Williams's honky-tonk classic "Cold, Cold Heart," a No. 1 pop smash for Tony Bennett and a song since recorded by everyone from Nat "King" Cole and Dinah Washington to Frankie Laine, Bill Haley, Jerry Lee Lewis, and Aretha Franklin. The sisters also covered Hank Snow's 1951 hit "Rhumba Boogie."

But the Fontane Sisters did not have their next hit, the Christmas song "Kissing Bridge," until 1954, after which they switched to the Dot label. Their first hit on Dot, a harmonized revival of Ruth Etting's 1928 hit "Happy Days and Lonely Nights," came out later in 1954. By the end of that year, the sisters had charted with their all-time best seller, a pop-style cover of the Charms' R&B chart-toppper "Hearts of Stone." The English historian Brian Ward comments:

> The producers of white covers . . . groped uncertainly for some of the musical magic which had initially made r&b popular with whites, but also sought to deepen their penetration of that white market by paring the music to its bare, functional, rhythmic bones and fleshing it out again according to "white" musical and lyrical specifications. These agendas were clearly audible in the differences between Otis Williams and the Charms' "Hearts of stone" [sic] on King, and the Fontane Sisters' cover on Dot. While the basic arrangements had much in common, the King record showcased Otis Williams' expressive lead tenor, which peeled away from the strict melody line and toyed with the basic rhythm. . . . By contrast, the Fontane Sisters abandoned the vocal and rhythmic

> fluidity of the original in favour of a rigid adherence to the melody and a more explicit statement of the dominant beat. A stolid male chorus sang in unison, anchoring the song to its melodic and rhythmic foundations, rather than providing the harmonic shadings offered by the Charms.[36]

Nevertheless, the Fontane Sisters' "Hearts of Stone" has enough rock 'n' roll feeling that its omission from the usual lists of first rock records is baffling. And the Charms' version managed to remain on the pop charts simultaneously with the sisters' record.

The Fontane Sisters' next hit, "Rock Love," was also a rhythm-and-blues cover. Written by Henry Glover and first recorded by Lula Reed for King, it charted in February 1955, a month before the movie *Blackboard Jungle* was released. But with lyrics such as "You got to have rock love within your heart / You got to have rock love before you start / So when temptation tries to move your soul / The rocks of love won't let you roll," it sounds as if the rock revolution were already in full swing. "Rock Love" was also covered by Teresa Brewer, Eddie Fontaine, Elaine Gay, Delores Gray, and Billy Farrell, all of them white. Later in 1955, the Fontanes scored the double-sided hit "Rollin' Stone"/"Playmates." "Rollin' Stone" is a cover of a Top 10 R&B hit by the Marigolds, a name taken by the reorganized Prisonaires; the song is a reworded version of the Drifters' "Honey Love" with the calypso influence emphasized further. "Playmates," a sort of mock children's song, is an update of Kay Kyser's 1940 hit, which borrows its melody from Charles L. Johnson's 1904 ragtime composition "Iola: Intermezzo Two-Step."

Still in 1955, the sisters covered Boyd Bennett's rockabilly-style pop hit "Seventeen," outselling the original. Next came the double-sided hit "Daddy-O"/"Adorable," combining a cover of Bonnie Lou's rockabilly-style pop hit with a cover of the Drifters' R&B-chart-topping cover of the Colts' original. The Fontanes' last record to chart in 1955 was "Nuttin' for Christmas," one of several hit versions of that song. In 1956, they had hits with covers of Fats Domino's "I'm in Love Again" and "Please Don't Leave Me," the Teen Queens' "Eddie My Love," LaVern Baker's "Still," and the Tarriers' "Banana Boat Song," as well as the strictly pop originals "Voices" and "Lonesome Lover Blues." Their only hit in 1957 was a cover of Jimmy Bowen's "I'm Stickin' with You," originally the flip side of Buddy Knox's "Party Doll." They had their final hits in 1958—a cover of Art and Dotty Todd's faux-French pop hit "Chanson D'Amour" and a cover of the country song "Jealous Heart," which was recorded by its composer, Jenny Lou Carson, in 1944, made into a country hit by Tex Ritter in 1945, and turned into a pop hit by Al Morgan in 1949. The Fontane Sisters quit performing in 1961, although they did record a final album and single for Dot in 1963.

The three McGuire Sisters began as church singers in their native Ohio. Inspired by the Andrews Sisters and the similar-sounding Dinning Sisters, they started singing pop songs at USO shows; discovered by a local bandleader, they performed with him at a hotel in Dayton, Ohio. In 1952, they traveled to New York to audition for *Arthur Godfrey's Talent Scouts* but wound up performing on Kate Smith's radio show; in 1953, they replaced the Chordettes on *Arthur Godfrey Time*, where they stayed for six years. They signed with Coral Records in 1952 but didn't have their first hit until 1954, when they teamed with Johnny Desmond and Eileen Barton on "Pine Tree, Pine Over Me." Most of their early records were pure pop, but they did cover Tennessee Ernie Ford's "Hey, Mister Cotton Picker" in 1953 and made the pop Top Ten in 1954 with a deracinated cover of the Spaniels' "Goodnite Sweetheart, Goodnite."

They had a No. 1 hit in early 1955 with a cover of Moonglows' "Sincerely," scrubbing the song nearly clean of doo-wop flavor; the flip side, a cover of the DeJohn Sisters' pop hit "No More," also charted. The McGuires' cover of "Hearts of Stone" the same year was not a hit, but their next release, a cover of Ivory Joe Hunter's R&B ballad "It May Sound Silly," was. Another of their 1955 hits, "Something's Gotta Give," has a flip side titled "Rhythm 'n' Blues (Mama's Got the Rhythm • Papa's Got the Blues)," but it's strictly a pop song. The McGuires had eleven more hits by the end of 1956, when they charted their next R&B cover, Jesse Belvin's ballad hit "Goodnight My Love (Pleasant Dreams)." One of their 1956 hits, "Weary Blues," is a version of Artie Matthews's 1915 composition with lyrics added and the boogie bass line omitted. The sisters had their second and last chart-topper in 1958 with "Sugartime," apparently based on a Chico Marx melody known as "I'm Daffy over You" or "Lucky Little Penny," which Chico performs to his brother Groucho's disdain in the movie *Animal Crackers* ("Say, if you get near a song, play it," Groucho cracks). Although "Sugartime" is a pop song through and through, it could almost have passed for one of the more saccharine rock songs of the day.

The McGuire Sisters enjoyed considerable popularity, with frequent television appearances that included their harmonized Coca-Cola commercials. They had their last hit as a group in 1961, although Phyllis McGuire, the lead singer, had a solo hit in 1964; Phyllis continued to perform after the group disbanded in 1968. The sisters made a comeback in 1985, playing Las Vegas and elsewhere before ultimately retiring. In 1995, a TV movie, *Sugartime,* was made about the romantic relationship between Phyllis McGuire and the Chicago mafia boss Sam Giancana.

The Chordettes had a more traditional background than most of the pop vocal groups of the 1950s, yet they adapted unusually well to the rise of rock 'n' roll. The group was formed in Wisconsin in 1946 by four friends, one of whose fathers was the president of the Society for the Preservation and Encouragement of Barber Shop Quartet Singing in America. After performing locally, they won the *Arthur Godfrey's Talent Scouts* competition in 1949 and became regulars on *Arthur Godfrey Time* and the nighttime television show *Arthur Godfrey and His Friends*. They recorded several singles and albums for Columbia in barbershop style, on their own and with Godfrey. But after Godfrey's musical director, Archie Bleyer, founded his own Cadence label, the Chordettes signed with Cadence and left Godfrey.[37]

Under Bleyer's sway, the group turned from barbershop to mainstream pop, although Bleyer's arrangements did make use of barbershop motifs such as the chiming arpeggios on the Chordettes' second Cadence single, "Mr. Sandman." A harmonized cover of a B-side by the middle-of-the-road singer Vaughn Monroe, "Mr. Sandman" was a No. 1 pop smash. After the group's next two singles failed to chart, they cracked *Billboard*'s Top 100 in early 1956 with a cover of "The Wedding," by the Harlem doo-wop group the Solitaires. Their next release, a cover of "Eddie My Love," sold about as well as the Teen Queens' original, though not quite as well as the Fontane Sisters' more faithful cover, with all three versions charting simultaneously. The Chordettes' follow-up single, "Born to Be with You," made the pop Top 5 and was covered for a country hit a decade later by Sonny James. After a pair of double-sided hits, they had a No. 2 pop smash in 1958 with "Lollipop," a cover of a record by the interracial duo Ronald and Ruby. Whereas the McGuire Sisters' "Sugartime" approaches rock 'n' roll, "Lollipop," with its shuffling backbeat, is well over the line, both the sumptuously sweet original and the Chordettes' close imitation, which maintains the street feel of lines such as "And when she does her shaky rockin' dance / Man, I haven't got a chance," substituting "he" and "his" for "she" and "her."

The Chordettes had a few more hits, of which the only rocker was "A Girl's Work Is Never Done," based on the Coasters' "Yakety Yak" and featuring King Curtis on saxophone. Curtis also plays on the flip side, "No Wheels," a campy jive-rock classic ("Man, like I'm way out in gaucheville") where the Chordettes essentially sing backup for Jeff Kron and Jackie Ertel (the latter a daughter of Janet Ertel, the Chordette who married Archie Bleyer). The group also cut respectable covers of such pop-rock and R&B hits as the Coasters' "Charlie Brown," the Teddy Bears' "To Know Him Is Love Him," Paul Anka's "Lonely Boy," Dodie Stevens's "Pink Shoelaces," and Lavern Baker's "I Cried a Tear." They continued to release records on Cadence almost until the label folded in 1964, by which time the Chordettes had broken up.

CARIBBEAN RHYTHMS

While white singers tended to make rhythm-and-blues sound bland, Caribbean influences gave the music additional spice. Even before the Andrews Sisters topped the charts with "Rum and Coca-Cola" in 1945, calypso had entered the popular mainstream. "Sly Mongoose," a Jamaican song that was absorbed into the Trinidadian tradition, had been recorded on Victor in 1923 by the Trinidadian violinist Cyril Monrose and by the Guyanese vaudeville singer Phil Madison; two years later, it was recorded on OKeh by the Trinidadian-born, New York–based vaudevillian Sam Manning. In 1938, Jack Sneed, seemingly an American of West Indian descent, cut "Sly Mongoose" for Decca with a band of black American jazz musicians.[38] Soon afterward, Benny Goodman performed "Sly Mongoose" on *The Camel Caravan.* In 1939, "Sly Mongoose" was recorded by the African American composer-arranger Edgar Sampson's band and by the black vocal group the Quintones, accompanied by Duke Ellington and members of his band.

Although the Andrews Sisters were white—as were the singer Vaughn Monroe and the bandleader Abe Lyman, both of whom also had hits with "Rum and Coca-Cola" in 1945—calypso was associated with blacks. Most of the calypsos popularized in the United States were recorded by black artists, whether covers of Trinidadian songs such as Ella Fitzgerald and Louis Jordan's "Stone Cold Dead in the Market (He Had It Coming)" in 1946 and Harry Belafonte's "Matilda, Matilda!" in 1953 (originally recorded as "Mathilda" by King Radio in 1938) or Tin Pan Alley imitations such as Nat "King" Cole's "Calypso Blues" in 1950 (the likely inspiration for Chuck Berry's "Havana Moon") and the Ravens' "Calypso Song" in 1952 (a Harold Arlen and Johnny Mercer composition from the movie *The Petty Girl*).

Belafonte did not have a hit with "Matilda, Matilda!" but did make the pop charts in 1954 with "Hold 'Em Joe," which had been recorded in 1926 as an instrumental titled "Hold Him Joe (My Donkey Wants Water)" by Sam Manning's Orchestra and in 1945, with lyrics, as "My Donkey Want Water" by Gerald Clark and His Original Calypsos featuring the Trinidadian-born, Harlem-based singer Macbeth the Great. An early version of the song had been collected by an English planter in Jamaica, Walter Jekyll, who published it as "Me Donkey Want Water" in his 1907 book *Jamaican Song And Story.*[39]

But calypso remained a minor undercurrent on the American scene until 1956, when Belafonte released his breakthrough album, *Calypso,* the first LP to sell over a million copies. Belafonte was born in New York to parents from Jamaica and Martinique and spent part of his childhood in Jamaica; much of his material consisted of semi-original compositions or adaptations of Jamaican songs rather than traditional Trinidadian calypsos. Nevertheless, his album not only touched off a calypso craze but helped revive the folk-music movement that had been launched by the Weavers, prompting three aspiring folkies to call themselves the Kingston Trio.

Written by the Brooklyn-born, Juilliard-trained calypsonian Lord Burgess to a melody taken from the Jamaican mento song "Iron Bar," "Jamaica Farewell," the first track from *Calypso* to be released as a single, became a Top

20 pop hit. "Day-O," the opening track on the album, was not released as single until after a white folk trio, the Tarriers, released a somewhat different version titled "The Banana Boat Song," the first of half a dozen recordings of the song to chart in 1957. The Tarriers' was the biggest seller, followed by Belafonte's and then the Fontane Sisters', which is plainly copied from the Tarriers' rather than Belfonte's version. Other versions were recorded by Steve Lawrence, Sarah Vaughan, Shirley Bassey, Stan Freberg, and Johnnie and Jack. "Banana Boat (Day-O)" originated as a Jamaican folk song, "Day Dah Light," in the mento tradition; first recorded, in a refined manner, by the British-based Trinidadian actor-singer Edric Connor on his 1954 album *Songs from Jamaica,* it was redone in authentic mento style by the Jamaican poet Louise Bennett on her album *Jamaican Folk Songs* the same year. Unlike Belafonte's version, the Tarriers' interpolates another Jamaican mento song, "Hill and Gully Rider," which is included on *Songs from Jamaica* but not *Jamaican Folk Songs*.

The calypso craze crested in 1957, when Belafonte had double-sided hits with "Mama Look at Bubu"/"Don't Ever Love Me" and "Cocoanut Woman"/"Island in the Sun." Originally recorded by Trinidad's Lord Melody around 1955 as "Boo-Boo" or "Boo Boo Man," the comic "Mama Look at Bubu" was also recorded, in an assumed Trinidadian accent, by the white actor Robert Mitchum on his 1957 album *Calypso Is Like So.* "Don't Ever Love Me" borrows its melody from the nineteenth-century Haitian song "Choucoune," as does "Yellow Bird," recorded by the Norman Luboff Choir in 1957. "Cocoanut Woman" and "Island in the Sun" were both cowritten by Belafonte and Lord Burgess.

Also in 1957, "Marianne" became a major pop hit for Terry Gilkyson (the composer of "The Cry of the Wild Goose") and for the Hilltoppers and a minor hit for the Lane Brothers and for Burl Ives. Originally recorded in the early 1940s as "Mary Ann" by Roaring Lion, the song was also recorded in 1947 by Xavier Cugat and in 1954 by the Charmer, later known as Louis Farrakhan.

While 1950s rock 'n' roll was largely the province of independent labels, many calypso hits were on major labels such as RCA Victor and Columbia. According to Charlie Gillett, "The general feeling of the major companies toward rock 'n' roll was probably expressed through their heavy promotion . . . of calypso music, which they believed—or anyway hoped—would be the new craze to replace rock 'n' roll." Nonetheless, as Gillett points out, "calypso was never more than a fad," although it left a lasting mark on rhythm-and-blues and rock 'n' roll through such calypso-influenced records as the Drifters' "Honey Love," from 1954; Richard Berry's "Louie Louie," from 1957; Little Anthony and the Imperials' "Shimmy, Shimmy, Ko-Ko-Bop," from 1959 (a cover of the El Capris' "[Shimmy, Shimmy] Ko Ko

Wop," from 1956); and Gary U.S. Bonds's "Twist, Twist Senora," from 1962.[40]

The mambo had a deeper and more enduring influence. Cuban music had been popular in the United States since the introduction of the habanera in the nineteenth century. After the bandleader Don Azpiazú introduced "The Peanut Vender (El Manicero)" [sic] in 1930, the Cuban *son,* mislabeled as the rumba or rhumba, became fashionable, showcased in Broadway musicals and Hollywood movies. Both swing and sweet bands featured "rhumbas" and, later, congas (line dances adapted from Afro-Cuban carnival processions); but with such exceptions as Cab Calloway's "Chili Con Conga," from 1939, these mostly lacked authentic Cuban rhythms, instead substituting ersatz Latin beats such as the one on Skeets Tolbert's "Rhumba Blues," from 1941.

The mambo developed in Cuba out of elements originated in the late 1930s by the bands of Arsenio Rodríguez and Antonio Arcaño, but it did not take the brassy big-band form by which it is now generally recognized until the mid-1940s.[41] In 1948, the Cuban pianist Dámaso Pérez Prado organized his own big band in Mexico City, where he began recording his brash, shrill, propulsive arrangements, punctuated by loud grunts, for RCA Victor. With the release of his 1950 single "Qué Rico el Mambo," backed with "Mambo No. 5" (a hit nearly fifty years later for Lou Bega), the mambo burst into international public consciousness.

Pérez Prado's "Qué Rico el Mambo" did not make the U.S. charts, but the American bandleader Dave Barbour's cover version, titled "Mambo Jambo," did. In early 1951, Johnny Otis cut the instrumental "Mambo Boogie," setting jump blues to a Cuban clave beat, as Louis Jordan had on his 1947 hit "Early in the Morning." In 1952, Sonny Thompson cut "Blues Mambo," an instrumental whose only Latin ingredient is a habanera bass line; Thompson's "Jumping with the Rhumba" is likewise scarcely Latin, but he also plays piano on the Swallows' doo-wopping "Roll Roll Pretty Baby," which opens to the rhythm of a bongo drum. Perhaps the best-known rhythm-and-blues recording of the early 1950s with a Latin or Latin-like beat is Big Mama Thornton's "Hound Dog," whose inauthentic rhythm is typical of the period.

The mambo craze had an impact on American pop, rhythm-and-blues, and even country music. It peaked in 1954, a year that saw the release of Perry Como's "Papa Loves Mambo," Vaughn Monroe's "They Were Doin' the Mambo," Rosemary Clooney's "Mambo Italiano," Ruth Brown's "Mambo Baby," the Platters' "Shake It Up Mambo," the Charms' "Mambo Sh-Mambo," and Hank Snow's "That Crazy Mambo Thing," all featuring at least some approximation of a mambo rhythm. In January 1955, Bill Haley recorded "Mambo Rock," a Top 20 pop hit with no Latin rhythm at all. But for the next few years, pop, rock, and R&B records by the likes of the

Coasters and the Four Freshmen would pulse with habanera bass lines and faux-Latin drumbeats. The most famous example is the Diamonds' pop hit "Little Darlin'," a cover of the Gladiolas' even more emphatically Latin-flavored 1957 R&B hit.

The American heyday of mambo and calypso music coincided with the eruption of rock 'n' roll, but while rock endured, calypso was supplanted in Trinidad by soca, which didn't make much of an impression in the United States, and mambo gave way in Cuba to the cha-cha-chá, which did. After Fidel Castro's 1959 revolution, however, Cuban music fell from stateside fashion, never to regain its former status. By the 1960s, the mambo had faded, but its afterglow lingered in songs such as the Beatles' "Twist and Shout" (a cover of the Isley Brothers' cover of the Top Notes' original) and the McCoys' "Hang On Sloopy" (a cover of the Vibrations' "My Girl Sloopy"). Other Latin-flavored rockers of that decade include the Yardbirds' "For Your Love" and the Rolling Stones' "Sympathy for the Devil." Since then, Latin music has broadened its influence on American pop, rock, and R&B, as various Caribbean and Brazilian rhythms have blended with rock and funk beats to produce an assortment of fusions.

Epilogue

Following the appearance of Bill Haley's "Rock Around the Clock" on the soundtrack of *Blackboard Jungle* in 1955, rock 'n' roll conquered America, or at least its teenage market. But "Rock Around the Clock" did not define the genre, despite its shuffling rhythm, boogie-ish bass line, and twelve-bar verse-and-refrain structure. Although many 1950s rock songs feature one or more of these characteristics, not to mention a backbeat, many do not. Some, such as "Hound Dog," are in blues form; of these, some, such as "Shake, Rattle and Roll," use the blues as both verse and refrain. Others, such as "Blue Suede Shoes" or "Jailhouse Rock," have a sixteen-bar verse-and-refrain structure; still others, such as "Great Balls of Fire," follow the thirty-two bar AABA pattern typical of ballads, complete with bridge. Along with up-tempo numbers, slow love songs were also part of the rock 'n' roll repertoire, distinguished from pure pop performances by adenoidal singing or doo-wop harmonies.

Upon its emergence, rock 'n' roll encountered a firestorm of criticism. "From 1958 to 1960 rock and roll lost much of its early drive and impetus, due largely to anti-rock pressures. From 1960 to 1962 rock was toned down to suit adult standards of propriety," write Linda Martin and Kerry Segrave in their book *Anti-Rock*.[1] It should be remembered, however, that rock 'n' roll had practically originated as a toned-down version of rhythm-and-blues. And in the 1950s, rock and R&B were not the only genres to come under pressure. According to *Billboard*, the disc jockey Martin Block refused to play Rosemary Clooney's "Mambo Italiano" on his WABC radio show in 1954 because the lyrics—presumably such lines as "Hey goombah, I love a how you dance a rhumba"—were offensive to Italian Americans.[2] The magazine reported earlier the same year that radio stations were denying airplay to Webb

Pierce's "There Stands the Glass," a No. 1 country hit, "because no punishment is meted out to the intemperate drinker."[3]

It is widely perceived that rock 'n' roll had become enervated by the time the Beatles arrived in the United States in 1964. A year-by-year comparison of top rock hits reveals a gradual debilitation but not a simple downslide; Jim Lowe's bland, sugary "The Green Door" was a No. 1 hit in 1956, for example, and the Kingsmen's raunchy, hard-edged "Louie Louie" reached the No. 2 spot in 1963. Still, in the wake of Elvis Presley's conscription in 1958, the death of Buddy Holly, Ritchie Valens, and the Big Bopper in a plane crash in 1959, and the payola scandal of 1959 and 1960, rock music grew noticeably milder.

Besides becoming softer and sweeter, the music changed in other ways. Vocal harmony groups did not disappear but became less prevalent. The twelve-bar verse-and-refrain song faded from fashion, except for oldies revivals such as the Beatles' "Everybody's Trying to Be My Baby." A slew of dance hits followed Chubby Checker's 1960 smash "The Twist," including "El Watusi," "The Loco-Motion," "Mashed Potato Time," "The Monkey Time," "Pony Time," "The Dog," "The Bird's the Word," and "The Jerk"; by 1962, Chris Kenner was singing of a "Land of 1000 Dances." Phil Spector's "wall of sound" was among the ingenious recording techniques that brought a new sophistication to rock 'n' roll, paving the way for ever more elaborate productions. The songwriters headquartered in Manhattan's Brill Building put their own distinctive stamp on the music, a kind of pop-rock update on Tin Pan Alley, while the surf music of southern California brought guitar instrumentals to the forefront.

The British Invasion streamed urban and rural blues (as opposed to jazz or pop blues) into rock 'n' roll. The blues-rock of the mid- to late 1960s turned psychedelic, then morphed into heavy metal. British rockers such as the Rolling Stones covered soul songs, but for the most part, rock 'n' roll and rhythm-and-blues diverged after the rise of soul music, never again to align as closely as they had in the mid-1950s. As it veered away from its R&B roots, rock increasingly departed from its original function as dance music. And as it adapted to the changing tastes of an upwardly mobile audience, the music grew more refined, with arrangements that borrowed from classical compositions and lyrics that aspired to be taken seriously as poetry.

Some aspects of rock have remained fairly constant. The celebration of teenage crushes and puppy love in early rock 'n' roll was novel, as juveniles had not previously been the focus of popular music. Since then, however, the travails of adolescence have become a rock staple, with endless variations on the themes of alienation and rejection.

After the mid-1970s, rock 'n' rollers sought inspiration less in outside sources such as blues, R&B, or country than in previous rock material. Punk rock arose as an attempt to recapture the spirit of early rock 'n' roll, in reaction to the pretentions of progressive rock and heavy metal.[4] But after several years of experimentation, innovation slowed to a crawl, and over the next couple of decades rock music ceded much of its audience to hip-hop, electronica, and R&B-flavored pop, as well as country. The remaining rock scene splintered into subgenres such as grindcore, post-grunge, pop punk, space rock, lo-fi, nu metal, and emo.

The demise of rock 'n' roll has been proclaimed at least since Don McLean's 1971 hit "American Pie" lamented the passing of Buddy Holly et al. on "the day the music died." Nevertheless, rock lives on, however feebly, having shown relatively little creative spark since the punk era. Geared to an audience that is overwhelmingly white and middle-class, it has become, in large part, a musically conservative genre, for all its radical posturing. What genuine inventiveness persists is mostly relegated to the fringes of the scene.

Paralleling the development of jazz, rock music has grown so distant from its original sound that modern rock hardly seems to belong to the same genre as vintage rock 'n' roll. Only the backbeat and amplified guitar-bass-and-drums instrumentation have endured, and even those elements are not always present. Today's rock musicians and fans may have little or no familiarity with old-school rock 'n' roll—regrettably, since reconnecting with the music's roots might help restore its vigor. Moreover, the recognition that rock 'n' roll and rhythm-and-blues grew mainly out of jazz and hokum rather than blues, country, pop, or gospel puts a new perspective on musical history. If rock drew its most characteristic song structure from hokum, that subgenre can no longer be regarded as a mere footnote. And if rhythm-and-blues derives primarily from jazz, then swing should be reevaluated as the root form of rock and not just of bebop.

Swing gave rise to both modern jazz and rhythm-and-blues, and rhythm-and-blues, largely through its appropriation by white country and pop artists, gave birth to rock 'n' roll. Neither rural nor urban blues—aside from the blues inherent in jazz, which passed into rhythm-and-blues—had much to do with rock music until the 1960s; swing and R&B had more influence on rural and urban blues than rural and urban blues had on swing or R&B. Hokum made its way into R&B and rock 'n' roll through blues, swing, and country music, providing the archetypal structure for some, though by no means all, of the most emblematic rock songs. But while many R&B and country singers had gospel-music backgrounds, gospel music per se did not make much of an impact on early rhythm-and-blues and rock 'n' roll except through doo-wop singing, although it was the primary source for the soul music of the 1960s and afterward.

The nascent sound of rock 'n' roll could be heard as early as the 1920s in a number of hokum songs, piano boogies, and jazz-band arrangements. The gestation of rock continued through the 1930s with hokum songs (in both blues and country style), jive songs, and boogie-woogies, some of which would be assimilated into western-swing. Rhythm-and-blues began to crystalize in the late 1930s, when artists such as Louis Jordan and the Harlem Hamfats blended blues and jazz; the boogie-woogie craze that began at the end of 1938 left its stamp on both rhythm-and-blues and country music. Wynonie Harris's 1948 smash "Good Rockin' Tonight" launched a wave of similar R&B songs that coincided with the rise of the hillbilly boogie, and by the early 1950s the rock 'n' roll revolution was well under way, as a musical if not a social phenomenon. But rock 'n' roll wasn't generally recognized as a distinct musical genre until 1955, when Alan Freed promoted his first New York concert and "Rock Around the Clock" was featured on the *Blackboard Jungle* soundtrack.

Rock 'n' roll showed its greatest verve in the mid-1950s, after which its vitality diminished and then revived several times, spiking during the British Invasion and the psychedelic, punk, and grunge movements. While the future of rock can't safely be predicted, its past should surely be known and not shrouded in mythology. Why, for example, does Robert Johnson's name come up so often when the roots of rock are discussed? Johnson deserves credit for his spine-tingling Delta blues, of course, but his contributions to the origins of rock 'n' roll are negligible. Sam Theard gave early rockers greater inspiration, if only because his recording of "Spo-Dee-O-Dee" in 1937 (the same year that Johnson cut "Hellhound on My Trail") formed the basis for Stick McGhee's pivotal hit "Drinkin' Wine Spo-Dee-O-Dee" a dozen years later. Yet Theard is all but unknown today.

Rock 'n' roll is quintessentially American music, drawing on a wider variety of sources than has previously been acknowledged—not only blues, country, and pop but jazz, hokum, boogie-woogie, mambo, calypso, and more. Besides absorbing external influences—everything from Mexican folk music to grand opera—rock possesses an intrinsic richness born of its diverse formative elements. The rediscovery of these constituents may enhance how rock 'n' roll is perceived and perhaps even how it will evolve in years to come. Much of this music remains to be explored—for example, the mingling of jazz and blues during the swing era, which laid the groundwork for rhythm-and-blues. The definitive study of rock 'n' roll origins has yet to be written.

Notes

INTRODUCTION

1. Christopher John Farley, "Elvis Rocks. But He's Not the First," *Time,* July 6, 2004, www.time.com/time/arts/article/0,8599,661084,00.html.

1. THAT'S ALL RIGHT

1. Nick Tosches, *Country: Living Legends and Dying Metaphors in America's Biggest Music* (New York: Scribner's, 1977), 45; Mike Callahan and David Edwards, "Randy Wood: The Dot Records Story," www.bsnpubs.com/dot/dotstory.html. Michel Ruppli, *The Decca Labels: A Discography; Volume 2: The Eastern and Southern Sessions (1934–1942)* (Westport, CT: Greenwood Press, 1996), 641. Tosches spells the name "Lamb," but Bob Lamm was the singer on bandleader Francis Craig's "Near You," which spent a record seventeen weeks at the top of *Billboard* magazine's pop chart in 1947. Lamm was also one of the first artists on the Tennessee-based Dot label in the early 1950s; in an e-mail response to my query, the discographer Mike Callahan confirmed that Lamm's "That's When Your Heartaches Begin" was issued on Dot 1050. Tosches credits the composition to the hillbilly-boogie guitarist Zeb Turner, which if true would make it a different song than the one written by Fred Fisher, William Raskin, and Billy Hill (under the pen name George Brown) that was recorded by the Ink Spots, Billy Bunn, and Elvis Presley. Although Fisher, Raskin, and Hill did not copyright the song until 1940, Shep Fields and his Rippling Rhythm Orchestra, featuring the singer Bob Goday, recorded it for Bluebird in 1937, crediting the songwriters on the label. Presley almost certainly copied the Ink Spots' reissued version, including the recited portion that's not found on Billy Bunn's or—it seems safe to presume—Bob Lamm's recording.

2. Jerry Hopkins, *Elvis: A Biography* (New York: Simon & Schuster, 1971), 66.

3. Albert Goldman, *Elvis,* 1st pbk. ed. (New York: Avon, 1982 [orig. McGraw-Hill, 1981]), 129.

4. Peter Guralnick, *Last Train to Memphis: The Rise of Elvis Presley,* 1st pbk. ed. (Boston: Back Bay Books/Little, Brown, 1994), 497.

5. Peter Guralnick, liner notes to *Elvis—The King of Rock 'n' Roll: The Complete 50's Masters,* RCA Records 07863 66050-2 (1992).

6. Hopkins, *Elvis: A Biography,* 68.

7. Guralnick, *Last Train to Memphis,* 84, 500.

8. Michael T. Bertrand, *Race, Rock, and Elvis,* 1st pbk. ed. (Urbana: University of Illinois Press, 2005 [orig. 2000]), 210, 211.

9. Guralnick, *Last Train to Memphis,* 147, 148, 368, 442, 507; Goldman, *Elvis,* 118. Both Guralnick and Goldman refer to statements by Nat D. Williams and Robert Henry quoted in Margaret McKee and Fred Chisenhall's 1981 book *Beale Black and Blue* (Louisiana State University Press).

10. Guralnick, *Last Train to Memphis,* 48, 92.

11. Guralnick, *Last Train to Memphis,* 95; Scotty Moore, as told to James Dickerson, *That's Alright, Elvis: The Untold Story of Elvis's First Guitarist and Manager, Scotty Moore,* 1st pbk. ed. (New York: Schirmer Books, 1997/1998), 58, 59.

12. Charlie Gillett, *The Sound of the City: The Rise of Rock 'n' Roll,* 3rd pbk. ed. (New York: Laurel/Dell, 1978 [orig. Outerbridge & Dienstfrey, 1970]), 39, 329, citing *Hit Parade,* January 1957.

13. Guralnick, *Last Train to Memphis*, 289.

14. Billy Altman, liner notes to Arthur "Big Boy" Crudup, *That's All Right Mama,* Bluebird/ BMG Music 61043-2 (1992).

15. John Broven, "Roy Brown, Part 2: Hard Luck Blues," *Blues Unlimited,* March/June 1977, 16; James Maycock, "Rocky Road to Rock and Roll," *The Daily Telegraph,* August 3, 2001, www.telegraph.co.uk/culture/4724825/Rocky-road-to-rock-and-roll.html. Maycock's story in the British *Daily Telegraph* quotes bandleader Ike Turner as saying that in 1952, Presley "was just a white boy that would come over to black clubs [in Memphis]. He would come in and stand behind the piano and watch me play. I never knew he was no musician." But this account is as dubious as Roy Brown's.

16. Joel Whitburn, *Joel Whitburn's Top R&B Singles 1942–1995,* (Menomonee Falls, WI: Record Research, 1996,), 99.

17. Guralnick, *Last Train to Memphis*, 45.

18. Stanley Booth, "A Hound Dog to the Manor Born," *Esquire,* February 1969, cited in Guralnick, *Last Train to Memphis*, 101, 502.

19. Colin Escott with Martin Hawkins, *Good Rockin' Tonight: Sun Records and the Birth of Rock 'n' Roll* (New York: St. Martin's Press, 1991), 67.

20. Escott, *Good Rockin' Tonight,* 72.

21. Hank Zevallos, "Elvis–Johnny Burnette Connection," www.biwa.ne.jp/~presley/elnews-JohnnyBurnette.htm. The Johnny Burnette Trio recorded "Oh Baby Babe" for the Coral label in May 1956, with virtually the same melody and the same "Come back baby, come" refrain as on "Baby Let's Play House." Zevallos, citing interviews with Burnette's widow Thurley and with Paul Burlison, claims that Burnette's trio wrote "Oh Baby Babe" in 1953 and that Presley heard the Memphis-based trio play it before he recorded "Baby Let's Play House." This, of course, would not explain how Arthur Gunter came to record "Baby Let's Play House."

22. Greil Marcus, *Mystery Train: Images of America in Rock 'n' Roll Music,* 4th rev. ed. (New York: Plume, 1997 [orig. Dutton/Penguin, 1975]), 141.

23. Mark Zwonitzer with Charles Hirshberg, *Will You Miss Me When I'm Gone? The Carter Family and Their Legacy in American Music* (New York: Simon & Schuster, 2002), 138.

24. Colin Escott and Martin Hawkins, *Sun Records: The Brief History of the Legendary Record Label* (New York: Quick Fox, 1980) [orig. published as *Catalyst: The Sun Records Story* (London: Aquarius Books, 1975)], 29.

25. Escott, *Good Rockin' Tonight*, 45.

26. Bill Ellis, "Sun Records' Sam Phillips talks Elvis, Johnny, Roy, Jerry Lee . . . ," *Memphis Commercial Appeal,* January 21, 2000, posted as "Walking through Musical History with Sam Phillips," www.talentondisplay.com/NewsArch01.html; Norm Shaw, "Sam Phillips Series, Part 3: Elvis' Early Years," *BlueSpeak,* August 1996, quoted in Louis Cantor, *Dewey and Elvis: The Life and Times of a Rock 'n' Roll Deejay* (Urbana: University of Illinois Press, 2005), 142, 143. Ellis quotes Phillips as saying, "When Elvis heard 'Mystery Train' by Little Junior Parker, he told me later that was the thing that gave him the courage to come in and get an audition." Shaw quotes Phillips as saying of Presley, "He told me right here in this room that

the thing that really got him interested in Sun Records was he loved 'Mystery Train' that I cut with Little Junior Parker."

27. "Charlie Feathers, Rockabilly's Main Man," attributed to Shane Hughes, *Tip Top Daddy: Charlie Feathers—His Life and His Music,* www.rockabilly.nl/artists/feathers.htm; "Charlie Feathers: 1932–1998," www.charliefeathers.com/bio/cfbio.html. According to the BlackCat Rockabilly Europe website, "The circumstances surrounding the evolution of 'I Forgot . . . ', though, are far from clear. Feathers himself claimed to have co-inked the song with Kesler, but Stan has since recounted that he wrote the song alone and gave fifty percent of the copyright to Charlie for singing the demo." Feathers is quoted on the Official Charlie Feathers Website as saying of "I Forgot to Remember to Forget": "I put the melody to it, and Stan put the biggest part of the words down."

28. "Review Spotlight on . . . Talent," *Billboard,* August 7, 1954, 39.

29. Marcus, *Mystery Train*, 141.

30. John Swenson, *Bill Haley: The Daddy of Rock and Roll* (New York: Scarborough House/Stein and Day, 1982), 27.

31. Swenson, *Bill Haley,* 37.

32. Jim Dawson, *Rock Around the Clock: The Record That Started the Rock Revolution!* (San Francisco: Backbeat Books, 2005), 61–63.

33. Jon Guyot Smith, liner notes to *Sing, Cowboy, Sing! The Gene Autry Collection,* Rhino Records 72630 (1997).

34. Swenson, *Bill Haley*, 45.

35. Dawson, *Rock Around the Clock*, 65; John W. Haley and John von Hoelle, *Sound and Glory: The Incredible Story of Bill Haley, the Father of Rock'n'Roll and the Music That Shook the World* (Wilmington, DE: Dyne-American Publishing, 1989/1990), 89; "Reviews of New R&B Records," *Billboard,* March 20, 1954, 43. Haley and Hoelle claim that it was Bill Haley who gave the song to his "old friend" Vennitti and that Haley was Jack Howard's "silent, but controlling" partner in Arcade Records.

36. Helge Thygesen, Mark Berresford, and Russ Shor, *Black Swan: The Record Label of the Harlem Renaissance* (Nottingham: VJM, 1996), 7, 65. Bernard helped popularize W. C. Handy's "St. Louis Blues" with recordings in 1919 and 1921, the latter with the Original Dixieland Jazz Band. In 1922, his recording of "I'm Looking for a Bluebird (to Chase My Blues Away)" was released under the pseudonym Slim White on the Black Swan label, which deceptively advertised its product as "the only records using exclusively negro voices."

37. Arnold Shaw, *Honkers and Shouters: The Golden Years of Rhythm and Blues* (New York: Collier/Macmillan, 1978), 64.

38. Shaw, *Honkers and Shouters,* 73.

39. Nick Tosches, *Unsung Heroes of Rock 'n' Roll* (New York: Scribner's, 1984), 1.

40. John A. Jackson, *Big Beat Heat: Alan Freed and the Early Years of Rock & Roll* (New York: Schirmer/Macmillan, 1991), 82.

41. Jackson, *Big Beat Heat*, 34, 52, 53.

42. Jackson, *Big Beat Heat*, 34, 85, 86.

43. Carl Belz, *The Story of Rock,* 2nd ed. (New York: Oxford University Press, 1972/1969), 13, 16.

44. Nik Cohn, *Rock from the Beginning* (New York: Stein and Day, 1969) [orig. published as *Pop from the Beginning* (London: Weidenfeld and Nicolson, 1969); also published as *Awopbopaloobop Alopbamboom* (St. Albans: Paladin Press, 1970)], 9.

45. Belz, *The Story of Rock*, 25.

46. Gillett, *The Sound of the City*, 139, 147.

47. Jim O'Neal, "Jackie Brenston," *Living Blues,* Spring 1980, 18.

48. Robert Palmer, *Deep Blues* (New York: Penguin Books, 1982 [orig. Viking Press, 1981]), 222.

49. Steve Tracy, "King of the Blues," *Blues Unlimited,* December 1971, 7.

50. Shaw, *Honkers and Shouters*, 243.

51. Tim Brooks, ed., *Little Wonder Records: A History and Discography* (St. Johnsbury, VT: New Amberola, 1999), 29.

52. Dena J. Epstein, *Sinful Tunes and Spirituals: Black Folk Music to the Civil War* (Urbana: University of Illinois Press, 1977), 233.

53. Robert M. W. Dixon, John Godrich, and Howard Rye, *Blues and Gospel Records 1890–1943,* 4th ed. (Oxford: Clarendon Press, 1977), 1252.

54. David Evans, liner notes to *Deep River of Song: Mississippi—Saints & Sinners,* Rounder Records 11661-1824-2 (1999)

55. M. H. Orodenker, "On the Records," *Billboard,* May 30, 1942, 25; M. H. Orodenker, "Record Reviews," *Billboard,* April 21, 1945, 66; M. H. Orodenker, "New Records," *Billboard,* June 22, 1946, 33. Reviewing Erskine Hawkins's recording of "Caldonia" in 1945, Orodenker writes, "It's right rhythmic rock and roll music"; he uses the identical phrase to describe Joe Liggins's "Sugar Lump" the following year.

56. Anthony Heilbut, *The Gospel Sound: Good News and Bad Times* (New York: Limelight, 1985 [orig. Simon & Schuster, 1971]), 27; Michael W. Harris, *The Rise of Gospel Blues: The Music of Thomas Andrew Dorsey in the Urban Church* (New York: Oxford University Press, 1992), 67–69, 151, 152; Bill C. Malone, *Singing Cowboys and Musical Mountaineers: Southern Culture and the Roots of Country Music,* pbk. ed. (Athens: University of Georgia Press, 2003 [orig. 1993]), 30, 31. Heilbut quotes Dorsey as saying, "In the early 1920s I coined the words 'gospel songs,'" but Harris quotes him disclaiming the first use of the word "gospel" and notes that he was influenced by a 1921 African American Baptist song book titled *Gospel Pearls.* In 1874, the white hymnodist Philip Bliss had published a book called *Gospel Songs,* after which the term "gospel song" was used for American hymns that had a popular flavor.

57. Dixon, Godrich, and Rye, *Blues and Gospel Records*, 765; Brian Rust, compiler, *Jazz Records 1897–1942,* 5th ed. (Chigwell, Essex: Storyville, 1982); Scott Yanow, review of the album *Scrapper Blackwell: Complete Recorded Works in Chronological Order, Volume 1 (1928–1932),* www.allmusic.com/cg/amg.dll?p=amg&sql=10:hvfuxqugldde. Dixon, Godrich, and Rye give the personnel as Robinson, Blythe, and Blackwell. Rust lists singer Teddy Moss as a possible alternative to Blackwell. Yanow gives the clarinetist as Arnett Nelson.

58. Dawson, *Rock Around the Clock,* 17. Dawson says that Richard Whiting and Sidney Clare originally wrote "Rock and Roll" for Shirley Temple, who sang their composition "On the Good Ship Lollipop" in the 1934 movie *Bright Eyes.* When Temple's studio, Fox Films, passed on "Rock and Roll," Whiting and Clare offered it to the Boswell Sisters.

59. Linda Martin and Kerry Segrave, *Anti-Rock: The Opposition to Rock 'n' Roll,* 1st pbk. ed. (New York: Da Capo Press, 1993 [orig. Archon Books, 1988]), 16–21.

60. Cohn, *Rock from the Beginning,* 10.

61. Frank Sinatra, "The Diplomacy of Music," *Western World* magazine, November 1957, 30. Sinatra's anti-rock diatribe has been widely misquoted and misattributed. It was first cited in an article in the *New York Times Magazine* of January 12, 1958, "Why They Rock 'n' Roll—And Should They?" by Gertrude Samuels, who says that Sinatra "was quoted in a Paris magazine." Others claim that Sinatra's comments were made at congressional hearings or give the date of the *Western World* article as 1958. In the second paragraph of his essay, which endorses American jazz and pop music as a means of promoting international goodwill toward the United States, Sinatra writes, "I have only one reservation here—rock 'n' roll—which I consider the martial music of every sideburned delinquent." He resumes his attack on rock later in the essay, repeating the "sideburned delinquent" remark with the ungrammatical preface "and as I said before," which has been replaced with ellipsis points.

62. Leonard Feather, *The Encyclopedia Yearbook of Jazz* (New York: Horizon Press, 1956), 24.

63. Duke Ellington, "Where Is Jazz Going?" *Music Journal,* March 1962, reprinted in *The Duke Ellington Reader,* ed. Mark Tucker (New York: Oxford University Press, 1993), 324, 325.

64. Bob Crosby, "Rock 'n' Roll Is Our Own Fault," *Music Journal,* September 1958, quoted in Martin and Segrave, *Anti-Rock,* 45.

65. Russell Sanjek, *American Popular Music and Its Business: The First Four Hundred Years; Vol. I: From the Beginning to 1790* (New York: Oxford University Press, 1988), 313.

66. Laurence Hutton, *Curiosities of the American Stage,* reprint ed. (New York: Johnson Reprint Corp., 1968 [orig. Harper & Brothers, 1891]), 99, 100; H. Earle Johnson, *Musical*

Interludes in Boston (New York: Columbia University Press, 1943),176, 177, www.archive.org/stream/musicalinterlude017691mbp/musicalinterlude017691mbp_djvu.txt; Shlomo Pestcoe, "Gottlieb Graupner: The First White Banjo Performer?" http://shlomo-sez.blogspot.com/2007/07/as-we-all-know-banjo-history-and-lore.html. Hutton attributes the Graupner story to "Charles White, an old Ethiopian comedian and manager" (the word "Ethiopian," in this context, refers to a white man who performed in blackface). However, he notes that another source, W. W. Clapp's book *History of the Boston Stage* (actually titled *A Record of the Boston Stage* and published in 1853 by J. Munroe and Company), says that the theater identified by White was closed in honor of George Washington's death at the time Graupner's performance supposedly took place. Johnson says that "the theater was hung with black in tribute to the Father of his Country" rather than closed and that at the performance of *Oroonoko,* "Mrs. Graupner, not Mr. Graupner, sang the popular ballad 'I Sold a Guiltless Negro Boy.'" Pestcoe cites a notice on page three of the December 21, 1799, edition of the *Columbian Centinel,* a Boston newspaper, announcing a December 23 performance of *Oroonoko* featuring "the Song of The Negro Boy," performed by Graupner's wife, the English-born singer Catherine Comerford Hillier (or Hellyer).

67. Hans Nathan, *Dan Emmett and the Rise of Early Negro Minstrelsy* (Norman: University of Oklahoma Press, 1962), 35; Russell Sanjek, *American Popular Music and Its Business: The First Four Hundred Years; Vol. II: From 1790 to 1909* (New York: Oxford University Press, 1988), 166.

68. Sanjek, *American Popular Music, Vol. II,* 163.

69. Two other minstrel performers, George Nichols and Bob Farrell, also claimed authorship of "Zip Coon."

70. Nick Tosches, *Where Dead Voices Gather,* 1st pbk. ed. (Boston: Back Bay Books/Little, Brown, 2002 [orig. 2001]), 20.

71. John Wesley Work, *Folk Song of the American Negro,* reprint ed. (New York: Negro Universities Press, 1969 [orig. Fisk University Press, 1915]), 106, (the author is John Wesley Work II, a member of the Fisk Jubilee Singers and the father of the John W. Work who made field recordings in Mississippi in 1941 together with Alan Lomax and Lewis Jones); Veit Erlman, liner notes to *Mbube Roots: Zulu Choral Music from South Africa, 1930s–1960s,* Rounder 5025 (1987). The tradition of black South African choral singing, best known through the song "The Lion Sleeps Tonight" and the work of the group Ladysmith Black Mambazo, is also traceable to the influence of the Fisk Jubilee Singers, whose style was taken up by both black and white American minstrel troupes. According to Veit Erlman, some of these troupes toured South Africa with great success in the late nineteenth century, most notably Orpheus McAdoo's Minstrel, Vaudeville and Concert Company, an African American group that spent more than five years in South Africa in the 1890s and inspired many imitators there.

72. Norm Cohen, liner notes to *Minstrels & Tunesmiths: The Commercial Roots of Early Country Music,* JEMF-109 (1981), 28; David Ewen, *The Life and Death of Tin Pan Alley* (New York: Funk and Wagnalls, 1964), 81–85.

73. W. C. Handy, *Father of the Blues: An Autobiography,* pbk. ed. (New York: Da Capo Press, 1991 [orig. Macmillan, 1941]), 118; Lynn Abbott and Doug Seroff, *Out of Sight: The Rise of African American Popular Music 1889–1895* (Jackson: University Press of Mississippi, 2002), 448.

74. Philip Furia, *Irving Berlin: A Life in Song* (New York: Schirmer, 1998), 41; Charles Hamm, *Irving Berlin, Songs from the Melting Pot: The Formative Years, 1907–1914* (New York: Oxford University Press, 1997), 117–119.

75. Tosches, *Where Dead Voices Gather,* 95.

76. Tosches, *Country,* 204; Charles Wolfe, "A Lighter Shade of Blue: White Country Blues," in *Nothing But the Blues: The Music and the Musicians,* ed. Lawrence Cohn (New York: Abbeville Press, 1993), 235, 236; Tony Russell, liner notes to the Allen Brothers, *Complete Recorded Works in Chronological Order, Vol. 1,* Document Records DOCD-8033 (1998). Tosches claims that the record in question was the Allen Brothers' first release, "Salty Dog Blues," backed with "Bow Wow Blues," and that the Allens filed and then dropped a lawsuit against Columbia. Wolfe agrees about the suit but identifies the disputed record as

"Chattanooga Blues," backed with "Laughin' and Cryin' Blues." Russell agrees with Wolfe about the record but is uncertain whether the suit, if there was one, was dropped or settled.

77. Gary Giddins, *Bing Crosby: A Pocket Full of Dreams, The Early Years 1903–1940* (Boston: Back Bay Books/Little, Brown, 2001), 81–85.

78. Donald Clarke, *Wishing on the Moon: The Life and Times of Billie Holiday* (New York: Viking Penguin, 1994), 429.

2. THE TRAIN KEPT A-ROLLIN'

1. Phil Cohen, liner notes to the Yardbirds, *Train Kept A-Rollin': The Complete Giorgio Gomelsky Productions,* Charly Records CD LIK BOX 3 (1993), 60; "Train Kept A Rollin' (Jimmy Page on Bass)," www.youtube.com/watch?v=lAwwwYpWKZM&feature=related. "There's been much discussion about who plays what on this track," asserts Cohen, who compiled the Yardbirds' boxed set. "For whatever it's worth, the late Keith Relf had stated that as for the great Beck/Page guitar duel that everyone imagines, 'That's Your Imagination.' He indicated in the same interview, that the second lead guitar was by Chris Dreja." Page can be seen playing bass while Dreja plays guitar on a 1966 performance of "The Train Kept A-Rollin'" for the French television program *Music Hall de France*.

2. Annette Carson, *Jeff Beck: Sticky Fingers* (San Francisco: Backbeat Books, 2001), 44; Giorgio Gomelsky, liner notes to The Yardbirds, *Train Kept A-Rollin',* 41.

3. Telephone interview with Giorgio Gomelsky, April 18, 2003.

4. Carson, *Jeff Beck*, 44.

5. Hank Zevallos, "Elvis–Johnny Burnette Connection," www.biwa.ne.jp/~presley/elnews-JohnnyBurnette.htm; Craig Morrison, *Go Cat Go! Rockabilly Music and Its Makers* (Urbana: University of Illinois Press, 1996), 37; Dennis West and John Blair, "Johnny Burnette & the Rock 'n Roll Trio," *Record Exchanger* 5, no. 4 (issue 26, 1978): 6; "1955," http://burnette-brothers.user.fr/ on The Johnny & Dorsey Burnette Discography website. Zevallos argues that Presley was influenced by Burnette's trio. Morrison, citing his own interview with Paul Burlison, says that the trio recorded for Von in 1953; Burlison also gave the 1953 date in other interviews. West and Blair give the Von recording date as 1954. The Johnny & Dorsey Burnette Discography website, compiled by the French researcher Marc Alesina, gives the date as November 1955.

6. Vince Gordon and Peter Dijkema, "Did Paul Burlison or Grady Martin play guitar for Johnny Burnette & the Rock'n'Roll Trio? And who 'invented guitar distortion'?" www.the-jime.dk/Rockabilly_Guitar/Johnny_Burnette_The_Rock-n-Roll_Trio.htm. Gordon and Dijkema dispute Burlison's "loose tube" explanation for the fuzz-tone guitar on "The Train Kept A-Rollin'" and "Honey Hush" and claim that the studio guitarist Grady Martin played the fuzz-tone parts using a different method. Martin certainly played one of the earliest fuzz-tone guitar solos on Marty Robbins's 1961 country smash "Don't Worry," where the fuzz effect is said to have been accidentally created by a defective channel in a mixing console.

7. Carson, *Jeff Beck*, 34.

8. Stephen Fratallone, "A Capitol Idea: Johnny Mercer's Dream of Capitol Records Waxing Great American Music Turns 60," March 2002, www.jazzconnectionmag.com/Capitol%20Records%2060th%20Anniversary%20Article.htm.

9. Morroe Berger, Edward Berger, and James Patrick, *Benny Carter: A Life in American Music, Vol. 1*, 2nd ed. (Lanham, MD: Scarecrow Press, 2002), 479.

10. Berger et al., *Benny Carter*, 469.

11. George T. Simon, *The Big Bands,* 4th ed. (New York: Schirmer1967/1981), 95.

12. Joel Whitburn, *Pop Memories 1890–1954: A History of American Popular Music* (Menomonee Falls, WI: Record Research, 1986), 7, 8, 27, 60.

13. Stuart Nicholson, *Ella Fitzgerald: A Biography of the First Lady of Jazz,* 2nd ed. (New York: Da Capo Press, 1995), 76–80, 269, 270. Nicholson refers to the group that backed Fitzgerald as the Three Keys, but other sources, including Phil Schaap's discography at the back of Nicholson's book, identify them as the Four Keys. Guitarist Slim Furness formed the

Four Keys with three of his brothers after the breakup of the Three Keys, a group founded in the early 1930s by Furness, pianist Bob Pease, and singer George "Bon Bon" Tunnell.

14. Fratallone, "A Capitol Idea."

15. Michael Corcoran, "The Morse Code," *Dallas Observer,* March 21, 1996, www.dallasobserver.com/1996-03-21/music/the-morse-code/2/.

16. Colin Larkin, ed., *The Encyclopedia of Popular Music,* 3rd. ed. (London: Muze, 1998), 1399.

17. "Boogie No. 1 (Cow Cow Boogie)," *Cow Cow Davenport—Volume 3: The Unissued 1940s Acetate Recordings,* Document Records DOCD-5586 (1997).

18. Peter J. Silvester, *A Left Hand Like God: A History of Boogie-Woogie Piano* (New York: Da Capo Press, 1989), 180; Cow Cow Davenport, "Cow-Cow and the Boogie-Woogie," *The Jazz Record,* April 15, 1945, 3; Cow Cow Davenport, "Mama Don't 'Low No Music," *The Jazz Record,* December 1944, 6–9.

19. Silvester, *A Left Hand Like God,* 63–66.

20. Cow Cow Davenport, "Mama Don't 'Low No Music," 7.

21. Cow Cow Davenport, "Mama Don't 'Low No Music," 9.

22. Carlton Brown, "Cow Cow Odyssey Colorful, but Tragic," *Down Beat,* December 1, 1945, 14.

23. Lynn Abbott and Doug Seroff, "'They Cert'ly Sound Good to Me': Sheet Music, Southern Vaudeville, and the Commercial Ascendancy of the Blues," *American Music* 14, no. 4 (Winter 1996): 437, 438.

24. W. C. Handy, *Father of the Blues: An Autobiography,* pbk ed. (New York: Da Capo Press, 1991 [orig. Macmillan, 1941]), 93.

25. W. C. Handy, *W. C. Handy: Father of the Blues,* DRG Records SL 5192 (1980).

26. Samuel B. Charters, *The Country Blues,* 2nd pbk. ed. (New York: Da Capo Press, 1977 [orig. Rinehart, 1959]), 38, 39.

27. Silvester, *A Left Hand Like God,* 182, 183.

28. David Evans, liner notes to *Cow Cow Davenport—Volume 3: The Unissued 1940s Acetate Recordings*; George Hoefer, "The Hot Box," *Down Beat,* January 25, 1956, 31. According to Hoefer, "Cow-Cow later claimed Leeds Music had given him $500 for the tune and removed his name from the sheet music."

29. Bruce Pegg, *Brown Eyed Handsome Man: The Life and Hard Times of Chuck Berry* (New York: Routledge, 2002), 247.

30. Gunther Schuller, *The Swing Era: The Development of Jazz, 1930–1945* (New York: Oxford University Press, 1989), 659.

31. Sammy Price, *What Do They Want? A Jazz Autobiography,* ed. Caroline Richmond (Urbana: University of Illinois Press, 1990), 51.

32. Morroe Berger, Edward Berger, and James Patrick, *Benny Carter: A Life in American Music, Vol. 2,* 2nd ed. (Lanham, MD: Scarecrow Press, 2001), 151.

33. Ernest Borneman, "Boogie Woogie," in *Just Jazz,* ed. Sinclair Traill and Gerald Lacelles (London: Peter Davies, 1957), 15.

34. David Wondrich, *Stomp and Swerve: American Music Gets Hot, 1843–1924* (Chicago: A Cappella Books/Chicago Review Press, 2003), 151; Anthony Slide, *The Encyclopedia of Vaudeville* (Westport, CT: Greenwood Press, 1994), 48; Peter C. Muir, "Before 'Crazy Blues': Commercial Blues in America 1850–1920" (PhD diss., City University of New York, 2004), 513; Samuel B. Charters and Leonard Kunstadt, *Jazz: A History of the New York Scene,* 1st pbk. ed. (New York: Da Capo Press, 1981 [orig. Doubleday, 1962]), 125. According to Wondrich, Haenschen and Schiffer, recording as Haenschen's Orchestra, made a personal Columbia record titled "Sunset Medley," which includes "A Bunch of Blues." The recording is included on *Stomp and Swerve: American Music Gets Hot* (Archeophone Records ARCH 1003, 2003), a companion CD to Wondrich's book. Little is known about Klass, but Slide mentions that he teamed with violinist Ben Bernie in 1910 in a vaudeville act called "Fiddle-Up-Boys." His recording of "A Bunch of Blues" on the Pathé label is listed in Muir's dissertation. The Original Memphis Five was one of the most successful and prolific of the groups that sprang up to capitalize on the success of the Original Dixieland Jazz Band, a white quintet that made the first jazz record ("Livery Stable Blues," backed with "Dixieland Jass Band One-Step") in early

1917. According to Charters and Kunstadt, the OMF was formed in New York later that year, taking its name from Handy's "Memphis Blues."

35. Telephone interview with Peter Muir, May 3, 2004.

36. Abbott and Seroff, "'They Cert'ly Sound Good to Me,'" 454.

37. Abbott and Seroff, "'They Cert'ly Sound Good to Me,'" 435.

38. Muir, "Before 'Crazy Blues,'" 394; David A. Jasen and Trebor Jay Tichenor, *Rags and Ragtime: A Musical History* (New York: Dover 1989 [orig. Seabury Press, 1978]), 213; "Trilby Rag" sheet music cover, http://digital.library.msstate.edu/cgi-bin/showfile.exe?CISOROOT=/SheetMusic&CISOPTR=26350&filename=26351.pdf; "Matrix C-16314. Trilby rag/Conway's Band," http://victor.library.ucsb.edu/index.php/matrix/detail/700001308/C-16314-Trilby_rag.

39. Jelly Roll Morton, "The Spanish Tinge," disc 6, track 8, *Jelly Roll Morton: The Complete Library of Congress Recordings by Alan Lomax,* Rounder 11661-1888-2 (2005). The quotation is transcribed on p. 104 of the PDF file on disc 8; Jelly Roll Morton, "I Created Jazz in 1902, Not W. C. Handy," *Down Beat*, August 1938, 3; Howard Reich and William Gaines, *Jelly's Blues: The Life, Music, and Redemption of Jelly Roll Morton* (New York: Da Capo Press, 2003), 36; Alan Lomax, *Mister Jelly Roll: The Fortunes of Jelly Roll Morton, New Orleans Creole and "Inventor of Jazz"* (Los Angeles: University of California Press, 2001 [orig. Pantheon Books, 1950]), 62. Morton told Lomax that "New Orleans Blues" was written "about nineteen-two"; in a letter published in *Down Beat* he said it was written in 1905. Reich and Gaines say that "as early as 1902 [Morton] had come up with a series of themes" that his piano teacher, Frank Richards, "helped him polish and develop" into the finished song by 1905. Lomax uses what appears to be the same quotation in edited form—"All the black bands in the city played it at that time"—in his book *Mister Jelly Roll.*

40. Jelly Roll Morton, "Game Kid Blues," disc 2, tracks 4, 5, *Jelly Roll Morton: The Complete Library of Congress Recordings by Alan Lomax.*

41. Reich and Gaines, *Jelly's Blues*, 271, 272; Peter Hanley, "Jelly Roll Morton: An Essay in Genealogy" (2002) (interpolating Peter Hanley and Prof. Lawrence Gushee, "Jelly Roll's Birth Year on the Mexican Visa," May 2005), www.doctorjazz.co.uk/genealogy.html. Reich and Gaines point out that the baptismal certificate, discovered by the Morton scholar Lawrence Gushee, is a 1984 copy that contains a number of errors. Hanley, an Australian researcher, cites a number of documents and attestations giving birth dates for Morton ranging from 1884 to 1894, concluding that September 20, 1890, is the most likely.

42. The cover of the first edition of Robert Hoffman's "I'm Alabama Bound," published in 1909, parenthetically notes that the song was "also known as the Alabama Blues."

43. "Unrecorded Interview Material and Research Notes by Alan Lomax, 1938–1946," PDF file, disc 8, *Jelly Roll Morton: The Complete Library of Congress Recordings by Alan Lomax,* Rounder 11661-1888-2 (2005), 189.

44. Reich and Gaines, *Jelly's Blues*, 43.

45. John Storm Roberts, *Latin Jazz: The First of the Fusions, 1880s to Today* (New York: Schirmer, 1999), 2, 3.

46. Al Rose, *Eubie Blake* (New York: Schirmer, 1979), 150; Peter Hanley, "Everybody's Just Wild about Eubie" (January 2003), www.doctorjazz.co.uk/portlater.html#eblake. Based on passport, census, and social security records, Hanley concludes that Blake was born in 1887 rather than 1883, as Blake had claimed. That would mean that Blake was only about eleven years old when he met Jesse Pickett.

47. David Cayer, liner notes to *The Original James P. Johnson, 1942–1945: Piano Solos,* Smithsonian Folkways 40812 (1996).

48. Robert E. Kimball, liner notes to *The Eighty-six Years of Eubie Blake,* Columbia Records C2S 847 (1969).

49. Fats Waller, playing organ, recorded a tune called "The Digah's Stomp" in 1927, but the melody is different and there's no Latin beat.

50. Larry Blumenfeld, notes to *Live Yardbirds! Featuring Jimmy Page,* www.8trackheaven.com/archive/yardbird.html.

51. Greg Russo, liner notes to *The Jimmy Page Collection: Have Guitar, Will Travel,* Fuel 2000 Records 302 061 291 2 (2003).

52. John Morthland, liner notes to *Texas Music Vol. 3: Garage Bands & Psychedelia*, Rhino Records R2 71783 (1994); Vernon Joynson, *Fuzz, Acid and Flowers: A Comprehensive Guide to American Garage, Psychedelic and Hippie-Rock (1964–1975)*, online edition (Wolverhampton, England: Borderline Books, 1994, http://alextsu.narod.ru/borderlinebooks/us6070s/index.html; Exotics bio, posted to the Exotics' MySpace page at http://www.myspace.com/tadrecords (2010).

53. John Sinclair, liner notes to *Killer Up!* Total Energy Records NER 3002 (1995).

54. Aerosmith with Stephen Davis, *Walk This Way: The Autobiography of Aerosmith,* 1st pbk. ed. (New York: Harper Entertainment, 2003 [orig. Avon Books, 1997]), 47, 48.

55. Alan di Perna, "Aerosmith: Classic Rocks," *Guitar World*, April 1997, 66.

56. Jeb Wright, "Classic Rock Revisited Presents an Exclusive Interview with . . . Dick Wagner," March 2000, www.classicrockrevisited.com (the interview no longer appears on this site but can be found in Italian on the web page www.loureed.it/articoli-e-interviste/intervista-a-dick-wagner-classic-rock-11-marzo-2000/).

57. Scott Alisoglu, "Classic Rock Revisited Presents an Exclusive Interview with . . . Dick Wagner," September 2002, http://www.classicrockrevisited.com/Dick%20Wags%202002.htm (the interview no longer appears on this page but can be found in Russian on the web page www.alicecooper5.narod.ru/staff/Dick_Wagner/Wagner-11.09.02.htm).

58. Greg Pedersen, "The Great Guitars of Dick Wagner and Steve Hunter," *Vintage Guitar,* May 15, 2001, www.vintageguitar.com/2795/dick-wagner-and-steve-hunter/.

3. ONE O' THEM THINGS!

1. Jelly Roll Morton, "See See Rider," disc 4, track 4, *Jelly Roll Morton: The Complete Library of Congress Recordings by Alan Lomax,* Rounder 11661-1888-2 (2005). The quotation is transcribed on p. 65 of the PDF file on disc 8; Big Bill Broonzy, portion of a taped interview with producer Bill Randle, July 12 or 13, 1957, included as track 3 of disc 2 on the three-CD set *The Bill Broonzy Story,* Verve 314 547 555-2 (1999 [orig. released as a 5-LP boxed set in 1960]). Although the authorship of "See See Rider" is credited to Lena Arrant (or Lina Arant), it is thought by some to be of folk origin. Jelly Roll Morton said he heard the song in his youth, and the version he recorded for Alan Lomax in 1938 contains verses—including bawdy ones—not found in other recordings. Big Bill Broonzy likewise said he heard the song as a youngster; in his interview with Bill Randle, Broonzy claimed that its originator was a former slave actually called See-See Rider, but he had earlier told Alan Lomax that this musician had taken his nickname from the song. Broonzy's 1934 recording also includes different verses, but later Broonzy recordings add still other verses, indicating that Broonzy, in true country blues tradition, simply threw in whatever lines came to mind at any given time. The song was also recorded by Ray Charles in 1949, at one of his first sessions, and by two traditional New Orleans jazzmen—clarinetist Emile Barnes in 1951 and trumpeter Kid Clayton in 1952—but it is unlikely that Chuck Willis heard those records. After Willis's hit, the song was recorded by dozens of blues, rock, pop, jazz, folk, R&B, and country artists—everyone from Lightnin' Hopkins, Muddy Waters, and B. B. King to Fats Domino, Jerry Lee Lewis, the Everly Brothers, Joey Dee and the Starlighters, Ian & Sylvia, Yusef Lateef, Cher, and Elvis Presley. A version by LaVern Baker made both the R&B and pop charts in 1963, as did one by the blind soul singer Bobby Powell in 1966; later in 1966, Eric Burdon and the Animals took the song to the pop Top 10.

2. Vic Fredericks, ed., *Who's Who in Rock 'n Roll: Facts, Fotos and Fan Gossip about the Performers in the World of Rock 'n Roll* (New York: Frederick Fell, 1958), 73. Although no writer is identified, the author is probably publisher Frederick Victor Fell, who takes editor's credit under a transparent pseudonym.

3. Big Bill Broonzy, interview with Bill Randle, included as track 8 of disc 1 on *The Bill Broonzy Story*.

4. James Dugan and John Hammond, program notes from the December 23, 1938, "From Spirituals to Swing" concert, 5, 11, and John Hammond, liner notes from the 1959 double

album *From Spirituals to Swing,* 8, both reproduced in separate booklets in the three-CD boxed set *From Spirituals to Swing: The Legendary 1938 & 1939 Concerts Produced by John Hammond,* Vanguard Records 169/71-2 (1999).

5. Charles Edward Smith, foreword to the American edition, Big Bill Broonzy with Yannick Bruynoghe, *Big Bill Blues: William Broonzy's Story* (New York: Oak Publications, 1964 [orig. Cassell & Co., 1955]), 13; William "Big Bill" Broonzy, "Baby, I Done Got Wise," *The Jazz Record,* March 1946, 9; Alan Lomax, *The Land Where the Blues Began,* 1st pbk. ed. (New York:The New Press, 2002 [orig. Pantheon, 1993]), 438, 443. Smith cites Papa Charlie Jackson as Broonzy's guitar mentor, although Jackson played six-string banjo, not guitar; Broonzy himself mentions Jim Jackson but not Charlie Jackson in the body of his sketchy "autobiography." In his article for *The Jazz Record,* Broonzy writes that he met Charlie Jackson in 1924 and that "Charlie first got me started on guitar." In a letter quoted by Lomax, Broonzy says he met both Jacksons in the early 1920s, but in a taped interview from the 1940s he tells Lomax that the one who "taught me how to make my music correspond to my singing" was Charlie Jackson, whom he identifies as the man who "had the first big blues hit with 'I'm Gonna Move to Kansas City.'" That, however, would have been Jim Jackson. Broonzy did record a couple of sides with Papa Charlie Jackson in 1935, but they were not released.

6. John A. Lomax and Alan Lomax, *American Ballads and Folk Songs* (New York: Macmillan, 1934), xxx.

7. Henry Edward Krehbiel, *Afro-American Folksongs: A Study in Racial and National Music* (Baltimore: Clearfield, 1996 [orig. G. Schirmer, 1914]), viii.

8. Howard W. Odum and Guy B. Johnson, *The Negro and His Songs: A Study of Typical Negro Songs in the South* (Westport, CT: Negro Universities Press, 1968 [orig. University of North Carolina Press, 1925]), 149.

9. Dorothy Scarborough, "The 'Blues' as Folk-Songs," *Coffee in the Gourd,* ed. J. Frank Dobie (Dallas: Southern Methodist University Press, 1969 [orig. Texas Folklore Society, 1923]), 52, 53, 58, 59. Scarborough published a slightly revised version of her essay as the "Blues" chapter of her 1925 book *On the Trail of Negro Folk-Songs.*

10. W. C. Handy, "How I Came to Write the 'Memphis Blues,'" *New York Age*, December 7, 1916, quoted in Elliott S. Hurwitt, "W. C. Handy as Music Publisher: Career and Reputation" (PhD diss., City University of New York, 2000), 113, 114.

11. Lynn Abbott and Doug Seroff, "'They Cert'ly Sound Good to Me': Sheet Music, Southern Vaudeville, and the Commercial Ascendancy of the Blues," *American Music* 14, no. 4 (Winter 1996): 425.

12. Stephen Calt and Gayle Wardlow, *King of the Delta Blues: The Life and Music of Charlie Patton* (Newton, NJ: Rock Chapel Press, 1988), 105, 107; W. C. Handy, *Father of the Blues: An Autobiography,* pbk. ed. (New York: Da Capo Press, 1991 [orig. Macmillan, 1941]), 73. Calt and Wardlow quote Willie Moore, an orphan who became Handy's ward, as saying that Handy "never played for no colored. . . . The colored folks didn't hire him 'cause they didn't have the money."

13. Handy, *Father of the Blues*, 73, 74; Max Haymes, "'This Cat's Got the Yellow Dog Blues'—Origins of the Term Yellow Dog," www.earlyblues.com/Yellow%20Dog.htm. Haymes, a British blues historian, suggests that the "Yellow Dog" rail line that Handy mentions was not the Yazoo Delta Railroad, as Handy believed, but the Yazoo and Mississippi Valley Railroad (a subsidiary of the Illinois Central Railroad), which had acquired the short-lived Yazoo Delta line by 1903.

14. Abbe Niles, "The Story of the Blues," in W. C. Handy, ed., *A Treasury of the Blues: Complete Words and Music of 67 Great Songs from* Memphis Blues *to the Present Day,* rev. 2nd ed. (New York: Charles Boni/Simon & Schuster, 1949 [rev. expanded ed. of *Blues: An Anthology,* New York: Albert and Charles Boni, 1926]), 17, 18 .

15. Hurwitt, "W. C. Handy as Music Publisher," 113, 114.

16. Gayle Dean Warlow, *Chasin' That Devil Music: Searching for the Blues* (San Francisco: Backbeat Books, 1998), 36.

17. Calt and Wardlow, *King of the Delta Blues*, 48, 85, 108. Calt and Wardlow say that Patton's parents gave the 1991 date to a census taker. Other sources date Patton's birth to 1887.

18. Calt and Wardlow, 87, 107, 307.

19. Handy, *Father of the Blues,* 99.
20. Lomax, *The Land Where the Blues Began,* 165, 166.
21. Niles, "Story of the Blues," 13.
22. Jelly Roll Morton, "I Created Jazz in 1902, Not W. C. Handy," *Down Beat,* August 1938, 3, 31; Jelly Roll Morton, "Jelly Roll Says He Was First to Play Jazz," *Down Beat,* September 1938, 4; Howard Reich and William Gaines, *Jelly's Blues: The Life, Music, and Redemption of Jelly Roll Morton* (New York: Da Capo Press, 2003), 152, 153. Reich and Gaines say that Morton's letter was actually written by Roy Carew, a white jazz fan who befriended Morton in 1938. They claim that "the mangled dates, spellings, and musicological errors affirm that the letter was Carew's handiwork," although letters known to have been written by Morton contain similar errors.
23. W. C. Handy, "I Would Not Play Jazz if I Could," *Down Beat,* September 1938, 5.
24. Jelly Roll Morton, "Mamie's Blues," disc 7, track 4, *Jelly Roll Morton: The Complete Library of Congress Recordings by Alan Lomax,* Rounder 11661-1888-2 (2005). The quotation is transcribed on p. 113 of the PDF file on disc 8.
25. Jelly Roll Morton, "Mamie's Blues," track 12, *Jelly Roll Morton: Last Session—The Complete General Recordings,* Commodore CMD-403 (1997); Alan Lomax, *Mister Jelly Roll: The Fortunes of Jelly Roll Morton, New Orleans Creole and "Inventor of Jazz"* (Los Angeles: University of California Press, 2001 [orig. Pantheon Books, 1950]), 21. In his book, which weaves Morton's Library of Congress interviews into a sort of autobiography, Lomax quotes Morton as saying, "Although I had heard them previously I guess it was Mamie first really sold me on the blues"; but this quotation does not appear in the Library of Congress transcripts.
26. Lomax, *Mister Jelly Roll,* 21; Alan Lomax, letter to *The Record Changer* in June 1949, cited by Peter Hanley, "Portraits from Jelly Roll's New Orleans," www.doctorjazz.co.uk/portnewor.html, as verifying the date of Lomax's interview with Bunk Johnson.
27. Abbott and Seroff, "'They Cert'ly Sound Good to Me,'" 407. Some sources place the recording of "I'm Alabama Bound" by Prince's Band (or Prince's Orchestra) in late 1909 rather than 1910.
28. Newman I. White, *American Negro Folk-Songs* (Cambridge: Harvard University Press, 1928), 306–308.
29. W. H. Thomas, *Some Current Folk-Songs of the Negro* (pamphlet) (Austin: Folk-Lore Society of Texas, 1912), 12.
30. R. J. Carew, "New Orleans Recollections" *The Record Changer,* May 1943, 11; Roy J. Carew, "Of This and That and Jelly Roll," *Jazz Journal* 10, no. 12 (December 1957): 10–12, www.doctorjazz.co.uk/thisthat.html.
31. Clarence Williams, *Clarence Williams Presents: The "Boogie Woogie" Blues Folio: First "Boogie Woogie" Tunes of Clarence Williams, George Thomas and Charles "Cow Cow" Davenport, with Annotations by Clarence Williams* (New York: Clarence Williams Publishing, 1940), 11.
32. "Unrecorded Interview Material and Research Notes by Alan Lomax, 1938–1946," PDF file, disc 8, *Jelly Roll Morton: The Complete Library of Congress Recordings by Alan Lomax,* Rounder 11661-1888-2 (2005), 189; Abbott and Seroff, "'They Cert'ly Sound Good to Me,'" 435, 452.
33. Howard W. Odum, "Folk-Song and Folk-Poetry as Found in the Secular Songs of the Southern Negroes," *Journal of American Folk-Lore* 24, no. 93 (July–September 1911): 278.
34. Donald M. Marquis, *In Search of Buddy Bolden: First Man of Jazz,* 1st pbk. ed. (New York: Da Capo Press, 1980 [orig. Louisiana State University Press, 1978]), 107, 108.
35. Marquis, *In Search of Buddy Bolden,* 100, 101, 105, 107–109; Jelly Roll Morton, "Buddy Bolden's Blues," disc 3, track 11, *Jelly Roll Morton: The Complete Library of Congress Recordings by Alan Lomax,* Rounder 11661-1888-2 (2005). The quotations are transcribed on pp. 51 and 52 of the PDF file on disc 8.
36. Marquis, *In Search of Buddy Bolden,* 2, 3.
37. White, *American Negro Folk-Songs,* 410.
38. John W. Work, *American Negro Songs: 230 Folk Songs and Spirituals, Religious and Secular* (Mineola, NY: Dover, 1998 [orig. Crown Publishers, 1940]), 32, 33.
39. Odum, "Folk-Song and Folk-Poetry," 270.

40. Calt and Wardlow, *King of the Delta Blues*, 63, 64, 275.
41. Lomax, *The Land Where the Blues Began*, 55.
42. Henry Townsend as told to Bill Greensmith, *A Blues Life* (Urbana: University of Illinois, 1999), 5.
43. Mississippi Fred McDowell, *I Do Not Play No Rock 'n' Roll,* Capitol ST-409 (1969).
44. Peter C. Muir, "Before 'Crazy Blues': Commercial Blues in America 1850–1920" (PhD diss., City University of New York, 2004), 404 [publication date of Maggio's "I Got the Blues"]; Abbott and Seroff, "'They Cert'ly Sound Good to Me,'" 405 [an "Up-to-Date Rag"]; "Stage," *Indianapolis Freeman,* August 30, 1902, quoted in Lynn Abbott and Doug Seroff, *Ragged but Right: Black Traveling Shows, "Coon Songs," and the Dark Pathway to Blues and Jazz* (Jackson: University Press of Mississippi, 2007), 252, 412. The *Indianapolis Freeman* mentions that the African American singer Will Goff Kennedy was performing a song called "I Got the Blues" in the traveling minstrel show *A Rabbit's Foot* in 1902, but it is not clear whether this is the same song as Smith and Bowman's "I've Got de Blues."
45. Anthony Maggio, quoted in the Personal News Notes column of *Overture* (journal of Local 47, American Federation of Musicians, Los Angeles) 35, no. 9 (December 1955): 13.
46. Abbe Niles, "Notes to the Collection," in Handy, ed., *A Treasury of the Blues*, 242 ["Handy . . . said he'd heard a church elder sing the figure"]; W. C. Handy, letter to William Grant Still (December 20, 1955), "Handy Letters to Still," part 2, *Black Perspective* 8, no. 1 (Spring 1980): 107, 108, quoted in Elliott S. Hurwitt, "W. C. Handy as Music Publisher: Career and Reputation" (PhD diss., City University of New York, 2000), 479–481 ["I haven't been in New Orleans since 1900"].
47. R. J. Carew, "New Orleans Recollections" *The Record Changer,* May 1943, 11.
48. Paul Oliver, *Conversation with the Blues* (London: Cassell, 1965), 96, 97; David A. Jasen and Gene Jones, *That American Rag: The Story of Ragtime from Coast to Coast* (New York: Schirmer, 2000), 36.
49. David A. Jasen and Trebor Jay Tichenor, *Rags and Ragtime: A Musical History* (New York: Dover, 1989 [orig. Seabury Press, 1978]), 71.
50. Peter C. Muir, *Long Lost Blues: Popular Blues in America, 1850–1920* (Urbana: University of Illinois Press, 2010), 207.
51. John Jacob Niles, "Shout, Coon, Shout!" *The Musical Quarterly* 16, no. 4 (October 1930): 519; Paul Oliver, *Songsters and Saints: Vocal Traditions on Race Records* (Cambridge: Cambridge University Press, 1984), 260–263.
52. William Barlow, *"Looking Up at Down": The Emergence of Blues Culture* (Philadelphia: Temple University Press, 1989), 64; Gates Thomas, "South Texas Negro Work-Songs: Collected and Uncollected," *Rainbow in the Morning: Publications of the Texas Folklore Society Number V,* J. Frank Dobie, ed. (Denton: University of North Texas Press, 1975 [orig. 1926]), 160.
53. Abbott and Seroff, "'They Cert'ly Sound Good to Me,'" 413.
54. Abbott and Seroff, "'They Cert'ly Sound Good to Me,'" 416, 429, 430.
55. Abbott and Seroff, "'They Cert'ly Sound Good to Me,'" 414–416.
56. Odum, "Folk-Song and Folk-Poetry," 272.
57. Odum, "Folk-Song and Folk-Poetry," 418, 421.
58. Charles Anderson, "Sing 'Em Blues," *Eddie Heywood & the Blues Singers,* Document Records DOCD-5380 (1995). Heywood, who accompanies Anderson on piano, was the father of Eddie Heywood Jr., a jazz pianist of the 1930s and 1940s who turned to pop music in the 1950s.
59. Samuel B. Charters, *The Country Blues,* 2nd pbk. ed. (New York: Da Capo Press, 1977 [orig. Rinehart, 1959]), 35, 36.
60. Handy, *Father of the Blues,* 106–110.
61. "George H. O'Connor Papers," *Library Associates Newsletter,* February 1986, Newsletter 18, http://old.library.georgetown.edu/advancement/newsletter/18/oconnor18.htm.
62. Muir, "Before 'Crazy Blues,'" 2, 74.
63. Handy, *Father of the Blues,* 200.
64. Tim Brooks, *Lost Sounds: Blacks and the Birth of the Recording Industry 1890–1919* (Urbana: University of Illinois Press, 2004), 17, 26–28, 254, 255, 486, 487; Rainer E. Lotz,

"Belle Davis and Her Piccaninnies: A Preliminary Bio-, Disco- and Filmography," *ARSC Journal* 25, no. 2 (Fall 1994): 179–183. Black male singers had been recorded since 1890, when George W. Johnson waxed "The Whistling Coon." The first black woman to record was Belle Davis, an American coon shouter who made a few recordings in 1902 while touring England, beginning with the operetta piece "The Honeysuckle and the Bee." Other early black female recording artists include Daisy Tapley, who recorded the hymn "I Surrender All" in a 1910 duet with the baritone C. Carroll Clark, and Florence Cole-Talbert, who recorded an African American spiritual and a French art song in 1919.

65. David A. Jasen and Gene Jones, *Spreadin' Rhythm Around: Black Popular Songwriters, 1880–1930* (New York: Schirmer, 1998), 259–263.

66. Jasen and Jones, *Spreadin' Rhythm Around*, 267.

67. Rudi Blesh, *Shining Trumpets: A History of Jazz* (New York: Knopf, 1946), 108–111.

68. Tony Russell, liner notes to *Male Blues of the Twenties, Vol. 1 (1922–1930),* Document Records DOCD-5482 (1996). Russell writes that a photograph of Du Pree appeared in the *New York Age* in 1912 and that "by the 1930s, if not earlier, he was based in Philadelphia." Other sources identify Du Pree (sometimes spelled Dupree) as a Philadelphia music promoter or booking agent who claimed credit for writing the song "Shortnin' Bread."

69. Jeff Todd Titon, *Early Downhome Blues: A Musical and Cultural Analysis* (Urbana: University of Illinois Press, 1977), 210.

70. Titon, *Early Downhome Blues*, 213.

71. Valerie Wilmer, "Lonnie Johnson Talks to Valerie Wilmer," *Jazz Monthly* 9, no. 10 (December 1963): 6.

72. Oliver, *Conversation with the Blues,* 78, 79.

73. Townsend, *A Blues Life*, 19.

74. Stephen C. LaVere, liner notes to Robert Johnson, *The Complete Recordings,* Columbia Records C2K 46222 (1990), 20.

75. Wilmer, "Lonnie Johnson Talks to Valerie Wilmer," 5.

76. Wardlow, *Chasin' That Devil Music,* 72.

77. Calt and Wardlow, *King of the Delta Blues*, 64.

78. Handy, *Father of the Blues,* 87.

79. Robert M. W. Dixon, John Godrich, and Howard Rye, *Blues & Gospel Records 1890–1943,* 4th ed. (Oxford: Clarendon Press, 1977), 966; Howard W. Odum and Guy B. Johnson, *Negro Workaday Songs* (Chapel Hill: University of North Carolina Press, 1926), 252; Marybeth Hamilton, *In Search of the Blues* (New York: Basic Books, 2008), 29, 45; Dorothy Scarborough with Ola Lee Gulledge, *On the Trail of Negro Folk-Songs* (Hatboro: PA: Folklore Associates, 1963 [orig. Harvard University Press, 1925]), 264, 265. Dixon, Godrich, and Rye cite the "phono-photographic" recordings made in North Carolina and Virginia in 1925 by Milton Metfessel and Howard Odum as "the earliest non-commercial field recordings of which we have knowledge." Odum describes these records in *Negro Workaday Songs*. According to Hamilton, Odum, using a type of phonograph called a graphophone, had recorded African American folk songs on wax cylinders as early as 1907 but lost or discarded the cylinders in the 1920s. Dorothy Scarborough also made recordings, which Ola Lee Gulledge transcribed for their book *On the Trail of Negro Folk-Songs*. Lawrence Gellert, a left-wing activist best known for his book *Negro Songs of Protest,* made field recordings in the Carolinas as early as 1924 that were discovered in the 1980s and released on the 1998 Document CD *Field Recordings, Vol. 9: Georgia, North Carolina, South Carolina, Virginia, Kentucky (1924–1939)*. And Natalie Curtis-Burlin made recordings of students at the Hampton Institute in Virginia, which she published in 1918 and 1919 in her four-volume series *Negro Folk-Songs*.

80. Stephen Calt, *I'd Rather Be the Devil: Skip James and the Blues* (Chicago: Chicago Review Press, 1994), 34–46; Dena J. Epstein, *Sinful Tunes and Spirituals: Black Folk Music to the Civil War* (Urbana: University of Illinois Press, 1977), 270. Lucy McKim first collected "Roll, Jordan, Roll" in the South Carolina Sea Islands in 1862 and published it at the end of that year. In 1867, her transcription, together with one collected by Charles Pickard Ware, was published as the first number in *Slave Songs of the United States*. But according to Epstein, "Neither version . . . has the tune now usually associated with 'Roll, Jordan, Roll' . . . That tune appears in *Slave Songs* as number 15, 'Lord, Remember Me.'"

81. Alan Lomax, liner notes to *Negro Prison Songs*, Tradition Records TLP 1020 (1957), reproduced in the CD booklet of *Prison Songs: Historical Recordings from Parchman Farm 1947–48, Vol. 1: Murderous Home*, Rounder Records CD 1714 (1997).

82. Son House, "I Can Make My Own Songs" (tape recorded and edited by Julius Lester), *Sing Out!* 15, no. 3 (July 1965): 45; Epstein, *Sinful Tunes and Spirituals,* 172; George Pullen Jackson, *White and Negro Spirituals: Their Life Span and Kinship* (Locust Valley, NY: J. J. Augustin, 1943), 252, 253. According to Epstein, the term "corn songs" usually refers to corn-shucking songs sung in chorus. According to Jackson, "long meter songs" are usually hymns or spirituals sung in slow tempo.

83. Frederick Law Olmsted, *A Journey in the Seaboard Slave States in the Years 1853–1854, with Remarks on Their Economy . . .* (New York: Putnam's, 1904 [orig. 1856]), 19, 20, quoted in Epstein, *Sinful Tunes and Spirituals*, 182.

84. Pete Welding, "'I Sing for the People': An Interview with Bluesman Howling Wolf," *Down Beat,* December 14, 1967, 21.

85. Charles Peabody, "Notes on Negro Music," *Journal of American Folk-Lore, Vol. 16,* (Millwood, NY: Kraus Reprint Co., 1979 [orig. Houghton, Mifflin, 1903]): 151, 152.

86. Lomax, *The Land Where the Blues Began*, 231.

87. Elijah Wald, *Escaping the Delta: Robert Johnson and the Invention of the Blues* (New York: Amistad/HarperCollins, 2004), 77.

88. Lotz, "Belle Davis and Her Piccaninnies," 183.

89. Dixon, Godrich, and Rye, *Blues and Gospel Records,* 859; Brooks, *Lost Sounds,* 92–102. Brooks says that the Standard Quartette rerecorded "Way Down Yonder in the Cornfield" for the U.S. Phonograph Company in 1896 or 1897, and that the Columbia Phonograph Company, which had produced the original 1894 recording, then had the Manhansett Quartette "remake a number of the Standard Quartette titles," presumably including "Way Down Yonder in the Cornfield."

90. Lynn Abbott, "'Play That Barber Shop Chord': A Case for the African-American Origin of Barbershop Harmony," *American Music* 10, no. 3 (Fall 1992): 304.

91. Carl Sandburg, *Cornhuskers* (Mineola, NY: Dover 2000 [orig. Henry Holt, 1918]), 30.

92. White, *American Negro Folk-Songs*, 370–372; Odum and Johnson, *Negro Workaday Songs*, 174.

93. White, *American Negro Folk-Songs*, 168, 169; Scarborough, *On the Trail of Negro Folk-Songs*, 12, 24, 25; John A. Lomax and Alan Lomax, *American Ballads and Folk Songs*, 228.

94. E. C. Perrow, "Songs and Rhymes from the South," *Journal of American Folk-Lore* 28 (1915): 135, 136, 138.

95. Joel Chandler Harris, *Uncle Remus: His Songs and His Sayings* (New York: Appleton-Century-Crofts, 1921 [orig. D. Appleton, 1880]), 32; Joel Chandler Harris, *Uncle Remus and His Friends* (Boston: Houghton Mifflin, 1892), 200, 201.

96. Lafcadio Hearn, "Levee Life," *Cincinnati Commercial,* March 17, 1876, reprinted in Henry Goodman, ed., *The Selected Writings of Lafcadio Hearn* (New York: Citadel Press, 1949), 224.

97. William Francis Allen, Charles Pickard Ware, and Lucy McKim Garrison, *Slave Songs of the United States* (New York: Dover, 1995 [orig. A. Simpson, 1867]), 89.

98. J. B. Harper, "Whar You Cum From," *The Negro Singer's Own Book* (Philadelphia: Turner & Fisher [1846?]), 411, cited in White, *American Negro Folk-Songs*, 370.

99. *White's Serenaders' Song Book* (Philadelphia: T.B. Peterson, 1851), 66–68, reproduced in the liner notes to Gid Tanner and His Skillet Lickers, *"Hear These New Southern Fiddle and Guitar Records!"* Rounder Records 1005 (1973).

100. Robert C. Toll, *Blacking Up: The Minstrel Show in Nineteenth-Century America* (New York: Oxford University Press, 1974), 50.

101. Howard L. Sacks and Judith Rose Sacks, *Way Up North in Dixie: A Black Family's Claim to the Confederate Anthem* (Washington, DC: Smithsonian Institution Press, 1993).

102. Epstein, *Sinful Tunes and Spirituals*, 241.

103. Allen, Ware, and Garrison, *Slave Songs of the United States*, vii, viii.

104. Richard Wallaschek, *Primitive Music: An Inquiry into the Origin and Development of Music, Songs, Instruments, Dances and Pantomimes of Savage Races* (New York: Da Capo Press, 1970 [orig. Longmans, Green, and Co., 1893]), 60, 61.

105. Julien Tiersot, *La musique chez les peuples indigènes de l'Amérique du Nord* (Paris: Librairie Fischbacher), cited in Krehbiel, *Afro-American Folksongs*, 32.

106. Krehbiel, *Afro-American Folksongs*, 22.

107. Krehbiel, *Afro-American Folksongs*, 69.

108. D. K. Wilgus, *Anglo-American Folksong Scholarship Since 1898* (New Brunswick, NJ: Rutgers University Press, 1959), 345–364.

109. Jackson, *White and Negro Spirituals,* 293.

110. Richard Alan Waterman, "African Influence on the Music of the Americas," *Acculturation in the Americas,* ed. Sol Tax (Chicago: University of Chicago Press, 1952), 207–18, quoted in Paul Oliver, *Savannah Syncopators: African Retentions in the Blues* (London: Studio Vista, 1970), republished in *Yonder Come the Blues* (Cambridge: Cambridge University Press, 2001), 26.

111. Henry Ratcliff/Bakari Badji, "Louisiana/Field Song from Senegal," *Roots of the Blues,* New World Records 80252 (1977).

112. Banning Eyre, *In Griot Time: An American Guitarist in Mali* (Philadelphia: Temple University Press, 2000), 55, 56.

113. Lucy Duran, liner notes to Ali Farka Touré, *Radio Mali,* Nonesuch Records 79569 (1999 [orig. World Circuit 044, 1996]).

114. Gerhard Kubik, *Africa and the Blues* (Jackson: University Press of Mississippi, 1999), 94.

115. Paul Oliver, *Savannah Syncopators,* 81–85.

116. Kubik, *Africa and the Blues*, 97–100.

117. Kubik, *Africa and the Blues*, 102.

118. Calt and Wardlow, *King of the Delta Blues*, 96.

119. Muir, *Long Lost Blues*, 195.

120. Cecil Brown, "We Did Them Wrong: The Ballad of Frankie and Albert," in *The Rose and the Briar: Death, Love and Liberty in the American Ballad,* ed. Sean Wilentz and Greil Marcus (New York: Norton, 2005), 126, 143, 144.

121. Peter van der Merwe, *Origins of the Popular Style: The Antecedents of Twentieth-Century Popular Music,* 1st pbk. ed. (Oxford: Clarendon Press, 1992 [orig. Oxford University Press, 1989]), 185, 186.

122. Abbe Niles, "Notes to the Collection," 244.

123. Broonzy, *Big Bill Blues,* 53–59; Big Bill Broonzy, tracks 13 and 14 on disc 1 of *The Bill Broonzy Story.*

124. Handy, *Father of the Blues,* 145–147; Howard W. Odum, "Folk-Song and Folk-Poetry as Found in the Secular Songs of the Southern Negroes—concluded," *Journal of American Folk-Lore* 24, no. 94 (October–December 1911): 351.

125. Van der Merwe, *Origins of the Popular Style*, 171–183

126. Cecil J. Sharp, *English Folk Song: Some Conclusions,* 4th rev. ed. (London: Mercury Books, 1965 [orig. Simpkin, Novello; Barnicott and Pearce, 1907]), 47–91.

127. Jackson, *White and Negro Spirituals*, 236–239.

128. Kubik, *Africa and the Blues*, 120, 121.

129. Don Palmer, "Baaba Maal and Ernest Ranglin: Fanta Seers," *Rhythm Music*, September 1998, 33, 34.

130. Van der Merwe, *Origins of the Popular Style*, 11–13.

131. Richard Nevins, liner notes to *Before the Blues: The Early American Black Music Scene as Captured on Classic Recordings from the 1920s and 30s,* Yazoo Records 2015, 2016, 2017 (1996), 2.

132. Thomas, *Some Current Folk-Songs of the Negro,* 11.

133. Tony Russell, *Blacks, Whites and Blues* [orig. Studio Vista, 1970], in *Yonder Come the Blues* (Cambridge: Cambridge University Press, 2001), 178. Russell notes that Uncle Dave Macon cut some of the same material that Thomas did and speculates that Brunswick, the company they both recorded for, "was attempting a sort of comparative issue programme—

Macon for the Whites, Thomas for the race." However, most of the songs they shared, such as "John Henry" and "The Fox and the Hounds" (also known as "Fox Chase"), were commonplace, and their renditions were, for the most part, radically different. The only song they performed similarly was "When the Train Comes Along," and Macon did not record that one until 1934, seven years after Thomas's version.

134. Wilgus, *Anglo-American Folksong Scholarship Since 1898*, 363

135. Titon, *Early Downhome Blues*, 215; Bruce Roberts, "'Blind' Lemon Jefferson Memorial," www.thebluehighway.com/blues/amazonx.html; Bruce Roberts, *Blues and Rhythm* 119 (May? 1997): 4, 5; Jonathan Black, "Draft Card Blues: A Newly Discovered Document Sheds Light on Blind Lemon Jefferson," *Living Blues*, October 2007, 66. Some sources give Jefferson's birth date as early as 1880, but the year 1897 was generally accepted until 1996, when Bruce Roberts discovered census records that gave the date as September 1893. More recently, a 1917 draft card was discovered in the National Archives that gives Jefferson's birth date as October 15, 1894.

4. THE ROCKS

1. Max Harrison, "Boogie-Woogie," in *Jazz: New Perspectives on the History of Jazz by Twelve of the World's Foremost Jazz Critics and Scholars,* ed. Nat Hentoff and Albert McCarthy, 2nd pbk. printing (New York: Da Capo Press, 1975 [orig. Holt, Rinehart and Winston, 1959]), 134.

2. Chuck Berry, *The Autobiography* (New York: Harmony Books, 1987), 142.

3. William Russell, "Boogie Woogie," *Jazzmen,* ed. Frederic Ramsey Jr. and Charles Edward Smith (New York: Limelight Editions, 1967 [orig. Harcourt Brace Jovanovich, 1939]), 183–205.

4. Ernest Borneman, "Boogie Woogie," *Just Jazz,* ed. Sinclair Traill and Gerald Lascelles (London: Peter Davies, 1957), 13–40.

5. Rudi Blesh and Harriet Janis, *They All Played Ragtime* (New York: Oak Publications, 1966 [orig. Alfred A. Knopf, 1950]), 192. If Eubie Blake was actually born in 1887, as Peter Hanley maintains, he would have been only nine years old, not thirteen, when he heard William Turk play boogie-woogie; alternatively, Blake may have heard Turk in 1900, not 1896. (See note 46, chapter 2.)

6. H. B. Kay, "8 to the Bar," *The Record Changer,* May 1949, 14, 20. Kay refers to Koster and Bial's Music Hall as "the Koster & Beals Music Hall."

7. Onah L. Spencer, "Boogie Piano Was Hot Stuff in 1904!" *Down Beat,* July 1939, 22.

8. Jelly Roll Morton, "Michigan Water Blues" disc 6, track 18, *The Complete Library of Congress Recordings by Alan Lomax,* Rounder 11661-1888-2 (2005). The quotation is transcribed on p. 110 of the PDF file on disc 8; Jelly Roll Morton, "Jelly Roll Says He Was First to Play Jazz," *Down Beat,* September 1938, 4.

9. Ross Russell, "Illuminating the Leadbelly Legend," *Down Beat,* August 6, 1970, 12; Charles E. Smith, "Leadbelly—King of the 12-String Guitar," *The Leadbelly Songbook,* ed. Moses Asch and Alan Lomax (New York: Oak Publications, 1962), 14; Charles Wolfe and Kip Lornell, *The Life and Legend of Leadbelly* (New York: HarperCollins, 1992), 35. Wolfe and Lornell quote Leadbelly, without attribution, as saying, "It was about 1904, 1903, piano players were walking the bases [sic]." Other sources claim that Leadbelly heard pianists play boogie-woogie bass lines as early as 1899.

10. Borneman, "Boogie Woogie," 17; Verne Streckfus, interview digest, September 22, 1960, Hogan Jazz Archives, Tulane University, New Orleans, cited on p. 197 of William Howland Kenney, *Jazz on the River* (Chicago: University of Chicago Press, 2005). Also Kenney, 40, 42, 125; Interview with William Howland Kenney, December 2005, www.jerryjazzmusician.com/linernotes/william_kenney.html. In his Jerry Jazz Musician interview, Kenney says that "Catalano was treated by *Down Beat* as the spokesperson for white jazz musicians who played on the river, and he was frequently interviewed about this when they wanted to write about jazz on the river."

11. Perry Bradford, *Born with the Blues: Perry Bradford's Own Story* (New York: Oak Publications, 1965), 31.

12. Borneman, "Boogie Woogie," 17; William Patton, *A Guide to Historic Downtown Memphis* (Charleston, SC: The History Press, 2010), 32; "Beale Street Memorabilia," http://historic-memphis.com/memphis-historic/beale/bealestreet.html; W. C. Handy, *Father of the Blues: An Autobiography,* pbk. ed. (New York: Da Capo Press, 1991 [orig. Macmillan, 1941]), xi, 152, 153. Patton says that the "Monarch Club," which "attracted all sorts of patrons, including W. C. Handy," did not open until 1910, but the Historic Memphis Beale Street web page displays an advertisement, said to date from 1908, for a "Monarch Saloon" at the same address. In his autobiography, Handy gives a notated example of the piano style that Benny French and Sonny Butts (but not Seymour Abernathy) played at the Monarch, citing it as the musical inspiration for his own "Beale Street Blues" and "Yellow Dog Blues." The example does not, however, include an "eight to the bar" bass pattern. In the book's foreword, Handy says that "Beale Street Blues" was inspired by a pianist at the Monarch whose name he didn't know. "Yellow Dog Blues," originally published as "Yellow Dog Rag" in 1914, does feature a boogie-style arpeggiated minor-third chord in the melody line, but not in the bass accompaniment. "Beale Street Blues," originally published as "Beale Street" in 1916, uses a brief, un-boogie-like walking bass figure at the ends of the blues choruses.

13. Jelly Roll Morton, "Benny Frenchy's Tune," disc 4, tracks 11, 12, *The Complete Library of Congress Recordings by Alan Lomax,* Rounder 11661-1888-2 (2005). Morton's comments are transcribed on pp. 75–79 of the PDF file on disc 8. He gives the year on track 8, "Jelly's Travels from Yazoo to Clarksdale," transcribed on p. 71.

14. Paul Oliver, *Conversation with the Blues* (London: Cassell, 1965), 95, 96.

15. Guido van Rijn and Hans Vergeer, liner notes to James "Stump" Johnson, *The Duck's Yas-Yas-Yas,* Agram Blues AB 2007 (1981).

16. Clarence Williams, *Clarence Williams Presents: The "Boogie Woogie" Blues Folio: First "Boogie Woogie" Tunes of Clarence Williams, George Thomas and Charles "Cow Cow" Davenport, with Annotations by Clarence Williams* (New York: Clarence Williams Publishing, 1940), 2.

17. Al Rose, *Eubie Blake* (New York: Schirmer Books, 1979), 26, 42, 43. If one takes Blake's word for his birth year, he would have been sixteen years old when he composed the complex, advanced, and highly original "Charleston Rag." If Peter Hanley's research is correct, Blake would have been only twelve. (See note 46, chapter 2.)

18. Judge Learned Hand, opinion in *Fred Fisher, Inc. v. Dillingham,* 298 F. 145 (S.D.N.Y. 1924), http://cip.law.ucla.edu/cases/1920-1929/Pages/fredfisherdillingham.aspx.

19. Peter J. Silvester, *A Left Hand Like God: A History of Boogie-Woogie Piano* (New York: Da Capo Press, 1989), 77, 78; Mike Rowe, liner notes to *Sippie Wallace, Complete Recorded Works in Chronological Order, Vol. 2,* Document Records DOCD-5400 (1995). Silvester mentions a rumor that Hersal Thomas was poisoned by a jilted girlfriend as well as Sippie Wallace's opinion that he died of accidental food poisoning; but Rowe notes that his death certificate identifies the cause of death as "acute gall-bladder."

20. Russell, "Boogie Woogie," 189.

21. "Meade Lux Lewis: A Blues Man's Story," *Down Beat,* February 19, 1959, 17.

22. Michael W. Harris, *The Rise of Gospel Blues: The Music of Thomas Andrew Dorsey* (New York: Oxford University Press, 1992), 40; John Chilton, *Who's Who of Jazz: Storyville to Swing Street* (New York: Time-Life Records Special Edition, 1978 [orig. Chilton Book Company, 1972]), 143. Quoting his own interviews with Dorsey, Harris identifies Heywood as one of Dorsey's early influences.

23. E. Simms Campbell, "Blues," *Jazzmen,* ed. Frederic Ramsey Jr. and Charles Edward Smith (New York: Limelight Editions, 1967 [orig. Harcourt Brace Jovanovich, 1939]), 112, 113.

24. Williams, *Clarence Williams Presents: The "Boogie Woogie" Blues Folio,* 2.

25. Williams, *Clarence Williams Presents: The "Boogie Woogie" Blues Folio,* 11.

26. David Evans, liner notes to *Texas Piano—Vol. 1 (1923–1935),* Document Records DOCD-5334 (1994).

27. Silvester, *A Left Hand Like God,* 22.

28. Karl Gert zur Heide, *Deep South Piano: The Story of Little Brother Montgomery* (London: Studio Vista, 1970), 16–18.

29. Heide, *Deep South Piano*, 18, 19.

30. Heide, *Deep South Piano,* 20, 21, 29, 30. Big Joe Williams, BBC interview, Chicago, 1976, cited in Giles Oakley, *The Devil's Music: A History of the Blues* (New York: Harvest/Harcourt Brace Jovanovich, 1978 [orig. British Broadcasting Corporation, 1976]), 79; Silvester, *A Left Hand Like God,* 29 ["barrelhouses"]. In the BBC interview, Williams says he played with Montgomery at a "camp" where "sometimes the women dance on top of the piano." In Heide's book, he identifies the venue as a brothel.

31. Silvester, *A Left Hand Like God,* 27. Silvester cites a 1960 recording of "Santa Fe Train" by the Texas pianist Buster Pickens, in which Pickens mentions playing at a sawmill, but Pickens was born in 1916, too late to have participated in the formative process of boogie-woogie.

32. Bob Hall, liner notes to *Shake Your Wicked Knees: Rent Parties and Good Times*, Yazoo Records 2035 (1998).

33. Silvester, *A Left Hand Like God,* 111, 112; Bob Koester, "The Saga of Speckled Red," *Jazz Report* (January 1962): 14, 15, 27. Silvester's account of Speckled Red's life is based on Koester's article, which in turn is based on an interview with Speckled Red, but Silvester appears to take some liberties. He tells how Red, having left Detroit, hopped freight trains during the time he was playing "the sawmill camps of the Piney Woods"; but Koester has Red riding the rails in the Midwest after World War I and makes no mention of sawmill camps at all, instead saying that Red left Detroit around 1929 and joined a medicine show in Tennessee shortly before recording "The Dirty Dozen" in Memphis.

34. David A. Jasen and Gene Jones, *That American Rag: The Story of Ragtime from Coast to Coast* (New York: Schirmer, 2000), 85).

35. "Boogie No. 1 (Cow Cow Boogie)," *Cow Cow Davenport—Volume 3: The Unissued 1940s Acetate Recordings,* Document Records DOCD-5586 (1997).

36. Borneman, "Boogie Woogie," 17.

37. Blesh and Janis, *They All Played Ragtime,* 192.

38. Silvester, *A Left Hand Like God,* 46, 47. Michael Montgomery, liner notes to Jimmy Blythe 1924–1931, RST Records JPCD-1510-2 (1994); "More Wonderful Ragtime in June," http://www.ragfest.com/ocrs_archives/2002_jun.html. "More Wonderful Ragtime in June," a review of the June 15, 2002, gathering of the Orange County Ragtime Society, describes a performance by pianist Bob Pinsker of "Syncophonic No. 4" and "Syncophonic No. 6" in which Pinsker says that "Christensen . . . didn't write any of the pieces [in 'Syncophonics'] but, rather, lifted 'bits and pieces' of them from various Jimmy Blythe piano rolls."

39. Sharon A. Pease, "I Saw Pinetop Spit Blood and Fall," *Down Beat,* October 1, 1939, 4, 18.

40. Jelly Roll Morton, "The Dirty Dozen," disc 5, track 1, *Jelly Roll Morton: The Complete Library of Congress Recordings by Alan Lomax,* Rounder 11661-1888-2 (2005). The quotation is transcribed on p. 83 of the PDF file on disc 8.

41. David A. Jasen and Gene Jones, *Spreadin' Rhythm Around: Black Popular Songwriters, 1880–1930* (New York: Schirmer, 1998), 58, 59, 130.

42. John Hammond, *John Hammond on Record: An Autobiography* (New York: Penguin, 1981 [orig. Ridge Press/Summit Books, 1977]), 164.

43. Judge Michael L. Igoe, opinion in *Shapiro, Bernstein v. Miracle Record,* 91 F. Supp. 473 (N.D. Ill. 1950), http://cip.law.ucla.edu/cases/1950-1959/Pages/shapiromiracle.aspx.

44. Russell, "Boogie Woogie," 188.

45. Robert Palmer, "Rock Begins," in *The Rolling Stone Illustrated History of Rock and Roll: The Definitive History of the Most Important Artists and Their Music,* ed. Anthony Decurtis and James Henke with Holly George-Warren (New York: Straight Arrow Publishers/Random House, 1992 [orig. Jim Miller, ed., Rolling Stone Press/Random House, 1976]), 4.

46. John Hammond, "Plenty of 'Swing' Talent Hidden in Chicago," *Down Beat,* May 1936, 2; "'Jitter-Bugs' Thrill at N.Y. Jam-Session: 17 Bands Swing for 3-Hours in Huge 'Clam-Bake,'" *Down Beat,* June 1936, 8, 9.

47. Ken Vail, *Count Basie: Swingin' the Blues, 1936–1950* (Lanham, MD: Scarecrow Press, 2003), 10. Most discographies give the recording date as October 9, 1936, but Vail's detailed chronology, illustrated with concert posters, has Basie playing his farewell show in Kansas City on October 3, making his Chicago debut on November 6, and cutting the Vocalion sides on November 9.

48. Linda Dahl, *Morning Glory: A Biography of Mary Lou Williams* (New York: Pantheon, 1999), 110.

49. Pete Johnson as told to Johnny Simmen, "My Life, My Music," *The Pete Johnson Story*, ed. Hans J. Mauerer (New York: private publication, 1965 [orig. *Jazz Journal* 12, no. 8 (August 1959)]), 22.

50. Dahl, *Morning Glory*, 110.

51. Peter J. Levinson, *Trumpet Blues: The Life of Harry James*, (New York: Oxford University Press, 1999), 60.

52. Maurice Waller and Anthony Calabrese, *Fats Waller* (New York: Schirmer, 1977), 126. Fats Waller did record a solo piano number featuring a boogie-woogie bass line—"Alligator Crawl," from November 1934, a Waller composition that Louis Armstrong and His Hot Seven had recorded (without the bass line) in 1927—but the short boogie passages contrast sharply with the more refined stride piano on the rest of the piece.

53. Gunther Schuller, *The Swing Era: The Development of Jazz, 1930–1945* (New York: Oxford University Press, 1989), 764.

54. Will Friedwald, liner notes to *Will Bradley & Ray McKinley: Best of the Big Bands*, Columbia Records CK 46151 (1990). Friedwald quotes drummer Ray McKinley, who sings the lyrics, giving Hammond credit for extending the song into a two-sided record.

55. Lionel Hampton with James Haskins, *Hamp: An Autobiography*, 1st pbk. ed. (New York: Amistad Press, 1993 [orig. Warner Books, 1989]), 91.

56. Arnold Shaw, *Honkers and Shouters: The Golden Years of Rhythm and Blues* (New York: Collier Books/Macmillan, 1978), 66.

57. John Chilton, *Let the Good Times Roll: The Story of Louis Jordan and His Music* (Ann Arbor: University of Michigan Press, 1994 [orig. Quartet Books, 1992]), 60.

58. Chilton, *Let the Good Times Roll*, 110; Todd Bryant Weeks, *Luck's in My Corner: The Life and Music of Hot Lips Page* (New York: Routledge, 2008), 172, 173. Weeks, citing an article in the December 15, 1945, edition of the *New York Amsterdam News*, says that Hot Lips Page claimed to have written "Caldonia."

59. Chilton, *Let the Good Times Roll*, 128.

60. Shaw, *Honkers and Shouters*, 64.

61. J. C. Marion, "Long Gone: Sonny Thompson," issue 43, *JammUpp Vol. 2*, http://home.earthlink.net/~v1tiger/sonnyt.html; Robert Pruter and Robert L. Campbell, "Sult1. 'Sonny' Thompson" on "The Sultan Label," http://hubcap.clemson.edu/~campber/sultan.html.

62. Robert Pruter and Robert L. Campbell, "Miracle Records," http://hubcap.clemson.edu/~campber/miracle.html.

63. Robert Pruter, *Chicago Soul* (Urbana: University of Illinois Press, 1991), 236.

64. "Little Richard Biography," http://rockhall.com/inductees/little-richard/bio/.

65. Charles Shaar Murray, *Boogie Man: The Adventures of John Lee Hooker in the American Twentieth Century* (New York: St. Martin's Griffin, 2002 [orig. 2000]), 127.

66. Murray, *Boogie Man*, 123, 127.

5. THE JUMPIN' JIVE

1. "'Jitter-Bugs' Thrill at N.Y. Jam-Session: 17 Bands Swing for 3-Hours in Huge 'Clam-Bake,'" *Down Beat*, June 1936, 1.

2. John Chilton, *Let the Good Times Roll: The Story of Louis Jordan and His Music* (Ann Arbor: University of Michigan Press, 1994 [orig. Quartet Books, 1992]), 64.

3. Allan Sutton, *Pseudonyms on American Records (1892–1942): A Guide to False Names and Label Errors*, 2nd ed. (Denver: Mainspring Press, 2005), 73, 167, 183, 288, 289, 304.

4. Sutton, *Pseudonyms*, 138; Jeffrey Magee, *The Uncrowned King of Swing: Fletcher Henderson and Big Band Jazz* (New York: Oxford University Press, 2005), 34. Henderson made his first recording on October 11, 1920, accompanying Lucille Hegamin on "Dallas Blues," but the record was never issued. Henderson's band is credited on a number of instrumental titles, including blues, issued by the Black Swan label as early as 1921, but some of these were actually recorded by white groups, and Henderson's name was used in order to keep up the pretense that Black Swan recorded only black artists.

5. Magee, *The Uncrowned King of Swing,* 76.

6. Rex Stewart, *Boy Meets Horn,* ed. Claire P. Gordon (Ann Arbor: University of Michigan Press, 1991), 65.

7. *Cab Calloway's Cat-ologue,* rev. 1939 ed., www.tcswing.com/PDFs/Hepsters%20Dictionary.pdf. This is an expanded update of the booklet Calloway originally published the previous year.

8. Marshall Stearns and Jean Stearns, *Jazz Dance: The Story of American Vernacular Dance* (New York: Da Capo Press, 1994 [orig. Macmillan, 1968]), 315, 316.

9. Stearns and Stearns, *Jazz Dance,* 126–129.

10. Stearns and Stearns, *Jazz Dance* , 329.

11. Samuel B. Charters, *The Country Blues,* 2nd pbk. ed. (New York: Da Capo Press, 1977 [orig. Rinehart, 1959]), 109.

12. Fred E. Cox, John Randolph, and John Harris, "The Jug Bands of Louisville," *Storyville,* September 1993, 166, 167, 175–177; Marshall Wyatt, liner notes to *Folks, He Sure Do Pull Some Bow! Vintage Fiddle Music 1927–1935: Blues, Jazz, Stomps, Shuffles & Rags,* Old Hat Records CD-1003 (2001). Cox, Randolph, and Harris base their tale of B. D. Tite on secondhand information gathered years after the events described and admit that this part of their account "may be called historical fiction." Wyatt cites Pen Bogert, a reference specialist at the Filson Club Historical Society in Louisville, as having been unable to verify the existence of some of the musicians identified as Tite's early colleagues by Cox et al.

13. David A. Jasen and Gene Jones, *Spreadin' Rhythm Around: Black Popular Songwriters, 1880–1930* (New York: Schirmer, 1998). 172.

14. *The Five Harmaniacs—1926–27,* Puritan Records 3004 (1978).

15. Jelly Roll Morton, "'Ungai Hai,' the Sign of the Indians," disc 6, track 7, *Jelly Roll Morton: The Complete Library of Congress Recordings by Alan Lomax,* Rounder 11661-1888-2 (2005). The song is transcribed on pages 102 and 103 of the PDF file on disc 8. "To-Wa-Bac-A-Wa" is the title of a traditional chant of the Mardi Gras "Indians" in New Orleans, recorded under such spellings as "Two-Way-Pak-E-Way" and "Two Way-Pocky-Way" by modern Indian troupes such as the Wild Magnolias, the Golden Eagles, and the Guardians of the Flame. Bits of the chant found their way onto R&B records by Dave Bartholomew ("Carnival Day," 1949) and Huey "Piano" Smith ("Don't You Know Yockomo," 1958), and the Dixie Cups, a female vocal trio from New Orleans, released "Two-Way-Poc-A-Way" as a would-be pop single in 1965. On his Library of Congress recordings, Jelly Roll Morton sings an older version of the chant, transcribed as "T'ouwais Bas Q'ouwais." But the "Bucket's Got a Hole in It" melody is heard only on the Louis Dumaine recording, which has nothing in common with the Indian chant besides the title.

16. Donald M. Marquis, *In Search of Buddy Bolden: First Man of Jazz,* 1st pbk. ed. (New York: Da Capo Press, 1980 [orig. Louisiana State University Press, 1978]), 108; Danny Barker with Alyn Shipton, *Buddy Bolden and the Last Days of Storyville* (London: Cassell, 1998), ix, 20, 21; Alyn Shipton, *A New History of Jazz* (London: Continuum, 2001), 83; Ingemar Wågerman, liner notes to Gota River Jazzmen, *". . . Thought I Heard Buddy Bolden Play,"* Grjcd Records GRJ06 (2003). Marquis says that Bolden "played 'Bucket [sic] Got a Hole in It' when he spotted friends or someone of the sporting crowd and wanted to liven things up" but gives no reference. Barker quotes a brother of Bolden's colleague Buddy Bottley, Dude Bottley, who says that "Bucket's Got a Hole in It" was part of Bolden's repertoire, but according to Alyn Shipton, Dude Bottley is a product of Barker's literary imagination. Wågerman, drawing his information from the Bolden web page formerly maintained by Carlos "Froggy" May at www.geocities.com/BourbonStreet/5135/Bolden.html, identifies the song as a "Bolden origi-

nal, according to Happy Schilling." George "Happy" Schilling was a white New Orleans trombonist, born in 1886, who led a band in the 1910s and 1920s.

17. In 1935, the white crooner Gene Austin wrote "I Hear You Knockin' but You Can't Come In (The Knock Song)," with a melody different from Lil Johnson's "Keep on Knockin'," for the Mae West movie *Klondike Annie,* but it was reportedly censored out. Austin filmed a Soundie of the song in 1942, and Tommy Dorsey recorded it as "The Knock Song" in 1949. Austin, meanwhile published "Keep A-Knockin', but You Can't Come In" under his own name in 1948.

18. Jelly Roll Morton, "The Origins of Scat and 'Scat Song,'" disc 3, track 10, *Jelly Roll Morton: The Complete Library of Congress Recordings by Alan Lomax,* Rounder 11661-1888-2 (2005). The quotation is transcribed on p. 51 of the PDF file on disc 8.

19. Louis Armstrong, "Jazz on a High Note," *Esquire,* December 1951, reprinted in *Louis Armstrong in His Own Words,* ed. Thomas Brothers (New York: Oxford University Press, 1999), 131, 132.

20. Cab Calloway and Bryant Rollins, *Of Minnie the Moocher and Me* (New York: Thomas Y. Crowell, 1976), 58, 59.

21. Calloway and Rollins, *Of Minnie the Moocher and Me,* 73.

22. Gunther Schuller, *The Swing Era: The Development of Jazz, 1930–1945* (New York: Oxford University Press, 1989), 327.

23. Sigmund Spaeth, *Read 'Em and Weep: The Songs You Forgot to Remember* (New York: Halcyon House, 1939 [orig. Doubleday, Page, 1926]), 116–119; Sigmund Spaeth, *Weep Some More, My Lady* (New York: Doubleday, Page, 1927), 122–127; Carl Sandburg, *The American Songbag* (New York: Harcourt, Brace, 1927), 204, 205.

24. Gary Giddins, *Bing Crosby: A Pocket Full of Dreams, The Early Years 1903–1940* (Boston: Back Bay Books/Little, Brown, 2001), 165, 639.

25. "A Strange Band," *New Orleans Weekly Pelican,* February 5, 1887, cited in Lynn Abbott, "Play That Barber Shop Chord: A Case for the African-American Origin of Barbershop Harmony," *American Music* 10, no. 3 (Autumn 1992): 303, 322.

26. "City Happenings," *Indianapolis Freeman,* April 7, 1894, referred to in Doug Seroff and Ray Funk, liner notes to *The Human Orchestra: Rhythm Quartets in the Thirties,* Clanka Lanka Records CL-144 (1985), cited in Lynn Abbott, "Play That Barber Shop Chord: A Case for the African-American Origin of Barbershop Harmony," *American Music* 10, no. 3 (Autumn 1992): 303, 322.

27. Billy Vera, "'Gloria': History of a Song," www.doowopcafe.net/Gloria.html.

28. "Ella Fitzgerald," *Tower Records Pulse!* April 1988, 74.

29. Richard M. Sudhalter, *Lost Chords: White Musicians and Their Contribution to Jazz, 1915–1945* (Oxford University Press, 1999), 372, 373.

30. Arnold Shaw, *52nd Street: The Street of Jazz* (New York: Da Capo Press, 1977 [orig. *The Street That Never Slept,* New York: Coward, McCann & Geoghegan, 1971]), 88, 90.

31. Will Friedwald, *Jazz Singing: America's Great Voices from Bessie Smith to Bebop and Beyond* (New York: Da Capo Press, 1992 [orig. Scribner's, 1990]), 141.

32. Marv Goldberg, *More Than Words Can Say: The Ink Spots and Their Music* (Lanham, MD: Scarecrow Press, 1998), 1–21.

33. Goldberg, *More Than Words Can Say*, 30.

34. Gayle F. Wald, *Shout, Sister, Shout! The Untold Story of Rock-and-Roll Trailblazer Sister Rosetta Tharpe* (Boston: Beacon Press, 2007), 68–70.

35. Around 1939, the Indiana-born trombonist Doc Wheeler, né Wheeler Moran, took over the leadership of the Sunset Royal Orchestra, which then changed its name to the Sunset Orchestra. The band, originally from Florida, had previously been known as the Sunset Royal Serenaders. Under the leadership of singer and banjo player Steve Washington, the Serenaders had come up with an innovative arrangement of Irving Berlin's "Marie" in which the musicians sang elaborate responses to Washington's simple vocal lines. After Washington died in 1936, the group was taken over by pianist Ace Harris, who later played in Erskine Hawkins's band. Meanwhile, Tommy Dorsey appropriated Washington's arrangement and scored a No. 1 hit with "Marie" in 1937, establishing the vocal technique as a fixture of swing, one that also influenced rhythm-and-blues.

36. John Broven, "Roy Brown, Part 1: Good Rockin' Tonight," *Blues Unlimited*, January/ February 1977, 6. "There's Good Blues Tonight," while not a major hit (and not a blues), was popular enough to have also been recorded by Erskine Hawkins, Hal McIntyre, Bobby Sherwood, Martha Tilton, and the Pied Pipers, all in 1946. Lightly seasoned with jive expressions such as "groovy," "chick," and "gate" (short for "alligator," with a meaning roughly equivalent to "cat"), the song has little in common with "Good Rockin' Tonight" besides the title and the line "So hold your baby tight." But on Millinder's version, which Brown probably heard, Annisteen Allen adds the introduction "I've got good news tonight" before the title phrase. Brown's first line goes, "I heard the news, there's good rockin' tonight."

37. Eddy Determeyer, *Rhythm Is Our Business: Jimmie Lunceford and the Harlem Express* (Ann Arbor: University of Michigan Press, 2006), 52, 86.

38. Determeyer, *Rhythm Is Our Business*, 91.

39. Larry Birnbaum, "Arnett Cobb: Soul Wrenching Sax," *Down Beat,* April 1981, 25.

40. George Barnes, a sixteen-year-old white jazz guitarist, recorded two tracks ("Sweetheart Land" and "It's a Low Down Dirty Shame") on electric guitar as an accompanist to Big Bill Broonzy on March 1, 1938, a couple of weeks before Durham made his first electrified recordings with the Kansas City Five. Jim Boyd recorded three tracks ("Slow and Easy," "Hot Dog Stomp," and Jimmie Lunceford's hit "Rhythm Is Our Business") with an electrified standard guitar as a member of the Dallas-based western swing band Roy Newman and His Boys on September 27 and 28, 1935.

41. Don Rayno, *Paul Whiteman: Pioneer in American Music, Volume I: 1890–1930* (Lanham, MD: Scarecrow Press, 2008), 188.

42. Carl Cons, "Busse & Kyser Grit Molars as Idea Thieves Cash In on Their Brain Kids," *Down Beat,* February 1938, 11; Patricia Willard, liner notes to *The Uncollected Henry Busse and His Orchestra 1935,* Hindsight Records HSR-122 (1978).

43. Stephen J. Danko, "A Brief Biography of the Joseph Sarvetnick Family," http://stephendanko.com/blog/403.

44. Cons, "Busse & Kyser Grit Molars," 1.

45. Shuffle Rhythm Used by Bach & Brahms," *Down Beat,* March 1938, 1, 15.

46. Schuller, *The Swing Era,* 765.

47. Chilton, *Let the Good Times Roll,* 32.

48. Chuck Berry, *The Autobiography* (New York: Harmony Books, 1987), 143.

49. James Lincoln Collier, *Jazz: The American Theme Song* (New York: Oxford University Press, 1993), 175; Paige Van Vorst, liner notes to Harlem Hamfats, *Hot Jazz, Blues & Jive 1936–1937,* Folklyric Records FL-9029 (1986), quoted in James Lincoln Collier, *Louis Armstrong: An American Genius* (New York: Oxford University Press, 1983), 349.

50. Paige Van Vorst, "The Harlem Hamfats, Part II," *The Mississippi Rag* IV, no. 5 (March 1977): 9.

51. Lynn Abbott and Doug Seroff, *Ragged but Right: Black Traveling Shows, "Coon Songs," and the Dark Pathway to Blues and Jazz* (Jackson: University Press of Mississippi, 2007), 178, 402 [Yankee Robinson's Circus].

52. Charters, *The Country Blues,* 182, 183 [brought country blues into the mainstream].

53. *Immortalia: An Anthology of American Ballads, Sailors' Songs, Cowboy Songs, College Songs, Parodies, Limericks, and Other Humorous Verses and Doggerel Now for the First Time Brought Together in Book Form* (privately published, 1927), 109, 110, www.horntip.com/html/books_&_MSS/1920s/1927_immortalia_(various)/index.htm.

54. Chilton, *Let the Good Times Roll,* 88.

55. Arnold Shaw, *Honkers and Shouters: The Golden Years of Rhythm and Blues* (New York: Collier Books/Macmillan, 1978), 78; Louis Jordan radio interview with Scott Ellsworth on the Los Angeles station KFI, April 26, 1971, quoted in Chilton, *Let the Good Times Roll,* 88. Chilton also writes that Lester Melrose "told *Music & Rhythm* that he had taken Weldon's recording to Jordan," but an examination of *Music and Rhythm*, a jazz magazine published in Chicago from November 1940 to August 1942, revealed no such statement. As a talent scout and producer for such labels as Columbia, Bluebird, OKeh, and Vocalion—but not Decca—Melrose was responsible for standardizing the blues sound by using studio bands, similar to the

ones that Williams employed, to back such artists as Big Bill Broonzy, Tampa Red, Jazz Gillum, Washboard Sam, Memphis Minnie, and Casey Bill Weldon.

56. Paul and Beth Garon, *Woman with Guitar: Memphis Minnie's Blues* (New York: Da Capo Press, 1992), 20, 21, 287.

57. "Hey Lawdy Mama (blues song)," http://en.wikipedia.org/wiki/Hey_Lawdy_Mama_(blues_song); Chris Welch, *Cream: The Legendary Sixties Supergroup—Ginger Baker, Jack Bruce, Eric Clapton* (San Francisco: Backbeat Books, 2000), 93. Another country blues that passed into the swing repertoire is "Hey Lawdy Mama," which was first recorded by the Atlanta bluesman Buddy Moss as "Oh Lordy Mama" in 1934. Another Atlanta bluesman, Curley Weaver, cut "Oh Lawdy Mama," accompanied by Blind Willie McTell, in 1935. The Georgia-born, Chicago-based bluesman Bumble Bee Slim recorded "Hey Lawdy Mama" in 1935 and a slightly different variation titled "Meet Me in the Bottom" in 1936. Count Basie cut an instrumental version of "Hey Lawdy Mama" with just a rhythm section in 1938, and Sammy Price sang "Oh Lawdy Mama" with his combo in 1940. Louis Armstrong recorded "Hey Lawdy Mama" with a septet in 1941, and Andy Kirk made *Billboard*'s R&B chart in 1952 with "Hey Lawdy Mama (Meet Me in the Bottom)," featuring singer June Richmond. Richmond recorded the song a few more times with Kirk's and other bands, including Roy Milton's Solid Senders, a pioneering rhythm-and-blues combo. Although "Hey Lawdy Mama" did not make its way into rock 'n' roll via early R&B, a 1965 version by the Chicago bluesman Junior Wells on his influential album *Hoodoo Man Blues* was transformed into the rock song "Strange Brew" by the British trio Cream.

58. Robert Pruter and Robert L. Campbell, "The Rhumboogie Label," http://hubcap.clemson.edu/~campber/rhumboogie.html. Citing the minutes of the musicians' union in Chicago, Pruter and Campbell give the October 1944 date for the Rhumboogie label's first session rather than May 1945, which is given in most discographies.

59. Tony Russell, liner notes to *Jazzin' the Blues, Vol. 3,* Document Records DOCD-5536 (1997).

60. Marshall and Jean Stearns, *Jazz Dance*, 296. A different song, "Lovin' Sam, the Sheik of Alabam," was written by Jack Yellen and Milton Ager in 1922 (the two later composed Ain't She Sweet" and "Happy Days Are Here Again") and recorded by several artists, most successfully by Nora Bayes. There was also a 1914 show called *Lucky Sam from Alabam'* staged by the Black Patti Troubadors, whose star, the opera singer Sissieretta Jones, was called the Black Patti after the white diva Adelina Patti.

61. Nick Tosches, *Unsung Heroes of Rock 'n' Roll* (New York: Scribner's, 1984), 71. According to Tosches, "Drinkin' Wine Spo-Dee-O-Dee" was originally sung by McGhee and his army buddies during World War II, with the chorus "Drinkin' wine, motherfucker, drinkin' wine! Goddam!" but this seems unlikely, given the song's strong melodic resemblance to Theard's "Spo-Dee-O-Dee."

62. Nick Tosches, *Hellfire: The Jerry Lee Lewis Story* (New York: Delta/Dell, 1982), 64, 65; Jimmy Guterman, *Rockin' My Life Away: Listening to Jerry Lee Lewis* (Nashville: Rutledge Hill Press, 1991), 39. According to Guterman, "Those at the event differ on what Jerry Lee played and sang."

63. Sammy Price, *What Do They Want? A Jazz Autobiography,* ed. Caroline Richmond (Urbana: University of Illinois Press, 1990), 96. The discography at the back of Price's autobiography, compiled by Bob Weir (not the Grateful Dead guitarist), lists Theard as the singer on "Lead Me Daddy Straight to the Bar." Other discographies tentatively identify Spo-De-O Sam as Price himself, which is not impossible, as Theard and Price had similar-sounding voices.

64. Chilton, *Let the Good Times Roll,* 128, 129.

65. "ACE Title Search," www.ascap.com/ace/search.cfm?requesttimeout=300&mode=results&searchstr=350008887&search_in=i&search_type=exact&search_det=tswpbv&results_pp=30&start=1; Mike Leadbitter, Leslie Fancourt, and Paul Pelletier, *Blues Records 1943–1970: "The Bible of the Blues,"* Volume Two (London: Record Information Services, 1994), 335. ASCAP gives Raphael Barrow, Henry Glover, and Sam Theard as the composers of "The Egg or the Hen." Leadbitter, Fancourt, and Pelletier's discography gives Theard as the singer on "Cheetie Bo Joe," another song recorded by Page at the same session. Other discogra-

phies do not include Theard on the session at all, and the singer on both songs sounds like Page rather than Theard.

66. Price, *What Do They Want?* 23, 28, 29. Price's autobiography is often unreliable. For example, he claims to have outplayed Hersal Thomas at shows in Houston and Galveston in 1927, a year after Thomas's death.

67. Douglas Henry Daniels, *One O'Clock Jump: The Unforgettable History of the Oklahoma City Blue Devils* (Boston: Beacon Press, 2006), 88.

68. Hot Lips Page as told to Kay C. Thompson, "Kansas City Man," *The Record Changer,* December 1949, 9; Todd Bryant Weeks, *Luck's in My Corner: the Life and Music of Hot Lips Page* (New York: Routledge, 2008), 31–35.

69. Paul S. Machlin, *Stride: The Music of Fats Waller* (Boston: Twayne, 1985), 4, 5.

70. Two 1929 recordings credited to Fats Waller and His Buddies also include backbeat sections—"Lookin' Good but Feelin' Bad," with drummer Gene Krupa, and "Won't You Get off It, Please?" with drummer Kaiser Marshall.

71. "Hold Barred," Radio, *Time,* April 24, 1939, 44.

72. John Chilton, *Sidney Bechet: The Wizard of Jazz* (New York: Oxford University Press, 1987 [orig. Macmillan Press, 1987]), 112.

73. Lou Levy, letter to the editor, *Time,* May 15, 1939, 2.

74. Chilton, *Sidney Bechet,* 116, 117.

75. William Ruhlmann, "The Andrews Sisters: Three Sides to Every Story," *Goldmine,* January 20, 1995, 28.

76. Jack Kerouac, *On the Road* (New York: Penguin, 1991 [orig. Viking Press, 1957]), 176, 177.

77. Shaw, *52nd Street*, 225, 226; Max Jones, *Jazz Talking: Profiles, Interviews, and Other Riffs on Jazz Musicians* (New York, Da Capo Press, 2000 [orig. Macmillan Press, 1987]), 229, 230; Joop Visser, liner notes to Slim Gaillard, *Laughing in Rhythm*, Proper Records, Properbox 62 (2003), 9–13; Arnold Passman, *The Deejays* (New York: Macmillan, 1971), 47–49. Although West Coast radio announcers had played records on the air, rather than presenting live music, as early as the mid-1920s, the sensational success of Martin Block's *Make Believe Ballroom* on the New York station WNEW, beginning in 1935, established the disc-jockey format as a staple of radio programming nationwide. Block based his show, where he would pretend that the musicians whose records he played were actually performing in the studio, on *The World's Largest Make Believe Ballroom*, which Al Jarvis had introduced in 1932 on a Los Angeles station where Block was working. Artists and record labels initially opposed the format, leading to the musicians'-union recording bans of 1942 and 1948.

78. Magee, *The Uncrowned King of Swing,* 148, 149.

79. Charles White, *The Life and Times of Little Richard: The Quasar of Rock* (New York: Da Capo Press, 1994 [orig. Harmony Books, 1984]), 40, 49–51.

80. M. H. Orodenker, "Cafe Creole, New York," "Night Club Reviews," *Billboard,* April 30, 1938, 20.

81. Nigel Haslewood, "The Jump Bands—No. 3, Part 1: Skeets Tolbert and the Gentlemen of Swing," *Storyville*, December 6, 1993, 220–231; Nigel Haslewood, "The Jump Bands—No. 3, Part 2: Skeets Tolbert and the Gentlemen of Swing," *Storyville*, March 1, 1994, 16–27.

82. Haslewood, "The Jump Bands—No. 3, Part 2," 19. Skeets Tolbert shares the writers' credit for "Hit That Jive, Jack" with John Alston, presumably the tenor saxophonist known as Johnnie Alston whose band backed Wynonie Harris on a December 1945 recording session. However, Tolbert told Nigel Haslewood that his co-composer was a different tenor saxophonist, Harold Austin, and that Austin played on the "Hit That Jive" session instead of Otis Hicks, who is listed in most discographies. The melody of "Hit That Jive, Jack" appears to have been adapted from a portion of Fletcher Henderson's 1936 hit "Christopher Columbus," a different portion of which was incorporated into Benny Goodman's anthem "Sing, Sing, Sing."

83. Hampton, *Hamp: An Autobiography,* 71.

84. Schuller, *The Swing Era,* 824.

85. Ray Charles and David Ritz, *Brother Ray: Ray Charles Own Story,* 2nd pbk. ed. (New York: Da Capo Press, 2003 [orig. Dial Press, 1978]), 44.

86. Berry, *The Autobiography,* 90.

87. Harry Gibson interview, 1991, text and audio clip, www.hyzercreek.com/harry.htm and www.hoyhoy.com/artists.htm.

88. Harry "the Hipster" Gibson, liner notes to *Everybody's Crazy But Me,* Progressive Records PRO 7042 (1986), www.hyzercreek.com/harryautobio.htm and "Harry's autobiography" link on the Harry Gibson section of www.hoyhoy.com/artists.htm.

89. "Be-bop Be-bopped," Radio, *Time,* March 25, 1946, 52.

90. Eric Townley, "The Man from Birmingham: An Interview with Paul Bascomb," *Storyville,* August/September 1979, 214.

91. The Rivingtons may have heard the cover version of "Mumbles Blues" cut by Bobby Lewis for Chess in September 1952 or the rerecording Lewis made for Mercury (and/or Spotlight) around 1958. Lewis is remembered mostly for his 1961 smash "Tossin' and Turnin'."

92. Hampton, *Hamp: An Autobiography,* 26.

93. John Hammond, letter to Rudi Blesh, July 1, 1970, quoted in Blesh, *Combo: USA; Eight Lives in Jazz* (Philadelphia: Chilton, 1971), 174, 223; Al Avakian and Bob Prince, liner notes to *Charlie Christian with the Benny Goodman Sextet and Orchestra,* Columbia CL 652 (1955). Hammond writes that on a broadcast of Benny Goodman's *Camel Caravan* radio show in August 1939, "Charlie came up with the riffs of 'Flying Home' which is erroneously listed as being composed jointly with Benny and Lionel Hampton." Avakian and Prince quote Mary Osborne, a white guitarist who went on to perform and record with both white and black jazz artists, describing a Christian performance with Alphonso Trent's band in Bismarck, North Dakota, that she witnessed in 1938: "I remember some of the figures Charlie played in his solos. They were exactly the same things that Benny recorded later on as *Flying Home* . . . and all the others."

94. Larry Birnbaum, "Illinois Jacquet: Still Flying Home," *Musician,* December 1988, 78.

95. Hampton, *Hamp: An Autobiography,* 38, 39.

96. Hampton, *Hamp: An Autobiography,* 78, 79; Ted Fox, *Showtime at the Apollo* (New York: Holt, Rinehart and Winston, 1983), 153; Malcolm X as told to Alex Haley, *The Autobiography of Malcolm X* (New York: Ballantine, 1987 [orig. Grove Press, 1964]), 77. In his 1989 autobiography, Hampton elaborates on the story he'd told to Fox. He also confirms Malcolm X's secondhand account of a pot-smoking fan at the Apollo Theatre who jumped off the second balcony during a performance of "Flying Home," inspiring trombonist Gerald Valentine to compose "Second Balcony Jump" for Earl Hines's band. That story is doubtful, however, not least because Hines recorded "Second Balcony Jump" in March 1942, two months before Hampton cut his landmark version of "Flying Home."

97. Schuller, *The Swing Era,* 394.

98. Hampton, *Hamp: An Autobiography,* 117.

99. John S. Wilson, "Buddy Johnson Shows How to Keep a Band Working," *Down Beat,* December 29, 1950, 4.

100. John A. Jackson, *Big Beat Heat: Alan Freed and the Early Years of Rock & Roll* (New York: Schirmer/Macmillan, 1991), 52, 64, 86, 97, 155.

101. Frank Driggs and Chuck Haddix, *Kansas City Jazz: From Ragtime to Bebop—A History* (New York: Oxford University Press, 2005), 212, 213.

102. Jay McShann as told to John Anthony Brisbin, "I Always Thought Blues and Jazz Went Together: Part One of a Two Part Interview," *Living Blues,* January/February 2000, 22.

103. Driggs and Haddix, *Kansas City Jazz,* 224.

104. Judge Charles L. Brieant, opinion in *Stratchborneo v. Arc Music,* 357 F. Supp. 1393 (S.D.N.Y. 1973), http://cip.law.ucla.edu/cases/1970-1979/Pages/strachborneoarc.aspx; Robert Gordon, *Can't Be Satisfied: The Life and Times of Muddy Waters* (Boston: Little, Brown, 2002), 149. Muddy Waters recorded his "Got My Mojo Working" for Chess on December 1, 1956, nearly two months before Ann Cole cut her version for Baton, but Waters had learned the song from Cole when his band accompanied her on a tour of the South. After Waters claimed the copyright for himself, Baton's proprietor, Saul Rabinowitz, who had acquired the rights to the song from its composer, Preston Foster, sued Chess's publishing arm, Arc Music. Arc settled out of court, conceding the composer's credit to Foster.

105. Jay McShann as told to John Anthony Brisbin, "Music Was a Good Life: Part Two of a Two Part Interview," *Living Blues,* March/April 2000, 54.

106. Shaw, *52nd Street,* 109.
107. Garry Boulard, *Louis Prima* (Urbana: University of Illinois Press, 2002 [orig. Center for Louisiana Studies, 1989]), 32, 33.
108. Shaw, *52nd Street,* 108.
109. Jerry Franken, "Rise of Jam Bands," *Billboard,* December 28, 1935, 49.
110. Boulard, *Louis Prima,* 60, 64, 65.
111. Boulard, *Louis Prima,* 63.
112. Sheet music for Frank Dumont's "The Dagoe Banana Peddler," copyright 1888, http://webapp1.dlib.indiana.edu/inharmony/detail.do?action=detail&fullItemID=/lilly/starr/LL-SSM-ALD3007&queryNumber=1.
113. "Lombardo Leads in Corn Contest," *Down Beat,* December 1937, 23; Barbara Hodgkins, "Louie Phooey," *Metronome* (June 1945), cited in Garry Boulard, *Louis Prima,* 76, 77.
114. John Tynan, "Heard in Person: Louis Prima–Keely Smith," *Down Beat,* October 31, 1957, 37.

6. GET WITH IT

1. John A. Lomax, *Cowboy Songs and Other Frontier Ballads* (New York: Macmillan, 1918 [orig. Sturgis & Walton, 1910]), xix.
2. A. H. Fox-Strangways with Maud Karpeles, *Cecil Sharp* (London: Oxford University Press, 1933), 129.
3. Fox-Strangways, *Cecil Sharp,* 143.
4. Olive Dame Campbell and Cecil J. Sharp, *English Folk Songs from the Southern Appalachians* (London: Putnam's, 1917), iv, vii–ix.
5. Norm Cohen, liner notes to *Minstrels & Tunesmiths: The Commercial Roots of Early Country Music,* JEMF LP-109 (1981)1.
6. Bill C. Malone, *Singing Cowboys and Musical Mountaineers: Southern Culture and the Roots of Country Music,* pbk. ed. (Athens: University of Georgia Press, 2003 [orig. 1993]), 14, 23, 29, 48.
7. Earl Scruggs, *Earl Scruggs and the Five-String Banjo* (New York: Peer International, 1968), 147, cited in Marshall Wyatt, liner notes to *Good for What Ails You: Music of the Medicine Shows 1926–1937,* Old Hat Records CD-1005 (2005), 42.
8. *Atlanta Constitution,* August 18, 1915, 7, cited in Wayne W. Daniel, *Pickin' on Peachtree: A History of Country Music in Atlanta, Georgia* (Urbana: University of Illinois Press, 1990), 90, 251.
9. Alfred P. Scott, "Wreck of the Old 97: The Origins of a Modern Traditional Ballad," www.rosegill.com/Old97/Old97.pdf.
10. Jack Palmer, *Vernon Dalhart: First Star of Country Music* (Denver: Mainspring Press, 2005), 116.
11. Mark Wilson, liner notes to Gid Tanner and His Skillet Lickers, *Hear These New Southern Fiddle and Guitar Records!* Rounder Records 1005 (1973).
12. Norman Cohen, "The Skillet Lickers: A Study of a Hillbilly String Band and Its Repertoire," *Journal of American Folklore* 78, no. 93 (July–September 1965): 229.
13. Dena J. Epstein, *Sinful Tunes and Spirituals: Black Folk Music to the Civil War* (Urbana: University of Illinois Press, 1977), 80.
14. Peter van der Merwe, *Origins of the Popular Style: The Antecedents of Twentieth-Century Popular Music,* 1st pbk. ed. (Oxford: Clarendon Press, 1992 [orig. Oxford University Press, 1989]), 191, 192.
15. Van der Merwe, *Origins of the Popular Style*, 84, 85.
16. Cohen, "The Skillet Lickers," 233.
17. First adapted in the 1860s from an eighteenth-century German lullaby, "Sleep, Baby, Sleep" had long been a vehicle for yodelers. A number of artists recorded it before Riley Puckett, most notably George P. Watson, who made several yodeling records of the song, beginning in 1897.

18. Abbe Niles, "Ballads, Songs and Snatches," *The Bookman: A Review of Books and Life* 67, no. 5 (July 1928): 566; Abbe Niles, "Ballads, Songs and Snatches," *The Bookman* 68, no. 1 (September 1928): 77; Abbe Niles, "Ballads, Songs and Snatches," *The Bookman* 68, no. 3 (November 1928): 328. Niles's monthly record-review column, which ran in *The Bookman* from February 1928 to January 1929, covered an unusually broad range of musical genres, from pop and jazz to blues and country—all the more surprising since Seward Collins, who had become the magazine's publisher in 1927, would later be known as an outspoken fascist who openly supported Hitler and Mussolini.

19. Carrie Rodgers, *My Husband Jimmie Rodgers,* 2nd ed. (Nashville: Country Music Foundation Press, 1995 [orig. San Antonio Southern Library Institute, 1935]), 27, 49.

20. Lynn Abbott and Doug Seroff, "America's Blue Yodel," *Musical Traditions* 11 (Late 1993): 5; Paul Oliver, *Songsters and Saints: Vocal Traditions on Race Records* (Cambridge: Cambridge University Press, 1984), 91; Nick Tosches, *Where Dead Voices Gather,* 1st pbk. ed. (Boston: Back Bay Books/Little, Brown, 2002 [orig. 2001]), 66. According to Abbott and Seroff, the *Indianapolis Freeman* reported that the black vaudeville team of Marshall and Davis performed a song called "He's in the Jail House Now" in Philadelphia in 1919; the same newspaper noted that in early 1920, a singer named Kid Thomas caused a "near riot" in Indianapolis with "his now famous song, 'He's in the Jail House Now.'" According to Oliver, the white Atlanta journalist and broadcaster Ernest Rogers "claimed to have sung it over the radio as early as 1922." And according to Tosches, Rody Jordan performed the song with the Al G. Field Minstrels, a white blackface troupe, during the 1924–1925 season.

21. Barry Gifford, "Couldn't Do No Yodeling, so I Turned to Howlin'," *Rolling Stone,* August 24, 1968, 6.

22. Mark Humphrey, "Johnny Shines: A Living Legacy of Delta Blues," *Frets*, November 1979, 37.

23. "Oscar 'Buddy' Woods Discography," www.wirz.de/music/woodsfrm.htm. The quoted lines are not found on the version of "She's a Hum Dum Dinger" that was issued by Victor but on an alternate version recorded the same day (with the same rhythm to the verses), which was released decades later on several CDs. Curiously, Gene Autry's 1931 version copies Davis's unissued take.

24. Kevin Coffey, liner notes to *Farewell Blues: Hot String Bands 1936–1941,* Krazy Kat Records KK CD 30 (2003), 6, 7. Coffey, a noted western swing historian, claims that "You Are My Sunshine" was adapted from "You Took My Sunshine," a song recorded for Vocalion in December 1938 by a South Carolina group called the Hi Neighbor Boys.

25. Holly George-Warren, *Public Cowboy No. 1: The Life and Times of Gene Autry* (New York: Oxford University Press, 2007), 39.

26. Rick Coleman, *Blue Monday: Fats Domino and the Lost Dawn of Rock 'n' Roll* (New York: Da Capo Press, 2006), 124.

27. Rosetta Wills, *The King of Western Swing: Bob Wills Remembered* (New York: Billboard Books, 2000), 111; Charles R. Townsend, *San Antonio Rose: The Life and Music of Bob Wills* (Urbana: University of Illinois Press, 1976), 40.

28. Gary Ginell, *Milton Brown and the Founding of Western Swing* (Urbana: University of Illinois Press, 1994), 56–61.

29. Pianist Alex Hill and guitarists Dan Roberts and Alex Robinson used the name Hokum Boys when they recorded "Somebody's Been Using That Thing" in June 1929. The African American singer and mandolin player Al Miller had originally recorded the song in February 1929, but Milton Brown probably took it from the April 1930 version by the same Famous Hokum Boys who cut "Nancy Jane." "Somebody's Been Using That Thing" was the flip side of the Famous Hokum Boys' "Eagle Riding Papa," recorded the following day. The Hokum Trio comprised Alex Hill, clarinetist Cecil Scott, and banjo player Ikey Robinson when the group cut "You're Bound to Look Like a Monkey When You Get Old" in May 1930.

30. Ginell, *Milton Brown,* xxi, 282.

31. Bill C. Malone, *Country Music, U.S.A.,* rev. ed. (Austin: University of Texas Press, 1968, 1985), 122.

32. Townsend, *San Antonio Rose,* 76, 77.

33. Townsend, *San Antonio Rose*, 59.

34. Townsend, *San Antonio Rose*, 113.

35. Townsend, *San Antonio Rose*, 127.

36. Gary Giddins, *Bing Crosby: A Pocket Full of Dreams, The Early Years 1903–1940* (Boston: Back Bay Books; Little, Brown, 2001), 338.

37. Townsend, *San Antonio Rose*, 268, 269.

38. Tony Russell, *Country Music Originals: The Legends and the Lost* (New York: Oxford University Press, 2007), 233.

39. Wayne W. Daniel, "'Are You Ready, Hezzie?' and Other Harmonious High Jinks of Those Hilarious Hoosier Hot Shots," *Nostalgia Digest*, October–November 1996, 26–30, www.hezzie.com/hhs/history.html.

40. Nick Tosches, *Country: Living Legends and Dying Metaphors in America's Biggest Music* (New York: Scribner's, 1977), 211, 212.

41. Tosches, *Country*, 186–188.

42. "Hillbillies Owe Rise to Jukes," *Billboard*, August 28, 1943, 70, 75.

43. "Bull Market in Corn," Music, *Time*, October 4, 1943, 49, 50.

44. Adam Komorowski, liner notes to *Hillbilly Boogie*, Proper Records, Properbox 50 (2002), p. 35.

45. Jim Dawson and Steve Propes, *What Was the First Rock 'n' Roll Record?* (Winchester, MA: Faber and Faber, 1992), 46.

46. Merle Travis, interview by William Lightfoot, September 15, 1979, cited in Jon Hartley Fox, *King of the Queen City: The Story of King Records* (Urbana: University of Illinois Press, 2009, 9.

47. Randy Fox, "A Shining Moment," *Nashville Scene*, November 8, 1999, www.nashvillescene.com/1999-11-04/stories/a-shining-moment; "100G Sought in Suit over 'Chattanoogie,'" *Billboard*, March 11, 1950, 16, 50. Fox says that the song publisher Fred Rose wrote "Chattanoogie Shoe Shine Boy" but signed the composer's credit over to WSM's station director Harry Stone and program director Jack Stapp (while retaining the publishing rights for himself and his partner Roy Acuff), "reportedly" in exchange for featuring his client Hank Williams on the *Grand Ole Opry*. However, the widow of the white blackface comedian Bunny Biggs claimed in a lawsuit that Stone and Stapp had simply reworded a song, "Shoe Shine Boogie," that Biggs had written in August 1947.

48. Ken Burke and Dan Griffin, *The Blue Moon Boys: The Story of Elvis Presley's Band* (Chicago: Chicago Review Press, 2006), 25.

49. "New Pop Records," Music, *Time*, June 27, 1955, 41.

50. Arnold Shaw, *Honkers and Shouters: The Golden Years of Rhythm and Blues* (New York: Collier/Macmillan, 1978), 164, 165.

51. Colin Escott with Martin Hawkins, *Good Rockin' Tonight: Sun Records and the Birth of Rock 'n' Roll* (New York: St. Martin's Press, 1991), 40.

52. James Smethurst, "How I Got to Memphis: The Blues and the Study of American Culture," in *American Popular Music: New Approaches to the Twentieth Century*, ed. Rachel Rubin and Jeffrey Melnick (Amherst: University of Massachusetts Press, 2001), 50.

53. Scotty Moore, as told to James Dickerson. *That's Alright, Elvis: The Untold Story of Elvis's First Guitarist and Manager, Scotty Moore*, 1st pbk. ed. (New York: Schirmer, 1997/1998), 123.

54. Coleman, *Blue Monday*, xiv, 307.

7. GOOD ROCKIN' TONIGHT

1. Gunther Schuller, *The Swing Era: The Development of Jazz, 1930–1945* (New York: Oxford University Press, 1989), 391.

2. Arnold Shaw, *Honkers and Shouters: The Golden Years of Rhythm and Blues* (New York: Collier/Macmillan, 1978), 89, 195.

3. Herb Abramson, "The Birth of Rhythm and Blues," *Rhythm and Blues*, December 1952, quoted in Big Al Pavlow, *The R&B Book: A Disc-History of Rhythm & Blues* (Providence, RI: Music House Publishing, 1983), 16.

4. Ed Pickering and Jim Dawson, "Bronze," *Goldmine*, May 12, 1995, 48, 52.

5. "Central Avenue Sounds: Leroy Hurte," interview by Steven L. Isoardi, tape number 1, side 2 (July 12, 1995), 46, 47, http://content.cdlib.org/view?docId=hb4m3nb6cj;NAAN=13030&doc.view=frames&chunk.id=div00016&toc.depth=1&toc.id=&brand=calisphere.

6. M. H. Orodenker, "Pop Record Reviews," *Billboard*, January 6, 1945, 69.

7. Jim Dawson and Steve Propes, *What Was the First Rock 'n' Roll Record?* (Winchester, MA: Faber and Faber, 1992), 5, 6.

8. Shaw, *Honkers and Shouters*, 183, 184; Sherrie Tucker, "West Coast Women: A Jazz Genealogy," *Pacific Review of Ethnomusicology* 8, no. 1 (Winter 1996/1997): 9, 11, www.ethnomusic.ucla.edu/pre/Vol1-10/Vol1-10pdf/PREvol8.pdf. Rupe probably did not name the Sepia Tones, originally an all-female trio comprising violinist Ginger Smock, pianist Mata Roy, and organist Nina Russell. The Sepia Tones group that recorded for Juke Box, however, was apparently a quartet, with Roy, Russell, clarinetist and tenor saxophonist Paul Howard, and drummer George Vann. Before Roy Milton joined the label, Vann also recorded for Juke Box as "The Blues Man," singing to the accompaniment of the other Sepia Tones, while Marion Abernathy recorded as "The Blues Woman," backed by the Buddy Banks Sextet.

9. Ted Hallock, "Roy Milton's One Squeal Shy of Jordan, a Beat from Hamp," *Down Beat*, May 21, 1952, 16.

10. "Coca in Calypso," Music, *Time*, January 29, 1945, 75.

11. "Rum and Coca-Cola" had been written in 1943 by the Trinidadian calypso singer Lord Invader, using a melody borrowed from "L'Année Passée," a song written in French Creole as early as 1906 by the Trinidadian bandleader Lionel Belasco. Later in 1943, the American comedian Morey Amsterdam, now remembered mostly for his 1960s television role on *The Dick Van Dyke Show*, heard "Rum and Coca-Cola" while entertaining American servicemen stationed in Trinidad. (The song is a veiled commentary about Trinidadian women prostituting themselves for the Yankee troops.) Returning to New York, Amsterdam gave "Rum and Coca-Cola" to the singer Jeri Sullavan [sic], who introduced it in her nightclub act. Amsterdam then copyrighted it his own name; following the Andrews Sisters' smash, however, he agreed to share the publishing credits with Sullavan and her arranger, Paul Baron. Lord Invader and Lionel Belasco each filed suit for copyright infringement, and in separate trials (with Belasco's case argued by the famous attorney Louis Nizer), both prevailed. But as part of the settlement, Amsterdam paid to retain the copyright.

12. Chip Deffaa, *Blue Rhythms: Six Lives in Rhythm and Blues* (Urbana: University of Illinois Press, 1996), 110.

13. Ray Charles and David Ritz, *Brother Ray: Ray Charles' Own Story*, 2nd pbk. ed. (New York: Da Capo Press, 2003 [orig. Dial Press, 1978]), 44.

14. Deffaa, *Blue Rhythms*, 122.

15. Norbert Hess, "Obituaries: Amos Milburn," *Living Blues*, Spring 1980, 92.

16. Steve Tracy, "That Chicken Shack Boogie Man," *Blues Unlimited*, July 1971, 7, 8.

17. Nick Tosches, *Unsung Heroes of Rock 'n' Roll* (New York: Scribner's, 1984), 52.

18. Pete Welding, liner notes to *The Original Johnny Otis Show*, Savoy 2230 (1978).

19. Lionel Hampton with James Haskins, *Hamp: An Autobiography*, 1st pbk. ed. (New York: Amistad Press, 1993 [orig. Warner Books, 1989]), 90. Herbie Fields played in Lionel Hampton's band in 1945. According to Hampton, Fields was "the first white cat I had in my band. When we performed onstage, he wore makeup to darken his face so he didn't stand out so much."

20. Shaw, *Honkers and Shouters*, 161.

21. Shaw, *Honkers and Shouters*, 168; Tony Douglas, *Jackie Wilson: The Man, The Music, The Mob* (Edinburgh: Mainstream Publishing, 2001 [orig. published as *Lonely Teardrops: The Jackie Wilson Story*, London: Sanctuary Publishing, 1997; also published as *Jackie Wilson: Lonely Teardrops*, New York: Routledge, 2005]), 27.

22. Shaw, *Honkers and Shouters*, 165.

23. George Lipsitz, introduction to *Upside Your Head! Rhythm and Blues on Central Avenue,* by Johnny Otis (Hanover, NH: Wesleyan University Press, 1993), xxvii.
24. "Open the Door, Richard," Music, *Time,* February 10, 1947, 45.
25. Jim Dawson, *Nervous Man Nervous: Big Jay McNeely and the Rise of the Honking Tenor Sax!* (Milford, NH: Big Nickel Publications, 1994), 19–21.
26. Ted Fox, *Showtime at the Apollo* (New York: Holt, Rinehart and Winston, 1983), 96.
27. RJ Smith, "Richard Speaks! Chasing a Tune from the Chitlin Circuit to the Mormon Tabernacle," *This Is Pop,* ed. Eric Weisbard (Cambridge: Harvard University Press, 2004), 79.
28. Dawson and Propes, *What Was the First Rock 'n' Roll Record?* 22, 23.
29. Smith, "Richard Speaks!" 82–84.
30. Smith, "Richard Speaks!" 78; Lynn Abbott and Doug Seroff, *Ragged but Right: Black Traveling Shows, "Coon Songs," and the Dark Pathway to Blues and Jazz* (Jackson: University Press of Mississippi, 2007), 303; Frank Cullen with Florence Hackman and Donald McNeilly, *Vaudeville, Old and New: An Encyclopedia of Variety Performers in America* (New York: Routledge, 2007), 388; "Pigmeat" Markham with Bill Levinson, *Here Come the Judge!* (New York: Popular Library, 1969), chapter 9, no pagination. Smith, citing a 1947 story in the *Baltimore Afro-American* weekly newspaper, gives the 1919 date for Mason's first performance of the "Open the Door, Richard!" sketch, but Abbott and Seroff note that a new show called *Oh You, Mr. Rareback* was produced by Bob Russell in 1923. Smith gives 1928 as the date for *Bamboola,* but Cullen and other sources say it was 1929.
31. Larry Birnbaum, "Eddie 'Cleanhead' Vinson," *Down Beat,* October 1982, 30.
32. Peter Grendysa, "Musin' with the Moose: Bull Moose Jackson," *Goldmine*, November 1979, 16, cited in Jon Hartley Fox, *King of the Queen City: The Story of King Records* (Urbana: University of Illinois Press, 2009), 23.
33. *Northern Music v. King Record Distributing,* 105 F. Supp. 393 (S.D.N.Y. 1952), http://cip.law.ucla.edu/cases/1950-1959/Pages/northernking.aspx.
34. John A. Jackson, *Big Beat Heat: Alan Freed and the Early Years of Rock & Roll* (New York: Schirmer/Macmillan, 1991), 42, 43.
35. Teddy Reig with Edward Berger, *Reminiscing in Tempo: The Life and Times of a Jazz Hustler* (Lanham, MD: Scarecrow Press and the Institute of Jazz Studies, Rutgers University, 1990), 98.
36. Reig, *Reminiscing in Tempo*, 100.
37. Arlette and Hal Singer, *Hal Singer: Jazz Roads* (Paris: Edition 1, 1990), 283–286; Hal Singer as told to Albert J. McCarthy, "The Hal Singer Story," *Jazz Monthly* 4, no. 11 (January 1959): 12, 13, 31.
38. Singer, *Hal Singer*, 286.
39. Dawson, *Nervous Man Nervous,* 15.
40. Dawson, *Nervous Man Nervous,* 11.
41. Dawson, *Nervous Man Nervous,* 87.
42. Bill Millar, "Big Jim Wynn: Saxman," *Let the Good Times Rock! A Fan's Notes on Post-War American Roots Music* (York, England: Music Mentor Books, 2004 [orig. published in *Record Mirror,* November 4, 1972]), 167.
43. Clora Bryant, Buddy Collette, William Green, Steven Isoardi, Jack Kelson, Horace Tapscott, Gerald Wilson, and Marl Young, eds., *Central Avenue Sounds: Jazz in Los Angeles* (Berkeley: University of California Press, 1998), 188.
44. Harry Shapiro and Caesar Glebbeek, *Jimi Hendrix: Electric Gypsy* (New York: St. Martin's Griffin, 1995 [orig. William Heinemann, 1990]), 41.
45. Tosches, *Unsung Heroes of Rock 'n' Roll,* 15.
46. John Coltrane with Don DeMicheal, "Coltrane on Coltrane," *Down Beat*, September 29, 1960, 26.
47. Larry Birnbaum, "Daddy G!" *Reader*, June 22, 1984, 12.
48. Ellen Blau with Dick Shurman, "Living Blues Interview: Pee Wee Crayton," *Living Blues*, Spring 1983, 11.
49. Jim and Amy O'Neal, "Living Blues Interview: Billy 'The Kid,' Emerson," *Living Blues*, Spring 1980, 35.
50. Shaw, *Honkers and Shouters,* 109, 110.

51. Jas Obrecht, "Clarence Gatemouth Brown: 40 Years on the Road as Picker, Fiddler, Bluesman, Jazzer," *Guitar Player,* May 1979, 44.

52. Obrecht, "Clarence Gatemouth Brown," 45. Brown told Obrecht, "I joined an old road band called W. M. Bimbo & The Brownskin Models," but the only references to W. M. Bimbo are in articles about Brown. There was, however, a well-known touring review called Irvin (or Irwin) C. Miller's Brown Skin (or Brownskin) Models.

53. Obrecht, "Clarence Gatemouth Brown," 45; Christopher Wilkinson, *Jazz on the Road: Don Albert's Musical Life,* pbk. ed. (Berkeley: University of California Press, 2001), 221, 222. Obrecht writes that Brown played at Albert's club—known as Don's Keyhole, the Keyhole Club, or the Key Hole—for two years with a twenty-three-piece band led by a French-horn player named Hort Hudge. Other sources—all pertaining to Brown—give the bandleader's name as Hart Hughes, Hoyt Hughes, or Hoyt Huge, but there seem to be no non-Brown-related references to this musician or band. Wilkinson, citing the *San Antonio Register,* an African American newspaper, writes that "on August 30 [1946], Dave Ogden and his seven-piece band, 'direct from Club Bali, New Orleans, La.,' began a month-long engagement [at Don's Keyhole], with blues man Clarence 'Gate Mouth' Brown joining the show on September 20." Wilkinson keeps a fairly detailed record of Keyhole bookings during this period but makes no other mention of Brown.

54. Obrecht, "Clarence Gatemouth Brown," 45; John Nova Lomax, "So Long, For Now So Long: RIP, Gatemouth Brown," *Houston Press,* September 29, 2005, www.houstonpress.com/2005-09-29/music/so-long-for-now-so-long.

55. Shaw, *Honkers and Shouters,* 479.

56. Obrecht, "Clarence Gatemouth Brown," 46.

57. Jas Obrecht, "Gatemouth Brown," in *Rollin' and Tumblin': The Postwar Blues Guitarists,* ed. Jas Obrecht (San Francisco: Miller Freeman Books, 2000), 82.

58. Stefan Grossman, "Whatever Happened to Mickey Baker," *Guitar Player,* January 1976, 10.

59. Bill Dahl, "Mickey Baker: The King of the Slip and Slide Guitar," *Living Blues*, November–December 2000, 40.

60. Dahl, "Mickey Baker," 45.

61. David Whiteis, "Jody Williams: An Unsung Guitar Hero Returns," *Living Blues*, February 2002, 15, 17.

62. Neil Slaven, liner notes to *Boogie Uproar: Texas Blues and R&B 1947–1954,* disc C, JSP Records (2006).

63. Jason Berry, Jonathan Foose, and Tad Jones, *Up from the Cradle of Jazz: New Orleans Music since World War II* (Athens: University of Georgia Press, 1986), 82, 84.

64. Jeff Hannusch, "Eddie 'Guitar Slim' Jones 1926–1959," *Guitar Player,* March 1984, 60.

65. Jas Obrecht, "Johnny 'Guitar' Watson: Razor-Blade-Totin' Guitar," *Guitar Player,* February 1982, 69.

66. Tony Collins, *Rock Mr. Blues: The Life and Music of Wynonie Harris* (Milford, NH: Big Nickel Publications, 1995), 29–39.

67. John Broven, "Roy Brown, Part 1: Good Rockin' Tonight," *Blues Unlimited,* January/February 1977, 6.

68. Collins, *Rock Mr. Blues,* 116, 117.

69. Aaron Fuchs, liner notes to *The Shouters: Roots of Rock 'n' Roll Vol. 9,* Savoy 2244 (1980).

70. Ruth Brown with Andrew Yule, *Miss Rhythm: The Autobiography of Ruth Brown, Rhythm and Blues Legend* (New York: Donald I. Fine Books, 1996), 60, 62, 63, 78, 79.

71. Arnold Shaw, liner notes to Dinah Washington, *A Slick Chick (on the Mellow Side): The Rhythm & Blues Years,* EmArcy Jazz Series 814 1841 (1983).

72. Frank Driggs and Chuck Haddix, *Kansas City Jazz: From Ragtime to Bebop—A History* (New York: Oxford University Press, 2005), 124, 132, 220.

73. Driggs and Haddix, *Kansas City Jazz,* 132, 257.

74. Brown, *Miss Rhythm*, 36.

75. Ahmet Ertegun with Perry Richardson, Greil Marcus, et al., *What'd I Say: The Atlantic Story, Fifty Years of Music* (New York: Welcome Rain Publishers, 2001), 15.

76. Brown, *Miss Rhythm*, 60.
77. Brown, *Miss Rhythm*, 123.
78. Brown, *Miss Rhythm*, 76, 77, 110.
79. "Lavern Baker Seeks Bill to Halt Arrangement 'Thefts,'" *Billboard,* March 5, 1955, 13.
80. Nick Tosches, *Hellfire: The Jerry Lee Lewis Story* (New York: Delta/Dell, 1982), 89, 95.
81. Myra Lewis with Murray Silver, *Great Balls of Fire: The Uncensored Story of Jerry Lee Lewis* (New York: Quill, 1982), 72, 73.
82. "Now Is the Hour" originated as a piano piece titled "Swiss Cradle Song" that was published in Australia in 1913, credited to Clement Scott. In New Zealand, Maori words were written to the opening theme, and the song, now called "Po Atarau," was sung as a farewell to Maori soldiers serving in World War I, leading to the mistaken belief that it was of folkloric provenance. The Maori singer-songwriter Maewa Kaihau added new lyrics in both English and Maori, and the resulting "Haere Ra Waltz Song" was heard by the English singer Gracie Fields on a visit to New Zealand in 1945. Fields's adaptation, "Now Is the Hour," was a worldwide hit and was covered in the United States by Bing Crosby, Margaret Whiting, Eddy Howard, Kate Smith, and others.
83. "Billy Williams Sings Blues in His Death," *Jet,* November 2, 1972, 58.
84. Marv Goldberg, "Yesterday's Memories: The Red Caps," *Discoveries* 4, no. 11 (November 1991): 120, 121.
85. M. H. Orodenker, "Popular Record Reviews," *Billboard,* January 22, 1944, 19, 61.
86. "Record Reviews," *Billboard,* March 25, 1950, 115.
87. "Treniers Stymied on 'Hi Yo, Silver,'" *Billboard*, January 24, 1953, 18.
88. Billy Vera, liner notes to the Ravens, *Their Complete National Recordings 1947–1950,* Savoy Jazz SVY 17304 (2003).
89. Marv Goldberg, "The Ravens," *Discoveries* 93 (February 1996): 23, 24.
90. Goldberg, "The Ravens," 27.
91. Marv Goldberg, "Marv Goldberg's R&B Notebooks: The Orioles—Part 1, The Early Jubilee Years 1948–1951," www.uncamarvy.com/Orioles/orioles1.html.
92. Goldberg, "Marv Goldberg's R&B Notebooks: The Orioles—Part 1."
93. Marv Goldberg, "Marv Goldberg's R&B Notebooks: The Dominoes—Part 1," www.uncamarvy.com/Dominoes/dom01.html (orig. published in *Discoveries* 89 [October 1995]).
94. Fox, *King of the Queen City*, 92.
95. Charlie Gillett, *The Sound of the City: The Rise of Rock 'n' Roll,* 3rd pbk. ed. (New York: Laurel/Dell, 1978 [orig. Outerbridge & Dienstfrey, 1970]), 167.
96. G. A. Moonoogian, "Wax Fax," *Record Collector's Monthly,* November/December 1991, 21.
97. Jackson, *Big Beat Heat,* 7.
98. Dawson and Propes, *What Was the First Rock 'n' Roll Record?* 95.
99. Charlie Gillett, *Making Tracks: Atlantic Records and the Growth of a Multi-Billion-Dollar Industry* (New York: E. F. Dutton, 1974), 93.
100. Douglas, *Jackie Wilson*, 214–241, 250–252.
101. "WXYZ Bars Versions of 'Such Night,'" *Billboard,* March 20, 1954, 19.
102. Marv Goldberg, "The Clovers: '50s Rhythm and Blues," *Discoveries* 113 (October 1997): 30.
103. Marv Goldberg, "Marv Goldberg's R&B Notebooks: The Chords," www.uncamarvy.com/Chords/chords.html.
104. Peter Grendysa liner notes to the Moonglows, *Blue Velvet: The Ultimate Collection,* Chess/MCA CHD2 9345 (1993), cited in Robert Pruter, *Doo-Wop: The Chicago Scene* (Urbana: University of Illinois Press, 1996), 35, 39, 269.
105. Dawson and Propes, *What Was the First Rock 'n' Roll Record?* 159, 160.
106. John Broven, liner notes to Paul Gayten and Annie Laurie, *Creole Gal,* Route 66 KIX-8 (1979). Most sources give Kentwood as Gayten's birthplace, but Broven quotes his own 1975 interview with Gayten where Gayten states, "I was born January 29, 1920 at Charity Hospital, New Orleans."

107. Broven, "Roy Brown, Part 1," 4–6; Jeff Hannusch, *I Hear You Knockin': The Sound of New Orleans Rhythm and Blues* (Ville Platte, LA: Swallow Publications, 1985), 73, 74; John Broven, *Rhythm & Blues in New Orleans,* 1st pbk. printing (Gretna, LA: Pelican, 1983 [originally published as *Walking to New Orleans: The Story of New Orleans Rhythm and Blues,* Bexhill, Sussex: Blues Unlimited, 1974]), 22. Hannusch quotes the Galveston pianist Candy Green as saying of "Good Rocking Tonight," "No, Roy [Brown] didn't write that tune. He had a pianist named Joel Harris who wrote it. Joel wasn't a full-time musician, he was a schoolteacher who just moonlighted for some extra bread. He wrote it and gave it to Roy." Broven also notes Harris's claim to authorship, adding that "Roy strongly denies this."

108. Hannusch, *I Hear You Knockin'*, 124.

109. Gillett, *The Sound of the City*, 140, 141.

110. John Broven, "Roy Brown, Part 2: Hard Luck Blues," *Blues Unlimited,* March/June 1977, 15, 16.

111. Hannusch, *I Hear You Knockin',* 245. Earlier sources say that Lewis was born in Union, Louisiana, in 1920, but Hannusch, who got his information from Lewis's first wife, says that the Union location and 1920 date were given by Lewis's second wife and are "certainly not true."

112. Hannusch, *I Hear You Knockin',* 246; George A. Moonoogian, "Blues with a Smile!" *Whiskey, Women, and . . . ,* November 1982. Hannusch states that Lewis joined Thomas Jefferson's band in the mid-1930s, while Moonoogian has him playing with Jefferson in the late 1930s. Jefferson was born in 1920, which would make him a teenager when he supposedly led his band with the considerably older Lewis and Tuts Washington (born in 1907).

113. Hannusch, *I Hear You Knockin',* 250.

114. Hannusch, *I Hear You Knockin',* 251.

115. Rick Coleman, *Blue Monday: Fats Domino and the Lost Dawn of Rock 'n' Roll* (New York: Da Capo Press, 2006), 24, 25.

116. Coleman, *Blue Monday*, 27.

117. In 1951, an obscure rhythm-and-blues singer, James "Wee Willie" Wayne, recorded a related song, "Junco Partner," with a habanera bass line and Caribbean-style percussion. Louis Jordan covered "Junco Partner" in 1952, and the white middle-of-the road singer Richard Hayes made it an unlikely pop hit the same year. The white New Orleans R&B singer Roland Stone reworked the song as "Preacher's Daughter" in 1959, and the Holy Modal Rounders did it as "Junko Partner" in 1965; by the 1970s, "Junco Partner" had become a Crescent City standard, recorded by James Booker, Professor Longhair, and Dr. John. In 1980, the British punk band the Clash set it to a reggae beat.

118. Coleman, *Blue Monday*, 105.

119. Pat Boone, *Pat Boone's America: 50 Years* (Nashville: B&H, 2006), 43, 44.

120. Coleman, *Blue Monday*, 125, 133.

121. Jackson, *Big Beat Heat,* 178, 179.

122. Jackson, *Big Beat Heat,* 165, 322; "Fats on Fire," Music, *Time,* June 10, 1957, 71.

123. Coleman, *Blue Monday*, 194, 326. Surprisingly, "I'm Ready" is the product of professional songwriters, although it's not clear which ones. Some sources, including the label on the original Imperial 45 rpm disc, attribute the song to Domino, Sylvester Bradford, and Al Lewis. Bradford was a black New York doo-wop singer, and Lewis was a white lyricist who cowrote "Blueberry Hill" (Bradford and Lewis also wrote Little Anthony and the Imperials' 1958 breakthrough hit, "Tears on My Pillow"). Coleman, citing a conversation with the author Colin Escott, says that the upstate New York rockabilly singer Ersel Hickey "was offered 'I'm Ready' on a demo sung by Bobby Darin." Other sources credit "I'm Ready" to three New Orleanians: Ruth Durand, an R&B singer who recorded mostly in a duo with Al Reed; Pearl King, a pseudonym used by Earl King; and Joe Robichaux, a traditional jazz pianist whose band had employed the teenage Dave Bartholomew.

124. Barry Miles, *Paul McCartney: Many Years from Now* (New York: Holt, 1988 [orig. Secker and Warburg, 1997]), 449.

125. Shaw, *Honkers and Shouters,* 261.

126. David Booth, "Lloyd Price: Mr. Personality," *Goldmine*, May 17, 1991, 108.

127. Seamus McGarvey, "Lloyd Price: Mr. Personality" [same as above title], *Juke Blues,* no. 24 (Autumn 1991): 6.

128. Shaw, *Honkers and Shouters,* 188; Dawson and Propes, *What Was the First Rock 'n' Roll Record?* 110; Booth, "Lloyd Price," 110; Peter Guralnick, *Dream Boogie: The Triumph of Sam Cooke* (Boston: Little, Brown, 2005), 87.

129. Charles White, *The Life and Times of Little Richard: The Quasar of Rock* (New York: Da Capo Press, 1994 [orig. Harmony Books, 1984]), 40, 41, 47; Booth, "Lloyd Price," 110. Price claims to have recommended Little Richard both to Don Robey, for whose Peacock label Richard recorded in 1953, and to Art Rupe. But as David Booth points out, Price said, "I had met Little Richard just before I went into the service [in late 1953], and I introduced him to Don Robey," for whom Richard first recorded in February 1953. Little Richard told Charles White that "I talked to Lloyd Price and he told me to send a tape to a guy called Art Rupe at Specialty Records in Los Angeles," then said that he sent Rupe a demo tape he'd recorded in February 1955 and that Specialty waited ten months to respond. Rupe, however, said, "We received the tape about seven or eight months before we recorded." Richard's first Specialty session was in September 1955.

130. Booth, "Lloyd Price," 112.

131. Booth, "Lloyd Price," 112.

132. White, *The Life and Times of Little Richard,* 188, 189.

133. Broven, *Rhythm & Blues in New Orleans,* 41, 42.

134. White, *The Life and Times of Little Richard,* 26, 39; James Brown with Bruce Tucker, *James Brown: The Godfather of Soul* (New York: Macmillan, 1986), 68.

135. Booth, "Lloyd Price," 110.

136. White, *The Life and Times of Little Richard,* 37, 38.

137. White, *The Life and Times of Little Richard,* 39, 40.

138. White, *The Life and Times of Little Richard,* 46.

139. White, *The Life and Times of Little Richard,* 47.

140. White, *The Life and Times of Little Richard,* 50.

141. Hannusch, *I Hear You Knockin',* 222.

142. Peter Guralnick, *Sweet Soul Music: Rhythm and Blues and the Southern Dream of Freedom* (New York: Harper & Row, 1986), 138.

143. White, *The Life and Times of Little Richard,* 60, 61; Eugene Chadbourne, "Enotris Johnson: Biography," www.allmusic.com/artist/enotris-johnson-p306206/biography; Phillip Ramati, "Little Richard Benefactor Dies at 82," *Macon Telegraph,* January 18, 2007, http://rollcallblog.blogspot.com/2008/12/little-richard-benefactor-dies-at-82-by.html. White quotes Bumps Blackwell telling how "a big disk jockey called Honey Chile" called him about Enortis Johnson, a girl who'd "walked all the way from Appaloosa, Mississippi, to sell this song to Richard." Chadbourne, however, identifies Enotris Johnson (not Enortis, as White spells it) as a white man who adopted Little Richard as a youth and whom Richard credited as co-composer of "Long Tall Sally," as well as "Miss Ann" and "Jenny, Jenny," simply out of generosity toward his adoptive parent. Other sources give Johnson's first name as Johnny and state that he and his wife, Ann, ran the Tick Tock Club in Macon, where Richard supposedly made his professional performance debut. All these accounts are dubious, Blackwell's because there is no such place as Appaloosa, Mississippi, and because there seems to have been no prominent disc jockey called Honey Chile, Chadbourne's because neither Richard nor any of the other Penniman family members interviewed for White's biography mentions an adoption. According to Ramati's obituary of Ann Howard, it was she who owned the Tick Tock Club—actually Ann's Tic-Toc, Macon's first openly gay bar. Howard, whose husband was named Johnny, is said to have inspired "Miss Ann."

144. Tony Scherman, *Backbeat: Earl Palmer's Story* (Washington, DC: Smithsonian Institution Press, 1999), 90, 91.

145. White, *The Life and Times of Little Richard,* 74.

146. White, *The Life and Times of Little Richard,* 239.

147. White, *The Life and Times of Little Richard,* 65, 66.

148. White, *The Life and Times of Little Richard,* 119.

149. "Morning Report: Movies," *Los Angeles Times,* February 5, 1987, http://articles.latimes.com/1987-02-05/entertainment/ca-1259_1; "Entertainment: Pop/Rock," *Los Angeles Times,* June 18, 1987, http://articles.latimes.com/keyword/richard-penniman; "Little Richard Sues over Ownership of New Hit Song," *Jet* magazine, March 9, 1987, http://books.google.com/books?id=qrMDAAAAMBAJ&pg=PA59&lpg=PA59&dq=%22matter+of+time%22+preston+penniman&source=bl&ots=LrxgcZnVB5&sig=RD-4HClMoHCJh_NUdjkL1ZrTX5A&hl=en&ei=Tgb4TOvUOIT7lwf81v2PAg&sa=X&oi=book_result&ct=result&resnum=2&ved=0CBoQ6AEwAQ#v=onepage&q=%22matter%20of%20time%22%20preston%20penniman&f=false. Billy Preston, Sylvia Smith, and John Schuller claimed that Little Richard adapted "Great Gosh A'Mighty! (It's a Matter of Time)" from a song they wrote. Richard sued them, maintaining that he had written the song himself and had only agreed to split the composer's credit with Preston after Preston suggested the phrase "Great gosh a'mighty." Preston, Smith, and Schuller then countersued for copyright infringement.

150. David J. Gallagher, comment posted on (and since removed from) the web page "Bunker Hill—The Girl Can't Dance" at www.youtube.com/watch?v=NIHO7OEzHQk.

151. David Kirby, *Little Richard: The Birth of Rock 'n' Roll* (New York: Continuum, 2009), 4.

8. ROCK LOVE

1. Michael Corcoran, "The Morse Code," *Dallas Observer,* March 21, 1996, www.dallasobserver.com/1996-03-21/music/the-morse-code/.

2. Jonny Whiteside, *Cry: The Johnnie Ray Story* (New York: Barricade Books, 1994), 40.

3. Frankie Laine and Joseph F. Laredo, *That Lucky Old Son: The Autobiography of Frankie Laine* (Ventura, CA: Pathfinder Publishing, 1993), 81, 82.

4. Laine and Laredo, *That Lucky Old Son,* 15.

5. Laine and Laredo, *That Lucky Old Son,* 76, 77.

6. Laine and Laredo, *That Lucky Old Son,* 94, 95.

7. Will Friedwald, *Jazz Singing: America's Great Voices from Bessie Smith to Bebop and Beyond* (New York: Da Capo Press, 1992 [orig. Scribner's, 1990]), 221.

8. Will Friedwald, *Sinatra! The Song Is You: A Singer's Art* (New York: Scribner's, 1995), 174.

9. Spencer Leigh, "Unfit for Auntie's Airwaves: The Artists Censored by the BBC," *The Independent,* December 14, 2007, www.independent.co.uk/arts-entertainment/music/features/unfit-for-aunties-airwaves-the-artists-censored-by-the-bbc-765106.html. It is widely reported, Leigh's article being one of many examples, that the BBC banned "Answer Me, Lord Above" as "a sentimental mockery of Christian prayer," whereupon Carl Sigman, the American songwriter responsible for the English lyrics, changed the song to "Answer Me, My Love," which was also recorded by Whitfield and later by Laine but which had its greatest U.S. success at the hands of Nat "King" Cole in 1954.

10. Friedwald, *Jazz Singing,* 214.

11. Friedwald, *Jazz Singing,* 215.

12. Friedwald, *Jazz Singing,* 216.

13. "Kay Starr 1993 April Love Tour—3," www.youtube.com/watch?v=W1n2PTLdmjI.

14. Whiteside, *Cry,* 68.

15. The tune of "It's All in the Game" was written as "Melody in A Major" in 1911 by Charles G. Dawes, who later became vice president of the United States under Calvin Coolidge. "Melody in A Major" was popularized by the classical violinist Fritz Kreisler in the 1920s and recorded as a trombone showcase by Tommy Dorsey during World War II. The lyrics were added in 1951 by Carl Sigman (see note 9).

16. Whiteside, *Cry,* 102, 103, 142, 143.

17. Peter Guralnick, *Last Train to Memphis: The Rise of Elvis Presley,* 1st pbk. ed. (Boston: Back Bay Books/Little, Brown, 1994), 131, 163. In 1951, Carson had recorded her first solo

single, "Satisfied," which has a strong handclapped backbeat at the beginning, middle, and end. Elvis Presley recorded "Satisfied" for Sun in 1954, but no disc was issued and the tape was presumably destroyed. Presley performed on the same bill as Carson in 1955 and, according to Carson, "just really idolized me."

18. Guralnick, *Last Train to Memphis,* 57, 58.

19. Whiteside, *Cry,* 223.

20. "Court Denies Williams Claim in 'Baby' Case," *Billboard,* December 8, 1951, 20; Tammy Lynn Kernodle, *Soul on Soul: The Life and Music of Mary Lou Williams* (Boston: Northeastern University Press, 2004), 150. Snub Mosley sued Mary Lou Williams in 1951, claiming that he had adapted her composition "Satchel Mouth Baby" as "Pretty Eyed Baby." Williams responded that William Johnson, a former member of Mosley's band, had misrepresented himself as having adapted the song, which she had neglected to copyright, and induced her to share the royalties with him. Ultimately, the composers' credit was divided among Williams, Mosley, and Johnson.

21. Jose, "Town & Country, Bklyn.," Night Club Reviews, *Variety,* December 11, 1957, 71.

22. "Pat Boone," interview with Stephen J. Abramson, September 10, 2010, www.emmytvlegends.org/interviews/people/pat-boone.

23. Ellen Willis, *Out of the Vinyl Deeps: Ellen Willis on Rock Music,* ed. Nona Willis Aronowitz (Minneapolis: University of Minnesota Press, 2001), 193, 194.

24. Bill Smith, "Paramount, New York," "Night Club-Vaude Reviews," *Billboard,* May 24, 1952, 45.

25. Benoit Vanhees, "Sunny Gale: Come Go with Me (English Version/Parts One and Two)," www.retroscoop.com/popcultuur.php?artikel=77 and www.retroscoop.com/popcultuur.php?artikel=85.

26. Tony Wilkinson and Klaus Kettner, "Bunny Paul," www.rockabilly.nl/references/messages/bunny_paul.htm.

27. Casey Stegall, "Vicki (Stegall) Young," www.saxonyrecordcompany.com/vicki-young.html.

28. "Reviews of New Pop Records," *Billboard,* May 8, 1954, 24.

29. David Ritz and Etta James, *Rage to Survive: The Etta James Story,* 2nd ed. (New York: Da Capo Press, 2003 [orig. Villard Books, 1995]), 49, 50.

30. Gale Storm with Bill Libby, *I Ain't Down Yet: The Autobiography of My Little Margie* (Indianapolis: Bobbs-Merrill, 1981), 81.

31. Jay Warner, *American Singing Groups: A History from 1940 to Today* (Milwaukee: Hal Leonard, 2006 [orig. *The Billboard Book of American Singing Groups: A History 1940–1990,* New York: Billboard Books, 1992]), 51, 52 .

32. Steven Gaines, *Heroes and Villains: The True Story of the Beach Boys,* pbk. ed. (New York: Da Capo Press, 1995 [orig. New American Library, 1986]), 51.

33. Ross Barbour, *Now You Know: The Story of the Four Freshmen* (Lake Geneva, WI: Balboa Books, 1995), 30–33.

34. Gary James, "Gary James' Interview with Frank Busseri of the Four Lads," www.classicbands.com/FourLadsInterview.html.

35. "Talent Corner," *Billboard,* January 15, 1955, 46.

36. Brian Ward, *Just My Soul Responding: Rhythm and Blues, Black Consciousness and Race* (London: Routledge, 2004 [orig. University College London Press, 1998]), 48.

37. Gage Averill, *Four Parts, No Waiting: A Social History of American Barbershop Harmony* (New York: Oxford University Press, 2003), 141.

38. John Crowley, "West Indies Blues: An Historical Overview, 1920s–1950s—Blues and Music from the English-speaking West Indies," in *Nobody Knows Where the Blues Come From: Lyrics and History,* ed. Robert Springer (Jackson: University Press of Mississippi, 2006), 240.

39. "Me Donkey Want Water," Walter Jekyll, ed., *Jamaican Song And Story: Annancy Stories, Digging Sings, Ring Tunes, and Dancing Tunes* (London: David Nutt, 1907), www.gutenberg.org/files/35410/35410-h/35410-h.htm.

40. Charlie Gillett, *The Sound of the City: The Rise of Rock 'n' Roll,* 3rd pbk. ed. (New York: Laurel/Dell, 1978 [orig. Outerbridge & Dienstfrey, 1970]), 76, 77.

41. Ned Sublette, *Cuba and Its Music: From the First Drums to the Mambo* (Chicago: Chicago Review Press, 2004), 507–510.

EPILOGUE

1. Linda Martin and Kerry Segrave, *Anti-Rock: The Opposition to Rock 'n' Roll,* 1st pbk. ed. (New York: Da Capo Press, 1993 [orig. Archon Books, 1988]), 103.
2. "Block Calls Tune 'Italiano' Offensive," *Billboard,* November 20, 1954, 16.
3. "Stations Turn Against No. 1 Drinker Song," *Billboard,* January 30, 1954, 22.
4. Andrew J. Edelstein and Kevin McDonough, *The Seventies: From Hot Pants to Hot Tubs* (New York: E. P. Dutton, 1990), 178.

Index

About the Author

Born in New York City to parents from Vienna, Austria, **Larry Birnbaum** was raised in Chicago, where he acquired a taste for blues, jazz, country, Latin, and classical music, as well as rock 'n' roll. For some thirty-five years, he has written about music for publications including *Stereophile*, *Down Beat*, *Newsday*, *Spin*, *Pulse!* and the *Village Voice*. He was the editor of Schirmer Trade Books, an imprint specializing in books about music; *Global Rhythm,* a world-music magazine; and *Ear,* a new-music magazine. He was also one of the hosts of the world-music radio show *New York International.* In 1988 he won the ASCAP Deems Taylor Award for his *New York Times* article "The Polka Continues to Thrive across America."